101. 22: 550 - 25

AREA HANDBOOK
for
ISRAEL

Co-Authors

Harvey H. Smith

Frederica M. Bunge
William W. Cover
William Giloane
Peyton Kerr
William Kinard
Aaron S. Klieman
Suzanne Teleki
Nancy E. Walstrom

Research and writing were completed on
June 15, 1969

Published
September 1970

(This pamphlet supersedes DA Pam 550-25,   May 1964)

DA Pam 550–25

For sale by the Superintendent of Documents, U.S. Government Printing Office
Washington, D.C. 20402—Price $3.50

FOREWORD

This volume is one of a series of handbooks prepared by Foreign Area Studies (FAS) of The American University, designed to be useful to military and other personnel who need a convenient compilation of basic facts about the social, economic, political and military institutions and practices of various countries. The emphasis is on objective description of the nation's present society and the kinds of possible or probable changes that might be expected in the future. The handbook seeks to present as full and as balanced an integrated exposition as limitations on space and research time permit. It was compiled from information available in openly published material. Extensive bibliographies are provided to permit recourse to other published sources for more detailed information. There has been no attempt to express any specific point of view or to make policy recommendations. The contents of the handbook represent the work of the authors and FAS and do not represent the official view of the United States Government.

An effort has been made to make the handbook as comprehensive as possible. It can be expected, however, that the material, interpretations and conclusions are subject to modification in the light of new information and developments. Such corrections, additions and suggestions for factual, interpretive or other change as readers may have will be welcomed for use in future revisions. Comments may be addressed to—

The Director
Foreign Area Studies
The American University
5010 Wisconsin Avenue, N.W.
Washington, D.C. 20016

iii

PREFACE

Modern Israel is a predominantly Jewish state in the midst of Arab neighbors. Geographically and topographically the country is a segment of the Middle East, but in most other respects its people are oriented toward the West, whence the great majority of its leaders, or their forefathers, have emigrated within the past century.

The Jewish people have been associated through the centuries with the civilizations of the area in which Israel now exists; but the country has been a sovereign state only since 1948. Because of the widespread ramifications of the continuing ferment in the Middle East, Israel plays an increasingly important role in world affairs related to this region.

This book is an attempt to provide, in compact, convenient, balanced, and objective form, an integrated exposition and analysis of the dominant, social, political, and economic aspects of the Israeli society. It is designed to give readers an understanding of the dynamics of the component elements of the society, and an insight into the ideas and goals of its people.

Grateful acknowledgment is owed to many persons within and outside the United States government, who gave their time and special knowledge to provide data and objective criticism of preliminary chapter drafts. Particular appreciation is extended to James K. Matter for his advice and perceptive comments on many chapters.

Appreciation is also extended to members of the staff of the Embassy of Israel, who were notably helpful in providing some of the needed sources and information. Likewise, special recognition is accorded to Sarah M. Thomas, Lecturer, School of Library and Information Services, University of Maryland, who furnished valuable source materials from her own personal collection.

An area of difficulty encountered in preparation of the study was the variety of transliteration systems used by different sources; inconsistencies often occurred within a single source. An effort was made to establish a common, simple system that would allow the general reader to approximate the pronunciation of the Hebrew word. Symbols and diacritical marks, uncommon in English usage, have been avoided. The spelling of Hebrew words and names has, in most instances, followed the transliteration system of *Webster's Third New*

International Dictionary (unabridged). Conventional spelling, however, was used for well-known personal names and some place names. The place names used are, wherever possible, those established for Israel by the Board on Geographic Names, United States Department of the Interior, in 1954 and 1962, or by *Webster's Geographical Dictionary* (revised edition, 1969), G. and C. Merriam Company, Springfield, Massachusetts.

A glossary is included as an appendix for the reader's convenience. Terms in the glossary are not in every case mentioned explicitly in the text but are likely to be encountered while reading the cited bibliographical sources.

COUNTRY SUMMARY

1. COUNTRY: Israel, with Jerusalem as its seat of government, was created in 1948 as a Jewish state in the territory previously known as Palestine. Independence, proclaimed on May 14, 1948, ended the British Palestine Mandate and formally established the state as a sovereign, parliamentary democracy.

2. GOVERNMENT: Political authority rests with the Knesset, a unicameral legislature of 120 members normally elected every 4 years by universal suffrage of citizens over 18 years of age. The president, official head of state, is elected by the Knesset for a 5-year term. To form a new government, he consults with the Knesset and political party leaders in the Knesset; he then calls upon a Knesset member to assemble a new cabinet and, as prime minister, to form a new government for Knesset approval. The prime minister and cabinet exercise executive authority and are collectively responsible to the Knesset. The Transition Law of 1949 prescribes in general terms the respective roles and powers of the president, of the legislature, and of the prime minister and cabinet; a written constitution has not been adopted. A series of Basic Laws passed by the Knesset serve as a constitutional framework.

3. POPULATION: Approximately 2.7 million by early 1968, with a Jewish population of almost 2.4 million. More than half of the total population is under the age of 25. Predominantly urban, only 18 percent classified as rural. Emigration low, while immigration continues from overseas Jewish communities. In the adjacent territories occupied by Israel during and since the Six-Day War of June 1967 there are about 1 million additional people, predominantly Arab.

4. SIZE: Before the Six-Day War of June 1967, area totaled 7,993 square miles on eastern shore of the Mediterranean. Occupied territories: Golan Heights (Syria), West Bank of Jordan River, including East Jerusalem (Jordan), and Sinai Peninsula (Egypt), constitute additional 25,600 square miles. Extreme length (north-south), approximately 265 miles; greatest width (east-west), 70 miles. Access to foreign areas is solely by way of the Mediterranean Sea and Red Sea port of Eilat on Gulf of Aqaba, or by air.

5. TOPOGRAHY: Three general areas: coastal plain, fertile and humid, thickly populated, stretching along the Mediterranean; hill

regions, including Hills of Galilee in north with highest elevation in country (3,963 feet) and Negev Hills in southern wastelands; Jordan Rift Valley with lowest point (1,302 feet below sea level) at Dead Sea.

6. LANGUAGES: Hebrew is official language and used in daily conversation. Arabic, predominant in the Arab minority, is also an official language and may be used in the Knesset, in the courts, and in approaches to the authorities. English is widely spoken and is taught in many public schools. Numerous other languages and dialects are spoken by smaller segments of the population, reflecting countries of origin.

7. RELIGION: Judaism is the predominant faith. Substantial Islamic and Christian communities are present. All three faiths are divided further into distinctive subgroups, such as the Karaites, the Sunnites, and the Catholics.

8. EDUCATION: High level of education with Jewish literacy rate of about 90 percent. Formal state education, free and compulsory in 1968 for all children aged 5 to 14, supplemented by religious schools, scouting and youth movements, and vocational training. Seven institutions of higher learning with 1968 enrollment of 28,520 students.

9. HEALTH: High level of health and of medical care, with average life expectancy of over 70 years and a steadily declining infant mortality rate. Widespread system of public health service helps in eradication and prevention of disease. In 1967 the country had 6,311 physicians, or one for every 429 citizens.

10. CLIMATE: Mediterranean, characterized by a long, hot, dry summer and a short, cool, rainy winter. Most of the land is arid or semiarid, with Negev region receiving minimum rainfall.

11. JUSTICE: Complete independence of judiciary guaranteed by law. Judges and magistrates of all courts appointed by president of the state. Judges sit as a panel; the jury system is not used. Supreme Court, highest of the land, consists of 10 members. Each major religious community has its own courts of first instance and appeal with exclusive jurisdiction in all matters of personal status coming before them.

12. ADMINISTRATIVE DIVISIONS: Country divided into six districts: Jerusalem, Northern, Haifa, Central, Tel Aviv, and Southern, and their respective administrative centers at Jerusalem, Nazareth, Haifa, Ramla, Tel Aviv, and Beersheba. Elected municipal, local, and regional councils, supervised by Ministry of Interior, provide public services and local self-rule. Occupied territories, as of mid-1969, were divided into four districts—Golan Heights, Judea and Samaria (West Bank of the Jordan River), the Gaza Strip and Northern Sinai, and Southern Sinai—each under a military governor responsible to the Ministry of Defense.

13. ECONOMY: Predominantly industrial, with emphasis upon exports. Raw materials and natural resources are limited, but skills of labor force, intensive agriculture, and outside financial aid are used to record a rapid growth rate. Government controls are extensive to promote national aims and objectives.

14. INDUSTRY: Expanding and diversified to provide for exports, defense needs, and consumer demands. Employs one-third of labor force. Ownership divided among private individuals, government, Histadrut (Histadrut Ha'ovdim Haklalit—General Federation of Labor) and other public bodies.

15. AGRICULTURE: Traditional nucleus of the economy is agriculture but its contribution to total production has declined to less than 10 percent. Sector is able to supply virtually all domestic needs, while providing a large volume of citrus fruits for export. Distinctive Jewish farm cooperatives, operated by communal and collective farm settlements (kibbutzim and moshavim), influence all walks of life.

16. LABOR: Labor force numbered over 1 million in 1969, growing at annual rate of about 4 percent. Of gainfully employed, 24.6 percent were in industry, 24.1 percent in public services, 14.9 percent in construction and transportation, 13.5 percent in commerce, finance and insurance, 12.6 percent in agriculture, 8.1 percent in personal services and 2.2 percent in public utilities. Workers highly organized within framework of the Histadrut trade unions.

17. EXPORTS: Increasing in volume and earnings, totaling over US$600 million net in 1968. Paced by polished diamonds, textiles, and citrus and other farm products. Sixty-three percent of exports went to Europe, 18 percent to the Americas, 13 percent to Asia, 4 percent to Africa, and the remainder to various other areas.

18. IMPORTS: Imports rising with growth of population and expansion of investment and production. Only 11 percent used for consumption in 1968. Net imports of goods rose to some US$950 million because of expansion of economic activity and defense requirements.

19. FINANCE: Government, represented by Bank of Israel, influences all financial institutions through investments, loans, and interest rates.

Currency. Basic unit is the Israeli pound (lira), divided into 100 agorot, and in mid-1969 was equivalent approximately to US$0.285. Government expenditures met by large capital imports. Chronic balance of payments deficit.

20. COMMUNICATIONS: Radio network, Kol Israel (Voice of Israel), and Israel Television are regulated by government. Radio broadcasts in Hebrew, Arabic, and seven other languages. Television, introduced on regular basis in 1968, is increasingly popular medium. Estimated about 610,000 radio sets and 30,500 television sets in the country in 1967.

21. PRESS: Twenty-two morning and two afternoon daily newspapers published; free of political censorship except in matters affecting military security; also, about 400 other periodicals, including over 70 government publications.

22. RAILROADS: State-owned, 454 miles, almost all standard gauge; mail lines link Jerusalem-Tel Aviv-Haifa. Extension of the system is underway to the Negev region in developing that area and extracting minerals.

23. ROADS: In 1967 about 2,500 miles of roads maintained, majority suitable for heavy transport, link Haifa with Eilat on the Red Sea. Buses, operated by cooperatives, are principal means of passenger travel; next in importance are railroads and taxis, with fares, routes, and frequency of services supervised by Ministry of Transport and Communications. Private cars increasingly in use, numbering over 100,000 by 1968.

24. PORTS: Haifa is major port for cargo and passenger service, whereas Ashdod and Eilat are being developed as important auxiliary harbors.

25. AIRFIELDS: One international airport at Lod (Lydda) near Tel Aviv. Airfields at Jerusalem, Haifa, Mahanaim, Herzliya, Masada, and Eilat are used for internal traffic.

26. CARRIER SERVICE: *Ships.* Zim (Israel Navigation Company) engages in shipping and passenger service. *Airlines.* El Al, Israel Airlines, government-owned company, with regular runs to 20 foreign cities. Arkia, Israel Inland Airlines, operates within country, scheduling tours.

27. INTERNATIONAL AGREEMENTS: Signatory to United Nations Charter. Not member of any formal bilateral treaty or regional alliance.

28. AID PROGRAMS: Engages in effective economic and technical assistance to developing countries. In period 1958–1968 over 10,500 trainees from over 80 countries in Africa, Asia, Latin America, and Mediterranean Basin, took professional courses and seminars in Israel. Experts were also sent to help in joint enterprises.

29. ARMED FORCES: Distinguished by citizen army with universal military training and reserve structure capable of rapid mobilization and by women participating. Permanent standing force of about 70,000. Emphasis upon armored units, air force, paratroops, border police. Budget for 1967–68 approximated 32 percent of total national budget.

ISRAEL

TABLE OF CONTENTS

xii

LIST OF ILLUSTRATIONS

LIST OF TABLES

LIST OF TABLES (Continued)

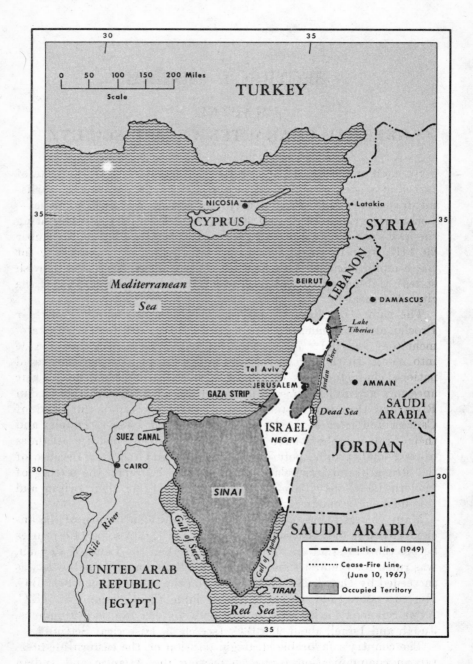

Figure 1. Position of Israel in the Eastern Mediterranean, 1968.

SECTION I. SOCIAL

CHAPTER 1
GENERAL CHARACTER OF THE SOCIETY

Situated at the eastern end of the Mediterranean Sea, the state of Israel, in existence only 21 years, is an independent sovereign, parliamentary democracy. The country borders on the Arab countries—Lebanon, Syria, Jordan, and Egypt. A major step toward creating the new state was taken by the United Nations (UN) on November 29, 1947, when its General Assembly adopted a resolution calling for the establishment in Palestine of "independent Arab and Jewish states" and for agreement on a special international status for the city of Jerusalem.

The name Israel was adopted by the country's founders in their Proclamation of Independence (May 14, 1948). In its opening statement they asserted: "In the Land of Israel the Jewish people came into being. In this Land was shaped their spiritual, religious and national character. Here they lived in sovereign independence." Their ancestors in Biblical times referred to this area between the Jordan River and the Mediterranean Sea as the Holy Land, the Land of Canaan and later as Eretz Yisrael (Land of Israel). Israelis and their Arab neighbors have all been influenced by historic attitudes toward land, people, political sovereignty, and religion. Because of the strength and interrelationship of these concepts, the setting of modern Israel may be understood by identifying their origin and tracing them from ancient to modern times.

Many changes have occured since the traditional return of the ancient Hebrews to this area after fleeing from Egypt some 14 centuries before the Christian era. The area, then called the Land of Canaan, was ruled for the first time, as a Hebrew Kingdom, by Saul, who was succeeded by David. He made Jerusalem the capital about 1000 B.C. His successor, Solomon, built the Temple there, around 960 B.C. After Solomon's death, his domain was divided into two kingdoms, Judah and Israel, about 930 B.C. (see ch. 3, Historical Setting).

The country's favorable strategic position on the eastern Mediterranean communication routes connecting the Atlantic and Indian oceans and three continents, Europe, Asia and Africa, has resulted in various foreign rulers competing for its control. Consequently over

1

the centuries suzerainty has passed from one power to another. Chronology of prominent changes and interruptions of rule include: Assyrian conquest of the area in 721 B.C. was succeeded by the Babylonian conquest and the destruction of Jerusalem in 586 B.C. The Greek invasion under Alexander the Great (333 B.C.) began more than a century-and-a-half of Hellenistic rule, ending with the revolt of the Maccabees and the introduction of the Hasmonaean dynasty in 168 B.C. Roman rule, starting in 163 B.C., shifted to rule by the Byzantines from Constantinople, dominant from A.D. 396 to 638 and terminating as a result of the Persian invasion (614) and the Muslim Arab conquest (636). Rule by the invading Seljuk Turks (1072) was interrupted by the Crusaders (1099). Egyptian rule under the Mamelukes, beginning in A.D. 1291, was succeeded by the Ottoman Turks in 1517 and finally by British military and civilian control (1917–23) and the British Palestine Mandate (1923–48) (see ch. 3, Historical Setting).

These incursions, many of them prolonged for several centuries, have left traces of foreign cultures. During these periods, the region, particularly Jerusalem, became a focal point for three prominent faiths: Jewish, Muslim, and Christian. As a result visitors from each, including theologians, students, researchers, and archeologists, continued to arrive.

The periods of domination were sometimes broken by revolts and interludes of independence, such as the revolt in 168 B.C. against the Seleucid Syrians by the Hasmonaean family, founders of the Hasmonaean dynasty whose members were known as Maccabeans. Their success introduced approximately a century of self-government, interrupted by the beginning of Roman rule in 63 B.C. Secret organizations developed among restless youths seeking Jewish independence. They eventually united, formed a revolutionary party known as the Zealots, and, in A.D. 66, initiated a strong revolt against Roman rule. The rebellion continued for 7 years. During that time civil war erupted in Jerusalem; casualties were high and the Zealots assumed command of the city. The forces of Titus, the Roman commander, besieged and finally took Jerusalem in A.D. 70 and destroyed the Temple. The last band of war-weakened Zealots perished in 73 after a final desperate stand at Masada on the western shore of the Dead Sea (see ch. 3, Historical Setting).

Roman rule was again threatened in A.D. 132, when several hundred thousand Jewish militant activists rebelled against repressive Roman edicts. Incited by the imaginative and enthusiastic warrior Bar Kochba, the rebellion continued until A.D. 135, when it was overwhelmingly crushed by Roman forces, after Bar Kochba was killed while defending his besieged fortified town southwest of Jerusalem. Considerable local autonomy was experienced by the few Jews remaining in the land from 1517 to 1917 under the Ottoman Turks; some Jews gained high posts in the Turkish government.

The invasions and periods of foreign domination resulted in worldwide dispersions of the Hebrew people, either as deportees under the Assyrians, as prisoners under the Babylonians, or as fugitives from subsequent periods of harsh rule. The whole body of dispersed Jews living outside Palestine after the Babylonian exile of 586–538 B.C. became known collectively as "the Diaspora." This term has become applicable also to the process of settling the dispersed Jews outside the area of ancient Israel; it also is frequently used in reference to the lands and places where they lived, and sometimes to the dispersed Jews themselves (see ch. 3, Historical Setting).

By the time of Egyptian and the later Ottoman domination in the Middle Ages, two major centers for dispersed Jews had developed. One was in eastern European areas, mainly Germany and Poland. These people became known as Ashkenazim (from the Hebrew for Germany), a name that became applied also to Yiddish-speaking Jews and their descendants living in central and northern Europe. The other center was in Spain until the time of the Spanish Inquisition in the 15th and 16th centuries, when many of them moved to North Africa and to the Middle East countries. This branch of the dispersed Jews became known as Sephardim (from the Hebrew for Spain), and the majority of them speak Ladino (a mixture of Spanish and Hebrew) or Arabic, depending largely on the language of the country in which they lived. A few went to England, the Netherlands, and the Americas (see ch. 5, Ethnic Groups and Languages).

The dispersed Jews, wherever they were in the world, generally retained a fervent sense of pride in their history, continued to practice their religion and customs, and preserved a strong emotional attachment to their ancient homeland. These factors were manifested in expressed desire to return to the Land of Israel as soon as circumstances permitted. Most of them, either individually or collectively, participated in the economic and political life of their new countries and, in western Europe in the 19th century, sought assimilation in the society. They were, however, usually regarded as a distinct minority group. On the whole, they maintained their historic hopes for a place of their own and for a society permitting free development of Jewish culture. Fulfillment of this desire, however, could not be attained by individuals alone. Resettlement in their avowed homeland seemed particularly urgent to those who realized the scant number of Jews remaining in Palestine at that time. In 1880 fewer than 25,000 Jews lived in what they regarded as the Holy Land (see ch. 4, Population).

As modern nationalistic ideas began to appear in Europe during the 19th century, and as the Ashkenazim began to absorb these ideas, the Jews gradually developed plans for combining their efforts towards returning to the ancient Land of Israel on a worldwide basis. In furtherance of this concept the World Zionist Organization, named after Mount Zion in Jerusalem, was founded in 1897 by Theodor Herzl at Basel, Switzerland. Its primary purpose, as stated in the Basel program announced by the organization, was "to create for the Jewish people a home in Palestine secured by Public Law." The organization expanded its program to include fostering unity among Jewish people, supporting Jewish welfare activities and raising funds for the promotion of world Jewry.

The return movement began on a large scale in 1882. Led by Ashkenazim from northern and eastern European countries, it became known as the First Aliyah (literally, First Ascent) a name applied to the succeeding waves of immigration, five in all. The Second Aliyah (1904–14) was curtailed by the beginning of World War I, when the total immigrants since 1882 amounted to more than 55,000. Because of deportations by Ottoman Turks and other privations during the war, the total Jewish population in Palestine was reduced to 36,000 by the end of 1918 (see ch. 4, Population).

British Foreign Secretary Arthur James Balfour, in the so-called Balfour Declaration of November 2, 1917, officially encouraged the concept of establishing a national home for the Jewish people, and mass arrivals started again in 1919. Immigrations were spurred by persecutions incident to Polish pogroms in the 1920's and by the rise to power of Adolf Hitler in Germany. During Hitler's regime between 1933 and 1945 extermination camps were established in which several million European Jews were executed. The total number of arrivals mounted to more than 364,000 by the end of the Fifth Aliyah at the beginning of World War II—an average of more than 17,000 per year during that 21-year period (see ch. 4, Population).

By the end of the war in 1945, immigrants were again arriving in large numbers, and at the termination of the British Mandate in 1948, the total number of immigrants since 1919 was almost 483,000. The great majority of these arrivals, almost 90 percent, continued to be Ashkenazim, mainly from Europe and the Americas. During the next 3 years (1948–51), however, the number of Ashkenazi and Sephardi arrivals were almost equal, with each slightly in excess of 330,000. These included an influx of post-World War II displaced persons and other refugees from Central and Eastern Europe, as well as immigrants from North Africa and refugees from Arab countries, such as Iraq and Yemen.

Jewish spokesmen and Jewish people at large were not unanimous in favoring the establishment of a separate national state. Further, the motivations of modern Israel's founders, proponents, and people were not entirely the same in kind or degree. To some, birth of the

4

new state was a religious event of transcending spiritual significance; to others, it was the supreme accomplishment of Zionist political nationalism; to still others, especially displaced European Jews in the wake of World War II, Israel represented primarily an opportunity for security and a new life.

Most Arabs in the Middle East are derived largely from the same Semitic base as the ancient Jews but are principally Muslim in religion. The Arab states opposed establishment of the Israeli state, arguing that it was a foreign intrusion that displaced their peoples, the Palestinian Arabs being the majority element of the population, and took lands that had been predominantly Arab for 13 centuries.

A major aspect of the general character of the society has been repeatedly manifested by the persistent determination of the people to cooperate with their military and political leaders in what they contend are efforts to survive as a national unit, generally described as a paramount goal. Arab policies and actions are carefully scrutinized and are copiously criticized if unfriendly intent is thought to be detected. This characteristic is evidenced by the dynamic reaction of the people against what they maintain are Arab aggressions, particularly along the country's borders, where major armed clashes have occurred on three outstanding occasions: 1948, 1956, and 1967.

On the first occasion, Israeli leaders found sympathetic response to their appeals for a common defensive attitude toward the antagonistic comments made by Arab journalists and political leaders regarding the presence of this new state in the area. This defensive attitude was intensified when Israel was attacked on May 14, 1948, the day after its proclamation of independence. The attack was mounted by the regular armed forces of Egypt, Iraq, Jordan, Syria, and Lebanon, as well as volunteer elements from Saudi Arabia, Yemen, and Libya. Israeli leaders encountered no difficulty in accelerating and expanding the organization of their staff and combat elements. The hastily assembled forces were based mainly upon the Jewish Brigade, composed of volunteers who had fought with Allied forces during World War II, and upon the Hagana, volunteer home guard groups formed during the Mandatory period to protect Jewish settlements against hostile bands (see ch. 26, The Armed Forces).

The Arab armies, nevertheless, were defeated and a month-long truce, June 11 to July 9, 1948, was arranged by UN representatives. After repeated violations, with each side blaming the other, a second truce, starting July 19, was also breached. Later, armistice talks were initiated. On February 24, 1949, the first armistice agreement was signed with Egypt, and subsequently agreements were signed with Lebanon, Syria, and Jordan.

The second major clash occurred in 1956 after continued border skirmishes resulted in further deterioration of the situation despite the armistice agreements. The country's press and leaders cited mounting pressure against Israel indicated by guerrilla raids emanating from the Egyptian-held Sinai Peninsula and by the concurrent formation of a new alliance (Egypt, Jordan, and Syria). At the same time, Egypt's expropriation of the Suez Canal Company alienated Great Britain and France. They landed military forces at Port Said in early November 1956 and neutralized Egypt's air forces. Meanwhile, commencing October 29, Israeli forces attacked in the Sinai region, overran the peninsula, and opened the Red Sea and Gulf of Aqaba to Israeli shipping through the Strait of Tiran.

Facing combined pressure of the United States and the Soviet Union in the UN, Israel withdrew from the Sinai early in 1957. In furtherance of quiet in the area, UN Emergency Forces (UNEF) were stationed on the Egyptian side along the Egyptian-Israeli frontier and the entrance to the Strait of Tiran.

Despite these measures, border clashes continued and tensions mounted, particularly between Israel and Syria. The early 1960's saw the formation of Arab guerrilla bands, such as Al Fatah (founded in December 1964 by Palestinians in Syria), and lesser groups of irregulars, aimed at Israel. Their efforts were publicly acclaimed by officials in Syria, Jordan, and Egypt as contributing to the goal of recovering Palestinian Arab lands and rights lost in the 1948 conflict.

The third large-scale hostilities occurred in 1967, after the United Nations secretary general unsuccessfully attempted to resolve the difficulties. In May President Gamal Abdul Nasser demanded that the UNEF leave Egyptian territory. He also declared a blockade on Israel's ships using the Strait of Tiran and signed a pact with Jordan, placing Jordanian armed forces under Egyptian command. Arab guerrilla activity continued at a high level along the borders; Israel responded with retaliatory raids. Repeatedly during May, Israeli leaders made warning pronouncements, asserting that continuation of the infiltrations and border guerrilla activity would result in serious confrontations.

Israeli air, ground, and armored forces, on June 5, launched a large-scale attack against Egypt, Jordan, and Syria. Within 6 days the Israeli forces had occupied the Sinai Peninsula and the Gaza Strip, Jordan west of the Jordan River (including East Jerusalem), and the Golan Heights in southwestern Syria. On June 8 Jordan signed a truce agreement effective on the lines held by the opposing forces, Egypt signed on June 9, and Syria the next day.

In mid-1969 ramifications of the Arab-Israeli issue extended worldwide in scope. Attempts at accommodation by the UN and by pressures from outside powers had not been successful. Border clashes continued almost daily. The Arabs continued to refuse recognition of the new state and to reject direct negotiation with it. Israeli leaders continued to maintain that their primary concerns were security and the attainment of settlements negotiated directly with the Arab states, objectives the Israelis have not achieved by the military victories of 1948, 1956, and 1967 (see ch. 15, Foreign Relations).

The country's boundaries have never been recognized internationally and, for the most part, are not demarcated by recognizable terrain features. When crossing from Israel into one of the neighboring countries, however, striking differences in language, religion, cultural orientation, economic practices, and political ideologies can be quickly discerned.

In general the political frontiers are the result of complicated historical developments. For example, the frontier with the Egyptian Sinai Peninsula originated in 1906 by an agreement between Turkey and Great Britain, outlining the area to be controlled by the Egyptian rulers who were, at that time, nominally subject to the Turkish sultan. The northern frontiers with Lebanon and Syria resulted from prolonged British-French discussions during and after World War I regarding the limits of their respective mandate areas.

Borders with Jordan along the Jordan River southward to the Dead Sea and Wadi Ha Arava, called Wadi al Araba in Arabic, to the Gulf of Aqaba, were traced in 1923, at the beginning of the British Palestine Mandate period, when British authorities outlined the eastern limits of the areas they intended to define as the "Jewish National Home," which had earlier been only broadly specified in the Balfour Declaration of 1917 as being "in Palestine." The Jordan River, between the Dead Sea and Lake Tiberias, served as a demarcation line until the Arab attack in 1948, when the frontiers in that area were moved some 25 to 30 miles westward to reflect the front line positions of the armistice arrangements, sponsored by the UN, that went into effect at that time (see ch. 2, Physical Environment).

These boundaries continued to define the limits of the area under Israeli administration until the Six-Day War of June 1967, when military controls were applied to the territory occupied by Israeli troops at the time of the truce. This again reflected the position of the opposing forces when fighting ceased.

The newly acquired occupied territory involved expanded administrative responsibilities derived from the holding of Golan Heights in southwestern Syria, all of the area west of the Jordan River that had been previously annexed by Jordan, the Gaza Strip, and all of the Sinai Peninsula. This occupied territory under military control totaled approximately 26,500 square miles and was populated by almost 1,100,000 people, mostly Arabs, including some 500,000 refugees.

The society, despite its heterogeneous origins and its segmentation between Ashkenazim, Sephardim, and their Israeli-born descendants, known as Sabras, tends to be cohesive, especially in face of external threats. The people, on the whole, are secular and nationalist but have a sense of mutual Jewishness and strong, general respect for Jewish cultural traditions and history. The non-Jewish minority of more than 324,000 persons (mostly Muslim Arabs) within the bounds of pre-1967 Israel is generally quiescent, but not culturally assimilated in the Israeli state (see ch. 6, Social Structure).

The social structure theoretically is based on socialist and classless principles. Certain hierarchical features, nevertheless, have developed in the Jewish majority population as a result of political background and other factors, such as length of residence in Israel, whether or not a person is a native-born citizen (Sabra), his age and, to a limited extent, his region of origin if he was born outside the country. By mid-1969 these factors did not represent cleavages of such severity as to endanger the state. They were recognized by the authorities and were being countered by various measures.

Outstanding among the effective unifying influences applied to the diverse components of the society is compulsory service in the national defense forces. All young people of military age, male and female alike (except women with children), undergo continuous disciplinary training on active duty for 20 months or more, and thereafter for 31 consecutive days annually on reserve duty until the age of 49 for men and 34 for childless women. Another important unifying influence is the school system. In 1968 education was free and compulsory for all children aged 5 to 15. In addition, approximately 125,000 youths were enrolled in secondary schools throughout the land. Both military and academic training systems merged all groups, minimized class, ethnic, and language differences, and emphasized the necessity for national unity against outside threats (see ch. 26, The Armed Forces; ch. 9, Education).

Politics is a dynamic force within all segments of the population. Political parties are numerous (16 parties campaigned for seats in the Seventh Knesset), and most of them are active in the central and local government, in the Zionist organizations, and in the labor unions. Despite the broadly based political awareness and the multiplicity of parties, none has been strong enough to win an absolute majority in national elections. The result has been a series of coalition governments. In general, all parties favor settlement of the Arab-Israeli issue by direct negotiations with the Arab powers involved. Differences and fragmentations, resulting in alignments and coalitions, are usually based on variations of viewpoints or policies pertaining to labor, religion, nationalism, foreign affairs, or welfare practices (see ch. 14, Political Dynamics).

The various shades of political thought represented in the early years of the World Zionist Organization and the Jewish Agency became the basis for political parties even before statehood was achieved in 1948. For example, the political nationalist ideology of Zionism and the interest of its leadership in labor-socialistic policies resulted in the organization of Histadrut (Histadrut Ha'ovdim Haklalit—General Federation of Labor, commonly known as Histadrut). Within a decade, in 1930, its leaders organized a political party known as MAPAI (Mifleget Poalei Eretz Yisrael—Workers' Party, Land of Israel), also known as the Israel Labor Party (see ch. 22, Labor).

From the beginning, MAPAI has been the strongest labor group and the largest single political party, deriving most of its strength from the ranks of employed labor, from the kibbutzim (collective farm settlements), and from the moshavim (cooperative smallholder settlements). Its leadership includes many respected persons, such as David Ben-Gurion, Zalman Shazar, Golda Meir, Abba Eban, and many other founders of the state. The party's moderately socialist platform aims at maintaining immigration and a planned economy but, at the same time, encouraging public and private initiatives. Its socialist-Zionist ideology is sufficiently flexible to cooperate occasionally with other groups coping with the country's problems. By cooperating with other parties, it has retained its dominant political position and has ruled through coalition governments since statehood.

Another strong socialist-oriented political party is MAPAM (Mifleget Poalim Meuchedet—United Workers' party). It was founded in 1948 by the combination of an early labor youth group and a left-wing political group that had previously broken away from MAPAI. More to the left than MAPAI in political ideology, the party advocates public-owned enterprises, guaranteed real wages, training of youth in pioneering settlements, Jewish-Arab solidarity of the working class, independence of the labor movement from government control, and a neutralist foreign policy. Early in 1969 it agreed to ally with MAPAI and submit a joint list of candidates for the general elections to be held later in the year.

Political power is vested in the unicameral legislative body of 120 elected members constituting the Knesset. Subject to its approval, this power is wielded by the prime minister and his cabinet, officially known as "the government." All prime ministers have been members of the MAPAI party and, reinforced by the powerful Histadrut, this party has been preeminent in all governments.

Despite vigorous political activity, with almost universal political consciousness and participation in one form or another, the government has been stable. Changes have been relatively few and have occurred without threat of coups or violent overthrows. For example, the first president, Chaim Weizmann, served until his death in November 1952. His successor, Itzhak Ben-Zvi, served until his death in April 1963. He was succeeded by Zalman Shazar, who was reelected to his second 5-year term by the Knesset on March 26, 1968. Since statehood, the country has had 14 cabinets and only four prime ministers, David Ben-Gurion, Moshe Sharett, Levi Eshkol (deceased in office February 26, 1969, and the incumbent in mid-1969, Golda Meir.

The main opposition grouping is the GAHAL (Gush Herut-Liberalim—Freedom-Liberal Bloc, also known as the Herut-Liberal Bloc). It was formed in 1965 by the nationalist Herut (Freedom) and Liberal parties. GAHAL advocates strong security measures, annexation of all or most of the occupied territories seized in the Six-Day War of June 1967, and private enterprise as opposed to the socialistic principles of the MAPAI and MAPAM parties.

Despite the differences, sometimes vociferous in nature, between the ruling coalition and the opposition groups, or within the fragmented coalition, virtually all parties are dedicated to the state itself and to the concept of a parliamentary democracy. Confrontation with the threat from superior Arab numerical strength has resulted repeatedly in consolidating positions, closing gaps between groups, compromises, and the formation in 1967 of a "government of national unity," which included two cabinet ministers from GAHAL.

Exceptions to this general attitude are the two Communist parties. The older is MAKI (Mifleget Ha Kommunisti Yisraeli—Communist Party of Israel). Founded in 1919, it is anti-Zionist in doctrine and closely follows Soviet Union leadership. The other is RAKAH (Reshima Kommunistit Hadasha—the New Communist List). It split away from MAKI in 1965, and it also supports Soviet policy in the Middle East and elsewhere, including peace with the Arab states and friendship with all Communist countries.

Economic power lies mainly in Histadrut and its subsidiaries, which include agencies for marketing, banking, insurance, transportation, welfare activities, and other functions relating to labor, its management and output. Founded in 1920, it has continued to maintain close relations with MAPAI. Key officials in both organizations are also in top echelons of government and often the same person holds a high post in all three bodies. Consequently Histadrut, with its strong trade union membership of more than a million workers in 1968, is the predominant economic power in the country. Favored with assured support within the government, Histadrut also has an important influence on the development and financing of economic programs. Because of its pervasiveness throughout all echelons of society, it virtually serves as the government's chief consultant in formulating national policies pertaining to foreign as well as domestic affairs (see ch. 19, Character and Structure of the Economy).

The country's economy, on the whole, is expanding while gradually changing from one based on production by small agricultural collective and cooperative settlements (kibbutzim and moshavim) to one with industrial production rising in prominence. An average annual rate of increase in gross national product, amounting to about 10 percent since 1950, has been achieved despite Arab boycott, difficulties involved in absorbing large numbers of immigrants, costs related to maintaining a sizable defense force (requiring about 39 percent of total budget in fiscal year 1969/70) and a lack or scarcity of raw materials, especially oil, coal, or satisfactory hydroelectric power sites. In addition the climate is dry and large areas of soil are unproductive.

The expansive Negev region is a desert wasteland. Rainfall is concentrated in the winter months and sparse or absent during the remainder of the year. Drought years are frequent. Through government planning and financing, agricultural production has kept pace with the increasing population by extended irrigation, intensive cultivation, and employment of advanced scientific farming methods. The country's scientists are among the world's pioneers in experiments with desalinization and artificial rain (see ch. 20, Agriculture).

Total agricultural production has expanded since 1948 and, in 1968, it supplied about 80 percent of domestic needs, despite a threefold increase in population and a rising level of nutrition. Agriculture's share of the total domestic product, however, decreased from about 15 percent in 1958 to less than 10 percent in 1966.

Industry has developed rapidly since 1955, with a widely diversified output ranging from simple consumer goods to trucks, aircraft, and complicated electronic equipment. This progress was assisted by reparations, from the Federal Republic of Germany (West Germany), both in funds and in capital goods. In addition, substantial aid was received in the form of remittances, loans, and investments from Jewish sources outside of Israel, particularly from North America and Europe (see ch. 21, Industry).

Dependence on international trade, because of scarcity of natural resources, has been increased by the influx of immigrants. The large trade deficit is financed by capital imports, a high proportion of which do not require repayment. To achieve a viable economy, the authorities consider that dependence on this type of capital imports must be reduced, primarily by increasing industrial exports.

This situation is reflected in the high priority given economic affairs in the country's foreign relations. By 1964 diplomatic relations had been established with 54 countries, and in most instances efforts were made to explore potentialities for trade development in various fields.

The primary goal of the country's foreign policy is to achieve a settlement of the issues with neighboring Arab countries by direct negotiations with them. Diplomatic representatives seek to retain political support for Israel and to preclude its isolation internationally by explaining its position and by countering Arab influences that would seem to weaken this position (see ch. 15, Foreign Relations).

Israeli leaders affirm that in their quest for peace and economic balance they are confronted with two outstanding problems. One is associated with the Arab refugees resulting from the 1948 and 1967 conflicts. The refugees, numbering approximately 1.4 million, demand resettlement in their former homes or payment of property loss claims. The other problem arises from the persistent Arab refusal to negotiate directly with Israel and to accord Israel a place in the community of nations. The resolutions adopted September 1, 1967, at the summit meeting of Arab leaders in Khartoum (Sudan) made no reference to military action or a need to destroy Israel, but it included the consistent Arab position of "no recognition of Israel." At mid-1969 this position had not been officially reversed by any of the participants.

CHAPTER 2
PHYSICAL ENVIRONMENT

Israel is situated on the eastern Mediterranean coast in the land of Palestine, known to Christians, Muslims, and Jews as the Holy Land. Geographically, it is part of a land area called the Fertile Crescent, which includes Lebanon, Syria, Iraq, and Jordan, and forms a semi-circle around the northern end of the Syrian Desert; it is also part of the Levant, the eastern Mediterranean coast (see fig. 1).

Israel derives its name from Jacob, the grandson of Abraham, who, according to the Bible, was given the name Israel (contender with God) after his struggle with the angel. Jacob's 12 sons became the founders of the 12 Hebrew tribes, which were collectively called the Beni Israel (the sons of Israel); the name eventually was applied to the Jewish people. The emotional and historical associations of the name led the Zionists to call their state Israel.

Israel's boundaries are not recognized internationally, but the armistice lines established by the armistice agreements of 1949 had functioned as borders until the Six-Day War of June 1967. Within these lines, it has a Mediterranean coastline of 118 miles, a Dead Sea shoreline of 33 miles, and a coastline on the Red Sea of 7 miles. The border with Lebanon is 51 miles long, with Syria 48 miles, with Jordan 349, with the Gaza Strip 37, and with Egypt (United Arab Republic) 128 miles long. The total area bounded is 7,993 square miles.

PHYSICAL FEATURES

The country can be divided into three general areas, each having distinctive geographic and climatic features. From west to east these areas are designated as the coastal plain, the hill region, and the Jordan Rift Valley.

The fertile and humid coastal plain, stretching along the Mediterranean Sea, is only about 5 miles wide in the north, but it gradually widens to about 15 miles towards the south as it approaches the Gaza Strip (see fig. 2). In the center of the country it is called the Plain of Sharon, famous for orange growing.

The second zone consists of uplands. In the north, the Hills of Galilee represent a lower and gentler continuation of the Lebanon Mountains. The highest elevation in the country, Mount Meiron, rising 3,963 feet above sea level, is in these hills, which are bordered on

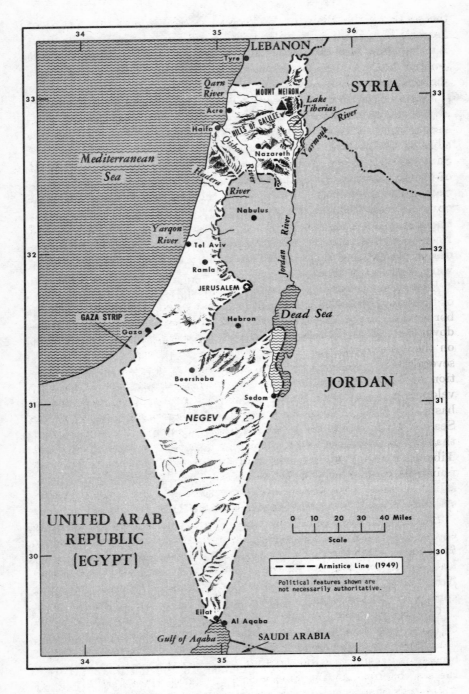

Figure 2. Topography and drainage of Israel.

14

the south by the Plain of Esdraelon, also known as the Valley of Jezreel. This Plain is 20 miles wide at the Bay of Haifa, only about 2 miles wide near the center, and wider again as it approaches the Jordan Valley. The Carmel Ridge, on the northwest of the Plain, shelters Haifa harbor, the only natural one in the country.

South of the Plain of Esdraelon lies another region of hills, generally divided into three sub-regions. The Shephela (Hashefela), consisting of foothills rising from the Plain of Sharon, forms the western edge of the central uplands. East of the Shephala lie the hills of Samaria and Judaea, former divisions of Palestine, the Biblical Land of Canaan, situated to the north and south of Jerusalem respectively. Samaria is more eroded into the hills than is Judaea, but there is no obvious break between them; most of this hill country lies within the Hashimite Kingdom of Jordan. A subsidence in the latitude of Beersheba separates the hills of Judaea from the hills of the Negev desert, an expansive spearhead-shaped wasteland, extending southward to the Gulf of Aqaba.

East of the central uplands lies the Jordan Rift Valley. It is part of the great Syrian-East African Rift that extends from the southern border of Turkey through Syria and Lebanon, Israel, and Jordan, down through the Red Sea, and through East Africa to Mozambique on the eastern coast of Africa. Within Israel it can be divided into several subsections. In the north, a basalt flow resulted in the formation of Lake Hula, which has been largely drained by Israeli developers to make room for farms and fish ponds. South of the Hula basin, the Jordan River flows into Lake Tiberias, also known as the Sea of Galilee, but to the Israelis as Lake Kinneret. It is much larger than the former Lake Hula, but is also formed by a basalt flow. Lake Tiberias is about 13 miles long, and about 7 miles wide at its broadest point; its surface lies 686 feet below sea level. Its waters are slightly saline because of the presence of underwater salt springs, but it nevertheless is used as an irrigation reservoir.

The Jordan flows south from Lake Tiberias and enters the northern end of the Dead Sea. Throughout this course it meanders through a floodplain called the Zor (Arabic, thicket) because of its thick tropical vegetation. The Zor is contained in a wider valley, the actual Rift Valley, which is called the Ghor (Arabic, depression); in the spring, the Jordan usually floods the Zor.

The surface of the Dead Sea is 1,302 feet below sea level. It is about 50 miles long, and its maximum width is about 11 miles. As the Jordan River nears the Dead Sea, its waters and the surrounding soils become increasingly saline because of the great amount of salts that the sea contains. At the surface each gallon of water contains 1.9 to 2.3 pounds of salts in solution, and at a depth of 360 feet, 2.7 pounds.

Between the Dead Sea and the Gulf of Aqaba lies a broad valley, the Wadi Ha Arava, called Wadi al Araba in Arabic. There are perennial streams to be found in this natural valley, but it forms the boundary between Israel and the Hashimite Kingdom of Jordan.

Occupied Territories

During the Six-Day War of June 1967, Israel occupied the Gaza Strip, the Sinai Peninsula, East Jerusalem, the entire West Bank area of Jordan, and the Golan Heights of southwestern Syria. After the war the territory newly brought under Israeli control totaled approximately 26,500 square miles, divided as follows: Gaza Strip, 140; Sinai, 23,622; East Jerusalem, 24; West Bank, 2,270; and Golan Heights, 444. The 1967 cease-fire lines stretched 523 miles, including 63 miles with Lebanon, 50 miles with Syria, 298 miles with Jordan (including 52 miles along the middle of the Dead Sea), and 112 miles with the United Arab Republic (including 104 miles along the Suez Canal). The occupied territories have a Mediterranean coastline of 142 miles, a Red Sea coastline of 393 miles and shoreline of 29 miles on the Dead Sea.

Rocks, Minerals, and Soils

Hill regions in the country are formed by simple upfolds, which in the north trend from north to south, but which in the Negev trend toward the southwest. Cross-faults and subsidences, some of them related to the Jordan Rift Valley system, divide the hills into sections.

Most of the rock series are sedimentary, although there are basalt outcroppings in Galilee, the Negev, and in the Jordan Valley. The principal rock type is a hard but permeable limestone. A chalky marl is frequently exposed in the central hill regions. In the Negev and along the coast, sandstone is common. The valleys and coastal regions contain recent alluvium and, in the Hula depression, deep deposits of peat are to be found.

Israel is not one of the mineral-rich regions of the world, but it nevertheless contains mineral deposits that are worthwhile exploiting commercially. A large deposit of low-grade copper ore is found at Timna, 15 miles north of Eilat at the tip of the Gulf of Aqaba and, since 1958, has been mined and concentrated there. Large quantities of gypsum are located in the Negev and in Galilee and are mined for use in cement production. Sands and clays for use in ceramic and glass manufacture are also mined in the Negev.

Phosphates are located at Oron and at several other places in the northeastern Negev. Phosphates containing exploitable traces of uranium are found southeast of Arad, also in the northeastern Negev. Only the Oron deposit is being worked, but there are plans to exploit the others.

Petroleum has been discovered in the coastal plain some 20 miles south of Ashdod at Helez, Beror, Hayil, and Kokhav, and a small percentage of the country's petroleum requirement is produced there. Other parts of the coastal plains, and offshore, and areas near the Dead Sea, seem favorable for the discovery of other petroleum reserves. Natural gas is extracted in the Arad region of the northeastern section of the Negev.

Limestone, suitable for both building stone and cement production, can be found in most parts of the country. Sufficient quantities of sand, gravel, and lime for building are also available. Good quality granite for building is located near Eilat, but quarrying has been discontinued because of technical and economic difficulties.

The Dead Sea is one of Israel's greatest mineral resources. Potassium chloride, bromides, and table salt are extracted from its waters, and plans are being made to extract magnesium and calcium chloride as well. Salt is quarried at Sedom, located at the southern end of the Dead Sea, but is extracted from the Mediterranean Sea near Haifa.

Other minerals, such as iron ore, sulphur, mica, manganese ore, barium sulphate, and orthoclase feldspar, all useful in industry, have also been found in the country. The small quantity of these ores, transportation difficulties and, in many cases, the poor quality of the ore have prevented their exploitation.

The best soil for agriculture occurs along the coastal plain and in the Plain of Esraelon. Along the coast, the soil is sand or sandy loam, except where a swamp has been created by sand dunes blocking the access of a stream to the sea. In the Plain of Esdraelon the soil is mainly heavy alluvium or swamp soil. In the limestone hills of Galilee, Judaea, and Samaria, a reddish soil called terro rossa is predominant; although easily eroded, it is fertile. The chalky base rock, also widespread, gives rise to a less fertile soil called rendzina, a reddish soil found in humid areas. The basalt soils, found in certain parts of Galilee, resemble the terra rossa.

In the Beersheba region of the Negev, a fine-grained soil called loess, which has been deposited by wind is common. Farther south the soil consists of sand and gravel; in many places, desert pavement, a hard aggregate of wind-driven pebbles, is present. In the Hula region of the Jordan Valley, the soil contains heavy amounts of organic matter, and toward the Dead Sea, it contains mineral salts.

Soil erosion is a problem throughout most of the country. The terra rossa and rendzina are easily eroded, and the loess forms a hard crust which is then eroded into badland topography. In limestone areas, ground water dissolves the rock giving rise to karat, a topography characterized by sinks, underground channels, caves, and sharp ridges. In Judaea, where the limestone and the more resistant marl alternate, natural terraces are formed in the hills.

In areas with sandy soil along the coast, as well as in terra rossa or rendzina regions, the interaction of solar heat and mineral-bearing ground waters produces below the surface a thick rock-like layer known as hardpan; this layer may inhibit the growing of deep-rooted crops. Along the coast, and in parts of the desert, sand dunes are formed. These dunes may be consolidated by minerals in solution, or they may drift with the wind.

Climate

Israel has a Mediterranean climate, characterized by a long, hot, dry summer and a short, cool, rainy winter. Fall is a transitional season, characterized by a gradual lowering of temperatures and little

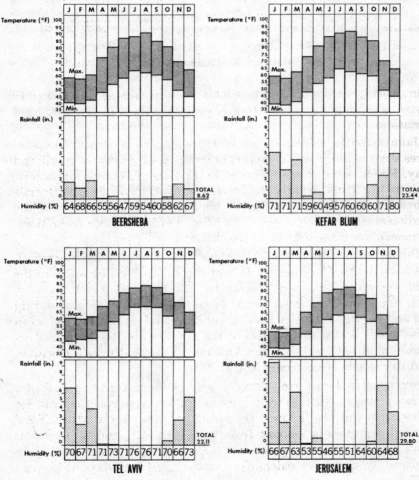

Figure 3. Israel weather data, 1967.

Source: Adapted from Israel, *Statistical Abstract of Israel, 1968*, No. 19, Jerusalem, 1968.

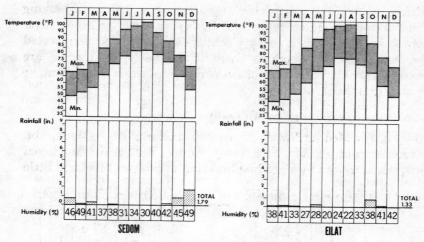

Figure 3.—Continued.

rain; spring occurs when the winter rains cause the vegetation to revive. The basic climatic pattern is locally modified by topographical variation.

January is the coldest month and August, the warmest. Temperatures drop rapidly in November, but rise more slowly in April and May. Frosts occur in the hills and in some sheltered interior valleys, such as the Hula depression. Summer temperatures frequently rise above 100°F. The daily range of temperature is narrowest for the Mediterranean coast and widest at Eilat, which is remote from Mediterranean maritime influences (see fig. 3).

During the summer, winds blow eastward from the Mediterranean Sea onto the land during the day; at night, the wind blows from the land westward out to sea. During the winter, wind directions vary. Hot, dry winds may enter Israel from the south or the east during fall and spring. Visibility may be impaired and crops damaged when these winds occur; the dryness of the air produces tenseness and irritability in both animals and humans. Occasionally in the winter, cold dry winds come from Central Asia.

Summers in Israel are virtually without rain. During the winter or rainy season, the rain usually comes in heavy storms that last for a few days and are followed by periods of clear dry weather. Total rainfall decreases in amount from north to south, and to an extent from west to east; it is greater at higher altitudes, where it may be replaced by snow; Jerusalem, for example, had four days of snow in 1967.

Dewfall provides moisture that is often of value to agriculture; it is heaviest along the coast, particularly at Mount Carmel near Haifa.

Humidity gradients tend to follow rainfall gradients. Most of the country is arid or semiarid with high rates of evaporation.

Climate in Israel is determined mainly by latitude, proximity to the sea, and topography. A salient feature is its variability. Several years of drought may be followed by a year with heavy precipitation; rainfall may vary widely from place to place in the same period. Within a single rainy season, the rainfall, although sufficient in quantity, may be so erratic as to adversely affect agriculture.

The government of Israel maintains 22 meteorological stations throughout the country; some of them have records going back as far as the 1930's. Since the main factors affecting climate are altitude, latitude, nearness to the sea, and geographic zone, representative samples of the country's climate can be obtained from data collected at six of these stations: Tel Aviv, Jerusalem, Beersheba, Kefar Blum, Sedom, and Eilat. Tel Aviv is on the central Mediterranean coast at an altitude of 10 feet above sea level; Jerusalem is in the central hill zone at an altitude of 2,660 feet; Beersheba is on the northern fringe of the Negev hill region, and is 920 feet above sea level; Kefar Blum is at the northern end of the Jordan Valley, surrounded by hills, and is 250 feet above sea level; Sedom is located on the southern end of the Dead Sea, within the Jordan Rift Valley, at an altitude of 1,280 feet below sea level; Eilat, on the Gulf of Aqaba, is also in the Jordan Rift Valley, and like the other stations in this valley, is remote from Mediterranean influences. It is 40 feet above sea level.

Humidity is highest along the Mediterranean coast and lowest in the Jordan Rift Valley. Precipitation, therefore, is the highest in the intervening hill regions, since rain-bearing clouds from the Mediterranean lose much of their moisture over the hills, and lowest in the rift valley. Temperatures respond to both altitude and latitude, so that they are highest in southern regions of low altitude, and lowest in northern hill regions.

Drainage

Israel is not endowed with abundant rivers. There are few springs and streams, most of which carry water after winter rainfalls. The Jordan River, which forms part of the boundary with the Hashimite Kingdom of Jordan, is the largest river. The only streams of importance are small, flowing out of the hills into the Mediterranean Sea. One is the Qishon, which drains the Plain of Esdraelon and empties into the Mediterranean Sea near Haifa; the other is the Yarqon, which flows into the sea at Tel Aviv, and is the southermost perennial stream in the Levant.

In the southern part of the country, the drainage system consists of empty stream channels (wadis) and dry lakes, which are filled only after the rare rainfalls. Much of the water that falls, even in the north, runs off and is not absorbed into the ground, especially at the beginning of the rainy season when the ground is hard. Nevertheless, where permeable strata crop out or where there are faults, springs emerge, even in the desert where they create oases.

PLANT AND ANIMAL LIFE

Native plant life in Israel is adapted to the Mediterranean climate of a short, rainy winter, and a long, hot, dry summer. There are two main types of adaptation. One type, exemplified in grasses and other annuals, completes its life cycle during the wet season and then dies, leaving its seeds in the soil to germinate during the next wet season. The other type has structural adaptations to the climate. Some plants spring up during the rainy season, and then lie dormant during the dry season while nutrients are stored in a bulb underground. Other plants reduce evaporation by decreasing the number of stomata (openings for loss of water), by the development of thicker and smaller leaves, or by acquisition of hairy, waxy, or cork-like coatings. Furthermore, some plants have made a special adaptation to the saline soils of the Jordan Rift Valley. A few of these, such as the tamarisk shrubs and trees, can eliminate surplus salt through the leaves.

Israel's plant life is varied, both because of the variation in climate and soil within the country and because of its position as a meeting ground of different geographic zones. In addition, the activities of man have added to the varieties of plants.

In the northern part of the country, hills in the uncultivated regions are covered with a low dense growth of thorny aromatic shrubs and small trees, such as buckthorn and dwarf oak; in a few places, remnants of evergreen forest remain. In the deserts and coastal sand dune areas the vegetation cover is sparse, and the plants, well adapted to drought conditions, are often entirely without leaves and have short growth cycles. For examples, the acacia is a common tree in the Negev. In the swampy areas along the coast, in the Jordan Rift Valley, and in desert oases, varieties of plants requiring high temperatures and large quantities of water are to be found, such as papyrus, palms, and rushes.

Cultivated plants include the citrus trees, wheat and other grains, cotton, olives, grapes, and vegetables, such as eggplant, onions, and squash. Agricultural conditions are variable enough to permit the introduction of plants from most parts of the world; numerous plants, such as corn, peanuts, sugar beets, tomatoes, and many others have been brought in from foreign countries.

Zionist settlers were eager to plant forests to replace those destroyed by overgrazing and from military activities over the centuries, as well as to aid in making land available for cultivation and in reducing erosion. One of the most important trees introduced from foreign lands is the eucalyptus from Australia, which in many regions has a Mediterranean climate similar to that of Israel. Tamarisks, in addition to the evergreen carobs and pines, are also used for erosion reducing purposes.

Centuries of human occupation have drastically altered the country's animal life, causing some species to become extinct and others to appear, either by deliberate introduction or by inadvertently creating a favorable environment. The establishment of Zionist settlements has hastened this process in the 20th century. One example is the Hula swamps, which have been drained but were once a vast wildlife preserve; the altered environment supports an entirely different animal population.

Invertebrates are the most numerous type of animal, especially since they are less apt to be disturbed by human occupation. There are spiders, some of them poisonous, and scorpions. Varieties of planteaters abound, such as grasshoppers and locusts, which are a threat to crops. Flies, mites, and ticks are still potential disease carriers, as are certain varieties of water snails. Disease carrying mosquitoes have largely been eliminated through swamp draining and spraying activities (see ch. 8, Living Conditions).

Amphibians are relatively scarce because the country is dry, and their numbers have been further reduced by swamp drainage. Reptiles are more abundant, and because of the warm dry climate, lizards and chameleons are common. There are many varieties of snakes, of which three species are poisonous, the most common being the Palestine viper.

Birdlife is abundant, but its character has been drastically altered by Zionist settlement activities. Hawks and owls have retreated to remote areas, whereas blackbirds, sparrows, and swallows have been attracted by the presence of new houses, fields, and gardens. Many bird species use the country as a passageway for their annual migrations.

There are many varieties of mammals, but their numbers are few because of the intense and long-standing human occupation of the country. Many species are adapted to the arid climate, with nocturnal habits and efficient utilization of available water. Gazelles, jackals, wild boars, and wildcats still survive in remote areas. Smaller mammals, such as bats, rodents, badgers, shrews, and foxes are more common. Black and Norway rats, which accompany human settlement, inhabit the coastal cities and may harbor disease-bearing organisms (see ch. 8, Living Conditions).

Marine life along the Mediteranean littoral is not abundant because of the salinity of the waters and the lack of nutrients; in general, it resembles that of the Atlantic. Tropical species are found along the

Red Sea coast. Various species of carp and catfish thrive in Lake Tiberias; they are also raised in fishponds, and constitute an important part of the food-producing industry.

CULTURAL FEATURES

Water Development

One of Israel's greatest problems is the acquisition, storage, control, and transport of water. Rainfall must be prevented from flooding and eroding the soil; it must be diverted into reservoirs, or allowed to enter the underground water table. Streams and rivers must be damned to store water and control floods. Water is most plentiful in the north, leaving the greatest amount of uncultivated land in the south, in the Negev desert. Both ground and surface waters may become contaminated by dissolved mineral salts, either from seepage from the sea along the coast, or by erosion.

The Israelis have had some success in restoring ancient cultivation methods and facilities, such as those of the Nabataeans people of an ancient Palestinan kingdom, and their Roman successors. Old dams and channels have been cleared and old wells restored. New wells have been dug, but pumping has drastically lowered the water table and permitted the ingress of sea water. Research has been carried out on the use of saline waters in agriculture and on the desalinization of sea water.

The terracing of hillsides to check erosion and provide level land for crops is an ancient practice in the country; in some hill regions, alternate horizontal hard and soft strata formations resulted in natural terraces. The Zionists, and later the Israeli land developers, have greatly expanded the amount of terraced land.

All water resources within the country are the property of the state, which regulates their distribution and use on a comprehensive national basis. Lake Tiberias is used as both a water source and as a reservoir. Water is pumped from it and led south and west into the northwestern part of the Negev along the government-owned and -operated water transportation system, the National Water Carrier, composed of canals, pipelines, and tunnels.

There are also smaller regional water development schemes. Water from springs at Rosh Ha Ayin (10 miles east of Tel Aviv) supplies the Tel Aviv area, and is also pumped into the National Water Carrier. Water is pumped from Nir Am (about 10 miles south of Ashqelon) to the northern part of the Negev. Jerusalem receives its water from Rehovot (about 15 miles southeast of Tel Aviv), Kefar Uriya (about 15 miles west of Jerusalem), and from Solomon's Pools (about 10 miles southwest of Jerusalem). Water from springs in Galilee is supplied to the Plain of Esdraelon; in the Plain, a lake at Kefar Barukh on the Qishon serves as a reservoir.

Transport

Despite the country's central location on the eastern Mediterranean coast, it does not serve as a regional transport center because of bad relations with its neighbors (see ch. 15, Foreign Relations). Land transport systems (roads and railways) are for internal use only since the borders are closed; only ships and airplanes communicate with more distant ports (see fig. 4).

In 1892 construction was completed on the first rail line (meter gauge) from Jaffa to Jerusalem. In 1905 a line was built from Haifa to the southern shore of Lake Tiberias. This line was later extended to link with the Hijaz Railway, connecting Damascus with the Muslim Holy Cities in Arabia.

Military requirements during World War I caused an intensification of railway building activity. In 1917 the British built a standard gauge line from Haifa southward into Sinai. The Turks, at about the same period, built a line from Nabulus (then in Palestine, subsequently in Jordan, but since 1967 in the Israeli occupied area) to Lod (10 miles southeast of Tel Aviv), then south to Beersheba and the Egyptian frontier. Turkish demands for railway fuel during World War I resulted in deforestation of much of Palestine and Lebanon.

During World War II, the British improved the line running from Haifa through Sinai to Egypt and, in 1942, continued it northward to Beirut and on to Tripoli in Lebanon. After the establishment of Israel in 1948, all rail links to other countries were closed. Some lines within the country have tended to fall into disuse, because they no longer connected important points.

Railroads are secondary to roads in the land transport system, since roads are less expensive to build and maintain and are much easier to construct over the rugged terrain characteristic of much of the country. Nevertheless, since 1948, new rail lines have been constructed. The one from Tel Aviv to Haifa is the heaviest-used line in the country. Another line connects Jerusalem and Haifa via Lod and Hadera. The second most important line connects Tel Aviv with Beersheba; it was built during the mid-1950's. A branch connects this line with the new port city of Ashdod about 20 miles south of Tel Aviv. In 1965 the line was extended to Dimona in the northeastern part of the Negev. Lines to other locations in the Negev were under construction in early 1969.

Israel has 472 miles of railway lines; all are standard gauge and all are owned and operated by the state. Despite the costs and the competition from other means of transportation, efforts have been made to modernize the equipment and facilities.

In 1967 the government maintained about 2,500 miles of roads. Some, although recent, follow ancient routes, but others are entirely

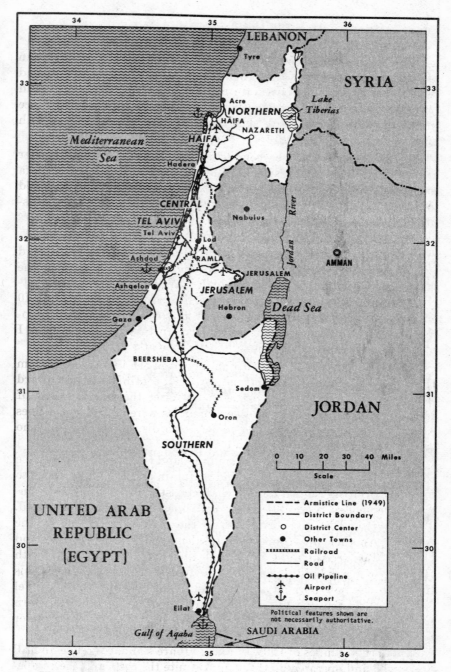

Figure 4. Transportation system and administrative districts, Israel.

new. International road linkages were severed after establishment of the state in 1948, and since then some roads have fallen into disuse.

The principal highways connect Tel Aviv, Jerusalem, and Haifa. Other important roads lead from Tel Aviv and Jerusalem to Beersheba and south to Eilat; also from Haifa and Tel Aviv to the Galilee region and the upper Jordan Valley. Other highways connect smaller cities and towns, and lead to developing areas, particularly in the Negev. Mining, industrial, port and pipeline construction, and operating activities in the southern part of the country have been a great impetus to road construction throughout the 1960's.

Initially, road-building emphasized speed of construction at the expense of quality. Roadbeds wore out quickly, driving conditions were often dangerous, and road size was not always adequate to carry the traffic. By the late 1960's the pace of development had slackened, and road improvement was emphasized. By early 1969 long stretches of the major highways in the center of the country had four lanes. Improvements and additions to the road system continued to be carried out.

The country has numerous airfields, most of them small and used only for local freight or crop dusting aircraft, or by the military forces. The principal international airport is at Lod (Lydda) near Tel Aviv. Other important airports are at Eilat, Haifa, and just north of Jerusalem. Air transport is important because international land communication is lacking. Improvements to Lod Airport have kept pace with the increases in air traffic.

Shipping is also important because of the absence of international land communications. In ancient times, Jaffa and Acre (later called Yafo and Akko, respectively) were busy ports; Acre, which has a natural harbor, became a stronghold for the crusaders but its importance decreased after their departure at the end of the Middle Ages, and Jaffa was traditionally the port for Jerusalem. There was no natural shelter at Jaffa, only a slight bend in the coastline. The water was so shallow that ships had to anchor well out to sea, using smaller vessels to transport passengers and freight. The port of Haifa was opened in 1933. It soon began to rival the Tel Aviv-Jaffa Harbor. Ports were opened at Eilat on the Gulf of Aqaba, providing egress to the Red Sea, and at Ashdod on the Mediterranean coast in 1965; at that time, the port facilities of Tel Aviv-Jaffa were closed because they were no longer needed. The state operates and develops the three ports of Eilat, Ashdod, and Haifa.

Before 1948 the Iraq Petroleum Company pipeline from the Kirkuk oilfields, north of Baghdad, crossed Jordan and Palestine and terminated at Haifa, where there was a refinery and oil-shipping facilities. After 1948 the Mediterranean outlet for the Kirkuk field and the company's refining operations were moved to Tripoli in

Lebanon, and the pipeline was abandoned. The Israelis constructed a 16-inch pipeline from Eilat to the installations at Haifa, which are now used by the Israeli state.

Since the closing of the Suez Canal in 1967, the Israeli government has begun construction on a 42-inch pipeline that is to extend from Eilat to Ziqim on the Mediterranean coast near Ashqelon, about 30 miles south of Tel Aviv. The new line is expected to be completed in late 1969. Eilat already has facilities for receiving and storing oil. Storage tanks are being built at Ziqim, and it is planned that oil tankers there will receive oil through floating pipelines while anchored offshore.

Political Divisions

Israel is divided into six administrative districts: Northern (center, at Nazareth), Haifa (center, at Haifa), Central (center, at Ramla), Tel Aviv (center at Tel Aviv), Jerusalem (center, at Jerusalem), and Southern (center at Beersheba). They are not equal in land area but vary in size in inverse proportion to population (see fig. 4). The administrative districts are divided into 14 subdistricts, which also serve as voting districts, although they are not constituencies (see ch. 13, The Government System).

Settlement Patterns

Historically, rural settlement patterns in Palestine resulted principally from the need for security. During centuries of external threats, settlements tended to be concentrated in the hill regions away from the coast and relatively inaccessible. At times, when internal conditions were unsettled, village communities tended to be clustered in small areas on hilltops and surrounded by their fields. At times the rural population declined sharply because of a movement to cities, or a change to nomadic life.

Toward the end of the Ottoman period, both internal and external security had improved. Farmers began to move down from the hills into the coastal plain. At the same time the first groups of Zionist settlers began to arrive. They settled in the coastal plain because it was more accessible, less densely populated, and because it resembled the plains of Central Europe from which many of them had come. By the 1960's those Arabs who remained in Israel tended to be concentrated in the hill regions as well as in the thickest Jewish settlements of the coastal plain.

Urban settlements have been distributed in response to communication routes and facilities, such as ports, accessibility to regions of importance in agriculture or mineral resources, and in the case of cities like Jerusalem, historical and religious associations. Israel's three principal cities are Haifa, a major port, Tel Aviv, a former port, centrally located on the coastal plain, and Jerusalem.

In the 20th century some new factors have influenced population distribution within the country. Because of the need to provide both space and livelihood for new immigrants, unsettled regions have been developed for industry and agriculture. Since Israeli statehood, the principal focus for new settlement has been the Negev. Another consideration that determined the location of new settlements was defense. Fortified villages were placed along the borders to ensure security.

CHAPTER 3
HISTORICAL SETTING

Israel is a young nation created as a Jewish state in 1948 within the territory of Palestine held by Great Britain under a League of Nations Mandate. Modern Israel's inhabitants are preponderantly Jews, principally immigrants since World War II or their descendants. The land and its associations with the Jewish people have a long and complex history, much of it interwoven with that of the people in other countries, particularly with the Arabs of the eastern Mediterranean region.

The earliest settlers with whom modern Israel identifies itself culturally and historically were from a Mesopotamian Semitic stock who established themselves in Canaan, later known as Palestine. After several generations, they became known as Jews. Over the centuries, interspersed with varying periods of Jewish independence, the land was ruled by foreign conquerors, and the people were subjected to deportation, exile, and dispersion. Consequently, sizable groups established communities in various countries throughout the world, particularly in Europe and around the Mediterranean.

Wherever they went, the Jewish people retained significant historical, cultural, and religious traditions, which contributed to a sense of common identity and to hopes for eventual return to the land of ancient Israel.

Creation of the modern state of Israel in 1948 was the culmination of 50 years of effort by the World Zionist Organization, the first significant outside impetus being given by the endorsement of a Jewish National Home in Palestine by Great Britain's Balfour Declaration in 1917. During the late 19th and early 20th centuries, the groundwork had been laid by the establishment of social welfare and economic institutions to enable and maintain Jewish immigration to Palestine. As a result, the small country has absorbed many people with a wide variety of languages and backgrounds.

Understanding of the new state is facilitated by knowledge of the origins and historical vicissitudes of the Jewish people, their strong cultural identification with the land of ancient Israel, the emergence of the Zionist movement and associated events of World War I, the experiences under the British Palestine Mandate (1923–48), as well as the major events subsequently influencing the development of the state.

The people and the government manifest a lively interest in Israel's antiquity and its history throughout the ages. In discussing modern issues and events, frequent references to the historic past serve to link it with the present and to draw benefits from its lessons while coping with modern developments.

JEWISH ORIGINS AND ANCIENT ISRAEL

Establishing modern Israel's concept of connection with the past, the Proclamation of Independence of May 14, 1948, declares at the start:

> In the land of Israel the Jewish people came into being. In this land was shaped their spiritual, religious, and national character. Here they lived in sovereign independence. Here they create a culture of national and universal import, and gave to the world the eternal Book of Books.

Occupation of the region west of the Jordan Rift, known in ancient times as Canaan, later both as Israel and Palestine, extends back to the Paleolithic era. Neanderthal remains from at least 100,000 years ago have been identified. The Jews of ancient Israel appear to have derived from an early Mesopotamian Semitic line, part of the population movements of the Middle Bronze Age from east and north into the previously settled, Egyptian-dominated area of Canaan. These migrations are not precisely dated, but are believed to have occurred in the 20th and 19th centuries B.C. In Biblical narratives the line of Jewish patriarchs headed by Abraham appears, vague in history but clear in cultural memory, and continues down through Moses, the Exodus from Egypt, and the Hebrew return to Canaan.

In this account Abraham led his family from Ur in Chaldaea, southern Mesopotamia, through Syria and southwest into Canaan. Here Abraham made the first Hebrew lodgment and received the divine covenant (Genesis 12:7): "Unto thy seed will I give this land." In return, Abraham was to serve only this single God of the covenant, and the rite of circumcision was instituted as the token of the contract. Later, possibly during the Hyksos invasions of Egypt in the late 18th century B.C., some of Abraham's Hebrew descendants migrated to Egypt, where they remained, according to tradition, for 400 years. After the Hyksos were expelled about 1570 B.C., the Hebrews fell under Egyptian bondage which lasted until the Exodus under Moses. This movement back to Canaan, the "Promised Land," may have occurred in the 13th century, B.C., during the reign of Pharoah Rameses II, circa 1304–1237 B.C. The central hero is Moses, traditionally portrayed in the dual role of leader and priest-prophet, maker of the nation and organizer of the Hebrew religion. During years of nomadic adversity in the Sinai wilderness, the Ten Commandments were written and Mosaic law was formed. Identity of people and religion was firmly established along with independence and a loose sovereignty linking them in their common effort to reenter the land.

Joshua, successor of Moses, led the people of Israel as they entered Canaan. The Canaanites were still in the land, and on the coast were the Philistines, from whom the word "Palestine" is derived. During the 13th to 11th centuries B.C., the Hebrew tribal peoples experienced only a loose political cohesion, usually for military purposes in times of stress, under a succession of tribal leaders known as judges. The Philistine and Canaanite peoples fought, lived with, and received tribute from or paid tribute to the Hebrews in fluctuating, uneasy accommodation. During this time, Jewish principles stressed unity of people and religion, rejected other gods (the idol worship and orgiastic rites of the Canaanite Baal cult), and maintained the ancient claim to the land. When times were good, the people tended to backslide and accommodate despite the denunciations of ancient prophets. In danger and bad times, the stern disciplines of their own Jewish law were reasserted for unity, self-preservation, and advancement.

History becomes more precise with establishment of the Kingdom of Israel under Saul, circa 1020 B.C. David, the Psalmist king (circa 1000–961 B.C.) conquered Jerusalem and established his capital there. Under Solomon his son (circa 961–922 B.C.), the first temple was built and ancient Israel reached its zenith. After Solomon, the kingdom split in two: Israel, to the north, had its capital at Samaria, near modern Nabulus, 30 miles north of Jerusalem, and encompassed 10 of the old twelve tribes; Judah, to the south, had its capital still at Jerusalem and encompassed the remaining two tribes. In 722 B.C. the northern kingdom fell to the Assyrian conqueror, Shalmaneser V (726–722 B.C.), whose successor Sargon deported its Jews in vast numbers and replaced them with people from Mesopotamia in an apparent effort to eliminate the Jews by exile and diffusion. The southern kingdom of Judah, although tributary to Assyria, preserved a shaky political independence until the Assyrian empire broke up before the growing power of Babylon.

In July 587 (or 586) Jerusalem was burned, and the walls and temple destroyed. The last king of Judah and thousands of selected Jews were carried off to captivity in Babylon by Nebuchadnezzar II (also known as Nebuchadrezzar II). Many of the remaining Jews migrated to Egypt. Among those in Babylon, some adapted themselves to the new surroundings and lost their identity, as did the northern Jews whom Sargon had deported more than a century earlier. A hard core in Babylon maintained the unity of people and religion; from these and later dispersions derived the Jewish communities of Mesopotamia, which remained to modern times.

Babylon, in its turn, fell before Cyrus II of Persia in 539 B.C. The liberal Cyrus, memorialized by the Hebrew prophet Isaiah, allowed voluntary return of the Jewish exiles to the ancestral land beginning in 538 B.C. and the temple was rebuilt at Jerusalem in the years 520–515 B.C. There followed a period of Jewish theocratic unity, with local autonomy under Persian suzerainty, until Alexander's conquest of the area in 332 B.C. With Alexander came the Greek language, literature, and ways of life. In Jerusalem, as elsewhere, Hellenistic tendencies gained a footing among the Jews in contention, like the earlier Canaanite Baal deviations, with orthodox Jewish tenets. After Alexander's death in 323 B.C., his eastern empire fell to rival Greek generals and became divided between the Ptolemies of Egypt and the Seleucids of Syria.

Judaea (formerly Judah) was at the strategic crossroads and was caught between Egypt and Syria. Ptolemaic overlordship was succeeded by Seleucid control in 198 B.C. In time, the practice of Jewish customs and religion was harshly repressed as constituting a source of disaffection and rebellion. After an interval of ineffectual passive resistance, the Jewish Revolt of the Maccabees broke out in 168 B.C. at the instigation of an aged priest named Mattathias and under the dynamic leadership of Judas Maccabaeus, his son. His victories over the Syrians led to rededication of the temple in Jerusalem in December 165 B.C., an event since celebrated annually by Jews as the Feast of Rededication (Hanukah). Judas fell in battle in 161 B.C., but the revolt continued under his brothers Jonathan (161–143 B.C.) and Simon (143–135 B.C.), the latter of whom was recognized as high priest and ruler of Judaea in 143 B.C. Jewish independence was thus reestablished, and the four identities—land, people, political sovereignty, and religion—were restored.

Under the Hasmonaean (Maccabean) line that followed, Judaea became in extent and power comparable to the ancient Davidic dominion. Rulers, however, became corrupt and oppressive. Internal political and religious discord ran high, especially between the Pharisees, fundamental interpreters of the Jewish law and tradition, and the Sadducee faction, supporters of imperialistic royal policies. In 64 B.C. dynastic contenders for the throne appealed for support to Pompey, who was then establishing Roman power in Asia Minor. In the next year Roman legions seized Jerusalem with much carnage, and Pompey installed one of the contenders for the throne as high priest, but without the title of king. Eighty years of independent Jewish sovereignty ended, and the period of Roman dominion began.

ROME AND BYZANTIUM IN PALESTINE

In the subsequent period of Roman wars, the half-Jew Herod was confirmed by the Roman Senate as King of Judaea in 39 B.C. and reigned from 37 B.C. until his death in 4 B.C. Nominally independent, Judaea was actually a client state of Rome, and the land was formally annexed in A.D. 6 as part of the Province of Syria. Among the Jews in Jerusalem, two councils, called Sanhedrins, developed. The political Sanhedrin was composed primarily of the Sadducee aristocracy and was charged by the Roman procurator with over-watching and reporting on civil order, specifically in matters involving imperial directives. The religious Sanhedrin of the Pharisees was concerned with the Jewish religious law and doctrine, which the Romans disregarded as long as civil order was not threatened. Foremost among the Pharisee leaders of the time were the noted teachers Hillel and Shammai. The era of Christianity began under the governorship of Pontius Pilate, who was Roman Procurator of Judaea from A.D. 26 to 36.

Chafing under foreign rule, the Jewish nationalist movement of the fanatical sect known as Zealots seriously challenged Roman control in a rebellion which broke out in A.D. 66. After a protracted siege begun by Vespasian, the Roman commander in Judaea, and completed under his son Titus in September A.D. 70, Jerusalem and the temple, which was the focus of Jewish life and culture, were seized and destroyed by the Roman legions. The last Zealot survivors perished in A.D. 73 at the mountain fortress of Masada, some 35 miles southeast of Jerusalem above the west coast of the Dead Sea.

During the siege of Jerusalem, Rabbi Yohannan Ben Zakki received Vespasian's permission to withdraw to the small Jewish school at the town of Jabneh on the coastal plain, about 15 miles southwest of present-day Tel Aviv. There an academic Sanhedrin was set up which soon established itself as the central religious authority, with jurisdiction recognized by Jews in Palestine and beyond. Roman rule, nevertheless, continued. The Emperor Hadrian (A.D. 117–138), endeavoring to establish cultural uniformity, issued several repressive edicts, including one against circumcision. These sparked the significant Bar Kochba-Rabbi Akiba revolt of A.D. 132–135, which was crushed by Severus, the Roman commander. Hadrian then suppressed the Sanhedrin, closed the center at Jabneh, and prohibited both the study of the Jewish Scripture (the Torah) and the observance of the Jewish pattern of life derived from it.

Judaea became Syria Palestina, Jerusalem was renamed Aelia Capitolina, and Jews were forbidden to come within sight of the city. Once a year, on the anniversary of the destruction of the temple, controlled entry was permitted allowing Jews to mourn at a remaining fragment on the temple site which became known as the "Wailing Wall." With these repressions by Hadrian, the political history of the Jewish state in antiquity ended. Jews were again dispersed throughout the known world. This movement became known as the Diaspora, literally the "Dispersion," a term applied collectively and referring in general to Jews living outside Palestine. Since 1948 it has referred to those living outside the state of Israel. By the end of the second century A.D., Jewish life in Palestine was on the verge of extinction, and a long period of exile had begun.

The Emperor Constantine (ca. 280–337) shifted his capital to Constantinople in 330 and made Christianity the official religion. Upon partition of the Roman Empire in A.D. 395, Palestine passed to eastern control, and the scholarly Jewish communities in Galilee continued with varying fortunes under Byzantine rule and dominant Christian influence until the Arab Conquest of A.D. 636. The period included, however, strong Jewish support of the briefly successful Persian invasion of A.D., 610–614. Principal Jewish accomplishments after Hadrian and during the Byzantine era were self-preservation and development and codification of Jewish law and learning in their far-dispersed communities, notably in Palestine, Mesopotamia, Egypt, and other centers around the Mediterranean littoral.

The Jewish people had been dispersed and had lost separate political sovereignty. Nevertheless, they retained their religion, literature, and culture. These preserved their identity and influenced the revival of their national consciousness twelve centuries later.

CONQUEST AND DISPERSION

From the Muslim Arab conquest of A.D. 636 to the end of World War I, Palestine was ruled, in whole or in part, by a succession of conquerors: the Arabs (A.D. 636–1072); Seljuk Turks (1072–99); Crusaders (1099–1291); Egyptian Mamelukes (1291–1517); and Ottoman Turks (1517–1917). The Mongol inroads under Tamerlane in 1400 and the Napoleonic invasion of 1798 were interludes of brief conquests.

In Palestine the four centuries from 1517 to 1917 were characterized principally by stagnation. Neither the Jewish presence, depleted again during the Crusades, nor the Christian presence, dispersed in its turn under Islamic rule, ever disappeared entirely, but both were small minorities. Knowledgeable sources estimate that the population of Palestine in 1880 was about 450,000, of whom only 24,000 were Jews. By 1898 the number of Jews in the land had increased only to approximately 50,000.

In Europe the medieval centuries were characterized by further Jewish dispersion and wandering imposed by varying political climates of repression or tolerance. From 1290 to 1496 edicts of expulsion, particularly from Spain in 1492, drove vast numbers of Western European Jews eastward into the receptive Kingdom of Poland and into the Ottoman Empire, particularly the Constantinople region.

The pattern of tolerance in Europe subsequently reversed. Eighteenth century enlightenment, with the consequent United States

Declaration of Independence, the French Declaration of the Rights of Man, and the spread of liberalism, promoted greater tolerance for the Jews in Western Europe; in the 19th century full legal equality was established in England, France, Germany, Holland, and Italy. In Eastern Europe, however, the 18th-century partitions of Poland had transferred the Polish Jews to German, Austrian, and Czarist Russian control. The Russian Empress Catherine II, in 1791, set up the territorial delimitation, known as the "Pale of Settlement," from the Baltic to the Black Sea and between the Oder and Dnieper Rivers, outside of which Jews were forbidden to reside. Within the Pale, they were increasingly confined to urban ghettoes.

Repressive policies continued under Catherine's successors. Discriminatory taxes and other restrictions were imposed, and the Jews lived as an unwanted minority in danger of oppression and periodic violence down into the 20th century. This situation led to some differences in attitude between Western and Eastern European Jews. The former were relatively well off and secure; with the latter the opposite was true. By 1900 extensive Jewish migration to the Americas was under way, but at that time 80 percent of world Jewry lived in Europe, the majority being in the Russian and Austro-Hungarian Empires.

During the centuries of dispersion the Jews had no separate sovereignty and were largely excluded from the land of ancient Israel. The identity, however, of people and religion was maintained not only by choice, but also by enforcement. The ghetto of the Christian and Muslim worlds has been described by Jewish historians as both a prison and a spiritual fortress. Even in Western Europe at the close of the 19th century, it seemed to many Jews that, despite efforts to identify themselves with their country of residence and despite their contributions to science, art, industry, and government, they remained aliens.

MODERN ZIONISM

Establishment of the modern state of Israel in 1948 climaxed 50 years of effort by Zionism, the Jewish political-nationalist movement founded by Theodor Herzl, which burst out of complementary scientific and political forces at work in Western Europe toward the close of the 19th century.

Scientifically, Jewish intellectuals of Europe were stimulated by the worldwide attention and controversy which followed publication of Charles Darwin's *Origin of Species*. Darwinism and other scientific and technical advances provoked a questioning of traditional texts and brought about revived interest in and reexamination of Jewish doctrines, religious laws, literature, and the Hebrew language. This revived interest materially influenced growth of Reform Judaism and a new spirit of Jewish identity and goals. Politically, Western Europe after 1870 was segmented into nation-states, some newly evolved and all characterized by intense nationalism which, in their drive for social uniformity, generated a new wave of anti-Semitism based not so much directly upon religion as upon culture and racism.

In 1862 Moses Hess, a German Jewish socialist, had argued in his book, *Rome and Jerusalem,* for the historical bases of Jewish nationalism and its indestructibility. In 1873 the writer Peretz Smolenskin declaimed that the Jews were a separate nation. Disassociating his theme from the old orthodox religious base, he held that self-abnegating hopes for the long-awaited Messianic era would be realized only when the Jews achieved their own political and moral emancipation. Also prominent among the precursors of Herzl was the Russian physician, Leo Pinsker, who stated, in his *Auto-Emancipation* of 1882, his disillusionment with any hope for full Jewish identification with the countries in which they lived. Stimulated by this revival, the society of Lovers of Zion (Hibbat Zion) was organized in Odessa and, by 1890, had spread elsewhere. Its original purpose was to encourage the movement of small bands of Jewish immigrants to Palestine and the establishment there of agricultural settlements. This movement, although financially supported by the wealth of Baron Edmond de Rothschild, encountered constant difficulty with Turkish governors and was not particularly successful. The missing impetus was supplied to European Jewish nationalism by Theodor Herzl.

Herzl, born in Budapest, Hungary, on May 2, 1860, was reared and educated in an environment of assimilation. Prepared for the bar in Vienna, he became a journalist and was well known as a columnist and playwright in Vienna by the time of the 1894 Dreyfus trial in Paris. Captain Alfred Dreyfus, a French officer of Jewish faith, was accused of, convicted of, and publicly disgraced for selling military information to Germany. He was later exonerated, but publicity at the time of his trial set off widespread anti-Semitic disturbances in France. Herzl's earlier life had not been strongly identified with Jewish culture or politics, and he is not known to have studied Hess, Pinsker, or other early nationalist spokesmen. In observing the Dreyfus trial as a Viennese correspondent, however, he bacame impressed with what he saw as basic Jewish insecurity in Europe. Shortly afterwards his concept of a Jewish homeland reportedly came to him like a revelation and, seized with enthusiasm, he wrote his classic pamphlet, *The Jewish State,* which was published in 1896.

Historically, since ancient times, anti-Semitism had been associated with Jewish separateness in religion or custom. Herzl saw the problem not as a religious or social one, but as a political-national question of international scope which remained despite the legal emancipation of Jews. He contended that the solution, in the best interest of all concerned, lay in establishing a separate Jewish national state. His plan was variously received.

In Western Europe and in the United States many Jews rejected the concept as dangerous to the assimilation they had gained and as generating charges of dual loyalties. Some Reform Jews insisted that Judaism had outgrown Palestine and the ancient identity with political sovereignty. Orthodox Jews retained the traditional Messianic ideas and maintained that Herzl was advocating a purely secular state. Still others argued that the scheme was impracticable (see ch. 11, Religion).

On the other hand, Eastern European Jewish nationalists welcomed Herzl's advent to leadership. Encouraged by this backing he convened in Basel, Switzerland, on August 27, 1897, the First Zionist Congress which founded the World Zionist Organization. In his pamphlet, *The Jewish State*, Herzl had left open the question of location of the state. The Eastern European group, however, insisted on the ancient identity, and the congress adopted the Basel Program with the stated aim: "To create for the Jewish people a home in Palestine secured by Public Law."

The World Zionist Organization established a General Council, a Central Executive, and a congress held either once a year or every 2 years. It developed member societies on a worldwide basis, continued to encourage the settlements in Palestine, registered a bank in London, and established the Jewish National Fund to buy land in Palestine. Acting from the premise that the state he envisioned could be brought about only by support of the European powers, Herzl spent the rest of his life in negotiations with the Turkish sultan, the German kaiser, the Pope, the Russian court, Austria, and Great Britain. With all but Great Britain, his efforts were nonproductive. After an initial discussion of settlement in the Sinai Peninsula, which was opposed by Egypt, Herzl came to the Sixth Zionist Congress in 1903 apparently willing to consider, as a temporary shelter, a British proposal for an autonomous Jewish entity in East Africa. The concept was vehemently rejected by Russian and Eastern European Zionists who, as before, insisted on the ancient political identity with Palestine. Exhausted, Herzl died of pneumonia in 1904 with no signal diplomatic victory. He had, however, created the World Zionist Organization and inspired its goals.

Zionism continued after Herzl's death. Parties arose within the movement, such as the Democratic Zionist Faction, from which came Dr. Chaim Weizmann, later first president of Israel, and the Workers of Zion party, which included David Ben-Gurion, first prime minister of Israel, and Itzhak Ben-Zvi, second president of Israel. While Herzl lived, the emphasis was on diplomacy. In the controversy be-

so-called "politicals" and "practicals" after his death, the bal-
shifted to the latter. The Eighth Zionist Congress in 1907 set up
onist Palestine Office in Jaffa, near which the Jewish city of
Tel Aviv was founded in 1909. The small Jewish settlements, which
became known as kibbutzim, evolved their distinctive system of communal living. Schools, publications, and labor movements developed
and, under stimulus of the second wave of immigration, known as
the second aliyah, Jewish population in Palestine rose to about 85,000
by the beginning of World War I. In the formulation of attitudes
and philosophy, a further modification was introduced by the writer
Ahad Ha'am, who saw the Zionist goal not simply as another political state, but as a home for Judaism. This emphasis on Palestine as a
center of culture appealed to those who were unenthusiastic about the
political nationalist program of Zionism.

Meanwhile, in Constantinople the Young Turk Nationalist Revolution of 1908 had driven out Sultan Abdul Hamid II and roused the
hopes of various nationalities of the Ottoman Empire. Ben-Gurion
pressed the Jewish claims for continued immigration and autonomy
in the Turkish state. Elsewhere, Arab opposition to Turkish rule
took two forms. One arose among Arab intellectuals of Beirut and
Damascus, who enunciated the ideas of a new Arab nationalism, but
who first sought autonomy within, rather than secession from, the
Ottoman Empire. The second lay in the turbulent spirit of the more
remote desert tribes, who were politically inarticulate, but resentful
of any outside control.

After 1908, however, it quickly became clear to Zionists and Arabs
alike that the nationalism of the successors of Abdul Hamid was
Turkish nationalism, bent on intensified Turkification of the Ottoman domain rather than granting local autonomies. The open Arab
committees of Beirut and Damascus were forced into clandestine
political conspiracy in the form of secret societies. The link between
them and the tribesmen of Arabia was Sharif Hussein Ibn Ali, the
Arab prince of Mecca and the Hijaz region of western Arabia who
was appointed to this position in 1908 by the Turkish government
but was closely watched by it. Prince Abdullah, son of Sharif Hussein, visited Lord Horatio H. Kitchener, British Agent and Consul
General in Egypt, at Cairo in February 1914 and inquired into the
possibility of British support should his father stage a revolt against
Turkey. Lord Kitchener's reply was noncommittal, since Turkey
was not then allied with Germany and World War I had not begun.
The Turkish government, at the outbreak of World War I in August
1914, also looked with disfavor on Zionism and its growing base in
Palestine, and prospects for Zionist continuity in the land were not
bright. The burden of the Zionist cause then fell on leadership outside

Palestine in the Diaspora, where the diplomatic breakthrough never accorded to Herzl was to be achieved by Dr. Weizmann.

WORLD WAR I AND THE BRITISH MANDATE TO 1939

Upon Great Britain's entry into World War I, Lord Kitchener was recalled to London as secretary of state for war and, in changed circumstances, sought from Sharif Hussein Arab support for the war against Turkey. In Cairo Sir Henry McMahon, the first British High Commissioner in Egypt, conducted an extensive correspondence from July 1915 to January 1916 with Sharif Hussein, two of whose sons—Abdullah, later king of Jordan, and Faisal, later king of Syria (ejected by the French in 1920) and of Iraq (1921–33)—were to figure prominently in subsequent events.

In a letter to McMahon, enclosed with a letter dated July 14, 1915, from Abdullah, Sharif Hussein specified an area for Arab independence under the "Sharifian Arab Government" consisting of the Arabian peninsula (except Aden) and the Fertile Crescent of Palestine, Lebanon, Syria, and Iraq. In his letter of October 24, 1915, to Sharif Hussein, McMahon, on behalf of the British government, declared British support for postwar Arab independence, subject to certain reservations and exclusions of territory not entirely Arab or concerning which Great Britain was not free ". . . to act without detriment to the interests of her ally, France." As with the later Balfour Declaration, the exact meaning was not clear, although Arab spokesmen since then have usually maintained that Palestine was within the pledged area of independence. In any event, on June 5, 1916, Sharif Hussein launched the Arab Revolt against Turkey and, in October, declared himself "King of the Arabs."

Meanwhile, on May 16, 1916, the British and French governments concluded the secret Sykes-Picot Agreement which, although allowing for a postwar Arab state on the Arabian peninsula and an ill-defined plan for an international arrangement over Jerusalem and part of Palestine, divided the rest of the Fertile Crescent between the two powers.

On December 7, 1916, David Lloyd George became British prime minister, with Arthur James Balfour as foreign secretary. Both of them regarded negotiation with the British Zionists, Dr. Weizmann and Lord Lionel Walter Rothschild, as of potential value to the pursuit of British war aims.

Weizmann, who was born in Russia in 1874 and educated in Berlin, had moved to England in 1904 and, as a chemist, had made notable contributions to the development of explosives. In support of the Zionist cause, his protracted and skillful negotiation with the British Foreign Office was climaxed on November 2, 1917 by the letter from the foreign secretary to Lord Rothschild which became known as the Balfour Declaration. This document declared the British government's ". . . sympathy with Jewish Zionist aspirations," viewed with favor ". . . the establishment in Palestine of a National Home for the Jewish People," and announced an intent

> to facilitate the achievement of this object, it being clearly understood that nothing shall be done which may prejudice the civil and religious rights of existing non Jewish communities in Palestine or the rights and political status enjoyed by Jews in any other country.

Although painstakingly devised, the wording of this declaration was interpreted differently by different people, according to their varied objectives and interests. Ultimately, it was found to contain two incompatible undertakings: establishment in Palestine of National Home for the Jews and preservation of the rights of existing non-Jewish communities, particularly the Arabs. This incompatibility sharpened over the succeeding years and became irreconcilable. Initially, however, there was no apparent substantial Arab nationalist sentiment in Palestine. The apprehensions of Sharif Hussein of Mecca and of his sons Faisal and Abdullah (not themselves Palestinians) were allayed by assurance that no one people in Palestine should be subject to another. Furthermore, the belief was widely held that Arabs and Jews could live there together peacefully under some arrangement not yet set forth.

Although the content of the Sykes-Picot Agreement was revealed in November 1917 by the Bolshevik Russian government, Arab misgivings as to Allied postwar intentions on this score were allayed by British and French reassurances and by the fact that Allied military operations in the Middle East were progressing favorably. Jerusalem was taken by Field Marshall Edmund Allenby on December 9, 1917, Turkish forces in Syria were subsequently defeated, and an armistice was concluded with Turkey on October 31, 1918.

On January 3, 1919, an agreement was signed by Prince Faisal, chief Arab delegate to the Paris Peace Conference, and Dr. Weizmann, representing the World Zionist Organization; it pledged the two parties to cordial cooporation, and by it Prince Faisal concurred with the Balfour Declaration. He wrote in Arabic on the document, however, a proviso that his signature was dependent upon fulfillment of Allied war pledges regarding Arab independence. Since these pledges were not fulfilled to Arab satisfaction after the war, most Arab leaders and spokesmen have not considered the Faisal-Weizmann agreement as having any validity. An American group known as the King-Crane Commission was appointed in 1919 by President Woodrow Wilson to investigate and report on the problem of dividing territory and assigning mandates. The commission's report of August 28, 1919, opposed unlimited Jewish immigration and a separate Jewish state in Palestine, but it was not considered by the Paris Peace Conference and was not widely published until 1922.

From the Paris Peace Conference of 1919 emerged the League of Nations Covenant and the Mandate system making Great Britain the Mandatory Power for Palestine. In the interim period Sir Herbert Samuel began his 5-year term as first British High Commissioner for Palestine on July 1, 1920. The terms of the Mandate were approved by the League Council on July 24, 1922, although they were technically not official until September 29, 1923. The United States was not a member of the League of Nations, but a joint resolution of the 76th Congress on June 30, 1922, endorsed the concept of the Jewish National Home.

The Mandate's terms recognized ". . . the historical connection of the Jewish people with Palestine," called upon the Mandatory Power to ". . . secure establishment of the Jewish National Home," and recognized ". . . an appropriate Jewish Agency" for advice and cooperation to that end. The World Zionist Organization was specifically recognized as that agency. Jewish immigration was to be facilitated, while ensuring that the ". . . rights and position of other sections of the population are not prejudiced." English, Arabic, and Hebrew were all to be official languages.

Arab spokesmen such as Sharif Hussein, who was then king of the Hijaz, and his sons, Abdullah and Faisal, although opposed to the Balfour Declaration, had accepted wartime assurances and had regarded it simply as providing a postwar refuge and home for Jews within an independent Arab state. Consequently, they opposed the Mandate's terms, since the overall League of Nations Covenant had endorsed popular determination and thereby, they maintained, supported the cause of the majority—namely, the Arabs—in Palestine. Further, the Covenant specifically declared that all other obligations and understandings inconsistent with it were abrogated. Therefore, Arab argument held that both the Balfour Declaration and the Sykes-Picot Agreements were actually null and void. Arab leaders particularly objected to the Mandate's numerous references to the "Jewish community," whereas the Arab people, then constituting about 90 percent of the Palestinian population, were acknowledged only as "the other sections."

The Arabs contended that it was unjust to allow a minority to overrule a large majority; that the continuous Arab occupation of Palestine from the seventh to the 20th century presented a more valid claim than that of Zionism; that one group cannot be bound by the differing religious beliefs of another group and is under no moral compulsion to accept them; that Europe and America, in attempting to correct social injustice in Europe, did so at Arab expense; and that the World War I pledges to the Arabs were formal agreements between states and thus superior to the position expressed in Lord Balfour's letter leading to the language of the Mandate.

To British authority, pressed with heavy responsibilities and commitments after World War I, the objective of Mandate administration was a peaceful accommodation in and development of Palestine by Arabs and Jews under British control. To the World Zionist Organization which, by 1921, had a worldwide membership of about 770,000, the recognition in the Mandate was seen as a welcome first step. Although not all Zionists and not all Jews were committed at that time to conversion of the Jewish National Home, set forth in the Mandate, into a separate political state, this conversion became firm Zionist policy during the next 25 years. The patterns developed during these years strongly influenced the state of Israel proclaimed in 1948.

The World Zionist Organization established in Palestine an executive office, thus implementing the language of the Mandate prescribing such an agency. In August 1929 a formalized Jewish Agency was established with a Council, Administrative Committee, and Executive. Each of these bodies consisted of an equal number of Zionist and nominally non-Zionist Jews. The president of the World Zionist Organization was, however, ex-officio president of the agency. Thereafter, the World Zionist Organization continued to conduct external diplomatic, information, and cultural activities, whereas the operational Jewish Agency took over fund raising, activities in Palestine, and local relations with the British Mandatory Authority. In the course of time, these became two different names for virtually the same organization.

Other landmark developments by the World Zionist Organization and the Jewish Agency under the Mandate included: establishment in December 1920 of the General Federation of Labor (Histadrut Ha'ovdim Haklalit), known as Histadrut; creation of a Jewish-elected assembly and National Council in 1920 to promote religious, educational, and welfare services; establishment of the Chief Rabbinate in 1921; centralized Zionist control of the Hebrew school system in 1919, opening of the Technion (Israel Institute of Technology) in Haifa in 1924, and dedication of the Hebrew University of Jerusalem in 1925; continued acquisition of land, largely through the Jewish National Fund, increasing from about 148,500 acres in 1922 to about 383,200 acres in 1939, and concurrent growth of Jewish urban and village centers; and establishment in the early 1920's of the Hagana, the semiunderground military arm of the Jewish Agency.

Politically the Jewish community in Palestine under the Mandate was divided within itself into many parties and factions differing in emphasis and outlook, ranging from extreme Zionist nationalists to strict Orthodox Jewish elements. Chief among these groups were the General Zionists, including many nonparty Zionists and initially the largest of the groupings; the Mizrahi, or religious Zionist party;

and the MAPAI (see Glossary), which grew out of two earlier labor groups to become the largest party by 1933. A left-wing, Marxist-Zionist party appeared after 1930. In 1925 a revisionist element developed under Vladimir Jabotinsky which favored more positivist measures and opposed Weizmann's leadership as too conciliatory toward British policy. In the heated controversy between the Hagana and the Revisionists, the Jewish guerrilla band known as the Irgun Group evolved in 1937, and from it the more extreme terrorist group, known to the British as the Stern Group, split off in 1939.

The formal name of the Irgun Group was the Irgun Zvai Leumi (National Military Organization), sometimes also called by the acronym ETZEL, from the initial letters of the Hebrew name. The Stern Group was formally known as the Lohamei Herut Yisrael (Fighters for Israel's Freedom), sometimes identified by the acronym LEHY or LEHI.

Despite internal differences, the Jewish community was in fundamental agreement as to its identity and aspirations. The Jewish Agency could point to many accomplishments, but it was, almost from the start, in continual dispute with the British Mandatory Authority (administered by the colonial secretary), which was caught between conflicting parties and denounced by both Jews and Arabs. Despite these disputes, the Jewish population in Palestine resulting from legal and illegal immigration and natural increase had risen sharply by 1939 (see table 1).

Table 1. Population of Palestine (later Israel), Selected Years, 1914–39

Year	Total*	Non-Jews*	Percentage of total	Jews*	Percentage of total	Immigrants in selected years*
1914	689.0	604.3	87.7	84.7	12.3	n.a.
1919	700.0	642.0	91.7	58.0	8.3	1.8
1922	752.1	668.3	88.9	83.8	11.1	8.7
1931	1,023.7	851.7	83.2	172.0	16.8	4.1
1935	1,261.2	940.8	74.6	320.4	25.4	66.5
1936	1,336.5	966.0	72.3	370.5	27.7	29.6
1939	1,501.8	1,056.3	70.3	445.5	29.7	31.2

n.a.—not available.
* Estimated in thousands.
Source: Adapted from Fred J. Khouri, The Arab-Israeli Dilemma, 1968.

Arab-Jewish conflict in Palestine developed early and continued at an erratically rising tempo throughout the Mandate period. The potential force of Palestinian Arab nationalism, whatever its effectiveness and leadership might be, had been underestimated. When Haj Amin al-Husseini, an anti-Zionist extremist, was appointed by Sir Herbert Samuel in 1921 as Grand Mufti of Jerusalem and head of the Supreme Muslim Council, increased intercommunal strife resulted. In March 1921 Winston Churchill, then colonial secretary, recognized Prince Abdullah as ruler of Transjordan under a separate

British Mandate. The Palestine Mandate as received by British had included Transjordan. This division, which was aimed, as was British support for Faisal in Iraq, at satisfying pledges to the Arabs, aroused strong Zionist objections and did not mollify the Arabs of Palestine; thus, violence continued.

Churchill's memorandum of July 1, 1922, reaffirmed the Balfour Declaration but, in the main, was directed at allaying Arab apprehensions regarding a Zionist seizure of political power. The World Zionist Organization saw this memorandum, subsequent commission reports, government White Papers, and regulation of immigration all as evidence of the Mandatory Authority's withdrawal from commitments and responsibilities. The Shaw and Hope-Simpson Royal Commissions of 1929 and 1930, respectively dispatched after outbreaks of violence in Palestine, both recognized, as did all later bodies, that the basic problem lay in the opposed positions of Zionist nationalism and Arab nationalism.

The rapid growth of anti-Semitism in Nazi Germany after 1933 accelerated Jewish movement, legal or underground, to Palestine. Greatly disturbed at the increase in Jewish immigration and land acquisition, Palestine Arabs formed a Supreme Arab Committee in April 1936, later known as the Arab Higher Committee, and declared a general strike, which assumed the proportions of a rebellion. The Arab Higher Committee was outlawed, and many of its leaders, including the Grand Mufti of Jerusalem, were forced out of Palestine. Great Britain dispatched the Peel Commission to Palestine, and its report, which was issued in July 1937, described the Arab and Zionist positions, and the British obligations to each, as irreconcilable and the existing Mandate as unworkable. It recommended partition of Palestine into Jewish and Arab states, with a retained British mandate over Nazareth, Bethlehem, and Jerusalem and a corridor from Jerusalem to the coast.

In 1937 the Twentieth Zionist Congress rejected the proposed boundaries, but agreed in principal to partition. Palestinian Arab nationalists rejected all considerations for partition, although some favorable earlier sentiment apparently existed in Jordan. The British government approved the idea of partition and sent a technical team to make a detailed plan. This group, the Woodhead Commission, reversed the Peel Commission's findings and reported in November 1937 that partition was impracticable; this view was in its turn accepted. The British government then returned to the concept of peaceful accommodation between Jews and Arabs and called for a conference in March 1938 in London between the Jewish and Arab representatives from Palestine and adjoining Arab states. The Jewish Agency objected to representatives from other Arab states on the grounds that they were not involved under provisions of the Mandate.

Arab supporters, however, approved the inclusion as a recognition of Pan-Arabism.

The conference failed to reach agreement, and the result was complicated by the fact that the Arab representatives refused to negotiate directly with the Jewish Agency representatives. Subsequently, on the eve of World War II, a new British White Paper was issued on May 17, 1939, extending British rule for 10 years; limiting Jewish immigration and land purchases in Palestine, and projecting a Palestinian government at the end of the 10-year period subject to Jewish-Arab accommodation. This White Paper met a mixed Arab reception and was rejected by the Palestinian Arab Higher Committee. The Jewish Agency rejected it emphatically, branding it as a total repudiation of Balfour and Mandate obligations. In September 1939, at the outset of World War II, David Ben-Gurion, then chairman of the Jewish Agency, declared: "We shall fight the war against Hitler as if there were no White Paper, and we shall fight the White Paper as if there were no war."

WORLD WAR II AND ESTABLISHMENT
OF THE STATE OF ISRAEL, 1939–49

Ben-Gurion's statement of 1939 set the tone for Jewish Agency policy and operations during the years of World War II. Thousands of Jewish volunteers served in the British Army, and on September 14, 1944, a separate Jewish Brigade was established. Palestinian Arab volunteers also served, and the British-officered Arab Legion of Transjordan played an effective role in Allied operations in Iraq and Syria. In Palestine the Jewish Agency promoted increased immigration in response to wartime pressure. In opposition, the Mandatory Authority sought to implement provisions of the 1939 White Paper by promulgating land transfer regulations and by regulating or attempting to regulate immigration.

Zionist policy and objectives were clarified in May 1942 at a conference of Zionist parties held in the Biltmore Hotel, New York. This conference was called at the initiative of Ben-Gurion, who had come to the United States to elicit the support of American Jews. It adopted a resolution known thereafter as the Biltmore Programme, which in turn was approved by the Zionist General Council in November 1942. Its provisions called for unlimited Jewish immigration into Palestine, control of immigration affairs by the Jewish Agency and, significantly and for the first time, for a so-called Jewish Commonwealth, the word "commonwealth" thus displacing "homeland." Weizmann, who had previously rejected an official commitment of this kind as inopportune, supported the resolution.

In 1943 information regarding Nazi persecutions in Europe was received, and the Irgun and Stern groups stepped up harassment of British forces in Palestine. Zionist leaders, especially Ben-Gurion, foresaw an ultimate end to the Mandate and estimated that they would then be engaged not only by the Arabs of Palestine, but also probably by the armies of neighboring Arab states, and that guerrilla methods would not be adequate. Preparations for larger forces were undertaken.

The end of World War II in Europe disclosed the scope of the Jewish plight. Approximately 6 million out of some 10 million European Jews had been exterminated. Immediately, the Allied Powers in Europe were confronted with the refugee, or displaced person, problem, which included large numbers of Jews. In Great Britain the Labour Party came to power in July 1945. Ernest Bevin, the new Secretary of State for Foreign Affairs, returned to implementation of the 1939 White Paper; limited Jewish immigration to Palestine; and, in January 1946, recognized Transjordan as a sovereign state with residual British influence. In the postwar atmosphere these actions were resented by the Zionists, and Palestine in effect became an armed camp.

The Jewish Resistance Movement was formed in an attempt to unite or at least coordinate the disparate Hagana, Irgun, and Stern groups. Reprisals and counterreprisals between Jews and the Mandate authorities, and between Arabs and the Mandate authorities continued. The Arab League was formed in 1945, and the Palestinian Arab Higher Committee reappeared to oppose renewals of immigration. There were, however, comparatively few Jewish-Arab clashes at this time. The Arab Higher Committee contended that the main objectives were elimination of the Mandate and withdrawal of British power, after which the Jewish Agency could be defeated. This estimate proved to be unsound.

In May 1946 an Anglo-American Committee of Inquiry unanimously declared its opposition to the White Paper of 1939 and proposed, among other recommendations, that the immigration of 100,000 European Jews be authorized at once. The Mandatory Authority rejected this report, specifying that admission of 100,000 new immigrants was impossible while armed organizations in Palestine were fighting the Mandate Authority and disrupting public order. Resistance and terrorism intensified, and the Twenty-Second Zionist Congress, meeting in Geneva in December 1946, named Ben-Gurion as executive chairman and defense minister of the Jewish Agency. Under his leadership, training, arming and expansion of the Hagana were accelerated in Palestine.

On February 18, 1947, Bevin informed the House of Commons of the government's decision to turn over the problem of Palestine to the United Nations, and on May 15, 1947, a special session of the United Nations General Assembly established the United Nations

Special Committee on Palestine (UNSCOP), consisting of 11 members. UNSCOP reported on August 31 that a majority of its members supported a geographically complex system of partition into separate Arab and Jewish states, a special international status for Jerusalem, and an economic union linking the three members. Backed by both the United States and the Soviet Union, the plan was adopted after 2 months of intensive deliberation as the United Nations General Assembly Resolution of November 29, 1947. This resolution is cited in Israel's Proclamation of Independence which was issued on May 14, 1948 (see ch. 13, The Governmental System).

On November 30, 1947, the Arab Higher Committee, rejecting the plan, called for a general strike in Palestine, and violence between Arabs and Jews mounted. Although considering the plan defective in terms of what they had expected from the League Mandate 25 years before, the Zionist General Council stated willingness in principle to accept partition. The Arab League Council, meeting in December 1947, said it would take whatever measures were required to prevent implementation of the resolution. The Arab League did not, at this time, approve sending forces into Palestine, but did endorse recruitment of volunteers to assist the Palestinian Arabs. Amid increasing conflict representatives of the newly formed United Nations Implementation Commission were unable to function. In January 1948 Great Britain, which had abstained from voting on the resolution, announced its intention to relinquish the Mandate on May 15, 1948. Withdrawal was completed, and the last British high commissioner, Sir Alan Cunningham, left from Haifa at midnight on May 14, 1948.

Almost simultaneously, forces of Egypt, Transjordan, Iraq, Syria, and Lebanon, with Saudi Arabian and Yemeni detachments, advanced into Palestine commencing May 15. Initially, these forces consisted of approximately 8,000 to 10,000 Egyptians, including a young officer named Gamal Abdel Nasser; 2,000 to 4,000 Iraqis; 4,000 to 5,000 Transjordanians; 3,000 to 4,000 Syrians; 1,000 to 2,000 Lebanese; and smaller numbers of Saudi Arabian and Yemeni troops; in all, about 25,000. The Israeli Hagana, irregulars such as the Irgun and Stern groups, and women auxiliaries numbered 35,000 or more. By October 14, deployed Arab forces had increased to about 55,000, including not more than 5,000 ineffective irregulars of Haj Amin al-Husseini's Palestine Liberation Force. The Israelis had increased to approximately 100,000. Except for the British-raised Arab Legion of Transjordan, Arab units were largely ill trained and had little experience. Israeli forces, usually operating with interior lines of communication, included an estimated 20,000 to 25,000 European World War II veterans in their numbers. The Arabs gained more initial success, but their advances were stemmed.

By January 1949 Israeli forces held the area that was to define Israel's territory until June 1967, although it was larger than the area contemplated by the United Nations resolution. The part of Palestine remaining in Arab hands was limited to that held by the Arab Legion of Transjordan and the Gaza area held by Egypt at the cessation of hostilities. The area held by the Arab Legion was subsequently annexed by Jordan and is commonly referred to as the West Bank. Jerusalem was divided. The Old City, the Wailing Wall, and the site of Solomon's temple, upon which stands the Muslim mosque called the Dome of the Rock, remained in Jordanian hands; the New City lay on the Israeli side of the line.

Early in the conflict, on May 29, 1948, the United Nations Security Council established a Truce Commission headed by a United Nations mediator, the Swedish diplomat Count Folke Bernadotte, who was assassinated in Jerusalem on September 17, 1948. He was succeeded by Dr. Ralph Bunche, an American, as Acting Mediator. The commission, which later evolved into the United Nations Truce Supervision Organization—Palestine (UNTSOP), attempted to devise new plans of settlement and arranged the truces of June 11–July 8 and July 19–October 14, 1948. Armistice talks were initiated with Egypt in January 1949 and an armistice agreement was established with Egypt on February 24, with Lebanon on March 23, with Transjordan on April 3, and with Syria on July 20. Iraq did not enter into an armistice agreement, but withdrew its forces after turning over their positions to Transjordanian units.

United States recognition was accorded immediately after proclamation of the state of Israel on May 14, 1948, and Soviet recognition was accorded on May 18. By April 1949, 53 nations, including Great Britain, had extended recognition, and on May 11, 1949, the United Nations General Assembly, on recommendation of the Security Council, admitted Israel to the United Nations membership.

The ancient Jewish identities of land, people, religion, and political sovereignty were again established. Recognition by Arab countries, however, has never been accorded; these countries considered that the state of war continued and had only been interrupted by an armistice. They regarded Israel as Occupied Palestine and have consistently refrained from dealing directly with or acknowledging the legitimacy of Israel. The nature of the Arab-Israeli hostility, with both sides declaring themselves to be in search of justice and independence, was the same as that prevailing after World War I, but magnified by the problem of some 900,000 Palestinian Arab refugees, of whom, about 500,000 were located mainly in Jordan, and with smaller numbers in Gaza, Syria, and Lebanon. The situation was further complicated by the currents of inter-Arab politics and by rising Arab nationalism.

ISRAEL FROM 1949 TO JULY 1967

Upon the founding of the state of Israel, a provisional government was formed, under Ben-Gurion, which set up provisional ministries and a civil service and conducted the war. The country's first Parliament, called the Knesset (assembly), was elected on January 25, 1949 (see ch. 13, The Governmental System; ch. 14, Political Dynamics). Dr. Weizmann was elected first president of the state by the Knesset on February 16, 1949, and continued in that office until his death on November 9, 1952. Ben-Gurion became the first prime minister, commencing his long tenure in that office and in the cabinet on March 10, 1949.

On June 13, 1950, the Knesset voted to adopt a constitution by evolution in the form of fundamental laws designated from time to time which, taken together, would form the constitutional base. Executive, legislative, and civil and religious judicial establishments are clearly defined in Israel, and the general mode of governmental operation resembles in many basic forms the systems common in Western Europe and in Great Britain (see ch. 13, The Governmental System).

Moving rapidly, the government and the country in the succeeding years absorbed refugees and immigrants; organized agriculture, industry, and transport; and developed national life, culture, education, and social services so effectively as to elicit widespread respect. Surrounded by hostile Arab states, Israel's military forces, based on a small, regular establishment, compulsory service, and a strong reserve, developed high levels of combat and technical effectiveness in all arms. The Weizmann Institute of Science, dedicated on November 2, 1949, gained international stature. An atomic reactor was built, and nuclear research was begun in 1960. Outside aid to Israel from the Diaspora, especially from private contributions from the United States, was a significant factor in the developmental years, although the official United States Aid Mission was withdrawn in 1963 as no longer necessary.

Internally, the longstanding characteristic of variety in political parties continued. The main groups were: the labor and the labor socialist parties, stemming from the original MAPAI; the liberal parties, emerging from the old General Zionists; and the orthodox religious parties. Among the more important internal issues have been the controversies between secular and Jewish orthodox interpretations of social patterns, and the need for adjustment and accommodation between Israelis of European origin or orientation, called Ashkenazic Jews, and those of Middle Eastern or North African origin, originally from Spain and Portugal, known as Sephardic Jews. The state and its power structure were developed and manned principally by the former. Before the Arab-Israeli hostilities of June 1967, a different problem, causing increasing concern, appeared in the sharp decline in annual immigration after 1951, 1957, and again after 1963 (see fig. 5).

The World Zionist Organization and the Jewish Agency continued in active operation after establishment of the state of Israel, although, as a natural consequence, they were modified in objectives and methods. The Twenty-Third Zionist Congress, meeting in Jerusalem in 1951, formulated a new program specifying that "The task of Zionism is: the consolidation of the State of Israel, the ingathering of exiles to the land of Israel, and the fostering of the unity of the Jewish people." This program was incorporated in the World Zionist Organization-Jewish Agency Status Law passed by the Knesset on November 24, 1952, and in the Covenant signed between the state of Israel and the Jewish Agency in July 1954. The Jewish Agency for Israel is the action arm of the World Zionist Organization for information and planning of immigration and for the reception, initial care, and placement of immigrants in Israel.

The hostile confrontation with the Arab states continued after 1949. President Gamal Abdel Nasser of Egypt became increasingly the symbol of Arab nationalism, especially to Arab revolutionary movements after 1955. After World War II, Arab nationalism entered a new stage and took on new characteristics. Previously, it had been aimed at securing independence for the emerging Arab states and was headed largely by traditional political, propertied, intellectual, and Western-oriented elites with the objective of developing modern national societies which they would direct. A unitary Arab state did not emerge from World War I, and nationalism in the interwar period took the form of separate national movements. After World War II, and with the achievement of independence by most Arab states, the nature of the leadership changed, tending to become mass-identified and to reject leadership by the older elites, who were viewed as dominated by outside, imperialist influences. The new Arab nationalism stood for nonalignment with world power blocs, and opposed the older Arab regimes and the nationalism of separate Arab states. It pursued the pan-Arab idea of the "Arab Nation," a concept embracing all Arab states and considered to represent the ultimate expression of Arab political life.

A common rejection of Israel and denial of its legal existence characterized the Arab states, and their spokesmen expressed the conviction that Israel would attempt further expansion. Internal and regional political differences, however, divided the Arab states, with some regimes, principally the monarchies, regarded as traditional or moderate, and others as radical. The Arab League had been founded in 1955. Being based on a multilateral pact, however, the league was dependent in practice on the actions of individual members, such as enforcement of the economic boycott of Israel. Arab nationalism was

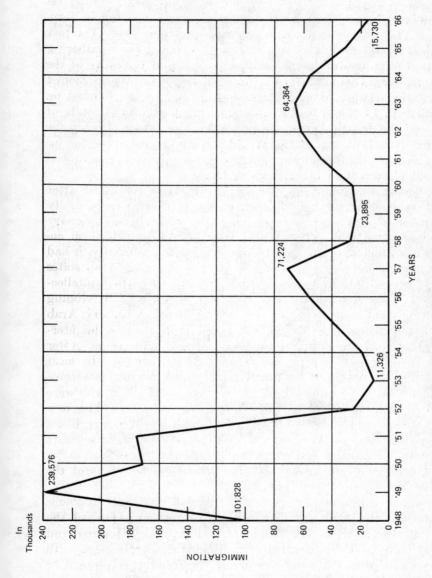

Figure 5. Immigration to Israel, 1948–66.

Source: Adapted from Israel, Ministry for Foreign Affairs, Information Division, *Facts About Israel, 1968.*

51

not a monolithic force, and Arab resources were in no way centrally controlled.

In the stress of inter-Arab political relationships, it became impracticable for any Arab government to initiate settlement action with Israel even if any of them had desired to do so. For its part, Israel denied expansionist ambitions. Arab governments have consistently refused to deal directly with the Israeli government, which they consider illegitimate; Israel, in turn, has maintained that a lasting settlement could be attained only by direct negotiations. Little progress was made in resolving the Arab refugee problem, a prime political as well as humanitarian issue. The humanitarian aspect was ameliorated by the administration of the United Nations Relief and Works Agency for Arab Palestinian refugees in the Near East (UNRWA), financed largely by the United States. Israeli drainage of Lake Hula, north of Lake Tiberias (the biblical Sea of Galilee), and use of the Jordan River engendered further Arab hostility.

An American plan for riparian distribution of the Jordan waters (the Eric Johnston plan) was accepted by Israel but, although recognized as technically sound, it was ultimately rejected by Jordan and the other Arab states since it would imply official recognition of the existence of Israel. Nonetheless, the allocations of the Johnston plan were respected in practice; and the plan continued to serve as a benchmark against which subsequent proposals were measured. Raids and violence along the border of some 600 miles by groups from both sides were common. During the early years after independence, Israel demonstrated a proclivity for sharp retaliation which, on several occasions, led to censure by the United Nations.

Guerrilla raids into Israel from the Sinai Peninsula by Egyptian-organized, commando-type raiders known as *fedayeen* became an increasingly common feature of the border conflict after 1949. These incursions and Egyptian army deployments into the Sinai Peninsula were regarded by Israel as a serious threat after President Nasser's nationalization of the Suez Canal on July 26, 1956. Israeli forces, under the leadership of Major General Moshe Dayan, attacked into Sinai on October 29, 1956, and by November 2 had routed the Egyptian forces and effectively dominated the entire peninsula. This action preceded the landing of British and French troops at Port Said on November 5, 1956. All were subsequently withdrawn; the British and French had departed by late December 1956, and the Israelis by the end of March 1957, after a United Nations Emergency Force (UNEF) had been stationed in Sinai and Gaza with Egyptian agreement. The Israeli military victory, and subsequent UNEF presence at the southern tip of the Sinai Peninsula, opened the Gulf of Aqaba to Israeli shipping.

Abroad, the Arab-Israeli problem, although not essentially linked to the confrontation between Western democracy and communism, became increasingly polarized between the great powers. The United States repeatedly endeavored to define a neutral position supporting peace and opposing the change of any Middle Eastern frontier by force. Expressing fears, whether justified or not, of Zionist expansionism, the regimes in Egypt, Syria, Iraq, Algeria, and Yemen sought aid from various sources. The Soviet Union, which had been second only to the United States in recognizing Israel, supported Arab positions, especially after 1956, and the extensive military and economic aid provided to these Arab states secured for the Soviet Union a position of influence in the Middle East which it had never previously held.

After 1956 comparative calm ensued, but no material change in the attitudes of the antagonists took place. A plan formulated at an Arab summit conference in January 1964 in Cairo led to formation of a Unified Arab Command as an attempt to coordinate military resources. The plan also initiated action to divert away from the Jordan River its headwaters in Syria and Lebanon as a counteraction to Israel's planned diversion of Jordan waters. Although extensive preparations were made by Syria for diversion of these headwaters, Israeli air attacks and ground fire on the digging site dissuaded the Arabs from continuing.

Border raids and incursions again mounted; Arab guerrilla organizations, difficult to identify but largely of Palestinian origin, grew in strength. The thrust of their operations came out of Syria and Jordan rather than from the Sinai Peninsula. On November 13, 1966, a severe Israeli retaliatory raid at the Jordanian village of Samu, near Hebron, resulted in United Nations censure and illustrated the hightening tension that continued into 1967. Tension mounted on the Syrian border in April, and in early May 1967 Egypt commenced an extensive military buildup on the Sinai Peninsula in response to Syria's allegations that it was in imminent danger of Israeli attack. President Nasser, on May 18, demanded removal of the UNEF from the Sinai Peninsula, which was acceded to by United Nations Secretary General U Thant and was promptly carried out; on May 22 President Nasser also announced a blockade against Israeli shipping in the Strait of Tiran at the entrance of the Gulf of Aqaba, which would have cut off the Israeli port of Eilat. Israel declared this action to be a cause of war, as it has publicly maintained since 1957. Jordan signed a military alliance with Egypt on May 30, in fulfillment of basic Pan-Arab commitments and in response to political pressure at home. Iraq and Egypt signed a similar pact on June 4, 1967.

The tempo of firing along the borders increased, and Egyptian, Jordanian, and Syrian forces were deployed in a state of increased readiness. In Israel Major General Yitzhak Rabin, Chief of Staff, stepped up Israel's military preparations; Prime Minister Levi Esh-kol, responding to public opinion, brought Major General Moshe Dayan into the cabinet as minister of defense; and Minister for Foreign Affairs Abba Eban informed the United States that Israel was determined to defend itself. Diplomatic efforts to relax tensions in the crisis were unavailing. On June 5, 1967, declaring itself surrounded with danger of attack increasing daily, Israel launched a massive air assault that eliminated Arab air power. This action immediately preceded Israeli ground invasions successively into the Sinai Peninsula and the Gaza Strip, Jordan, and finally Syria.

In the 6-day conflict that followed, Israeli forces defeated forces of the United Arab Republic, Jordan, and Syria; they also seized the entire Sinai Peninsula (except Port Fuad in the extreme northwest) to the East bank of the Suez Canal, Jordan's West Bank, including all of Jerusalem, and the Golan Heights of Syria overlooking Lake Tiberias. By evening on June 11, a cease-fire had been established. This striking victory secured for Israel a military position that could be more easily defended, and, particularly in the unification of Jerusalem, it provided to Israelis and to Zionism at large a major psychological impetus as well as the sense of national confirmation. Morale, confidence, and pride soared. New problems, however, appeared; old problems remained, and were in many cases magnified. The basic political issues with the Arab states and Arab nationalism were unresolved and, by mid-1969, had proven as intractable as ever.

CHAPTER 4
POPULATION

The most striking characteristic of the population in mid-1969 was its dynamic rate of growth during the two decades after the country attained statehood on May 15, 1948. The total population on January 1, 1968, as estimated by the Israeli Central Bureau of Statistics, was 2,708,100, an increase of about 239 percent over the 799,600 estimated by the same source to be the population on May 15, 1948, the date Israel attained statehood (see table 2). During this 20-year period, the Jewish population mounted from an estimated total of 649,600 to 2,383,600, an increase of approximately 267 percent. This Jewish increase was caused mainly by immigration.

Table 2. Population of Israel, for Selected Years, 1948–68
(in thousands)

Population	May 15 1948	January 1 1950	1956	1962	1968
Jews _____	649.6	1,013.9	1,590.5	1,981.7	2,383.6
Non-Jews _____	150.0	160.0	198.6	252.5	390.3*
Muslims _____	____	(111.5)	(136.3)	(174.9)	(286.6)
Christians _____	____	(34.0)	(43.3)	(51.3)	(70.6)
Druzes and others _____	____	(14.5)	(19.0)	(26.3)	(33.1)
Total _____	799.6	1,173.9	1,789.1	2,234.2	2,773.9*

* Includes population of East Jerusalem (about 65,800).

Source: Adapted from Israel, Central Bureau of Statistics, *Statistical Abstract of Israel, 1968*, p. 17.

Meanwhile, the number of non-Jews more than doubled (approximately 324,500 in 1968 compared to about 150,000 in 1948), almost entirely as the result of natural increase caused by the excess of births over deaths. The annexation of East Jerusalem, on June 29, 1967, added another 65,800 to increase the total non-Jewish population to about 390,300 and the country's total to about 2,773,900.

Non-Jews comprise almost 12 percent of the population, excluding East Jerusalem; nearly all are Arabs. The only non-Arab minority of significance is a small group of Circassians, numbering perhaps 2,000 (see ch. 5, Ethnic Groups and Languages). About 72 percent of the non-Jewish population is classified as Muslim and about 18 percent as Christians; Druzes account for most of the remainder (see ch. 11, Religion).

Since 1882, when the modern period of immigration began, some 2 million Jews have moved to Palestine and Israel. Up to the time of independence, the new arrivals were overwhelmingly European in origin. During the mass movement of 1948–51, the number of immigrants was about evenly divided between those that came from countries in the Middle East and North Africa and those that came from countries in Europe and America. After 1951 immigration was predominantly from the Middle East and North Africa.

Ashkenazim (see Glossary) have played a dominant role in national life, and they still occupy a position of leadership in the country (see ch. 17, Political Values and Attitudes). In numbers, however, the Ashkenazim are gradually being overtaken by the Sephardim (see Glossary), and both groups are being challenged by the growing proportion of the younger, Israeli-born element, the Sabras. Of the total population, slightly fewer than 30 percent were born in Europe and America, more than 27 percent in the Middle East and North Africa, and almost 43 percent in Israel or Palestine. Including native-born descendants, persons of Sephardic origin slightly outnumber those of Ashkenazic origin, 47 percent to 46 percent; the remaining 7 percent were native-born of native-born fathers.

With more than half of the population under the age of 25, Israel is a relatively young country. The crude birth rate averaged 25.2 per thousand population in 1963–67; with a death rate of 6.3; the rate of natural increase was 18.9 per thousand. The birth rate for Jews has been declining in recent years, but in 1968 it jumped 1.4 per thousand over the rate for 1967 and at 22.9 was the highest since 1960, when it was 23.9 per thousand. The birth rate for non-Jews was 45.0 per thousand in 1968, up only 0.1 per thousand over 1967 and still below the 1963–67 average of 49.1 per thousand.

The population is predominantly urban, with only about 18 percent classified as rural. The most notable change in settlement patterns since 1948 has been the growth of small- and middle-sized towns. Accompanying this change has been a decrease in the proportion of the population concentrated in the Tel Aviv, Haifa, and Jerusalem districts.

Over a million persons, virtually all Arabs, live in areas occupied by Israel during the Six-Day War of June 1967. According to an Israeli census, there are 599,000 in Judaea and Samaria, including 61,000 in refugee camps; 66,000 in East Jerusalem; 356,000 in the Gaza Strip, including 175,000 in refugee camps; 43,000 in northern Sinai; 7,000 in southern Sinai; and 6,400 on the Golan Heights. Of the total, about 1,015,000 were Muslims; Christians numbered about 43,000; and Druzes, about 7,000. These figures exclude an estimated 400,000 persons who had lived in these areas before the war but who fled during the fighting or thereafter, principally to East Jordan, though significant numbers also went to unoccupied Syria and the United Arab Republic.

IMMIGRATION

Jews first began to return to Palestine in significant numbers in 1882, and, by the time the British Palestine Mandate came to an end in 1948, over half a million Jews had immigrated to Palestine (see table 3). During this period Palestine's Jewish population rose from an estimated 24,000 to nearly 650,000, roughly a twenty-fivefold increase. On a worldwide basis, this represented an increase from 0.3 percent to 5.7 percent of the total world Jewish population. Independence brought even greater numbers of immigrants, and by January 1, 1968, Israel, with about 17.5 percent of the world's total, had become the world's third largest nation of Jews, exceeded only by the United States, with 42.6 percent, and the Soviet Union, with 18.8 percent.

Table 3. Jewish Immigration to Palestine, Selected Periods, 1882–1948
(in thousands)

Period	Number of immigrants
First Aliyah, 1882–1903	20.0 – 30.0
Second Aliyah, 1904–14	35.0 – 40.0
Subtotal	55.0 – 70.0
Third Aliyah, 1919–23	35.2
Fourth Aliyah, 1924–31	81.6
Fifth Aliyah, 1932–39	247.7
1940 – May 14, 1948	118.3
Subtotal	482.8
TOTAL	537.8 – 552.8

Source: Adapted from Israel, Central Bureau of Statistics, *Statistical Abstract of Israel, 1968*, p. 90.

Palestine (1882–1948)

The impetus for the first wave of immigration, or *aliyah* (plural, *aliyot*), came from the persecution of Jews in Czarist Russia. Beginning in 1880 a series of pogroms forced hundreds of thousands of Russian Jews to seek refuge in countries of central and western Europe, with many eventually moving to the United States. The number immigrating to Palestine in the first wave, commonly called the First Aliyah, including some from Rumania as well, is variously estimated between 20,000 and 30,000.

The Second Aliyah followed in the wake of renewed anti-Jewish pogroms in Russia. Beginning in 1904 and lasting until the outbreak of World War I, the Second Aliyah brought an additional 35,000 to 40,000 immigrants to Palestine. Many of these were organized groups of Russian and Polish Jews motivated and encouraged by the World Zionist Organization, which had by then come into existence, to establish their homes in Palestine (see ch. 3, Historical Setting).

In 1914 the Jewish population in Palestine had reached 85,000, but by the end of World War I, it had been reduced to about 36,000. Immigration virtually ceased during the war, and many emigrated because of conditions in Palestine. Others were expelled by the Ottoman government. Political developments toward the end of the war, however, notably the Balfour Declaration and its subsequent endorsement by the United States and the League of Nations, stimulated a new wave of immigration, the Third Aliyah. Immigrants were again primarily Russian; by the end of 1923 they numbered about 36,000. The Palestine census of October 23, 1922, showed 83,800 Jews, almost the prewar number and about 11 percent of Palestine's total population.

The Fourth Aliyah witnessed the arrival of almost 82,000 Jewish immigrants between 1924 and 1931. Most were from Poland, where discrimnation against Jews had become widespread, but for the first time sizable numbers came from countries outside Europe. America, mainly the United States, furnished about 2,000, and there were about 9,000 from countries of the Middle East. Immigration curbs adopted in the United States formed one of the factors that prompted many Jews to turn to Palestine. According to the census of November 18, 1931, Jews in Palestine numbered 174,600, about 17 percent of the total population.

The period of the Fifth Aliyah, 1932–1939, coincided with the rise of Adolf Hitler to power in Germany and the beginning of World War II. Persecution of Central European Jews was intensified, and by the end of the period, 90,000 from Poland and 40,000 from Germany and Austria had immigrated to Palestine. In all more than 247,000 came to Palestine during the Fifth Aliyah. Included were 16,000 from the Soviet Union, 11,000 from Rumania, and 7,000 from Yemen and Aden. At the end of 1939 the Jewish population in Palestine was estimated to be 445,500; at that time it constituted about 30 percent of the total population.

Towards the end of the Fifth Aliyah, immigration was slowed by the Arab revolt in Palestine and, in May 1939, the British limited further immigration to a maximum of 45,000 over the next 5 years, with the number after that to be decided in agreement with the Arabs. World War II was itself a limiting factor and, by the end of 1945, additional immigrants had numbered about 120,000. Many of these entered illegally, as they continued to do in the period immediately after the war. Estimates for 1946 show 608,200 Jews, approximately one-third of that year's total population, 1,845,500. Immigration from 1946 until the date that Israel proclaimed its statehood in 1948 totaled about 58,000.

Of the more than 4 million Jews who emigrated from their native countries between 1882 and 1948, those who came to Palestine were only a fraction. Their number was nevertheless substantial, and their impact was historic. Each major immigrant group after the first was either a driving force or an important catalyst in the establishment and development of a Jewish community that was eventually to emerge as a nation-state (see ch. 12, Social Values).

The First Aliyah left little heritage that was tangible, but it advanced an idea, without benefit of Zionism, and thus served as a precedent and ideological example. The pioneers of the First Aliyah met resistance from the existing Jewish community, most of whom had become integrated, except for religion, within the native society and who shared neither the idealistic nor agricultural zeal of the newcomers. Faced with this opposition along with difficulties posed by an alien and physically inhospitable environment, the new arrivals gradually lost their own pioneer fervor and ended up by living mainly on the philanthropy of the wealthy French Baron Edmond de Rothschild.

Immigrants of the Second and Third Aliyot, however, were deeply motivated by the idea of a national home in Palestine, and they are credited with laying the foundations for many of the country's basic economic and social institutions. One of their major contributions was the establishment of an educational system focused on the primary role of the Hebrew language (see ch. 9, Education). They created a new pattern of collective and communal agricultural settlements known as moshavim and kibbutzim (see ch. 7, Family; ch. 20, Agriculture). They also established Histadrut (Histadrut Ha'ovdim Haklalit—General Federation of Labor), a massive organization that eventually played a preeminent role in economic, social welfare, and educational affairs (see ch. 22, Labor).

The Fourth and Fifth Aliyot consisted mainly of immigrants with an urban, middle-class background. Most were also refugees, and their primary motivations could scarcely be considered ideological. As a group, however, they complemented the existing societal structure with qualifications and skills previously lacking or in short supply. The various professions were well represented, and many immigrants were businessmen and financiers, some with substantial capital. The economy as a whole benefited, and there were still sufficient numbers of immigrants influenced by Zionist principles and imbued with a pioneering spirit to carry forward the political, cultural, and sociological ideas and work of their predecessors.

When the British Mandate came to an end in 1948, the Jewish community in Palestine was overwhelmingly European in origin.

Countries in the Middle East and in North Africa furnished only about 10 percent of the total number of immigrants between 1919 and 1948; in 1948, of the approximately 65 percent foreign-born in the population, about 85 percent were born in Europe and America. Anglicization of the law under the Mandate contributed further to a Western orientation, and the nature and character of the Jewish community clearly reflected the dominance of its European members.

Israel (1948–68)

Establishment of the state and passage of the Law of Return (1950) opened the gates to a new surge of immigrants. The Declaration of Independence proclaimed that "the State of Israel will be open for Jewish immigration and for the Ingathering of the Exiles"; the Law of Return set forth in legal terms the right of every Jew to come to Israel as an immigrant. Military success was the galvanic force that gave substance to these principles (see ch. 26, The Armed Forces).

Between May 15, 1948, and January 1, 1952, it is estimated that over 684,000 Jews immigrated to Israel, a number greater than the entire Jewish population at the time of independence and more than those who had come during all the years of the preceding century. The initial group of immigrants consisted mainly of volunteers to fight against invading Arab military forces, but by September 1948 thousands began to arrive from Displaced Persons Camps in Germany, Austria, and Italy. The camps were subsequently used as staging areas for other Jews wishing to immigrate to Israel. Principal European sources were Poland, Rumania, Bulgaria, and Yugoslavia. Nearly one-half of all immigrants during the period were from the Middle East and North Africa. About 35 percent of the total came from the Middle East, mainly Iraq, Iran, Turkey, and Yemen; about 14 percent were from Morocco, Algeria, Tunisia, and Libya.

On May 15, 1948, the Jewish population was 649,600; on January 1, 1952, it was 1,404,400, an increase of 116 percent in a little more than 3½ years. Other effects of this mass immigration were equally significant: the number of persons born in Israel declined to a little over one-fourth of the total, and the number born in the Middle East and North Africa increased from less than 10 percent to nearly 27 percent of the total and from about 15 to 37 percent of all foreign-born.

Immigration slowed considerably in 1952 and has never since approached the rates attained in 1948–51. A main cause for the slowdown was the fact that potential sources of immigrants had largely been exhausted, except for those countries that had reinstituted curbs on emigration; also, those who had become assimilated into the affluent societies of the West were increasingly reluctant to leave their established homes.

Annual rates since 1952 have fluctuated considerably; in 1953 there was a migratory imbalance of 1,528 persons. A notable feature has been a marked change in immigration sources (see table 4). The number of immigrants from the Middle East and North Africa during the 1952–66 period outnumbered those from Europe and America by more than 50 percent and, at the end of 1966, they constituted about 43 percent of all immigrants since 1919, up from their preindependence ratio of about 10 percent.

Table 4. Jewish Immigration to Israel by Region of Birth, May 15, 1948–December 31, 1966*

(in thousands)

Year	Absolute Numbers		Percentages	
	Europe-America	Middle East–North Africa	Europe–America	Middle East–North Africa
1948–51	335.0	330.5	50.3	49.7
1952–54	11.2	40.0	21.9	78.1
1955–57	49.6	110.7	30.9	69.1
1958–60	46.5	25.9	64.2	35.8
1961–63	56.4	111.7	33.5	66.5
1964–66	52.9	41.2	56.3	43.7
Subtotal 1952–66	216.6	329.5	39.7	60.3
TOTAL 1948–66	551.6	660.0	45.5	54.5

* Immigrants, region of birth unknown, totaled 19,400 during the period 1948–66; of these, 18,800 arrived in 1948–51.

Source: Adapted from Israel, Central Bureau of Statistics, Statistical Abstract of Israel, 1968, p. 91.

The population registration of November 8, 1948, conducted as a prelude to elections for the First Knesset, revealed that 65 percent of the Jews were foreign-born; of these, most were from Europe and, together with those from America and Oceania (islands of the South Pacific, including Australia and New Zealand), they constituted 85 percent of those born overseas. About 12 percent were from Middle Eastern countries and about 3 percent from North African countries. On January 1, 1968, about 57 percent of the Jewish population was foreign-born; the European-American majority among these was reduced to 52 percent, and the proportions for the Middle East and for North Africa increased to 23 percent and 25 percent, respectively (see table 5).

The Jewish population born in Palestine and Israel was 253,700 on November 8, 1948; by January 1, 1968, it had risen to 1,020,500, a fourfold increase. The greatest increase was among those of eastern descent and, by 1968, together with those born in the Middle East

Table 5. *Jewish Population in Israel by Region of Birth, 1948–68*
(in thousands)

Region of Birth	November 8, 1948		January 1, 1958		January 1, 1968	
	Number	Percentage	Number	Percentage	Number	Percentage
Foreign born _____	463.0	----	1,165.8	----	1,363.1	----
Europe–America _	(393.0)	54.8	(654.9)	37.1	(708.6)	29.7
Middle East _____	(57.8)	8.1	(293.2)	16.6	(310.3)	13.0
North Africa _____	(12.2)	1.7	(217.7)	12.4	(344.2)	14.5
Israeli born _____	253.7	35.4	597.0	33.9	1,020.5*	42.8
TOTAL _____	716.7	100.0	1,762.8	100.0	2,383.6	100.0

* Israeli-born persons whose fathers were born in Israel and Palestine, 162.5 ; in Europe or America, 392.6 ; and in the Middle East or North Africa, 465.4.

Source : Adapted from Israel, Central Bureau of Statistics, *Statistical Abstract of Israel, 1968*, pp. 40–42.

and in North Africa, they comprised about 47 percent of the total Jewish population, as compared to 46 percent for those of Western descent or origin. The remaining 7 percent consisted of those whose fathers were also born in the country.

VITAL STATISTICS

Net migration accounted for 63.4 percent from 1948 through 1967 ; 99.4 percent of the growth in non-Jewish population was by natural increase, the number by which births exceed deaths (see table 6).

With the sharp decline in immigration, natural increase has become the predominant factor in population growth. The rate of natural increase, however, has also slowed considerably since the early years of statehood. The main cause for the slowdown has been a declining Jewish birth rate. Birth rates among non-Jews have remained consistently high, whereas the death rate has substantially decreased because of improved health conditions.

Table 6. *Sources of Population Growth in Israel, 1948–67*
(in thousands)

	Jews			Non-Jews		
	Population[1]	Net Migration	Natural Increase	Population[1]	Net Migration	Natural Increase
1948–52[2]	649.6	666.4	88.4	150.0	--	--
1950–51	--	--	--	160.0	2.0	11.4
1952–54	1,404.4	20.2	101.4	173.4	0.2	18.2
1955–57	1,526.0	136.1	100.7	191.8	0.2	21.2
1958–60	1,762.8	46.9	101.5	213.2	—0.1	26.1
1961–63	1,911.2	145.8	98.6	243.3[3]	—0.2	31.4
1964–66	2,155.6	79.2	110.1	274.5	—0.9	38.9
1967	2,344.9	4.3	34.4	312.5	—0.3	12.3

[1] At beginning of period.
[2] Beginning May 15, 1948.
[3] Revised upward by 4,100 on basis of 1961 census data.

Source : Adapted from Israel, Central Bureau of Statistics, *Statistical Abstract of Israel, 1968*, p. 18.

For the entire population, the crude birth rate averaged 25.2 per thousand in 1963–67. The crude death rate was 6.3 per thousand. The rate of natural increase was 18.9 per thousand. Birth rates for 1967, a year of mobilization and the Six-Day War, were slightly lower than the average.

The 1963–67 birth rate for Jews averaged 22.2 per thousand. It was 31.5 in 1949–53, 26.3 in 1954–58, and 22.9 in 1959–63; death rates during the same periods were 6.4, 6.1, and 5.8, respectively. Corresponding rates of natural increase were 25.1, 20.2, and 17.1. With a 1963–67 death rate of 6.3, the rate of natural increase had fallen to 15.9.

The death rate for non-Jews has declined steadily from an average 10.0 per thousand in 1951–53 to 8.2 in 1954–58, to 7.0 in 1959–63, and to 6.2 in 1963–67. The birth rate, on the other hand, has shown a slight upward trend. For the entire 1951–62 period, it averaged 47.6, as compared to 49.1 in 1963–67. Rates of natural increase were 36.8 in 1951–53, 38.4 in 1954–58, and 42.3 in 1959–63. The 1963–67 average was 42.9.

Vital statistics reflect the wide difference in fertility between Jewish and non-Jewish women. Total fertility—the average number of children a woman may bear during her lifetime—is about 3.4 for Jews and 8.2 for non-Jews. Total fertility also varies widely within each group. Among Jews, it is 5.0 for those born in the Middle East and in North Africa and 2.3 for those born in Europe and America; for native-born Jewish women, it is 2.7. Among non-Jews, total fertility is highest for Muslims, 9.7, and lowest for Christians, 4.3; it is 7.4 for Druzes and others.

Gross and net reproduction rates provide a more meaningful device for measuring population trends. The gross reproduction rate is the average number of females born to a woman during her lifetime; the net reproduction rate takes into account the mortality of women during their childbearing years, age 15 to 49 inclusive. Other things being equal, a net reproduction rate of 1.0 would indicate continued replacement of the population at its present level. The gross reproduction rate for Jews in 1966 was 1.65, and the net reproduction rate was 1.59. The gross reproduction rate for non-Jews was 4.0.

AGE-SEX DISTRIBUTION

Israel is one of a relatively small number of countries where there are more males than females in the population. Females on the average constitute about 48.5 percent of all births, but the main cause of the disparity was the predominance of males among immigrants. The margin has been decreasing steadily, however, and the sex ratio declined from about 107:100 in 1948 to about 102:100 in 1967.

Immigration has also exerted a major influence on the distribution of the population by age. Before independence, immigrants were for the most part younger adults. Afterward, however, the number of older persons rose sharply as whole communities, or large parts of them, were transplanted to Israel. The average age of the Jewish population increased from 28.9 years in 1948 to 29.8 at the end of 1967, and the proportion aged 50 and over rose from 13.0 percent to 21.0 percent. The trends were accelerated somewhat by an improved life expectancy of 70.4 years for males and 73.6 for females, up by more than 5 years for each (see table 7).

Table 7. Israel, Age Distribution of the Population, January 1, 1968
(in percent)

Age Groups	Jews	Non-Jews	Muslims	Christians	Druzes	Total
0–14 _____	31.0	50.5	53.3	39.9	49.1	33.4
15–29 _____	25.2	23.9	23.6	25.3	23.8	25.0
30–44 _____	17.3	13.5	12.4	17.5	14.2	16.8
45–64 _____	19.8	8.3	7.2	12.1	8.9	18.5
65 and over _____	6.7	3.8	3.5	5.2	4.0	6.3

Source: Adapted from Israel, Central Bureau of Statistics, Statistical Abstract of Israel, 1968, pp. 34–35.

Meanwhile, however, immigration was having a similar effect at the other end of the age spectrum. As immigrants became settled, married, and raised families, the median age began to drop. The median age for Jews was 27.1 in 1948, but by the end of 1968 it had fallen to 24.7. The number of children aged 14 and under increased from 28.6 percent of the Jewish population in 1948 to 31.0 percent by 1968. The other postindependence age group, those from 15 to 19 years old also increased slightly, from 8.4 percent to 10.8 percent. Each of the other 5-year age groups from 20 to 49 declined, as a percentage of the total, and the labor potential represented by these groups was reduced from 58.4 percent to 48.0 percent (see ch. 22, Labor). The average age of non-Jews at the end of 1967 was 20.9 years, and more than one-half were children under 15.

GEOGRAPHICAL DISTRIBUTION

On January 1, 1968, the country had a population density of 354 persons per square mile. The majority of the people, however, were concentrated in the Tel Aviv, Haifa, and Jerusalem districts (see table 8). Together these districts comprise only a little more than 8 percent of the country's total land area, but they contain 55.2 percent of the population. Along with the Central District, they comprise about 14.2 percent of the land area but contain nearly three-quarters of the population.

Density is highest in the Tel Aviv District, with 12,517 persons per square mile. It is lowest in the largely desert Southern District,

Table 8. Population of Israeli Districts, 1948, 1961, and 1968
(in thousands)

District	November 8, 1948 Jews	November 8, 1948 Others	May 22, 1961 Jews	May 22, 1961 Others	January 1, 1968 Jews	January 1, 1968 Others
Central	106.2	16.1	380.1	26.9	459.5	35.9
Haifa	147.7	27.4	322.3	48.0	378.2	54.3
Jerusalem	84.2	2.9	187.7	4.2	225.7	4.9
Northern	53.4	90.6	194.3	142.8	238.6	186.7
Southern	6.0	15.4	155.3	18.6	267.6	25.1
Tel Aviv	302.1	3.6	692.6	6.7	814.0	7.6
Unknown	17.1	---	---	---	---	---
Total	716.7	156.0	1,932.3	247.2	2,383.6	314.5

Source: Adapted from Israel, Central Bureau of Statistics, *Statistical Abstract of Israel*, pp. 20–21.

where there are 54 persons per square mile. The Northern District, with a density of 331, most nearly approaches the country's average. Density is 1,342 in the Haifa District; within the Haifa Subdistrict, it rises to 3,009. It is 1,225 in the Jerusalem District, including East Jerusalem, and 1,033 in the Central District.

The population, including Jews and non-Jews, is 82.2 percent urban, as determined by type of settlement (see ch. 13, The Governmental System). Urban types of settlements include towns (municipalities); settlements with a population greater than 10,000; settlements with 5,000 to 10,000 inhabitants in which less than one-half the labor force is employed in agriculture; and settlements with 2,000 to 5,000 inhabitants in which less than one-third of the labor force is engaged in agriculture. Settlements between 2,000 and 10,000 not designated as urban, and all settlements with fewer than 2,000 residents are classified as rural.

Although the population was also predominantly urban in 1948, there have been significant changes in the geographical pattern of distribution. In 1948 there were only nine settlements in all Israel with a population greater than 10,000 persons; by 1968 the number had grown to 47 settlements (see table 9). Ten of the 47 had populations in excess of 50,000; eight others had 30,000 to 50,000.

The metropolitan areas of Tel Aviv, Haifa, and Jerusalem also continued to expand at a rapid rate, but their combined population dropped as a percentage of the total. The proportion living within the three districts declined from 66.4 percent in 1948 to 55.2 percent in 1968, whereas the proportion living within the municipal limits declined from 49.4 percent to 29.5 percent.

The Tel Aviv District experienced the largest population gain, with 28 percent of the total 1948–68 increase. The Central District had 20 percent. The Haifa and Northern districts had 15 percent each; the Southern District, 14 percent; and the Jerusalem District, 8 percent.

Table 9. *Israel, Cities and Towns With a Population of 30,000 or Over* (in thousands)

City or town	January 1, 1951	May 22, 1961	January 1, 1968
Akko (Acre)	12.2	25.2	32.8
Ashqelon	5.1	24.3	37.4
Beersheba	8.3	43.5	69.5
Benei Beraq	14.4	47.0	64.7
Bat Yam	5.5	31.7	62.0
Givatayim	12.0	30.9	40.9
Herzliya	12.2	26.9	35.6
Hadera	15.0	25.6	30.0
Haifa	140.0	183.0	209.9
Holon	17.1	49.0	75.9
Jerusalem	123.0	167.4	200.5
Nazareth	30.0	25.0	30.9
Netanya	23.0	41.3	57.9
Petah Tigra	31.8	54.0	73.5
Ramat Gan	30.0	90.8	106.8
Rehovot	18.2	29.0	34.0
Rishon Le Zion	18.0	27.9	40.0
Tel Aviv-Jaffa	335.0	386.1	388.0

Source: Adapted from Israel, Central Bureau of Statistics, *Statistical Abstract of Israel, 1968*, pp. 30–31.

The bulk of the increase went to medium-sized towns, principally in districts already urbanized. In other areas the most important changes took place in the Southern District, where the number of Jews increased dramatically. In 1948 there were only 6,000 Jews in the Southern District; by 1968 the number had risen to 267,600, an increase from less than 1 percent to more than 11 percent of the total Jewish population.

The Jewish population is 88.6 percent urban. There are 24 towns and 48 urban areas classified as Jewish. Rural settlements number 705; of these, 233 are kibbutzim, 345 moshavim, and 22 collective moshavim, comprising a majority of the rural population (see ch. 20, Agriculture). There are 60 Jewish villages.

At the extremes, more than one-third of all Jews but less than 2.5 percent of the non-Jews live in the Tel Aviv District, whereas well over one-half the non-Jewish population but only 10 percent of the Jews inhabit the Northern District.

In contrast to the Jews, non-Jews are predominantly rural. Including East Jerusalem, the proportion is 56.8 percent; excluding East Jerusalem, the ratio rises to more than two-thirds. The village is the principal form of settlement pattern. Non-Jewish settlements include two towns, three urban areas, and 99 villages. A sizable number of non-Jews also live in six urban localities where a great majority of the population is Jewish. The remainder of the non-Jewish population consists of 43 Bedouin tribes, numbering about 33,900 persons.

CHAPTER 5
ETHNIC GROUPS AND LANGUAGES

The major ethnic divisions are Jews and non-Jews, with both subdivided into distinct groups on the basis of language, culture, and national origin. A group is more likely to be considered a separate one if it is highly visible by virtue of physical appearance, customs, number of its members, coresidence, and socioeconomic status.

Religious conversion is possible, but not frequent; intermarriage between Jews and non-Jews is difficult and is not common among the various Jewish groups. Individuals rarely transcend their national origins, although their descendants may do so. Informal social relationships tend to take place within an ethnic group.

ETHNIC GROUPS

The Jews

The Jewish population is divided into three major groups; the Sabras, native born, before or after the creation of the state of Israel; the Ashkenazim, of European origin; and the Sephardim, or Oriental Jews of North African or Middle Eastern origin. The latter two terms originally referred to European Jews speaking Yiddish and Ladino, respectively. After the Jews were forced to leave the Iberian Peninsula, in the 1490's many of them settled in the Middle East and North Africa; Jews from these areas are generally referred to as Sephardim, even if they are not descended from the Iberian Jews. The Ashkenazim and Sephardim also differ in the pronunciation of Hebrew and in certain minor ritual details. Each group has its own chief rabbi (see ch. 11, Religion).

Government statistics for the end of 1967 indicate that 708,600 persons were born in Europe or the Americas, and 654,500 in the Middle East or North Africa. Of the Sabras, 392,600 had fathers from Europe or the Americas, 465,400 from Asia or Africa, and 162,400 born in Israel. The total Jewish population was 2,383,600.

A small Jewish community had remained in Palestine since ancient times, but the major part of Jewish immigrations (*aliyah*—from the Hebrew word meaning "ascent"—see Glossary) did not begin until the 19th century. The earliest settlers were either religious persons who wished to spend their declining years in the Holy Land, or were

Zionists, who hoped to promote a Jewish revival in Palestine; in the main, both groups were of European, particularly East European, origin (see ch. 3, Historical Setting).

The second significant period of immigration occurred in the early years of the 20th century, composed largely of Zionists from Europe. Immigration, which resumed after World War I, was also mainly from Europe, and the years immediately preceding and during World War II saw a great increase in the numbers of Jewish settlers. After the establishment of the State of Israel in 1948, a great influx of immigrants came from the Middle East and North Africa.

The most recent census (1961) enumerated individuals according to their country of birth. The largest Middle Eastern group was from Iraq, including both Arab city dwellers and villagers from Kurdistan. The next largest group was from Aden and Yemen in South Arabia. Turkish Jews included those of Sephardic origin and those from rural areas. Another group came from Iran. Indian Jews came from Bombay and from the southwestern district of Cochin; a third Indian group was of Iraqi origin. Other Jews came from Syria, Lebanon, and Soviet Central Asia.

Morocco yielded the largest group from North Africa. Algeria and Tunisia contributed a large group, mainly French-speaking. Egypt and Libya were also sources in Africa. A few immigrated from South Africa, but they were largely of European origin. Finally, a small group came from Ethiopia.

Polish Jews constituted the largest European group, followed by Jews from Rumania, Czarist Russia, and the Soviet Union. Germany, Austria, Czechoslovakia, and Hungary also contributed substantial numbers. Many Sephardic Jews came from Bulgaria, Greece, and Yugoslavia. Relatively few Jews have immigrated from North and South America, or Australia.

The principal ethnic division among Israeli Jews is between Europeans (whether or not born in Israel, and including Americans, South Africans, and Australians) and Orientals (whether or not born in Israel, and including Middle Eastern and North Africans), inaccurately referred to as Ashkenazim and Sephardim, respectively. There is great variety within both of these groups, but the differences between them are still greater than their internal differences. The Middle Eastern and North African Jews have more in common with the Arabs than the with the European Jews, except for religion.

Jews all over the world have adopted the culture of the people among whom they lived, often making modifications to fit religious beliefs and practices. They have also converted and intermarried with those people, so that they have come to resemble them physically. There is no universal Jewish physical or cultural type.

Middle Eastern and North African Jews, for example, tend to be more kin-oriented than European Jews, have more children, live in larger family household units, and have more social relationships with relatives. On the whole, they have less formal secular education, and more of them have relatively unskilled occupations. Their attitudes are more traditional, manifesting less interest in social and technological experiment and innovation. They have demonstrated, however, their capability to adapt to numerous and far-reaching changes.

As a consequence of their education and occupations, together with the larger size of their families, many Middle Eastern and North African Jews are concentrated in the lower socioeconomic levels. Many of them had to abandon property and occupations when they immigrated to Israel, where they had to start over again.

The Middle Eastern and North African Jews tend to be Orthodox. In social relations, they are characteristically polite, hospitable, and leisurely. They take a relatively inactive approach toward governmental and civic affairs. Physically, they are usually darker-skinned than European Jews and, at least when they first arrive, they wear different types of clothing. They have firm opinions about propriety in social affairs and hold to a firm division of labor between men and women, as well as upholding feminine modesty. Folkloric beliefs and customs are different from those familiar in Europe.

Middle Eastern and North African Jews from the large cities of the Levant and North Africa, however, do not fit these generalizations, as many had acquired a secular European education and had attained middle class or higher status. In Israel, nevertheless, they still tend to be classed with other Jews from the same two regions.

One minor Jewish group, the Samaritans, is unique. At one time they were numerous, but their numbers have dwindled to only a few hundred adherents. They have lived in Palestine at Nabulus continuously since ancient times and have formed an inbreeding population. Culturally, they are part of the Arab world (see ch. 11, Religion).

Non-Jewish Groups

The non-Jewish population is largely Arab. At least since the period of the Ottoman Empire it has been divided into numerous religious communities, and the Israeli government has preserved the communal structure. As a religious minority, it is acutely aware of its status.

Up to 1948, the non-Jews constituted an overwhelmingly majority of the population (see ch. 4, Population). During and after the conflict against Arab forces in 1948, large numbers of Arabs fled or were expelled, leaving a minority of about 18 percent in late 1948 (see ch. 3, Historical Setting). Since 1948, their rate of natural increase has been greater than that of the Jewish sector, but Jewish immigration was heavier, so that by the end of 1967, non-Jews constituted about 12 percent of the country's total population (excluding East Jerusalem). The total non-Jewish population at the end of 1967 was approximately 324,500, including about 232,900 Muslims, 59,600 Christians, and 32,000 Druzes, and others.

The Arabs in Israel are mainly descendants of the ancient inhabitants of the country. After the Arab-Islamic conquest of the seventh century, they gradually adopted the Arabic language and culture, and most of them became Muslims. Most of the Palestinian Arabs were either small farmers, or businessmen and professionals in the cities; a relatively small number were Bedouins, either in the Galilee or Negev regions. The greater part of the Arab population has concentrated in the Galilee region. The Muslims are the largest religious community among the Arabs, and almost all of them are adherents of the Sunni branch of Islam (see ch. 11, Religion).

Among the Christians, the Melkites are the largest community, followed by the Greek Orthodox, Roman Catholics, Maronites, Protestants, and members of various Oriental churches. The Druzes follow the Christians in number. They are unique among Arab groups in their greater willingness to deal with the Israeli state. There are a few adherents to Ahmadiyya Islam and to the Bahai faith; only a small number of these are Arabs (see ch. 11, Religion).

A few thousand of the Muslim minority are not Arabs, but Circassians who came from the Caucasus in the 19th century when the Czarist Russians occupied their lands and were settled by the Ottoman government in various regions of the Levant. Their language is unrelated to Arabic, and they preserve their national identity. Like the Arab Druzes, the Circassians in Israel have been more willing to take part in Israel affairs.

A few Armenians still remain in the cities. There are also a few non-Arab representatives of various religious communities, most of them European.

Interrelations of Groups

In general, interrelations of groups are characterized by cooperation in economic and governmental affairs, but by aloofness in informal social relations. Individuals tend to seek out members of their own groups for friends and neighbors, although they may work with members of many national groups. The groups tend to marry within themselves, although intermarriage, at least with coreligionists, is increasing.

The government maintains principles of equality in social and political rights for all citizens, regardless of nationality or religion. Although it is a Jewish state, except for certain types of immigration, non-Jews are given equality with Jews before the law in secular affairs, with exceptions in instances where security is concerned (see ch. 26, The Armed Forces; ch. 27, Public Order and Internal Security).

Economic development of the country has brought about increased social mobility. Despite the persistence of the old pioneering ethic of egalitarianism, persons are increasingly differentiated by socioeconomic status, which is connected with nationality of origin because of such features as education and family size. Strains of adjustment to the new environment have created tension between groups. Within the Jewish population, however, there is still the common religion that is a strong bond, especially in times of national crisis.

The government is concerned with integrating its citizens culturally and socially. To this end it promotes mass education on a European model, including adult education, and the use of Hebrew as a spoken language. Housing policies are designed to promote integration of nationalities, and to encourage European-style family life. Folklore is modified and used to promote national unity (see ch. 9, Education; ch. 10, Artistic and Intellectual Expression).

LANGUAGES

Hebrew is the principal language used in the country. Both Hebrew and Arabic are official languages and may be used in the Knesset, in the courts, and in approaches to officials. English is also widely used on street signs and in government publications; it is the foreign language most frequently taught in the schools (see ch. 9, Education). Both Arabic and English were official languages, together with Hebrew, during the British Mandate period (1923–1948). Other foreign languages are spoken by immigrants; the chief of these are Yiddish and Ladino.

Hebrew

Hebrew is a Semitic language, related to Aramaic and Arabic. It was first spoken by the ancient Canaanites of Palestine, and the nomadic ancestors of the Hebrews learned it there. Records of Hebrew from the 14th century B.C. have been found in Egypt. The Hebrew alphabet was derived from the same Phoenician alphabet from which English derives its alphabet; it is written in a noncursive style from right to left. Like Arabic, the alphabet is consonantal, with the vowels being indicated by optional small marks above and below the line. Word formation is based on a system of triconsonantal roots.

From the time of the Hebrew invasion of Palestine, Hebrew was both the spoken and the written language of the people. After the conquest by Alexander the Great (333 B.C.), the use of Hebrew began to decline, being replaced by Greek and Aramaic. After the final destruction of the Jewish state in A.D. 73, Hebrew survived only as a sacred language.

Jews all over the world came to speak the language of whatever country they inhabited, interspersing it perhaps with a few Hebrew words, and often speaking a distinct dialect. Sometimes the Hebrew alphabet was used to write the language of the country, however unrelated it might be to Hebrew. The Jewish people began to think of Hebrew as sacred, raised above the level of everyday affairs; in Israel, some of the Orthodox still refuse to use Hebrew in their everyday speech, because they regard it as a holy language.

Jewish scholars often use Hebrew for some of their works. The language continued to serve as a lingua franca among the different Jewish communities throughout the world. In Europe its use, never universal among Jews, began to decline with the expansion of mass secular education. The modernizing Haskalah (Enlightenment) movement of the 19th century was a Jewish response to European progress, which aimed at a Jewish-Hebrew renaissance. Early Zionists also promoted the Hebrew revival. Biblical Hebrew was revived, and in 1886 a daily Hebrew press was established.

One early Zionist, Eliezer Ben-Yehuda, a Polish Jew, is responsible for the use of Hebrew as the national language of Israel. He emigrated to Palestine in 1880, and immediately began to promote the use of Hebrew as a spoken language. Central to his campaign was the use of Hebrew as the medium of instruction in the schools. Gradually the Jewish schools in Palestine began to teach in Hebrew. By 1913 the idea was so popular that when a technical high school, the precursor of the Israel Institute of Technology (commonly known as Technion), was opened in Haifa, it was obligated to teach in Hebrew, despite the undeveloped state of the language for technical subjects.

Hebrew in the 1880's was not well suited for use in everyday life, nor for technological and scientific subjects, although it served well for religion, philosophy, and literature. Ben-Yehuda and others compiled a number of comprehensive dictionaries. In 1904 the Vaad ha-Lashon (Language Council) was founded to settle matters of spelling and grammar and to create new words for new objects. In many cases, old but little used words were revived with new meanings. Other words were formed from preexisting roots, borrowed from Biblical Aramaic, or by translating the elements of foreign words. In 1954 the Vaad ha-Lashon was given status as the official Academy of the Hebrew Language. The Israel Defense Forces and other government agencies also have responsibilities regarding word formation; popular writers also play a role in the creation of new words.

In 1921 the Mandate Authority recognized Hebrew as one of the three official languages of the country. After the founding of the state of Israel in 1948, Hebrew was installed as the official language. Great efforts have been made to teach immigrants the language and to use it throughout the country.

Israeli Hebrew is a mixture of styles and eras. It follows the Sephardic pronunciation because Ben-Yehuda felt that it was the closest to the original form of the language. Many Israelis contract words in rapid speech. The Middle Eastern and North African Jews use an Arabic pronunciation in their Hebrew.

Others

Many immigrants from Europe still speak Yiddish or Ladino. Yiddish is a variant of the German language that has a large Hebrew-derived vocabulary and is generally written in the Hebrew alphabet. It developed as the speech of Jews in Germany, who later migrated into Eastern Europe. Ladino, a variant of medieval Spanish, developed in the Iberian Peninsula and spread into North Africa and Southern Europe after the Jews were forced to leave Spain in 1492.

Most of the immigrants from North Africa and the Middle East speak Arabic, as do the indigenous Palestinian inhabitants of the country. Although spoken Arabic has a number of dialects, the written language is a common standard. Arabic is closely related to Hebrew in syntax and vocabulary; the alphabet is similar, but in cursive style. Arabic possesses a vast literature, and many of the Arabic speakers keep up with it.

Other language are also spoken by immigrants, including English, French, and German, as well as Russian, Rumanian, Bulgarian, and Polish; Aramaic is spoken by many Persian and Kurdish Jews as well as by some Christian groups.

CHAPTER 6
SOCIAL STRUCTURE

The society, drawn from heterogeneous origins, is complex but cohesive and is deeply conscious of history and tradition though subject to change. It is democratic and egalitarian but confronted with the unique problems of a large, unassimilated minority differentiated by religion and political factors. The society is characterized more distinctly in terms of segments, or groupings than by rigid forms of stratification. Mobility is possible in all directions, but not with equal ease in all, and is more likely to occur within major groupings than across them.

The principal structural division is between the Jewish majority and the non-Jewish minority. The important subgroupings within the majority are the Ashkenazi Jews of European origin, who were dominant in the prestate Jewish community in Palestine, in the initial immigrations after statehood in 1948, and in the subsequent leadership of the state; and the Sephardic Jews of Middle Eastern and North African background who were the most numerous immigrants after 1952. The latter, with their progeny, formed the largest segment of the population in 1969 (see ch. 4, Population). Native-born Israelis, known as Sabras, are generally identifiable with either an Ashkenazi or Sephardic background, but are forming a new stratum that will ultimately be predominant in the society. Also within the Jewish sector, and mostly of Western background, is the small grouping of ultra-Orthodox Jews, identifiable by distinctive customs and representing one of the main stresses in the society, that of secular versus religious interpretation and determination (see ch. 17, Political Values and Attitudes; ch. 12, Social Values).

The non-Jewish minority is indigenous. It consists of Arab Muslims and Arab Christians, plus small numbers of Circassian Muslims and of Druzes, and their descendants, who remained in Israel at the time of statehood in 1948 or later gained readmission.

The state was founded under the influence of an ideology dedicated to the socialist principles of a classless society functioning by teamwork (as in the kibbutz), in which the role of the individual should be encompassed within and subordinate to the society in all its phases. These concepts are apparent in the general informality of Israeli society, with its easy communication between individuals; in the highly organized form of the multiparty political system; in the strong party discipline maintained; and in the stylized language of the founding ideology, still used by most of these parties.

The original nature of the society changed, however, after statehood was attained. With the passage of time and the confrontation with pragmatic requirements, there occurred an evolutionary shift in status criteria, that is, in the general concept of what was recognized, respected, and admired. By 1969 it appeared that at the top of the strata was not wealth or political position or ideological identification, but individual achievement in a predominantly urbanized, industrial society. This criterion was not necessarily restricted to a particular occupation, but was heavily weighted in favor of professional achievement in science or technology, especially if furbished by distinguished war service. A degree of class consciousness appeared to be developing with distinctions based on professional status. The kibbutz farmer, as such, was no longer seen so much as the personification of the ideal Israeli, but rather simply as a rural person. The war hero, even if undistinguished by other achievements, ranked higher in popular recognition.

Background of birth, family status, wealth, and influence were not necessarily determinant criteria for recognition of individual achievers. The operation of background factors, however, appeared to facilitate the development and emergence to recognition of able individuals having certain characteristics. For example, a hypothetical army reservist colonel of early middle-age who had fought with distinction in all three wars (1948, 1956, and 1967), who had been born in a kibbutz of Second Aliyah (1904–14) Ashkenazi parents, and later became a professor at the Israel Institute of Technology (known as Technion) or The Weizmann Institute of Science, and who had developed an electronic process of wide scientific and commercial applicability, and had won an international professional award, would stand on or near the top rung of the status stratification ladder.

In the social structure, as in the political structure, the founding ethic of equality was in competition with the concurrent founding ethic of a Jewish state with regard to the non-Jewish minority. Although the Arab enjoyed legal equality and might, in fact, attain higher levels of education, professional status, and even Knesset membership, he necessarily remained an Arab in a minority for which accommodation was possible but full assimilation unlikely. Ultimate resolution of this societal problem was dependent upon political rather than sociological developments.

SEGMENTS IN THE SOCIETY

Although characterized by a powerful political elite, the society is not constricted by rigid traditional forms of hereditary aristocracy or class (see ch. 14, Political Dynamics). It may be described in terms of segments cut across by transverse strata, reflecting various criteria of status, such as education, income, or other determinants. Through these strata the individual may move according to his ability and inclination, modified by conditions of relative advantage and subject to some constraints not always under his control.

The principal recognizable segments of the society are non-Jews, Jews, and ultra-Orthodox Jews. The dominant center grouping of secular to moderately religious Jews accounts for about 80 percent of the society and determines its character and direction. The other two categories, although much smaller, exhibit such distinctive differences as to enable separate initial delineation (see ch. 4, Population).

Non-Jews, constituting about 12 percent of the population, include those Arab Muslims, Christians, Circassian Muslims, Druzes, and other non-Jews within pre-June 1967 borders. Their number at the beginning of 1968 was about 324,400 divided into subgroupings of 72 percent Muslims, 18.5 percent Christians, and 9.5 percent Druzes and others. Almost one-half of the total lived in some one hundred villages, with two-fifths in towns and the balance being seminomadic Bedouins.

Characterization as part of the non-Jewish community and its subgroupings is determined by birth in a nonproselyting society. Identifications may become attenuated in individual relevance and practice, but formal change is virtually unknown. The non-Jewish community is indigenous, rather than immigrant, and grew, along with minor numbers of readmissions, at a rate of natural increase with excess of births over deaths two to three times greater than that of the Jewish population, from the approximately 150,000 non-Jews who remained in the country at the time of Israel's establishment in 1948.

Ultra-Orthodox Jews represent only about 6 percent of the total population, but are governed by distinctive life styles, separating them in the social structure from fellow Israelis. Politically they are represented by the Agudat Israel (Association of Israel) and Poalei Agudat Israel (Workers of the Association of Israel) parties (see ch. 14, Political Dynamics). Some, such as the small sect in Jerusalem called the Neturei Karta (Custodians of the Town), regard the state merely as a man-made, worldly arrangement not constituting the true Israel, which they contend must come about by divine intervention. The ultra-Orthodox interpret the nature of a Jewish state in terms of religion, and religion is interpreted in terms of strict, fundamentalist observance of the Judaic law as it pertains to social behavior, dietary restrictions, Sabbath observance, forms of worship, and matters of personal status, such as marriage and divorce (see ch. 11, Religion; ch. 13, The Governmental System).

The ultra-Orthodox element in Israeli society was identified early in the life of the state in a proportion that varied little thereafter. There is no restriction preventing or impeding their entry into the mainstream of Israeli social and political life other than their own patterns of religious belief and practice. To those in the Israeli society for whom the idea of a Jewish state was not defined in religious terms or, if so defined, then not in the sense of strict fundamentalist practices, the "ultras" represented an anachronistic mode of life. By their insistence on the forms of observance as the embodiment of spiritual values and ethical principles, the ultra-Orthodox constituted what to many other Israelis seemed a harassment of the general society. The problem of the "ultras" was seen by some Israeli sociologists as part of the larger problem of defining the national identity and nature of a Jewish state. Whether the social grouping of the ultra-Orthodox would attenuate to remnant status or continue to maintain its strength at about a 5 to 6 percent level of the whole population was not clear. In 1969 their numbers did not appear to be declining rapidly, and some evidence indicated that ultra-Orthodox youth might become even more fundamentalist than their elders (see ch. 12, Social Values).

Besides non-Jews and ultra-Orthodox Jews, the most distinctive and commonly perceived divisions of Israeli society consist of Jews of European or American origin, often roughly collectivized by the term Ashkenazi Jews; those of Middle Eastern and North African origin, referred to as Sephardic Jews; and native-born Jews, called Sabras. Even among the native-born, an identification with either the European tradition and background or the Middle Eastern and North African tradition and style can usually be made (see ch. 5, Ethnic Groups and Languages). Although the Sephardim and their descendants by 1969 had attained an increased numerical preponderance, it was the earlier and better-educated Ashkenazic immigrants who had provided the leadership and organization of the state (see ch. 4, Population). In consequence, and partly because of patterns established under the British Palestine Mandate, as well as the later barriers erected by hostile Arab states, the principal economic connections were with Europe and the Americas. The founding ideology of the state had visualized a classless, rural, agricultural society based on socialist principles, but the general form to which the society had evolved by 1969 was urban, industrial, and increasingly capitalist in a mixed economy. The values of the younger generation, while basically close to those of their elders and equally or more nationalistic, were less specifically ideological than the old socialist Zionism. They were less involved with religious commitment, more concerned with technology and current Western cultural forms, more inclined to a tough policy toward the Arab states and, on the European-type spectrum of left-center-right values, were politically and economically more to the Center or to the Right (see ch. 12, Social Values; ch. 17, Political Values and Attitudes).

FORMS OF STRATIFICATION

In a young state, established in recent history after long preparation climaxed by dramatic conflict and difficulty, a number of Israel's founding fathers were still living in 1969 and enjoyed a special elite status of esteem and respect. Their numbers, however, were few and decreasing, and at no time did they or their descendants constitute a rigid or formal aristocracy. In the highly organized political and economic life of the nation, pervading all levels and segments of society, the hierarchy of political and bureaucratic control in the government and Histadrut (Histadrut Ha'ovdim Haklalit — General Federation of Labor) similarly did not constitute an aristocracy, although its members held power and influence in an essentially conservative system, manned in the main by apprenticeship, training, and succession in service (see ch. 14, Political Dynamics).

Transverse strata cutting across the segments of society could be identified in terms of density of regional settlement, occupation, age levels, education, income, and urban and rural habitation (see table 10). Examination of data shows that the Jewish population is predominantly urban, with heaviest concentration in the Tel Aviv Dis-

Table 10. Rural-Urban Distribution of the Population by Type of Settlement, Israel, 1968

(in thousands and percentages)

Habitation	Jews		Non-Jews[1]		Total	
	Number	Percent	Number	Percent	Number	Percent
Urban	2,110.7	88.6	168.5	43.2	2,279.2	82.2
Towns	(1,665.4)	(69.9)	(144.8)	(37.1)	(1,810.2)	(65.3)
Urban areas	(445.3)	(18.7)	(23.7)	(6.1)	(469.0)	(16.9)
Rural	272.9	11.4	221.8	56.8	494.7	17.8
Large villages	21.6	0.9	133.4	34.2	155.0	5.6
Small villages	27.7	1.1	52.1	13.4	79.8	2.9
Moshavim	121.3	5.1	0.3	--	121.6	4.4
Collective moshavim	4.9	0.2	-0.1	0.1	5.0	0.2
Kibbutzim	83.1	3.5	-0.2	--	83.3	3.0
Bedouin	--	--	33.9	8.7	33.9	1.2
Institutions	12.0	0.5	0.1	--	12.1	0.4
Other	2.3	0.1	1.7	0.4	4.0	0.1
Total	2,383.6	100.0	390.3	100.0	2,773.9[2]	100.0

[1] Includes about 65,800 in East Jerusalem.
[2] Breakdown of total population in percent: urban Jews 76.1, rural 9.8, total 85.9; urban non-Jews 6.1, rural 8.0, total 14.1.

Source: Adapted from Israel, Ministry for Foreign Affairs, Information Division, *Facts About Israel, 1969.*

trict, and is engaged mainly in industry, the professions, commerce, finance, and public services, with only about 10.3 percent in agriculture. On the other hand, the non-Jewish population is predominantly rural and agricultural, with its principal concentrations in the Northern District in the Galilee region and in the Haifa and Central districts. In the country's labor force as a whole, only some 12.6 percent were engaged in agriculture; but in the non-Jewish portion of the labor force, 41.2 percent were in agriculture, and the next highest category was construction (se ch. 22, Labor).

As to age levels, the proportion of young people among the non-Jewish population was distinctly higher than among the Jewish majority, 74.4 percent of the former being in the age group of 30 years or less in 1968 and only 56.2 percent of the latter. Within the Jewish sector, those of Sephardic background constituted more than half of the same age bracket. The birth rate in the non-Jewish population exceeded that of Sephardic Jews, which in turn exceeded that of Ashkenazic Jews. Whereas non-Jewish and Sephardic families typically have been larger than Ashkenazi, some evidence pointed to an apparent trend toward a decrease in Sephardic family size (see ch. 7, Family). It appeared, however, that the Sephardic sector would expand more rapidly and continue to increase its numerical preponderance in relation to the Ashkenazi grouping. The non-Jewish community of pre-1967 Israel, by statistical studies made in early 1967, could theoretically constitute a majority in the country by the year 2000 (see ch. 4, Population).

In terms of education, the general level among Ashkenazim was higher than among Sephardim and the non-Jewish element. For example, among the immigrants of 1963, 98 percent of the males from Europe and America were literate in at least one language compared to 82 percent of those from the Middle East and North Africa; the former group had a median level of about 10 years' schooling, and the latter had about 7. Disparities among females in the same groups and categories were even greater. In the whole group of immigrants, 23 percent of those from Europe and the Americas had an occupational background in the professions or technical skills compared to 6 percent of those from the Middle East and North Africa. Nationwide literacy in Israel of persons over 14 years of age was about 88 percent in 1968, that of the Jewish population being 90 percent or more. Among Jews of European and American background, 96 percent were literate; among those of Middle Eastern and North African background, about 57 percent. In the non-Jewish population, literacy was estimated at about 50 percent. At the higher levels of education, the cleavage was even more marked. Of college and university undergraduates in 1966, 59 percent were born in Israel, 30 percent in Europe, and 10 percent in North Africa or the Middle East. Among the native-born students, only 4 percent were of Sephardic background (see ch. 9, Education).

Income is still another factor affecting status in the society. Annual salaries and wages for 1967 ranged from more than I£16,000 (I£1 equals approximately US$0.285—see Glossary) for highly skilled engineers and self-employed professional persons, down to I£6,000 for workers and to about I£3,500 for temporary unskilled farm labor. The higher positions were filled mainly by Ashkenazim, whereas Sephardim and non-Jewish elements were found in the lower levels.

Because the founding leadership and the early population base were predominantly of European origin and because of the higher education levels of this sector, the better jobs and controlling positions in the society remained in Ashkenazi hands. Although numerous exceptions could be adduced, the Sephardim were characterized by entry into the unskilled or low-skilled labor pool and small business. Non-Jews were characterized as being rural and agricultural. The situation tended to be self-perpetuating, but changes in the composition of the population numerically favoring non-Jews and Sephardic Jews, plus the slowly rising levels of education in these groups and the growth of a full Sabra generation to legal age, portended future change.

RECOGNITION AND EMULATION CRITERIA

The principal criterion for social recognition and esteem is that of individual achievement and performance in peace and war. In the active, industrial-technical, urbanized, security-conscious, and nationalistic society of Israel, this criterion defined the upper stratum of prestige. Not necessarily confined to any one occupation, the criterion was perhaps most marked in the realm of science and technology where individual attainment was clearly recognized and highly esteemed, especially among the younger, nonideological generation.

Neither wealth nor political activity is necessarily highly regarded as prestigious in itself. It is likely that material reward will be associated with accomplishment. The professional politician must, like everyone else, demonstrate tangible results to attain recognition and prominence.

Distinguished war service is a badge of the highest prestige. The war hero is clearly recognized in the general esteem after the trials of three wars and almost continual interim conflict; the jet pilot, paratrooper, or tank driver image is more generally identified as a hero role than that of the tractor-driver in the old kibbutz ideology. A combination in one individual of scientific learning, technical accomplishment, and distinction on the battlefield would, in the Israeli society of 1969, place such an individual at the pinnacle of prestige.

The criterion of personal accomplishment appeared to be a guideline for the future and has been described by Israeli spokesmen as foreshadowing development of a society led by a "meritocracy," as opposed to a political ideocracy. Proponents of this view wanted not a "chosen society" but an open and competitive one based on industry and science. The past contributions of Zionism and its utopian principles were respected and valued, but nostalgia was rejected. Promotion and recognition based on merit were seen to be the keys to a modernized definition of the society, with less political rhetoric but more equalized education and access opportunities for all to become "meritocrats." In economic terms productivity as a measure of accomplishment was the standard for recognition, not ideology.

The recognition role of individual accomplishment in a society defined as a "meritocracy" was in sharp contrast to the tenets of the founding socialist-Zionist ideology. This older doctrine had held the individual subordinate to society and glorified the collectivized agricultural worker in the ideological bastion of the kibbutz. On the other hand, it disparaged nondoctrinaire, pragmatic effort, no matter how intense or brilliant, that appeared not to be organized under Zionist ideology (see ch. 17, Political Values and Attitudes). Despite the legacy of the past and the genuine respect in which its accomplishments were held, the societal recognition determinant of prestige in 1969 had become individualized achievement, and this development was described by Israeli commentators as a logical expectation. Closely associated is the Israeli principle of *ein breyra*, a Hebrew expression signifying "no alternative," which meant that the state had to succeed, that problems had to be solved, and that security had to be maintained. This principle engendered a spirit of positive pragmatism and determination (see ch. 12, Social Values).

SOCIAL MOBILITY

Basically, Jewish society is an open and informal one where public figures may be called by their first names and treated with good-natured irreverence, thus reflecting the old ideal of a classless society. It appeared in 1969, however, that there was developing a greater class consciousness based on distinctions of professional status. All citizens, including non-Jews, are equal before the law, and there are no legally fixed barriers to social mobility. Ability and performance were the key determinants. The idea of equality specifically included equality of women, as shown by the Equal Rights for Women Law of 1951, by the position of women in the kibbutzim, by the fact that women may be called for military training and service and by the example at the national level of Prime Minister Golda Meir, herself a founder of Israel and longtime holder of high office in the state. The equality of women, however, was less firmly established among

Sephardic and non-Jewish populations, where the traditionally inferior role of women was often maintained.

In practice certain inhibitory or accelerative factors of mobility applied within the groupings of Ashkenazim, Sephardim, and non-Jews, including education, training, wealth, and access to influence. In consequence, it was, in general, more likely that a youth from an educated Ashkenazic family of some means and repute would himself attain higher levels of education and access to position at or above his family background status than for a Sephardic youth of the same ability to attain the same levels. Research studies showed strong aspirations for upward mobility among Sephardim, but these aspirations were visualized more in terms of improved status or skills rather than the highest offices or professional positions. Among Ashkenazim, aspirations were found to be somewhat less strong and directed more at maintenance of the same or somewhat higher levels of occupation and status as found in their families, a finding considered to reflect the fact that Ashkenazim were already predominant in the professions and leadership positions (including the military services) and, in consequence, did not perceive a need to emphasize strong mobility aspirations. The non-Jew, affected like the Sephardic by disparities in education and starting point, was also confronted with the irrefutable ethnopolitical fact that he was a non-Jew in a Jewish state.

The Israeli government has been keenly aware of these problems. The great influx of Sephardic Jews after statehood produced tensions reflecting the segments of Jewish society sometimes referred to informally as the "First Israel," or Ashkenazim, especially those of the earlier immigrations, and the "Second Israel," or Sephardim of the immigrations after 1948. Coming mostly from Arab or other Islamic countries of the Middle East and North Africa, they brought with them life styles of dress, manner, and attitude different from the Jews of Europe or even those of the Yishuv (see Glossary) of the British Palestine Mandate period. Heads of the typically patriarchal Sephardic families often found themselves at a loss, with their children usually acquiring new languages, especially the modern Hebrew established in Israel, and new skills faster than they. The Sephardim most demonstrably responded to the call for immigration to Israel after statehood, known in Zionist terminology as the "ingathering from the Diaspora," and they expressed resentment at sometimes seeming to be regarded as "less useful" citizens than the "more useful" types of higher skill and education sought by the state from Europe and the Americas for tasks of development.

Further, there was Sephardic resentment over the payments from the Federal Republic of Germany (West Germany) of restitutions to individual Israelis and families who had been victimized in World

War II. These payments were in addition to the national-level, state-to-state restitutions. It was clear that the Sephardim were not eligible for the individual restitution payments and that the Israeli government could not alter the situation; it was regarded among Sephardim, however, as a further aggravation of already existing Ashkenazi advantages.

During the second decade of Israeli statehood, the problem of absorption, assimilation, and acculturation of the Sephardim was one of the major preoccupations of the state. Public health efforts decreased the overall death rate and infant mortality. Educational levels commenced a slow rise. Government establishment of new towns and villages by 1969 had improved population dispersal ratios in comparison to the high concentrations in major cities that prevailed in 1949. Although it remained true that marriages occurred principally within the respective Ashkenazi and Sephardic sectors, a slow but apparently rising degree of intermarriage was recorded. This trend was small in numbers but significant in that it appeared to be increasing, even if slowly. Ultimately this trend to exogamy, the rise in education levels, and the emergence of the younger generation to control of the society were visualized by sociologists as producing an undifferentiated Israel in which the compartments of Ashkenazim and Sephardim would be merged (see fig. 6).

In the case of non-Jews, mostly Muslim or Christian Arabs, living conditions improved in the years after 1948. Both their overall death rate and infant mortality rates declined sharply, education levels rose markedly and were continuing to rise, and Arab citizens were afforded freedom to maintain their Arabic culture. Arabic and Hebrew are the two official languages of Israel. Never barred from political life, 85 percent of eligible Arab voters went to the polls in the 1965 elections for the Sixth Knesset and elected six Arab members and one Druze. More than half of the Arab labor force belongs to the Histadrut (see ch. 22, Labor).

Civil marriage in Israel, however, is not possible for Israeli citizens. Although some assertions of the occurrence of mixed marriage between Jews and non-Jews have been recorded, no quantification is available and the evidence is insubstantial. Such unions would necessarily result either from religious conversion of one of the parties or would not be legally recognized. Because of ethnic and political antipathies, exogamy between Arab and Jew did not hold promise as a possible solution to the minority problem.

COHESION AND COMMUNICATIONS

Despite its heterogeneity and its groupings differentiated by background, culture, and attitudes toward ideology and religion, the dominant Jewish majority is cohesive. It is united in dedication to

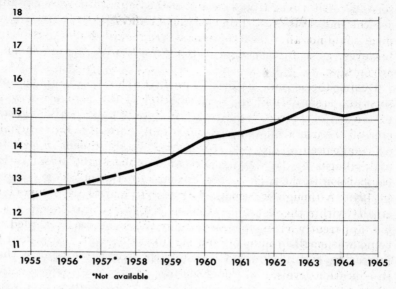

Intermarriage by Percent

Not available

Year	Ashkenazic-Groom		Sephardic-Groom		
	Ashken Bride	Seph. Bride	Ashken. Bride	Seph. Bride	TOTAL
1955	6,466	1,001	581	5,301	13,349
1958	6,372	1,275	698	6,314	14,659
1959	6,245	1,329	673	6,190	14,437
1960	6,214	1,370	723	6,104	14,411
1961	5,915	1,273	777	6,076	14,041
1962	6,065	1,335	855	6,477	14,732
1963	6,296	1,424	1,042	7,268	16,030
1964	6,873	1,369	1,216	7,754	17,212
1965	7,329	1,340	1,425	8,002	18,096
TOTAL	57,775	11,716	7,990	59,486	136,967

Figure 6. Marriage and intermarriage of Ashkenazic and Sephardic Jews, Israel, 1955–65.

Source: Adapted from Government of Israel, Central Bureau of Statistics, *Statistical Abstract of Israel, 1968*, Jerusalem, Government Press, 1968.

the state, in its overriding if not precisely defined awareness of mutual Jewishness, in its pride in the accomplishments of the state in peace and war, and in its common perception of having no alternative. The tensions between Ashkenazim and Sephardim are social and internal. Even internally they are not political, as Jewish ethnopolitical parties have never been strong and have not attained a Knesset seat since the first election in 1949. Further, as demonstrated by historical experience, these tensions are not subject to exploitation by foreign interests.

One of the main factors in establishing a cohesive Israeli Jewish society, and one which continually assisted in promoting a blending of its diverse elements, was the revival of Hebrew and its successful adaptation as a modern language. Not native either to the Ashkenazi or Sephardic Jew, the acquisition and use of this common language created a link of communication and mutual identification (see ch. 5, Ethnic Groups and Languages).

Between the young, middle, and older generations a strong cohesion also exists, for the same reasons that establish the overall bonds between Ashkenazim and Sephardim. Methodology and specific applications of doctrinaire ideology changed, but the society, except for the differentiated non-Jewish minority, remained horizontally and vertically cohesive and open. The nuclear family as a socializing unit, despite an apparent slow decrease in size, remained basic and strong through all groupings, and its importance was apparently increasing in the kibbutzim. In 1968, however, the kibbutzim included only about 3.5 percent of the population (see ch. 7, Family).

Other major factors conducive to societal unity were the small size of the country, the well-developed system of communications, the leveling and educational influence of general military service, and the fact that governmental and political affairs are intensively and extensively identified in the society. The relationship is so close that it is difficult to distinguish between social and political matters in the national life, since there is no insulation from the world of politics and government.

Finally, the general cohesion of the society was reemphasized by the stress and victories of the Six-Day War of June 1967, which engendered increased respect and sense of mutual identification between old and young and between Sephardim and Ashkenazim. Internally social problems were recognized and serious efforts were underway to bring about developmental social changes to allow ability and performance full play in the individual and general majority interest.

SOCIAL CONTRADICTIONS

The non-Jewish minority experienced a growth from about 150,000 persons to some 324,400 during the years 1948 through 1968. Standards of living were raised, income and education increased, and health and life expectancy improved. Birth rates soared to more than twice that of the Jewish population. The last remaining areas under Israeli military administration in the Arab community of pre-1967 Israel were turned over to civil government in 1966. Arabs had legal equality and religious freedom. They remained, however, a differentiated minority in the society, and it was not clear how full assimilation into that society might be attained or whether such assimilation might, in fact, ever be possible.

Basically the problem was seen to be political and closely related to the continuing general crisis of security and settlement with the Arab states, including determinations regarding the original Arab refugees of 1948. In Israel a small sector of public opinion, as represented by the Ha'olam Hazeh party (literally, This World—also known as New Force), with one seat in the Sixth Knesset, advocated positive separation in Israel of religion and state and peace based upon integrated cooperation between Arab and Hebrew nationalism. Ha'olam Hazeh's view included the heretical concept of Israel as a Levantine state (see Glossary) of the Middle East rather than an extension of Europe.

The older political elite formed under the socialist-Zionist-kibbutz ideology typically has rejected the Levantine state concept, as shown in the stands taken on this subject by David Ben-Gurion and Pinhas Lavon, political opponents who shared in common an intense rejection of Levantism. Likewise, periodic proposals for some form of binational Jewish-Palestinian Arab state had met with no success by early 1969. Other opinion suggested that a solution might lie in a broader philosophical and practical view of the nature of Judaism and the definition of the term "Jewish state."

Meanwhile the Palestinian Arab minority of Israel in 1969 remained socially differentiated. With regard to this minority, the Israeli national ethic of equality, in the sociological sense if not in the strictly legal sense, continued to be in competition and contradiction with the "Jewish state" principle—equally a founding ethic of the nation.

CHAPTER 7
FAMILY

In the late 1960's the prevailing form of family organization and the dominant pattern of domestic life were those of the urban European-derived and native-born majority, which comprised about 72 percent of the population. The usual type of family structure was the nuclear family, composed of a man, his wife, and their children. Family members followed the same general style of domestic life as their counterparts in Europe or the United States; that is, the family was an independent economic unit in which husband and wife had a generally equal relationship, sharing the management of family funds and the making of decisions. Discipline of children was usually moderate, and early signs of independence were encouraged.

The family performed an important social role. It gave its members a sense of social identity, served as focal point of emotional and physical security, and was the chief instrument for the socialization of the young. At the same time, however, it shared with other social institutions, such as the schools, youth groups, and the army, certain traditional functions which, in less complex societies, lay within its scope.

Patterns of domestic life varied in accordance with a number of criteria. The two most significant were the size and type of community in which the family lived and the national origin of the head of the household. Of secondary importance were the family's religious behavior and its financial resources. The urban centers accounted for about 82 percent of the population. European-born (Ashkenazic) and native (Sabra) Israelis were concentrated in the three largest cities, Tel Aviv, Haifa, and Jerusalem, with only a few in the smaller towns. On the other hand, Sephardic Jews, tracing their origins mainly to Iraq, Iran, Yemen, Turkey, and North Africa, were settled primarily in medium-size and smaller urban centers.

Urban families headed by a European or Sabra husband were typically of the middle-income level, with adult members engaged in managerial or professional pursuits. Despite the fact that family members spent a good deal of time away from each other at work, in school, or in civic activities, the domestic unit was generally close-knit. Parents spent much of their leisure time in the company of their children. Nominally adherents of Judaism, most members of this urban European-derived and Sabra majority were, nevertheless, secularly oriented and gave little time or attention to the details of orthodox religious behavior.

A small number of Orthodox Jews, however, were found in the major cities, especially Jerusalem, where their forebears had been merchants and traders for many centuries (see ch. 11, Religion). Family life and customs in this community departed substantially from the norm in such patterns as average family size and the distribution of authority within the household.

In smaller urban centers, especially so-called development towns, patterns of domestic life, to some extent, reflected the non-Western cultural tradition of the Sephardic majority. As immigrants to Israel, the predominantly Sephardic inhabitants of these towns had brought with them a system of family organization in which connections and obligations among kinsmen were far more extensive than in Western societies. Since their arrival, however, these groups had felt the impact of very great pressure for change, caused both by the forces of modernization and the process of adaptation to a new environment. The result had been a continuing process of fission of the extended family and a trend toward reallocation of family roles.

In rural areas the nuclear family was also the prevailing form of family organization. In the moshavim (smallholders' cooperative settlements), the nuclear family was the basic social and economic unit. Each family had its own household and was an independent economic unit. In the kibbutzim (collective settlements), the nuclear family existed in a modified form. Extended family organization had been maintained in non-Jewish communities but has been undergoing a process of structural change.

THE SETTING

Trends of development in family structure and behavior over the past several decades have resulted less from conscious social planning than from the pressures and trends in other spheres. Both the Zionist colonizing movements and, since 1948, the policies of the government have given less emphasis to the family than to other social institutions. The kibbutz movement deliberately attempted to limit the role of the family, and the moshav program offered a framework in which it could expand. These movements, however, have involved only a small minority of the population.

Rabbinical courts have exclusive jurisdiction in matters of marriage and divorce of Jewish citizens or residents. Other religious communities—Muslims, Christians, and the Druzes—have their own courts which apply their own laws (see ch. 13, The Governmental System). There is no provision for civil marriage or divorce, except in the case of non-Jewish foreign residents, who may be married by their consuls if their national law permits such a marriage. Grounds for divorce include sterility in women, impotence in men, adultery by either partner, mental defect, or a serious disease that was contracted before marriage and concealed.

In general, the laws of the society uphold the elevation of women to full equality with men. The Women's Equal Rights Law (5711–1951), annuls any law that discriminates against women and states that a man and woman shall have equal status with regard to any legal proceeding. This law supersedes any religious law that discriminates against married women in regard to property rights. It also gives equal rights of guardianship to both parents and makes the mother the natural guardian of the children in the event of the death of her husband. This contrasted with previously existing laws by which the father was the sole natural guardian of the person and property of the children, and the mother did not become guardian in the event of his death.

The stress on equality of women can be seen in all spheres of the national life. Women have the right to vote and are prominent in national affairs. The country's minister of foreign affairs from 1956 to 1966 was Mrs. Golda Meir, the first woman to hold such a post in the non-Communist world and the third to serve as head of government (see ch. 18, Biographies of Selected (*Key Personalities*). Women engage in a wide variety of occupational pursuits and have risen to prominence in a number of professions. If unmarried or childless, they are subject to compulsory army training along with the young men of the country; but their term of service is shorter (see ch. 26, The Armed Forces).

In the initial period after independence in 1948, great social emphasis was given to women's role as childbearers. A high birth rate was considered in the national interest; children symbolized the promise of the future. Traditional Jewish teaching underlined the virtues of procreation, and the prime minister himself awarded motherhood prizes to women after their 10th delivery.

Clerical and political opposition to birth control continued during the 1960's. The ministry of health had no official policy on birth control, but family planning centers were few, and most were operated by local authorities. Despite this, however, the birth rate has been steadily declining.

The number of births per thousand mean population in 1967 was 24.2 as compared with 26.6 in 1960, 29.2 in 1955, and 33.8 in 1951. Available statistics indicate a correlation between the length of residence in Israel of the wife and the number of children; the longer she had lived in the country, the fewer children she was likely to have. The urban middle-class norm was two children.

The major exception to this general trend toward low fertility

ars among Sephardic women, many of whom adhere to tradi-
il cultural norms and produce a large number of children. In the
traditional ideal of family life, among Sephardic Jews, women are
limited in their activities and concerns to the domestic circle, and
their value as women is in large part a reflection of their ability to
produce many heirs.

STRUCTURE

The basic structural unit of the family system is the two-generation
nuclear family. Husband, wife, and children typically maintain an
independent household, with one or both adults employed outside the
home. In the urban centers the nuclear family is most prevalent
among urban organized and skilled workers, professional persons,
civil servants, and those engaged in business. It is also found, however, in rural areas, both in the moshavim and, in modified form, in
the kibbutzim.

Among Sephardic Jews, the basic structural unit of the traditional system of family organization was the extended family. This
consisted of three generations—parents, their sons and their sons'
wives, and their sons' children—all living in one household or adjacent households. The oldest man was head of the family, managed its
properties and had the final voice in all decisions. Beyond the extended family, kinsmen were organized into still larger groups, or
lineages, known as *hamulas*. These *hamulas* were composed of all persons, male and female, who traced their descent in a single line from
a common male ancestor. The number of generations by which this
ancestor was removed from the oldest living one varied, though a
depth of four to six generations was usual.

THE MODERN URBAN FAMILY

In 1967 the average family size for the country as a whole was 3.8,
including single persons, or 4.2 without single persons. Family size,
however, showed a considerable divergence in relation to the size of
the community. Reported figures for 1967 were 3.2 persons per family
in Tel Aviv-Jaffa, 3.3 for Haifa, 3.8 for Jerusalem, and 3.8 for other
towns. The discrepancy was even greater in comparison with rural
settlements. Average family size, including single persons, in Jewish
villages was 4.3; in kibbutzim, 2.3; and in the moshavim, 5.1.

Within these various types of settlement, family size also varied
in relation to ethnic origin. Families in which the heads of household
were European-born averaged 2.9 persons, those headed by Sabras
averaged 3.2, and those headed by Middle Eastern- or North African-
born Israelis averaged 4.8 persons. For non-Jewish families, the average family size was 5.9, including single persons, or 6.2 without single
persons.

Major Cities

The pattern of domestic life among European-born Jews in the major metropolitan centers was that which they had brought with them from their countries of origin. The family, typically made up of a couple and their children, was established in its own separate household and was an independent economic unit. Husbands and wives had a partnership type of relationship, with neither having greater authority than the other and each sharing equally in family responsibilities. Both contributed to the social development of the children and were mutually accountable in representing the family in dealing with outsiders.

As the children of these European-born parents grew to adulthood and married, they too established the same pattern in their domestic lives. They lived apart from their parents and beyond their control. Most managed to maintain a fairly close relationship with their parents and with their siblings, but the degree to which they turned to them for advice and assistance varied from individual to individual. Ties with married brothers and sisters and parents were maintained through such activities as the giving of mutual assistance in times of sickness or stress and the exchange of visits. Religious and secular holidays, such as Passover and Independence Day, were made the occasion of family get-togethers, usually at the home of the oldest couple.

Parent-child relationships were generally characterized by great warmth and affection. Most parents devoted a great deal of their leisure time to their children. Mothers gave help with homework before serving the midday meal, which brought all the family members together to recount and share the activities of the day. Afterwards, many fathers provided companionship for their children, reading aloud or playing games with them. The Saturday break in the workweek was a special time when families often joined together for such pursuits as hiking, nature study, and amateur archeology. Short automobile trips were popular. Sometimes children spent nonschool nights at their grandparents' homes.

In child training, which was generally permissive, a premium was laid on early social development. Parents took special pride in evidences of self-reliance and independence in their children at a young age.

The household was generally supported largely by the father's earnings. Wives in the middle-income group, however, were often employed on a part-time basis. They might, for example, teach, serve as a museum guide, or work in an office or a hospital. Typically, a portion of their salaries went toward the wages of a domestic servant, a reflection of the frequent preference of such women for outside employment as against household duties. Such servants typically were drawn from lower-income urban families, many of whom were North African-born or had emigrated from other Middle Eastern countries.

The ideal of family life among extreme orthodox groups, found in small numbers in the major cities, was drawn from a tradition that stressed the authority of males and the importance of the group over that of the individual. Overt behavior between husband and wife was relatively formal and gave little evidence of a strong personal attachment. At the same time, however, it was essential to the ideal that there be a large number of offspring, for children were regarded as the real meaning of marriage.

Other Towns

Because of decisions made by settlement authorities, most of the inhabitants of the so-called development towns, such as Ashdod and Eilat, were immigrants from Iraq, Yemen, other Middle Eastern countries, and part of North Africa. These persons, who made up what was termed the Oriental community, were also found in moderate numbers in other urban centers. A handful had been settled in moshavim, the smallholders cooperatives in the rural areas.

Among a substantial segment of the Jewish population from Middle Eastern and North African countries, the extended family structure had experienced varying degrees of disintegration and the mode of domestic life that had accompanied it was changed. In many instances the senior male, whose authority traditionally had gone unquestioned, no longer had a real place. His sons had physical mobility, had served in the army, and had economic resources or possibilities of employment on their own. The cultural emphasis on self-reliance served to reinforce the deterioration of traditional relationships between father and son. In general, however, enough continuity had been maintained in the process of change to prevent the development of serious social disorganization.

Another departure from tradition was the fact that many women of these communities commonly worked outside their own homes. Many such families lived in public housing projects. The number of children was usually large, and in order to provide for them parents sometimes had to place one or more in a public institution.

RURAL FAMILY PATTERNS

The kibbutz movement dates back 60 years, during which time the position of the family within it has been considerably transformed. In the initial period the scope and functions of the family were radically curtailed, reflecting the intent of the founders as well as the political and economic exigencies that mitigated against the emergence of a family-centered group. More recently, however, a partial restitution of family functions has taken place.

The kibbutzim, settled almost entirely by European-born Israelis or Sabras, are governed by a general assembly of all members. Populations range from 60 to 2,000. Production and consumption are communally organized, and no member owns any private property other than a few personal belongings. The adults all work, and children are cared for by specially trained members of the community. They live in their own so-called Children's Houses. In sum, the community is run as a single economic unit and as one household.

Initially the kibbutzim curtailed the scope and structure of the family almost to the point of disappearance. Many kibbutz members were unmarried youths. Married couples were permitted to live together, but often only after a waiting period, and then occasionally being asked to share their single room with one or two other persons. They ate their meals in a communal dining hall, and worked in different parts of the kibbutz, in accordance with regulations forbidding their being assigned to the same place of work. There was no economic relationship between husbands and wives, nor did they share the task of rearing their children, which was basically that of the kibbutz. The birth rate was far below the level of replacement.

The keynote of the relationship between a man and his wife and between them and their children was comradeship on easy terms. While there was strong emphasis on personal autonomy and freedom in the sphere of sexual relations, this was counterbalanced by the value placed on ascetic dedication to collective goals. Differences between the sexes were deemphasized. Women wore a masculine style of dress and did little to enhance their femininity. Family tasks were performed on the basis of strict sexual equality and neither partner had any authority over the other. Relations with children were characterized by permissiveness.

By the late 1960's there had been a partial reversal of these early trends, and the family had regained some of its primacy. In daily living, greater privacy was accorded to family members, who might have a two-room dwelling unit with its own kitchenette and private sanitary facilities. In some kibbutzim, families shared meals at home rather than in a communal dining room. Family size was increasing, some couples having three or four children, and parents were taking over the duties of child care and social upbringing to a greater extent. There was increased occupational specialization by sex. More women did the work that kept them close to home or in touch with the children; some occupations were almost completely sex-segregated.

In terms of Israeli society as a whole, other important trends were indicated. Members strengthened their ties with kinsmen, and young persons started to look for marriage partners outside the kibbutz. Some collective settlements were making a place for their founders and for aging or sick parents.

About 5 percent of Israelis live in moshavim, as compared with 3 percent in kibbutzim. The moshav is made up of a community of families engaged in agriculture on a cooperative basis. Two types of moshavim have evolved, distinguished by different economic arrangements, but in each the nuclear family is the basic social and economic unit.

Each family lives in its own small house, which has at least two rooms, plus a kitchen and an inside bath. Wives and children care for flower and vegetable gardens adjoining the house. Children live with their parents, attending a moshav-run kindergarten after reaching the age of 4 years and the village school or a regional school after reaching 5 or 6 years of age.

Families must meet certain qualifications in order to be admitted to a moshav. In general, they must be in good physical health. In many moshavim the settlers are predominantly young married couples with children under 10 years of age, and couples over 40 years of age with older children are not accepted. Older-than-average children involve the moshav with the additional expense of arranging schooling in another village. Some moshavim accept responsibility for parents of members, providing them with housing and all services they need.

The scope of family functions is relatively broad. The family has the basic responsibility of socializing the child, although the schools, youth groups and, eventually, the army share in this process. Parents are expected to assist children in making decisions and to offer them moral support and protection. Apart from working arrangements, the family is completely independent and arranges its private life as it sees fit.

Moshavism that are organized on a collective farm basis are called moshavim shitufiim. They assume complete responsibility for the economic welfare of members. All persons are entitled to the same payments and services whether or not they are healthy and working. Even those called on for army duty continue to receive their payments. It is anticipated that they will also provide for all members in their old age.

In Arab villages social life is based on interrelationships between a small number of extended families. The senior male asserts ultimate authority within the family and is its leader and principal spokesman. An underlying principle is that of the inequality of the sexes, with women having inferior status and few rights of their own.

In such villages the nuclear family is not independent but functions as part of a larger extended family, which is the basic family unit in terms of production, consumption, and socialization. Extended families are joined into hamulas, which serve as the major source of social status.

Most persons in the traditional village follow centuries-old occupational pursuits, in agriculture or trade. The domestic unit includes several generations, sometimes as may as four. Husbands control their wives, and parents exercise complete authority over their children. Marriages are arranged by the parents, with payment of a bride-price, a characteristic feature of the contract.

The Arab village family is adapting to new conditions at a rapid pace. The extended family is weakening, inasmuch as fewer sons are remaining in their parents' household after marriage, and the period for which they remain before leaving is becoming shorter.

TRENDS IN MARRIAGE AND DIVORCE

The rates of both marriage and divorce have been declining steadily during the past two decades. The number of marriages per thousand mean population was 11.4 in 1951, as compared with 7.5 in 1967. Approximately 1.7 divorces per thousand mean population were legalized in 1951, as compared to 0.8 in 1967. Although the marriage rate is declining, it is, nevertheless, relatively high, and the number of unmarried persons of marriageable age is therefore low. The comparatively high marriage rate can be ascribed both to the youthfulness of the immigrant population and to Jewish tradition that strongly approves of marriage, and remarriage in the case of widows and widowers.

The reasons for the declining divorce rate were not indicated in any studies completed by early 1969. Possibly the decline was a general reflection of the increasing stability of the society. Divorce was relatively more frequent among urban than rural inhabitants, among European-born than among Asian-, or African-born persons, and among secularly oriented families, than among orthodox families.

In the late 1960's the great majority of marriages united persons born in Europe, or of European descent, with persons of like origins. Similarly, North African- and Middle Eastern-born Jews usually married persons of the same background. Nevertheless, there was a small but significant trend toward intercommunal marriage, especially noticeable among Sabras. Both within and between the two broad divisions—Ashkenazic and Sephardic—there was an upward trend in marriages between persons of different origins.

CHAPTER 8
LIVING CONDITIONS

The differences between the living standards of various sectors of the population in the late 1960's were, for the most part, moderate. In general, the urban population, representing over 80 percent of the total, was slightly better off than the rural component, who found nonessential commodities less readily available than in the towns. In many developing areas, however, hardship conditions prevailed. Cutting across this broad division was the disparity in living conditions existing between both the European-and native-born Israelis and the minority of persons born in the Middle East or North Africa, the so-called Oriental Jews. The latter group was generally less educated than the remainder of the populaiton, and its members had somewhat lower incomes and a less well-balanced diet than other Israelis.

The level of health and of available medical care was high, in comparison with neighboring countries and with conditions existing at the time of independence. Life expectancy at birth for Jewish male children in 1967 was 70.4 years for males and 73.6 years for females.

The infant mortality rate had declined steadily during the previous decade falling to 25.9 per thousand in 1967. Malaria and a number of other communicable diseases had been eliminated or reduced to negligible incidence. The country, moreover, had a higher ratio of physicians to inhabitants than any other nation, and a widespread system of public health services brought modern medical care to all parts of the country.

This progress had been made despite the great difficulties that had faced the government in the early years of independence. Mass migration had brought together thousands of persons from widely scattered parts of Europe, North Africa, and the Middle East. A substantial number of the new arrivals had been in poor physical health. Many of them had never had any kind of medical or dental care and were unfamiliar with the basic fundamentals of hygiene. Besides this, it had been necessary to house temporarily many immigrants in overcrowded quarters that lacked sanitation facilities. At first, health services, both preventive and curative, had been unable to keep up with immigration, but during the next two decades the situation was altered markedly.

Although most of the major health problems had been overcome by the late 1960's, some still remained. Of these, probably the most pressing was the need for improvement in sanitary facilities in many parts of the country.

The social welfare activities of public and voluntary agencies were extensive. Programs were in effect for the care of the aged, children, and young persons, the chronically ill, the handicapped, and new arrivals in the country. Many of these programs received substantial financial support from organizations abroad, especially from the United States. About 72 percent of the total population participated in the health insurance fund of the Histadrut (Histadrut Ha'ovdim Haklalit—General Federation of Labor). The entire adult population was covered by a pension plan that was of a comprehensive national insurance scheme.

LIVING STANDARDS

Most of the population lived in moderately comfortable circumstances. A survey taken in the mid-1960's among urban-dwelling Jews, who constituted about 80 percent of the population, revealed that the average annual net income of individuals in the group was I£6,790 (I£1 at that time equaled approximately US$0.333—see Glossary). Within this group, averages for persons in different occupational groups ranged from a high of I£12,504 for self-employed persons in the liberal professions to a low of I£5,916 for workers in various privately owned or cooperative enterprises. Deductions for income taxes, pension funds, union dues, and other purposes yielded a net income which was an average of 85 percent of the gross figures.

A family expenditure survey on consumption patterns among Jewish urban employees was done by the government in 1963–64. According to the study, the average family spent about 30 percent of its monthly income on food, 22 percent on housing and household maintenance, and 10 percent on clothing. The remainder was spent in more or less equal portions of health, education, and culture; transportation and special services furniture and household equipment; with a smaller percentage going to organization dues and donations.

The steady refiniement of living conditions was reflected in the growing numbers of families that had acquired labor-saving devices and other personal possessions in the previous decade. In 1967, for example, electric refrigertors and gas ranges were owned by four families in five, whereas in 1958 only about one family in three had owned them. Also, in 1967 about a third of all families owned an electric washing machine, as compared with only a tenth in 1958.

Among the European-born and Sabra (native-born) majority, the family's most prized possession was likely to be its personal library. Collections of books were carefully chosen and displayed with pride, and in many households a great deal of living space was given over to their shelving. Almost every family had at least one radio, and a substantial number had two. One family in three had a record player; one in ten had a tape recorder. The number of privately owned automobiles was increasing. In 1967, 13 percent of all Israeli families owned an automobile, as compared with 5 percent in 1963.

Nutrition

Domestic food production in the first years after independence fell short of consumption requirements, because of the rapid growth of the population and of the limited development of agriculture. Despite this setback, most persons appeared to have had an adequate diet. In 1949/50 daily per capita caloric intake averaged 2,610.

Domestic production of foodstuffs expanded rapidly, and by 1952 both the rationing system and price controls had been eliminated. Foods were available in greater variety and most could be obtained on the open market. Since then, production has risen still further, and by early 1969 it covered about four-fifths of consumption.

In 1966/67 Israelis consumed an average of 2,925 calories per day. In general, daily intake of various nutrients was at an acceptable level. Clear signs of nutritional deficiency, however, were encountered among certain groups. A study of urban women done in the early 1960's revealed that the diet of lower income families was considerably below estimated requirements for animal protein, calcium, iron, and vitamins A, B_2, and C. This was linked partly to low income and partly to culturally-derived food preferences. Most of the women in the lower income group were of Middle Eastern or North African origin.

Clothing

Western dress is the usual mode of attire, with emphasis on informality and suitability to a warm climate. Traditional garments are still worn by the Bedouins, by the ultraorthodox Jewish communities and, on special occasions, particularly national holidays, by some other Jewish groups.

In the major cities middle-aged and younger men generally dress in slacks with a long- or short-sleeved shirt. When more formal attire is called for, a necktie and jacket may be added. Women wear simple dresses, often sleeveless, or skirts and blouses during the day. Hats provide protection from the hot sun. Slacks and shorts are sometimes seen. At an evening concert or the theater, the usual female attire is less casual, and the temperature may call for a light sweater. The wardrobes of the wives of some prosperous urban professionals and businessmen include garments designed by European or Israeli couturiers.

In rural areas the universal working attire for both men and women consists of a pair of shorts, usually worn with a shirt or blouse, and a pair of sandals. Children, both boys and girls, wear identical attire—a pair of shorts, with perhaps a shirt, or a blouse or undershirt. In the kibbutzim (collective farms or settlements), there is a conscious attempt to deemphasize personal adornment.

Housing

At the time of its establishment in 1948, Israel faced a critical housing shortage. Immigrants entered the country at a pace that far exceeded the rate at which new construction could be accomplished. Housing abandoned by Arabs who had left the country met only a small portion of the need. The Jewish Agency, which was responsible for the absorption of immigrants, and the government undertook a vast building program. Private construction efforts played a second-ary role. Both temporary shelters and permanent dwellings were erected. Many new immigrants were at first housed in tent camps; later they moved to one-room, corrugated iron or frame houses with outside toilets and showers.

By the mid-1960's, however, the housing shortage had been largely alleviated, and there was no longer any need for the *ma'abarot* (temporary dwellings). Newcomers were moved immediately into permanent residential units, of which more than half a million had been built. Many of them were located in accordance with a com-prehensive plan for population dispersal (see ch. 4, Population).

About two-thirds of all the houses built during the first 15 years after independence were put up under public auspices on a nonprofit basis. Permanent housing for immigrants was made available to tenants for purchase at moderate prices. Mortgage terms varied with individual requirements. Retired persons and others who could not afford to buy a house could rent one at a modest monthly rate.

Prosperous families could participate in the government's so-called Save-for-Housing Scheme. Prospective purchasers made a minimum deposit to register for the plan, then accumulated the cost-price of the house they intended to buy through gradual savings, which earned 4 to 6 percent yearly interest tax-exempt. When they had saved 75 percent of the purchase price, they could buy a house, with the government taking a mortgage for the rest.

The most recent census of housing, taken in 1961, provides some data on home ownership. At that time it was revealed that in urban areas the ratio of home ownership to renting was about two to one. The percentage of persons owning their own dwelling units was

higher among the European-born Jews than among North Afric[...]
and Middle Eastern Jews. Non-Jews in urban areas were more like[...]
to rent than to own their houses, but the reverse was true in the
countryside. Among various occupational groups, the percentage of
home ownership was highest for administrative personnel, merchants,
and farmers, and lowest among persons in service occupations.

Urban

Of the residential construction undertaken in urban areas, the
greater part consisted of apartment complexes rather than single-
family dwellings. Accordingly, in the late 1960's most of the inhabitants of the major cities occupied small apartments in buildings designed to house from six to 12 families. The buildings were usually
identical and no more than three stories high. Floor space in each
apartment averaged more than 500 square feet, divided into two or
three rooms, plus kitchen and bath. Single-family houses were about
equivalent to apartments in size and living space. In the hot climate
the ubiquitous awning-shaped balcony is an important adjunct to
indoor living space.

Houses and apartments built by private construction firms were
more spacious and more generously equipped with amenities than
those built under public auspices. Many, for example, had tiled baths
and kitchens and, in service areas, custom-built cabinets.

Rural

Many rural inhabitants live in moshavim (cooperative settlements), in which they have their own private dwelling units. Typical
of many such single-family units is a prefabricated frame house,
consisting of two rooms, a kitchen, a bathroom, and a small porch.
Total interior space amounts to somewhat more than 625 square feet.
Such a house usually stands on half an acre of land, on which there
are also some outbuildings to shelter a small number of dairy cattle
and broodhouses for poultry. Many permanent settlers have added
rooms to the original structure.

A smaller number of rural inhabitants belong to the kibbutzim,
where housing arrangements are entirely different. These vary from
one settlement to another, but basically the pattern is for each adult
couple to have one room, with meals taken in a communal dining hall.
Public toilets and bathing facilities are located nearby. Children are
housed separately according to their age groups, visiting with the
parents in evenings during special hours set aside for this purpose.
The trend toward greater privacy in some kibbutzim has led to an
arrangement allowing each couple private living quarters, with
cooking and bathing facilities.

Although the housing in collective and communal villages is all relatively new, since these settlements have all been organized in this century, other villages consist primarily of old houses, many of which have been standing for generations. These are usually made of stone or brick, with tile roofs and with thick walls to keep out the heat.

PUBLIC HEALTH

Environmental Sanitation

The level of sanitation in the late 1960's showed marked improvement over conditions existing before 1948. A Sanitation Division has been developed in the Ministry of Health; the division is staffed by more than 20 entomologists, chemists, bacterologists, and sanitary engineers, in addition to more than 120 specially trained aids who assist in carrying out educational and other programs in the field.

Food sanitation has improved measurably with the widespread use of modern refrigeration equipment, the growing emphasis on hygienic packaging, and the stress on cleanliness among food handlers, especially those in restaurant kitchens. Representative from the Ministry of Agriculture were assigned to oversee milk production methods to assure cleanliness and engaged in with the eradication of cattle diseases.

Especially noteworthy has been progress in provision of an adequate and safe drinking-water supply, a problem that has been crucial for the development of the country. In the late 1960's the coastal plains areas were drawing their supplies chiefly from deep wells, whereas in the highlands the supply came from springs or rainwater cisterns. More than 90 percent of townspeople and nearly 85 percent of rural inhabitants were served by central water distribution networks. In most urban areas the water was chlorinated before distribution, and in many places bacteriologic monitoring was maintained. Transmission of contagious disease through impure drinking water became rare.

Despite this progress, the level of sanitation continued to fall short in certain respects. High standards of cleanliness were not uniformly maintained in either small retail food markets or by street vendors. An acute gastrointestinal type of food poisoning caused by salmonella contamination of meat and eggs was fairly common. Cases of accidental food poisoning attributable to improper food additives and toxic food contaminants also occurred from time to time.

Sewage disposal presented a serious health problem. In the early years of the state, the development of central disposal plants could not keep pace with the rate of urban growth. Many temporary installations, such as septic tanks, were introduced, but some functioned ineffectively because of poor ground absorption. With construction of housing and factories, the volume of waste matter rose rapidly. No natural riverbeds or lakes suitable for its disposal existed, so that much sewage poured into open channels or *wadis* (the watercourse or valley of an intermittent stream, or the stream itself).

By the mid-1960's, however, the major cities had at least partial sewage systems, and many smaller centers, temporarily depending on cesspools, were developing their own. Modern sewage-disposal plants existed in Tel Aviv and Haifa. In Jerusalem the central system was not fully operative and much sewage ran into open watercourses, which were breeding grounds for mosquitoes. Wells in the area frequently became polluted and had to be closed.

Sanitary facilities were generally more available in the towns than in the countryside. Official statistics revealed that nearly all urban dwellings had an inside toilet and either a bathtub or a shower, and that most had some water-heating system. This contrasted with rural dwellings, among which fewer than half had inside toilets, a slightly larger portion had an inside bath or shower, and fewer than half had hot water available.

Another health problem was the presence of various pests—among them rats and spiders—that, directly or indirectly, interfered with the well being of the population. Malaria eradication programs had wiped out the anopheles mosquito, but other types of mosquitoes were a public nuisance. Two prevalent species were identified as carriers of West Nile fever, or encephalitis, and possibly filariasis (infestation with parasitic worms).

Causes of Death

The crude death rate in 1967 was 6.6 per thousand for Jews and 6.2 per thousand for non-Jews. The leading causes of death were heart disease and cancer, followed by strokes, accidents, and pneumonia. Heart disease was roughly three times more prevalent among European-born Jews than among those born in the Middle East and North Africa. In 1967 maternity deaths averaged 0.30 per thousand live births. Infant mortality was 20.8 per thousand live births among Jews and 44.3 among non-Jews. Infant deaths were attributable chiefly to congenital malformations, asphyxia, birth injuries, pneumonia, and undefined causes.

Diseases

During the early 1950's both chronic and communicable diseases contributed to the relatively unfavorable state of public health in the country. During this period, malaria and intestinal infections were widespread. Typhoid fever, poliomyelitis, and dysentery were commonplace, at times reaching epidemic proportions in some areas. The incidence of other diseases, including diphtheria, pneumonia, measles, and whooping cough, was high.

Although certain diseases presented a medical problem to the entire population, others were associated mainly with persons of particular national origin. European-born concentration camp survivors, for example, were highly susceptible to tuberculosis. Jews from Yemen, because of their health habits, suffered from various illnesses including trachoma and liver flukes.

By the late 1960's, however, many of these diseases had been virtually wiped out. In part, this was attributed to a system of routine immunizations of children, the scope of which had been expanding over a 20-year period. By 1968 the diseases for which routine immunization was taking place included: smallpox, tuberculosis, typhoid, diphtheria, tetanus, whooping cough, poliomyelitis, and measles.

Another aspect of the improved situation was the success of the Malaria Eradication Program, which had been launched in 1960 with the assistance of the World Health Program. Earlier control efforts, dating back as far as the British Mandate period, had been only moderately effective, partly because immigration had brought carriers of the disease in an unbroken flow. By 1965, however, the incidence rate had dropped so markedly that only one new indigenous case (a rate of 0.004 per 10,000 population) was reported in 1965 (none in 1966 and 1967). The total number of new malaria cases in 1967 was 13 (a rate of 0.05 per 1,000), compared to 842 in 1950 (a rate of 6.6 per 1,000). A more gradual decline was registered in respect to newly reported cases of tuberculosis. Some 610 new active cases were reported (2.3 per 10,000) in 1966, as compared with 1,500 (10.5 per 10,000) in 1952.

This progress notwithstanding, infectious diseases continued to be responsible for a major share of acute illnesses in all age groups. Upper respiratory infections, such as tonsilitis, bronchitis, and pneumonia, were widespread. Immunization against measles as a routine procedure has been in effect since 1966, but outbreaks of the disease are still common.

In the early 1960's mortality rates from acute intestinal infections had fallen significantly because of improved housing and sanitation, but such infections were still common, and severe cases were sometimes seen among the Middle Eastern and North African Jewish community and the Arabs. Trachoma also afflicted this group. Infectious hepatitis was endemic, particularly as an autumn-winter disease. Reported cases of syphilis among the population as a whole had risen. Among the European-born Jewish community, certain chronic diseases, notably cancer and heart disease, were major causes of illness.

Medical Personnel

In 1967 the country, with 6,311 physicians (one for every 429 inhabitants), had a higher proportion of doctors than any other country. There were, in addition, 1,255 dentists or one for every 2,158 inhabitants. Other medical personnel licensed by the Ministry of Health included 658 dental technicians, 1,539 pharmacists, 554 pharmaceutical assistants, and 462 midwives. Trained nurses were required to register with the Ministry of Health but did not need a license.

A great many physicians were older men who had immigrated from Europe in the 1930's and 1940's, having already obtained their degrees in medicine before coming to Israel. Younger Israeli doctors were educated either in the Hebrew University-Hadassah Medical School in Jerusalem or at universities abroad. In 1964 a medical school was opened at Tel Aviv University.

Most of the doctors were concentrated in the urban areas, however, and modern medical care in the rural areas was less readily available than in the towns. In 1963 over 44 percent of all licensed physicians lived in Tel Aviv and its environs. Another 26 percent was evenly divided between Jerusalem and Haifa, and an additional 20 percent was found in smaller urban centers. The remainder practiced in rural areas and towns with a population of fewer than 15,000.

Health Services

Government control of matters relating to public health is vested in the Ministry of Health, which is the supreme administrative and coordinating authority and serves as the licensing body for the medical and allied professions. The chief official, the minister, has cabinet rank and is responsible to the Knesset (Parliament). His deputy is the director-general, a civil service physician. The staff is composed of almost 9,000 persons, including more than 900 doctors and 3,500 nurses.

The ministry has two major divisions, reflecting its basic functions. One of these is the Division of Curative Services, which operates the government hospitals and is responsible for licensing and supervising nongovernment hospitals. The other is the Public Health Division, concerned with environmental sanitation, communicable disease control, maternal and child health, mental health, and the rehabilitation of persons suffering from chronic disease. In addition, it coordinates the work of units at headquarters with that of six district and 15 subdistrict offices, and various health centers and clinics in the field.

Although the principal responsibility for public health services rests with the Ministry of Health, other agencies play a major role. The Kupat Holim, the health insurance fund of the General Federation of Labor, usually known as the Histadrut or Histadrut Ha'ovdim Haklalit, is Israel's largest medical organization, with a membership of more than 1.9 million persons. It maintains hospitals and health facilities throughout the country. The Hadassah Medical Organization operates the Hebrew University-Hadassah Medical Center in Jerusalem.

Hospitals

In 1967 the country had 147 hospitals, of which private agencies maintained 65; the government, 34; and the Kupat Holim, 14. Additional hospitals were operated by Hadassah; various missions groups; by Malben, the American Joint Distribution Committee in Israel; and other agencies. The Hebrew University-Hadassah Hospital, Jerusalem, was one of the most modern institutions of its kind in the world, with 500 beds and an outpatient department that can care for 250,000 persons per year. Its staff of 1,500 included the faculty of the medical school, which compared favorably with those in leading universities anywhere. Many of the other institutions also provided a high level of care, but the multiplicity of independent operating agencies gave rise to problems for the government in organizing and coordinating hospital services to make maximum use of the country's facilities.

The 147 hospitals provided a total of 21,610 beds, including 9,175 for general care, 8,874 for mental illness, and 2,647 for chronic disease. More beds were needed, particularly for the chronically ill. Most of those available were in profit-making institutions.

Other Facilities

Besides hospitals, the government maintained a variety of other medical facilities. Among them were 450 maternal and child health centers, providing care to pregnant women, infants, and preschool children. The centers gave physical examinations to expectant mothers and provided them and their infants with postnatal care. They also gave health education courses, as well as routine vaccinations to children.

The government operated facilities for the diagnosis, care, and rehabilitation of handicapped children, including victims of poliomyelitis, cerebral palsy, rheumatic fever, and visual, speech, and hearing disorders. In addition, it operated a number of diagnostic laboratories and various schools for training of paramedical personnel.

Modern medical care was brought to all parts of the country not only through the network of government clinics and welfare centers but also by other facilities run by the Kupat Holim. In the late 1960's the Kupat Holim maintained, apart from its hospitals, over 1,000 clinics, 15 convalescent and rest homes, nearly 150 laboratories, 100 physiotherapeutic institutes, and over 200 pharmacies. It also maintained a highly respected medical research institute, the Rogoff Medical Research Institute.

Rehabilitation services are carried on by a number of agencies, both public and private. One of the most renowned of such facilities is the Weizmann Rehabilitation Center at the Tel Hashomer Government Hospital near Tel Aviv, where cardiac patients and persons who have lost the use of one or more limbs are rehabilitated.

The country's physicians have demonstrated a particular interest in medical research. The Weizmann Institute near Tel Aviv, for example, sponsors various projects of interest to medical science, such as research or the synthesis of proteins and the causes of cancer.

The government also provided medical care in the field of mental health. The circumstances of the country's establishment, involving rapid population growth and an unusual demographic composition, had created exceptional demands for such services. European-born immigrants, among whom were many concentration camp survivors, included a number of persons afflicted with chronic schizophrenia or involutional depression.

Long-range government planning for treatment of the mentally ill was based on a policy of early diagnosis, continuity of care, if possible in the local community, and an interdisciplinary approach to the problems of the patient and his family. Each of four internal regions into which the country was divided was to be provided with a related group of specialized-care facilities: psychiatric wards in general hospitals; short-term care psychiatric hospitals; work villages for long-term rehabilitation; centers for treatment of neurotic patients; custodial services; geriatric services; and child psychiatry clinics. In the late 1960's services of each type were in operation, and more were being developed.

Health services for Arabs are provided in many of the same facilities that serve the Jewish population. Where the need arises, however, special services are provided. A separate division within the Ministry of Health had been established especially to deal with the Arab population, and in the mid-1960's a total of 85 clinics and health centers were located in Arab villages.

Health Insurance

Voluntary health insurance is offered by the Histadrut-affiliated Kupat Holim and by five smaller agencies. Founded in 1911, the Kupat Holim had grown by the late 1960's to an extensive organization whose insurance covered roughly 75 percent of the country's population. Initially, the agency had limited its services to Histadrut members exclusively, and patients were treated by different physicians with no reference to personal choice.

For that reason, several smaller insurance groups were formed in the late 1930's: the National Workers' Sickness Fund, the General Zionists Sickness Fund, and the People's Sickness Fund. In 1968 these funds insured populations, respectively, of 219,000, 71,000, and 45,000. The Maccabi Sickness Fund, founded in 1940, and the Assaf Sickness Fund, formed in 1962, operated on the basis of free choice of physicians, of service facilities, and of pharmacies. They had memberships of 155,000 and 31,000, respectively.

In the late 1960's the Kupat Holim included members of the religious workers' organizations and self-employed craftsmen and farmers, who joined individually, as well as all Histadrut members. It also provided free insurance for the first three months to all immigrants. Income was derived from sources including members dues and government grants. Members and their families received medical care in the agency's own institutions, where they existed, or in government facilities. In 1959 a family physician system was introduced under which a single physician became responsible on a continuing basis for the medical needs of an entire family, which could choose its physician.

SOCIAL WELFARE

Israeli society stresses the responsibility of the community in promoting and ensuring the welfare of its members. Much emphasis is given to the obligation of providing mutual aid, not only in the collective and cooperative settlements but also in the society as a whole. Accordingly, in the late 1960's social welfare programs were being undertaken by a multiplicity of organizations, both public and private. The scope of their activities was such that assistance was generally available to any individual who found himself in economic or personal difficulty.

The focal point and central authority for matters in this field was the Ministry of Social Welfare, which coordinated, supervised, and supported the efforts of other agencies and organizations involved in welfare. Under its jurisdiction were local welfare bureaus, manned by professional staffs, under the guidance of the central ministry and with varying degrees of financial assistance from it.

The ministry maintained institutional care facilities for wayward, deaf, and homeless children and supervised thousands of children in private institutions or foster homes. It ran clubs, youth centers, and workshops for delinquent children. These activities were carried out by a trained staff that included welfare and probation officers. The ministry also maintained sheltered workshops for the handicapped and provided special services for the aged, the blind, and the mentally retarded.

Several other government ministries were engaged with welfare activities within their own contexts. The Ministry of Defense, for example, took an active role in the rehabilitation of war invalids and the care of war widows and orphans. Apart from the government, the two principal welfare organizations were the Jewish Agency, representing the World Zionist Organization in Israel, in particular its Absorption and Youth Aliyah departments, and Malben, an agency for the care of handicapped immigrants that received its funds from a philanthropic group in the United States, the American Joint Distribution Committee.

Youth Aliyah, founded in 1934, was originally established to assist in bringing to Israel children from countries where their physical or cultural existence as Jews was threatened, and to insure their well-being thereafter. Since independence it has continued the operation of children's villages, helping boys and girls acclimatize to a new way of life. In 1969 youth movements had a combined membership of more than 200,000. Roughly a dozen separate organizations were in existence, each with specific goals of its own. Of these, the largest was the Association of Working and Student Youth, affiliated with the Histadrut, with nearly 100,000 members. This group laid special emphasis on agricultural training and pioneer village work, but also offered vocational training courses in various trades.

Malben engaged in a variety of welfare activities, principally involved with providing medical, social, and vocational rehabilitation to sick, aged, and handicapped persons, and new immigrants. By 1968 it had assisted over 250,000 persons.

Large numbers of other civic and social groups, some in Israel, some based in countries abroad, were also active in welfare work. Among them were: the Women's International Zionist Organization; the Israel affiliate of the World Organization for Rehabilitation through Training (ORT); and the Mo'etzet Hapo'alot (Women Workers Council), a Histadrut affiliate, with 490,000 members as of 1969.

Since 1954 the country has had a comprehensive system of social insurance. Administered by the National Insurance Institute, the system encompasses three types of benefits: old-age and survivor's benefits; work injuries insurance; and maternity insurance, including allowances for large families. The rate of pensions is relatively low. Tied to the cost of living, the number of dependents of the insured, and the outside income of the insured, it varied in 1968 from approximately I£68 for single persons to I£210 for a couple with three dependents. The age of eligibility was 65 to 70 years for men and 60 to 65 for women. Pensions and grants for the disabled included medical treatment and rehabilitation and about three-fourths of full pay for up to 26 weeks during treatment. Maternity insurance provides a benefit of I£280 to new mothers whose confinement takes place in a hospital, and 6 to 12 weeks' maternity leave at 75 percent of normal earnings. Family allowances for children under eighteen are paid on the basis of I£12.50 per month for the first four children. After the fourth child, they are scaled in increasing amounts, starting at I£13.50 for the fifth and rising to I£17.50 for the eighth and each additional child thereafter.

CHAPTER 9
EDUCATION

Education has developed rapidly since the attainment of state-hood in 1948, and by 1969 school facilities or informal educational services outside the school system were available to almost everyone. The literacy rate among the Jewish population was estimated at 88 percent. Education is free and compulsory for all children aged 5 to 15. The 10 years of compulsory education include one year of preprimary schooling for 5-year-old children. About 98 percent of the Jewish children of ages 6 to 13 attend primary schools, and an estimated 62 percent of Jewish youths 14 to 17 years of age are enrolled in secondary schools or secondary preparatory courses. The country's seven institutions of higher learning enrolled about 6.6 percent of young men and women in the 20- to 24-year-old group. Adult education programs included Hebrew-language instruction, primary school classes, and a variety of academic and practical courses. The services of schools and of adult education facilities were complemented by the Israeli army and by various paramilitary and youth organizations (see ch. 26, The Armed Forces).

During the late 1960's the extent of participation in the formal educational process varied among groups of different cultural back-grounds. Because of the lack of early educational experiences and the low income earned by their families, immigrants from North African and Middle Eastern countries, and their first-generation descendants, the so-called Oriental Jews, constituted only a small percentage of the student body in secondary schools and in the universities. In 1965 these children accounted for about 15 percent of the students in academic secondary schools and for approximately 12 percent of those attending institutions of higher learning. To encourage the cultural integration and to facilitate the academic advancement of these students, the government introduced simplified curricula and special examination standards for them in the primary and secondary schools.

The period since independence has been marked by growing government initiative in education. The importance of education in furthering national goals has been emphasized by cabinet members, regardless of party affiliation. Government programs initiated during the 1960's were designed to raise the general level of education and to furnish professionals and skilled workers needed by the economy. Equal official emphasis has been placed, however, on the role of the schools in promoting the integration of groups with varying cultural backgrounds, in fostering patriotism and the spirit of pioneering, and in encouraging national unity. Primary and secondary curricula were redesigned to include subjects that focus the student's attention on elements of the Jewish spiritual and historical heritage.

Official efforts to facilitate cultural and political integration through education have been hampered by the presence of competing religious and political influences within the school system. Despite the generally centralized administration of public education, the Ministry of Education and Culture shares the operation and financing of many schools with religious associations and with other groups representing various ideologies within the Zionist movement. The Mizrahi (National Religious party), for example, which has partial supervision of public religious schools, opposes the secularizing trend in official educational policies and favors the adoption of a strictly religious curriculum to prepare students for a life based on the strict observance of Jewish law and ritual. The pedagogical philosophies of the Histadrut (Histadrut Ha'ovdim Haklalit—General Federation of Labor), and of moderate and militant socialist or nationalist parties assert themselves in the kibbutz (collective settlement) school and in some vocational training institutions.

Government plans announced during the mid-1960's emphasized the development of secondary, especially vocational, education. The plans called for the doubling of enrollment in vocational training schools between 1966 and 1971. A substantial portion of the funds for the expansion of secondary education facilities were to be made available by the United Jewish Appeal, a fund-raising organization for Jews in the United States. This organization announced a fund drive to raise more than US $27 million to build 72 secondary schools in Israel, to contribute to the financing of teacher training, and to purchase laboratory and teaching equipment.

Because of linguistic and religious differences, education facilities for the Arab minority were administered separately from the Jewish schools, although both operated within the general framework of the public educational system. Some Arab students, however, were enrolled in Jewish schools, notably in the universities and in vocational training institutions. About 84 percent of Arab children from 6 to 13 years of age attend primary schools, but only 23 percent of those in the 14- through 17-year-old age bracket are in school. About 5,000 were enrolled in 1968 in secondary schools, some of which were operated by Christian religious missions.

After extensive debate, the government adopted an important reform in 1968. It decided to move from the hitherto dominant eight-

114

four grade division (eight primary and four secondary grades) of primary and secondary schools toward a six-three-three grade division (six primary, three intermediate secondary, and three upper secondary grades). At the same time it made the ninth grade (10th year of compulsory schooling) free and compulsory for all students.

BACKGROUND

Jewish schools in Palestine during the early 19th century were dedicated exclusively to religious studies. Located mainly in the cities of Jerusalem, Hebron (about 15 miles southwest of Jerusalem), Tiberias, and Safad (about 8 miles northwest of Lake Tiberias), these schools were maintained by funds collected from Jews abroad. Many secular schools were established during the first major influx of immigrants during the 1880's and were financed and operated by Jewish philanthropic and Zionist organizations in the United Kingdom, Germany, and France.

The basis of the school system dates back to the British Mandate period (1922–48). During that time, the Jewish community in Palestine operated its own schools, under the general supervision of the Department of Education of the Palestine government. Until 1932 school administration was entrusted to the World Zionist Organization. Subsequently it was turned over to the Va'ad Leumi (National Council of the Jewish Community in Palestine), an autonomous body that had been empowered to exercise certain governmental functions. The system itself included three separate groups of schools, each group following a religious or political trend reflecting the political trend reflecting the philosophies of one of the three major Zionist parties that sponsored and operated them, notably the General Zionist party, the Mizrahi, and the Histadrut. The institutions within this system became known as trend schools. Each trend enjoyed full autonomy in determining its curriculum, teaching practices, and methods of inspection. The trend schools were represented in the Department of Education of the Va'ad Leumi (see ch. 14, Political Dynamics).

The proliferation of separate political parties within the Zionist and the labor movements during the late 1940's was reflected in the school system. Several new subtrends emerged, notably in the schools operated by the agricultural collectives and cooperatives, the kibbutzim and moshavim (see ch. 20, Agriculture). These subtrend schools represented the political and religious views of about nine federations and movements with which the respective collectives and cooperatives were affiliated.

The trend system continued after the establishment of independent Israel in 1948. During the same year, the schools operated by the orthodox Agudat Israel (Association of Israel), which had held aloof from the Va'ad Leumi, were recognized as a fourth trend, coequal with the rest. During the early 1950's institutions representing the views of the Histadrut enrolled 44.2 percent of Jewish primary and secondary school students and those of the General Zionist Party, 26.5 percent. The schools of the religious Mizrahi and the Agudat Israel enrolled 17.8 and 7.8 percent, respectively. The rest of the students attended unaffiliated schools.

Education experts and several members of the government coalition party, however, criticized the trend schools as sources of national disunity and religious discord. The use of the schools by various groups in competition for the political allegiance of newly arrived immigrants, as well as quarrels among religious groups over questions of education, together with the administrative and financial complexities of the system, all contributed to several major controversies within the cabinet in 1950 and 1951.

The trend schools were finally abolished by the State Education Act promulgated in August 1953. This law provided for the establishment of a unified system of secular and religious state education under general supervision of the Ministry of Education and Culture. It also prohibited teachers from disseminating the views of any political organization.

THE SCHOOL SYSTEM

In 1968 the school system included three groups of schools. By far the largest group was comprised of public religious and public secular schools. The educational institutions of the orthodox Agudat Israel functioned essentially outside the framework of public schools but received government subsidies. The third group included public schools for Arabs and a few private institutions, mostly on the secondary level, operated by Catholic teaching orders and by Protestant missionary societies. These private schools served chiefly the Arab population and other non-Jewish communities.

Supervision of the religious public schools is shared between the Ministry of Education and Culture and the Mizrahi. These schools follow the same curriculum as the public schools but place more emphasis on studies of Jewish law and on the observance of rituals. The public religious schools enrolled 28.8 percent of primary school students in 1968, as compared to 26.5 percent in 1960. Public religious schools on the secondary level enrolled 16.7 percent of secondary students in 1965, according to the latest available statistics.

Public schools are government supervised, but many are operated and partially financed by Zionist, civic and philanthropic organizations, and by the collective and cooperative settlements. Nearly all kibbutzim and moshavim maintain a preprimary and primary school, and some also offer secondary courses. Many secondary schools, notably the vocational training institutions, are under the auspices of the Histadrut, the Women's International Zionist Organization, and the Jewish Agency for Israel. Despite the abolition of the trend system, political and religious influences are still noted in the schools. Views of the Mizrahi prevail in the state religious schools, and the political philosophies of left- and right-wing Zionist parties and of the Histadrut are noted in many of the kibbutz schools.

The school system is divided into preprimary, primary, and secondary levels. Variations exist in the duration of the respective levels and in the designation of grades within them. In 1968 more than 625,000 Jewish students were enrolled in 4,982 preprimary, primary and secondary institutions, including special schools, such as those serving handicapped children and those designed to complement the primary-level schools and the teacher-training colleges.

The curriculum of each Jewish public secular and public religious school must include Bible studies in all grades, complemented by Jewish history and literature. In accordance with educational policies initiated during the late 1950's, the historical and literary subjects must include elements of the spiritual heritage and Jewish customs. They must also emphasize religious and historical values associated with the major festivals. The subjects must be taught with a view to encourage the students' awareness of the Jewish past and to foster their consciousness of Jewish values.

For Jewish students the school year includes about 210 schooldays, from early September to the last days of June. Schools are open 6 days a week, Sunday through Friday, classes beginning at 8:00 A.M., lasting to noon or 1:00 P.M. Hebrew is the language of instruction. Arabic is taught as an elective language in many secondary schools and in some primary schools. English and, in some cases, French are required foreign languages in the upper primary grades and in the secondary schools.

For Arab students, as of 1968 there were 373 preprimary, primary, and secondary schools and one teacher-training college. These institutions enrolled a total of about 83,000 students, of whom about 13,200 attended private schools. The language of instruction is Arabic, but Hebrew is taught as a second language from the fourth primary grade upward. The school week lasts from Sunday through Thursday in Arab institutions, which are attended mainly by Muslim students. Where the student body includes Christians, classes are held from Monday through Thursday and on Saturdays.

Administration and Finance

The Ministry of Education and Culture directs and plans the country's educational system, provides pedagogical guidance, supervises all secular and religious public schools, drafts curricula, administers public examinations, and employs and pay public school teachers. The senior staff of the ministry, operating under a director-general, is comprised of six assistant directors, each respectively in charge of administration, primary education, teacher training, Arab education, extracurricular programs, and examinations and teachers' affairs. The jurisdiction of the assistant director for examinations and teachers' affairs includes the Department of Religious Education, which is designed to represent the interests of religious public schools. Two pedagogical secretariats deal with policy guidance and curricula affecting primary education and teaching training, and postprimary education, respectively. Each of these secretariats is headed by a chairman who holds the position of assistant director. Approximately 14 major departments and divisions of the ministry, each headed by a director, deal with tasks in various areas of education and culture.

For the purposes of school inspection, the country is divided into six administrative districts, each under a district inspector. The inspectors are responsible for carrying out directives of the Ministry of Education and Culture, for reporting on the academic, administrative, and financial status of the institutions under their jurisdiction, and for assigning school inspectors. Specifically, district inspectors are charged with investigating academic and teaching standards, maintenance of buildings and teaching equipment, and cleanliness and discipline in the schools.

The government provides most of the funds for education. Expenditures, however, for school construction and for the development of secondary and higher education are shared by local authorities and private organizations, notably the Jewish Agency for Israel.

During the 1960's the education budget accounted for about 8.5 percent of the national income and for over 11 percent of the national budget. The budget of the Ministry of Education and Culture for 1967–68 totaled I£485 million (I£1 equals approximately US$0.285—see Glossary).

Preprimary Education

Preprimary schools offer training for children 4 to 6 years of age. In accordance with the Compulsory Education Act of 1949, the attendance for 5-year-old children is free and compulsory. Most preprimary schools are public, but some operate under the auspices of voluntary women's organizations, kibbutzim, or private individuals. The curricula are informal, stressing the overall development of the child's personality. Special efforts are made to help the integration of children of European and Oriental backgrounds. Some of the institutions combine preprimary with first-year primary school training, in order to provide a transition between the two school levels.

In 1968 there were 2,797 preprimary schools for Jewish children with an enrollment of 93,395. During the same year, 9,243 Arab children attended some 159 preprimary schools.

Primary Education

In 1968 there were 1,247 primary schools for Jewish children offering instruction in grades one through eight to children from 6 to 14 years of age. The total primary school enrollment during the same year was 385,589. The majority, or 248,010, of the children attended secular public schools, and 110,887 were enrolled in religious public schools. The rest (26,692) attended schools of the orthodox Agudat Israel. Because of the constant flow of immigration and the varying educational background of the students, the percentage of those above the normal age for the respective grades is relatively high. In 1967 more than 20 percent of the students in grades six, seven, and eight were over-age. This percentage, however, represents an improvement since 1957, when the comparable share was over 34 percent.

Towns are divided into zones, with a public secular or public religious school serving each zone. In rural areas the children of five to 10 small villages are conveyed by bus to a regional school, serving a certain district. Wide variations exist in the physical condition of school buildings and equipment. In schools built before 1948, the classrooms are often small and poorly lighted. Many also lack furniture, teaching aids, and playgrounds. The number of pupils per class varies, depending on the location of the school, but in most primary classes there are about 30 to 40 children. In 1968 the average class size for Jewish primary schools was 29.1.

The primary curriculum includes Bible study, arithmetic, geography, Hebrew language and literature, Jewish history, foreign languages (in the upper grades), music, art, science and nature studies, physical education, and social activities. Manual training, woodwork, and metalwork for boys and domestic science for girls are also offered. In addition, both boys and girls are trained in the fundamentals of agriculture; schools in rural areas have their own small gardens or plots, whereas pupils from urban schools are taken by bus to farms outside the towns.

Regulations of the Ministry of Education and Culture prescribe the number of weekly lesson periods for each subject in each grade. In schools attended mainly by Oriental children who have difficulty mastering verbal subjects, the time devoted to manual training may be increased to twelve periods a week, in order to encourage these children to take interest in crafts and technical skills.

Regulations also determine what subject material must be presented in the course taught in the respective grades. Adjustments are made,

119

however, for the level on which the subjects may be presented, depending on the early educational and cultural experiences of certain students. Consequently, a so-called bracketed syllabus may be followed in which some subjects are taught on the level of an essential minimum, and others may be omitted altogether. Gifted pupils, on the other hand, may follow an "enriched" curriculum offered in mathematics and science in grades seven and eight.

Legislation promulgated in 1962 provides for extended school-days for Oriental children who need additional tutoring. These children attend 7- or 8-hour schooldays instead of the standard 5 to 6 hours. The extra time is devoted to remedial reading exercises and tutoring in various academic and manual subjects.

After completing the eighth grade, pupils must take the *seker* examination (terminal examination for the primary grades) administered throughout the country by the Ministry of Education and Culture. In some cases, the examination may be taken at the end of the sixth grade. The passing grade for this examination has been determined at 80 percent or above for children of European origin and at 60 percent or above for Oriental children. The student's performance in these examinations serves as a basis for choosing from the various types of secondary education. It also provides a criterion for the amount of government scholarship awarded to those who enter secondary schools.

In 1968 primary education for Arabs was offered in 192 schools. Enrollment in these schools totaled about 56,946, as compared to 24,659 in 1957. A slight majority, or 58 percent, of the students enrolled in 1968 were boys. The curriculum was similar to that in Jewish schools, with special emphasis on Arab history and literature. Religion was taught by Christian or Muslim instructors. Special primary schools, located mostly in Galilee and in the environs of Haifa, served the Druze population. Some schools were also operated for Bedouins, but the enrollment in these schools was low. One of the Bedouin schools, located in the desert country near Beersheba, enrolled about 180 students in 1965.

Special Schools

According to the Compulsory Education Law of 1949, young people 14 to 17 years of age, who have not completed the primary grades, must enroll in schools for working youth. The law, however, is not fully enforced, and the Jewish enrollment in these schools declined from 11,341 in 1957 to 6,691 in 1968.

Schools for working youth, established originally during the late 1940's and early 1950's, were intended to serve the large numbers of immigrant youths whose primary education had been interrupted. In 1968 there were 149 such schools, attended mostly by youths of

Oriental background. Some of them had never been to school, and others had left after completing a few years of the primary course in order to earn wages. For Arabs, there were six schools for working youth, with an enrollment of 239 during 1968.

Because of the great disparities in the pupils' ages, education, and social background, the schools for working youth offer a flexible curriculum, featuring language studies, the Old Testament, arithmetic, civics, and nature studies. Classes meet in the late afternoon or evening, three or four times a week. Students who have never attended primary school are grouped into preparatory classes; others, according to their educational background, attend classes corresponding to the primary school levels.

In 1968 the government maintained 146 special schools, with an enrollment of 12,570, for the education of Jewish children who were physically handicapped or mentally retarded. These institutions also cared for children who were orphaned, delinquent, or abandoned by their parents. There was one school for handicapped Arab children, with an enrollment of 52. Depending on the nature of their disability, some of the handicapped children were taught in special classes operating in conjunction with primary schools. Statistics for 1963 indicate that, of a total of 22,600 children in schools for the handicapped, 12,400 were mentally retarded; the rest were physically disabled or suffered from emotional maladjustments.

Secondary Education

Secondary education, open to youths 14 to 17 years old, is offered in three types of institutions: academic, vocational, and agricultural. Admission requirements are variable, but the completion of eight primary grades is required by most secondary schools. The secondary course usually lasts 4 years (divided into grades nine to 12), but some institutions offer courses extending over 2, 3, or 6 years. Tuition and fees represent the main source of income for most of the schools. Vocational and agricultural schools supplement this income by the sale of products. In addition, secondary schools receive subsidies from the government and from various organizations sponsoring them. During the late 1960's most secondary schools charged between I£875 and I£1,025 annually for tuition and fees.

In 1968 academic, vocational, and agricultural secondary instruction was offered in 595 institutions. In many rural areas, however, notably in the development towns, secondary school facilities are still lacking or are inadequate. Nearly all academic and agricultural schools are coeducational, but separate vocational schools operate for boys and girls.

In the same year, secondary school enrollment in Jewish schools totaled 107,023. Of the total, 58,114 were in academic secondary;

41,044, in vocational; and 7,865, in agricultural schools. In addition, more than 16,000 students attended secondary courses in kibbutz schools, preparatory courses for teachers' colleges, and secondary courses in evening schools. Attrition rates were high, especially in the upper grades, and more than 60 percent of secondary school students were enrolled in grades nine and ten.

Academic secondary schools are the choice of a large majority of students. In 1968 more than half of the secondary students were enrolled in academic schools. To encourage interest in vocational training, the government, during the mid-1960's, initiated a new type of secondary education in the so-called comprehensive schools. These schools offer courses comprising two, three, or four years of study, incorporating academic as well as vocational subjects. The students are at liberty to choose between academic or vocational specialization, but all must learn a trade during their courses. In 1968 the government announced plans to open two comprehensive schools in each of the large towns and to introduce a curriculum of vocational specialization in fifty academic secondary schools.

The government operates an extensive scholarship program for students who are qualified to enter secondary school but who lack financial resources. The amount of the scholarship varies, depending on the student's academic ability, the parents' economic situation, and the number of children in the family. The children of newly arrived immigrants receive additional aid to cover the cost of transportation, boarding, textbooks, and school supplies. In 1968, 45 percent of the students enrolled in secondary schools were totally exempt from paying tuition; 35 percent received scholarships covering from 20 to 80 percent of the tuition; and the rest paid full fees.

Also, in 1968 a total of 2,909 Arab students attended 15 institutions offering secondary education. The large majority, or 2,357, were enrolled in academic secondary schools; 267 attended vocational, and 285, agricultural schools.

Seven of the 10 Arab academic secondary schools and all four of the vocational schools were located in and around Nazareth. All except one of the 7 secondary schools were private, operated by Catholic or Protestant religious missions. The curriculum was similar to that offered in the Jewish secondary schools, but with an emphasis on Arabic cultural background in the social science subjects.

Academic Secondary Schools

Completion of the secondary academic course takes 4 years for graduates of the eight primary grades. These students may also take 2-year secondary courses in lieu of the 4-year courses. Some of the schools offer 6-year courses to students who have completed 6 years of primary schooling. Both types of academic secondary schools sometimes form part of an institution offering all 12 grades.

The four- and 6-year academic secondary schools prepare the students for entrance into institutions of higher learning. A general liberal arts curriculum is offered up to the 10th grade. From the 10th grade on, students may follow specialized programs, depending on their intended professional field. Six specialized programs are offered: agriculture; biology; humanities, which may be combined with a foreign language; mathematics and physics; Oriental studies; and social sciences. Geography, civics, and history are included in all the specialized programs. Since 1965 courses in modern history and modern Jewish history have also been made compulsory subjects.

Completion of the 4- or 6-year course of the academic secondary schools leads to a terminal examination called the *bagrut*, which is required for university admission. Since the early 1960's a secondary school certificate has been issued to students who have completed the secondary school cycle but do not wish to take the *bagrut*. The *bagrut* is a comprehensive examination based on the entire primary and secondary curriculum. The students are tested in seven subjects, including all the courses of specialization. Questions in the chosen field of specialization are given on an expanded level. Since 1965 questions on ancient and modern Jewish history have also been included in the examination.

The *bagrut* is generally open only to those who have attended academic secondary schools, but it may also be taken on an individual basis by graduates of vocational and agricultural schools. These are called external candidates and must furnish proof of evidence of 10 years of education, or they must pass a preliminary test. The number of Jewish candidates who passed the *bagrut* increased from 3,464 in 1961 to 10,588 in 1967. Examinations are difficult, as reflected in the relatively high percentages of failure. According to the latest statistics available, some 27.3 percent of the candidates in 1964 failed. In previous years, however, the rate of failure ranged between 30 and 40 percent.

Secondary schools of the kibbutzim and moshavim have 2-year programs, representing the equivalent of grades nine through 10, and of grades nine through 12, respectively. These schools, however, do not prepare the students for the *bagrut* examination.

There are also special secondary level institutions (*yeshivot*) under the supervision of the Ministry of Religious Affairs, dedicated mainly to the study of the Talmudic law. Since the early 1960's some of these schools have combined religious studies with part of the standard academic secondary curriculum (see ch. 11, Religion).

In 1967, 144 Arab students passed the terminal secondary school examination as compared to 94 in 1961. Arabic languages and literature were substituted for Bible studies and Jewish history as major subjects in the examination.

Vocational and Agricultural Secondary Education

In 1968 a total of 216 vocational training schools offered courses in machine and construction technology, marine mechanics, automobile and aviation mechanics, metalwork, electronics and communication, photography, printing, and textile technology. Automobile and aviation mechanics, metalwork, and electronics and communication attracted the largest number of male vocational students. Girls were enrolled mostly in sewing, home economics, and handicrafts, including interior decoration.

Most vocational schools are owned and operated by the Histadrut; others are under the auspices of the Organization for Rehabilitation Through Training, an international organization dedicated to the vocational training of refugees and immigrants. The schools offer programs lasting 3 or 4 years to graduates of the eighth primary grade. The curriculum is divided between theoretical secondary school subjects, totaling 21 to 26 hours a week, and practical training. There are also 2-year vocational training schools devoting full time to practical instruction.

Some institutions offer courses in commercial subjects. In a few of these institutions, the course is sometimes combined with academic subjects and qualifies for the *bagrut* examination. Others specialize in a typing and stenography course, lasting several months.

Some 30 institutions offer agricultural training, combined with secondary academic courses. A few of the students graduating from these schools qualify to take the *bagrut* examination as external candidates and proceed to study agricultural technology at one of the universities.

Agricultural training concurrent with secondary schooling is also offered by many of the kibbutzim and moshavim and by agricultural boarding schools. Most of the students enrolled in these programs are recent immigrants, sponsored by the Aliyat Hanoar (Youth Immigration) organization or by various social welfare agencies (see ch. 8, Living Conditions).

Teacher Training

In 1968 teachers for preprimary and primary schools were trained in 48 colleges with a total enrollment of 7,502. Most of these institutions were maintained by the government. Others were operated by private organizations and received government subsidies. Tuition fees were nominal in the public teacher-training colleges. Government loans and scholarships were granted to those students who were unable to pay the cost of fees and boarding in private institutions.

There are special training colleges for persons wishing to teach in preprimary and primary state religious or secular schools, in schools of the orthodox Agudat Israel, kibbutzim, or in immigrant village schools. Within the general curriculum, students may acquire special qualifications to teach the lower or upper primary grades, vocational subjects, music, or agriculture. The course leading to the primary teacher's certificate lasts 3 years, but in 1967 completion of the 3d year was not compulsory in all colleges.

The large majority of teachers and teacher trainees are women. In 1968 men accounted for only about 13 percent of the students in these training colleges. Preprimary and primary school teacher-training institutions during the mid-1960's graduated between 1,500 and 1,800 students annually, a number considered by education experts to be adequate for the demand. The number of persons available to fill teaching positions, however, was much less, since many of the graduates were married before commencing a career. To fill teaching posts, the schools have often had to hire candidates who have not completed their training. In 1964, for example, about 25 percent of the preprimary and primary school teachers were not fully qualified. By 1968, however, the supply of teachers had caught up with the demand, and the number of teacher-training colleges was being reduced.

Teachers' salaries tend to be relatively low, despite raises granted during the 1960's. The maximum salary is only about double the basic rate, and promotions tend to be slow. The brevity of the training period and the inadequate qualifications of many persons in the profession have contributed to the declining social status of teachers. Among Oriental Jews, the teaching profession is still highly regarded, but women teachers are generally frowned upon.

Secondary school teachers are trained at institutions of higher learning. Courses leading to undergraduate and graduate degrees in education are offered at the Hebrew University of Jerusalem; the Israel Institute of Technology, known as Technion, in Haifa; Tel Aviv University; and at Bar Ilan University in Ramat Gan, near Tel Aviv. The latter is the principal institution for the training of school teachers for religious schools. Courses leading to a secondary teacher's certificate are open to students who have completed the academic requirements for the bachelor's degree.

At the Hebrew University, the course lasts 2 years and includes about 20 hours a week of lectures and seminars, in addition to practice teaching. At the Technion and Bar Ilan University, 10 to 16 weekly lecture hours are required, and these may be taken concurrently with the courses leading to the bachelor's degree. Students graduating from the Tel Aviv University must continue to attend an education seminar during their first year of teaching, before the teacher's certificate is conferred upon them.

About 1,000 secondary school teachers are needed each year. Education departments of the various universities admit an estimated 500 students annually, but many of these discontinue their studies before earning the bachelor's degree in education, or they choose another major field. In 1964 only about half of the secondary school teachers held education degrees. During the same year, about 1,200 persons were enrolled in secondary teacher courses, but education experts estimated that only some 200 would enter the teaching profession.

There was one training college for Arab primary teachers with an enrollment of 316 in 1968. Completion of secondary schooling is an admission requirement, although female applicants who have graduated from the 11th secondary school grade are sometimes admitted. Arab students wishing to teach special subjects are also enrolled in Jewish teacher-training colleges, and those wishing to teach secondary school may attend one of the universities. There was a total of 1,830 Arab primary school teachers in 1967, and approximately 170 Arab secondary school teachers. Their social status among the Arab population is high, and the profession is usually practiced by men.

Higher Education

There were seven institutions of higher learning in 1968: the Hebrew University of Jerusalem; the Israel Institute of Technology (Technion) in Haifa; Bar-Ilan University in Ramat Gan, near Tel Aviv; the University of Tel Aviv; the Weizmann Institute of Science, located in Rehovot about 15 miles south of Tel Aviv; the Institute of Higher Education in the Negev at Beersheba; and Haifa University College. Most of these institutions offer 4-year undergraduate courses and graduate programs leading to the master's and doctor of philosophy degrees. The university operate under the general supervision of the Council for Higher Education. Established in 1958, the Council determines the standards of accreditation required for institutions of higher learning and deals with various questions relating to their general development. It is headed by the Minister of Education and Culture and comprises 19 members, six of whom are appointed by the government and thirteen appointed in consultation with the recognized academic institutions. The universities are financed by tuition fees and grants and also receive large government subsidies. Many of the schools and departments of the respective institutions are sponsored and supported by Jewish civic groups and their counterparts in the United States, notably the Hadassah Women's Zionist Organization.

In 1968 there were 28,520 university students as compared to 10,-836 in 1961. The total included 1,893 foreign students. Women accounted for somewhat less than half of the student body. During the same year the universities conferred degrees upon 3,700 persons. The majority of students were enrolled in the humanities (33.7 percent) and the social sciences (22.6 percent). The natural sciences (16.2 percent) and engineering (14.1 percent) were the next preferred choices. The remaining students studied law (6.7 percent), medicine (3.8 percent), architecture (1.4 percent), or agriculture (1.4).

The largest and oldest institution is the Hebrew University of Jerusalem, opened in 1925. It has faculties of humanities, social sciences, law, natural sciences, medicine, dental medicine, and agriculture, and schools of social work, education, graduate librarianship, and pharmacy. The faculties of medicine and dental medicine and the school of pharmacy were established by the Hadassah Women's Zionist Organization. In 1968 the university enrolled a total of 11,-586 students, including about 250 Arabs and Druzes and nearly 1,400 foreign students, and employed a teaching staff of 1,371.

The Tel Aviv University was the second largest institution of higher learning, with an enrollment of 6,308 and a teaching staff of 1,312 in 1968. Its campus, consolidated and renovated in 1964, includes more than 20 buildings. The university has faculties of natural sciences, law, humanities, social sciences, business administration, medicine, and continuing medical education, and schools of education, music, and technical training. It also has six research institutes, including one for research into the Middle East and Africa.

The Israel Institute of Technology (Technion) was opened in 1924 under the auspices of a fraternal association of German Jews. Located in the suburbs of Haifa, it has faculties or departments of architecture and town planning, chemical engineering, civil engineering, electrical engineering, mechanical engineering, food technology and biotechnology, materials engineering, aeronautical engineering, agricultural engineering, industrial and management engineering, mathematics, physics, chemistry, mechanics, nuclear science, computer sciences, teacher training, and general studies. The course of study for the bachelor of science degree lasts 4 years in most departments; an engineering diploma is awarded after an additional year of practical work. In 1968 the Technion enrolled 5,115 students and had an academic staff of 863. The largest numbers were enrolled in the departments of electrical and civil engineering.

Bar-Ilan University, opened in 1955, was founded and operates under the auspices of the Mizrahi. It is a distinctly religious institution that requires all students, regardless of their major field of specialization, to study the Old Testament and Jewish law in the orthodox spirit. In 1968 the university had a total enrollment of 3,-111, including about 300 foreign students, and a faculty of 454. The university has faculties of Jewish studies, natural sciences and mathematics, humanities and social sciences, and languages and literatures, schools of education and social work, and an institute of criminology. Special sources, under joint sponsorship with the government, are offered in pedagogy, criminology, and teacher training.

The Weizman Institute of Science, founded under a different name in 1934, is one of the world's leading research institutes in the natural sciences. Its graduate school, which was opened in 1958, offers 3-year courses leading to the doctoral degree to students holding a master's degree in science. In 1968 the graduate school had an academic staff of 114 and enrolled a total of 307 students, many of whom were from abroad (see ch. 10, Artistic and Intellectual Expression).

The Haifa University College operates under the auspices of the Adult Education Center of the Hebrew University and of the Histadrut. It offers undergraduate programs in the humanities and in the social sciences. In 1968 it had an academic staff of 216 and enrolled 1,829 students, mostly women. The Institute for Higher Education in the Negev offers undergraduate courses in engineering, natural sciences, humanities, and the social sciences. The Technion is aiding the institute in engineering and the natural sciences, by providing teaching staff, advice on curriculum development, and other support. In 1968 the institute had an academic staff of 169 and enrolled a total of 264 students. Haifa College and the Negev institute are new institutions still getting started. In time they are expected to grow into universities.

ADULT EDUCATION

Adult education programs operate under the auspices of the various ministries, including the Ministry of Education and Culture, the army, and civic organizations, notably the Histadrut.

Most popular among the programs are the intensive Hebrew-language courses, known as *ulpanim*. Designed to impart to students a good working knowledge of Hebrew within the shortest time possible, these 6-month courses are offered in resident colleges where students take language lessons and are encouraged to converse in Hebrew. Social activities and excursions are part of the curriculum. Subsidized by the Jewish Agency for Israel, the colleges charge nominal fees for tuition and boarding costs. In some cases the *ulpanim* are located in a kibbutz where students may work a certain number of hours instead of paying fees.

In addition to the *ulpanim*, evening language courses in Hebrew are available in nearly every town and rural community. Classes are held two to four times a week, and the total length of the course is usually 2 years. According to estimates by education experts, some 14,000 persons a year during the late 1960's acquired a working knowledge of Hebrew by attending *ulpanim* or evening language courses.

Primary school instruction in evening classes and boarding schools is available to adults who have never attended school. Home classes are also held for farmers by women teachers in lieu of military service. Farmers may receive primary instruction at special centers in rural areas.

The Ministry of Labor sponsors vocational training courses on beginning and advanced levels, designed to expedite the economic adjustment of recently arrived immigrants. Courses offered in building construction, technician training metalwork, woodwork, clerical subjects, and home economics enrolled a total of 14,339 in late 1967.

Military training in the army is complemented by an extensive educational program. Primary school subjects are taught to men and women in the service who have not completed that school level. Those who are eligible and interested may enroll in secondary-level courses in various subjects (see ch. 26, The Armed Forces).

LITERACY

In 1961 literacy was officially defined as "the knowledge of reading and writing in any language at least for simple, everyday purposes." According to this definition, 88 percent of Jews aged 14 years and over and 48 percent of adult non-Jews were classified as literate in that year. Among the adult Jews, 7 percent of the men and 17 percent of the women were illiterate. Among non-Jews, the illiteracy rate was 32 percent for men and 71 percent for women. The rate of literacy was highest among Jews born in Europe and among Jews born in Israel, with 98 and 97 percent, respectively.

Literacy among the Jewish population in 1967 was estimated by United States sources at 88 percent, with an overall rate for the country of approximately 70 percent. In the absence of other statistics, inferences may be made from data published in 1967 on the number of years of school attendance. This information indicated that only 11.3 percent of the Jewish population has never attended school; the comparable percentage for the non-Jewish population was 44.9 percent.

EDUCATION AND SOCIETY

Education is valued by all Israelis as the key to scholarship, knowledge, and piety and as an essential requisite for personal development. Depending on the intensity of religious views, however, different attitudes exist among various groups on the merits of different types of education. Some favor an exclusively secular curriculum designed to provide the foundation for a general, humanistic knowledge, and sound scholarship. Others favor an education that seeks to adapt Jewish religious values and the elements of the Talmudic law to modern social and scientific thought. A third, orthodox religious groups, would exclude virtually all secular subjects and dedicate the entire educational process to the study of the Old Testament and Jewish oral law, as presented in the Talmud and in other sacred books.

During the late 1960's education was a principal requirement for economic advancement and for the attainment of social status. Completion of secondary education has become essential in order to qualify for positions offered by expanding industrial enterprises and by government offices and projects. Rapidly developing research institutions place a high premium on professional competence and scholarly creativity. Despite some ideological influences stressing collective effort and deemphasizing actions for the sake of individual achievement and reward, most Israelis are eager to secure for themselves the economic advantages and social prestige available to those who have educational qualifications. The people expect their government to show vigorous initiative in developing the school system but are also willing to contribute substantially toward the financing of public and private education. Most Israelis who study plan to acquire a professional degree or to qualify for entrance into institutions of higher learning, but many take courses to satisfy their personal interest in a subject or to raise their general educational level. People hurrying to evening classes after a day's work are a common sight in the cities and towns. There has been enthusiastic response to adult education programs and to similar opportunities available through youth organizations and private clubs.

CHAPTER 10

ARTISTIC AND INTELLECTUAL EXPRESSION

The arts and scholarship in Israel reflect the influence of varied cultural traditions bound together by a common religious heritage. The main avenues of creative expression are dominated by European (Ashkenazic) Jews. Most of these have been raised in the universal, humanistic culture of Europe to which Jewish philosophers, writers, artists, and scientists have contributed for many centuries. A narrower cultural tradition represented by Orthodox Jews who lived in religious and social distinctness in the small towns of Eastern Europe and who have drawn exclusively from the heritage of Jewish religion, history, and lore. Middle Eastern and North African (Sephardic) Jews represent Mediterranean and Eastern cultural influences, noted mostly in the decorative arts and in some forms of music and dance.

The religious heritage and the political and social experiences in the countries of their origin have exerted a powerful influence upon the artistic output of immigrants from Europe. The encased existence of Jewish communities, the persecutions before and during World War II, and the feeling of separateness have been treated in literature, portrayed in the interpretive and visual arts, and analyzed in sociological studies. Against the background of these experiences life in Israel has been presented both as a symbol of unrestrained existence and also as a secular contrast to spiritually oriented past traditions. The experience of Israeli statehood has also contributed to the revival of Hasidism, a religious tradition that exalts the virtues of outdoor life and encourages the expression of free, joyful feelings in music and dance (see ch. 11, Religion).

The development of an Israeli national style in the arts and letters has been the subject of much public discussion by scholars, linguists, and art critics. Poets and writers who immigrated during their early youth or who were born in Israel before the establishment of statehood appeared to be the precursors of such a style. Their works were permeated with the socialist-Zionist ideology, with religious zeal, and with exaltations of the pioneer kibbutz spirit. Young native-born Israeli (Sabra) writers, however, have departed from these themes. Devoid of ideological and religious messages, their works deal in depth with the universal problems of human existence. This trend has been criticized by many older immigrants who had hoped for an eloquent restatement of the Israeli national ethos in the young Sabra literature. In the visual arts painters and sculptors have drawn mainly from European art forms. Some have expressed the essence of Israel's physical and human landscape in dynamic colors and abstract forms, others in the more traditional figurative styles.

Scholars, scientists, and intellectuals are highly regarded and share considerable influence in formulating social policies and determining the orientation of scientific research. Intellectual activities are addressed to contemporary political and social problems relevant to Israel. Scholars have sought to examine the roots of Israeli nationalism, problems, related to the integration of Middle Eastern and North African Jews (sometimes called the Oriental Jews), the social impact of industrialization, and the role of Israel in the Arab Middle East. The experiences of Jews during and before World War II have prompted sociologists and psychologists to study the origins and causes of naziism and anti-Semitism. Religious scholars and philosophers were engaged in a reexamination of Judaic moral and legal tenets that were to furnish the basis of moral values for a new society.

Social thought also reflects a strong preoccupation with attempts at defining Jewish identity and the essence of Jewish culture (see ch. 9, Education). This quest expresses itself through Biblical and historical studies and the revival of the Hebrew language. Archeology, a main link with the past, has been vigorously developed and has attained the status of a national hobby.

The main thrust of scientific investigations is directed towards problems presented by the country's physical environment and the fullest development of its resources. Research activities designed to promote the development of science-based industries have also been given high priority by the National Council for Research and Development, Israel's highest official body for scientific planning. The country has attracted worldwide attention with the quality of its top-level science personnel and its modern research facilities and with progress in such scientific endeavors of universal interest as arid-zone agriculture, the uses of solar energy, and innovations in industrial chemistry. Scientific activity receives significant support from the international research program of the United States government. Some 7 million dollars have been earmarked for the United States fiscal year 1969 to finance almost 300 Israeli research projects. Most of these were in the medical, biological, and agricultural sciences.

Israelis are noted for their intense interest in cultural activities. They eagerly participate in the creative process, both as spectators and audience and as amateur participants. Professional artists and those for whom art is only an avocation compete in the production of plays, novels, poems, and theater and dance productions. Paintings and sculptures decorate many homes. Artistic members of agricultural settlements are freed from work during part of the day to pursue their vocation. Books, plays, and paintings are subjects of lively critical comment in discussions that take place in coffeehouses and homes among young and old.

LITERATURE

Novels, short stories, and poetry in Hebrew are produced by authors representing several generations. The country's outstanding writer is Shmuel Yosef Agnon (1888–), winner of the Nobel Prize for Literature in 1966. His early works show deep attachment to the traditional religious culture of Jews living in the small towns of Eastern Europe. Novels and short stories written in his middle years deal with the changing relationship of the modern generation with religious and cultural traditions (see ch. 18, Biographies of Selected Key Personalities). Problems arising from the confrontation of the spiritual tradition with secular values regulating daily life in contemporary society are treated in the works of Hayyim Hazaz (1897–). His stories deal with the past experiences of immigrants but emphasize their new life situation in Israel. Several of his works portray the resettlement of the Yemenite Jewish community.

The religious heritage and the situation confronting Jews outside Israel were still prominent themes in the works of a younger group of writers who came to Israel during the 1920's, although they were raised in the largely secular, communal-pioneering spirit of the country's early kibbutz settlers. The impact of the Jewish experience in Europe before and during World War II has been responsible for the preoccupation with Jewish destiny in the works of the poets Shin Shalom (1905–), Uri Zvi Greenberg (1894–), and Avraham Shlonsky (1900–). The resolution of conflict in Shlonsky's poetry reflects the socialistic idealism of the early Zionists, whereas Greenberg envisaged Jewish salvation in the reenactment of the ancient battles for the Jews' promised land. Nathan Alterman (1910–) was the most influential writer in this group and, during the late 1960's, was still regarded as one of the country's most accomplished writers. His works emphasize universal, humanistic, and religious themes set against the Israeli background of nation building and warfare. Alterman is also noted for his compassionate literary treatment of the Arab minority.

Ideological and religious themes are less prominent in the writings of authors born in Israel, including S. Yizhar (1916–), Yigael Mossinson (1917–), and Moshe Shamir (1921–). Most of them fought in the hostilities preceding the establishment of the state in 1948 and belonged to socialist-Zionist youth movements. Their writings show deep concern for the political and military problems of national revival, but these problems are not resolved in ideological or religious terms. The favorite literary form of these authors is the short story that provides the framework for descriptions of events and personal experiences in wartime and during the early days of independence. Heroes are often portrayed in the midst of personal conflicts arising from the demands of nation building and the striving for individual choices and free development. Some writers expressed themselves through social criticism, occasionally in a satirical vein, as they witnessed the problems of resettlement and immigration and the position of Middle Eastern and North African Jews in a society dominated mostly by Western cultural values.

Introspective humanism characterizes the works of the youngest writers who have grown up in an already organized state of Israel. Detached from ideology and religion, they have shown little sympathy for the experiences and ideological convictions of the early Sabras and of those older immigrants who have survived persecutions in Europe and elsewhere. Plays, short stories, poems, and novels of these authors examine personal conflicts resulting from guilt, anxiety, and suffering. The complexities of everyday life in a modern society and the fighting in the country's border areas are presented in the background, but the works focus on the heroes' subjective feelings in the presence of a critical situation. Several short stories have been written about the Six-Day War of June 1967, dealing with the personal experiences of soldiers who fought in it and with the effects of that war on the lives of individuals and families. Novelist Yael Dayan, daughter of the minister of defense, Moshe Dayan, is a popular representative of the new Sabra literature.

Religious themes and those dealing with problems of Jews living abroad are occasionally revived by both old and young Sabra authors. Such revivals are usually prompted by events recalling the losses suffered by Jews during World War II, such as the Adolph Eichmann trial in 1962, and by visits of these authors to countries where Jews live in religious and cultural distinctness.

THEATER

Theater performances are offered by three repertory companies of countrywide recognition. Habimah, the first modern Hebrew theater, produces mainly classical and contemporary drama. It was founded abroad in 1917 and in 1958 became the national theater of Israel. Others include the Ohel Theater Company, founded in 1935 as a workers' theater; the Cameri Theater, started in 1944; and the Haifa

Municipal Theater, in 1961. Cameri is noted for its production of modern plays and is much favored by the younger generation.

All four major theater companies regularly tour the country, reaching even small collective settlements and development towns. Performances at these locations are subsidized by the Ministry of Education, the American Israel Cultural Foundation, the Histadrut Ha'ovdim Haklalit (General Federation of Labor, commonly known as Histadrut) and are offered to the audience at reduced admission fees. The companies have also given performances abroad.

Smaller theater groups founded during the mid-1960's include Bimat Hasachkanim (Actors' Stage), noted for its experimental plays and modern staging and acting techniques, and the Godik Theater, which features adaptations of American musicals.

In addition there are several smaller professional companies in the cities and some 200 amateur groups throughout the country. Theatergoers in the major cities may select from a variety of productions, ranging from Shakespearean drama to modern plays by Bertholt Brecht. An average of about 25 new plays are staged each year by the various theater companies. They are seen by about 1.5 million Israelis. In the cities many hold seasonal subscriptions; others attend the theater about three to four times a year.

There is a tradition of theater plays in the Yiddish language, originating mainly in Poland and Russia. These plays are still performed and are favored by older immigrants from Eastern Europe. Some plays are produced by Israeli authors in Hebrew. Most of these deal with modern social problems relevant to Israel, such as the conflict between generations, the transition from pioneering to a modern industrial society, and the Arab-Israeli controversy.

The government-sponsored Public Council for Culture encourages local playwrights by offering fellowships and prizes to the authors of outstanding Hebrew language plays. Acting is a respected profession, and the people take pride in those Israeli artists of the stage who have attained international fame. The government sponsors a School of Drama in Ramat Gan, a northeastern suburb of Tel Aviv. Training for the stage is also offered at the Department of Theater Arts of Tel Aviv University and at the Hebrew University in Jerusalem (see ch. 9, Education).

THE ARTS

Music and Dance

Israelis are noted for their intense interest in music. Most of them have had some musical training during childhood and are amateur performers on at least one instrument. Musical education is also emphasized in schools and by youth groups. Musical performances offered throughout the country by local and visiting symphony and chamber orchestras, soloists, and opera companies are attended by knowledgeable and enthusiastic audiences. Amateur performers regularly practice their talents with one of the many informal music ensembles established by members of enterprises, kibbutzim, and civic groups.

The Israel Festival of Music held each year during the late summer months features outstanding local and international musicians. The annual music festival held at Ein Gev kibbutz, on the shores of Lake Tiberias, is a major musical event that attracts many Israelis and visiting foreign tourists.

The Israel Philharmonic Orchestra, the country's outstanding musical group, offers more than 200 concerts a year to audiences in the cities and rural areas. In the large cities each program has to be repeated several times to satisfy some 36,000 holders of season tickets. Internationally known conductors and soloists from other countries regularly perform with the orchestra. The late Brazilian composer Hector Villa Lobos wrote and dedicated to the state of Israel a symphonic poem entitled *L'Odyssee d'une Race*, which was first performed by the Israeli Philharmonic Orchestra in 1954. Established in 1936 by the celebrated violinist Bronislav Hubermann as the Palestine Symphony, the orchestra included among its original members many outstanding Jewish musicians who had fled persecutions in Nazi Germany during 1933–45. By 1968 over 40 percent of the orchestra's musicians were born and trained in Israel.

The Kol Israel Orchestra is maintained by the Kol Israel Broadcasting Authority. Its programs emphasize works by Israeli composers, played by local performers. In addition there are municipal orchestras in Haifa, Ramat Gan, and other cities, 2 chamber music groups, several smaller ensembles, and approximately 120 choirs. The Israeli National Opera in Tel Aviv has a repertory of some 53 Italian and French operas and of 35 ballets. The repertory also includes *David*, an opera by the French composer Darius Milhaud, commemorating the foundation of Israel, and *Alexandra Hasmoneon*, by the Israeli composer Menahem Avidon.

Israeli composers have drawn from various musical traditions. Their works reflect the influence of folk songs from Eastern and Western Europe, Ashkenazic and Sephardic religious chants, and Near Eastern and modern European musical forms. Paul Ben Haim has written symphonies, chamber music, piano music, and choral works; Joseph Kaminsky is noted for his compositions for solo instruments; and Oedoen Partos for his symphonic work dedicated to the Ein Gev kibbutz. In the writing of vocal music, composers have frequently followed the inflections and melody patterns of spoken Hebrew.

There has been a vigorous revival of folk song, especially among the young generation. Written in a composite of Western and Middle Eastern musical modes, these songs may be gay or sentimental, commemorating harvests, celebrations, and various events of kibbutz life. Others are of an epic character, originating in the days of the first pioneer settlers, commemorating their deeds and the tribulations of their daily lives. Songs composed since the establishment of statehood celebrate the freedom of the Israeli countryside; still others are based on Biblical songs and modern Hebrew poems. The songs are sometimes accompanied by the *chalil*, a Near Eastern, flute-like instrument. A new type of folk song, popularized mostly by army music bands, expresses the moods of the Six-Day War of June 1967.

The hora is Israel's national dance. It originated in the agricultural settlements of the 1920's and expresses the communal spirit of kibbutz life. It is danced in a circle by men and women, moving to a quickening tempo. Couples may break away to perform a solo but, toward the end of the dance, return to the circle, expressing the communality of the group. Traditional dances and choreographic forms of Yemenite Jews are interpreted by a group of Yemenite folk dancers performing regularly in Israel and abroad.

Painting and Sculpture

Biblical themes and religious ritual were the principal subjects of painters working in Palestine before the large-scale immigration of the 1920's. The plastic arts were largely limited to the making of ornamental objects including candelabra and elaborately decorated prayer books. After the founding in 1906 of the Bezalel Art School in Jerusalem by the painter Boris Schatz (1862–1932), younger artists, some of them Israeli born, sought to develop a specifically national art based on themes inspired by the local landscape and history and to revive ancient crafts characteristic to the region. During the late 1960's the Bezalel Art School was the country's principal institution for the training of painters, sculptors, and decorative artists.

Western European art styles dominated the works of painters who immigrated to Israel since the 1930's. Chaim Atar (1902–1953) and Moshe Mokady (1902–) used the symbolic forms and exaggerated dimensions of French expressionism to portray their emotions evoked by Israel's scenery and its human characters. Mordechai Ardon (1896–) was noted for his symbolistic paintings expressing religious mysticism.

Since the late 1940's there has been a marked tendency towards abstraction and other modernistic styles, including cubism. Joseph Zaritzky (1891–) was noted for the lyric quality of his semi-abstract watercolors representing the scenery around Jerusalem and Tel Aviv. Dynamic colors and bold forms marked the abstract and figurative painting of Marcel Janco (1895–). Exclusively abstract shapes, less dependent on a concrete, visible world, asserted themselves in the paintings of Jacob Wechsler and Aharon Kahana.

Oriental and folkloristic motifs appear in the paintings of Joseph Halevy, a young Yemenite, and of Shalom Moskowitz (1883–). The latter, commonly known as Shalom of Safad (Zefat), is noted for his paintings of Biblical scenes and of episodes from ancient Jewish history, executed in a primitive style on a miniature scale.

Sculpture plays a distinct social role in expressing Israel's national ethos. The countryside is dotted with public monuments erected in remembrance of the country's heroes and martyrs. The abstract, monolithic forms, executed on a large scale, are placed in public parks or mark scenic sites. Many of them imitate striking natural phenomena, such as the stratified ravines and rock formations of the Negev region. Public buildings, schools, and hotels also incorporate many examples of modern sculpture.

Most of the country's representative sculptors were trained in Europe and have held exhibitions abroad. Yitzhak Danziger is noted for his large-scale sandstone statues and his abstract bronze-iron sculptures. He executed the Monument to Fallen Soldiers, which stands in Holon near Tel Aviv. Jehiel Shem's metal sculptures are inspired by the country's flora. The sculptures of David Palumbo emphasize forms and textures as they occur in nature. He executed the decorative details on the Heroes' and Martyrs' Memorial in Jerusalem, one of the country's most distinctive monuments.

Artists work on a private basis, showing and selling their works through art galleries located in the principal cities. Ein Hod, a village near Haifa, is a well known art colony. Another similar settlement is Safad, located in the town of the same name, in the northernmost part of the country. Sculptures, paintings, and craft objects made in these artists' colonies are shown in special exhibitions; some of them are exported for sale abroad.

Yemenite immigrants have brought to Israel a long tradition of folk arts and crafts. Their silver filigree, embroidery, copperware, brassware, and woven fabrics made notable contributions to the country's handicrafts. Arab, Bedouin, and Druze craft products, including sewn baskets of plaited straw, and traditional Arab pottery are available in the bazaars of the major cities. Israeli craftsmen who have immigrated from Europe learned their skills in their countries of origin and adapted these skills to shapes, forms, and colors traditional in the Middle East.

Architecture

Functionalism has been the primary concern in the country's contemporary architecture. Consequently, most of the dwellings lack distinction, but a few public buildings of good design have been erected. The Israel Museum in Jerusalem, designed by Alfred Mansfeld, includes a complex of buildings dedicated to the respective arts and is built of indigenous pink-streaked or yellow sandstone, quarried near Jerusalem. The same material has been used for the new Knesset building, which has been decorated with mosaics and tapestries designed by Marc Chagall. The building was designed by Joseph Klarwein in collaboration with other architects.

Israelis also take pride in the architectural efficiency of the Hebrew University-Hadassah Medical Center in Jerusalem. The large modernistic building houses a hospital, a medical school, a research center, and a nursing school. It is decorated by 12 stained-glass windows designed by Marc Chagall, with designs symbolizing the twelve tribes of Israel.

INTELLECTUAL EXPRESSION

The Old Testament is a subject of interest to virtually all Israelis. It is regarded as the broad foundation of Israeli culture and is widely studied either as a source of spiritual reading or as historic literature. Quizzes relating to the Old Testament are conducted regularly by newspapers and by the Kol Israel Broadcasting Authority. The Israel Society for Biblical Research maintains a network of study circles throughout the country. President Zalman Shazar is regarded as an eminent Old Testament scholar, participating actively in the research and study of the sacred texts.

Many scholars have attained international reputation. Martin Buber (1878–1965) was one of the world's outstanding religious philosophers. Yehuda Talmon is noted for his works on totalitarianism and on Israeli statehood; Shmuel N. Eisenstadt for his analysis of Israeli society.

Scholars, educators, authors, and journalists seek to develop and to expand Hebrew terminology and to adapt it for use in modern science, literature, and daily speech. Linguistic research is guided by the Hebrew Language Academy. Its decisions regarding grammar, orthography, and transliteration are published in the official government gazette and are binding on research institutions and government departments.

Science

The country takes pride in the achievements of its scientists and devotes extensive funds to the development of pure and applied research. Scientific activity in Israel carries much prestige abroad, and numerous research grants by foreign governments are awarded to Israeli institutions.

The National Council for Research and Development, operating under the Prime Minister's Office, advises the government on national policies guiding scientific activity, administers government funds earmarked for research, manages public scientific institutions, and coordinates public and private research activities.

Activities in this field are conducted by scientific institutes and research groups operating in conjunction with the country's seven institutions of higher learning and by some eight major organizations under public and private auspices. Probably the most prestigious research organization is the Weizmann Institute of Science, devoted to basic research in the natural sciences. During the late 1960's some 400 research projects were under progress at the institute, covering genetics, nuclear physics, biochemistry, and related fields. The Hebrew University-Hadassah Medical Center is internationally known for its accomplishments in medical research. The Israel Institute of Technology, known as the Technion, is noted for applied research related to industry and for its testing services available to enterprises in all sectors of the economy (see ch. 9, Education).

Environmental and medical research are the main activities of scientific institutions. Because of the rapid expansion of science-based industries, notably chemistry and electronics, industrial research also has high priority. According to government sources the National Council for Research and Development has set aside for the advancement of industrial research during the 5-year period 1966–1972 more than I£100 million (I£1 equals approximately US$0.285—see Glossary).

Scientific investigations in the field of medicine have centered on sclerotic heart disease, diabetes, anemia and other blood diseases, and tooth decay. Immigrants from the various regions of Europe and from the Middle East have served as control groups in studies on the effects of genetic factors, diet, climate, and physical environment on health. Extensive studies of the causative factors of cancer have been conducted at the Weizmann Institute. Researchers from the Hadassah Medical Center are engaged in a long-term study of arteriosclerosis, conducted jointly with their counterparts at the United States National Institute of Health. Applied research projects in progress at the center have been devoted to the development of electronic equipment for diagnostic medicine and to problems relating to the large-scale production of artificial kidneys. In April 1969 the Weizmann Institute and the Volcani Institute of the Ministry of Agriculture announced the discovery of a new immunizing substance derived from proteins and enzymes that may soon be used to prevent severe infectious diseases in humans.

The country has two nuclear reactors, one located at Nahal Soreq near Yavne, about 25 miles south of Tel Aviv, and the other at Dimona in the Negev. Studies in atomic physics relate to radiation,

140

radiobiology, the application of isotopes in medicine, and the use of nuclear energy in desalinization processes. The National Physics Laboratory in Jerusalem maintains a laboratory to measure and establish physical standards and is engaged in applied research on the uses of solar energy as a substitute for electrical power.

Problems related specifically to the country's physical environment are the main endeavors of the Negev Institute for Arid Zone Research at Beersheba. Research projects conducted by the institute include plant ecology, environmental physiology, and meteorology of the Negev region. A major research effort relates to the improvement of the Negev's brackish water resources by means of electro-dialysis. The Volcani Institute conducts research in plant biology, soil chemistry, irrigation, and veterinary medicine through a network of laboratories and regional experimental stations. The Israel Mining Institute at Haifa has developed a new process for producing a phosphoric acid fertilizer from low-grade phosphate rocks occurring in abundance in the Negev. Studies in desalinization and hydrology are also conducted at the Weizmann Institute.

In the field of industrial research, the Technion has conducted extensive investigations of the properties of cement, the country's main construction material, under high temperatures and humidity. Through its Research and Development Foundation, the Technion also carries out extensive applied research in food processing, electronics, and the industrial uses of soils and metals. The Yeda Research and Development Company, an affiliate of the Weizmann Institute, is engaged in the commercial promotion of industrially promising research findings. Synthetic amino acids, for example, discovered by the institute's scientists have been supplied to chemical and medical laboratories in foreign countries. Research on cotton and other fibers used in the textile industry has been carried out by the Institute of Fibers and Forest Products in Jerusalem.

Archeology

Archeological explorations associated with Jewish history, confirming Biblical stories or writings of the Talmud and other sacred books, are in the center of public interest. Crowds of citizens often gather at the site of public works where bulldozers may accidentally uncover valuable remnants from ancient times, including roads, bridges, buildings, or artifacts. Such accidental discoveries have frequently been made since 1948. Extensive traces of habitation and cultivation from ancient times have been found in the Negev region, for example, in the course of development work in that area. Some discoveries predate historic times. Human skull fragments more than 5 million years old have been uncovered in the Jordan River valley, south of Lake Tiberias. Village sites, cave dwellings, burial grounds, and tools from ancient times have been found throughout the country.

Among the major archeological discoveries are the Judaean royal fortresses from the 10th century B.C., south of Jerusalem, and at Megiddo in the north. A temple, also from the days of the Judaean Monarchy, was found at Arad, 20 miles west of the Dead Sea. The palace of King Herod (37 B.C.–4 B.C.) has been uncovered at Masada, located in the desert by the Dead Sea. Lakhish, 40 miles southwest of Jerusalem, contains a walled town conquered by the prophet Joshua during the 13th century B.C. Sites recalling the days of the New Testament include Kefar Nahum (conventional Capernaum), on the shores of Lake Tiberias (Sea of Galilee), where Jesus preached. The foundations of an agricultural development, including irrigation systems, were uncovered and restored at Avdat, in the desert of the Negev. They were built by the Nabateans, a people living in that area more than 2,000 years ago. Port facilities used by the Romans and Roman statuary were found in the port of Ashqelon, south of Tel Aviv.

The western shore of the Dead Sea has been the site of perhaps the most significant archeological discoveries. In 1947 the famous Dead Sea Scrolls were discovered near the northern end of the Dead Sea's western shores. Some of the scrolls include Biblical descriptions portraying life and everyday affairs of Israel before the Christian era. Among them was found the oldest known text of part of the Old Testament, the Book of Isaiah, in Hebrew. In the course of archeological research in 1961, relating to the revolt of the Jews against the Romans under the leadership of Bar Kochba (A.D. 132–135), Professor Yigael Yadin discovered about 50 documents representing the administrative correspondence of the Jewish revolutionary government, some signed by Bar Kochba himself.

Archeological and artistic treasures are preserved at the Israel Museum in Jerusalem opened in 1965. The Museum is also noted for its large collection of Jewish folk art. The Museum includes the Bronfman Biblical and Archeological Museum and the Shrine of the Book. The latter contains the Bar Kochba letters and the Dead Sea Scrolls. Many towns and settlements have their own archeological collections of discoveries of local interest.

Archeological explorations are conducted by numerous groups headed by the Department of Antiquities and Museums in the Ministry of Education and Culture, the Hebrew University in Jerusalem, and the Israel Exploration Society. The government also extends financial and technical assistance to foreign archeological expeditions.

CHAPTER 11
RELIGION

Judaism is the predominant faith. Orthodox Jewry, however, comprises only a minor segment of the population. Most members of the European and native-born Israeli majority, while nominally adherents of Judaism, devote little time to the observance of religious ceremonies or ritual. Nonetheless, Judaism as religion or tradition is a powerful source of cohesion in Israeli society. With its orientation of return to Palestine (Zion), maintained over two millennia, it was an underlying force in the establishment of the state. More than 85 percent of Israelis identify themselves as Jews; Jewish cultural and intellectual influences have been a dominant force in shaping the values and attitudes of contemporary society.

Over the centuries, return to Zion had been inextricably interwoven into Jewish faith and tradition. An ancient proverb declared that it is better to dwell in the waste places and deserts of the land of Israel than in palaces outside it. The yearly cycle of prayers and ceremonies constantly stressed return to the land that, according to Biblical narratives, God had given to the descendants of Abraham. Jewish law indicated that the duty of the faithful to live in Israel was greater than the rest of the law and that certain commandments could be fulfilled only by persons living there. Hence the Jewish community in Palestine had always been treated with special respect by other Jews, who considered it a sacred duty to contribute to their support.

In the new state of Israel, most observant Jews belonged to specifically religous political parties that sought to bring public law and institutions into conformity with principles of the Jewish faith. Whereas orthodox Jews were in a minority, the political balance of power worked to their advantage, so that despite the strong secularist current, religious influence was much evident in political and social institutions.

Religious parties numbered among their achievements state recognition of the Chief Rabbinate, of the Sabbath, and of the holy days. Other achievements were the continued observance of Jewish dietary laws by public agencies and the continued jurisdiction of rabbinical courts over personal status matters for Jews. The parties were also responsible for the influence of religion within the educational system. In addition to private religious schools, there were religious schools operated by the state as part of the public educational system (see ch. 9, Education).

Owing to the great divergence of religious commitment within the population and the strong feelings associated with them, the appropriateness of ecclesiastical control over personal status matters and related issues is the subject of frequent debate. The nature and meaning of Jewishness itself is sometimes publicly explored. Topics of this nature generate intense interest among all Israeli Jews, from the most orthodox to the least confirmed believers, and active discussion of such issues is a characteristic part of the national life.

Despite the paramount position of Judaism, the country has no official state religion, and minority communities have their rights guaranteed. Within the territory comprising the modern state of Israel are ancient historic shrines not only of Judaism but also of Christianity and Islam. Most of Israel's Arba minority, comprising about 12 percent of the population in early 1968, were Muslims, almost all adherents of the Sunni branch of Islam (see Glossary). A few were Christians. Druzes, whose traditions derive partly from Islam, constituted another small minority.

JUDAISM

Origins

Judaism is the oldest of the great monotheistic religions. The Hebrew Scriptures, usually referred to by Christians as the Old Testament, ascribe its earliest beginnings to the age of the ancient patriarchs, between the 20th and 16th centuries B.C. The first patriarch of the people that were destined to become monotheistic was Abraham, who, according to Biblical narratives, journeyed at God's command with his family from his birthplace in Mesopotamia through Syria and southwest to the Egyptian-dominated land of Canaan. In Canaan, the scriptural account told, God entered into a covenant with Abraham, giving the land to his people and promising them personal protection and future material blessing. The covenant was sealed symbolically by performance of the rite of circumcision.

The Biblical narrative describes later experiences of the Hebrew people in Egypt, a miraculous deliverance, and further wanderings in the barren Sinai desert under the leadership of the Prophet Moses. At the foot of Mount Sinai came a renewal of the covenant and new teachings from God, who had revealed himself to Moses in the name of Yahweh. The Biblical account passes on to the conquest of Canaan under Joshua, the unsettled period of continual contests with Canaanites, Philistines and other peoples, and finally the consolidation of Israelite territory under Saul, David, and his son Solomon, who built the First Temple in Jerusalem (see ch. 3, Historical Setting).

From the 10th to the sixth century B.C., belief in the covenant manifested itself in a growing sense of ethnic and cultural distinctiveness among the people of Israel as well as an increasing conviction that God had given them a unique religious mission. Their prophetically foretold deportation to Babylonia, after the fall of the Kingdom of Judah in 586 B.C., was regarded as indicative of God's displeasure with them. Likewise, subsequent restoration to Palestine by the Persians in the fifth century B.C. was deemed a sign that they had regained his grace.

The birth of Jesus of Nazareth at Bethlehem in Palestine and the subsequent beginnings of Christianity occurred toward the end of the Second Commonwealth period, which lasted from several centuries before the Christian era to A.D. 70. After the Roman destruction in that year of Jerusalem and of the Second Temple, which had been the focal point of Jewish life and culture, Jewish dispersion from Palestine reached the proportions of a national migration. Some Jews fled to Egypt, Syria, or Babylonia, others to Arabia, where Islam, third of the great monotheistic faiths, was to be founded by Mohammed in the seventh century A.D. Other Jews joined established Jewish communities in more distant points in Asia Minor, Italy, North Africa, and Spain. A few retired to outlying parts of Palestine, hoping some day to go back to Jerusalem.

In the widespread dispersion of Jews from Palestine, often called the Diaspora, two major Judaic traditions developed—that of the Ashkenazic Jews, who settled mainly in Western, Central, and Eastern Europe, and that of the Sephardic Jews, who settled mainly in Spain and other Mediterranean lands. The two traditions came to differ somewhat in liturgy, custom, and ritual, surrounding prescribed forms of worship. Nonetheless, throughout the centuries that followed, belief in the covenant continued to act as a unifying force among Jews throughout the world, regardless of whatever tradition they represented.

Principles of Faith

In broad terms, Judaism can be said to be a way of life, one that seeks to govern every human action. The devout believers strive to follow the rules of right and wrong, so as to have a meaningful life and share in bringing about the establishment of the Kingdom of God and the brotherhood of men on earth. Ceremonial disciplines are binding only on Jews, but the ethical element in the faith is regarded as universal in its application. Judaism thus blends religion and morality into an indissoluble entity and provides the moral and ethical underpinnings for the entire society of which it is a part.

The basic concepts of Judaism are rooted in the law and the teachings of the Prophets. The faithful believe that the written law, consisting of the Hebrew Scriptures, was given by divine inspiration at Mount Sinai. The Scriptures include the Five Books of Moses (also referred to as the Torah), the Prophets, and a third and less familiar section, called the Hagiographa.

Oral law supplements and elaborates upon the written law. It is a large and somewhat fluid body of amplifications of that law, also originating at Mount Sinai. Contrary to the written law, however, it was handed down by word-of-mouth for centuries and only later put into writing. The traditionalist accepts the view that the whole body of oral law as well as the written law was divinely inspired.

Since ancient times, there have been substantial variations in the interpretation of the law and teachings of the prophets among Hebrew scholars. Oral law in particular, because of the manner of its development, has invited widespread differences of opinion. These varying interpretations gave rise to internal divisions early in the history of Judaism. During the Second Commonwealth, the most generally accepted interpretation was represented by the community known as the Pharisees, but other groups, including the Samaritans, Sadducees, and Essenes competed with them.

After the destruction of the Second Temple in Jerusalem in A.D. 70 and the loss of political autonomy by the Jews, the set of beliefs and practices upheld by the Pharisees, later known as Rabbinic Judaism achieved complete ascendancy. Other Jewish groups disappeared with the single exception of the Karaites in Babylonia. In modern times, some new trends developed, but Rabbinic Judaism has continued to be the most representative form of the faith.

Even among rabbinical scholars, there is variation of interpretation regarding Judaic concepts. The differences in some cases are so great that it is difficult to characterize any concept as being universally Jewish or rabbinic. This has led to the assertion that Judaism has no dogmas. Although there has never been a central authority in Judaism that has formulated a creed, there have nonetheless been attempts to outline articles of faith.

Among them the best known is the creed of Maimonides, the medieval Jewish philosopher (1135–1204), incorporating 13 fundamental principles. These principles are: belief in the existence of a single supreme being; in His unity; in His incorporeality; in His timelessness; in His approachability through prayer; belief in prophecy; in the superiority of Moses to all other prophets; in the revelation of the Law and that the Law, as contained in the Torah, is that revealed to Moses; in the immutability of the Law; belief in Divine providence; in Divine justice; in the coming of the Messiah; and in the resurrection and human immortality.

Ultimate reward and punishment are associated with attainment of or denial of immortality. The supreme reward is eventual reunion with God, a circumstance in which man is no longer subject to the rivalries and antagonisms that he experiences in his physical existence. Wickedness, on the other hand, brings harm to a man in this life and, more importantly, denies him the possibility of immortality.

Judaism makes no claim to universal allegiance. It accepts converts, but somewhat reluctantly, and only after the candidate has demonstrated strong conviction. Candidates must be told of all the difficulties attached to being a Jew and must show that they are not motivated by mundane considerations. It is regarded as improper for a Jew to urge someone to become a convert, partly because the obligations assumed by such persons are considered to be binding not only on them but also upon all their descendants. The ritual of conversion demands circumcision and immersion for the male and the latter for the female.

Modern Judaism is tolerant of other monotheistic faiths, holding that each makes a distinctive contribution toward the realization of the kingdom of God on earth. Because Islam is dogmatically unequivocal in its monotheism, Judaism was somewhat more lenient toward it than toward Christianity, which at first was regarded as simply another form of idolatry. Over the centuries, however, there has been increasing acceptance of Christianity, especially since the Jewish philosopher, Maimonides, declared that the spread of Christianity had paved the way for the ultimate universal acceptance of true faith.

Besides Rabbinic Judaism, which provides the dominant set of beliefs in the country today, there are two small Jewish communities representing other points of view. Neither group has at any time rejected the basic conception of Judaism as a revealed religion whose observance is incumbent on all the Jewish people, and each remains linked to the faith. They are nevertheless considered distinct from the mainstream of Judaic thought. One is the Karaite community, numbering about 10,000 persons. The Karaites reject the authority of oral law and accept only the literal law of the Scriptures as they interpret it. The other is the Samaritan community, whose origins date back to the eighth century B.C. Samaritans, of whom there are only a few hundred, recognize only the authority of the Five Books of Moses and the Book of Joshua. Their High Priest lives in Nabulus, about 30 miles north of Jerusalem. They regard nearby Mount Gerizim, where they anciently had a temple, as sacred.

Observance and Conduct

Religious expression is viewed both as a communal, social activity and as a private, individual experience. Devout behavior is associated with loyal participation in the life of the Jewish community as it finds expression in the home, synagogue, and school. Religious observance differs for men and women.

Women do not participate in communal rites, although they may attend services in the synagogue, and they are not required to engage in study of the law, which Rabbinic Judaism regards as one of the most basic of religious duties. Wives and mothers fulfill special religious functions in the home, however, such as lighting the candles on Sabbath Eve. They are also expected to help their husbands and sons meet their religious obligations.

Rules for the conduct of life according to religious precepts are traditionally divided into negative and positive commandments, each thought to be equally important. There are, for example, dietary laws calling for the abstinence from meat of certain animals that are termed unclean, and dictating the manner of preparation of certain foods. *Kashrut*, Jewish religious dietary observance, is the rule in the armed forces and other public institutions. Pious Jews abstain from leaven for the 7 days of Passover in commemoration of the Exodus from Egypt. Other negative regulations pertain to aspects of personal hygiene and sexual activity and to idol worship.

Prayer, preferably recited together with the community in the synagogue, occupied a central place in religious observance. The faithful are expected to pray three times daily—in the morning, afternoon, and evening. An additional element is included in the morning prayer on the Sabbath and during festivals. Services on the Sabbath, festivals, fast days, and other special occasions also call for readings from portions of the Torah, arranged so that the whole Pentateuch is covered within a year. Traditional services are conducted in Hebrew. All devout male believers are expected to devote considerable time to the mastery of the basic texts of Rabbinic Judaism, since these sources are believed to be the means through which God revealed his will to mankind.

Special rites are performed on the most important occasions of the religious calendar, which are the holy days and the fast days. In addition to the Sabbath (Hebrew, Shabbat), which is celebrated on the 7th day of the week (Saturday), the holy days are: Pesach (Passover); Shabouth (Pentecost); Rosh Hashanah (New Year's Day); Yom Kippur (Day of Atonement); and Sukkoth (Feast of Tabernacles). Yom Kippur, dedicated to repentance, calls for a full day of fasting and of prayers.

Various occasions in the course of life are marked by other special rites. No ceremony of admittance to the faith is necessary for the child of a Jewish mother, who is regarded as a Jew by birth; male children, however, undergo the rite of circumcision on the 8th day of life. Later, on the Sabbath following the boy's 13th birthday, he participates in the formal reading of the Torah at services in the synagogue, a ceremony commonly called the bar mitzvah.

The proportion of the country's Jewish population represented by persons who observe traditional rites and customs is not precisely known. Estimates based on votes won by religious political parties suggest a total of about 15 percent; estimates based on enrollment in religious schools suggest a higher percentage, somewhat more than 35 percent. Within the observant group itself, there are varying degrees of commitment to traditional rites and customs, as evident in the existence of Ultra-Orthodox, Modern Orthodox, and Progressive congregations.

For the great majority of devout Jews, the religion is identified with Orthodoxy. In Tel Aviv alone, there are some 700 Orthodox synagogues, attended regularly by some 100,000 persons. Orthodox Jews believe in careful observance of Judaic law, which regulates every area of daily life as well as birth, marriage, and death. Even among this group, however, there are those who reject the emphasis on strict observance of ritual law as outdated and who think of themselves as practicing the traditional faith in a manner appropriate to the contemporary setting.

Ultra-Orthodox Jews, by contrast, are uncompromising in their efforts to abide by the 613 commandments of Judaic law. They adhere rigidly to the *halacha* (Rabbinical Code), preparing all food according to dietary laws, immersing themselves regularly in ritual baths, and refraining from travel, labor, and other forms of activity considered to be a violation of the Sabbath. Most Ultra-Orthodox Jews are concentrated in the so-called Mea Shearim section of the new city of Jerusalem. One extremist group (the Neturei Kartas) denies the authority of the state, claiming that it came into being without the sanction of God (see ch. 17, Political Values and Attitudes).

A special development of Orthodox Judaism is the mystical movement known as Hasidism that emerged in late 18th-century Poland. Hasidism lessened the ascetic tendencies in Jewish living, sanctioned the hard realities of life, and encouraged self-expression in the form of storytelling and song. Hasidic groups have been in Israel since the middle of the 19th century.

The Reform and Conservative movements, which are major trends of modern Judaism in Europe and the United States, have no status in Israel. Recently, however, small congregations of Progressive Judaism have emerged in major urban centers. Progressive congregations have developed slowly, representing only a few thousand believers in the late 1960's and have met with strong opposition from Orthodox leadership .They receive no official support. Their rabbis are not recognized as such, and they are neither paid from public funds nor permitted to officiate at weddings or funerals.

Institutions

Government administration of religious and related matters is vested in the Ministry of Religious Affairs. Functions of the ministry include the supervision of the Jewish, Muslim, Christian, and Druze communities and their courts, the regulation of the production and sale of kosher food, the enforcement of Sabbath restrictions and burial procedures, and the maintenance or restoration of sacred shrines.

There is no hierarchical organization or central authority in Judaism, nor is there any sharp distinction in status between rabbi and layman. A rabbi is especially knowledgeable about the Scriptures and the Talmud, one of the basic texts of Rabbinic Judaism, and his advice is sought on points of law and practice. For Jews in Israel, supreme religious authority rests with the Chief Rabbinate, made up of the chief rabbis, for the Ashkenazic and Sephardic communities and members of the Supreme Rabbinical Council. The major responsibility of the Rabbinate is to interpret Judaic law and to supervise the eight rabbinical courts. It also certifies rabbinical fitness, approves textbooks for religious schools, and supervises ritual circumcisions. Activities on a local level are performed by several hunderd religious councils or committees. In late 1968 the country had nearly 400 officially appointed rabbis, but the number was insufficient and many positions for rabbis were vacant.

Reflecting the supreme importance Judaism assigns to the study of Talmudic law, Israel itself has become a world center for Jewish religious studies. The country has a religious university (Bar Ilan University, near Tel Aviv) that provides instruction in Jewish and related studies to some 3,800 students (see ch. 9, Education). There are about 267 *yeshivot* (Talmudic colleges), secondary-level institutions, whose curricula focus on Jewish law and history. Almost 18,000 students are enrolled in them.

Judaism as a religion and tradition receives varying degrees of emphasis in different types of elementary schools. State education is oriented by law to emphasize the values of Jewish culture, love of the homeland, and devotion to the Jewish people. Of the two types of state schools, secular and religious, both offer instruction in Jewish history; basic texts of Rabbinic Judaism and the Scriptures are taught in literature courses. State religious schools, however, give greater emphasis to religious studies than do the secular schools. Besides the state religious schools, there are also Orthodox religious schools, with an almost exclusively religious curriculum (see ch. 9, Education).

Judaism has many shrines in Israel, of which the most venerated include the Western Wall of the Temple Court in Jerusalem, sometimes referred to as the Wailing Wall. Other centers of tradition and sanctity include David's tomb on Mount Zion in Jerusalem, the tombs of the Patriarchs in Hebron, and the Cave of Elijah on Mount Carmel. Another sacred site is that of the tomb of Rachel, one of the wives of Jacob, located on the northern edge of Bethlehem.

Judaism and Society

There is no consensus among Israelis regarding the role that Judaism should fill in the national life. Orthodox and Ultra-Orthodox Jews seek by educational means as well as by political action and legislative efforts to bring both private and public life into conformity with religious law. Secularly oriented Jews, on the other hand, comprising by far the majority of the population, see such action as an infringement of individual liberty and are often critical of the rulings of the rabbinical councils. Despite the fundamentality of this issue to Israeli society, political leaders of all shades of opinion have avoided a direct confrontation on the subject, considering the active pursuit of its resolution not to be in the national interest.

Nonetheless, the practical morality of the people as a whole appears to be still strongly influenced by the teachings of Judaism and by the stream of Jewish historical consciousness. For many secularly oriented Israelis, the accent of religion has shifted from theology and ritual to the social sphere, with emphasis on the universal character and ethics of Judaism rather than strict observance of ritual law. The emergence of the kibbutz (collective settlement), in which there is no private property and everything is shared in common by the group, for example, is closely linked with the Judaic emphasis on social justice.

OTHER FAITHS

Adherents of Islam, a development of the Judeo-Christian religious tradition, represent the principal religious minority. Islam means in Arabic "submission to the will of God" and believers refer to themselves as Muslims. The founder of the faith, Mohammed, is regarded as the last in a series of prophets that included Moses and Jesus. The faith is divided into two major branches, followers of which are called Sunnites and Shiites (see Glossary). The great majority of the roughly 233,000 Muslims in the country in mid-1968 belonged to the Sunni branch. Nearly all were Arabs, although there were a few thousand Circassians among them.

Muslim prayer leaders numbered about 180 and there were some 80 mosques. Muslim tradition holds that one point in his life, Mohammed, on departing the earth, left the imprint of his foot on the boulder that the Dome of the Rock encloses. Jerusalem is, therefore, the third most holy city of Islam, after Mecca and Medina, in Saudi Arabia.

Muslims had full autonomy in their internal affairs. Their own courts dealt with matters of personal status within the community. Their spiritual leaders, or imams, were paid by the state, as were those of other religious communities. Trusteeship committees administered the *waqf* (plural *awaqf*), the Muslim charitable foundations.

Christians form the second largest religious minority, numbering about 60,000 in 1968. About 11,000 are Roman Catholics, including about 3,000 foreigners, most of whom are associated with religious houses. Some 23,000 belong to the Greek Catholic (Melkite) community, whose church is in full communion with Rome, but is organized separately; their chief religious dignitary is an archbishop, whose seat is in Haifa. Another Uniate church, that of the Maronites, has about 3,000 followers. Eastern churches, not in communion with Rome, are represented in Israel principally by the Greek Orthodox community, which has about 17,000 members. Besides these, there are various other small Christian groups, including about 2,000 Protestants.

The historical link of Christians with Israel is the fact that the country was the scene of the earthly life of Jesus. Churches, monasteries, convents, and shrines are numerous, and the sacred places have been identified and taken into custody and care by the Christian community.

The Druzes form another religious minority. Their monotheistic faith is in part a historical derivative of Shia Islam. They do not, however, regard themselves, nor are they regarded by others, as Muslims. They reject part of the most important article of the Islamic faith—the supreme prophethood of Mohammed. They live mainly in the mountains of Syria and Lebanon, but there are some 32,000 in Israel, principally in the Galilee hill region, west and north of Lake Tiberias. The community has its own religious courts and schools.

The Bahai faith has only about 200 adherents in Israel, but the country is, nevertheless, its world center, with the principal shrines in Acre (Akko) and Haifa. The faith, which arose in Iran in the 19th century, is a synthesis of elements drawn from a wide range of religious and philosophical sources. It gives emphasis to the development of moral relationships between men rather than to the observance of strict rituals.

CHAPTER 12
SOCIAL VALUES

Pragmatism, straightforwardness, and dynamism, terms often used in portraying the citizens of Israel, may be applied as well to the set of values that they share. The people, and their attitudes toward those fundamental social questions that confront any society, have been shaped by a diversity of historical factors, producing a value system that is distinctively Israeli. Drawn in the first instance from the Jewish legacy of three millenia, it has been supplemented by the more recent experience of Zionism in Palestine.

The resultant value system offers certain standards for desired behavior. It encourages application of insights from the past in dealing with current problems. Israelis believe it commands the blending of idealism with reality, emotion with firmness, physical labor with respect for the intellectual and spiritual realms, and a strong military posture with a sincere desire for peace.

Whereas specific values, either of substance or of style, may have changed during the initial 21 years of statehood, a core of Israeli values has not only endured but has been reinforced. These basic premises and assumptions are perpetuated through their endorsement by both the younger Sabra (native-born) generation and new immigrants. There is, above all, a deep sense of national consciousness. This concern for the community, in its larger context of the State, and strong attachment to the land of Israel, Eretz Yisrael, overrides such divisive tendencies as doctrinaire partisanship and party affiliation. Similarly, maintenance of the Jewish character of the society in some meaningful form is regarded by an overwhelming majority of the inhabitants as intrinsically valuable and essential.

On the level of interpersonal relations, one's advancement and social standing to a major extent is determined by individual achievement, characteristic of a society imbued with the pioneering spirit for over 50 years, rather than on the basis of prescribed class status, personal connections, or ancestral lineage. Initiative, knowledge, efficiency, sincerity, and candidness are all regarded as admirable virtues. Fulfillment by a person of his duties is expected no less than the exercise of his rights. Freedom of expression, being the primary avenue for dialogue between ruling elite and general population, is preserved in its many forms. Democratic government and social welfare programs are safeguarded as tangible expressions of basic human rights.

Whereas these values are permanent features of the system, others, such as informality and simplicity, have been challenged under the impact of technological change. Further evidence of the transitional nature of the society has been the decline of the kibbutz, or collective settlement, its former role in defining tastes and values being assumed instead by the complex urban centers. The population has become more abundant and less homogeneous in terms of ambition, needs, and desires.

Nevertheless, because the value system and those who subscribe most earnestly to it have been receptive to change, the system has succeeded in providing the tacit consensus essential to domestic order and national purpose. The values operate constantly to govern daily activities; yet their strength and utility as a positive force for cohesion and stability have been more readily apparent to the outside observer at times of national emergency such as occurred during the security crisis in May–June 1967.

FACTORS INFLUENCING THE VALUE SYSTEM

Diverse forces, ranging from history to geography and from economic and military necessity to cultural preferences, have contributed to the set of values that guide life in Israel. When Theodor Herzl, founder of the modern Zionist movement, wrote a book in 1902, describing his vision of the Jewish future in Palestine, he entitled it *Altneuland*, "old-new land." Current values reflect this emphasis upon both the old and the new, integrated to create an Israeli synthesis.

History is an important part of the psychological makeup of every Jew living in the country. The subject was stressed as part of the traditional course of Judaic studies in all those countries, oriental or occidental, from which Jews have emigrated to Israel over the years. It is now incorporated in the educational system, so that members of the younger, native generation are also steeped in the main themes of this long history (see ch. 3, Historical Setting). The brief periods of Jewish sovereignty are contrasted with the more dominant condition of exile and persecution. The significance of an independent Israel is made apparent through frequent reference in textbooks, speeches, and literary works to the negative impact of foreign rule or minority status—discrimination and wandering, pogroms, and cultural stagnation. Periodic evidence of anti-Semitism and the tragic experience of naziism have led the leaders and general public to view their state as an act of redemption and as perhaps the last hope for Jewish survival. As a result, Israel, unlike many of the emergent nations of Asia and Africa, possesses in this historical heritage an asset that serves to unify a heterogeneous population and to instill a sense of national identity (see ch. 4, Population).

Israelis, perhaps conscious that generations of their ancestors were never able to reach the Holy Land, regard *aliyah* (immigration) as not merely a physical act of coming but, as the word implies, an ascent, a spiritual experience. This identification with the land of Israel finds expression in several ways. Young and old alike participate in the national pastimes of hiking and archaeology, visiting those famous sites referred to in the Old Testament (see ch. 2, Physical Environment).

An early manifestation of this quest for ancient roots in Palestine and need to renew the Jewish association with the land occurred as early as the late 19th century. The first pioneers (*chalutzim*), reacting to the confinement of Jews in Eastern European ghettoes, glorified farming and direct contact with the soil. Early folk songs and Hebrew poetry also alluded to the beauty of the land and to the opportunities it offered for material and spiritual fulfillment. Planting trees came to symbolize this sentiment. Since 1948 this claim to inalienable possession of the land has been intensified.

The moral teachings and religious inheritance of Judaism are a third major determinant of values within the society. Although many people are secularists in terms of religious observance, the majority value the Torah and related writings for their historical content, ethical guidelines, and traditions (see ch. 11, Religion). Because of the need to create and then to defend and develop the state, to which secularist and Orthodox alike have contributed, and because of the emotions that the subject evokes, the role of religion has not been fully clarified. Yet it has been the cause for intense public debate, and the government, through its educational policy, sought to encourage "Jewish consciousness" among the youth (see ch. 9, Education). In 1969 the impact of the Six-Day War led many of its participants to a new awareness of their Jewishness and to reassess the possible importance of religious observances for them.

If the bond between Jewish history, the land, and Judaism, established many centuries ago, is still relevant, more recent events in the history of the Palestine Jewish community, the Yishuv, during the past 70 years have had an equal impact upon value formation. Each successive influx of immigrants, by emphasizing certain virtues and by its ability to institutionalize them, contributed to the evolution of a value system that prevailed throughout the period of the British Palestine Mandate, with traces still evident in 1969. Consequently, by the 1930's, and certainly before 1948, there existed a basic framework for social activities. All subsequent settlers as well as the children had to adjust to and conduct themselves within an established system of values.

155

Those pioneers of the First Aliyah (1882–1904), reflecting their Russian origin, set out to transform themselves into a landed Jewish agricultural working class through individual enterprise. Motivated by romantic sentiment, they favored absorption into the indigenous cultural life of the Middle East; this goal, as opposed to erecting a Westernized society, comparable to Switzerland, still found many advocates in 1969.

The Second Aliyah (1904–1914) brought a more rigorous and conscientiously ideological approach. Its members, advocates of labor Zionism, called for the use of cooperative methods, which were applied to the founding of the first kibbutz, Degania, and the first all-Jewish city, Tel Aviv. Their efforts were strengthened during the Third Aliyah (1919–1923) when many new collective settlements were established and the main outline of kibbutz life and ideology were formed. Among these ideas were a commitment to Zionism, the benefits of "a return to the soil" found only in farming, group guidance and mutual aid, self reliance, simplicity of living standards, and equal sharing of the benefits of production. At the same time similar ideas guided the creation of Jewish communities as urban socialist institutions, such as the Histadrut (Histadrut Ha'ovdim Haklalit—General Federation of Labor).

The fourth (1924–31) and fifth (1932–39) waves of immigration upset the initial socialist homogeneity of the Jewish community. The new arrivals, fleeing from the threat of naziism in Germany or unable to enter other countries, were not necessarily socialists or even Zionists. Agricultural work and collective life were alien to them; nor were they suited by temperament or professional experience to other than city-dwelling and private enterprise. Consequently, they resided in the cities, transforming Tel Aviv into a metropolis, and opened small businesses. A large percentage of those who came in the 1930's were professionals or entrepreneurs. These doctors, teachers, lawyers, and shopkeepers made an imprint upon the economy, institutions of higher learning, and culture. Their capitalism and attention to materialism also competed with the socialist idealism of the kibbutzim as an alternative way of life.

The socialists and the capitalists, despite sharp ideological differences, nevertheless had a common denominator: their European origin and appreciation for Western culture. This was reinforced by such things as belief in the need for a Zionist state, the revival of Hebrew as a language, and the need to defend the state. As a result, when large numbers of Sephardim (Oriental Jews) from North Africa and Yemen arrived after 1949, they had little choice except to fit themselves into the existing, essentially Western, social framework.

The institution most immediately and drastically affected was the family. Family relations among the Sephardic communities had centered upon the two pillars of the patriarch and the extended family. Once in Israel, however, the senior male in each family found himself alien to the dominant culture and unskilled for any well-paying job. His children, instead, became the providers, learning Hebrew quickly, going through military service, acquiring a trade and abandoning the larger family unit for opportunities afforded only in the cities. Similarly, the difficulties of earning a living worked to preclude retaining several wives or maintaining more than the immediate family under one roof. It was still unclear in 1969 to what extent the Sephardim have been able to retain some of their Oriental values while adjusting to life in Israel.

The harsh realities of Palestine ultimately determined basic values and life style. Scarcity of water, financial resources, and fertile land emphasized the need for communal cooperation. The threat of raids by Arab bedouin and the opposition on the part of the native Palestinian Arabs to displacement by Israelis meant that the settlers had to be prepared to defend their interests by force. The militia groups formed in the early years of the 20th century were the precursors of the present Israel Defense Forces (see ch. 26, The Armed Forces). The fact that the *chalutzim* were engaged primarily in physical labor, as well as the warm climate, dictated simplicity in dress and tastes. Because the Jewish population was comparatively small until the 1940's, it meant that most of the inhabitants knew each other, were often related by marriage, felt no need for formalities, and addressed each other on a first-name basis.

DOMINANT VALUES

Statehood, three major military confrontations with the Arab world, expanded industrialization, and the absorption of over 1 million immigrants, all within the short span of 20 years, have either reinforced or modified the earlier set of values. As a result of these most recent influences, the dominant value system at the end of the 1960's comprised a wide range of features.

One such feature was known to Israelis as the principle of *ein breyra*. It implied a sense of "no alternative" and permeated every aspect of life. Viewing themselves politically with their backs to the sea in the face of Arab hostility, the people were resolute in facing whatever challenges presented themselves. The Negev wasteland had to be recultivated at great expense, since there was a shortage of otherwise fertile soil. A channel, the National Water Carrier, was built to enable waters from the northern Jordan River to flow the long distance to the south. Provision had to be made for the destitute immigrants, so there was no choice except to restrict domestic consumption and to raise local taxes, two policies that were accepted by the public as necessary for many years (see ch. 25, Financial and Monetary System). The constant possibility of attack was met by youths settling in isolated frontier outposts; by maintaining a large military defense budget; and by inaugurating a new foreign relations thrust towards the countries of Asia and Africa in order to escape diplomatic containment by the Arabs (see ch. 15, Foreign Relations).

Thus the essential negativism of *ein breyra* has been elevated to the status of a virtue and is responsible to a considerable extent for dynamism of the people, their positive attitude and determination.

Another feature of Israeli society was the strong attitude toward independence. Having gained sovereignty with great difficulty and having accomplished much since then, despite the skepticism of many foreign experts, the typical Israeli was not prepared in 1969 to relinquish any of this independence.

The shift of the economy from agriculture to industry has pushed fresh values to the surface. Recognition was given to the individual possessing *yeda*, technical know-how. Scientific, technical, and managerial skills were esteemed for their potential contribution to industrial growth (see ch. 21, Industry). Education, in consequence, was increasingly vocational and technical rather than general and humanistic. Greater emphasis was being placed upon preparing students to contribute meaningfully to the expanding, more complex and, therefore, more sophisticated economy.

Efficiency was yet another by-product of industrialization. It involved greater attention to planning, research and development, and science. Efficiency, and belief in the superiority of quality over quantity, stemmed from the fact that Israel's population was vastly outnumbered by that of the adjoining Arab countries. This emphasis upon efficiency was most apparent in the Israel Defense Forces.

The people took a keen interest in current events, although there was less ideological commitment and party identification on the part of the young. Because of pride in the existence of a Jewish government, service by most men and women in the citizen army, and an awareness that the government held the key to their security and economic future, the people helped to make Israel a participatory government. Despite this concern, they tended to treat public figures with good-natured irreverence, still calling military officers and politicians by their first name, and to criticize the pervasive bureaucracy (see ch. 17, Political Values and Attitudes). The former tended to make government more intimate whereas the latter tended to make government more remote by expanding the distance between the people and their leaders.

A final value of great significance for understanding the Israeli and his society is the high premium put upon the life of each individual citizen. Jewish history again asserts itself, for the loss of almost 6 million Jews in the Nazi era is still a vivid part of the collective national memory. Many middle-aged Israelis are former inmates of the Nazi extermination camps; others, after 1948, left inhospitable conditions in the Arab countries to seek safety. In 1969 their children were responsible for guarding the uneasy borders. Even with approximately 2.4 million Jews, the community still remained closely knit, so that weekly casualty figures affected many households by virtue of family, business, social, or neigborly contacts.

The comparatively small size of the population from the very outset of the Yishuv had been conducive to the equality of women. They did a full share of work on the kibbutzim, had a role in decision-making, and even performed military service; the biography of Mrs. Golda Meir reflected the important role of women throughout (see ch. 18, Biographies of Selected Key Personalities).

The dominance of these individual and collective values benefited from the educative influence of several decentralized yet nontheless effective institutions. Schools, youth movements, settlement organizations, Gadna (a paramilitary organization), and Nahal (Noar Halutz Lochaim—Fighting Pioneer Youth) all functioned to inculcate the basic values in the young Sabras during the several stages of their maturation (see ch. 9, Education). Cultural activities, displays, and commemorations shared in this process. The trial of Adolf Eichmann, for example, held in Jerusalem in 1962, exposed the younger generation to a traumatic period of Jewish history that was a prelude to establishment of the state. In the case of young immigrants, the army plays a role in integrating newcomers into the society and its value system, while blending together Sabras from the city and farm.

CHALLENGES TO THE DOMINANT VALUES

Although the essential value system has been stable, there was growing concern in recent years that particular components within the system had either become obsolete or else deemphasized. Initially the land had produced farmers and had determined the economy. The struggle against the British and Arabs had produced Jewish fighters, in defiance of the traditional stereotype of the Jew as meek and passive, while determining the central position of the defense establishment. The state, in turn, produced men of leadership ability and determined the nature of the political system. At the end of the 1960's, the drive toward modernization was beginning to affect markedly the society, producing a new class of technocrats, and in the process creating a different amalgam of individual and social values.

By 1969 city-dwelling had surpassed the kibbutz and moshav as the dominant way of life for Israelis (see ch. 8, Living Conditions).

More people lived in the three major cities of Jerusalem, Tel Aviv, and Haifa, the intermediate cities and the development towns, than in the two major forms of communal rural settlement. Agriculture contributed less to the gross national product than industry and service-oriented professions. Tel Aviv was the pacemaker of social standards and tastes; no longer were the members of Degania (the first kibbutz) or Nahalal (the first moshav) being looked to as models of social behavior. Values of individual consumption superseded the earlier phase of collective production. The jet pilot, or the paratrooper with his red beret, rather than the kibbutz dweller, was the hero of Israeli youth. The kibbutz ethic, in short, was certainly no longer quite as relevant because of the complexity and needs of the society as a whole.

Materialism, an emphasis upon the accumulation of tangible goods by the individual, was endorsed, by young and old alike, in varying degrees. Many of the younger generation, exposed by press and television to the higher standards of living found in Western Europe and the United States, sought for comparable conditions inside Israel. Feeling that their contribution to the community had been fulfilled through 2 or 3 years of military service, these men and women became preoccupied with their own education and career advancement as the key to financial success. Entrance to the universities was limited by lack of facilities, and study was taken extreme seriously.

The unrelenting demand for consumer goods influenced a revision of official economic policy in favor of removing restrictions on the import of goods. The older generation, the *vatikim* or veterans, arrived at the same goal, although by a longer path. They are reaching an advanced age after years of personal sacrifice for the sake of their dream of a Jewish state, which has become a reality. In the past they had also lived by modest means for the sake of an ideology that no longer seems as absolute. These elders wish to retire as comfortably as possible and to enjoy some of the fruits of their labor.

Much of the idealism had diminished. "Old guard" members, who had conquered the soil, built cities, fought the British, and lived in wooden shacks, were now pursuing a mundane, normal existence. Perhaps because of this there existed a growing nostalgia for the old Yishuv days, a sentiment captured by Nathan Alterman in his popular play, *Kinneret, Kinneret*, or by the slow passing away of former prominent figures of the pre-1948 Yishuv.

Not only has modernization led to impressive economic growth, but it has also contributed, along with the mingling of Ashkenazi and Sephardi, to a social malaise. The cities suffered from overcrowding, as the youth were lured by the cultural and material attractions otherwise unavailable to them in the rural areas. Thus by 1969 there existed a phenomenon referred to by Israelis derisively as the "Expresso generation." Its members, emulating their Western European counterparts in fashions, music, and intellectual interest, amounted to an idle class in a society that had always frowned upon laziness, soft-living, and any refusal to contribute toward the common good. The urgent appeals by former Prime Minister David Ben-Gurion for a renewal of *chalutziut* (the old pioneering spirit), in order to populate the Negev, often seemed to go unheeded. Readiness to volunteer, to sacrifice one's private life, to personally implement the aims of Zionism had diminished as obvious social traits; yet willingness to defend the state, tested by crisis, was the salient feature of the entire value system at the end of the 1960's.

This patriotism, however, was also a cause for concern. It, like loyalty to the state and a sense of national identity, had been strengthened rather than weakened under the constant external threat. What the leadership sought to avoid was an excess of patriotism, of an Israeli ethnocentrism. Many of the young gave greater emphasis to their being Israeli than to their Jewishness. Such patriotism was not without paradox. On the one hand citizens retained the hope of a further *kibbutz galuyot* (ingathering of the exiles), especially from the United States and the Soviet Union. On the other hand disappointed at the only moderate response to the call for *aliyah*, these Israelis sharpened the distinction between themselves and the Jews in the Diaspora. Similarly, Israelis were worldly, largely because of concern for the welfare of these Jewish communities overseas and because of the importance of world opinion for the Arab-Israeli dispute. Yet disappointment with the United Nations, frustration with the complexities of big power diplomacy, and skepticism in general at the ability of world opinion to persuade the Arabs to end their hostility have led to disillusionment and to the possibility of a drift towards isolationism and self-reliance.

Another concern, related to patriotism, was that of excessive emphasis upon militarism and the use of force. Any Sabra under age 25 in 1969 had grown up in a social milieu dominated by the necessity of using forceful means to protect the continued existence of the state and its inhabitants. More than 20 years in a virtual state of siege has left a deep impact upon all of the people, particularly the young. It has encouraged toughness, trust in the utility of force, and respect for the martial skills.

This introspective younger generation presented other problems for the "old guard" and its established values. Egalitarianism was being abandoned slowly in favor of greater class consciousness, with distinctions based upon professional status; the army, as a leveler, was perhaps the single exception to this trend. The straightforward manner of the Sabra was taken at times to be due to a lack of refinement, or, at worst, outright arrogance. Contact with the Arabs in situations of conflict was gradually replacing the historical memory of Arab-Jewish compatibility with a tendency to speak of the Arab as the enemy, as incompetent, culturally backward, and vengeful.

The young, in their desire for economic development, have even loosened the romantic hold of the Hebrew language. Ephraim Kishon, Israel's leading humorist, often referred to Israel as being the only country where parents learned the mother tongue, Hebrew, from their children. The veterans had built an aura of romanticism around speaking Hebrew, viewing the process as a revival of the ancient, holy language of the Bible after centuries of disuse. In 1969 their children, with characteristic pragmatism, spoke Hebrew matter-of-factly, liberally absorbed foreign words, and sought to learn English, the newest international lingua franca, as a tool for professional advancement.

The Sabra, inheritor of a well-developed and clearly defined value system and building an industrialized society upon this traditional foundation, looked with confidence to Israel's third decade. Yet he was uncertain of the relevance for him and the state of Judaism, Zionism, and socialism. He felt exasperation at times at the elusiveness of peace in the Middle East. Having been entrusted with the Jewish state as a going concern, nevertheless, he lacked the perspective of his elders. Ghetto mentality and minority status were alien to him; the experience with Nazi Germany, life in Yemen or Morocco, the era of pioneering were history to be learned of in textbooks and novels; neither he nor many of his peers had gone through a traditional religious upbringing. Many of this age group had yet to visit overseas and thereby to evaluate the status of their society and values by comparison with other countries.

The challenge, therefore, to the "old guard," on the one hand, was not so much the retention of political power. Their reputation depended in the long run on success in perpetuating the essence of the earlier values by alerting their children to the enduring relevance of these values. For the young generation, on the other hand, their role in shaping the evolving value system depended upon an ability to discriminate between values suggested to them by their Judaic and Israeli background and those values that accompany Westernization. Both generations drew comfort and confidence from their united performance during the crisis of June 1967, which illustrated great national solidarity. Both generations pointed with satisfaction to the subsequent 2 years in which, despite heavy pressures, they were able to maintain political stability, economic growth, military preparedness, and social cohesion.

SECTION II. POLITICAL
CHAPTER 13
THE GOVERNMENTAL SYSTEM

The governmental system is embodied in a series of basic laws having constitutional status and in other legislation that in sum established a parliamentary democracy, employing the principle of cabinet responsibility to the legislature. These laws control and guide governmental procedure, structure, and operation in the absence of a formal constitution. After the proclamation of independence on May 14, 1948, Israel was at first governed by the Provisional Government and Provisional Council of State drawn from the Zionist Jewish Agency and Jewish National Council, existing in Palestine under the British Mandate. Nationwide elections were conducted in January 1949, and on February 14, 1949, the Constituent Assembly held its inaugural meeting. On February 16, 1949, this body, by the Transition Law, designated itself as the First Knesset and laid the foundation of the permanent government of Israel.

Paramount authority is vested in the Knesset, a unicameral legislature of 120 members, sitting in Jerusalem and chosen by popular suffrage, under a system of proportional party representation. The head of state is the president, elected by majority vote of the Knesset. Executive authority, however, as in the British parliamentary system, is exercised by the prime minister and ministers of the cabinet who direct the civil service and armed forces. The prime minister and the cabinet are collectively designated as "the government," and are continuously responsible to the Knesset. An independent judiciary is guaranteed by law. The Supreme Court is the highest court of the land, having both appellate and original jurisdiction, but not the power of judicial review of laws passed by the Knesset. Lower judicial echelons include district and magistrates courts, religious courts, courts-martial, and certain administrative tribunals.

Local government takes the form of municipalities, local councils, and regional councils within a national administrative system of six districts supervised by the Ministry of the Interior. Certain other national institutions or major organizations, such as the Jewish Agency and the Histadrut Ha'ovdim Haklalit (General Federation of Labor), are either quasi-governmental in nature or are closely related to governmental operations. Scrutiny of all government agencies is performed by the state comptroller, an appointed official nominated by and responsible only to the Knesset.

Political authority and power, as applied in 1969, have developed from a variety of both external and internal sources. Among the principal sources are the United Nations (UN) General Assembly Resolution of November 29, 1947, which called for the creation of a Jewish state in Palestine; the Proclamation of Independence, May 14, 1948, which was set forth in implementation of the UN Resolution; attainment of UN membership on May 11, 1949, which attested to the acceptance and viability of Israel as an independent state; and the enactment by the Knesset of specially designated Basic Laws that serve as a constitution. Many laws and local governmental forms, applicable at the termination of the British Mandate in 1948, were retained with appropriate revisions and recodification by the Knesset. Various systems of religious law and religious courts determine many matters relating to personal status, such as marriage and divorce, applying doctrine and procedures rooted in ancient religious codes.

The goals, principles, and orientation of the governmental system include promotion of the general welfare, maintenance of individual rights, internal and external security of the state, efficient administration at home, and peaceful cooperation abroad. An outline of goals, principles, and orientation is contained in Israel's Proclamation of Independence. It includes the natural right of the Jewish people to political sovereignty; definition of the country as "a Jewish state in the Land of Israel"; encouragement of immigration, with Israel open to all Jews of the world; establishment of a state to "rest upon foundations of liberty, justice and peace as envisioned by the Prophets of Israel"; freedom of religion, conscience, language, education, and culture with equality of social and political rights for all citizens; protection of the holy places of all religions; loyalty to principles of the Charter; full citizenship for Arabs living in Israel, calling upon them to "keep the peace and to play their part in building the State"; peace with adjoining states and their peoples, calling upon them to cooperate "with the independent Jewish nation in its Land"; and readiness to contribute to "a concerted effort for advancement of the entire Middle East."

These goals and principles have been reaffirmed frequently in whole or in part by Israeli leaders, and the governmental system is firmly established in its basic nature and form. It is not rigid and is subject to and capable of change, especially through the continuing development of law.

THE PROVISIONAL SYSTEM AND THE TRANSITION

On May 14, 1948, the Jewish National Council, consisting of 37 persons representing the Yishuv (Jewish Community in Palestine) and the Zionist Movement, proclaimed at Tel Aviv the independence of Israel, to take effect concurrently with the termination of the British Palestine Mandate on the next day. The Jewish National Council further declared that it would act as Provisional Council of State until elected permanent authorities were set up under a constitution, which was to be adopted by an elected constituent assembly not later than October 1, 1948. The Jewish Agency's national executive, headed by David Ben-Gurion, was designated as the Provisional Government of the new state. This provisional arrangement prevailed for the next 9 months. Under it, the proclamation of independence was successfully defended against Arab forces, and basic steps were taken to establish the permanent government and set its future course.

Initially the Provisional Council of State declared itself to be the legislative authority and repealed the provisions of laws deriving from the British government's White Paper of 1939, in particular those dealing with Jewish immigration and transfers of land. At the same time the council proclaimed that the law in force in Palestine on May 14, 1948, should remain in force in Israel, except where it was inconsistent with or modified or revoked by the proclamation or any future laws. The proclamation was amplified and interpreted by the Provisional Council of State's first law, the Law and Administration Ordinance, in effect from May 15, 1948. The word "ordinance" continues to be used for enactments of the Mandate Authority and the Provisional Council of State; the word "law" is used for later enactments by the Israeli Knesset.

The Law and Administration Ordinance has remained in effect. An amendment of June 27, 1967, added a new section providing that "the law, jurisdiction, and administration of the State shall apply in every area of Eretz Yisrael, which the Government prescribes by order." On June 28, 1967, the Old City of Jerusalem and certain adjoining villages were placed under these provisions by the government.

The same ordinance also allowed for declaration of a state of emergency by the Provisional Council of State, under which the prime minister, as head of the government, and the cabinet ministers should have broad powers to make "emergency regulations" for defense, public security, and essential supplies and services. The Provisional Council of State then issued a further declaration that such an emergency in fact existed. This declaration continued in force and early in 1969 had not been withdrawn.

In all the Provisional Council of State enacted 98 ordinances, including one on November 18, 1948, 10 days after completion of a population census, providing for elections to a constituent assembly to be composed of 120 members. The election was held on January 25, 1949, and on February 14, 1949, the Constituent Assembly held its first meeting, thus terminating the interim roles of the Provisional Council of State and the Provisional Government. On February 16, 1949, the Constituent Assembly passed its first law, the Transition Law, upon which the permanent governmental system of Israel is based. The Transition Law, subsequently modified and amended, established the offices of president, prime minister (head of the government), and the cabinet. It designated the legislature of Israel as the Knesset, and the Constituent Assembly as the First Knesset. It also provided that legislative enactments henceforth should be known as laws, not ordinances. It further required that laws must be signed by the head of the government, the particular ministers charged with implementation, and by the president of the state unless the presidential office is concerned; and that they must be published in the *Reshumot* (Official Gazette) within 10 days of enactment by the Knesset. Laws as a rule become effective from the date of such publication, unless otherwise specified.

The First Knesset on February 16, 1949, elected Dr. Chaim Weizmann as first president of Israel. He, in turn, called upon David Ben-Gurion to form a government under the Transition Law; and, on March 10, 1949, after approval by the Knesset, Ben-Gurion became the first prime minister.

THE CONSTITUTIONAL SYSTEM

Israel's Proclamation of Independence specifically mentions "a Constitution to be adopted by the Elected Constituent Assembly." The form that this constitution should take occasioned one of the significant early debates in the Knesset. It occurred after the report in 1949 by the committee that had met to consider whether or not the constitution should be a unit document. Opinion was sharply divided between those favoring a unitary, written constitution and those favoring the unwritten constitutional system of Great Britain based on tradition, precedent, and longstanding statutes applicable in particular cases. In June 1950 a compromise was reached, and the Knesset resolved to enact from time to time special legislation officially designated as the Basic Laws. Each of these laws would be complete in itself and would constitute a separate chapter of a compendium that, taken as a whole, would form the constitution.

By early 1969 three Basic Laws had been passed. Their titles are: The Knesset, February 12, 1958; Israel Lands, July 10, 1960; and the President of the State, June 16, 1964. A fourth basic law, the government, had been submitted to the Knesset in 1966 by the Constitution, Law, and Justice Committee and was still under consideration at the end of 1968. With some specific and partial exceptions, no special legislative procedures are required to pass, change, or revoke a Basic Law different from those applicable to other laws, a condition not regarded as desirable by all Israeli spokesmen.

Other legislation that is intended for ultimate constitutional incorporation as Basic Law includes the Law of Human Rights, the State Comptroller Law, and Law of Return (opening Israel to all Jews who wish to live there), the Equal Rights for Women Law, the Judges Law, the Nationality Law, and others of a fundamental and constitutional nature.

The Knesset is the sovereign body of Israel and there is no appeal from its decisions. It can, however, regulate itself, and by new law add to or change the constitutional structure.

THE PRESIDENT

The president of Israel is the official head of state, but not head of the executive arm. He is elected by majority vote of the Knesset for a term of 5 years, and may be reelected for one additional term. The seat of the president is prescribed by law as Jerusalem. Any resident citizen of Israel is eligible for consideration as a candidate for the office. Since the term of the president is 5 years and that of the Knesset is 4 years, the presidential tenure is not keyed to that of the Knesset.

The President receives and accepts the accreditation of foreign diplomatic representatives of Israel, appoints diplomatic representatives (recommended by the foreign minister), and must sign all treaties ratified by the Knesset and all laws, except those concerning presidential powers. He does not, however, have the power of veto. He also appoints judges (on recommendation of a nominating committee) and the state comptroller (on recommendation of the Knesset House Committee) and has the power of pardon and commutation of court sentences. When a new government is formed, the president consults with representatives of the political parties in the Knesset (as required by law) and then calls upon a Knesset member to assemble a new cabinet and form a new government subject to Knesset acceptance.

After election, the president is sworn in at a ceremony in the Knesset where he makes and signs the following declaration: "I undertake to preserve allegiance to the State of Israel and its laws and to perform faithfully my functions as President of the State." His term of office dates from the time of this declaration. He has legal immunity and cannot be called to account before any court or tribunal during his term of office. He may, however, be removed from office by action of a three-quarters majority of the Knesset. When a vacancy occurs in the office or when a new president has not yet been sworn in, the speaker of the Knesset is acting president of the state. Should the president be incapacitated or for some other reason temporarily cease to perform his function, the speaker of the Knesset officates during such periods instead of the president.

Detailed definition of the presidency and its related powers and procedures are set forth in a constitutional document, the Basic Law, President of the State. This law includes the safeguard that it may not be changed or suspended by the emergency regulations authorized under the Law and Administration Ordinance.

THE GOVERNMENT

Separation of powers between the executive and legislative branches and the manner of designating the prime minister and cabinet follow British precedent. The executive branch was established in Sections 9 and 10 of the Transition Law of 1949: "Section 9: After consultation with the representatives of the parties in the Knesset, the President of the State shall assign to one of the Members of the Knesset the task of forming a Government"; "Section 10: The Government shall be composed of a Prime Minister and a number of Ministers from amongst the Members of the Knesset or from without." The prime minister is officially called the "Head of the Government"; he and his cabinet constitute "The Government" during their term in office. As indicated in Section 9 of the Transition Law, the prime minister must be a member of the Knesset, but under Section 10, this is not a requirement for ministers. In practice, however, most ministers have been Knesset members. Deputy ministers may be appointed; all must be members of the Knesset.

As soon as a government is constituted it must appear in the presence of the Knesset and receive a vote of confidence before beginning to function. When this vote is secured, the government members, each separately, take the following oath before the chamber: "I, as a member of the Government pledge myself to be loyal to the State of Israel, and to its laws, and to comply with the decision of the Knesset."

The government is thereafter responsible to the Knesset for all its acts. A government's term in office may be terminated in one of four ways: by a vote of no confidence in the Knesset; by the ending of the Knesset's tenure of 4 years as prescribed by law; by a decision of the government itself to resign; by resignation of the prime minister. Such action on his part, as head of the government, is held to invalidate the government (resignations of individual ministers do not have this effect). Historically, no one party has ever commanded a majority in the Knesset. Consequently, all governments have been formed by coalitions.

The Transition Law was amended in 1951, 1952, 1956, and 1962. In consolidation and further revision of these actions, the draft basic law, the government, when passed, will become one of Israel's constitutional documents.

Comparing the government of Israel with the government of Palestine under the British Mandate, all powers held by the latter were assumed by the Provisional Government of Israel except those conferred by the Law and Administration Ordinance upon the Provisional Council of State. The Provisional Government's powers, under the Transition Law, then devolved to the government of Israel. Consequently, the prime minister and cabinet, although subordinate to the Knesset, have extensive authority. They formulate domestic and foreign policy and allocate resources under existing law, propose and defend new laws in the Knesset, and direct the operations of government through the administration of the various ministries.

At mid-1969 under the Sixth Knesset (elected in November 1965), the government included, in addition to the prime minister, four ministers without portfolio and 20 specific ministries: Agriculture, Commerce and Industry, Communications, Defense, Development, Education and Culture, Finance, Foreign Affairs, Health, Housing, Immigrant Absorption, Interior, Justice, Labor, Police, Posts, Religious Affairs, Social Welfare, Tourism, and Transport and Communications. In addition, deputy ministers were designated in the Prime Ministry, and in the ministries of Agriculture, Development, Education and Culture (two), Finance, Immigrant Absorption, Interior, and Religious Affairs, as authorized by the 1951 and 1956 amendments to the Transition Law. The creation of ministries of Information and of Science and Technology had been proposed by mid-1969, but not yet adopted.

The prime minister receives a monthly salary of I£1,959; ministers, I£1,850 to I£1,872; and deputy ministers, I£1,550 (I£1 equals approximately US$0.285—see Glossary).

THE CIVIL SERVICE

State employees are organized under a civil service recruited by a merit system, with the method of appointment regulated by law, which also restricts political activities. Civil servants constitute about 3 percent of the total population, excluding the Administered Territories. In 1967 they numbered about 59,000. This figure does not include teachers, civilian employees in the defense establishment, or regular military personnel of the Israel Defense Forces. It does include some 640 in offices of the president of the state, the Knesset, and the state comptroller, the balance being assigned to the various ministries.

The civil service is headed by a commissioner appointed by the cabinet and directly responsible to the minister of finance. The commissioner manages recruitment and appointments, job classifications and approvals, training and education, organization and methods, pensions, and discipline. He is assisted by a Civil Service Board consisting of three directors-general of ministries and three public members. In addition, the commissioner controls the Central School of Administration, run jointly by the Civil Service Commission and the Ministry of Finance, and furnishes administrative services to the civil service disciplinary court provided for by law.

Uniform salary scales cover 75 percent of the civil service establishment, the balance being under professional or technical scales. Typical monthly salaries range from I£560 for an experienced typist to I£1,500 for an assistant director-general of a ministry. In addition, cost-of-living and family allowances are provided for, along with paid annual leave, ranging from 13 to 26 days, plus public holidays and an allowance of annual sick leave up to 1 month per year. The compulsory retirement age is 65. Pensions are paid from the state budget, without employee contribution, and are automatically adjusted upward with any rise in salaries and allowances. Pensions amount to from 20 to 70 percent of terminal salary, according to length of service. Survivors' benefits are provided at 25 to 70 percent of terminal salaries, according to the number of dependents, without regard to length of service.

THE LEGISLATIVE ARM

The Knesset sits at Jerusalem and is the supreme authority of the state. The president of the state and the government hold no powers that are not provided in law by the Knesset or subject to its review. The Supreme Court, not holding the power of judicial review, cannot invalidate laws of the Knesset and is composed as determined by that body. Its authority, definition, and detailed description are contained in the Basic Law, The Knesset.

Procedure in the Knesset has been determined by four main influences: parliamentary practice in Western Europe; British procedure, especially as reflected in the Mandate period; traditions of ancient Israel; and Israeli experience since 1948. The name Knesset is taken from the Knesset Hag'dolah, or Great Knesset, which was the legislative body of ancient Israel after the return of the Jews from captivity in Babylon. The modern Knesset stems from the Palestine Jewish community's National Council under the Mandate (the body that proclaimed independence), and then in sequential stages from the provisional Council of State and the Constituent Assembly (see ch. 3, Historical Setting).

The Knesset is composed of 120 members elected by popular suffrage from party lists according to proportional percentages of votes received. The term of election is 4 years; the Knesset itself may, however, decide on new elections before the end of its normal term. It cannot be dissolved by the president of the state or by the prime minister, nor can either of them veto its laws. Each new Knesset assembles on the second Monday after the week during which election results are published, and the 120 members take the following oath: "I pledge myself to bear allegiance to the State of Israel and faithfully to discharge my mandate in the Knesset."

The first task of a new Knesset is to elect a speaker, whose main duties as set forth in standing orders are to direct the affairs of the Knesset, to represent it, to preserve its dignity and decorum, and to uphold the standing orders. The speaker is assisted by a presidium of eight deputies drawn from the principal parties represented. He has powers of arrest and control in the Knesset building area and is supported by a distinctively uniformed Knesset Guard.

Duration of sessions and recesses are set by law. As a minimum the Knesset is required to sit not less than 8 months per year and meets at least 3 times a week under weekly agendas, fixed by the speaker, to question ministries and consider proposals from the government or motions from members. Allocations of time are made in advance by the speaker to individuals and parties, thereby precluding filibuster or cloture rules. The first half-hour of each meeting is devoted to "question time," during which any member may submit written questions directed to a particular minister or minsters, who must then reply orally from the rostrum of the Knesset within 21 days. Other than a national emergency, the most important item that is dealt with by the Knesset at any session is the budget. After careful scrutiny, it is processed and passed in the same manner as laws.

The Knesset operates through a system of nine committees of 19 members each. These committees are: House; Constitution; Finance; Economic; Foreign Affairs and Security; Interior; Public Services; Education and Culture; and Labor. Committees are made up to reflect as far as possible the same party composition as the Knesset membership.

In becoming law a bill goes through seven stages: publication of the draft by the government in the Official Gazette and registering it in the Knesset; first reading in the Knesset, which includes an explanatory speech by the responsible minister, and debate; reference of the bill, if not defeated at first reading, to the appropriate committee; second reading, which includes a report by committee chairman, introduction of amendments, debate, and vote on amendments;

third reading, in which the bill in revised form is submitted to a vote; signature of the approved legislation by the responsible minister, the prime minister, and president of the state; and publication in the Official Gazette. As a rule this publication is taken as the effective date of the law. Any number of Knesset members present constitutes a quorum, and bills are passed by a simple majority of those present and voting. Exceptions to this rule apply in election or removal of the president of the state, removal of the state comptroller, changes to the proportional elections system, and changes to the Basic Law, The Knesset. In these cases required majorities are specified by law.

Six Knessets have functioned since Israel became a state: the First elected in February 1949; the Second, in August 1951; the Third, in August 1955; the Fourth, in August 1959; the Fifth, in August 1961; and the Sixth, in November 1965. Elections for the Seventh Knesset were scheduled for late October 1969. No single party has ever held a majority of seats, and the majority position depends, as does composition of the government, upon a temporary or long-term coalition of parties. For example, on January 29, 1969, the Israel Labor party (a fusion formed on January 21, 1968, by MAPAI, Ahdut Ha-Avoda, and RAFI) and the United Workers' party (MAPAM) entered into a "covenant of alliance," giving the resultant combination 62 seats. Those parties not belonging to the coalition in power or not in support of coalition policy constitute the Knesset opposition.

Knesset members have certain legal immunities and privileges, designed to facilitate performance of their duties. Members are paid monthly salaries of I£1,267; deputy speakers, I£1,550; and the speaker, I£1,941—supplemented by family alowances. Official language of the Knesset is Hebrew, although Arab members may address the house in Arabic, simultaneous translation being provided in each case. The Knesset is housed at Jerusalem in a building, completed in 1966, built with funds bequeathed by the late James A. de Rothschild of Great Britain, eldest son of Baron Edmond de Rothschild (see ch. 3, Historical Setting). Knesset sittings are recorded and published in the weekly *Divrei Ha'Knesset* (Proceedings of the Knesset).

THE ELECTORAL SYSTEM

Early in its history, Israel implemented a provision of the UN Resolution of 1947, which stated that national elections were to be held for a constituent assembly in the new state envisioned by the resolution, and that qualified voters were to be over 18 years of age, either Palestinian citizens or Jewish and Arab residents declaring intention to become citizens. The resolution also prescribed that the constituent assembly should establish a permanent legislative body based on universal suffrage, the secret ballot, and proportional representation.

On November 18, 1948, the provisional Council of State passed the Constituent Assembly Elections Ordinance. The basic system established by this ordinance has continued in effect, with several modifications. Permanent law was set forth in the Knesset Elections Law of 1955, which, with the Basic Law, The Knesset, contains all fundamental legislation covering qualification of Knesset members and the manner of their election. Since the Knesset is the paramount sovereign authority of the state, on which all other state organizations and operations ultimately depend, the principal function of the electoral system is the election of the Knesset.

Chief characteristics of the system, as set forth in the Constituent Assembly Elections Ordinance, are a proportional representation system similar to that used by World Zionist Congresses and the single national constituency party candidate list procedure, deriving from the Jewish community experience in Palestine under the British Mandate. The voter votes for a party list of candidates arranged in an order of priority, predetermined by each party according to its own procedures, with each list standing for the entire nation as a single constituency. According to its proportion of valid votes received, each party wins a corresponding number of the 120 Knesset seats. These are then filled by individual candidates from each party list, working down from the top.

Elections to the Knesset are held regularly at 4-year intervals, unless the Knesset votes to dissolve itself before the end of its normal term, and thereby require an earlier election, as in the case of the Second and Fifth Knessets. Elections to the Knesset must be held nationwide on the same day, and votes must be cast directly for party lists of choice, not for individuals. Every citizen eligible to vote has one vote, and voting procedures must be secret, with legal supervision and safeguards.

All Israeli citizens 18 years of age or older on December 31 preceding the election year have the right to vote in Knesset elections, unless legally deprived of this right by the courts. Voting is limited, however, to the land area of Israel and its ships. Each voter may vote only at the particular polling station where he is listed on the official Register of Voters and after presentation of proper identification. To facilitate voting, party list ballots are identified by distinctive letter symbols.

To be eligible as a candidate for the Knesset and listed on the party ticket, an individual must be an Israeli citizen 21 years of age as of the date on which party lists are submitted. The important sequence of listing is a matter of party determination, normally the first name on a list being that of the party's leader. Judges may not become candidates; members of the armed forces and civil service, although not precluded, are subject to certain restrictions. It is not necessary to conduct by-elections for or make appointments to any vacancies created by death or resignation. Such a vacancy is automatically filled by the next person on the same party list at the last election.

Supervision of elections is in the hands of a Central Election Committee composed of 30 to 35 members formed by the political parties on the basis of one member for every four seats each party holds in the outgoing Knesset, providing that each party represented in the Knesset shall have at least one member on the Central Election Committee. The chairman of the committee is a judge of the Supreme Court chosen by the court and additional to the party members. Ministers, members of the armed forces, and state officials generally may not be members of the committee.

Committee functions include accepting or rejecting the party lists that must be submitted prior to each electoral campaign; designation of election districts (14 in 1968); appointment of district committees that supervise the more than 2,500 polling stations and local polling committees; devising election procedures and administrative arrangements; monitoring the campaign to ensure that pertinent laws and rules are observed; and certifying and publishing the election results in the Official Gazette. Polling stations are set up by the Ministry of the Interior, but conduct of the election is supervised by the polling committees and by the district committees under the Central Election Committee. Complaints and appeals can be made through the same channel of committees, with provision for final appeal to the Knesset itself.

The people are highly conscious of political rights and the electoral process. Party competition is characterized by year-round vigor, intensified in the election year. Election day is a legal holiday on which, except for public services, business and industry are closed, and sale of alcoholic beverages is prohibited. Polling arrangements are provided for members of the armed forces, but campaigning is forbidden in military installations or by military personnel. Furthermore, the use of certain public display and entertainment media in campaigning is restricted by the Elections Law of July 6, 1959.

In the history of Israel's electoral system, proposals for major changes have not been favorably received in the Knesset. In particular proposals supported by the larger parties from time to time for abandoning the proportional list system in favor of area constituencies have been defeated by combined votes of the smaller parties. These parties have argued that, without a unitary written constitution or long parliamentary tradition, a constituency system would give a majority party too much power.

THE JUDICIARY, COURT SYSTEM, AND LEGAL CODES

The judicial system comprises secular civil courts (including certain judicial and administrative tribunals), religious courts, and military courts. The minister of justice is responsible for administration of the system and, except for the Supreme Court, has broad powers under law to establish the composition and jurisdiction of the courts. Independence of the judiciary is guaranteed by law. As during the Mandate period, courts do not use the jury system; and all questions of fact and law are determined by the judge or judges of the court concerned. The fundamental principle of innocence until proved guilty is maintained.

Initially the Law and Administration Ordinance of 1948 provided that the existing court system of Palestine should be retained unless legally changed in whole or part. No fundamental or far-reaching change has been made. Status of the judiciary and definition and authority of the court structure were, however, spelled out in Knesset legislation by the Judges Law of August 28, 1953, and the Courts Law of July 23, 1957.

In accordance with the Judges Law, all judges are appointed, under a uniform system, by the president of the state on recommendation of a broadly based nominations committee chaired by the minister of justice and composed of two members of the Knesset, three members of the Supreme Court, including the president, one cabinet member in addition to the minister of justice, and two members of the Chamber of Advocates, the body certifying lawyers to the practice of law.

Judges hold office from the day of appointment, with tenure ending only upon death, resignation, mandatory retirement at age 70, or removal from office by disciplinary judgment as specified in the law. Permanent transfers of judges from one locality to another require consent of the president of the Supreme Court. Salaries of judges are determined by the Knesset. Judges may not be members of the Knesset or engage in partisan political activity. Upon appointment, judges make the following declaration of allegiance: "I pledge myself to bear allegiance to the State of Israel and to its Laws, to dispense justice fairly, not to pervert the Law and to show no favor."

At the top of the court system is the Supreme Court, sitting at Jerusalem and composed of such number of judges as is determined by a Knesset resolution. This number in 1968 and early 1969 was 10, consisting of a president, a specifically designated deputy president, and eight associate judges. Cases are normally heard by three judges; in exceptional cases, by five. The Supreme Court has both appellate and original jurisdiction. It hears appeals from lower courts in civil and criminal cases and sits as a court of first instance in matters of relief and justice not within the jurisdiction of lower courts. In the later role it is known as the High Court of Justice and may restrain or direct government agencies by writs, such as mandamus and habeas corpus, customary under English common law, and also may rule on the applicability of law to specific cases.

By these powers, the Court protects the individual from arbitrary action by agencies of the state and exemplifies the principle of rule of law in a parliamentary democracy. The Supreme Court, however, does not have the power of judicial review and cannot invalidate Knesset law. It can, however, nullify local ordinances and government administrative regulations on grounds of illegality. As the highest court of the land, the Supreme Court rules on the applicability of law and questions of respective jurisdiction between lower civil courts and the religious courts.

Directly below the Supreme Court in the civil structure are the four district courts located at Jerusalem; at Tel Aviv, with jurisdiction in both the Tel Aviv and Central Administrative Districts; at Haifa, having jurisdiction in the Haifa and Northern Administrative Districts; and at Beersheba for the Southern Administrative District. While the number of members of the Supreme Court is specifically determined by the Knesset, the composition, location, and membership of the district courts and lower courts are established by the minister of justice under the Courts Law. As courts of first instance, district courts hear cases in civil and criminal law not within the authority of lower courts, although some matters of personal status fall within concurrent jurisdiction of the religious courts. District courts also hear appeals from lower echelons. The district court sits as a bench of one or of three judges; in capital cases, as three, including a judge of the Supreme Court as presiding justice.

The third principal form in the civil category is the magistrate court, one or more being located in each administrative district and subdistrict. Magistrates courts also have both civil and criminal jurisdiction, but are limited to categories of offenses in which the maximum sentence is not more than 3 years imprisonment or property claims not exceeding I£3,000. Most such courts have three assigned judges, but cases may be heard by one.

The civil structure also includes bodies of special jurisdiction under the minister of justice. Principal among these are the municipal courts in large cities, which enforce local ordinances and regulations; tribal courts specific to the Southern Administrative District and having jurisdiction in whatever civil or criminal cases may be assigned to them by the president of the district court or the district commissioner; the maritime court sitting as a court of admiralty in Haifa, with appeal directly to the Supreme Court; and administrative tribunals concerning profiteering, tenancy, water, national insurance, and infiltration.

Religious courts have jurisdiction in the broad area of matters pertaining to personal status, such as marriage, divorce, alimony, or inheritance according to respective religious codes and traditions. This role has been defined in extensive legislation and regulation since the early days of the Mandate period. For the majority Jewish community, the highest religious court is the Supreme Rabbinical Council, which supervises local rabbinical offices and rabbis of communities, and is headed by two chief rabbis, one representing the Ashkenazim and one the Sephardim (see ch. 11, Religion). Other religious courts are Muslim (Shari'a), Druze, and Christian. The recognized Christian communities are Eastern Orthodox, Roman Catholic, Gregorian Armenians, Armenian Catholic, Syrian Catholic, Babylonian, Greek Catholic, Maronite, and Syrian Orthodox. Of these, recognized courts are maintained by the Eastern Orthodox, Greek Catholic, Armenian Orthodox, Roman Catholic, and Maronite groups. In certain cases jurisdiction by religious or civil courts may be elected by the individual. When borderline cases are appealed to the Supreme Court, it has tended to support the civil structure and, in any event, the civil law of the Knesset is the ultimate authority. For example, appeals to the Supreme Court, as High Court of Justice, against the prohibition of polygamy were rejected as not contravening freedom of religion since Muslim codes allow but do not require polygamy. The minister of religious affairs is responsible for the administration of the religious courts.

Courts-martial in the military services are administered by the minister of defense and are governed by the Military Justice Law of December 31, 1955, replacing the Army Code of 1948 issued by the minister of defense under the emergency regulations power. Distinct from courts-martial are the military courts, having jurisdiction over civilians in offenses against defense emergency regulations, as provided under the Military Courts Appeals Amendment Law of July 18, 1963 (see ch. 26, The Armed Forces).

Law codes are based on the law of the British Palestine Mandate, drawn from English law and utilizing English common law in any case not covered by existing law. The Mandate Authority also retained large parts of the earlier Ottoman codes, known as the Mejelle, which in turn were in part based on French codes. Consequently, the lawyer must be familiar with all these systems as well as that evolved by Israel itself since 1948. In general, however, British law has provided the main base on which Israel has built its court procedure, criminal law, and civil law, whereas practice in the

United States has strongly influenced Israeli law regarding civil rights and liberties, as well as the system of appeals to the Supreme Court. The main representative of the government in the enforcement of both criminal and civil law is the attorney general, under the minister of justice.

Among the innovations introduced in Israeli jurisprudence is the provision in the Courts Law for retrial of criminal cases in the Supreme Court or district courts if the original verdict becomes questionable because of new evidence likely to favor the accused, subject to the requirement that no more severe penalties may be imposed at retrial than those originally given. This law may be applied also in reviewing cases of petition for pardon made to the president of the state if the minister of justice determines that a question exists that should be referred for consideration to the Supreme Court. The Court then decides if it should consider the question, and if it so decides, proceeds as for retrial. In any case, however, the presidential power of pardon is a separate power.

The general pattern of punishment and parole is established in the Penal Law Revision Law of September 8, 1954; earlier, punishment by whipping had been specifically prohibited by a law of July 25, 1950. Capital punishment for murder was abolished by law on February 16, 1954. The death penalty may be awarded only for high treason or serious crimes involving enemy infiltration in times of actual hostilities and for crimes under the Nazis and Nazi Collaborators Law of 1950 and the associated Crime of Genocide (Prevention and Punishment) Law of 1950, invoked in the Eichmann Trial of 1961–62. The second act was promulgated in implementation of the UN General Assembly approval on December 9, 1948, of the "Covenant for Prevention and Punishment of the Crime of Genocide." Death sentences for treason and Nazi-associated crimes must be confirmed both by the minister of justice and president of the state; in cases of enemy infiltration, the sentence is handed down only by military courts. The Criminal Procedures Law of 1965 established and codified criminal codes in Israel, replacing earlier codes still in use at that time.

Two distinctive Israeli laws are of particular interest in the challenge posed to the judiciary and legal system: the Law of Return of July 5, 1950, and the Nationality Law of 1952. The former provided for admission to the state of all Jews (other than any specifically judged to be a danger to the state) immigrating from anywhere in the world. The latter provided that Israeli nationality is gained, or may be gained, by birth, immigration, residence, or naturalization. It may be lost only through revocation for cause by a district court or higher, or by renunciation. Adjudication of nationality, inheritance, custody and related problems peculiar to Israel is a continuing and evolving task of the court system.

THE STATE COMPTROLLER

The state comptroller, under the State Comptroller Law (Consolidated Version) of March 17, 1958, is appointed by the president of the state on recommendation of the House Committee of the Knesset for a renewable term of 5 years. He is responsible to the Knesset alone and may be relieved only by that body, or by his own resignation or demise.

Functions of the state comptroller include inspection of the financial accounts and activities of all ministries, the armed forces and security services, local authorities, and any companies or organizations in which the government has a management role. The Office of the State Comptroller publishes an annual report containing statements of assets and liabilities, reports on local authorities and corporations, and special findings and opinion on specific matters. The state comptroller acts in liaison with the Finance Committee of the Knesset, and reports to it whenever he or the Committee finds it desirable to do so. During his term, he may not be a member of the Knesset or otherwise active in politics and is excluded from any public or private activity that could in any way create a conflict of interest with the proper performance of the duties of his office.

LOCAL GOVERNMENT

Local control of public services, such as health and sanitation, water, roads and parks, education, recreation, and welfare, is exercised by locally elected authorities. Large urban areas are classified as municipalities and have municipal councils. Other areas are grouped under local councils or regional councils. In 1968, excluding the occupied territories, there were 26 classified municipalities (including 2 Arab), 115 local councils (41 Arab), and 47 regional councils, covering 670 small villages. The function of local authority is supervised by the Ministry of the Interior, which drafts legislation pertaining to local government and approves the tax rates, budgets, and by-laws set up by local bodies.

For the purpose of administration of national law and to facilitate the operation of local government, the country is divided into six administrative districts and 14 subdistricts. In each district, the minister of the interior is represented by an appointed district commissioner, assisted by district officers, who exercises the minister's authority in the district. Functions specific to other ministries and the staff personnel who implement them are not under control of the minister of the interior but may with his agreement be transferred to him and to respective district commissioners by the minister primarily concerned with a particular law or function.

The district commissioner, consequently, has extensive local powers. He is not, however, a provincial governor, but rather an executive officer, representing the minister of the interior, exercising executive and administrative controls under national law. Statutory authority for the system of administrative districts and role of ministries and of district commissioners is based on the British 1922 Orders-in-Council issued in Palestine. These have been confirmed by the Israeli Law and Administration Ordinance of 1948, updated in a government executive order of April 13, 1957, and by the Delegation of Powers (District Commissioner and District Officer) Law of 1964.

Local government is still based on two key ordinances from the period of British administration: the Municipal Corporations Ordinance of 1934 and the Local Councils Ordinance of 1941. These were, however, amended and modified by law in 1949, 1957, 1964, and 1965 and by the Government (Ministry of the Interior) Orders of 1950, 1953, and 1962.

Under the Mandate distinct differences existed between laws and regulations pertaining to municipalities and local councils from one place to another, especially between Jewish and Arab communities, as regarded voter qualification and manner of election of local bodies. Increasingly, standardization has taken place since 1948. Remaining distinctions between Jewish, Arab, and mixed communities as to age, nationality, sex, and fiscal qualification requirements for voting in local elections were eliminated in 1949. Previously the Constituent Assembly Elections Ordinance of 1948 had granted the right to vote in Knesset elections at age 18 and the right to be elected to the Knesset at 21. This had a wide standardizing effect, since it was not then feasible for local government to impose stricter requirements for voting or candidacy to local bodies.

Elections to municipal, local, and regional councils are standardized in being general, direct, equal, secret, and on the proportional list system. On the whole, local election procedures and principles are a reflection of national procedures and principles at a lower level, including election committees to supervise the process similar to the Central Election Committee. Under the Mandate, mayors were appointed from municipal councils by the high commissioner, who could also dismiss them. Since 1950 selection for these offices is made by election of the councils from their membership, although the minister of the interior has appointive powers in special circumstances.

Formerly distinctions were made in law and practice by the Mandate Authority between urban (municipal) and rural (local) administrations because of widely differing conditions. These differences have increasingly narrowed since 1948; the form of municipality administration, however, continues to be extremely detailed in law not subject to alteration by the minister of the interior, whereas ministerial latitude to make internal changes in local and regional council procedures is considerably broader.

Designation of new municipalities and local and regional councils is a function of the minister of the interior, who in the case of municipalities must first conduct a survey, to include desires of the majority, in order to determine if such designation should be made or withdrawn. These restrictions on the minister's authority do not pertain to local and regional council designation or termination, which the minister may accomplish without formally consulting the affected electorate. After a new designation of a municipality, local, or regional council, the first council body is appointed by the minister of the interior. Local councils are designated class "A" (larger) or class "B" (smaller), but differences in legal status are minor. Regional councils, do not, in fact, constitute a distinct administrative form but are rather local councils covering a number of villages or settlements, including the economic cooperatives known as kibbutzim and moshavim (see ch. 20, Agriculture).

The office of mayor is distinctive to municipalities, the headman in the local and regional council being designated as chairman. The work of municipal, local, and regional councils is done by committee system, under approved by-laws. Council functions are classed as "duties," required by law unless specifically exempted by the minister of the interior, and "powers," which cover activities authorized so long as authority is not withdrawn by the minister. All councils are legal entities; mayors, deputy mayors, chairmen, and deputy chairmen, and deputy chairmen receive salaries fixed by the minister of the interior.

The size of the municipal and local councils is determined by the population within their boundaries (see table 11). Regional councils are composed of elected delegates from settlements represented according to their size. The size of the regional council is determined by the minister of the interior in consultation with local representatives.

The extensive powers of the minister of the interior in respect to local government include the power to dissolve municipal councils in extraordinary circumstances to ensure continuity of lawful and orderly administration. In such cases he may call for new municipal elections or set up a nominated council with full council powers. In like circumstances the district commissioner has the same power in respect to local councils.

The police and prisons service functions under the Ministry of Police. The police service is a centralized agency controlled by a national headquarters and administered in three districts, Northern, Tel Aviv, and Southern, with headquarters at Nazareth, Tel Aviv,

Table 11. *Municipal and Local Council Size, Israel, 1967*

Population	Number of Council Members [1]	
	Minimum	Maximum
Municipalities:		
Up to 5,000 _____	9 [2]	9
5,000 to 25,000 _____	9	15
25,000 to 100,000 _____	15	21
Above 100,000 _____	21	31
Local Councils:		
Up to 1,000 _____	5 [3]	5
1,000 to 3,000 _____	7	9
3,000 to 25,000 _____	9	15
Above 25,000 _____	15	21

[1] Established by the minister of the interior under the laws pertaining to local governments of 1934, 1941, 1949, 1964, and 1965 and subject to change at his review.

[2] Number fixed by the municipality law of 1934.

[3] Number fixed by the local council law of 1941.

Source: Adapted from Yehoshua Freudenheim, *Government in Israel*, 1967.

and Jerusalem, respectively. The prison service, in 1966, operated seven installations, caring for almost 1,700 inmates (see ch. 27, Public Order and Internal Security).

NATIONAL INSTITUTIONS

Related to governmental system and virtually part of it are certain quasi-governmental bodies established by statute and long practice. Concerned with immigration, fund raising, welfare, historical commemoration, land and labor, these organizations are prominent in the national life.

The World Zionist Organization's connection and continuing identification with Israel was legally established in the World Zionist Organization Status Law passed by the Knesset in 1952. This law defines the main task of Zionism as "consolidation of the State of Israel; the ingathering of the exiles to the Land of Israel; and the fostering of the unity of the Jewish people."

The Jewish Agency operates under a covenant signed with the government of Israel in 1954. It contains the same statement of objective as that of the World Zionist Organization Status Law. It represents the World Zionist Organization as its action arm for the promotion of Jewish immigration and works in close cooperation with the government. In 1968 a new government Ministry for Immigrant Absorption was established, taking over from the Jewish Agency the primary responsibility for immigrants during their first few years in Israel.

The Foundation Fund, sometimes called the United Israel Appeal, or Keren Hayesod, is the financial office for Jewish Agency operations. It is devoted to fund raising through voluntary contributions at home and abroad.

The Jewish National Fund, or Keren Kayemeth Le-Israel, was originally a Zionist instrumentality for buying land in Palestine (see ch. 3, Historical Setting). Since establishment of the state, it has been responsible for land development and reclamation in Israel. Work of the Fund has made notable contributions, especially in the Negev and Galilee regions.

The Youth Aliyah organization, activated in 1934, is concerned with bringing into Israel, educating, and training children and young people from abroad who have the status of wards. It cooperates closely with the Ministry of Social Welfare.

The Martyrs and Heroes Remembrance Authority, or Yad Vashem, is established by law to study and record the history of Jewish persecutions in Europe. Its center in Jerusalem attracts many visitors from abroad.

The General Federation of Labor, or Histadrut, is not a national institution in the same sense as those named above. Its membership, however, includes more than half the adult population and its services cover directly or indirectly about 90 percent of all workers. This extensive organization is a major factor in Israel's national life and has had significant influence on labor legislation. It works in close cooperation with several ministries, particularly the Ministry of Labor, the Ministry of Agriculture, and the Ministry of Commerce and Industry (see ch. 21, Industry; ch. 22, Labor).

GOVERNMENT RELATIONSHIPS TO INDIVIDUALS AND GROUPS

Since the governmental system's inception, it and the individual Israeli citizen have been closely identified. Because of the historical factors of its establishment, the nature of the system itself—a parliamentary democracy, the small size of the country, and the fact that the country, since the state was formed, has either been at war or under not more than armistice conditions with its Arab neighbors, the governmental structure has never been remote from the individual. Israelis are government-conscious (see ch. 17, Political Values and Attitudes).

The Proclamation of Independence not only contains basic undertakings in the interest of individual freedoms and the "complete equality of social and political rights for all its citizens" but also commits the state to "developing the land for the good of all its inhabitants." In furtherance of these principles, the National Insurance Law of April 1, 1954, initiated a comprehensive plan of social security. The insurance provided includes retirement pensions, survivors and disability benefits, maternity benefits, and family allowances.

183

Individuals participate by contribution of a percentage of income. In 1968 more than 900,000 persons were insured by the National Insurance Institute which administers the law. Other acts closely relating the state to the individual are the Compulsory Education Act of 1949, making schooling free and obligatory from the age of 5 to 14 years, and the State Education Law of 1953, which placed all schools under supervision of the state (see ch. 9, Education). Additional services are provided for guidance and assistance to the blind, aged, retarded, and other handicapped persons. The Ministry of Social Welfare maintains its own Social Work Training Institute and assists the Hebrew University in its degree program in social work.

The relationship of government to the many political, economic, social, and religious groups in the population is close, being featured by considerations of public interest and security, balanced with considerations of rights under the democratic form.

Although established by its own proclamation as "a Jewish state," the country contained about 300,000 Arabs before the Arab-Israeli hostilities of June 1967. This minority group, composed primarily of villagers, but including urban dwellers and some tribal peoples, was not a source of significant internal disturbance but remained under security scrutiny. Except for the Druze element, Arabs in Israel do not serve in the military forces. They posses all other legal rights, however, and participate in local and national government. In the executive arm at the national level, the prime minister is assisted by an adviser on Arab affairs.

Among Jewish groups, the state has taken cognizance from time to time of special educational and developmental needs of certain groups in its heterogeneous population. Further, the detailed provisions in law for religious court jurisdiction in matters of personal status illustrate state attention to diverse cultural backgrounds, while encompassing them within the overall state jurisdiction. Military groups have not exerted dominating influence in governmental experience, for the principle of civilian control of the military establishment has been maintained from the outset (see ch. 17, Political Values and Attitudes; ch. 26, The Armed Forces).

GOVERNMENT IN OCCUPIED TERRITORIES

In the Arab-Israeli hostilities June 1967, Israel seized control of the Sinai Peninsula, the area of Jordan west of the Jordan River, and the Golan Heights of southwest Syria. These areas and their approximately 1 million Arab inhabitants were placed under a military government administration of the minister of defense, whose office includes a staff section for occupied areas and a secretary to an interministerial committee having cognizance of these areas.

Government policy regarding occupied areas had not been finally determined, and settlements with the Arab states concerned had not been attained by mid-1969. Consequently, the areas remained under local semiautonomy, subject to Israeli military authority under the minister of defense. The regular law of Israel, however, was extended on June 28, 1967, to the Old City of Jerusalem and neighboring villages under the Law and Administration Ordinance Amendment Law of June 27, 1967. This act stated that "the law, jurisdiction, and administration of the State shall apply in every area of Eretz Yisrael, which the Government prescribes by order."

CHAPTER 14
POLITICAL DYNAMICS

After the Israeli military victory in the Six-Day War of June 1967, political changes of comparable magnitude did not result. Discussions then became centered on a long-term policy for management and administration of the territories seized in the war, on attitudes toward the continued problem of a negotiated settlement with the Arab states, and on measures for coping with the Arab guerrilla campaign mounted from the border areas by Palestinian Arab groups owing allegiance to no legally constituted Arab state (see ch. 15, Foreign Relations; ch. 27, Public Order and Internal Security). External and internal political ramifications of these problems were extensive. There was general agreement in Israel that a settlement could not be accepted that was imposed or managed by external great-power arrangements and there was continued affirmation of the long-standing Israeli position calling for solution by direct negotiations with the Arab states. Differences within Israel, however, prevailed between those favoring the maintenance of some degree of flexibility in which diplomatic or political maneuver might be possible and those favoring a harder line of independent Israeli action.

Although the need for policy determination on these questions was recognized as urgent, decisionmaking was inhibited by the approach of elections to the Seventh Knesset scheduled for October 28, 1969, and further by the death of Prime Minister Levi Eshkol on February 26, 1969 (see ch. 13, The Governmental System). Internal political cleavages were revealed but were suppressed in the process of leadership succession and confirmation of Golda Meir as prime minister on March 17, 1969. The Meir cabinet, unchanged in representation from that of Eshkol, was, in consequence, a continuity government of national unity. Although prepared to explore and develop any situation that might arise favorable to the national interest, the cabinet was charged primarily to maintain security and status quo in the interim before the election.

Political life in Israel is characterized by a long-standing fragmentation into multiple parties, falling into four broad categories: labor, nationalist, religious, and other, or miscellaneous, parties. Alignments and coalitions have frequently formed and shifted from time to time. The labor parties, basically socialist and secular in nature, have been dominant in every government. Of them, MAPAI (see Glossary) has always been strongest; all prime ministers have been members of MAPAI.

Reinforced by its ties with the powerful Histadrut (Histadrut Ha'ovdim Haklalit—General Federation of Labor), this party has led all cabinets, which, in all cases, have been coalitions. Since 1965, and especially after June 1967, both in the pressing interest of national unity and from a basic desire for labor unanimity, the smaller labor parties in a sequence of separate actions joined with MAPAI. This adaptation finally produced, on January 20, 1969, a labor alignment, the strongest in Israel's history, holding 62 of the 120 Knesset seats. The continued viability of the long-standing MAPAI power structure was, in fact, illustrated by the selection and approval of Golda Meir to succeed Levi Eshkol (see ch. 22, Labor).

Certain other issues, distinctively Israeli in nature, arose early in the history of the state and appeared likely to continue as grounds for political differences as to means and methods. Among these have been the debates concerning educational systems, problems in promoting and processing Jewish immigration, relationships between the government and the quasi-governmental organizations, determinations of nationality and controversy between secular and religious views of life in a Jewish state, and problems of a planned economy versus free enterprise. The Israeli economy during 1968 showed a strong rise after the recession of 1965–67 and, in consequence, economic issues did not immediately constitute difficulties comparable with political and military problems (see ch. 19, Character and Structure of the Economy).

Changed conditions and the progress of national development since the early years after 1948 have generated pressures for change, but working against these pressures is a widespread tendency to traditionalize older pragmatic methods and forms. Political change has followed orderly processes within an overall system of law and custom. The basic ideology of the state is vigorous, but the pace and style of political change have been cautious and nonvolatile.

Concurrent with all other issues is the inexorable aging of the elite generation of Eastern European "founding fathers," which could be seen in the characteristics of the Knesset membership as well as among widely known Israeli personalities. A transition of power, therefore, to younger, native-born Israelis (Sabras) is inevitable in the not-too-distant future. This transition will require an indeterminate span of time, which could also include the exercise of greater influence by Israelis of Sephardic background and some possible reorientation of national attitudes and concepts of national identity as factors of political dynamics. None of these issue, from those of immediate security and settlement with the Arabs to those concerning the ultimate nature of the state, had been clearly resolved by mid-1969.

POLITICAL PARTIES AND KNESSET CHARACTERISTICS

Political life is characterized by a fragmentation of multiple parties, differing in emphasis and aims, a condition accentuated by the diverse origins of a heterogeneous, largely immigrant population. Twenty-one distinct parties submitted lists for election to the Constituent Assembly of 1949 (which became the First Knesset), 18 to the Second Knesset in 1951, 18 to the Third Knesset in 1955, and 24 to the Fourth Knesset elections in 1959. Only 12 parties, however, secured seats in the Fourth Knesset. In the Fifth Knesset of 1961, seats were gained by 11 of 14 parties, and in the Sixth Knesset of 1965, by 13 of 17.

Major parties and groups did not newly emerge at the time of the establishment of the State in 1948 but are traceable to origins in European branches of the World Zionist Organization, founded by Theodor Herzl in 1897, and to the Jewish Agency and other political elements in the Palestine Jewish community of the British Palestine Mandate period (1923–48). For example, a faction called the Democratic Zionists, including Dr. Chaim Weizmann in its membership, was active in 1900; the Mizrahi (Mer Kaz Ruhani—Spiritual Center), a moderate Orthodox religious Zionist movement, was founded in 1902; and Poalei Zion (Workers of Zion), including in its membership David Ben-Gurion and Itzhak Ben-Zvi, was founded in 1907.

This early experience produced three broad groupings: General Zionists, deriving from the so-called Western European "politicals" of Herzl's time; Labor parties, deriving from the Eastern European "practicals"; and religious Zionists of Orthodox Jewish persuasion (see ch. 3, Historical Setting). These groupings continued to be identifiable, but numerous internal shifts and realignments occurred in the years after 1948. A fourth, or miscellaneous category of diverse groups was added to the scene including the Arab parties, MAKI (Mifleget Ha Kommunisti Yisraeli—Communist Party of Israel, see Glossary), the older Communist party, RAKAH (Reshima Kommunistit Hadasha—the New Communist List, see Glossary), independent factions, and small regional or special interest elements emerging from time to time that exercised influence only in association with the major parties.

Particularly after election of the Sixth Knesset in 1965 and the subsequent shifts through mid-1969, the parties could be categorized broadly as labor, nationalist, religious, and other parties. The government established on March 17, 1969 by Golda Meir did not represent a new alignment, since it was essentially a continuation of the Eshkol cabinet. This action, however, illustrated and reconfirmed the internal political lines existing at that time and foreshadowed the issues of the Seventh Knesset elections, scheduled for October 1969.

Numerous variations in identification, strength, and alliance among political parties have occurred. The most significant grouping of recent years took place in three stages. In Israel's 13th cabinet, headed by the late Levi Eshkol and accepted on January 12, 1966 by the Sixth Knesset, the majority was composed of a group representing MAPAI and the Ahdut Ha-Avoda (Unity of Labor) party, the combination of which became known as the Alignment. On January 21, 1968 the Alignment and nine of the 10 Knesset members of the RAFI party coalesced to form the Israeli Labor Party, with a total of 54 seats. On January 21, 1969 MAPAM (see Glossary) joined this grouping in a "covenant of alliance," hailed by Levi Eshkol as an important element of national unity pointing the way to elimination of old factional differences. This alliance brought into being the strongest political grouping in Israel's history to that date, holding 62 Knesset seats—the first political party alliance ever to hold a clear majority of the 120-member house.

Most of the Israeli political parties do not operate in practice in the manner of parties in Western Europe. In addition to political organization and campaigning, they frequently engage in economic enterprises, operate insurance companies, publish newspapers, and maintain specific clubs, theaters, and recreation centers. Consequently, voters tend to support parties not only as voters but also often as clients or fraternal brothers as well. Membership in a registered party is not a requirement for voting, but, although varying from time to time, formal party membership is high and accounts for 25 to 50 percent of the vote.

Except for the small Arab and Communist political groups, parties have a common characteristic of being basically Zionist in nature, since Zionism sought the objectives of a Jewish state in Palestine (achieved in 1948) and the development of the country by immigration of Jews throughout the world. Zionism is not necessarily capitalist, or socialist, and in its own shades of allowable interpretation may include adherents who are religious, nonreligious, or antireligious. In general, attempts to organize parties on the basis of specific origin, such as Yemeni or Moroccan Jews, have not developed significant political power.

MAPAI, a moderate, non-Marxist, Socialist-Zionist organization, founded in 1930, has been the strongest single party in Israel's political life, which has always been dominated by a coalition of labor parties headed by MAPAI. Historically, the names of David Ben-Gurion, Zalman Shazar, Levi Eshkol, Golda Meir, Pinhas Sapir,

Kadish Luz, and Abba Eban are associated with this party. Ben-Gurion left it, however, in 1965 to form RAFI, whose Knesset members (excluding Ben-Gurion, but including Minister of Defense Moshe Dayan) regrouped with MAPAI in 1968.

The dominant position of MAPAI and party changes in alignment over the years are indicated by the voting patterns for election of the six Knessets and consequent distribution of seats won by the parties (see table 12). Personnel statistics on Knesset members show that their principal place of origin is Eastern Europe; that the occupations principally represented are party workers, civil servants, farmers, and lawyers; that the main places of residence are Tel Aviv or Jerusalem or in the rural settlements known as kibbutzim and moshavim; and that the average age has increased—almost 50 percent of the Sixth Knesset members were over 55 years of age in the 1965 election year. These broad characteristics were established early and, on the whole, have since held good. The main shift that has occurred was the increase of ten seats held by native-born Israelis (Sabras) in the Sixth Knesset compared to the Fifth and at the same time a decrease of 14 seats held by members of Eastern European origin. It appeared also that a trend to an increase in Middle Eastern- and North African-born (Sephardic) members might be developing (see table 13).

PARTY PLATFORMS

Basic principles and politics advocated by the various parties were stated in platforms announced in 1966 or later. Many of these principles, however, can be identified from the days of the Mandate or earlier. In the Sixth Knesset, parties and platforms may for convenience be grouped under the four headings of labor, nationalist, religious, and other or miscellaneous parties.

Labor

Labor parties were led by the Alignment for the Unity of Israel's Workers, usually referred to as the Alignment. It was formed on May 19, 1965 by MAPAI and Ahdut Ha-Avoda and was joined by RAFI on January 21, 1968 to form the United Labor party. MAPAM merged with this group a year later, January 21, 1969.

MAPAI, founded in 1930 in Palestine, has a platform aimed at immigration of the Jewish people, a planned economy, encouragement of public and private developmental initiatives, peace with the Arab states based on negotiation and territorial integrity of all Middle Eastern states, friendly relations with all countries, and development cooperation with new countries.

Ahdut Ha-Avoda, formed in 1919 by the older Poalei Zion and certain nonparty workers, is a pioneering Zionist organization stand-

Table 12. Knesset Election Results, Israel, 1949–65

Party	First Percent[1]	First Seats	Second Percent[1]	Second Seats	Third Percent[1]	Third Seats	Fourth Percent[1]	Fourth Seats	Fifth Percent[1]	Fifth Seats	Sixth Percent[1]	Sixth Seats
MAPAI	35.7	46	37.3	45	32.2	40	38.2	47	34.7	42	36.7[2]	45[3]
Ahdut Ha-Avoda	14.7[4]	19	12.5[4]	15	8.2	10	6.0	7	6.6	8	*(merged w/ MAPAI)*	
MAPAM	*(merged)*		*(merged)*		7.3	9	7.2	9	7.5	9	6.6	8[2]
RAFI[5]	---	---	---	---	---	---	---	---	---	---	7.9	10[2]
Herut	11.5	14	6.7	8	12.6	15	13.6	17	13.8	17	21.3[6]	26[7]
Liberals[8]	5.2	7	18.9	23	10.2	13	6.1	8	13.6	17	*(w/ Herut)*	
	4.1	5	3.2	4	4.4	5	4.6	6	---	---	3.8[9]	5
National Religious Party	12.2[10]	16	8.3	10	9.1	11	9.9	12	9.8	12	9.0	11
Agudat Israel	*(merged)*		3.7[11]	5	4.7	6	4.7	6	3.7	4	3.3	4
Poalei Agudat Israel	---	---	---	---	---	---	---	---	1.9	2	1.8	2
Communists	3.5	4	4.0	5	4.5	6	2.8	3	4.2	5	3.4	4[12]
Arab Lists	3.0	2	4.7	5	4.9	5	3.5	5	3.5	4	3.3	4
Others	10.1	7[13]	0.7	---	1.9	---	3.4	---	0.7	---	2.9	1[14]

Electoral Data	First	Second	Third	Fourth	Fifth	Sixth
	1949	1951	1955	1959	1961	1965
	January 25	July 30	July 26	November 3	August 15	November 2
Number of registered voters	506,567	924,885	1,057,795	1,218,483	1,274,280	1,449,709
Percent voting	86.8	75	82.8	81.5	81.3	82.9
Valid votes cast	434,684	687,492	853,219	964,337	1,006,964	1,206,728
Official number of votes cast required for one seat[15]	3,592	5,692	6,938	7,800	8,332	9,881

[1] Percentage of valid vote.

[2] Alignment (MAPAI and Ahdut Ha-Avoda).

[3] On January 21, 1968, MAPAI, Ahdut Ha-Avoda, and nine members of RAFI combined to form the Israel Labor Party, joined in political convenant of alliance by MAPAM on January 21, 1969.

[4] In 1949 and 1951 MAPAM included Ahdut Ha-Avoda.

[5] RAFI—Israel Labor List, formed in 1965 after a split in MAPAI.

[6] Herut-Liberal Bloc (GAHAL).

[7] In 1967 three Herut Knesset members formed the Independent Free Center Faction.

[8] Figures for first four Knessets refer respectively to General Zionists and Progressives, who merged in 1961 to form the Liberal Party. See also footnotes six and nine.

[9] Independent Liberals.

[10] In 1949 these parties constituted the United Religious Front.

[11] In 1951, 1955, and 1959, these constituted the Torah Religious Front.

[12] Three seats, RAKAH (New Communist List) and one seat, MAKI (Israel Communist Party).

[13] Four seats, Sephardim; one seat, Yemenite; one seat, Women's International Zionist Organization (WIZO); one seat, Fighters for Israel's Freedom (former LEHI resistance group).

[14] Ha'olam Hazeh—New Force.

[15] Seats are allocated based upon number of valid votes received by each party list compared to a voting quotient for one seat obtained by dividing total valid vote by 120, and further allocation based on proportional arithmetical remainders. For this reason, and since percents received as shown in this table are rounded off, the final number of votes required for one seat do not correspond exactly to the raw percentages shown.

Source: Adapted from Israel, Ministry for Foreign Affairs, *Facts About Israel, 1968*; and Moshe Rosetti, *The Knesset: Its Origins, Forms and Procedures*, 1966.

193

Table 13. Characteristics of Knesset Members, Israel

Characteristic	First 1949	Second 1951	Third 1955	Fourth 1959	Fifth 1961	Sixth 1965
Origin:						
Native-born _____	16	18	17	22	19	29
Eastern Europe* ____	87	89	84	80	83	69
Western Europe and Americas _____	14	9	13	9	11	8
Middle East and Africa _____	3	4	6	9	7	14
Total _____	120	120	120	120	120	120
Occupation:						
Party workers and civil servants _____	56	39	35	36	34	30
Farmers _____	21	28	28	27	25	27
Lawyers and journalists _____	22	21	21	29	27	30
Others, various _____	21	32	32	28	34	33
Total _____	120	120	120	120	120	120
Residence:						
Tel Aviv or Jerusalem	84	86	84	82	80	87
Kibbutzim and Moshavim _____	28	21	27	23	24	20
Other _____	8	13	9	15	16	13
Total _____	120	120	120	120	120	120
Age group:						
24–44 _____	39	35	32	26	18	17
45–64 _____	72	80	77	83	83	86
65 and above _____	9	5	11	11	19	17
Total _____	120	120	120	120	120	120
Average age (year of election) _____	49.1	49.2	50.9	51.9	53.9	54.2

* Includes Bulgaria, Czechoslovakia, Hungary, Latvia, Lithuania, Poland, Rumania, and the Soviet Union.

Source: Adapted from Asher Zidon, *Knesset: The Parliament of Israel*, 1967.

ing for planned economy, encouragement of agricultural settlements, activist defense policy, nonidentification with foreign blocs, and friendship with all peace-loving states, particularly those in Asia. Yigal Allon, deputy prime minister in the Eshkol and Meir cabinets, is a leader of the Ahdut Ha-Avoda, which aligned with MAPAI.

RAFI was formed by Ben-Gurion with Moshe Dayan and a MAPAI minority in 1965, in a split with the Alignment leadership of the late Prime Minister Eshkol, Deputy Prime Minister Yigal Allon, and the then MAPAI secretary-general, Golda Meir. RAFI advocated increased self-reliance in national security matters, peace with neighboring countries from a position of defensive strength based on flexible military initiatives, electoral reforms aimed at a constituency system, universal secondary education, social justice, and greater division of governmental powers.

MAPAM, a left-wing Zionist Socialist party, was formed in 1948 from the Ahdut Ha-Avoda group that had broken away from MAPAI in 1944 and the Poalei Zion and an early labor youth group, called the Hashomer Hatzair (The Young Watchman). During the first two Knessets, MAPAM included Ahdut Ha-Avoda but the latter then separated from MAPAM and in the Sixth Knesset rejoined MAPAI. The MAPAM party stands for development of socialist political and economic procedures, inflow of Jews into the country, training of youth in pioneering settlements, Jewish-Arab working class solidarity, and peace in the Middle East, based on neutrality of the whole region.

Nationalist

The main nationalist parties are found in GAHAL (Gush Herut-Liberalim—Freedom-Liberal bloc, also known as Herut-Liberal bloc, see Glossary), formed in 1965. GAHAL resulted from an alignment in 1961 of the Herut (Freedom) and the Liberal parties, the latter encompassing the earlier Progressive and General Zionist parties. In the Sixth Knesset of 1965, GAHAL attained 26 seats.

Herut, at the right of the Israeli political spectrum, was formed in 1948 as a direct descendant of the Revisionist movement organized in 1925 by Vladimir Jabotinsky (see ch. 3, Historical Setting). Menahem Begin, former Irgun leader and minister without portfolio in the Eshkol and Meir cabinets, is the party leader. Herut advocates territorial integrity of Israel in the historic boundaries of Eretz Yisrael (Land of Israel), strong secular Zionist nationalism, positive security measures, and private initiative in the state's economic and social structure, with a minimum of essential governmental controls.

The Liberal party has stood for enactment of a written constitution, reforms in the civil service and electoral systems and, while supporting social welfare concepts, it has favored a free enterprise economy of individuals and organizations based on fair competition.

Religious

The religious parties are conservative in nature, but distinct from the secular GAHAL. In the time of the First Knesset, they were grouped together under the name of the United Religious Front. They are based on principles of religious Zionism and have a common dedication to Jewish Orthodox patterns of life. The three principal religious parties held a total of 17 seats in the Sixth Knesset but were not formally aligned and did not necessarily vote together.

The National Religious party, formed in 1956, encompasses the earlier Mizrahi and Hapoel Ha-Mizrahi (Mizrahi Workers) and seeks to promote the ethical and social principles of Judaism. It fosters legislation based on the Hebrew Scriptures and favors development of immigration, settlement, and trade union activities in a religious context.

Agudat Israel (Association of Israel) is Ultra-Orthodox and strictest in advocating national life based on the Scriptures. It supports administration of the state under rabbinical authority, calls for traditional Jewish educational forms and methods in schools at all levels, and proposes state control of health and welfare funds.

Poalei Agudat Israel (Workers of the Association of Israel) is a religious labor movement, advocating development of the state, land pioneering, and protection of workers' rights in the spirit of Orthodox Judaism.

Others

Other party platforms show great variations of doctrine being advanced by factions miscellaneous in nature and secular rather than religious. They represent minority or special interest groups and, although they held a total of nine seats in the Sixth Knesset, did not act together or wield substantial power.

The MAKI party, founded in 1919, and the RAKAH, which split off in 1965, are based on Marxist-Leninist theory; they support independence and neutrality, equal rights for the Arab population, peace with the Arab states, and friendship with Communist countries. MAKI's style of communism is Soviet oriented and its members are mostly Jewish; RAKAH is Peking oriented and is largely Arab. The percentage of popular support for the Communists was established early in Israel's life as a state and has remained almost constant, varying only in the narrow range of 2.8 percent to 4.5 percent of the vote in the six Knesset elections. Leaders of the MAKI have included Moshe Sneh and Samuel Mikunis; of the RAKAH, Meir Wilner, Tewfik Tubi, and Emile Habibi.

Arab parties in the Sixth Knesset consisted of the Cooperation and Fraternity party, representing Muslims and Druzes in the Mount Carmel and Galilee hill areas, east of Haifa, and the Progress and Development party, representing mainly Muslims and Christians in central Galilee. These parties, or earlier forms, such as the Arab Independents and Arab Workers, have functioned in the Israeli system since the First Knesset and have not constituted a source of internal disorder. They have operated on a local rather than a national basis. They advocate greater local autonomy and abolition of military rule where it exists in Arab areas and have frequently supported MAPAI or MAPAM in the Knesset, except on matters of Arab refugee property or military rules. After the mid-1960's, the

Arab parties showed an increased tendency to support independent factions.

The Independent Liberal party, not part of GAHAL, separated from the Liberal party and won five seats in the Sixth Knesset. It is similar to the Liberal party in its aims but places stronger emphasis on development of a welfare state.

The Free Center movement was formed by three Herut members of the Knesset in 1967 and, consequently, had not submitted a party list in a Knesset election prior to 1969. It stands for various policies, including: peace with the Arab states within the boundaries held by Israel after the Six-Day War of June 1967 and for the settlement of refugees living there; national identification with Western ways of life; free enterprise, but with state ownership of health and social services; and for a constituency election system.

Ha'olam Hazeh (New Force), with one seat in the Sixth Knesset, is an independent reform movement. Created in 1965, by the weekly newspaper of the same name, it stands for democratization, a written constitution, firm separation of religion and state, Arab minority equality, neutralism abroad, and peace by cooperation between Arab and Jewish national movements.

Jewish community parties, such as the Sephardim party, the Yemenites, or the North African Union, have arisen from time to time. In addition, the LEHI and the Women's International Zionist Organization (WIZO) submitted a party list in 1949. Except in the First Knesset, none of these small parties has mustered enough support to gain a seat in the Parliament.

RECURRING ISSUES AND CABINET CHARACTERISTICS

The nature of the Israeli state and its background embodies certain basic attitudes and issues (see ch. 3, Historical Setting; ch. 17, Political Values and Attitudes). These are reflected in the four categories of political grouping that evolved. The nature of these categories and their components also illustrates typical positions taken on recurring specific issues.

The principal specific issues are in the form the elementary and secondary educational system should take in a Jewish state, the degree to which Jewish tradition and observance of religious laws should prevail in the social, political, and economic life of the state— the issue of separation of church and state, and the extent that the national economy should be planned and state controlled or operate by free enterprise.

Other recurring specific issues include debate as to what form the constitution should take—written, unwritten, or the compromise system of Basic Laws; the use of the party list system in national and local elections and the question of representational constituency versus national constituency; the control of health and welfare funds; the relationship of the government and other sectors of the political and social structure to the Histadrut; the role of, and government relation to, the quasi-governmental World Zionist Organization and the Jewish Agency; attitudes toward the Arab minority in Israel; questions of national security policy in relation to the Arab states and the problem of settlement with them; and policy toward other foreign nations, external commitments, and international bodies (see ch. 13, The Governmental System; ch. 15, Foreign Relations).

Prominent as foreign policy issues have been relationships with the Federal Republic of Germany (West Germany), questions concerning trials arising from the Nazi persecutions of World War II, problems of state identification or non identification with particular countries or regions, and determination of attitudes towards the United Nations (UN).

Alignments of political convenience may occur from time to time, but the long-standing political parties have in the main taken consistent positions on these issues. For example, the religious parties would oppose distribution of health and welfare funds by the Histadrut, since they hold that such distribution should be made by a national government administered under rabbinical guidance. Distribution by a secular agency gives that agency power and influence, which is correspondingly denied to the religious leadership who, in their view, should be shaping the state and its people.

The state has in some cases taken over functions performed during the Mandate period by the Histadrut. This widespread organization, however, still has a dominant voice in determining labor legislation and and the national wages policy, not only in the private sector but also in the public service as well (see ch. 22, Labor). In addition to being an organ of workers' self-government, it comprises many economic enterprises, runs a publishing house and three daily newspapers, operates a medical insurance program, and conducts a wide variety of cultural and athletic activities. Elections to the Histadrut's governing body, known as the General Convention, are conducted every 4 years by direct vote of the entire membership and are second in importance only to elections for the Knesset. Political parties, other than the religious parties, customarily submit lists of candidates to the Histadrut elections, which are held in the same manner and on the same system of proportional representation as the national elections. Consequently, if MAPAI is the strongest single party in the government, it is likely also to be predominant in the Histadrut General Convention and has been so since founding of the state. This arrangement has maintained a strong labor-socialist orientation in the economy and throughout the national life but has not been immune from political criticism and question as to its continuing desirability.

Further, questions have been raised as to the continued relevance of the World Zionist Organization and the Jewish Agency and the division of functions and patterns of cooperation prevailing between these organizations and the state. There is strong general agreement that a link must be maintained between Israel and world Jewry at large. The need for increased Jewish immigration, especially from the Americas, and particularly in view of the Soviet Union's restrictions on Jewish emigration from that country, has been repeatedly mentioned by Israeli political leaders as a problem of the most serious nature.

After the wide Jewish response to the crisis of 1967, Levi Eshkol, in March 1968, asserting that this support was a "renewal of our covenant with world Jewry," stated that the government was committed to "strengthening our links with the Diaspora." He announced a search for new ways among Jewish people abroad "to halt assimilation" and "to foster *aliyah* (immigration)" since "the central problem for the State and the People of Israel is copious *aliyah* from the affluent provenances." He added, "We must double our numbers within a generation by births and mass *aliyah*." The task of promotion and management of immigration has historically belonged to the World Zionist Organization and the Jewish Agency; their internal organization and methods were, however, subject to reevaluation by the government. The establishment of the Ministry for Immigrant Absorption in mid-1968, under Deputy Prime Minister Yigal Allon, is one fruit of Prime Minister Eshkol's pledge, and it was widely held to reflect dissatisfaction with the recent performance of the World Zionist Organization and Jewish Agency in promoting *aliyah*.

In addition, tensions have existed between occidental or Ashkenazic Israelis, and the Oriental, or Sephardic immigrants, who include a higher percentage of the unskilled and lesser educated. From 1948 to 1969 these tensions were more economic and sociological than political in character, but it was by no means certain this would remain so in view of the higher Sephardic birthrate and growing acclimatization of the Sephardim to the essentially Western-oriented Israeli society.

A factor acting to restrain political change, and one which may cut across all parties, is the tendency to traditionalize and venerate established forms or procedures that worked under stress and danger in the earlier days of the state, despite later developments and changing conditions. This factor has been particularly strong in Israel, whose people and culture have been strongly influenced by respect for the body of detailed, traditional law and procedure represented in the historic Jewish mode of life. The political party or parties in power, typically MAPAI and its close associates, tend to preserve their position and the status quo, marshaling their power to perpetuate existing systems in face of pressures for change in the older pragmatic and historical methods.

Pressures for political change have typically been manifested by the separation of a faction from a larger, powerful party or by the formation of a new, outside group into an independent party. The former pattern is illustrated by Ben-Gurion's split with MAPAI and formation of RAFI in 1965, having, as one objective, the clearer definition and acceleration of the national programs that RAFI held to be lagging. Another illustration is the Free Center movement of 1967 resulting from a split from the Herut branch of GAHAL. The second form is exemplified by the independent appearance of movements, such as Ha'olam Hazeh, created by a weekly newspaper.

Customarily, such factional parties or new parties have been sharply definitive in articulating specific aims but lacked the position, power, and broad base of support needed for implementation. They also have not carried the weight of government decision-making and administrative responsibilities that must be borne by a party in power and make it less receptive to and less likely to initiate change. Although Israel is a new nation in the Middle East, change of government by subversion or violent overthrow by coup groups has not been a feature of its political life.

In Israel's history until March 1968 14 governments (cabinets) had been in office, under six Knessets (see table 14). An incumbent government terminates and a new one is formed under one of four conditions: vote of no confidence by the Knesset, end of a Knesset term, resignation of the government as a cabinet action, or the individual resignation or demise of the prime minister. Therefore, the term of a Knesset may encompass terms of several cabinets. Any Knesset terminates in one of only two ways: at the expiration of a normal 4-year term or by voting its own dissolution and directing new elections to be held on a date that it designates. In any case the incumbent government continues in caretaker or interim status, until relieved by its successor. Both the Second and Fifth Knessets were elected and constituted early, occasioned in each case by a cabinet crisis of such magnitude as to cause not only the fall of the government but also the dissolution of the existing Knesset (see ch. 13, The Governmental System).

During the First Knesset serious questions arose regarding the religious education of children in immigrant camps, the assertion being that secular education was being forced on children from strictly Orthodox families. This dispute, coupled with argumentation on economic policies, was sufficient to bring down the First Cabinet. Under the Second Cabinet, confirmed on November 1, 1950 and, again, headed by Ben-Gurion, the problem of religious education and of other forms of partisan-oriented schools, known as trend schools and recognized by the Compulsory Education Law of 1949, became magnified (see ch. 9, Education). The issue involved was whether or not youth should be educated in a politically directed school environment along one of the lines of Zionist thought—the general-nationalist, the labor-socialist, the Orthodox-religious, or a modified religious form. The resultant political controversy caused the First Knesset to call for new elections. Resolution of the problem was finally attained in law by the State Education Act of August 12, 1953, under the Second Knesset and Fourth Cabinet.

The second political crisis causing Knesset dissolution was the so-called Lavon Affair that brought down the Ninth Cabinet on January 31, 1961, followed on March 28, 1961, by Knesset vote for new elections to be held August 15, 1961. This affair centered on Pinhas Lavon, who had resigned as minister of defense from the Fifth Cabinet on February 21, 1955 in an issue involving proposals that he had made for changes in the defense structure. He was replaced as minister of defense by Ben-Gurion, who at that time was a member of the Knesset, but not a member of the government, since he had withdrawn after resigning from the Fourth Cabinet on December 6, 1953.

The circumstances of 1955 were exhumed in 1960 by Lavon, then secretary general of Histadrut. The matter involved security affairs and the validity of certain prior testimony and investigations as well as the original substance. Further investigation generated severe political strains within the MAPAI party, the cabinet, and the Knesset. Ben-Gurion, then prime minister, resigned on January 31, 1961; and the Knesset, on March 28, scheduled new elections. The succeeding Tenth Cabinet was organized by Levi Eshkol of MAPAI, who had been minister of finance in every cabinet since the Fourth one. He retained the same portfolio; and Ben-Gurion, on November 2, 1961, resumed the office of prime minister for the eighth time. On June 16, 1963, however, Ben-Gurion resigned for personal reasons and was succeeded on June 24, 1963 by Levi Eshkol, who began continuous tenure in that office, at the head of the Eleventh, Twelfth, and Thirteenth cabinets, terminating with his death on February 26, 1969.

The Fourteenth Cabinet, headed by Golda Meir, took office essentially as a continuity government on March 17, 1969, with a strong approving Knesset vote of 84 to 12. Ben-Gurion abstained from voting, declaring that he would continue to support the RAFI movement under that name. The Communist, Ha'olam Hazeh, Free Center, and Agudat Israel parties remained in opposition. GAHAL continued to support the national unity government, although its cabinet representatives were ministers without portfolio.

Table 14. Cabinets and Leaders, Israel

Cabinet	Tenure [1]	Prime Minister [2]	Parties Supporting Government [3]	Termination	Knesset
1	March 8, 1949– October 15, 1950	David Ben-Gurion	MAPAI, Religious Front Progressives, Sephardim, Arabs	Cabinet resigned on religious education issue.	1
2	November 1, 1950– July 30, 1951	David Ben-Gurion	Same, plus one nonparty minister	Education issue became magnified, cabinet resigned. (Knesset set new elections for July 30, 1951.)	1
3	October 8, 1951– December 19, 1952	David Ben-Gurion	MAPAI, Hapoel, HA-Mizrahi-Mizrahi, Agudat Israel, Arabs	Cabinet again resigned on the education issue.	2
4	December 23, 1952– December 6, 1953	David Ben-Gurion	MAPAI, Hapoel, Ha-Mizrahi-Mizrahi, General Zionists, Progressives, Arabs	Ben-Gurion resigned for personal reasons.	2
5	January 26, 1954– June 29, 1955	Moshe Sharett	Same composition as Fourth Cabinet	Moshe Sharett resigned after dispute between General Zionists and Herut on Nazi trials issue.	2
6	July 1, 1955– July 26, 1955	Moshe Sharett	MAPAI, Hapoel, Ha-Mizrahi-Mizrahi, Progressives, Arabs	Caretaker government interval before elections of July 26.	2
7	November 3, 1955– December 31, 1957 (Ben-Gurion designated, August 18, 1955; cabinet not approved until November 3.)	David Ben-Gurion	Same as Sixth Cabinet, plus Ahdut Ha-Avoda and MAPAM	Ben-Gurion resigned in dispute with Ahdut Ha-Avoda on alleged press leaks.	3

Table 14.—Continued.

Cabinet	Tenure [1]	Prime Minister [2]	Parties Supporting Government [3]	Termination	Knesset
8	January 7, 1958– July 5, 1959 (December 15, 1959)	David Ben-Gurion ----------	Same as Seventh Cabinet	Ben-Gurion resigned on July 5, 1959 in dispute with MA-PAM and Ahdut Ha-Avoda on sale of arms to Germany. Cabinet continued in caretaker status till elections.	3
9	December 17, 1959– January 31, 1961 (November 1, 1961)	David Ben-Gurion ----------	MAPAI, National Religious Party, MAPAM, Ahdut Ha-Avoda, Progressives, Arabs, one nonparty minister	Political stresses of Lavon Affair caused resignation of Ben-Gurion on January 31, 1961. Knesset on March 28, 1961, directed new elections to be held August 15, 1961. Cabinet continued in interim as caretaker.	4
10	November 2, 1961– June 16, 1963	David Ben-Gurion ----------	MAPAI, Ahdut Ha-Avoda, National Religious Party, Poalei Agudat Israel, and Arabs	Ben-Gurion resigned for personal reasons.	5
11	June 24, 1963– December 14, 1964	Levi Eshkol ----------	Same as Tenth Cabinet	Eshkol resigned because of intraparty controversy in MAPAI.	5
12	December 22, 1964– November 2, 1965	Levi Eshkol ----------	Same as Eleventh Cabinet	End of normal term of Fifth Knesset.	5
13	January 12, 1966– February 26, 1969	Levi Eshkol ----------	Alignment (MAPAI and Ahdut Ha-Avoda), MAPAM, National Religious Party,	Death of Levi Eshkol on February 26, 1969. Deputy Prime Minister Yigal Allon	6

Table 14.—Continued.

Cabinet	Tenure [1]	Prime Minister [2]	Parties Supporting Government [3]	Termination	Knesset
			Poalei Agudat Israel, Arabs, and Independent Liberals. (RAFI and GAHAL also in support effective June 5, 1967.)	became acting prime minister until Fourteenth Cabinet.	
14	March 17, 1969–	Golda Meir ————————	Same as Thirteenth Cabinet	(Elections for Seventh Knesset scheduled for November 1969.)	6

[1] Terminated cabinets continue in caretaker status until Knesset approves new government cabinet.
[2] All prime ministers have been members of MAPAI (Ben-Gurion not in office when he formed RAFI in 1965).
[3] Initial support at time of Knesset approval of new prime minister's government. Parties not shown constituted Knesset opposition.

Source: Adapted from Asher Zidon, *Knesset: The Parliament of Israel,* 1967.

Although it did not cause dissolution of a Knesset or downfall of a cabinet, still another issue illustrates the political dynamics growing from basic issues peculiar to Israel. This is the problem of nationality, or "Who Is A Jew?" arising from the proclaimed nature of the state, the Law of Return of 1950, and the Nationality Law of 1952. Under the Eighth Cabinet, 1958–59, a sharp controversy on this matter developed not only in the government, the Knesset, and the Israeli populace but also in Jewish communities throughout the world. The problem in its immediate legal and administrative context was resolved in a ruling by the minister of the interior in 1958, stating that "any person who declares in good faith that he is a Jew is to be registered as a Jew, and no other proof is to be required of him." Particular cases involving this problem continued to arise, however, and a comprehensive judicial determination continued to emerge in an evolutionary manner (see ch. 13, The Governmental System).

MAIN EVENTS AND ISSUES SINCE JUNE 1967

Victory in the Six-Day War and seizure of the Sinai Peninsula, the Gaza Strip, the West Bank of the Jordan River, and the Golan Heights of Syria provided Israel with a greatly enhanced position of military security against conventional attack. In addition, it evoked a surge of national pride, uplifted morale, and enhanced the already high reputation of its military forces. This victory did not, however, bring about the solution of any political issue. The Arab states continued to refuse to negotiate directly with Israel either on a settlement of the war of June 1967 or on the larger issues of recognition, refugees, and delineation of boundaries.

On November 22, 1967 the United Nations Security Council adopted a resolution calling for withdrawal of Israeli forces from the occupied Arab areas, mutual guarantees of borders by the states concerned, open passage of the Straits of Tiran, and Israeli transit of the Suez Canal (see ch. 15, Foreign Relations). A UN Special Representative, Gunnar Jarring of Sweden, was designated by the secretary general in accordance with the resolution "to establish and maintain contact with the states concerned in order to promote agreement and assist efforts to achieve a peaceful and accepted settlement in accordance with the provisions and principles in this resolution." The Arab-Israeli situation, however, still stalemated after the Six-Day War began again to deteriorate with increased border incidents. Shortly after the war, the Soviet Union began the rapid replacement of the massive material losses suffered by Egypt, and by mid-1968 these losses had been replaced to a substantial degree.

Simultaneously, all political parties were seriously concerned with the Arab (chiefly Palestinian) guerrilla groups owing allegiance to no constituted Arab government, as these groups grew in strength and increased the frequency of terrorist attacks against Israel. Best known of these was the organization calling itself Al Fatah, headed by the Palestinian Yasir Arafat, who also became Chairman of the Palestinian Liberation Organization (PLO). Labeling their effort a "War of National Liberation" Arab guerrilla leaders proclaimed that they aimed at attrition of the Israeli state by terror and turmoil with the objective of disrupting Israeli society, overthrowing the state, and establishing Palestinian Arab control of the land. The Fatah and PLO have also advocated as a replacement for Israel a multinational state in Palestine in which the Palestinians, Jews, and other groups would reside. With regard to great power consultations on the Arab-Israeli issue, Arafat stated in Algiers on February 1, 1969, that "the Palestinian people have made their own decision and this springs from the gun."

As Arab guerrillas increased their raids and incursions into Israel, their activities were further highlighted by attacks against Israeli flag airliners in Athens, Greece, and Zurich, Switzerland, in late 1968 and early 1969. Concurrently, the pattern of Israeli retaliation by land and air more than kept pace, most notably, the raid of December 28, 1968 against the airport at Beirut, Lebanon (see ch. 27, Public Order and Internal Security).

In February 1969 heavy exchanges of artillery fire broke out and continued sporadically along the Suez Canal. The Egyptian chief of staff, Lieutenant General Abdel Munim Riad, was killed by artillery fire on March 9, 1969. After Prime Minister Levi Eshkol's death on February 26, 1969, Deputy Prime Minister Yigal Allon became acting prime minister and on March 17, 1969, Golda Meir, former minister of foreign affairs, became prime minister, and her cabinet was approved by the Knesset. This transition reflected the continued viability of the traditional MAPAI political power structure despite some public pressure in favor of the well-known minister of defense and former chief of staff, Moshe Dayan.

During the 1965–67 period the Israeli economy underwent a recession that proved to be only temporary; and, in the recovery of 1968, industry and the economy generally rose to new levels (see ch. 19, Character and Structure of the Economy; ch. 21, Industry; ch. 24, Foreign Economic Relations). Economic problems remained in early 1969, the most serious being that of financing large military expenditures, including expenditures abroad.

In basic attitudes the Israeli political structure and society in general showed strong unanimity and cohesion (see ch. 17, Political Values and Attitudes). These general views included a common dedication to the state and an intense determination to survive, preferably through negotiated accommodation with the Arab neighbors, but, if necessary, as a garrison state maintained by its own military strength. Likewise, there was a common rejection, restated by Prime Minister Meir after taking office, of an Arab-Israeli settlement imposed or, in some manner, managed from the outside by the great powers. There was broad endorsement of Golda Meir's reaffirmation of the basic Israeli position calling for direct talks with the Arab states. The internal political issues were ones of methodology and degree.

During the buildup to the Six-Day War, the Israeli public favored a more aggressive military stance in what was seen as a worsening situation. Public demand developed such strength as to oblige Levi Eshkol to bring Moshe Dayan into the government as minister of defense. The Eshkol cabinet had been criticized for relying excessively on diplomatic efforts. Eshkol, however, approved Israel's resort to war when he judged diplomacy had become unavailing and after the announced Egyptian closure of the Straits of Tiran. Nevertheless, differences remain between interpretations as to the degree of military readiness and preparation that constitutes a provocation endangering diplomatic settlement or the amount of military strength required for security reasons.

Similarly policy for retaliation against terrorists and methods for coping with the guerrilla bands, such as Al Fatah, constitute an issue in the political spectrum. Ben-Gurion and his adherents, such as Moshe Dayan, have customarily favored a flexible, mobile strategy of strategic defense based on tactical initiatives not necessarily confined to border areas or static border exchanges of a minor nature. Associated with these determinations, especially in context of the guerrilla war waged against Israel in 1968 and early 1969, was the matter of attitude toward the Arab minority within pre-1967 Israel. Security demanded close surveillance of this minority. On the other hand a pattern of firm evidence had not appeared in Israeli-held areas of widespread, concerted Arab civilian collaboration with the guerrilla raiders. As the occupation continued into 1969, however, recurring incidents suggested that the Arabs who lived in Israel before the hostilities of June 1967 were becoming radicalized by contact with the Arabs of occupied territories.

Closely related was the larger problem of disposition of the occupied territories and the more than 1 million Arabs in them. The "hard line" view held that, since the Arabs were bent on the ultimate destruction of Israel in any case, security and reason required that the territories be held and that the people within them be drawn into the Israeli state either by attractions of efficient government, education, industry, commerce, and trade, or by whatever measures were necessary. This view, however, had to accept the idea of a probable future Arab majority within what its founders had declared to be a "Jewish state."

A different view, more widely held by those still hopeful of negotiated settlement, looked on the occupied territories as a subject for
negotiation and bargaining in the channels of diplomacy. In their
view annexation of the territories by Israel and absorption of the inhabitants by the Israeli state would be a premature action, endangering chances for a long-term settlement. This commitment, they contended, could compromise the inhabitant, who would likely not cooperate, and it could also cast Israel into the permanent mold of a
garrison state. Instead they favored a measure of diplomatic flexibility, regarded as more important in the long-run than a strong military posture, that, while essential for survival, was not the key to an
ultimate solution. The status of Jerusalem did not appear to be readily negotiable, but the development of a formula for custody of the
holy places by an international arrangement of some kind was not
entirely ruled out by Israeli leaders. The Israelis, moreover, had not
yet been confronted with a choice between compromising on the
status of Jerusalem as part of a settlement of the Arab-Israeli problem, or acceptance of indefinite warfare. The idea of another division of the city was unacceptable to the government and public.

Arab hostility was manifested by strengthened Arab forces in conventional engagements and by the growing guerrilla threat of Al
Fatah and similar organizations. These added to the growing pressures for determination of policy regarding the occupied areas, and
they constituted problems of the most serious nature for the state.
Confronted with these pressing requirements, decision-making was
inhibited, however, by the imminence of elections for the Seventh
Knesset, scheduled for October 1969.

Simultaneous with the grave political-military problems and
approach of elections was still another factor, that of aging leadership. Political leaders since the inception of the state had been drawn
from an Eastern European power elite of "founding fathers," such
as Weizmann, Ben-Gurion, Ben-Zvi, Moshe Sharett, Zalman Shazar,
Levi Eshkol, and Golda Meir. By mid-1969 many of this elite had
died. Those who remained were aging and an inevitable transition of
leadership generations became a factor of political dynamics. Increasingly the influence was apparent of native-born Israelis, such as
Moshe Dayan and Yigal Allon, both representatives of the newer
kibbutz-born, indigenous elite. In addition, among Israeli-born youth
now coming of age in the generation after Dayan and Allon, attitudes other than loyalty toward the state were not yet clear.

CHAPTER 15
FOREIGN RELATIONS

Resolution of the Arab-Israeli conflict and attainment of broad international relations are among the fixed goals of Israel's foreign policy. They have been reiterated and elaborated upon by official spokesmen since the inception of statehood in 1948. Given the absence of such a durable, contractual peace, however, Israeli diplomacy has sought to avoid, at a minimum, political isolation from the international community.

Relations are conducted in terms of at least five specific policy objectives: to secure recognition and diplomatic support by the greatest possible number of states; to promote friendly economic and cultural exchanges; to defend the existence of the state by explaining its governmental policies and by publicizing its social development; to counteract Arab influence while inducing the neighboring Arab states by various means to enter into negotiations aimed toward peace; and to strengthen ties between Israel and world Jewry. Diplomatic skill combines with military preparedness to form the principal components of security for the state, which has had to live for the most part in an atmosphere of neither war nor peace.

THE MINISTRY FOR FOREIGN AFFAIRS
Diplomatic Traditions

Those who represent the country abroad benefit from a diplomatic tradition that predates 1948. This historical legacy may be traced, in the first instance, to the Biblical period. Its most contemporary phase began in the early years of the 20th century when Theodor Herzl, soliciting support for an autonomous Jewish settlement, conferred unsuccessfully with the rulers of Europe. Dr. Chaim Weizmann, his successor, concentrated instead upon Great Britain and was rewarded in 1917 with the Balfour Declaration, regarded as the outstanding achievement of Zionist diplomacy until 1947–48 (see ch. 3, Historical Setting).

When British determination to retain the mandate for Palestine weakened in the 1940's, the Zionist leaders turned their attention instead to multilateral diplomacy and also to the United States and the Soviet Union, both then emerging as world powers. These efforts culminated in the resolution adopted in November 1947 by the United Nations (UN) General Assembly supporting partition of Palestine into separate Arab and Jewish states and in the recognition accorded Israel by Washington and Moscow in May 1948.

Structure

The Ministry for Foreign Affairs came into existence immediately upon statehood, its entire staff initially comprising a director, his secretary, and a personal assistant. Additional members were drawn from the Political Department of the Jewish Agency for Palestine, which had presented the case for Jewish sovereignty before the UN. Moshe Sharett became the first minister for foreign affairs; Eliahn Elath was appointed ambassador to the United States; and Mrs. Golda Meir served as the first minister to the Soviet Union. Positions within the ministry were filled almost exclusively at the outset by Jews of European origin because of their language aptitudes, educational background, and familiarity with Europe. Since then, however, more Sephardim (Oriental Jews) and Sabras (native-born Israelis) are entering into professional diplomatic service (see ch. 5, Ethnic Groups and Languages).

The Ministry for Foreign Affairs expanded considerably in the 1960's, reflecting the growth and diversification of Israel's foreign relations. Its 31 divisions are classified into eight geographical and 14 functional units, the remainder being involved in administration. The permanent staff amounts to nearly 1,000 persons, divided almost equally between Jerusalem and overseas posts. In 1968 there were 92 permanent missions (63 having embassy status) in 70 countries: nine in Asia, 29 in Africa, one in Eastern Europe, 22 in Western Europe, 13 in North America, 16 in Latin America, one in Australia, and one in New Zealand. A permanent delegation was in residence at both centers of UN activity in New York and Geneva. Missions were attached to the European Economic Community (EEC), International Atomic Energy Agency (IAEA), the Food and Agriculture Organization (FAO), and the UN Educational, Scientific and Cultural Organization (UNESCO).

Techniques

Policy is implemented by Israel's emissaries through a variety of means, conforming to the belief of the Minister for Foreign Affairs Abba Eban that "international solidarity is composed of countless links which transcend national frontiers." Foreign trade, assuming a more prominent position within the economic sector, is one such link (see ch. 24, Foreign Economic Relations). Economic cooperation with countries all over the globe has been facilitated by formal bilateral trade agreements that were being phased out by mid-1969. Pavilions were present at 35 international trade fairs in 1967, and many countries exhibit regularly at the biennial International Trade Fair in Tel-Aviv.

Participation in the work of the UN specialized agencies is regarded as another such link. Exchange of scientists, medical experts, and scholars takes place regularly, while the program of technical assistance has played a central role in expanding relations with Asia, Africa, and Latin America since 1955 (see ch. 24, Foreign Economic Relations). Tourism similarly fulfills a dual function of strengthening the economy while making the country more meaningful to foreign visitors.

Visits abroad by artistic troupes, such as the Israel Philharmonic Orchestra, actors of Habimah (the Israel National Theater), and sports teams, or by individual performers, musicians, lecturers, and literary figures are also significant for cultural relations. Personal diplomacy has also been practiced effectively. In June and July of 1966, for example, President Zalman Shazar paid state visits to Uruguay, Chile, and Brazil; at the same time, the late Prime Minister Levi Eshkol completed a 3-week tour of seven African countries. Minister for Foreign Affairs Abba Eban has made frequent trips to various capitals in order to consult personally with world leaders. Because they enhance Israel's prestige, reciprocal visits by foreign dignitaries are also encouraged.

Despite the publicity attending such high-level contacts, the fundamental work of diplomacy is conducted daily on a routine basis at the diplomatic consular and unofficial levels. A consular service functions to expedite travel through issuance of passports or visas. An information service disseminates material about facets of life in the country. Brochures and booklets of a general character, totaling more than 2 million copies, were distributed in a variety of languages during 1967. Newsreels, films, displays, and answers to requests for specific items of information are provided, as are speakers to address public or professional audiences (see ch. 16, Public Information).

PHASES OF POLICY

Statehood (1948) to Suez Crisis (1956)

In 1948 the United States and the Soviet Union recognized the state of Israel, whereas the Arab states opposed it forcibly. These two salient features challenged the ingenuity of former Minister for Foreign Affairs Moshe Sharett and his staff in the initial phase of national diplomacy. Relations with the Soviet Union became strained by 1953. Hopes of ending Arab hostility fell short of expectation despite serious attention to the problem. Envoys were able to sign separate armistice agreements with Egypt, Jordan, Syria, and Lebanon in 1949 at Rhodes with the assistance of Dr. Ralph Bunche, UN acting mediator for Palestine. The armistice was interpreted by most members of the UN as an intermediate step in the transition from temporary truce to permanent peace.

Contrary to these expectations, further progress toward peaceful relations with the Arabs was not made after 1949; the situation, instead, became rigid. Certain features, as a result, became fixed and were still in evidence during 1969. The UN sought, often without success, to exert a moderating influence upon the dispute. The Arab-Israeli dispute became a more crucial part of the larger confrontation between East and West. Plans for regional Arab unity foundered on nationalistic issues. The loss of territory in Palestine compounded Arab frustration and led to hardened attitudes opposing compromise with Israel, while Israel rejected any solution that might question its right to full sovereignty.

The persistent hostility found expression in diverse ways. The foundation of official Arab policy was no direct negotiation with or recognition of Israel. Ships enroute to or from Israel were prevented from passing through the Suez Canal. Merchants and corporations investing in Israel were boycotted. Information media within the Arab world warned of the prospect of further war. Jerusalem in 1949 became a city divided into Jordanian and Israeli sectors along battle lines perpetuated in armistice agreements. The Palestinian Arab refugees (some 40 percent in camps) in Gaza, Jordan, Syria, and Lebanon were assisted by the UN Relief and Works Agency (UNRWA), whereas most Jews from the Arab countries immigrated into Israel. The number of border incidents increased despite the efforts of UN personnel assigned to the several mixed armistice commissions under the UN Truce Supervision Organization (UNTSO). Both sides expended large sums for purchasing modern weapons.

Israel, despite such pressing problems, nevertheless recorded several successes during the 1949–56 period. On May 11, 1949, membership in the UN was approved by both the Security Council and the General Assembly. In 1950 the "new city," the portion of Jerusalem under Israel's control, was declared the country's official capital, although the majority of nations did not recognize this act because it contradicted the 1947 UN decision calling for internationalization of the city. In September 1951 ths Security Council formally called upon Egypt to terminate its restrictions, regarded as "unjustified interference," on the passage of goods through the Suez Canal. In spite of the general Arab boycott, Israel established economic, cultural, and political relations with a number of countries, particularly those in Western Europe. In 1952, a reparations agreement was negotiated with the Federal Republic of Germany (West Germany), which, even in the face of Arab objections, was ratified in March 1953.

212

The security problem, however, remained foremost. The situation, always uneasy, deteriorated in 1955. Repeated incursions by armed Arab commandos, called fedayeen, and strong retaliatory measures by the Israel Defense forces contributed to increased tension. Weapons deliveries to Egypt from Eastern Europe and signs of military co-ordination among the Arab countries produced a sense of crisis in Jerusalem, and the Ministry for Foreign Affairs sought for possible allies. The interests of France and Great Britain paralleled those of Israel against President Gamal Abdel Nasser of Egypt; the result was the launching of an offensive by the three allies directed at the Suez Canal in the fall of 1956.

Suez Crisis to Six-Day War

The second phase of Israel's diplomatic history began after the Suez Crisis of 1956 (see ch. 3, Historical Setting). Previously empha-sis had been placed on transit rights through the Suez Canal; after 1956 greater concern was given to freedom of navigation in the Gulf of Aqaba, the Strait of Tiran, and the Red Sea. There was a related shift in emphasis from Europe to the new opportunities for diplo-matic activity offered by the independent countries of Asia and Africa.

Until 1956 the government still maintained hope of restoring friendly relations with the Soviet Union; after 1956 this was no longer regarded as an immediate possibility. Israel subsequently be-came more closely associated with the West, the United States and France in particular.

The state's existence had been institutionalized between 1948 and 1956, and during the subsequent 11 years it enjoyed a period of nor-malcy, in spite of the fluid political situation in the Middle East. The primary gain from the war of 1956 was the comparative tranquility along the borders that lasted until the third military confrontation in June 1967. During this interim the Ministry for Foreign Affairs, headed by Mrs. Golda Meir until 1966, was able to broaden its scope. Growing foreign trade and tourism, the originality of the assistance program to developing countries, the visit by Pope Paul VI in Janu-ary 1964, and the selection of Shmuel Yosef Agnon as recipient of the Nobel Prize for Literature in 1966 — all enhanced the country's international status (see ch. 18, Biographies of Key Personalities). Further evidence of this normalization was the formal exchange of ambassadors between West Germany and Israel in 1965.

After the Six-Day War

Abba Eban succeeded Mrs. Meir as minister for foreign affairs at the beginning of 1966. Maintaining the tradition of active, flexible diplomacy and serving as an eloquent spokesman for Israel's interests, he began by exploring opportunities with the countries of Eastern Europe. Romania, in particular, was receptive to the idea of strengthening relations, and a series of modest trade agreements was undertaken with it and with other Communist countries. Any hopes of improving relations with the Soviet Union through improved relations with the other Communist bloc members ended prematurely, however, when a crisis emerged in May and June 1967 in which the Soviet Union again sided with the Arabs (see ch. 3, Historical Setting).

At the height of the crisis, the Ministry for Foreign Affairs was engaged in formulating, explaining and defending official policy. It regarded as provocative Egypt's mobilization in Sinai, the request for the immediate removal of the UNEF contingents, as well as the general Arab call for renewed war against Israel, and it considered the blockade of the Gulf of Aqaba an act of war. In taking this stand and in justifying Israel's military action on the morning of June 5, 1967, as defensive, the country derived wide support from world opinion, evidenced by press comment and public demonstrations. Israel was viewed popularly as the underdog, whose very existence was menaced.

Victory in the Six-Day War of June 1967 produced a set of new circumstances in which Israel found itself occupying large territories. It also created diplomatic challenges and opportunities; government policy in 1969 was to deal forcefully with any resistance in the administered territories or with Arab efforts to alter the status quo by other than peaceful means, holding the Arab governments directly responsible. Activities by guerrilla forces operating from bases in neighboring countries represented a specific problem. Sporadic attacks on border settlements or patrols, planting of bombs in places of public assembly, and attempts at interfering with operations of the El Al Israel Airlines were answered by strong reprisals, such as the raid upon Beirut airport in December 1968, which were often viewed critically by other nations. Reunification of Jerusalem under Israeli control in June 1967, opposition to reopening of the Suez Canal without guarantees for Israel shipping, and opening settlements in the occupied territories (a violation of the Geneva Convention on Occupied Territories, which Israel had ratified), all tended to alienate some who had supported Israel's position previously.

Mrs. Meir, who became prime minister in March 1969 upon the death of Levi Eshkol, reaffirmed official policy. This policy was to seek peace treaties with the Arab states through direct negotiations; it rejected any withdrawal prior to a directly negotiated peace and opposed the idea of the Big Powers (United States, Great Britain, France, and the Soviet Union) imposing a settlement.

Although preoccupied with the problem of Arab hostility, the coun-

214

try had adopted positions on other substantive issues affecting the international community at the end of the 1960's. It expressed shock at the Soviet military occupation of Czechoslovakia in 1968 and welcomed the opening of negotiations in Paris aimed at ending the fighting in Vietnam. Having supported the Africans in their pursuit of national independence, Israel voiced concern at the personal suffering in the Nigerian civil war and made a contribution toward the relief of impoverished Biafrans.

On the complicated question of the nuclear nonproliferation treaty, the government on May 9, 1968, expressed the view that the treaty would be an important part of the universal effort toward general disarmament. In 1963 it was among the first nations to adhere to the atomic test ban treaty. Nevertheless, because of its sensitivity to the security aspect, and being a party to an unresolved conflict, the government had reservations about guarantees. Israel is one of several states considered to have the capability of making nuclear weapons, but it has not signed the nonproliferation treaty. Perhaps more than any other nation, Israel is sensitive to the limitations in the UN capacity to play a more positive, effective role in preserving peace in the world. With regard to the overriding international issue of the cold war, the policy has been to endorse the principles of peaceful coexistence and nonintervention.

RELATIONS WITH FOREIGN GROUPS

World Jewry

Israel tends to regard the 11 million Jews living outside the country as its greatest ally. Consequently, it seeks to strengthen the emotional, religious, cultural, and historical bonds between itself and world Jewry. This goal has several motivations. Based on the concept that Israel is the spiritual center for Judaism, the country's leadership affirms that it has a responsibility to increase Jewish consciousness among dispersed communities by such means as providing teachers and textbooks and by fostering the study of Hebrew. Moreover, by increasing the sense of identification of Jews in the Diaspora with Israel, the goal of achieving active political and economic support is also served.

Another motivation is concern for the physical safety of Jews in the Arab countries, South America, and the Soviet Union. The government encourages *aliyah*, immigration to Israel, as a means of fulfilling Zionist ideology and of increasing the Jewish State's security. Accordingly, early in its history, in 1950–51, Israel absorbed 45,000 Jews from Yemen and 110,000 from Iraq. Although in smaller numbers, absorption of immigrants was continuing in the late 1960's; 15,730 persons settled in the country in 1966. The large concentration of Jews in Europe and North America also offers the opportunity to build support, both political and economic, by promoting travel to and investment in the country.

The West

Mutual interests between the United States and Israel were most pronounced in the 1960–68 period. Israel's commitment to democratic values and anti-Communist orientation, its ability to defend itself, and its achievement in all spheres of national life contributed to the basis for an understanding. This was exemplified in personal meetings between former President Lyndon B. Johnson and the late Prime Minister Levi Eshkol in June 1964 and in January 1968. The beginning of a new administration under President Richard M. Nixon in 1969 offered an opportunity for both countries to reassess their relationship. The United States was motivated by a desire to exert greater influence upon the Arab-Israeli dispute in order to avoid a direct East-West military confrontation, to facilitate a return to peace and stability, and to resume normal relations with the Arab world.

Western Europe as a region has been given considerable attention by the Ministry for Foreign Affairs, and relations with its individual countries have fluctuated. Contact with West Germany was kept to a minimum in earlier years because of painful memories of the Hitler era and focused primarily on transfer of German reparation and restitution payments. Since the establishment of diplomatic relations in 1965 and the popular demonstration of support for Israel during the Six-Day War of June 1967, contacts between the two countries have increased. Relations with Great Britain have also improved since the early years of independence, as unpleasant memories of the Palestine Mandate have receded.

The converse was true of the French government in 1969. Whereas France was one of Israel's closest friends from 1956 to 1967, the crisis in 1967 caused an estrangement when General Charles de Gaulle took the position that Israel was responsible for the hostilities and suspended the delivery of military equipment, most importantly the fifty Mirage jet aircraft, purchased by Israel Defense Forces. Relations with the other governments of Western Europe have been more stable. The Scandinavian countries, the Netherlands, and Italy have extended diplomatic support while intensifying cultural and commercial intercourse. Since at least the early 1960's, Israel has sought an agreement with the European Economic Community (EEC) providing preferential access to the EEC market for Israel goods.

The East

Little opportunity has been found to moderate the anti-Israel policy of the Soviet Union or of those countries aligned with it. Diplomatic relations, at no time firm and stable since 1952, were broken by the

Soviet Union as well as other Eastern European Communist countries (Romania excepted), because of the June 1967 war; trade agreements, previously negotiated, were canceled as well. The Communist nations have generally supported the Arab cause in the UN, and the Soviet Union has served as the leading supplier of arms and economic aid to several of Israel's neighbors; Romania has been the single exception to this policy of isolation, and relations have been maintained also by Cuba. The Soviet Union has also objected to what it contends is Israel's attempt to involve itself in Soviet internal affairs through expressions of concern for the safety and welfare of Soviet Jewry and by the demand that they be permitted to emigrate to Israel.

Arab States

Israel's policy toward the Arab states is conditioned by their hostility and dominated by a determination to win from them recognition of Israel's legitimacy. Although early in its history Israel proposed to allow some of the Arab refugees to return, persisting Arab hostility has hardened Israel's attitude. It now insists that to take the refugees back would be paramount to admitting a fifth column. Some observers believe that, given a free choice, few Arabs would desire to return to live as citizens of a Jewish state. Many of the refugees insist, however, that they might have a right to return under UN resolutions, which also provide that those choosing resettlement elsewhere would be compensated for their lost properties.

Israel contends that the Arab states could absorb the refugees, as Israel absorbed Jewish refugees from Arab lands, and that in fact an exchange of populations has occurred. Meanwhile, Israel seeks to minimize the refugee problem, which is much worse since the 1967 war, as additional hundreds of thousands were displaced from refugee camps and villages in occupied territories and from the west bank of the Suez Canal. Despite exhortations from the UN, supported by the United States, to permit the newly displaced persons to return, Israel has allowed back only some 25,000 persons.

Since 1967 Israel has been faced by a growth of Palestinian nationalism. With no stake in the status quo and a future clouded by an indefinite refugee status, the refugees with other Palestinians are turning increasingly to guerrilla warfare and terrorist attacks against Israel. Though they have sustained heavy losses, terrorism continues. Even some of the Israeli Arabs appear to have been affected.

In the face of this provocation, Israeli retaliations and security measures in the occupied areas have become increasingly severe. Israel argues that this is the only effective means of discouraging Arab attacks. The respite in the wake of retaliation has never been more than temporary, however, and since the June 1967 war, there has been even less relief gained through reprisal.

217

Acceptance by neighboring states, except Syria, of the November 1967 Security Council resolution constituted recognition of Israel's legitimacy by those states for the first time. The lack of progress toward a settlement, however, has eroded this position. Concurrently Palestinian Arab nationalism now seeks a Palestine where Jews, Christians, and Muslims would live without distinction. Israel recognizes that Palestinian nationalism poses a severe threat.

Peripheral Middle Eastern Countries

Israeli foreign policy has sought to circumvent the existing isolation by its immediate neighbors by establishing contacts at least with those states bordering on the outer periphery of the Middle East. To the north and west, Israel has succeeded in establishing relations with Turkey, Cyprus, and Greece. Iran does not have diplomatic relations with Israel, but economic relations are important, as Iran is the source of most of Israel's petroleum supply. To the south, the government maintains cordial relations with Ethiopia. Tunisian President Habib Bourguiba, upon occasion, has expressed his feeling that the existence of Israel should be acknowledged by the Arab states; he has not gone so far, however, as to establish formal diplomatic relations and has coupled his remarks with demands that Israel deal justly with the refugees.

Others

With the development of Eilat as a "gateway to the East" in 1957, Israel placed new emphasis upon establishing friendly ties with the underdeveloped, former colonial countries. This initiative was partially a reaction to the Afro-Asian Conference that took place in Bandung, Indonesia, in April 1955. At this conference delegates from the Arab or Muslim countries supported an anti-Israel resolution that was passed. Israel responded vigorously in competing for the support of these newly independent countries, which, in addition, formed a substantial bloc within the UN General Assembly.

Evidence of this initiative was given in September 1957 when the first Israeli ambassador to an African country presented his credentials in Ghana and negotiated the contract for a joint endeavor that established the Black Star Shipping Line. Diplomatic and economic relations grew rapidly as new African countries attained independence. In March 1961 another milestone was reached when 64 students from 24 countries graduated from the first course of the Afro-Asian Institute in Tel Aviv, where students from developing countries receive training in agriculture, health, and community development (see ch. 24, Foreign Economic Relations).

In cultivating relations with the Third World countries, the Israeli government has been confronted by the fact that many of these are heavily populated by Muslims who are predisposed in favor of their Arab coreligionists. The response has been to stress several factors in Israel's favor: a shared experience in opposition to colonial rule; impressive economic and social progress in the short period of independence that might prove useful to the more recent sovereign states; the absence of color prejudice and the assimilation of Sephardic minorities; and a willingness to cooperate for the benefit of both sides.

CHAPTER 16
PUBLIC INFORMATION

In 1968 the country had a well-developed network of communications media. According to official sources, more than 74 percent of all households had radios. The 24 daily newspapers circulated some 150 copies for every 1,000 inhabitants and were available even in relatively isolated areas. Each person attended an average of 25.5 film shows a year; they were offered by commercial theaters and by mobile film units operating throughout the country. According to the United Nations Educational, Scientific and Cultural Organization (UNESCO), the country ranked second in the world for the number of book titles published in proportion to the population.

In addition to furnishing news and information, the media are extensively used to further the assimilation of the diverse cultural backgrounds of the inhabitants, to promote the study of Hebrew, to aid in the adjustment of new immigrants, and to enhance feelings of national cohesion and patriotism. This information policy, exercised through the Cenrtal Office of Information and the Government Press Office, is fully supported by newspaper editors, film producers, and book publishers.

Newspapers are privately owned and are free to express a variety of political, ideological, and religious views. They are responsive to government guidance, however, in matters relating to national security and to the country's foreign relations. Publication of items affecting military security is forbidden. Newspapermen cooperate in exercising voluntary restraint to exclude material that may jeopardize the country's interests.

The skills of communications media are put to intensive use by a highly literate (about 90 percent in at least one language among the Jewish population) and interested public. The press provides intellectual stimulation for political debates and offers a wide range of educational and cultural information. A little less than half of the daily newspapers are published in foreign languages to serve the needs of their recently immigrated readers, whose knowledge of Hebrew is in the beginning stages. In the cities most Israelis read, in addition to the major dailies, one or more newspapers reflecting their political views or printed in the language of their country of origin. Many, however, prefer the radio as a source of news.

Kol Israel (The Voice of Israel), the country's one civilian radio station, operates under the administrative jurisdiction of the government, and has extensive transmission facilities. Its multilingual programs, beamed to all parts of the coutry, reach nine out of 10 persons over 18 years of age. The Israeli armed forces operate their own radio stations (see ch. 26, The Armed Forces).

Understanding and support of foreign nations for Israel's policies are solicited through a multitude of foreign-language publications and documentary films. These are published and produced mainly by the Government Press Office and the Central Office of Information but may appear under private auspices as well. Of primary importance in this effort are the foreign-language broadcasts of Kol Israel, reaching virtually all countries in the Middle East and many others in Europe and in North and South America.

Information from foreign countries is available to Israelis from foreign wire services represented in Tel Aviv and from broadcasts of foreign radio networks, including the Voice of America. In addition, information is also obtained from numerous foreign publications on sale in bookshops and on newsstands.

GOVERNMENT AND FREEDOM OF THE PRESS

The Central Office of Information and Government Press Office are in charge of guiding and overseeing the information media. In 1968 both were under the Prime Minister's Office and were supervised by a minister without portfolio in charge of information services, who is minister of information in all but name. The Kol Israel Broadcasting Authority also was under the administrative jurisdiction of the Prime Minister's Office. To coordinate information policies, frequent meetings are held between officials of the Government Press Office, the Information Division of the Ministry of Foreign Affairs, and representatives of the Broadcasting Authority.

Close contact is maintained between government agencies dealing with news media and with members of the press represented by the Committee of Editors. The Government Press Office gives regular briefings to members of the Committee. The newspaper editors are also briefed by cabinet members, including the prime minister, on major national issues including foreign affairs. In the course of these briefiings, newspapermen occasionally are asked to treat certain items of information as background only and refrain from submitting them for publication.

Strict censorship governs the publication of material relating to national security, including military operations, activities in occupied areas, and matters relating to foreign affairs. Provisions and procedures are spelled out in the Censorship Laws that formed part of the emergency regulations promulgated by the British authorities in 1945 and still in force. Articles dealing with subjects affecting national security are reviewed by a board of military censors. Material that is regarded as endangering the nation's safety is deleted, and offending newspapers are liable to be fined. The Committee of Editors represents the press before the military censors. Appeals against the actions of the censors may be lodged with a three-man committee comprised of an army officer, an editor, and the president of the Bar Association. In general every effort is made by editors to refrain from publishing material that is subject to censorship. Occasional deviations result mainly from the censors' expansion of the subject matter included in the category of material affecting national security.

A Defamation Law passed in July 1965 was designed to protect from slander organized bodies and communities as well as individuals; these groups sometimes come into conflict in Israeli society, which is composed of persons of diverse ethnic origins. The law provided that persons publishing, writing, or distributing information regarded as defamatory must furnish proof that such information is true and that it was published in the public interest. In case of conviction under the terms of the law, penalties are imposed not only on journalists and publishers, but on newspaper office employees, printers, and news vendors as well. Because of the vigorous protest of journalists and newspaper employees against the Defamation Law, its provisions have been under review by the Knesset (literally "place of assembly"), Israel's unicameral parliament.

INFORMATION MEDIA

The Press

Character and Scope

Newspapers published during the British Mandate period (1922–48) were primarily journals of opinion and religious publications. Some of them printed local and international news items, but their main purpose was the exposition and propagation of Zionism. Their solemn and didactic tone was addressed to a small group of readers who expected newspapers to furnish background material for ideological debates rather than a record of daily events.

Since 1948 newspapers have proliferated, and their character and format have undergond marked changes. Dailies and weeklies published in 1968 still vigorously expressed ideological, partisan, and religious views, but most of them have made adjustments to the growing demand of readers for more news with less commentary. The standards of journalism are generally high, especially in the leading dailies, some of which are independent or mildly partisan. News coverage, including that of international news, is extensive. Many dailies have their own correspondents abroad. The keen competition for readers also prompted many newspapers, including the strongly partisan ones, to devote more space to sports and women's news and to general interest features.

Because of the objections of religious groups to the publishing of stories involving violence and scandal, most newspapers consistently avoid the sensational reporting of crimes and of intrigues relating to the private lives of public figures and of celebrities. Events of this type are sparsely reported or are omitted altogether in all but a few newspapers.

Newspapers reflect the diverse ethnic and cultural backgrounds of Israeli journalists and of their readers. Editorials and political articles are written in the polemic style of Eastern and Central European newspapers before World War II. Reports and news stories show the marked influence of British and American journalism. Feature sections are modeled after those in the Swiss and the West German press. Many of the leading newspapers are published in the original mother tongue of the immigrants (see table 15). During the 1960's, however, the Hebrew-language press has been gaining in circulation and prestige as more of the older immigrants become familiar with Hebrew and as youths born and educated in Israel join the ranks of newspaper readers.

In 1968 there were about 128 newspapers and general interest periodicals, including 24 daily newspapers, of which 22 were published in the morning and 2 in the afternoon. Of the morning newspapers, 13 were printed in Hebrew; the rest, in English, Hungarian, German, Romanian, Yiddish, Polish, Bulgarian, French, and Arabic. The major morning newspapers have weekly circulations of about 40,000; circulations of the smaller morning dailies range between 2,000 and 20,000. The two afternoon Hebrew newspapers have the largest circulations; they sell between 115,000 and 160,00 copies daily. On Fridays the circulation of morning newspapers rises to over 60,000 and that of afternoon newspapers to over 200,000. The morning newspapers and the smaller weeklies are sold largely by subscription, but the two afternoon newspapers are sold mostly on the street.

The daily newspapers print from six to twenty pages but, on Fridays, when cutural, religious, and literary supplements are featured, the number of pages usually is doubled. No newspapers are published on Saturday, the Jewish Sabbath. Photographs are rarely used. Editorial cartoons, however, are featured regularly and are popular with many readers. Advertising is an important source of revenue to the major dailies and weeklies, but most of the smaller newspapers rely on the financial suport of political or religious groups. Advertisements occupy less than one-third of a newspaper's total space. Some columns are also devoted to family announcements and to con-

Table 15. *Major Metropolitan Hebrew and Foreign-Language Dailies of Israel, 1968* *

Name of Newspaper and English Translation	Circulation (estimated)	Language	Editor	Remarks
MORNING DAILIES:				
Al Hamishmar (The Guardian)	18,000	Hebrew	Yakov Amit	Organ of militant socialist MAPAM (United Workers' Party).
Al Yaum (The Day)	5,000	Arabic	Tuviah Shamosh	
Davar (The Word)	43,000	Hebrew	Jehua Gotthelf	Organ of Histadrut (General Federation of Labor).
Haaretz (The Land)	43,000 (weekdays) 63,000 (Fridays)	Hebrew	Gershom Schocken	Independent, liberal; most prestigious daily.
Hatzofe (The Observer)	11,000	Hebrew	S. Daniel	Organ of National Religious Front.
Hayom (The Day)	n.a.	Hebrew	J. Kremmerman	Organ of GAHAL, a right-wing coalition.
The Jerusalem Post	23,000	English	Ted Lurie	Independent; best-informed foreign-language daily.
Lamerchar (The Wide World)	18,000	Hebrew	David Padahzur	Organ of moderate Marxist Ahdut Ha-Avoda Poalei Zion (Unity of Labor).
Letzte Nayes (Latest News)	11,000	Yiddish	M. Zouia	Independent.
L'Information d'Israel	4,000–8,000	French	Nathaniel Green	Published by the governing Israel Labor party (MAPAI).
Izraelskie Noviny i Kurier (Israel News and Messenger)	10,000	Polish	S. Yedidyah	Independent.

Table 15.—Continued

Name of Newspaper and English Translation	Circulation (estimated)	Language	Editor	Remarks
MORNING DAILIES:				
Omer (Saying)	11,000	Hebrew (voweled)	Zvi Rotem	Published by Histadrut (General Federation of Labor) for beginners in Hebrew.
Uj Kelet (New East)	20,000	Hungarian	E. Marton	Independent.
Viata Noastra (Our Life)	16,000	Rumanian	Meir Zait	Published by the governing Israel Labor party (MAPAI).
Yediot Chadashot (New News)	18,000	German	I. Lilienfeld	Independent.
AFTERNOON DAILIES:				
Maariv (Evening)	118,000 (weekdays) 133,000 (Fridays)	Hebrew	A. Dissentshik	Leading afternoon paper; has the highest circulation; independent.
Yediot Achronot (Latest News)	85,000 (weekdays) 102,000 (Fridays)	Hebrew	H. Rosenblum	Independent.

n.a.—not available.

* All published in Tel Aviv, except *The Jerusalem Post.*

Source: Adapted from Europa Publications, *Europa Year Book, 1968*; and Israel, Ministry of Information, *Newspapers and Periodicals Appearing in Israel, 1966.*

gratulations or expressions of sympathy in response to such announcements. Until about 1956 newsprint was often in short supply and most of it had to be imported. During the 1960's, however, the country has produced about 75 percent of its newsprint needs. The total per capita newsprint consumption increased from 8.3 pounds in 1962 to 16.0 pounds in 1965.

The great majority of newspapers are published in Tel Aviv; others, in Jerusalem and Haifa. Because of the high cost of production and limited advertising potential, newspapers are not published in the smaller towns. Communal settlements, on the other hand, have their own newspapers, mostly weeklies. They are primarily interpretative and ideological organs, but they also feature news and present problems affecting the communal group. These newspapers are written and edited by nonprofessionals and are distributed free of charge.

Dailies, Weeklies, and Periodicals

Several of the major dailies published in 1968 were founded during or before the British Mandate period; others first published during the early 1950's. Despite occasional financial straits most of them have proved durable and have had relatively little fluctuation in their circulations.

Haaretz (The Land), the country's oldest and most prestigious newspaper, was founded in 1918. Noted for thorough news coverage and for the moderate and sober tone of its editorials, *Haaretz* generally is regarded as a mouthpiece of informed public opinion. Its circulation, about 43,000 on weekdays and 63,000 on Fridays, is the largest among the morning dailies. *Davar* (The Word), the other leading morning daily with a circulation of also about 43,000, is the organ of the Histadrut Ha'ovdim Hakalit, the General Federation of Labor, commonly known as Histadrut (see ch. 22, Labor). *Davar* generaly reflects the views of the governing Israel Labor party. It is sometimes described as semiofficial. Almost every issue features essays or articles by a leading government figure; the extensive use of political cartoons has also contributed much to the newspaper's popularity. Histadrut also publishes *Omer* (Saying), a small daily printed in easy-to-read voweled Hebrew for new immigrants.

Lamerchav (The Wide World), with a circulation of about 18,000, is published under the auspices of the moderately Marxist Ahdut Ha-Avoda (Unity of Labor) wing of the Israel Labor party. *Al Hamishmar* (The Guardian), founded in 1943, is an organ of the militant socialist MAPAM (see Glossary), and also has a circulation of about 18,000. Strongly partisan, it has many readers in the communal settlements. *Hayom* (The Day), relatively new among the morning dailies, was founded in 1966, under the auspices of GAHAL, a right-wing coalition bloc (see ch. 14, Political Dynamics).

The religious parties are represented by three dailies. *She'arim* (Gate), founded in 1951, is an organ of the ultraorthodox Poalei Agudat Israel (Workers of the Association of Israel); *Hatzofe* (The Observer) with a circulation of about 11,000 is published by the Mizrahi (National Religious Front). *Hamodia* (The Herold) is published by Agudat Israel (Association of Israel).

Most influential among the foreign-language morning dailies is *The Jerusalem Post*, published in English, with a circulation of about 23,000. Carefully edited and noted for its concise and informative articles, *The Jerusalem Post* serves as a principal source of information to many foreign observers of Israeli affairs. Next most popular is the Hungarian-language *Uj Kelet* (New East), with an approximate circulation of 20,000. Both *The Jerusalem Post* and *Uj Kelet* are politically independent. Other popular foreign-language dailies, including the German *Yediot Chadashot* (New News), with a circulation of 18,000, the Polish *Izraelskie Noviny i Kurier* (Israel News and Courier), and the Yiddish *Letzte Nayes* (Latest News) are also published under independent auspices. The French-language *L'Information d'Israel* and the Rumanian *Viata Noastra* (Our Life) are published by the governing Israel Labor party. There are two Arabic newspapers, *Al Ariba* (The News) and *Al Quds* (Jerusalem), both begun in 1968. *Al Quds* is published by a Palestinian Arab of Jordanian nationality.

The two afternoon dailies, both published in Hebrew, have steadily gained in popularity during the 1960's. *Maariv* (Evening) attracts many well-informed readers with its lively style, colorful features, and a daily column of satirical comments on public life. It prints four regional editions, each adapting its dominant news coverage to local interests. *Yediot Achronot* (Latest News) is noted for its independent opinion and the daily lead article of its editor. Thorough news coverage, human interest stories, and a gossip column contribute to its popularity.

About 400 periodicals, including over 70 government organs, were published in 1968. Most of them were weeklies, biweeklies, and monthlies; others were published quarterly or irregularly. Three-fourths of the periodicals were published in Hebrew, the rest in Arabic, English, French, Hungarian, Polish, Spanish, Bulgarian, Rumanian, Ladino (Judeo-Spanish), Persian, and Yiddish. They include political weeklies, picture magazines, and publications catering to a variety of specialized interests, such as literature, art, religion, technology, philately, and chess. About 30 of the periodicals are intended for children and youth. Scholarly journals, many of them in the fields of science, medicine, and engineering, are published by learned societies and universities (see ch. 10, Artistic and Intellectual Expression).

The best-known weekly is *Haolam Hazeh* (This World), an illustrated news magazine with a circulation of 30,000 to 40,000. It is perhaps the only news magazine in the country that features sensational items, with the lavish use of photographs and large headlines. The Israel Labor party publishes several weeklies, including *Hapoel Hatzair* (Young Workers) and the Rumanian-language *Facla* (The Torch). *Hamis'har* (Commerce) is a widely read business weekly with a circulation of about 39,000. *La'Isha* (For the Woman) a popular women's magazine, has a circulation of about 30,000. *Bamachane* (The Camp), another illustrated weekly, is published by the Israeli defense forces, mainly for military personnel, although it has many readers among the general population; its circulation is an estimated 30,000.

Most of the monthly, twice monthly, and quarterly publications have small circulations ranging between 2,000 and 7,000. The monthly *Gazit* (Gazette) features articles in literature and art. *Moznaim* (Balance) is a literary and cultural monthly; *Mada* (Science), published every other month, features poplar scientific articles.

Journalists and Professional Associations

Most journalists have completed academic secondary schools, and some have university educations. Modern news reporting techniques are learned mostly on the job, although many journalists were employed on the staffs of newspapers in other countries before coming to Israel. Courses in journalism are offered at Tel Aviv University and at Hebrew University in Jerusalem.

The professional interests of newspapermen are represented by the Israeli Journalists Association. The Israeli Press Council, established in 1963, deals with matters relating to press freedom and to professional ethics. The Daily Newspaper Publishers' Association of Israel, an affiliate of the International Federation of Newspaper Publishers, negotiates on behalf of publishers with official groups and with labor unions. It is also in charge of the purchase and distribution of newsprint.

News Agencies

Domestic news is furnished to the press by the Associated Israel Press Limited, known at ITIM (Itonout Israel Meougedet). It is the country's national news agency with bureaus in Tel Aviv and Jerusalem. Founded in 1950 by a group of newspapermen, ITIM is controlled by a board of managers representing the dailies that hold shares in the agency. Local news to the newspapers and to the Kol Israel Broadcasting Authority are furnished by a network of staff reporters who cover various areas of the country. Some of ITIM's news material originates with the Government Press Office. The agency publishes a weekly *Airmail Bulletin* and a daily *Financial Bulletin*, both in English.

For international news coverage the press relies on the British Reuters Bureau, the Agence France Press, the Associated Press, and United Press International. The last-mentioned has its own fully staffed bureau. Reuters is the one most widely used. The other news services are represented by local correspondents. Bureaus of the London-based Jewish Telegraphic Agency and of its local affiliate, the Israeli News Agency, are located in Jerusalem and Tel Aviv, respectively. Other foreign news agencies have local correspondents for dispatching outgoing news but have not distribution services to Israeli newspapers. These agencies include the Catholic News Service, the World Union News, the Hearst Headline Service, and the Religious News Agency, all from the United States. Also included are the Dutch Press Syndicate from the Netherlands and the Greek News Agency. News from the Communist bloc is furnished by the Amtliche Deutsche Nachrichten of the German Democratic Republic, the Czechoslovak Ceŝkoslovenska Tiskova Kancelar, the New China News Agency of the Chinese People's Republic, and by the Soviet Union's Telegrafnoe Agentsvo Sovietskovo Soyuza (TASS).

Radio

Kol Israel is operated by the Broadcasting Authority, which is headed by a 5-member Management Board; its senior staff includes an Assistant Director General for Planning and directors for operations, news and current events, light programs, music, external broadcasts, and Arabic programs. The 25 members of the Broadcasting Authority are appointed by the president, upon the recommendation of the government. The budget of Kol Israel is financed by license, advertisement, and announcement fees, and by government grants.

The four networks of Kol Israel broadcast on 22 medium and short wavelengths for a total of 327 hours a week in Hebrew, Arabic, English, Yiddish, Ladino, Rumanian, Hungarian, Spanish, Moroccan-Arabic, Persian, French, and Russian. There are a total of 19 studios in Jerusalem, Tel Aviv, and Haifa, and an additional mobile unit. Technical facilities are located in Jerusalem, Bet Hillel (21 miles north of the Sea of Galilee), Eilat (at the head of the Gulf of Aqaba), Zefat (30 miles northeast of Haifa), Yavne (about 15 miles south of Tel Aviv), Acre (on the Mediterranean coast, about 10 miles north of Haifa), Qadima (16 miles north of Tel Aviv), and Ram Allah (about 8 miles north of Jerusalem in the occupied West Bank). The power of transmitters ranges from 0.05 to 200 kilowatts (see table 16).

Table 16. The Kol Israel (Voice of Israel) Broadcasting Authority, 1968

Network	Station Name	Location	Power (in kilowatts)	Frequency (in kilocycles)	Wavelength
A[1]	Kol Israel _____	Jerusalem, Tel Aviv	50	575	522
	____ do _____	Zefat _____	1	845	355
	____ do _____	Bet Hillel ___	0.05	881	340.5
	____ do _____	Jerusalem ___	1	1169	256
	____ do _____	Acre _____	10	1205	249
	____ do _____	Eilat _____	1	1358	220
B[2]	Kol Israel _____	Jerusalem, Tel Aviv	100	656	457
	____ do _____	Jerusalem ___	2.5	710	423
	____ do _____	Haifa _____	1	1097	273
C	Kol Israel Kol Tzion Yeru- sholayim (Voice of Is- rael, Voice of Zion in Jeru- salem)	Yavne _____	50/7.5	9009	33.3
		Yavne _____	100	9625	32.1
	____ do _____	Qadima _____	100	9725	30.8
	____ do _____	Qadima _____	100	11910	25.2
D	Dar Al-Idha'ah Al Isralliyah (Israel Broad- casting Sta- tion)	Ram Allah __	200	677	443
	____ do _____	Qadima _____	100	737	292
	____ do _____	Yavne _____	100/200	737	407
	____ do _____	Yavne _____	20	7189	42

[1] This network also broadcasts on FM with frequencies of 91300 kilocycles (from Jerusalem) and 96600 kilocycles (from Haifa).

[2] This network also broadcasts on FM with frequencies of 95500 kilocycles (from Jerusalem and Haifa) and 88800 kilocycles (from Jerusalem).

Source: Adapted from Israel, Central Office of Information, Prime Minister's Office, *Israel Government Yearbook, 5728(1967–68); World Radio-Television Handbook, 1968;* and U.S. government sources.

Network A of the domestic service broadcasts on mediumwave in Hebrew only. The network provides a program of music, entertainment, and news. The light musical programs often include new and old Hebrew songs; they are interspersed with quiz programs and with features on art, science, literature, and geography. Network B, the other main domestic service, also broadcasts on mediumwave. The programs of this network are intended mainly for new immigrants. Newscasts and commentary in Yiddish, Ladino, French, English, Rumanian, Hungarian, Russian, Moghrabi (the Arabic dialect of North Africa), alternate with popular music, educational programs, Hebrew-language lessons, and comical entertainment. Network D broadcasts in Arabic on mediumwave and shortwave to listeners in

Israel and in the neighboring countries. The Arabic program consists of political commentary, press reviews, entertainment, and 15 newscasts each day. Educational broadcasts are beamed to the country's Arab schools. In addition, there are religious programs and a daily hour of Arab music.

According to the latest statistics available, there were about 610,000 radio sets in the country. Owners of radio sets must pay a small license fee. The sets are produced within the country, but there is a general preference for imported transistor sets that are sold at small cost. Most Israelis in the cities have their own radio sets, but group listening is popular in the communal settlements and in the coffeehouses.

Kol Israel's programming emphasizes public service and educational broadcasts. Newscasts and commentary are supplemented by special weekly programs on activities of the Knesset and of the United Nations. Public service features, including live broadcasts on the life of communal settlements, provide insights into the country's social, educational, and cultural problems. Educational programs include a People's University on the Air, Hebrew-language lessons, and a science program. Educational quizzes, serialized radio plays, and religious broadcasts are regularly featured. Programs of music and entertainment are geared to the diverse cultural backgrounds of the listeners. At the same time, an effort is made to popularize the works of native-born Israeli composers, poets, and playwrights.

Many Israelis prefer news that is broadcast over the radio to that available in the newspapers. According to a public opinion survey conducted in 1968, about 31 percent of a group questioned listened to more than five news programs a day. Radio reports were regarded as more reliable than press reports by more than half of the group questioned; about one-third of the respondents believed that all news broadcast by Kol Israel was truthful.

Television

Television is in the beginning stages. The Instructional Television Trust, founded and supported by the Rothschild Memorial Group, introduced educational telecasts in 1966 to about 30 schools on a pilot study basis. Television for general audiences began in May 1968 over the strong opposition of orthodox religious groups which object to programs generally shown on commercial television. The Columbia Broadcasting System (CBS) has provided technical assistance, and Israeli television technicians have been sent for training to the United States.

Telecasts from neighboring Arab countries may be viewed in Israel. By the end of 1968 there were over 125,000 television sets in the country; 16.6 percent of households had one. The demand for sets has been rapidly increasing since May 1968.

Films

Films are extremely popular. The country has one of the largest film audiences in the world in proportion to its total population. In 1968 there were approximately 46.9 million admissions, or more than 25 per person. There was a total of 301 film theaters with a seating capacity of 201,536. Most of the theaters were located in the cities, but mobile film units regularly served the isolated villages and communal settlements. The Histadrut, for example, showed educational and other documentary films in the rural areas.

The great demand for films has helped to develop a small but active domestic motion picture industry. The government encourages Israeli film makers by granting them tax refunds, subsidies, and customs exemptions. Film production in Israel by foreign producers, for showing in foreign countries, is also welcomed and is encouraged by the granting of favorable rates of currency exchange. The developing domestic film industry receives vigorous assistance from the motion picture industry in the United States. In June 1963 an agreement was signed between the Israeli Ministry of Commerce and Industry and representatives of film-making establishments in Hollywood for the establishment of large-scale film production in Israel.

During 1967 Israeli film makers produced seven full-length feature films, one of which, entitled *Three Days of a Child*, won critical acclaim at the Cannes Film Festival in France. In 1968 they produced 13 feature films and two feature-length documentaries, while foreign producers made an additional four feature films and two full-length documentaries. Documentaries and entertainment films on short subjects are produced in large quantities. The production of films emphasizing the artistic and cultural contributions of the country is subsidized by the Ministry of Education and Culture. During 1967 several short films were made on the Arab-Israeli hostilities of June 1967, some of them by foreign producers.

Approximately two newsreels are produced each week, and their showing in commercial film theaters is obligatory by law. A government-appointed board edits the films in order to determine the proportion of time to be allotted to the showing of domestic and international events.

Foreign films are popular and are imported in large numbers. In 1967 a total of 430 films were imported, of which 155 originated in the United States, 73 in Italy, 49 in France, 35 in the United Kingdom, 12 in the Soviet Union, 6 in Poland, 3 in Sweden, and 97 in other countries. Before release to the exhibitors, foreign films are censored for scenes featuring violence and other subjects affecting public morality.

Book Publishing and Libraries

Reading is a favorite recreation of Israelis. In 1967, 1,471 new book titles were published. Most of them were literary works, school texts, and works in the humanities, religion, and science.

The demand for foreign translations is great. In 1965, 499 titles were translated, mostly from English, Russian, French, and German. Book sales averaging from 2,000 to 5,000 copies are customary; those selling more than 6,000 copies are regarded as bestsellers.

There are about 40 major book publishers in Tel Aviv and Jerusalem. The best known are the United Hebrew Book Publishers of Israel, located in Tel Aviv, and the Bialik Institute in Jerusalem. The latter is a nonprofit organization, noted for publishing classical works, encyclopedias, and books on archaeology, art, history, religion, and children's literature. There is also an Arabic Publishing House, operated by the Histadrut.

In 1967 there were about 1,000 libraries with holdings of about 8 million volumes. The total included libraries of institutions of higher learning, primary and secondary school libraries, and public libraries in urban and rural settlements. Largest among them is the National Library of the Hebrew University in Jerusalem, with holdings exceeding 1.5 million volumes.

In 1968 government statistics show that there was a total of 206 public libraries in urban settlements, visited by a total of 177,000 readers. Holdings per library averaged 9,880 volumes, featuring titles on religion, agriculture, Zionism, and works on technology. The majority, or 149, of the libraries were located in urban settlements established before 1948. The rest were in the three largest cities, Tel Aviv, Jerusalem, and Haifa, in other towns and urban settlements, and in development towns established after 1948.

INFORMAL CHANNELS

Formal communications media are gradually reaching most areas of the country, but much information is transmitted by word of mouth. Israelis, especially youths, readily strike up conversations with each other or with visiting foreigners in public places, on the road, and on buses. Journeying to places of historical interest is popular among many groups, and news readily travels in the brisk traffic of visitors.

Communal living also facilitates the exchange of news. The mess-halls of kibbutz and moshav settlements and the meeting halls in the development townships are important centers for the transmission of news and rumors. Young people exchange opinions as they meet in youth organizations, scout groups, and hobby clubs. News and political commentary are subjects of lively discussions in the urban coffeehouses visited daily by many men and women.

Arabs rely heavily on word-of-mouth for news and information, but many of them also listen regularly to radio and television broadcasts. News communicated by the head of the family often is given credence even though it may be at variance with that originating in one of the formal media.

DOMESTIC INFORMATION PROGRAMS

The Central Office of Information and the Government Press Office are the principal agencies for the dissemination of government information. In general the topics featured in lectures, films, and publications intended for domestic audiences and readers are designed to supplement general education, to impart training in civics, to facilitate communication between groups of varying cultural backgrounds, and to explain Israel's role in the Middle Eastern conflict.

The Central Office of Information organizes lecture series and documentary film showings and disseminates special publications. Many of the programs and publications are intended for new immigrants. Residents of collective agricultural settlements and of new development townships are among the main target audiences. Lectures held for these groups are often presented in conjunction with theater, musical, and folk performances. Special information programs are offered in towns and villages inhabited by Arabs.

The Film Service of the Central Office of Information produces documentary films and distributes them to government agencies, civic organizations, and to Israeli representatives abroad. Commercial distribution of these films on a worldwide basis was initiated in 1967. Subjects featured in the educational documentaries of the Film Service during the same year included Israel's fauna and flora, driver education, accident prevention, water and soil research, and the role of government bonds. Other films dealt with progress in public housing and irrigation projects and with employment conditions.

Information material presented by the Government Press Office and by the Central Office of Information in 1968 focused mainly on the Arab-Israeli hostilities of June 1967. A full-length documentary film was devoted to the origins and aftermath of that war. A pamphlet entitled *Know What to Answer*, designed to meet questions and criticism relating to Israel's policies in its conflict with the Arab world, was issued to schoolteachers, lecturers, and to personnel traveling abroad. A standard lecturer's kit on the same subject included materials illustrating the Israeli position. Many publications of the Government Press Office are intended for foreign readers.

Foreign correspondents receive translations of communiques by government officials as well as an illustrated fortnightly news publication distributed by the office. Pamphlets and annual publications in English and French present the history of the state of Israel; its social and economic progress since 1948; and Israeli cultural, artistic, and scientific achievements. Among these are *Facts About Israel*, an illustrated booklet, and the *Israel Government Yearbook*, both published annually in English; *Faites et Chiffres* (Facts and Figures) is published annually in French. In addition, there are various bilingual statistical publications, including the annual *Statistical Abstract of Israel* and the monthly *Statistical Bulletin of Israel*, published both in Hebrew and English by the Central Bureau of Statistics.

Kol Israel broadcasts directed at foreign audiences are beamed on Network C on shortwave for 40 hours a week on 9009, 9725, and 7189 kilocycles. Programs in French, English, Hungarian, Rumanian, Russian, Yiddish, Ladino, and Moghrabi to Europe and to North and South Africa are broadcast between 6:30 A.M. and 8:45 A.M. and between 5:30 P.M. and 12:00 P.M. A special program entitled "This is Israel" is taped and sent weekly to the United States and Canada, where it is broadcast by certain radio stations to Jewish audiences. Kol Israel also has a Transcription Service that sends taped radio programs, including music, lectures, and commentary to broadcasting stations in Europe, North and South America, Australia, Africa, and Asia. The tapes are in French, English, Spanish, Portuguese, Yiddish, and Hebrew.

The Arabic service of the domestic Network D also reaches Arab audiences outside Israel. The programs, beamed for 14¼ hours a day in both the Palestinian and Egyptian dialects, include newscasts, music, and special features entitled "Falsehood and Truth," "Spot Reactions," and "Weekly Talk in Spoken Iraqi."

FOREIGN GOVERNMENT INFORMATION PROGRAMS

Information about the United States is available through the offices of the United States Information Service in Tel Aviv. It has a 32,000-volume library in Tel Aviv, with an 8,000-volume branch in Jerusalem. Film shows and lectures are offered, and exhibitions are held under its auspices. It produces information material that is placed regularly in the Israeli media. News items are supplied to ITIM and to the major newspapers; Kol Israel receives taped broadcasts, and documentary films are shown in many of the theaters. In addition to presentations of events in the United States, the United States Information Service material also includes information and commentary on the activities of the United Nations. Information on the United States and the free world is also available through the

English-language broadcasts of the Voice of America, directed at countries of the Middle East.

The United Kingdom and France supply cultural information through the British Council and the Alliance Française, respectively. The British Council has library services in Tel Aviv, Haifa, and Jerusalem. It offers language courses, arranges lectures by British authors and scientists, and secures scholarships to British universities for qualified candidates. The Alliance Française offers French-language instruction and also cooperates with the school system in organizing French-language teaching programs.

In 1968 Arabs in Israel could listen to the Palestinian Program of the Voice of Arabs, broadcast by the United Arab Republic. It was transmitted daily from 6:00 A.M. to 8:00 A.M. and from 2:00 P.M. to 3:00 P.M. on shortwave. Also directed toward Israel were the Voice of Al Fatah broadcasts by the Arab commando organization. Featuring mainly accounts of guerrilla activities against Israel and political commentary on the Arab-Israeli conflict, Al Fatah broadcasts began daily at 7:29 P.M. on the same medium wavelengths as Radio Cairo's Middle East Program. Broadcasts of the Palestine Liberation Organization, composed maily of Palestinian refugees, also originated in the United Arab Republic.

In 1968 Communist information efforts had relatively little impact because of the Soviet Union's pro-Arab stand in the conflict between the Arab countries and Israel. Communist diplomatic missions to Israel (those of Bulgaria, Rumania, Hungary, Yugoslavia, Czechosolvakia, Poland, and the Soviet Union) were important centers for the dissemination of Communist information, but these missions (except for that of Rumania) were closed after the outbreak of the Arab-Israeli hostilities of June 1967. Information is lacking regarding the status of friendship societies maintained by some of these countries in Israel before June 1967. Rumania, which has not joined the Soviet Union and the other countries of the Communist bloc in condemning Israel, retained its legation in Tel Aviv. A scientific exchange agreement between Israel and Rumania also remained in force, and the Rumanian-Israeli Friendship Society continued to be active.

The Soviet Union broadcasts 7 hours a week in Hebrew and Yiddish to Israeli audiences. Hungarian language broadcasts of Hungary's Radio Budapest are also broadcast into the area for ten and a half hours a week.

CHAPTER 17
POLITICAL VALUES AND ATTITUDES

Intensive introspection and self-criticism concerning national identity and direction were widespread among articulate elements of Israeli society preceding the Six-Day War of June 1967. The military victories of that war, however, confirmed and strengthened national commitment to the state and brought about a new sense of unity and confidence.

Within the society the political values and attitudes of the younger generation and of the growing Sephardic population were not identical with the concepts of the original socialist-Zionist-Kibbutz ideology. This traditional ideology was seen to be losing relevance or becoming transformed in meaning but continued to be used as the ritual language of the still powerful, Ashkenazic leadership elite.

Urbanization and industrialization became dominant in the social and economic life in contrast to the older dedication to agriculture and pioneering proclaimed in kibbutz ideology. Israeli nationalism appeared to be supplanting Zionism and Judaism as a more relevant basic ideology. Symbols and tokens of Zionism and Judaism were, in effect, adapted by the state and have become symbols of nationalism. Although a consensus of attitude on certain fundamental questions regarding the state and its institutions was yet to emerge and become translated into political action, the value of the state itself was almost unanimously unquestioned by the Jewish population of Israel.

Because of the passage of time and the patterns of immigration and natural population increase, determinitive attitude groups consisted of the younger, native-born (Sabra) generation and the Sephardic population, which together constituted a growing majority of the general population. The younger generation showed in its political attitudes a strong nationalism, a trend away from socialism in general and Zionist socialism in particular, and a preference for Western education and modes of life. Among the older Sephardim, typical attitudes had been formed under patterns of authoritarian, traditional Middle Eastern societies in state, kin group, and family; and these attitudes also were not congenial with socialism or hard-line political Zionism.

The long-entrenched MAPAI-Histadrut (see Glossary) power

combination, managed by an older Eastern European elite leadership, often acted pragmatically but always spoke in the ritual language of Zionist ideology. The middle generation succeeding to power was confronted with an array of internal and external security problems. In meeting these problems leaders recognized that the successor leadership would necessarily have to find its base of political support among emerging population groups, certain to become dominant sooner or later, whose attitudes differed, at least in part, from the traditional official ideology of the state.

POLITICAL VALUES HELD BY THE SOCIETY

Basic common values held by the society include a general sense of respect for law, for the rights of man, and for education. The Israeli Proclamation of Independence of May 14, 1948 dedicated the state to the ideals of liberty, justice, and peace "as envisioned by the Prophets of Israel;" to equality of social and political rights; to freedom of religion, conscience, language, education, and culture. It also asserted the common right to "a life of dignity, freedom, and honest toil." These commitments and principles have wide acceptance, being reinforced by the ancient Jewish Orthodox concept of life ordered by law, the Jewish cultural tradition of regard for learning, and by pragmatic experience in the national life.

At the founding of the state, the Zionist leadership and the Jewish population of Palestine that they represented were not confronted with a vacuum of political ideology. The principles of the Proclamation of Independence (always seen in the context of a Jewish state), the doctrines of socialist Zionism, and the initial implementing forms of government already had acceptance through the long background years of organization, indoctrination, and effort by the World Zionist Organization and the Jewish Agency (see ch. 3, Historical Setting). The system survived and succeeded; and later immigrants were encompassed within it, although not always without stress.

Despite internal political and social cleavages, the Jewish majority population is characterized by a strong dedication to the state itself and to its general form as a parliamentary democracy. Two exceptions may be noted to this basic unity. First, a small but sometimes violent fringe group of the Orthodox Jewish Community, itself a minority, which is known as Neturei Karta (Custodians of the Town) and located in Jerusalem, holds that the state itself is spurious because it did not come about through messianic intervention. Second, strict doctrinal Communists within the MAKI and RAKAH parties (see Glossary) would materially alter the form and alignments of the state. Neither of these extreme elements has a substantial following nor wields significant power. The Arab

240

Muslim, Christian, Druze, and Circassian minorities within pre-June 1967 Israel do not manifest the same dedication to the state as the Jewish Population; neither, however, have they constituted a major source of active disaffection and civil disturbance (see ch. 5, Ethnic Groups and Languages; ch. 14, Political Dynamics).

National pride in the state and its achievements is high. The armed forces, regarded as the nonpolitical guardians of the country, are held in high esteem, based on their performance and victories in 1948 and 1956 and magnified in 1967. This esteem further derives from the close identification of the people with the armed forces through national conscription and reliance on the reserve system and through the civic action role of the forces (see ch. 26, The Armed Forces). Similarly, the national police force enjoys public confidence. In the earlier years of the state, immigrants and Sabras tended by habit to look upon the police as representatives of oppression rather than as fellow citizens. This reaction, however, was overcome by police efficiency functioning under law and by growth of national consciousness and confidence in the law of the new state (see ch. 27, Public Order and Internal Security).

Dedication to the state, national pride in accomplishments, memories of heroic episodes and efforts in both the ancient and recent past, a general sense of mutual, although not precisely defined, Jewishness, a mutual realization of danger shared in the face of continued hostilities, and a sense that for the Israeli society at large there is no alternative to the state—all are factors contributing to a common determination to survive. Symbols and tokens from the Jewish past, the Zionist tradition, and Israeli history have been adopted by the state, as seen in the flag and national anthem, in military insignia, and in public buildings, monuments, memorials, and ceremonies (see ch. 14, Political Dynamics). Along with the strength of nationalism and confidence in military and technical prowess, however, extensive attitude surveys among the Israeli population both at large and in the kibbutzim have shown a strong desire for peace and settlement with the Arab states (see table 17).

Commonly held values among the Jewish population thus include endorsement of the state, national pride, and a desire for peace, counterbalanced by an intense, deep-seated determination to survive politically as a nation. Also included is a widespread perception of a basic political dilemma concerning the nature of the state and definition of the national identity. The founders of Israel were primarily secular Zionists, among them David Ben-Gurion, former prime minister. Nevertheless, while proclaiming principles of equal opportunity and full political equality, they also proclaimed that Israel was to be a "Jewish state." Consequently, the ethic of equality competes with the ethic of a Jewish state.

Table 17. Public Attitudes in Israel, 1962

Public Attitudes	General Sample (percent)[1]	Kibbutz Sample (percent)[2]
Hopes Expressed for the Nation[3]:		
Peace with the Arabs	55	73
Peace, general	16	19
Population increase	36	52
Technological advance	47	59
Improve living standard	34	40
Military strength	14	8
Maintain independence	18	33
National unity	8	22
Fears Expressed for the Nation[3]:		
War with Arabs	49	56
War, general	30	37
Population problems	10	20
No technological advance	9	17
No improved living standard	12	15
Military weakness	5	6
Lose independence	9	23
National disunity	6	16

[1] Number of persons interviewed, 1,170; spread by age, sex, income, education, and residence.

[2] Number of persons interviewed, 300; kibbutz members from 10 kibbutzim; spread by age, sex, and education.

[3] Data from 1962, not additive, respondents could express multiple attitudes.

Source: Adapted from Hadley Cantril, *The Pattern of Human Concerns*, 1965.

How this problem was to be resolved and the definition of what was meant by a Jewish state in view of the rapidly growing Arab minority in pre-1967 Israel, as well as the lands and people of the occupied areas, was not yet clear in 1969. An important internal effect of the successes in the Six-Day War of June 1967 was the upsurge in confidence of the people in themselves and the state. From the Israeli viewpoint the problem of whether there would be a national identity was resolved in the affirmative; the problem of what it would be, the old dilemma of commitment to a Jewish state, and the question of "Who is a Jew?" remained to be determined within the overall protective aegis of nationalism (see ch. 13, The Governmental System).

DEGREE AND MEANS OF POLITICAL INVOLVEMENT

National political life is active, highly organized, and controlled by the long-established system of multiple political parties (see ch. 14, Political Dynamics). This strong, pervasive party system encompasses well-disciplined political structures controlled from the top that may be regarded not only as vote-getting organizations but also as ideological movement and primary subculture groups. In casting his vote the Israeli citizen, consequently, expresses at least ostensibly his political values and attitudes rather than support for individual personalities.

Between elections, political matters are dealt with by party structures and party consensus. Party membership is high. Individual expression of values and attitudes, to be effective, typically has had to move through party channels, and attainment of leadership roles has depended upon working up through a long period of party apprenticeship. The preeminence of the party system is maintained by Israeli political institutional forms, including party representation by proportional vote received, the voting for lists of party candidates rather than individuals (split-ticket voting or individual designation is not possible), and the national constituency concept under which each party list stands for the entire country.

In consequence the Israeli electorate, although politically conscious, expresses itself primarily at the national elections normally held every 4 years. Meanwhile values and attitudes are expressed through party channels. A notable exception to this established and essentially conservative form occurred prior to the Six-Day War of June 1967 when popular opinion, expressed through the press and public media, caused the appointment of Moshe Dayan as minister of defense—an action not initiated by the prime minister or by consensus of the party coalition in power.

THE TRADITIONAL IDEOLOGY AND POWER ELITE

Informed observers have estimated that in 1935, 40 percent of the world's Jews lived in Eastern Europe and 30 percent in the Americas, but that in 1880 these figures had been 75 percent in Eastern Europe, especially Czarist Russia, and only 3 percent in the Americas. At this time the Eastern European populist-socialist movements aimed at social justice, elimination of classes in the society, and common ownership of means of production were gaining strength. Simultaneously but separately a European impetus for Jewish enlightenment and emancipation developed. Precursors of Zionism appeared in the first pioneering Jewish agricultural settlement, set up in Palestine in 1878, and in the Russian Leo Pinsker's pamphlet *Auto-Emancipation* of 1882 (see ch. 3, Historical Setting).

In the Jewish ghettoes of the Russian Pale of Settlement, existing under severe oppressive discrimination and in constant danger of destructive pogroms, the concepts of socialism seemed to offer to many Russian Jewish thinkers and leaders political values that could improve the Jewish condition. Their experience with Russian populists, however, did not provide convincing proof that the Russian socialist movement (which culminated in the Bolshevik victory of 1917) included Jews, as such, in its "classless society." Neither did they accept the Western European trend to emancipation and assimilation of Jews in their countries of residence as a genuine solution.

In Western Europe Theodor Herzl also concluded, after the Dreyfus trial of 1894 in Paris, that antisemitism was so deeply rooted in the society that he knew that Jews could not live in peace by assimilation. He described the problem, not primarily as religious or social, but as a secular, political problem of international magnitude, with the true solution seen in terms of Jewish nationalism in a national homeland. Herzl provided the inspiration and dynamism that brought about the World Zionist Organization; but he and Chaim Weizmann after him remained essentially nationalists, operating by diplomacy and nonviolent political means (see ch. 3, Historical Setting).

In Eastern Europe, especially in Russia, three trends characterized the life of Jewish people at the close of the 19th century: the static condition of those who remained behind; the trend of emigration to the Americas; and the Zionist trend of Eastern European "practicals" who assumed the dominating role in the World Zionist Organization and promoted the successive waves of *aliyah* to Palestine, especially the key Second Aliyah of 1904–14 and the Third commencing in 1920. The Russian Zionist leadership brought into the movement the values and methodology of socialism, thus forming a synthesis that was to provide the founding ideology of Israel. It also provided a powerful implementing elite, which included David Ben-Gurion, Itzhak Ben-Zvi, Moshe Sharett, Levi Eshkol, and Golda Meir, who exercised paramount influence from the earliest days to the present.

This synthesis was a compound of nationalism and socialism in a Jewish society to be established in a land identified by a cultural and religious tradition as being ancestral to the Jews, that is, in Palestine. Associated with this synthesized ideology was the objective of elevating the pride and dignity of the Jew through a secure environment in which the status or personality-image of the Jew as a landless merchant, mendicant peddler, or soft intellectual might be changed by hard work. Also associated was the attitude that life is serious, and that true ideological values could not be realized in the pursuit of pleasure or of selfish self-aggrandizement.

In Israel national politics became party politics conducted by a political elite who, although frequently acting pragmatically, spoke and politicized the nation with a value system expressed in the ritual ideological language of socialist Zionism. The communal agricultural settlement called the kibbutz became the personification of this ideology and was considered to exemplify its values in purest form.

The socialist-Zionist-kibbutz ideology, or value system, may be expressed in terms of ten fundamental themes. Four of these are essentially socialist in nature: mutual responsibility in society under the principle of "from each according to his ability, to each according to his needs"; equality in society without difference in privilege because of material possession; abolition of private ownership of the means of production; and the idea that man's character is formed by society and that, in consequence, society encompasses and is above the individual. Two themes express both socialist and Zionist-nationalist concepts: well-to-do Jews in the Diaspora should form the base of the state in Israel, and the image of the Jews must be that of a laboring nation. Related to the latter was the distinctively Zionist corollary theme that the Jewish laboring nation should be developed in an agricultural framework, that is, in the kibbutz. Zionism as a political value is a nationalism uniquely characterized by two further themes: the Jews of the world constitute not only a religion but a nationality, and the Jews of the world should immigrate to Israel.

Finally there is an overall motivating concept in the socialist-Zionist-kibbutz ideology holding that attainment of these values will provide an example of right action to the rest of mankind, which should adopt them. Ideological spokesmen indicate that of these 10 principles the socialist values are those deserving universal acceptance; the entire ideology is to regulate a peaceful and prosperous life for the Jewish people and the state of Israel. This final theme, although it was enunciated in a secular context, was also compatible with the traditional Jewish messianic belief in the ultimate perfectability of human society in relation to God through the example and agency of a select, or covenanted people (see ch. 3, Historical Setting).

None of these principles has at any time been unanimously accepted or fully realized in the political life of Israel; interpretation and implementation have been relative to changing times and conditions and to pragmatic situations. The hierarchy of the 10 traditionally respected ideological values, however, has provided a pattern of basic guidance and only one element—the primacy of agriculture —has undergone serious change, as shown in the government policy of shifting emphasis from agriculture to industry (see ch. 21, Industry; ch. 24, Foreign Economic Relations). The original socialist-Zionist-kibbutz values remain identifiable, especially governing the style if not the substance of action, and forming a ritual language in which debate is conducted or pronouncements are made by the political elite. The intensity of demonstrated general acceptance of the original ideology, however, had declined by 1960. In 1968 only about 3.5 percent of the Jewish population lived in kibbutzim and only about 8.8 percent in kibbutzim and moshavim combined. The kibbutz, however, continued to be the citadel of original ideology and, as shown in political attitude surveys, kibbutz inhabitants were more conscious of and concerned with the old ideological socialist themes than the population at large.

PREEMINENCE OF THE MAPAI-HISTADRUT CONJUNCTION

Zionism before 1948 provided not only a political-nationalist ideology and an elite leadership subscribing to its principles but a socioeconomic structure and political machine as well. The commitment of the Eastern European leadership to labor-socialism brought forth the Histadrut (General Federation of Labor) in 1920 and the MAPAI party (see Glossary) in 1930; Ben-Gurion was the first secretary general of Histadrut, as well as being leader of MAPAI until 1965. Since MAPAI as a party has always been dominant both in government and in Histadrut, the expression of political values by MAPAI has greatly influenced the political consciousness of the public and has tended to preserve the ideology, perpetuate a power structure, and to set the tone of the state (see ch. 14, Political Dynamics; ch. 22, Labor).

From the start this pervasive influence has been reinforced by the absence of challenges from coup groups, personality cults, or military overthrow. In part, this stability has been the result of political institutional forms, such as party-list voting, and in part stems from the traditional ideological themes stressing mutual cooperation and the supremacy of society over the individual. This view has meant that egoistic self-interest, accomplishment aimed merely at personal advancement, and even assertive technological expertise have been regarded as ideologically and politically suspect.

Civilian control over the military was established early in the history of the state. The minister of defense of the prestate Jewish Agency was Ben-Gurion, who unified diverse military elements during and after the 1948 War of Independence, including disestablishment of the elite Palmach (see ch. 26, The Armed Forces). Thereafter, in his long tenure as prime minister and minister of defense, Ben-Gurion maintained between his office and the armed forces a relationship of harmony and mutual identification, but one in which he held final power. Other factors operating against military intrusion in politics have been the broad base of popular support for and identification with the armed forces cutting across all group and party lines and the character of the senior Israeli military leadership.

246

SPECTRUM OF IDEOLOGICAL VARIATIONS

The MAPAI party has been the leading single party in Israeli political life. It has not, however, at any time been a monopoly or even a majority party; the span of variation in political values and ideology is illustrated by the vigor of the multiparty system (see ch. 14, Political Dynamics). This system is historically derived from the continental European parliamentary tradition. As a base of reference the stated values of Israeli political parties, other than the religious and Arab non-Communist parties, may be arranged on the traditional left-right spectrum placing degrees of socialist values on the Left and capitalist free enterprise values on the Right with allowance for specific Israeli manifestations.

At the extreme left is the Communist party, known as MAKI, which is strongly socialist, pro-Histadrut, nonactivist with respect to the Arab states and the only anti-Western element on this scale. Of the long-established parties, MAPAM (see Glossary) is to the right of MAKI, and the socialist-oriented Ahdut Ha-Avoda (Unity of Labor, commonly called Ahdut) is to the right of MAPAM. At left of center, in terms of stated ideology and not of numbers, is MAPAI;· it is pro-West but committed to a moderate socialism. The ideology of RAFI (see Glossary) was identified with MAPAI, although more activist with respect to the Arab states and even less socialist. Next on the scale are the small parties of the center, such as the Independent Liberals and Independent Free Center, with the Liberal party next. At the far Right is Herut (Freedom party): pro-Western, anti-socialist, anti-Histadrut, and favoring a tough policy toward the Arab states to include retention of much of the occupied areas in order to reestablish the ancient boundaries of Eretz Yisrael (Land of Israel). New Force, a secular party list proposing a semitic ideology of peace between Hebrew and Arab nationalisms was advanced by the weekly magazine *Ha'olam Hazeh*. This party received enough support to win one seat in the Sixth Knesset. While neither religious nor Communist, it also cannot be placed in this scale (see ch. 14, Political Dynamics).

Utilizing this base of reference, election returns for the Fifth Knesset in 1961 can be examined as indicators of the apparent distribution of left-right continuum value acceptance among the electorate. The Fifth Knesset is used since the major parties were last identifiable in election returns at that time, prior to the later trend to merger and alliance as well as the split of the Communist movement into MAKI and RAKAH (see table 18). Based on these election returns, about 11.7 percent of the electorate ostensibly favored the stated values of the far-left positions held by MAKI and MAPAM; about 41.3 percent supported the Left and left of center area of Ahdut and MAPAI (including the element that would later became RAFI); and only about 27.4 percent supported the center to right-wing concepts of the Independent Liberals, Independent Free Center, Liberals, and Herut. For the Sixth Knesset elected in 1965, these same blocks of apparent value support were respectively 10 percent, 44.6 percent, and 25.1 percent.

Table 18. Political Value Spectrum and Apparent Support in Fifth Knesset, Israel, 1961

| Spectrum | | Fifth Knesset—1961 | |
value	Party [1]	Seats	Percent of valid vote
Far-left _____	MAKI _____	5	4.2
	MAPAM _____	9	7.5
Left _____	Ahdut Ha-Avoda _____	8	6.6
Left-of-center _____	MAPAI[2] _____	42	34.7
Center _____	Liberals _____	17	13.6
Right _____	Herut _____	17	13.8

[1] Religious parties and Arab parties not included.

[2] Includes minority that became RAFI in 1965.

Source: Adapted from Alan Arian, *Ideological Change in Israel*, 1968; and Israel, Ministry for Foreign Affairs, Information Division, *Facts About Israel*, 1968.

Between elections to the Fifth and Six Knessets, detailed attitude research studies of cross sections of the nonkibbutz Israeli adult population and of the elite revealed a different distribution. In response to value questions not specifically labeled "left," "center," or "right" and also not tied to political parties by name, 2.8 percent of the sample identified themselves with ideas and values characteristic of the far Left, only 28.6 percent with those of the Left and left of center, and 43.7 percent with the values of the Center and Right, with 24.9 percent being of mixed ideology or not identifiable by ideology. This research suggested to Israeli analysts that the older stated values of the socialist-Zionist ideology were becoming less relevant, that the electorate was in fact more at the Center or Right than the old ideology's precepts and that it voted by party organization and campaign influence or for pragmatic issues (or combinations of these) rather than for the traditional ritual positions (see table 19).

MAPAI in its membership became increasingly pluralistic as the state developed. In addition to its traditional support from the kibbutzim and urban workers it also attracted urban middle classes, Sephardic immigrants, and some businessmen. The broadening base and trend to larger secular parties was illustrated, despite the withdrawal of Ben-Gurion, by the association of MAPAI, with Ahdut in 1965. This association became known as the Alignment and in 1968 was followed by formation of the Israel Labor party made up of the Alignment and RAFI. This action in turn was followed by the alliance between the Israel Labor party and MAPAM in 1969 (see ch. 14, Political Dynamics). This trend was apparent also in the 1965 GAHAL (see Glossary) alliance of the Liberal and right-wing Herut parties.

Table 19. *Political Value Spectrum and Popular Sample Analysis, Israel, 1962 and 1964*

(percentages)

Spectrum value [1]	General Sample [2]	Elite Sample [3]	Merged Sample [4]
Far-left	2.0	6.0	2.8
Left	7.7	3.0	6.9
Left-of-center	22.4	18.0	21.7
Center	23.4	34.8	25.2
Right	18.5	18.5	18.5
Mixed or nonideological	26.0	19.7	24.9

[1] Questionnaire containing ideological questions not specifically labeled as Left or Right or by party name.

[2] Number of persons interviewed, 1,170; nonkibbutz persons spread by age, sex, income, education and residence, 1962.

[3] Number of persons interviewed, 233; elite spread between Knesset members, civil servants, and university students, 1964.

[4] Merged sample is arithmetic combination of general and elite samples.

Source: Adapted from Alan Arian, *Ideological Change in Israel*, 1968.

Distinguishing political values held by adherents of the religious parties are uniquely Israeli, being identified with the Jewish religion and not readily placed in the secular spectrum. They are, however, characterized by degrees of orthodoxy. Arab political values, other than Communist, as shown by their parties within pre-1967 Israel, also cannot validly be placed in the secular Israeli scale, since this element of the population is considered to remain indifferent if not hostile to Israel. For example, the national symbology, both religious- and secular-based, is either culturally meaningless to the Arabs or an active irritant.

DIFFERENTIATION OF ATTITUDE GROUPS

The elder generation in Israel, represented by such figures as Ben-Gurion and the late Levi Eshkol, survives from the Yishuv, or pre-state Jewish community in Palestine. Cultural homogeneity outweighed diversity among the Yishuv; their life style was predominantly European, and their dominant ideology, particularly among the critical elite, was pioneering socialist Zionism. There was no comparable competing ideology. In their view mere accomplishment without reference to a governing ideological framework was not only unsound but wrong. Their expressed attitude was one of re-

249

gret that their grandchildren did not appear to have a comparable creed or set of ideological beliefs regarding Israel.

In the middle generation, characterized by Abba Eban and native-born leaders, such as Moshe Dayan, Yigal Allon, and Yitzhak Rabin, long apprenticeships in public life had been served in the two decades of statehood or even longer as they rose to positions of high influence (see ch. 18, Biographies of Selected Key Personalities). Thoroughly familiar with the older generation's ideology, their views and methodology were influenced by their own experience and changing conditions. As the middle generation succeeded to power, it was equally inevitable that the people they would lead and who would furnish their base of political support would be from the young Sabra generation, about 300,000 of whom became eligible to vote in a Knesset election for the first time in 1969.

The main political attitude, or governing rationale, of the young generation prior to the Seventh Knesset elections was not definitely established except in the one essential and demonstrated element of loyalty to the state. Israeli spokesmen affirmed, and these views were supported by social research studies, that the younger generation's concept of the state was seen in terms of self-reliant nationalism, that the tenets of socialist Zionism and Orthodox Judaism as well had to them decreasing motivational appeal, and they would favor a strong, industrialized, capitalist, Western-style, middle-class society as the national norm; in short, on the traditional European spectrum their ideology would be of the Center or right wing. Regarding the old political value attachment to Diaspora Jews, Israeli youth had appeared to be less conscious than their elders of this concept. The strong support from abroad during the period of the Six-Day War of June 1967, hailed by Levi Eshkol as the "renewal of our covenant with world Jewry," revived this issue. Jewish immigration was, in any event, one of the nationalist rather than socialist themes of the traditional ideology.

After statehood the heavy influx of Sephardic Jews from North Africa and the Middle East produced an attitude group whose background differed sharply from that of the European, socialist-Zionist values of the Yishuv. Although their skill and educational levels were lower than those of European background, their natural increase was greater, and by 1969 Sephardic immigrants and their descendants in the Israeli population outnumbered Ashkenazic immigrants and their descendants (see ch. 4, Population). The older Sephardim were, in general, from authoritarian, tradition-organized societies in which the European left-wing political value spectrum had scant practical relevance. They were not familiar with the tenets of secular socialist-Zionism and showed little interest in it; they were accustomed to individuality and to strong personality leader-

250

ship in the patriarchal family or kin group rather than to the collective leadership and subordination of the individual postulated in socialist ideology. These immigrants, nevertheless, as shown in research studies, were basically committed to the Jewish homeland as their proper place despite those themes in the state ideology that were unfamiliar and foreign to them.

In terms of education the level in the Sephardic background rose steadily but slowly. In 1966, 59 percent of university and college undergraduates were Israeli born, 30 percent were born in Europe, and only 10 percent in Africa or the Middle East. Among the native-born 59 percent, only 4 percent were of Sephardic background.

In consequence leadership in the society was broadly projected to remain in the hands of Israelis of Western background, represented and supported by a Jewish population mainly from a North African-Middle Eastern background. The political values of those with Sephardic background differed from the apparent emerging values of Israeli youth, but were compatible at least to the extent of a common commitment to the nation and a nonidentification with the doctinaire socialist themes of the founding Zionist ideology.

Those in the Israeli population for whom Jewish religious principles formed the main frame of value reference accounted for about 15 percent of the electorate, an apparent proportion that was established early in the life of the state and has varied little since then. They constitute an attitude group in national political life, expressing their values through their political parties and in the cabinet by a minister of religious affairs (see ch. 13, The Governmental System; ch. 14, Political Dynamics). Among this group the adherents of the moderate National Religious party outnumbered the strictly orthodox by two to one. This evidence and the party's record of working with and frequently influencing the dominant MAPAI coalitions suggested that Israel's Jews for whom religion is important may increasingly have found satisfactory religious values in more moderate forms of observance and in accommodation with a secular society. Some Israeli spokesmen have estimated that the supporters of the ancient, severely orthodox forms may, by the attrition of time, become remnant groups (see ch. 11, Religion). Public resistance to imposition of ultraorthodox life patterns is extensive, as shown by the League for Prevention of Religious Discrimination, a secularist organization that by 1966 had become a significant private interest group. As expressed by the secular Sabra of the young generation, in what both old Zionist and orthodox representatives for different reasons deprecate as short-sighted pragmatism, the Sabra is an Israeli; this encompasses Jewishness and he has no "Jewish problem."

The Arab minority, about 300,000 in pre-1967 Israel, had a rate of natural increase in 1967 of about 2.5 times that of the Jewish

251

sector (see ch. 4, Population). Arab attitudes were seen as local and passive or enigmatic but potentially hostile on the whole. Social and political connections with Arabs in adjoining states became attenuated after the separation in 1948 when Israel was established. Widespread support for Arab guerrilla movements had not been identified among the Arabs of pre-1967 Israel, and individual instances of collaboration were subject to prosecution and heavy penalties. These Arabs remained cognizant of Arab political values, however, as shown by their attention to radio and television broadcasts from the surrounding Arab states. A demographic report by the Central Bureau of Statistics in 1967 prior to the Six-Day War showed that a statistical projection of 1966 birth rates would result in an Israel with an Arab majority by the year 2000. Government leaders have asserted that this rate of increase and the basic fact that this population group remains Arab may pose questions of security and political attitudes of particular importance.

All attitude groups, regardless of political party, were confronted with internal value issues regarding the identity of the state, the socialist-capitalist nature of the political and economic life, and the secular versus religious question. Externally, attitude groups faced the critical problems of security, of long-term policy for the occupied areas and, growing from that policy, of settlement and peace with the Arabs.

TRENDS IN ATTITUDE PATTERNS

The Six-Day War of June 1967 has demonstrated to the older generation that the younger generation could be counted upon in emergency. Similar experiences, shared danger, and sacrifice have formed a bridge of mutual respect between generations. The strength and continued viability of the basic national commitment to the state and its survival, in whatever manner that state might finally be defined, outweighed differences of age, ethnic background, and political details.

In a nation faced with a continuing security problem but becoming increasingly industrialized, urbanized, and economically successful, the value system of socialist-Zionist-kibbutz ideology espoused by the founding East European leadership elite remained identifiable. It was, however, less intensely perceived as relevant by the younger generation in a society of which a majority were of Middle Eastern and North African backgrounds not identified with the pioneering ethic of the kibbutz. Educational and economic trends indicated that the general patterns of life would be European in form. In the middle generation of Israeli leadership, debate might be conducted in the familiar ritual language of the old ideology, but attitudes were influenced by pragmatic requirements in changed circumstances to maintain and improve the state rather than to found it.

Political change occurred slowly (see ch. 14, Political Dynamics). The trend in determinant values and attitudes, however, appeared to be in the direction of Israeli nationalism in an increasingly secular, Western-style state of fewer but larger political parties and away from the original socialist-Zionist-kibbutz ideology.

CHAPTER 18

BIOGRAPHIES OF SELECTED KEY PERSONALITIES

The country's topmost positions in the political, governmental, military, financial, and literary fields include 12 outstanding leaders. In 1969 they ranged in age from 44 to 83; half of them were 60 years old or older and only two were under 50. Seven were born in Eastern Europe (in Poland or in Czarist Russia), one in Yuogslavia, another in South Africa, and three in Palestine. At an early age all were engaged in various forms of Jewish organizational activities, at or near their place of residence, and by the beginning of World War II all, except one, had moved to Palestine where their efforts in furtherance of unified Jewish action were intensified.

AGNON, Shmuel Yosef. Leading Hebrew author and the only Israeli Nobel Literature Prize winner.

Born on July 17, 1888, at Buczacz (Bochatz), in Galicia, then a province in the Austro-Hungarian Empire, later a part of southern Poland and the Soviet Ukraine. He is descended, through his father, from a long line of Talmudic scholars. Received his early education at a religious school and a teachers' seminary. Moved to Palestine in 1907.

His first works were verses written in Hebrew and Yiddish at his birthplace but published in Yiddish in 1908. His later volumes, however, were customarily written and published in Hebrew.

In 1913 he went to Berlin to study and resided there until 1924. Meanwhile, in 1919, he married Esther Marx. They have a son and a daughter. Except for a few brief periods of travel, including a tour of Eastern Europe between 1929 and 1932, he has continued to reside in Jerusalem.

A prolific writer, he is the author of more than a dozen books. In addition he has contributed many short articles to newspapers and periodicals, and his stories have been translated into as many as 16 languages. He has not become actively involved in governmental programs, but his published and orally expressed ideas are respected by Israeli leaders in all fields. His works, attaining the status of classics in Israel, are required reading in the schools and universities. In 1935 he became the first recipient of the Bialik Prize for Literature, named after Chaim Nachman Bialik, an earlier Hebrew literary personality. Besides receiving the Bialik Prize on several subsequent occasions, he was awarded the Nobel Prize for Literature on October 20, 1966, for his "profoundly characteristic and narrative art with motifs from the life of the Jewish people."

Among his best-known books are *The Bridal Canopy*, appearing in 1935; *In the Heart of the Seas*, published in 1947, and *Days of Awe*, in 1948. Later works include *Betrothed*, an autobiographical account; *You Have Seen*, a collection of writings on the Divine revelation at Mount Sinai; particularly well known is *A Guest in the Night*, which is the story of a visit to the war-ruined town of his childhood. Another important work, *Only Yesterday*, is a philosophic introduction to the problems and thoughts of immigrant Jews in the post-World War I period.

Critics assert that his style bridges the gap between traditional Hebrew and European literature. An Orthodox Jew, his novels draw liberally on Biblical and Talmudic stories, and his mysterious plots, some spiced with earthy humor, appeal particularly to young readers among Israeli Orthodox religious groups. Many of his stories are based on his knowledge of Jewish life in Eastern Europe or in Palestine. His large library contains an excellent collection of literary works of the 17th, 18th, and 19th centuries dealing with Palestine.

ALLON, Yigal. Deputy prime minister and concurrently minister for immigrant absorption since July 1, 1968.

Born on October 10, 1918, in a village of southern Galilee. He is the youngest son of five brothers and two sisters. His father, an immigrant from Russia and a carpenter who took up farming, organized the neighboring youths, including his young son, into a group that guarded their fields at night. Early education was received at the Kadoury Agricultural School, 12 miles southeast of Haifa; later he attended the University of Oxford, the London School of Economics, and the Hebrew University of Jerusalem. He speaks Hebrew, English, and Arabic learned from Arab companions living near his farm. Married Ruth Appesdorf, and they have three children. He became a founding member of Kibbutz Ginnosar on the western shore of Lake Tiberias.

Began serving in the Hagana at age 18 and took military training in school as an extra curricular activity. He soon was selected to attend noncommissioned officer classes and, in 1938, was admitted to a three-month officer's course. By the spring of 1939 he commanded a noncommissioned officer's school, where he introduced the use of live ammunition in field exercises and headed long marches with full packs.

In 1941 he helped establish the Palmach, shock troops of the

Hagana. By 1943 he was assistant commander of the Palmach and was its commander during operations against the Arab forces in 1948. In the same year he was also commander of Israeli forces in three areas—upper Galilee, Central Israel, and the Negev. After release from army service in 1950 with the rank of brigadier general, he continued his schooling at Hebrew University.

Since August 1955 he has been a member of the Knesset on the socialistic Ahdut Ha-Avodah (Unity of Labor) party list (see ch. 14, Political Dynamics). Became minister of labor in David Ben-Gurion's cabinet formed on November 2, 1961, and was reappointed to the same position on June 26, 1963, in the new cabinet headed by Prime Minister Levi Eshkol. After serving in this post until July 1, 1968, he was appointed deputy prime minister and concurrently minister for immigrant absorption.

His appointment to these new positions was widely regarded by Israeli political observers as a step towards his selection as successor to Prime Minister Eshkol, on competition with Minister of Defense Moshe Dayan, the prime minister's political opponent. In a dispute with the prime minister on policies regarding the occupied areas, he caused a cabinet crisis on January 11, 1969, by submitting a letter of resignation from four key ministerial committees. The prime minister did not respond to the letter and the crisis ended.

After the sudden death of Prime Minister Eshkol on February 26, 1969, he was selected by the cabinet to head the interim caretaker government as acting prime minister, and he served in this capacity until March 17, 1969, when Golda Meir accepted the nomination as prime minister from President Zalman Shazar. All former ministers retained their posts in the new government.

His political ability to attract a significant following is indicated by the wide support accorded his proposed policy announced in 1968, known as the Allon Plan, for establishing Israeli settlements in the sparsely populated occupied area immediately west of the Jordan River. The plan would leave the Arabs a corridor through Jericho, connecting Transjordan with heavily Arab parts of the West Bank, while providing Israel with outposts along the river for security purposes. He has published at least two books, *The Story of Palmach*, in 1951, and *Curtain of Sand*, in 1960.

BARLEV, Haim. Chief of staff, Israel Defense Forces, since January 1, 1968.

Born at Zagreb, Yugoslavia, November 16, 1924, as Haim Bratzlavsky. Moved to Palestine in 1932. Married Tamar Marshak, whom he met in the Palmach; they have one daughter, Zohar, and one son, Omri. Attended the Mikveh Yisrael Agricultural School in the southern outskirts of Tel Aviv. Subsequent education, academic and military, received at various periods during his career. He speaks Hebrew, English fairly well, and some French.

After completing his agricultural studies he joined the Palmach at age 18 and enrolled in a course for section leaders and, then, in one for platoon commanders. As a participant in the resistance movement, he headed the group that blew up the Allenby Bridge across the Jordan River in mid-1948.

After fighting against the Arab forces ceased late in 1948, he became an instructor in a battalion commander's course before being transferred to the staff of the Northern Command in the Haifa-Lake Tiberias area. While on these duties, he took leave at times to study academic subjects, obtaining sufficient credits to graduate from Hebrew University.

Appointed head of the training department of the Israeli Defense Forces, with the rank of colonel, early in 1956; in October, just before the Sinai Campaign started, he was placed in command of an armored unit. His troops were among the first to reach the Suez Canal. Within a year he was appointed commander of the Armor Corps and, in 1958, was promoted to brigadier general. As chief of the Armor Corps he expanded and reorganized it according to his concepts so that armored units could be used not only as an infantry supporting arm but also would be capable of thrusting forward with their own facilities. He asserts with pride that Israeli armor employment methods are purely Sabra (native-born), meaning they are applicable to local conditions and were developed without the aid of foreign experts.

Upon completing his service in the Armor Corps in 1961, he went to the United States, where, after two and a half years of study at Columbia University he received a master of arts degree in economics and administration (1963).

Returning to Israel, he was appointed director of operations of the Defense Forces, a post ranking just below that of chief of staff. In 1966 he went to Paris for further studies but was recalled in May 1967 to be appointed as deputy chief of staff on June 1, under Chief of Staff Major General Yitzhak Rabin. This appointment was made just before the outbreak of the Six-Day War of June 1967. On January 1, 1968, he became chief of staff, with rank of major (later lieutenant) general, succeeding Major General Rabin whose 4-year tenure had expired.

In addition to academic studies in the United States, London, and Paris, he has taken senior officer's courses in Great Britain and at the Ecole de Guerre, Paris. Later he completed a parachutist course and, in November 1968, he qualified for flying advanced types of airplane.

BEGIN, Menahem. Journalist and politician. Chairman of the

Central Council of the Herut (Freedom) party; minister without portfolio since June 1, 1967.

Born August 16, 1913, at Brest Litovsk, about 110 miles east of Warsaw. He is married and has one son and two daughters. Attended the Faculty of Law at Warsaw University. At an early age he joined a nationalist youth movement, called Betar, that later became associated with Herut and, by the outbreak of World War II, he headed this movement in Poland. Arrested in 1940 by the Soviet authorities, who detained him in Siberian concentration camps, until released in 1941. After joining the Polish army, he went to Israel in 1942 and took command of ETZEL (see Glossary). As commander he led the underground operations against the British Palestine Mandate Authority.

After proclamation of the state of Israel in 1948, he and his friends founded the Herut movement, which became a political party (see ch. 14, Political Dynamics). On fund-raising trips in the movement's behalf, he visited the United States later in 1948 and South America in 1949, and again in 1952. In addition to journalistic writings he continued to be active in Herut affairs and, by 1956, was chairman of the movement's Central Council. Reelected to the Knesset on August 15, 1961, and on April 26, 1965, he signed an electoral pact with Joseph Saphir, the Liberal party leader, to present a joint list of candidates to run in the November general elections and in the local elections, held simultaneously. The party combination, actually a political coalition group, became known by the acronym GAHAL (see Glossary).

The GAHAL coalition elected 26 members to the Knesset in 1965. Its program advocated that the head of state should be the head of the armed forces; that friendship with the German people should be discouraged; that return of the Arab refugees should be opposed; that free enterprise economy should be fostered; and government enterprise should be restricted to areas where private enterprise is unable to operate.

In Prime Minister Eshkol's new cabinet formed in January 1966, the government's principal opposition stemmed from GAHAL under the leadership of Begin. On June 1, 1967, he was taken into the government as minister without portfolio during the prewar crisis. Since 1967 he has been one of the leading advocates of retaining all the occupied territories. In Janury 1969 he was chairman of the Israel-France Association.

BEN-GURION, David. Veteran Israeli statesman.

Born on December 16, 1886, at Plonsk, 35 miles northwest of Warsaw, Poland. Married to Paula Munweis. They have one son and two daughters. Early education at a religious school, was supplemented (1912-1914) by law studies at the University of Istanbul. He speaks Hebrew, Yiddish, English, Turkish, Arabic, and Russian.

After actively promoting Zionism in Poland and Russia, he went to Palestine in 1906 and worked 1 year as an agricultural laborer and watchman in different parts of the country. Helped organize the Zionist Labor party in 1910. His persistent Zionist activities, after he returned from law studies in Istanbul, attracted attention of the Turkish authorities who exiled him from Palestine in 1915, when he went to the United States and founded the Hehalutz movement, designed to prepare Jewish youths for life in Palestine; he also recruited for the Jewish Legion.

After returning to Palestine in 1918, he served in the Jewish Legion until it was disbanded. At the end of World War I, he became interested in labor affairs and was a key figure in organizing Histadrut (Histadrut Ha'ovdim Haklalit—General Federation of Labor). Since 1920 he has been prominent in all its institutions and was its secretary-general from 1921 to 1935.

In the mid-1920's he drafted a basic ordinance called Knesset Yisrael (the Israeli Community), designed to serve as a representative governing institution. The draft, with certain changes, was officially adopted by the British Palestine Mandate Authority in 1928. Was a founder of MAPAI (see Glossary), the Israel Labor party, in 1930. From 1935 to 1948 he was chairman of the Jewish Agency Executive, became an aggressive personality in the Labor Section of the World Zionist Organization, and was generally regarded at home and abroad as Israel's predominant leader.

After the country statehood in 1948, he became head of the Provisional State Council, then the first prime minister and minister of defense and, on February 17, 1949, was entrusted with forming the country's first cabinet. He held these posts concurrently until December 1953, when he resigned and retired to Sede Boqer, 25 miles south of Beersheba in the Negev.

Returned to the cabinet as minister of defense late in February 1955, under Prime Minister Moshe Sharett. After the general elections of October 1955, was selected to form the coalition government, thus becoming the country's political leader during the Sinai Campaign in 1956. Formed a new cabinet in December 1959 and continued as prime minister until June 16, 1963, when he unexpectedly announced his resignation, stating that it was solely for personal reasons. Observers generally agreed that at age 76, he was seeking quietude and an opportunity to write and use his influence toward raising the educational standards of immigrants from backward countries.

His continued interest in political activities, however, soon became evident. On June 16, 1965, after a disagreement with Levi Eshkol, his successor as prime minister, he called upon his supporters to leave MAPAI, the party he helped to create and had headed for more than three decades. With the help of Moshe Dayan and other supporters he formed a new party, the RAFI (see Glossary). It won only 10 Knesset seats in the 1965 elections and initially placed no members in Prime Minister Levi Eshkol's new cabinet announced on January 10, 1966. In response to public pressure, however, Moshe Dayan was brought into the cabinet as minister of defense just before the Six-Day War of June 1967. On January 21, 1968, RAFI joined with the Alignment, an association of MAPAI and Ahdut Ha-Avoda, to form the Israeli Labor party. Ben-Gurion opposed the merger and was left to represent RAFI alone in the Knesset (see ch. 14, Political Dynamics).

During his tenure as prime minister, totaling approximately 12 years, his trips to foreign countries included two important extended visits, both in 1960. In March, on an unofficial trip to the United States, he delivered a lecture at Brandeis University, Waltham, Massachusetts, and received an honorary doctor of laws degree. He then went to Washington, D.C., and met with President Dwight D. Eisenhower and Vice President Richard M. Nixon; in New York he talked with United Nations (UN) leaders and with Doctor Konrad Adenauer, then chancellor of West Germany. On returning, he visited one week in London. In mid-June, on an informal 7-day visit to Paris, he talked with President Charles de Gaulle; this was followed by a week in Brussels and The Hague, where he was received by King Baudouin and Queen Juliana.

After leaving the office of prime minister, he made several semi-official trips. He attended the state funeral of Sir Winston Churchill, on January 29, 1965, in London. On April 25, 1967, he was an Israeli representative at the funeral of former chancellor, Doctor Konrad Adenauer, in Cologne. In May and June 1969, on a 5-week tour of South Africa, Latin America, and Europe, he met with Jewish communities and talked to Jewish youths about the importance of Hebrew education and urged them to "return to Israel." Known as a dynamic and vigorous political figure rather than an author, he also is particularly interested in philosophy and Buddhism. His writings are numerous and well known, however, and include *Palestine Historical, Geographical, and Economic Survey*, written in Yiddish in 1917 in cooperation with Itzhak Ben-Zvi. Other books published in 1920, 1933, and 1935 are on socialistic and Jewish problems. His latest book, *Years of Challenge*, was published in 1963.

DAYAN, Moshe. Minister of defense, since June 1, 1967.

Born May 20, 1915, at Degania, near Lake Tiberias (Sea of Galilee), on the first kibbutz (collective farm), created in Israel. His parents, born in Russia, helped to found the MAPAI. His father, a prominent author, was a former member of the Knesset. He was married in 1935 to Ruth Shwarz, daughter of a Jerusalem lawyer; she became a leader in the Israeli fashion industry. They have one daughter, Yael, a well-known novelist, and two sons.

His early education was received at the Kadoury Agricultural School, 12 miles southeast of Haifa, where he was trained to be a farmer. He speaks Hebrew, English, and Arabic. Finds relaxation in amateur archeological work, and his home and garden are filled with collections.

Entered the Hagana in 1929, at age 14 and, at age 22, he joined one of Captain Orde Wingate's commando units formed to guard agricultural settlements (see ch. 26, The Armed Forces). In 1939, when the Hagana was declared illegal, he was arrested and sentenced to 10 years imprisonment by British authorities for his underground activities. After 2 years detention at Akko (Acre), he was released to help the British against Vichy-French forces in Syria, where he lost his left eye, which has forced him to wear a distinctive black eye-patch.

After World War II he returned to farming but remained with the Hagana as a lieutenant colonel in the reserve corps. Recalled to active duty early in 1948, he headed a commando unit operating against Arab forces in the Negev. When the Palestine Mandate ended in 1948, he was a brigadier general commanding Jewish troops in the Jerusalem area. In 1949 he headed the Israeli armistice negotiations delegation on Rhodes and was one of the signatories to the armistice with Jordan on April 3, 1949. He then became chief liaison officer with various mixed armistice commissions.

In 1952, after attending a senior officer's course in the British Staff College at Camberley, he served briefly as chief of staff of the Southern Command and, in 1953, of the Northern Command. Late in 1953, was appointed chief of staff of the army.

He directed operations against Egyptian forces in the Sinai Campaign of October-November 1956 and is generally regarded by his countrymen as mainly responsible for the rapid victory of Israeli forces.

After withdrawal from the Sinai area, he resigned as chief of staff on January 26, 1958, reverted to the rank of brigadier general and was given a 2-year leave of absence to study political science at Hebrew University in Jerusalem. This marked the beginning of a new career, featured by strong support of MAPAI politicians, led by Prime Minister David Ben-Gurion. Elected to the Knesset on the MAPAI electoral list, he promtly entered Ben-Gurion's cabinet on December 17, 1959 as minister of agriculture. After reappointment to this post by Ben-Gurion on November 2, 1961, and by his successor, Levi Eshkol, on January 26, 1963, Dayan resigned, at his own request, on November 4, 1964, assertedly because of policy differences with the prime minister.

In July 1965 he was a leading member of Ben-Gurion's new RAFI party, formed by breaking away from MAPAI (see ch. 14, Political Dynamics).

As tension in neighboring Arab states mounted in 1966–67, Prime Minister Eshkol, pressured by pronouncements of political leaders, appointed Dayan, then a popular war hero, as minister of defense on June 1, 1967. He still retained this post in mid-1969, while being mentioned as a strong contender to become prime minister after the elections scheduled to be held late in 1969. Despite political activities, he found time in 1965 to publish a book, *Diary of the Sinai Campaign*, his account of the operations against Egypt. Preoccupation with military and internal political affairs has limited his visits outside the country. He visited Burma in 1957 and on his return stopped at the Taj Mahal in India. In 1966 he visited the Republic of Vietnam, accredited as a war correspondent, and toured the combat area with United States forces. In December 1968, accompanied by his wife, he went to the United States where he met president-elect Richard M. Nixon and addressed a banquet sponsored by the United Jewish Appeal.

EBAN, Abba. Diplomat and politician; minister of foreign affairs since January 10, 1966.

Born on February 2, 1915, in Cape Town, South Africa. His father, a businessman, died soon after the birth of his son, who was then taken by his mother to England where he was educated in public and private schools and at the University of Cambridge. There he studied the Hebrew, Arabic, and Persian languages and was an honor student.

Enlisting in the British army at the outbreak of World War II, he became an officer and, at his request, was sent to the Middle East to serve in Palestine. In 1940 he was appointed liaison officer of the Allied Headquarters with the Jewish population of Jerusalem, where he encouraged them to engage in war efforts.

In 1945 he married Susan Ambach, a literature major at American University in Cairo, Egypt. They have one son, born in 1950, and a daughter.

He entered the service of the Jewish Agency in 1946, was appointed liaison officer with the UN Special Committee on Palestine in 1947 and became a member of the Jewish Agency delegation to the UN General Assembly. On May 18, 1948, was appointed by the provisional government of Israel as its representative to the UN, where he sought international intervention to check Arab attacks on the new nation. On May 11, 1949, he became the permanent representative, with the rank of minister. Appointed ambassador to the

263

United States in September 1950 and served concurrently as a permanent representative to the UN until late in 1959.

In November 1959, was elected to the Fourth Knesset on the MAPAI electoral list, and served in four successive cabinet positions: minister without portfolio, 1959–60; minister of education and culture, 1960–63; deputy prime minister in Prime Minister Levi Eshkol's cabinet, 1963–66; and on January 10, 1966, succeeded Golda Meir as minister of foreign affairs, a post he was still holding in mid-1969.

While serving as permanent representative in the UN, he staunchly defended his country's position, particularly on issues pertaining to Arab matters. In January 1959 he expressed Israel's willingness to compensate the Palestine Arab refugees without waiting for a peace settlement, provided they would be integrated into the host countries and international financial help would become available to Israel to pay their claims.

As minister of education and culture and president of the Weizmann Institute of Science, in August 1960, he initiated an international conference on the Role of Science in the Advancement of New States. The conference was held at the institute, near Tel Aviv, and resulted in requests for Israeli technical and scientific help from 15 African and Asian countries.

While deputy prime minister, he denounced the Federal Government of Germany (West Germany) before the Knesset in November 1964, for refusing to extend the time limit under the statute of limitations for Nazi war crimes beyond 1965. After becoming minister of foreign affairs, he started an extended official tour, on January 28, 1966, to visit France, the United States, Canada, the UN, and England.

In 1967 he attended the funeral of former chancellor Doctor Konrad Adenauer, on April 25, at Cologne. In May he instructed his ambassadors to countries represented on the UN Security Council to bring the gravity of the Israeli-Arab situation to their attention, stating that Israel could not remain inactive "in the face of constant aggression." In July, after the Six-Day War, as chief spokesman for Israel, he presented his country's case before the UN Special Emergency Session on the Middle East War.

During 1968 he visited Scandinavian countries in May and, in June, at Bucharest, he signed an agreement on economic, scientific, and technical cooperation with Rumania. In January 1969 he visited the Netherlands; in March, he went to the United States, where he conferred with President Richard M. Nixon, with Secretary of State William Rogers, and with United States permanent representative to the UN, Charles Yost and, in addition, attended the funeral services for former President Dwight D. Eisenhower.

Besides maintaining a moderate position on the Arab issue, he has avoided positive statements regarding permanent retention of the occupied areas or of withdrawal from them. He speaks in favor of direct negotiations with Arab countries and argues against a settlement imposed by big powers.

In addition to a master's degree from the University of Cambridge, he has been awarded honorary doctorate degrees from several universities in the United States, including New York, Boston, Maryland, Cincinnati, and Temple. He is also a Fellow of the American Academy of Arts and Sciences and a Fellow of the World Academy of Arts and Sciences.

His publications are mainly on literary or political subjects, such as *The Modern Literary Movement in Egypt* (1944), *Maze of Justice* (1946), *Voice of Israel* (1957), *Tide of Nationalism* (1959), *Israel in The World* (1966), and *My People: The Story of the Jews* (1968). His latest book, *To Be or Not To Be*, political memoirs of the Six-Day War, was scheduled to be published in 1969.

HOROWITZ, David. Economist; governor, Bank of Israel since 1954.

Born on February 15, 1899, at Drogobych, about 40 miles southwest of Lvov (Lemberg), in western Ukraine. Educated at Lvov and Vienna. He speaks Russian, German, Hebrew, and English. Emigrated to Palestine in 1920. Married to Riva Bobkoff; they have one son.

Became a member of the Executive Committee of Histadrut in 1923. From 1932 to 1935 he was economic adviser and secretary on the American Economic Committee for Palestine, a private organization interested in aiding Jewish-American immigrants. From 1935 to the end of the British Palestine Mandate in 1948, he directed several enterprises, served on various governmental committees under the mandate regime and became director of the Economic Department of the Jewish Agency for Palestine, administrative body of the World Zionist Organization.

After establishment of the government, he was appointed director general of the Ministry of Finance but resigned in 1952, when he became governor-designate of the Bank of Israel. In 1954 he became governor of the bank, a post he still retained in mid-1969.

His rise to the top in Israeli financial affairs was paralleled by expanding participation in international economic matters. After serving as liaison officer to the UN Special Commission on Palestine in 1946, he became a member of the Jewish Agency Delegation to the UN at Lake Success in 1947. In 1948 he headed the Israeli representatives to the UN Economic Survey Commission. The next year he was chief of Israel's delegation to the financial talks on sterling releases between Israel and Great Britain, held in London. He also participated in negotiations between Israel and Great Britain on economic and financial affairs in connection with termination of the mandate. Afterwards he represented Israel in the International Finance Corporation and the International Bank for Reconstruction and Development. He also became chairman of the board of directors of The Eliezer Kaplan School of Economics and Social Sciences at Hebrew University and a member of the State Council for Higher Education. In 1964 he headed Israel's delegation to the UN Conference on Trade and Development, at Geneva.

As governor of the Bank of Israel he is responsible for the stability of the country's currency at home and abroad, for the maintenance of production, employment, national income, and capital investments, and for management of the public debt. In addition the bank acts as the government's sole fiscal and banking agent. He is a strong advocate for membership in the European Common Market, regarding it as essential for the country's economic development (see ch. 24, Foreign Economic Relations; ch. 25, Financial and Monetary System).

He has written numerous articles on economic subjects, including: *Aspects of Economic Policy in Palestine*, 1936; *Jewish Colonization in Palestine*, 1937; *Economic Survey of Palestine*, 1938; *Palestine Jewry's Economic War Effort*, 1942; *Post War Reconstruction*, 1942; *Palestine and the Middle East, an Essay on Regional Economy*, 1943; *Production and Reality in Palestine*, 1945; *State in the Making*, 1953; *Anatomie Unserer Zeit* (Anatomy of Our Time), 1964; *Hemispheres, North and South*, 1966; and *The Economics of Israel*, 1967.

MEIR, Golda. Politician and labor leader; former minister of labor and social insurance and of foreign affairs; prime minister since March 17, 1969.

Born Golda Mabovitch on May 3, 1898, at Kiev, capital of the Ukraine, in Czarist Russia. Father was a skilled carpenter. In 1903 the family moved to Pinsk, where revolutionary activity and anti-Semitism prevailed. They emigrated to the United States, the father leaving first in 1906, to find work and earn funds to enable the mother and the three young daughters, Shaineh, Golda, and the baby, Tsipke, to follow. After staying a short period with grandparents in Pinsk, they joined the father in Milwaukee, where he worked as a railway carpenter and the mother ran a grocery store.

At age 12, she organized a group of girls, known as the Young Sisters Society, to provide textbooks for needy children. At age 14, she left home to join her older sister, who was then married and living in Denver, but parental objections finally induced her to return to Milwaukee in 1916.

After graduating from a Milwaukee teachers' seminary in 1917, she married Morris Myerson, but only after he had agreed to emigrate to Palestine. From 1917 to 1920 she was busily engaged in war-relief work and other activities, such as the Poalei Zion (Workers of Zion) party and the Jewish People's Relief for East European Jewry. She was a party delegate to the American Jewish Congress and then toured the United States to organize party branches and raise funds for its newspaper (see ch. 14, Political Dynamics). She also worked in a library and taught in Yiddish language folk schools, attracting attention as a forceful speaker in both Yiddish and English.

In 1921 she emigrated to Palestine with her husband and sister Shaineh and settled first in Merhavia, a kibbutz in the Yizre'el Valley, southeast of Haifa. There she changed her name to Meir, conforming to David Ben-Gurion's idea that immigrants should adopt Hebrew-sounding names. At Merhavia she operated a poultry farm and within a year was the kibbutz delegate to the council of Histadrut. Meanwhile she studied Hebrew and Arabic. Her husband was unable to stand kibbutz hardships. Consequently, they moved to Tel Aviv in 1923 and, in 1924, to Jerusalem, where their two children, Menahem and Sara, were born. He was employed as a bookkeeper, and she worked as a cashier and laundress to pay for the children's kindergarten expenses. The son became a cellist in Tel Aviv, and the daughter settled on a kibbutz in the Negev.

In 1928 she became secretary of the Women Workers' Council of Histadrut and, thereafter, worked her way to the top of the organization, while serving in various responsible positions from 1929 to 1946 (see ch. 22, Labor). Meanwhile in 1930, she was a founding member of MAPAI and a delegate to the British Labor Council in London. In 1932 she was sent to New York for 2 years as a delegate to the Pioneer Women's Organization, a branch of Histadrut concerned primarily with child education and with welfare activities. After returning in 1934, was selected to serve on the Executive Committee and in 1935 was elected to the Secretariat. By 1936 she was in charge of Histadrut's mutual aid services and chairman of the board of directors of Kupat Holim (Workers' Sick Fund).

Her positions involved increasing participation in political leadership and in negotiations with the British Palestine Mandate administrators. In 1939 she became head of Histadrut's Political Department and a member of MAPAI's delegation on the Action Committee of the World Zionist Organization. At the outbreak of World War II, she became a member of the War Economic Advisory Council of the Palestine government. From 1946 to 1948 she headed the Political Department of the Jewish Agency for Palestine, replacing Moshe Sharett in this post. Early in 1948, on a fund-raising trip to the United States, she raised $50 million in two-and-a-half months. She then went to Amman, Transjordan, disguised as an Arab woman, to plead with King Abdullah in an unsuccessful effort to prevent an Arab attack against the new state of Israel.

After termination of the mandate on May 15, 1948, she was sent to the United States as an Israeli representative and while there was informed of her appointment as minister to the Soviet Union. She was recalled from Moscow in April 1949 to become minister of labor in Prime Minister David Ben-Gurion's cabinet. While serving 7 years in this post, she formulated the country's first labor code, stressed employment and home construction for immigrants and answered demands to speak at home and abroad. Her husband died in 1951 while she was on a speaking trip to the United States.

During her 10-year tenure as minister for foreign affairs (1956–66), she played a key role in the diplomatic struggles resulting from the Sinai Campaign, less than 6 months after she took office. Making numerous foreign visits she prepared the way for diplomatic ties with the newly independent states of Africa and Asia. In March 1958 she returned from a 4-week tour of Western Africa and set up an International Cooperation Department in her ministry, under whose sponsorship Israeli youths and experts have been sent to some 60 developing countries. In mid-1960 she handled the secret transfer of Adolf Eichmann from Argentina to Israel for his war-crime trial. In March 1965 she arranged the details for establishment of diplomatic relations with the Federal Republic of Germany. When Levi Eshkol became prime minister in 1963, she retained her post but decided to retire in January 1966 in order to relax and rest.

Within a year, however, she became secretary general of MAPAI and guided the party through negotiations, combining it with Ahdut Ha-Avoda and RAFI, to form the Israel Labor party in January 1968 (see ch. 14, Political Dynamics). She resigned as secretary general in August of that year.

After the death of Prime Minister Eshkol on February 26, 1969, leaders of labor party groups urged her to accept nomination as prime minister. She accepted and was confirmed on March 17, 1969, and announced that her policies would remain the same as those of her predecessor. Both inside and outside party circles, her opinions are respected, and her influence is still strong.

RABIN, Yitzhak. Army officer and diplomat; ambassador to United States since January, 1968.

Born on March 1, 1922, at Jerusalem; he is the son of parents who had immigrated to Palestine from Chicago during World War I and were prominent in political and literary fields. His father, Nehemiah, had lived 15 years in New York, Saint Louis, and Chicago and went to Palestine as a soldier in the Jewish Legion. His mother, the former Rosa Cohen, became a labor leader in Tel Aviv after 1922. His academic education was received at the Kadoury Agricultural School,

12 miles southeast of Haifa, also attended by Moshe Dayan, and earlier by Yigal Allon. He is married and has one daughter, Dalia, born in 1951, and one son, Yuval, born in 1956. His wife, a former member of the Hagana and Palmach, is interested in army welfare activities, particularly in rehabilitation camps.

After leaving school, he was recruited for the Hagana, an underground striking force trained by the British for sabotage and partisan activities. At age 19, he led a Jewish scouting unit 10 miles behind the Vichy-French lines in Syria to intercept the retreat of their forces. Urged by Yigal Allon in 1941, he joined the Palmach, the commando section of the Jewish military forces then being organized to provide the Hagana with a mobile combat unit (see ch. 26, The Armed Forces). By 1944 he was a deputy battalion commander, but in June 1946 the British placed him in a detention camp along with other Zionist political and underground leaders. He was released when the British Palestine Mandate ended in 1948 and was appointed the Palmach's deputy commander.

Early in the operations against invading Arab forces, beginning in May 1948, he became a Palmach brigade commander and helped raise the siege of Jerusalem. Later, after fighting the Egyptians in the Negev and at Eilat, he represented the Israeli Defense Forces in the armistice negotiations held in Rhodes in February 1949.

In 1953, after attending courses at the Royal Staff College, Camberley, England, and at Fort Bliss, Texas, he was appointed head of the Training Branch of the armed forces and, in 1954, was promoted to brigadier general. He introduced a compulsory parachute training course for all senior officers in the army and wears the parachutist pin himself.

At the outbreak of the Sinai Campaign in 1956, he headed the Northern Command. In 1959 and part of 1960 he was chief of the Armed Forces' Manpower Branch and, later in 1960, was appointed deputy to the chief of staff and head of the General Staff Branch (see ch. 26, The Armed Forces).

On January 1, 1964 he became chief of staff of the armed forces with the rank of major general, which was later advanced to lieutenant general for this post. He continued to serve in this position through the Six-Day War of June 1967 and until the end of his 4-year term in January 1, 1968, when he was appointed ambassador to the United States. Meanwhile, on December 3, 1967, he ended a 4-day visit to England where he addressed the 50th anniversary banquet of the Jewish Legion and lectured before the Institute of Strategic Studies in London. On June 26, 1967, he received an honorary doctor of philosophy degree from Hebrew University.

A military tactician rather than a political activist, he was credited by former Prime Minister Levi Eshkol with planning the tactics used in the Six-Day War, in which he sought indirect approaches instead of direct assaults, using air units in cooperation with armored forces and artillery.

SAPIR, Pinhas. Politician; minister without portfolio; secretary general of MAPAI since July 1968.

Born in 1909, in Lithuania. Went to Palestine in 1929 and worked as an agricultural laborer. From 1934 to 1947 he was assistant director of the Mekorot Water Company, Limited, Palestine's major water development company. After establishment of statehood in 1948, he became director general of the Ministry of Defense and, subsequently, director general of the Ministry of Finance.

Was appointed minister of commerce and industry in 1955 and, in June 1963, he succeeded Levi Eshkol as minister of finance but retained his post as minister of commerce and industry until January 1966, when it went to another appointee in Prime Minister Eshkol's new cabinet. He resigned as minister of finance in July 1968 to accept the position of secretary general of MAPAI, a post held during the previous 2 years by Golda Meir. Retained a seat in the cabinet as minister without portfolio.

During the period when he was a minister in the cabinet, he was usually designated as acting prime minister when Prime Minister Eshkol was absent from the country. As minister of finance, he headed a trade delegation in April 1967 to Rumania, where he signed economic, technical cooperation, and long-term trade agreements. He announced that Israel would be the first non-Communist country to open a trade office in Bucharest, apart from its embassy, and that these agreements were opening the way for relations with other Communist countries (see ch. 24, Foreign Economic Relations).

In a radio broadcast in November 1967, he stated that devaluation of the British pound necessitated devaluation of the Israeli pound to avoid decreased exports and an unemployment crisis. A conservative attitude toward government finances was indicated in December 1967, during a talk to the Tel Aviv Branch of the Council of MAPAI, opposing any increase in cost-of-living allowances before 1969 and recommending a reduction in Jewish Agency officials to make more funds available for immigrants.

Continuous experience in high public office since statehood in 1948 has resulted in his profound influence on the country's economy. He is reputed to be a hard worker and a clever politician. Aside from his long-standing support of Golda Meir, his moderation and political shrewdness make him known as the strong man in the dominant MAPAI party. He has avoided political wrangling, limiting his public statements mainly to matters affecting the country's economy and finances, or to party affairs.

SHAZAR, Shneur Zalman. President of Israel since 1963; historian and journalist. Born October 6, 1889, at Mir in Czarist Russia about 450 miles southwest of Moscow.

Entered the Zionist labor movement at age 16 and was a delegate to the Zionist Labor Conference at Minsk, in 1906. For a brief period, worked for a Zionist publishing firm at nearby Vilna. Was arrested with the rest of the publishing staff by the Czarist police. After release he entered the Academy at Saint Petersburg (later Leningrad). The academy selected him to study history and philosophy in Germany, where he specialized in historical research, particularly the messianic movement, at the Universities of Berlin, Strasbourg, and Freiburg.

After visiting Palestine in 1911 and 1920, he settled there and, in 1925, joined the editorial staff of *Davar*, a daily paper published by Histadrut. While rising to the position of chief editor, he was a prominent organizer in the labor movement and a member of the Israeli delegation to the UN General Assembly at Lake Success, New York.

He remained with *Davar* until elected to the First Knesset in 1949 as a member of MAPAI. Became Israel's first minister of education and introduced compulsory education in the public schools.

After resigning from the cabinet in 1950, he became a member of the Executive Committee of the Jewish Agency in charge of its Information Department and was its acting chairman in 1956. Meanwhile, he headed the Zionist Organization Department of Education and Culture from 1954 to 1963.

On May 21, 1963, he was elected as Israel's third president by the Fifth Knesset, succeeding Itzhak Ben-Zvi who had died the previous month. On March 26, 1968, was reelected for a second 5-year term by the Sixth Knesset, receiving 86 votes from the 110 deputies present.

As chief of state he has made numerous trips abroad on official visits and as delegate to Zionist congresses. He attended Sir Winston Churchill's state funeral on January 29, 1965, at London, and early in May 1966, he received West Germany's chancellor, Doctor Konrad Adenauer, during his 9-day private visit to Israel. In the summer of 1966, on state visits to Uruguay, Chile, and Brazil, he was awarded an honorary doctorate degree by the University of Rio de Janeiro. He made an official visit to Washington on August 1 and 2, 1966. On March 31, 1969, he attended the funeral services for former President Dwight D. Eisenhower at Washington.

Despite his age, 80 years in 1969, he appears to be in excellent health, performs his duties assiduously and participates regularly in the many required functions of his office.

He speaks Hebrew, Russian, German, and English. His major interests are educational matters, Jewish history, and mysticism. His principal publications are *Kochvei Boker* (*Morning Stars*—autobiographical sketches), published in 1950, with an English translation appearing in 1967, and *Or Ishim* (The Light of Personalities-biographical and historical studies), published in 1955.

SECTION III. ECONOMIC

CHAPTER 19
CHARACTER AND STRUCTURE OF THE ECONOMY

In its brief history as a state, Israel has been required to deal with many exceptional economic difficulties. The country is poor in natural resources; in addition to the limited supply of arable land and water resources, there is no coal or iron and only a very limited amount of oil. Between 1948 and 1968 approximately 1.25 million Jews immigrated to Israel. Mass immigration and the natural increase in population caused the labor force to increase from approximately 450,000 in 1950 to slightly over 1 million in 1969. A large proportion of the immigrants was required to learn new occupations. Very large expenditures were necessary for housing, health, education, and vocational training in addition to heavy defense expenditures and investments to create sources of employment. The restricted scope of the domestic market does not permit economies of scale in industry, and the boycott and blockade practices of neighboring Arab countries have caused difficulties in the development of foreign trade.

Despite these difficulties, the economic position has greatly improved. During the period from 1950 to 1967, the gross national product (GNP) increased at an average annual rate of 9.3 percent, as compared with 7.5 percent for the Federal Republic of Germany (West Germany), 4.5 percent for Holland, and 3.3 percent for the United States. The massive inflow of immigrants has been absorbed, there has been a shift from an agricultural to an industrial economy, per capita income has risen rapidly, and there has been a substantial accumulation of foreign exchange reserves. The standard of living is high for a country that is poor in natural resources. The average level of private consumption is similar to that of such developed countries as Norway and Holland and exceeds that of Italy.

The economy is unusually diverse in its structure and is subject to extensive government control to promote national aims and objectives. Large capital imports have been derived mainly from public and semipublic sources abroad and have passed through government channels or through public organizations, such as the semiautono-

273

mous Jewish Agency, representing the World Zionist Organization. As a result the public sector has had control of a large part of capital available for investment. These circumstances are responsible for the creation of a large sector of public and semipublic enterprises in almost every branch of the economy. Cooperative enterprise is highly developed; most agricultural production, important parts of industry and trade, and almost all transportation of passengers and freight by road are conducted by cooperatives. Partnerships are frequent between groups belonging to the private and cooperative sectors, or between these sectors and the government sector.

The public sector includes the central government, the national institutions, and the local authorities. The central government is by far the most important. The national institutions are the World Zionist Organization, the Jewish Agency for Israel, the Jewish National Fund (Keren Kayemet le-Israel), and the Foundation Fund (Keren Hayesod). The major part of their funds has come from abroad. Their main function has been to contribute to the financing of immigration and the absorption of immigrants into the economy. The Jewish Agency has also been prominent in financing housing and agricultural settlements and owns a substantial interest in the largest commercial bank and the national shipping line.

The local authorities enjoy considerable autonomy, but are dependent on the government for about one-fifth of their revenue and are responsive to the economic policy of the government.

There are more than 5,000 nonprofit institutions that are engaged in activities similar to those of the public sector in the fields of health, education, and welfare. Their services are generally provided without payment or for a price below cost. Like the national institutions, some of them are financed from abroad and are connected with international Jewish organizations. Since 1948 many of their fields of activity have been transferred gradually to the state. The distinction between the public sector and certain major nonprofit institutions is based more on legal than on economic criteria; in fact, the services of the nonprofit institutions complement those provided by the government. For example, 60 percent of the cost of their educational activities is financed by transfers of funds from the public sector, and the major health fund, connected with the Histadrut (Histadrut Ha'ovdim Haklalit—General Federation of Labor) and financed by members' fees, is in fact a national health service.

The Histadrut is a multipurpose organization that is one of the most powerful institutions in the country (see ch. 22, Labor). It is primarily a giant federation of labor unions representing at least 75 percent of all wage earners, but its entprepreneurial activities are numerous and important in almost every branch of the economy. It administers the major health fund, is the owner of the third largest

274

bank, and owns and operates, often on a cooperative basis, between 20 and 25 percent of the industrial plants. Companies owned by the Histadrut are also active in mining, construction, commerce, transportation, and other services. Some of its companies are wholly owned, and some are joint ventures with public or private interests. About 90 percent of agricultural collective settlements are affiliated with the Histadrut, and almost all the produce of these settlements is marketed by an affiliate of the Histadrut. In undertaking an activity, Histadrut enterprises seek to serve a national or group interest. The relationship between the Histadrut and the government is such that the Histadrut sector may be said to occupy a position somewhere between the public and the private sector.

The private sector accounts for about 60 percent of the net domestic product, and the remaining 40 percent is attributable to the public and Histadrut sectors in about equal proportions. There has been no consistent and well-defined policy as to what fields the government should enter. The role of the government has been determined more by economic factors, such as absorption of immigrants and the inflow of foreign capital through government channels, than by ideology. In terms of the profit motive as distinguished from other motives, it is not clear how much of the 40 percent of domestic product originating in the public and Histadrut sectors deviates in fact from the economic criteria of the private sector. Many public-sector enterprises are owned jointly by the government, the national institutions, the Histadrut, and private entrepreneurs.

The public sector's share of total investment is probably higher than in any other non-Communist country. At the beginning of the 1950's, approximately two-thirds of total investment involved participation by the government or financial institutions in the public sector. During 1960–1966 this proportion declined to approximately 43 perecent. In agriculture and irrigation, however, the government financed 83 percent of the total investment during 1958–66.

The principal sectors of private investment are industry, construction, and trade. A majority of industrial enterprises are privately owned, although there are sizable government holdings in the fertilizer industry and in mining companies, particularly those exploiting mineral resources in the Negev.

In addition to its direct influence in economic activity through financing investment, the government has exerted extensive indirect influence in the course of administering incentives to economic development, such as tax concessions, differential export incentives, and commercial bank loans authorized by the Bank of Israel for specified purposes at low interest rates. Continuous inflation, combined with foreign exchange control, has given rise to a complicated mechanism of government interference with free-market prices.

AGRICULTURE

Nine-tenths of the land is owned by the state or the Jewish National Fund established in 1901 for purchasing land in Palestine to be held in trust for the people. The land is leased to collective farms and to members of cooperative settlements at rates that have been estimated to average less than 0.4 percent of the value of gross farm output. Public ownership of the land has facilitated agricultural planning. The government and the Jewish Agency have assumed responsibility for financing of agricultural investments and determination of the pattern of farm production. Broad control over the pattern of agricultural output is exercised by fixing production quotas for a number of commodities; for example, sugar beets, tomatoes, and poultry. The government has provided credit on easy terms, has assumed the major share of the cost of irrigation water, and has controlled prices through price supports and subsidies. Subsidies have represented a significant share of agricultural income. The cost of irrigation is very high because most water resources are in the north and most of the cultivated land is in the central and southern parts of the country. Shortage of water is probably the most important barrier to further development.

There are two types of farming: citriculture, based on modern technical methods and high capital investment and producing mostly for export; and mixed farming, based on intensive cultivation and irrigation and directed toward supplying the urban population. In the latter type, production is concentrated on dairy farming, poultry breeding, and fruits and vegetables, with some mechanized production of cereals.

In 1948 only about 30 percent of food needs were supplied by domestic production; by 1968, despite a tripling of population, domestic production covered about four-fifths of domestic consumption, the level of nutrition was much higher, and agricultural exports balanced the cost of food imports that consisted primarily of grains, beef, and fats. Agricultural exports consist mostly of citrus, citrus products, and off-season fruits and vegetables. Production of these export commodities has been raised to a high level of efficiency. Citrus and citrus products are second only to diamonds as a source of export earnings.

Despite the prominent position of agriculture in national life, its share of the total domestic product declined from a peak of 15 percent in 1958 to less than 10 percent by 1966. The average annual growth rate declined from 16 percent during 1949–1954 to about 4.5 percent during 1964–1967 because of limitations of land and water and in domestic demand for agricultural products. The proportion of total employment provided by agriculture was 17 to 18 percent up to 1960, but had declined to about 13 percent by 1966.

INDUSTRY

Industry developed more slowly than other branches of the economy during the early 1950's, but industrialization has been rapid since 1955. German reparations, primarily in the form of machinery and related items, made it possible to develop new industries and replace obsolete equipment, and also facilitated rapid development in land and sea transportation and modernization of communication facilities.

In recent years industry, excluding construction, has accounted for about one-fourth of total employment and one-fourth of the GNP. In 1965 private industry accounted for 76 percent of total industrial employment; Histadrut-affiliated enterprises, for 15 percent; and publicly owned establishments, other than defense plants, for the remaining 9 percent.

Industrial output ranges from consumer goods to complicated electronic equipment. Defense plants produce a variety of arms and ammunition. Despite increasing diversification, food products and textiles have continued to account for about 21 percent and 10 percent, respectively, of the total industrial production.

Because of the small domestic market, industry is predominantly small-scale. In 1966, among industrial establishments employing five or more persons, only about 10 percent employed 50 or more, and only about 1 percent had a labor force of 300 or more; the latter were primarily government-operated mining and mineral-processing plants. In addition to small-scale operations, difficulties faced by plants in the private sector include lack of specialization, limited competition, and underutilization of capacity.

With the exception of the cement, ceramics, glass, and food-processing branches, processing industries work with imported raw materials whose transportation costs represent a small part of the values of the finished products. Examples are diamonds, precision tools, electrical appliances, and the fashion trade. In the case of diamonds, the value added to imported rough diamonds by cutting and polishing is only about 20 percent.

The government has actively influenced the direction of industrial development by providing various incentives on a selective basis, such as grants, low-interest loans, tax exemption, and export subsidies. A very high level of protection has been provided by tariffs and quantitative restrictions on imports, and production in some sectors has expanded to the point where a range of products is produced in such small quantities as to be uneconomical. The level of protection is being reduced gradually to stimulate greater efficiency. Having achieved substantial self-sufficiency in agriculture, government policies are aimed at developing and modernizing the industrial sector, particularly those industries with export potential that can be developed to reduce the large trade deficit. The share of industrial exports in total exports rose from 50 percent in 1950 to 67 percent in 1959 and to 80 percent in 1967. A substantial part of production of the following industrial products is exported: diamonds, citrus and citrus products, automobile tires, copper, phosphates, potash, textiles, and clothing.

In addition to employment provided by industry, construction has accounted for about 10 percent of total employment, except during the recession of 1966–67. This is a larger proportion than in most developed countries because of the need to provide housing for immigrants and plants and facilities for industrialization. The contribution of construction to the GNP has fluctuated between 8.5 percent and 9.5 percent, except during the recession starting in 1966.

LABOR

In the employment structure, there is a concentration of employment in services that is similar to that in countries with much higher per capita incomes. Over one-fifth of all workers are employed in government and other public services. The proportion engaged in trade and personal services is not particularly high. Professional and technical workers increased from 11 percent of the total in 1958 to 14 percent in 1966. The main trend in employment by economic branch has been a decline in the proportion of workers in agriculture and an increase in the proportion of industrial workers.

The level of unemployment has fluctuated with the waves of immigration as well as with changes in the level of economic activity; for example, 11.5 percent in 1950, an average of less than 3 percent between 1960 and 1966, and 10 percent in 1967. In the early years of the state, unemployment was fairly high because of the difficulty of adapting the economy to the rapid increase in the labor force. Throughout the 1960's there were shortages of skilled manpower and, at times, of unskilled labor.

Wages and working conditions are regulated by collective agreements, negotiated in most cases by the Histadrut, representing labor, and the Manufacturers' Association, representing management. These negotiations are undertaken at the same time for all sections of industry, and the agreements set the wage patterns that cover workers in all sectors, including those not members of the Histadrut. The basic wage is supplemented by a cost-of-living allowance that has been subject to renegotiation every year and by a family allowance and various fringe benefits that include annual bonuses, severance pay, and employer contributions to union welfare plans.

The wage structure has been strongly influenced by the equalitarian principle, and differentials between wages of skilled and unskilled labor have been relatively narrow though recently the gap has been widening. Rapid economic expansion has tended to widen such differentials, however, by placing a premium on technical skills and higher levels of education. Increasing inequity of personal income has been particularly pronounced between the group of European origin and the group of Middle Eastern origin.

FINANCIAL AND MONETARY SYSTEM

There are three categories of financial institutions with assets divided as follows: the central bank and the commercial banks, 47 percent; institutions providing long-term credit, 34 percent; and social insurance funds and insurance companies, 19 percent. In addition, there are credit cooperatives that specialize in extending credit to a particular branch of the economy. In 1968 there were 24 commercial banks with the bulk of transactions concentrated in the three largest banks that operate numerous branches. Institutions providing long-term credit include mortgage banks, which deal chiefly in loans to home buyers and builders, industrial development banks, and institutions lending to agriculture.

A large proportion of private saving consists of contributions by employers and employees to social insurance funds that amount to about 8 percent of the total wage bill. This form of saving is an important factor in government financing, since social insurance funds are required to invest half of their resources in government securities.

The government exercises extensive influence in the operations of all types of financial institutions. A significant proportion of short-term commercial bank credit is extended to enterprises or branches of the economy in accordance with government directives at specified interest rates. During the mid-1960's credit controlled directly or indirectly by the government represented about 30 percent of all outstanding bank credit to the private sector.

The government has also played a decisive role in the mobilization and allocation of long-term capital, having financed directly about 40 percent of total domestic investment and controlled indirectly a large additional proportion. Agricultural settlements, irrigation works, and electric power facilities have been financed primarily from public funds, and construction of housing and transportion facilities has relied heavily on public finance. Most of the important institutions providing long-term credit are subject to such a degree of governmental direction that they function as quasi-governmental financing agencies, even when they are not government-owned. All new issues of securities by both public and private corporations must be authorized by the government.

FOREIGN TRADE

Principal export products are diamonds, citrus and citrus products, other foodstuffs, textiles, chemicals, and minerals and mineral products. In 1968 diamonds and citrus and citrus products accounted for 54 percent of total exports. Other exports include a variety of goods, each accounting for only a small proportion of the total.

Dependence on imports is unusually large because of the scarcity of raw materials. Imports are composed primarily of raw materials and capital goods required for economic development; only about 11 percent are used for direct consumption. Imports have amounted to 35 to 40 percent of the GNP, and the rate of growth of imports has been close to the rate of growth of the GNP.

Most trade is conducted with the industrial countries of Western Europe and the United States. During 1963–66 these countries provided 80 percent of commodity imports and absorbed 70 percent of commodity exports. South America and Africa accounted for only about 9 percent of exports. Israel's natural market, the neighboring Arab countries, is closed to her.

Trade policy is predicated on the assumption that future economic growth will depend increasingly on export earnings. In 1962 a policy of gradual import liberalization was adopted to expose Israeli goods to foreign competition and render them more competitive in world markets. Import licensing has been substantially eliminated and customs duties are being progressively reduced. Because of the heavy dependence on exports to the developed countries, especially in Western Europe, Israel has applied for associate membership in the European Economic Community, which provides a market for 29 percent of its exports. This application was still under consideration in 1969. Since 1964 Israel has had an agreement with the European communities providing preferences for Israeli citrus.

BALANCE OF PAYMENTS

The salient feature of the balance of payments is a substantial excess of imports over exports. The deficit on goods and services reached a peak of US$696 million in 1968 as compared with the previous peak of US$573 million in 1964. This deficit has been financed by capital imports.

Large amounts of capital have been obtained from abroad in forms requiring no repayment: gifts from world Jewry, German reparations and personal restitution payments, and grants-in-aid from the United States government. During the period from 1949 through 1965, these unilateral transfers financed approximately 70 percent of the import surplus. The remainder was financed by loans from the United States government and the World Bank, by purchases of State of Israel bonds by world Jewry, and by foreign equity capital. World Jewry covered 59 percent of the import surplus; the government of West Germany, 29 percent; and the United States government, 12 percent.

This large capital inflow not only financed the import surplus, but also permitted the accumulation of substantial foreign exchange reserves. During 1960–67 net capital imports averaged US$561 million annually as compared with an annual average import surplus of US$459 million.

Since the termination of reparations in 1966, the government of West Germany has extended development loans of about $35 million per year. The inflow of capital from the United States government, under P.L. 480 (see Glossary) and from the Agency for International Development and the Export-Import Bank, had declined to US$40 million by 1966.

DEVELOPMENT PLANNING

Development planning has faced major economic uncertainties and formidable political obstacles. As a small country with few natural resources, Israel is heavily dependent on foreign trade and hence is exceptionally vulnerable to declines in demand for its exports in world markets. Two key factors in the growth of the economy, the annual volume of immigrants and the inflow of foreign capital, are largely beyond the government's control. Another uncertainty has been the level of defense expenditures. The coalition structure of the government and the consequent need for compromise and consensus have also impeded adoption of a comprehensive and integrated development plan that goes beyond a statement of desirable goals (see ch. 13, The Governmental System). Under the circumstances, the authorities have adopted a problem-by-problem approach as the only feasible procedure, and planning has been essentially sectoral rather than integrated.

Progress toward coordinated planning was achieved through establishment of the Economic Planning Authority in 1962. This agency has gained experience and a stronger administrative position by being placed in the Prime Minister's Office and has prepared three plans covering periods of 4 or 5 years. The last, a 4-year plan for 1968–71, was published in March 1968. It is based on sector plans prepared by individual ministries within terms of reference outlined by the cabinet. It includes a thorough survey of the economy from 1950 through 1967 and an analysis of projected development in each sector during 1968–71. It also proposes ways and means to achieve the following objectives: reduction of the import surplus from US$532 million in

1967 to approximately US$400 million in 1971; an annual average increase in the GNP of 7 to 9 percent; full employment; improvement in the welfare of the less privileged; and dispersal of the population from the present concentration in the coastal area. In mid-1969 it did not seem likely that the projected reduction in the import surplus would be achieved, whereas the GNP was clearly growing faster than the plan projected.

It is acknowledged in the plan that this is a difficult combination of goals. Rapid growth is essential to generate the tax revenue that will be required to achieve welfare objectives and to reduce quickly the relatively heavy defense burden, but it complicates the problem of reducing the trade deficit by generating pressure for increased imports. The basic conflict is between economic growth and economic independence. To the authorities, economic independence implies a balance of payments in which the import surplus will be reduced to a level that will not require long-term capital imports, particularly in the form of unilateral transfers. In their view, if investment at the level required for rapid growth is to become gradually independent of unilateral transfers, domestic savings must increase. This will require a budget surplus and a wages-and-incomes policy that will restrain the increase in per capita consumption.

Growth targets have been determined on the assumption that there will continue to be substantial reliance on capital imports during 1968–71. The prospective ratio of service payments on external debt to disposable foreign exchange income indicates that there will be no difficulty in servicing foreign debt during this period. Nevertheless, with the decline in immigration and the prospect of a gradual reduction in unilateral transfers of capital from abroad, it has been the aim of the authorities since the mid-1960's to adapt the economy to more normal conditions. The authorities consider that efforts to reduce the trade deficit will have to be concentrated on increasing exports, since import substitution has already been pushed very far, as evidenced by the fact that production of some commodities now being manufactured in Israel is not economic. Furthermore, a high level of imports, particularly of raw materials, is required to sustain production.

A substantial expansion of exports will require alignment with world prices. Rapid economic growth has been accompanied by price distortions associated with inflation, price supports, subsidies, protective tariffs, and other restrictions on imports. To promote alignment with world prices and close integration into the world economy, the government plans to continue its policy, begun in 1962, of exposing producers to competitive imports by gradually reducing the level of protection and by relating the degree of protection to the value added to raw materials in the course of producing finished goods.

The government will continue to encourage exports by grants, tax concessions, loans at low interest rates, and various other incentives. Preference will be given to industries that export a considerable portion of their output, industries processing local raw materials, science-based industries, and industries manufacturing nonstandard products or products with a low transportation component.

If goals are realized, industry will account for 26 percent of the GNP in 1971 compared with 23 percent in 1967, about 21 percent of industrial output will be exported compared with 16 percent in 1966, and industrial exports will constitute about 81 percent of total commodity exports compared with 74 percent in 1967.

Because of limited land and water resources, agricultural output is expected to increase by only 5 percent annually, which is less than the projected growth of the GNP, so that the share of agriculture in total production will be somewhat smaller. There is only a limited potential for further import substitution, since production of grains, fodder, sugar, oilseeds, meat, and dairy products, which are imported in large quantities, involves relatively high production costs. About one-fifth of agricultural output will continue to be exported. The limit of development of citrus production has almost been reached, since practically all suitable areas have been planted. Exports of other products, for which Israel has an advantage because of climate and techniques, are expected to increase. Examples are winter vegetables and subtropical fruits. It is anticipated in the plan that the productivity of labor in agriculture will increase at the same rate as production, so that no additional manpower will be required in agriculture.

CHAPTER 20
AGRICULTURE

Agriculture has occupied a position of eminence in national life far greater than is warranted by its contribution of less than 10 percent to the nation's total production and less than 13 percent to employment. It provides, however, almost 20 percent of the total merchandise exports. Its central place in Zionist ideology, its dominant role in the settlement of the country, and its vital security aspects have assured it the highest priority in the economic policies of the government and of other public bodies. In the years 1960 to 1967, the public sector provided from 81 to 97 percent of the annual investment in agriculture and irrigation (see ch. 12, Social Values; ch. 13, The Governmental System).

As a consequence of the country's settlement history, agriculture of the Jewish farmers is highly organized. Communal or cooperative action is nearly universal, although less prominent in the small private sector. Agricultural research is of a high order and its findings are quickly translated into advanced technology on the farms, with the aid of a competent extension service. Farmers are literate and enterprising. The role of the government in guiding and financing agricultural development and in securing parity of income for farmers is pervasive.

Agricultural land is national property and is let to farmers on favorable terms. The cultivable area is small and cannot readily be expanded. Because of insufficient rainfall, irrigation is essential to maintain farm output. Water resources, however, suffice to irrigate less than half the cultivated acreage, and the remainder must be dry farmed. Intensive efforts, therefore, are directed toward further nationalization of the use of water resources for agriculture.

The variation in topographical and climatic conditions allow the cultivation of a wide range of crops. The prevailing pattern of agriculture, promoted by the government and by the settlement authorities, has been one of mixed farming, but a shift in the direction of specialization is being encouraged in the interest of greater efficiency and to stimulate the output of high-value export crops.

Domestic production, having expanded sixfold since the establishment of the state in 1948, covers about four-fifths of consumption and provides a large volume of citrus fruits for export. Import requirements continue primarily for grains, beef, and fats.

Apart from the private sector, Jewish farm settlements take the form of collective farms or of cooperative smallholders' villages. All farming activities are guided by comprehensive national plans, carried down to the level of the individual farm and buttressed by the government's policies concerning resource allocation, prices, subsidies, loans, and production quotas. The purchasing of farm requisites and the marketing of farm products are cooperatively organized.

Arab villages constitute an important, though less developed, segment of the country's agriculture. Despite significant advances in their living conditions and production methods since the establishment of the state, these villages are less productive than Jewish farms, in part because of a relative dearth of irrigated land. With about one-fifth of the cultivated land area and one-fourth of the agricultural labor force, the non-Jewish segment produced less than one-tenth of the farm output in the 1967 agricultural year, October 1, 1966, to September 30, 1967.

LAND USE

Land use is conditioned by the great diversity of climatic and topographical conditions (see ch. 2, Physical Environment). Availability of water is the most important single factor.

The climate is subtropical, characterized by long, dry, and hot summers and by short, mild winters. Precipitation is concentrated in a few winter months. The amount of rainfall varies widely in different parts of the country and fluctuates from year to year. About 90 percent of the precipitation occurs during the 5 months of November through March, with roughly 45 to 70 percent of the total in December and January.

Precipitation decreases rapidly from north to south; from a long-term annual average of about 30 inches in Kefar Giladi in the Galilee Region, to 21 inches in Tel Aviv, 8 inches in Beersheba, and only 1 inch in Eilat, on the Gulf of Aqaba, at the Negev's southern tip. Over half the country receives less than 7 inches of rain per year. Annual fluctuations in the amount of precipitation range from 25 percent of normal during years of drought to 160 percent of normal in good years. Under these conditions irrigation is indispensable for the development of a stable agriculture.

An area of about 2 million acres is suitable for the development of natural pastures, but little of this area was being used in the late 1960's. Natural forests cover about 86,000 acres. In addition, there were about 114,000 acres of reforested land in 1967, compared with only 13,000 acres in 1949. This increase reflects the systematic tree-planting program of the Jewish National Fund and the government.

In 1967 coniferous trees covered about 63,000 acres of the reforested land, and eucalytus trees about 30,000 acres. The balance of some 21,000 acres was under acacias and various other species. Ownership of the reforested land is vested primarily in the Jewish National Fund, which controlled almost 74 percent of it in 1967. About 23 percent of the area was in the government's possession. Owners of the remaining 3 percent have not been identified.

Irrigation

The bulk of the cultivated and cultivable land is located in the central part of the country and in the northern Negev, north and northwest of Beersheba, but the major water sources are in the north. This handicap has been partially overcome through the construction of an integrated national irrigation system, which comprises most of the major waterworks and regulates most of the water resources. It allows planned distribution of water over a large part of the country's 410,000 irrigated acres and carried water through pipelines all the way from Lake Tiberias to the northern Negev.

Most of the water sources lie at a low elevation, and the pipeline extends over a distance of nearly 140 miles. This necessitates expensive pumping, and the cost of irrigation is consequently high. A portion of these costs is absorbed by the government through sale of water to farmers at subsidized prices.

Continuing research on irrigation techniques and equipment has yielded results that made it possible to expand the irrigated acreage by one-third between 1959 and 1967, with an increase of only 11 percent in the amount of water consumed. Water sprinklers have been found better adapted to prevailing conditions than surface irrigation. This method is used on about 90 percent of the irigated acreage. A more efficient method of drop-irrigation through perforated plastic pipes laid along the rows of plants or trees has been developed since 1963. It is being introduced for general use and is expected eventually to replace the sprinkler system.

In an effort to overcome the water shortage, extensive research and experimentation has been carried on for the desalinization of sea and brackish water. Although a small desalting plant (1 million gallons per day) is already supplying the city of Eilat with most of its water requirements, none of the methods studied to early 1969 could produce sweet water on a large scale cheaply enough for use in agriculture.

Water remains the single most important limiting factor in the development of agriculture. Beginning in 1967 emphasis in the government's irrigation policy shifted from the development of new water resources to water conservation measures.

Cultivated Area

The cultivated area has been stable at slightly over 1 million acres since 1960, having increased two and a half times since 1948. The reported cultivated acreage is larger than the physical area of land available for cultivation because of double-counting of acreages supporting more than one crop per year. It varies somewhat from year to year, depending upon the amount of precipitation. Irrigated acreage totaled 410,000 acres in 1968, compared with only 74,000 acres 20 years earlier. Excluding the Negev, half of all farm land was irrigated in that year. The remainder had to depend upon dry-farming methods and was subject to the vagaries of weather.

Over 40 percent of the cropped acreage, amounting to about 420,000 acres, is located in the northern Negev and in the Lakhish area, northwest of Beersheba. Another 25 percent is situated in the coastal plain between Mount Carmel, just south of Haifa, and Ashdod, about 20 miles south of Tel Aviv, and about 17 percent in the four northern valleys skirting the hills of Galilee—Acre, Yizreel, Beit Shean, and Kinneret. The remaining cropland is in the Galilee Region, the Hula Valley, and in the area west of Jerusalem.

Soils in the interior valleys and in the coastal plain, reclaimed and improved at great economic and human cost over a period of many years, are deep and fertile. They provide the basis for the country's intensive and diversified modern agriculture. On hillsides, reforestation, contour plowing, terracing, and other conservation methods have been practiced to restore the soil destroyed by centuries of neglect. This land is used largely for fruit orchards and for pasture.

Unirrigated land is devoted primarily to the production of grains, pulses, and feed crops. Melons, tobacco, oilseeds, and small acreages of orchards, vineyards, cotton, and sugar beets are also grown without irrigation. Irrigated acreage is used to grow all potatoes, vegetables, and flowers. It is also used to grow more than four-fifths of the cotton, orchard trees, and vineyards, and almost three-fourths of the sugar beets. An acre of irrigated land yields crops of up to five times higher value than the same land without irrigation.

The great variation in topographic and climatic conditions throughout the country gives rise to a variety of ecological zones. As many as 36 distinct natural regions are officially recognized, and agricultural planning is based on 17 zones with a much larger number of subzones. Drastic differences in growing conditions exist within short distances, so that apples in the Hula Valley and bananas in the Kinneret Valley can be grown only 30 miles apart.

The central coastal plain is the most productive area. It contains nearly half the country's irrigated land, and over three-fourths of its acreage is irrigated. Of the country's total acreages under irrigation, this plain accounts for almost all the hothouse vegetable acreage, and nearly three-fourths of the acreage under citrus, wine grapes, and avocadoes. The plain also has more than half the acreage of peanuts, flowers, and feed crops, and from one-third to half the acreages under grains, cotton, potatoes, and vegetables.

LAND TENURE

Agricultural land constitutes inalienable national property, except for land owned by non-Jews and about 150,000 acres in private Jewish ownership. The land belongs to the state and to the Jewish National Fund, which holds the land in trust for the nation. It is let to collective farms and to members of cooperative settlements on automatically renewable 49-year leases. Short-term leases of up to 3 years may also be arranged.

Rentals vary, depending upon location, type of soil, and availability of irrigation but are, in fact, nominal. Israeli economists have estimated rental payments to average less than 0.4 percent of gross farm output. In 1967 the combined rentals and interest charges amounted to 3.1 percent of total farm output and 8.7 percent of net farm income.

Individual farmers or farm communities cannot own the land they work, but the terms of the lease provide them security of tenure and assure them ownership of the improvements they make. Buildings and equipment may be mortgaged. Leaseholds may be sublet or transferred, but only as integral units without subdivision, and tenants may receive payment for their investment. Leaseholds must also be passed in their entirety to a single heir. These provisions of the lease prevent fragmentation of the land into uneconomic units. National ownership of the land facilitates agricultural planning and the establishment of new farm settlements in accordance with national needs.

Absentee landownership exists to some extent, but other information on the tenancy system prevailing in the small private Jewish sector is unavailable. In Arab villages the traditional Muslim land tenure system was modified after the establishment of the state, so that most Arab farmers work their own land. Information is available only on one provision of the law: land need no longer be divided equally among all heirs but may be passed on by will of the testator.

FARM ORGANIZATION

There are four basic types of Jewish rural settlement in the country: the moshava (plural, moshavot); the kibbutz (also known as the kvutza; plural, kibbutzim or kvutzot); the moshav (plural, moshavim); and the moshav shitufi (plural, moshavim shitufiim). They differ in the form of property ownership, in the organization

duction, and in social organization. There is also a substantial
r of non-Jewish villages in existence, predominantly Muslim
and Druze (see ch. 2, Physical Environment; ch. 7, Family).

Types of Settlement

The moshava is a European-type village of privately owned farms.
The farmers are free to buy, sell, and rent land, to decide upon the
nature of the crops to be grown, and to employ hired labor. Some of
the older moshavot in the coastal plain have developed into prosperous towns and cities, such at Petah Tiqva, Rehovot, and Hadera, in
which agriculture remains an important activity. In 1967 there were
64 rural moshavot with a total population of almost 50,000 persons.

The kibbutz is a collective rural settlement, the main features of
which are voluntary association, common ownership of all property
other than land, and communal organization of production and consumption. It is run as a single economic unit and as one household.
For purposes of land settlement, the normal size of a kibbutz is considered to be from 100 to 120 families, although existing kibbutzim
may vary in size from as few as 60 members in new settlements to
2,000 or so in long-established ones.

In 1967 there were 233 kibbutzim having a total population of
83,300 persons and 287,000 acres of arable land. This constituted
about 30 percent of the Jewish rural population and 50 percent of
the arable land in Jewish farms. The kibbutz labor force consisted
of 51,000 persons, 20,400 of whom worked in agriculture.

A moshav is a cooperative smallholders' settlement, in which each
family lives in its own household and operates its own farm on its
allotment of national land. Purchasing of machinery and supplies,
the sale of farm produce, and mutual help are organized on a cooperative basis. Hired labor, in general, may not be employed.

Moshavim range in size from some 40 to 50 families for the smallest to about 100 to 120 families for the largest, with an average of
80 to 100 families. They constitute the bulk of the settlements in all
newly developed regions. In 1967 moshavim numbered 345, with a
population of about 121,600 persons and 174,000 acres of arable land,
equivalent to about 45 and 30 percent, respectively, of the population
and arable acreage in Jewish farms. The moshavim had a total labor
force of 43,700 persons, 39,600 of whom worked in agriculture.

The moshav shitufi is a collective village that combines economic
features of the kibbutz with social features of the moshav. Farming
is conducted as a collective enterprise and profits are shared equally,
on the model of the kibbutz. Living arrangements are those of a
moshav. This form of settlement provides farmers with collective
economic security, while preserving their individual family life.

290

There were 22,000 collective villages in 1967 with a populati
about 5,000 and 16,500 acres or arable land.

Non-Jewish villages, mostly in the hill regions, numbered 9§
1967, with a population of more than 185,500 Muslims, Druze, a
Christians. These non-Jewish rural people living in villages constituted about 37 percent of the total rural population. Only 25,000
persons were actively engaged in farming. The villagers worked
about 215,000 acres of cultivated land, not quite 21 percent of the
country's total. About 167,000 acres of this land were used for field
crops, 31,000 acres were in orchards, and 11,000 acres were used for
vegetables, potatoes, and peanuts. Irrigated acreage amounted to
10,000 acres, a fivefold increase since 1948. The organization and
production methods of these villages have been undergoing a change
from a traditional toward a Western pattern.

Cropping Pattern

Except for private farms, which specialize largely in citriculture
and winegrowing, mixed farming is the prevalent pattern. It includes
field crops, vegetable, dairy, poultry, and fruit production. Depending upon the natural conditions at the settlement site, however, one
branch or another of farming may predominate. A difference in
emphasis also exists between kibbutzim and moshavim.

Generally kibbutzim concentrate on capital-intensive and moshavim on labor-intensive production. The large size of the kibbutzim
enables them to use machinery effectively, whereas small farmers rely
primarily on their own and their families' labor. Kibbutzim therefore predominate in field crop production and moshavim in the growing of vegetables, potatoes, and peanuts. In 1967 kibbutzim accounted
for 54 percent of the field crop acreage in Jewish farms and moshavim for 28 percent. By contrast kibbutzim cultivated only 15 percent of the vegetable, potato, and peanut acreage, and the moshavim
over 63 percent.

The cultivation of cotton provides an illustration of the difference
between kibbutzim and moshavim. During the early years after its
introduction, when harvesting was done by hand, most of the cotton
was grown in moshavim and on private farms. With the appearance
of the mechanical cotton picker, the kibbutzim became the dominant
producers.

The economic advantages of large-scale production enabled kibbutzim to raise their share of the milk output to 50 percent of the
total, at the expense of the moshavim. Within the moshavim a process
of concentrating larger herds in a smaller number of farms is taking
place. Kibbutzim have also acquired a dominant position in the production of deciduous fruits, bananas, and the recently introduced
avocadoes and mangoes.

PRODUCTION

In 1968 agricultural production totaled over I£1.7 billion (I£1 equals approximately US$0.285—see Glossary), a sixfold increase (in comparable prices) over the 1949 output of I£275 million. This increase represents a cumulative annual growth rate of 10 percent. The rate of expansion has been steadily declining, from an annual average of 16 percent during the 1949–54 period to only about 4.5 percent during the 1964–67 period. The year-to-year rates of increase varied rather widely, largely in response to climatic conditions, but at no time did output fall below the level of the preceding year.

The initial spurt in output was caused by the urgent need of the newly established state to provide food for its rapidly growing population in the face of a severe shortage precipitated by the total cessation of shipments from the neighboring Arab countries. It was facilitated by the acquisition of new lands, the influx of immigrants (many of whom were directed into agriculture), and by massive investments in agricultural development and irrigation. Productivity rose rapidly in response to large-scale mechanization and intensive use of fertilizers and pesticides (see table 20).

With declining immigration in subsequent years, the expanding output caught up with the domestic demand for most products by 1960. The demand for vegetables had been met 5 years earlier. Because of inadequate foreign market outlets, surpluses actually developed in a number of commodities, including vegetables, poultry, milk, and eggs. The consequent pressure on farm prices and adjustments in the government's price supports brought about a slowing down in the growth of output.

In terms of value, plant products constituted 57.5 percent of the total farm output in 1968 and livestock products, 42.5 percent. The major products in that year were citrus fruits, field crops, and meats, followed by fruits other than citrus, milk, eggs, and vegetables. The output included about 1.3 million metric tons of citrus; 265,000 metric tons of grain, including 190,000 metric tons of wheat; 450,000 metric tons of vegetables and potatoes; 114,000 metric tons of meat; 117 million gallons of milk; and 1.1 billion eggs.

Citriculture is one of the oldest branches of the country's agriculture. Developed as an export industry before the establishment of the state, it suffered a severe decline as a result of World War II and the War of Independence in 1948. After the wars, old orchards were rehabilitated and new ones planted in moshavim and kibbutzim, with a consequent growth in output and export volume. The 1968 production constituted about 22 percent of total farm output. It was 4.7 times larger than output in 1949, and citrus exports of US$88.4 million were almost 5 times higher.

Table 20. Agricultural Production of Israel for Selected Years, 1949–67 [1]
(in thousands of metric tons) [2]

Major Item	Average		
	1949–51	1957–59	1965–67

Field Crops:

Grains:

Wheat	21	73	157
Barley	28	64	48
Sorghum	3	38	35

Industrial Crops:

Peanuts (unshelled)	1	15	13
Cotton (lint)	---	5	25
Cottonseed	---	9	41
Tobacco	1	2	2
Sugar beets	0 [3]	91	272

Melons and Pumpkins	24	71	93

Vegetables and Potatoes:

Potatoes	33	93	102
Vegetables	116	259	331
Tomatoes [4]	(20)	(69)	(83)
Cucumbers [4]	(10)	(18)	(27)
Carrots [4]	(7)	(19)	(21)
Onions [4]	(2)	(16)	(24)
Others	(77)	(137)	(176)

Fruit:

Citrus Fruit:

Oranges	249 [5]	383	682
Grapefruit	42 [5]	64	192
Lemons	7 [5]	16	38

Deciduous Fruit (including nuts):

Apples [4]	1 [3]	6	54
Pears [4]	0 [3]	0 [3]	13
Peaches [4]	0 [3]	1	10
Plums [4]	2	6	7

Other Fruit:

Olives	6	11	15
Bananas	4	26	49
Table grapes	9	23	44
Wine grapes	7	27	36

Table 20.—Continued

Major Item	Average		
	1949–51	1957–59	1965–67
Livestock Products:			
Eggs (millions)	321	848	1,310
Milk (million gallons) :			
Cows' milk	24	58	93
Sheep and goat milk	3	11	12
Meat (live weight) :			
Poultry	7	32	82
Cattle	2	13	30
Sheep and goats	1	4	7
Fish	6	12	22

[1] Agricultural years ending September 30; for example, agricultural year 1949 is from October 1, 1948 through September 30, 1949.

[2] Except where otherwise specified.

[3] Less than 500 metric tons.

[4] Organized marketing.

[5] Citrus fruit figure is average of 1949–51, but the breakdown for 1949 and 1950 is lacking. The breakdown here was prorated in accordance with the 1951 figures.

Source: Adapted from Israel, Central Bureau of Statistics, *Statistical Abstract of Israel, 1968*, pp. 324–325, 336–337, 340.

Fruit production other than citrus, including nuts, accounted for about 9.5 percent of farm output in 1968. Nearly all the orchards were planted since the establishment of the state, in response to a strong domestic demand for fruits. More than 20 varieties are grown, ranging from types produced in temperate climates to those native to the tropics. Apples, grapes, and bananas constitute about two-thirds of the total volume; pears, peaches, apricots, and olives about one-fourth. Avocadoes, guavas, mangoes, pineapples, persimmons, loquats, dates, figs, and a few other varieties are produced in smaller amounts. Increasing quantities of these fruits are being exported, partly in processed form.

During the first 5 years of the state's existence, grain production nearly tripled, encouraged by the government in a drive for self-sufficiency. Vulnerability of the crop to droughts, with consequent heavy costs to the government for drought insurance payments, and availability of United States surplus grain on concessionary terms, resulted in the eventual restriction of grain growing to areas where the probability of droughts is low. Although the grain acreage has hardly expanded since 1954, grain output increased about 260 percent, mainly because better seeds and production methods were used. During this period wheat replaced barley as the major grain crop. Grains cannot be grown in sufficient quantity to satisfy domestic needs.

Among important field crops, other than grains, are cotton and sugar beet. Commercial production of cotton began in 1955 and output rose to 33,000 metric tons of medium-staple fiber and 55,000 metric tons of seed by 1968. The output supplies all domestic needs for this length of staple and provides increasing quantities for export, which reached a level of US$5.2 million in that year. Attempts to grow long-staple Pima cotton have not been successful.

Production of sugar beets was introduced about the same time as cotton to supply the needs of local refineries. Output rose to almost 295,000 metric tons in 1965, surpassing the available refining capacity, but declined to about 274,000 metric tons by 1968 through the imposition of production quotas. Local production of sugar covers about 35 percent of consumption.

Output of livestock products is in excess of domestic demand, except for beef, and eggs since 1968. Beef accounts for only about one-fifth of the domestic meat supply, but poultry provides two-thirds of the total volume. Lamb, mutton, goat, and camel meat make up the balance. All but a small portion of this output is obtained from Jewish farms, which raised livestock herds totaling about 196,000 head of cattle and 156,000 sheep and goats in 1967, and poultry flocks totaling 8.1 million birds, including 6.7 million laying hens. These numbers reflected a sixfold increase in livestock and an almost fivefold increase in poultry since 1958. Poultry flocks have been hard hit by Newcastle disease (virus disease resembling bronchitis), since the Six-Day War of June 1967 brought contact with infected flocks in the occupied areas.

The largest increase has been in the number of beef cattle, which grew from only 410 in 1950 to almost 68,000 in 1963. In the next 4 years the number declined somewhat, reaching 56,950 in 1967. These fluctuations, caused by changes in the relative profitability of beef and milk production, were brought about in part through the operation of the government's subsidy program. The absence of pastures and the high cost of home-grown and imported feed make beef production expensive. Domestic beef output, therefore, is not expected to cover consumption needs in the foreseeable future.

ROLE OF GOVERNMENT

The government has exercised a broad control over the development of agriculture. Almost all activities concerned with rural settlement, such as the channeling of manpower, allocation of land and water, and financing of investments, have been carried out by the Jewish Agency and the government, which have thus determined the location of the settlements and the direction and scope of their activities.

Agricultural policy has been shaped in response to several objectives, not all of which are compatible. Among the major objectives are rapid settlement of the land for social and strategic reasons, maximum satisfaction of the country's food requirements through domestic production and the development of farm exports to reduce the foreign trade gap, increased productivity to lower costs and make farm products competitive in foreign markets, low food prices to consumers, equality of incomes among farmers, and parity of farm income with incomes in other sectors of the economy. In pursuit of these aims, the government has intervened both in the production and marketing of farm products.

The government and the Jewish Agency determine the scope and details of the farm production program through a joint planning center in the Ministry of Agriculture. In cooperation with regional and local bodies, this office prepares long-range overall plans for agriculture as a whole and for specific branches, as well as regional and detailed annual plans.

Production and prices have been influenced by selective controls over imports of farm products and through government-supported marketing boards in all branches of agriculture. Exempt from anti-trust laws, these boards enjoy broad powers, including the allocation of production among farmers in accordance with the exigencies of the market.

A more direct method used to stimulate production and to maintain farm prices and incomes, while keeping consumer prices reasonably low, involves the payment of subsidies out of the government budget for various farm products and input items such as feeds, water, and fertilizer. These subsidies favor the weaker, that is, the less efficient producers. Over the years, price supports have been extended to a larger share of the total output and a greater number of products.

In 1968 price-support payments amounted to I£161.5 million, including direct subsidies of I£109.5 million on output and I£42.0 million on input. The largest direct subsidies by far were paid for cows' milk and eggs, amounting to I£35.4 million and I£22.7 million, respectively. Wheat was a poor third, with I£9.4 million, followed by vegetables and potatoes, sugar beets, beef, poultry, and seven or more other commodities. Direct and indirect subsidies on livestock products, exclusive of water and fertilizer payments, accounted for about 57 percent of the total.

Substantial additional subsidies are provided by the government through the provision of credit on easy terms and through the assumption by the government of the major share of the cost of irrigation water. This share has been estimated by Israeli economists to be more than two-thirds of the total cost.

The drive for increased output and the income-support policy have stimulated production of several items to a level which exceeds domestic needs and export possibilities. To cope with this surplus problem, a system of production quotas has been introduced. Among the products subject to quota allocation are milk, eggs, certain vegetables, and sugar beets.

The government is aware of the shortcomings of its price- and income-support measures in regulating production and of their negative effect on productive efficiency. It is equally aware of the desirability of placing agriculture on a more sound economic basis. The authorities realize that their commitment to the maintenance of farm incomes and the importance of the noneconomic aspects of agriculture preclude any major change in policies under present conditions. Hope is placed in the development of specialized production for export. In this context, substantial funds have been made available for incentive payments in the form of grants and loans, in addition to the regular subsidies.

CHAPTER 21
INDUSTRY

As of early 1969 the country's industry, expanded and diversified since the mid-1950's, has been called upon by the government to spearhead further economic development and to assure the supply of essential defense needs. It has also been urged to intensify production for export and for import substitution in order to help reduce the large foreign trade deficit. Industrial export expansion is to be founded in large part on chemicals and on new science-based industries to be developed in cooperation with the research institutes and universities. As an inducement for industry to respond to this challenge, the government liberalized incentives for domestic and foreign investors and outlined a broadened program of financial and fiscal support for export industries.

Despite a scarcity of indigenous raw materials, industry, including construction, has grown at a rapid pace, with a brief slowdown during the 1965–67 economic recession (see ch. 19, Character and Structure of the Economy). It has provided employment for a little more than one-third of the labor force and has contributed an equal share to the national income. Manufactures, ranging from simple consumer goods to complicated electronic equipment, reached a level of about I£8 billion (I£1 equals approximately US$0.285—see Glossary), and industrial exports rose to US$490 million in 1968.

Industrial ownership is divided among private individuals, the government, the Histadrut (Histadrut Ha'ovdim Haklalit—General Federation of Labor), and other public bodies. With the exception of government-operated mining and mineral-processing plants, industrial establishments, heavily concentrated in the coastal plains, are generally small scale and nonspecialized. Much of the labor force has had no previous industrial experience and, despite intensive training programs, essential technical and managerial skills are in short supply. In a number of instances, particularly in the outlying areas that are being newly developed, purely economic considerations have had to be subordinated to broader national goals. These conditions, accompanied by a general lack of active competition, have militated against the achievement of high productive efficiency, with consequent high costs of production.

The government has played an active role in the direction of industrial development in three ways: provision of substantial financial support on a selective basis to individual plants and industries; granting of varying degrees of protection against imports and subsidies for exports; and authorization of the formation of cartels under certain circumstances. To stimulate greater efficiency, however, and thus make domestic goods more competitive in world markets, the government has progressively, though not substantially, reduced the level of protection against imports.

The directing role of government and the government's participation in industrial production have been intensified by the urgent need arising from the Six-Day War of June 1967 to develop domestic manufacture of complex defense equipment. The country's substantial research resources have been mobilized in support of this production program. Authorities expect these developments to provide a strong stimulus to the metals, machinery, aviation, optical, and electronic industries, which would raise the country's capability to export industrial goods.

Building construction, a key element in the country's economy, is reported to have recovered from the severe slump it suffered in 1965–67 and to be booming in 1968–69. Electric generating capacity and power production have kept pace with the rising needs.

RAW MATERIALS

Industrial development is hampered by a scarcity of raw materials and cheap sources of energy. Aside from an adequate supply of building materials, minerals are limited to potash in the Dead Sea and to small, low-grade phosphate rock and copper ore deposits. Only minor crude oil and natural gas deposits have been discovered. Agriculture provides citrus fruits and some sugar beets for the food-processing industry and a portion of the cotton requirements for the textile mills. The great bulk of raw materials must be imported. Imports of raw materials for industry averaged about I£414 million per year in 1964–67, including over I£112 million in rough diamonds (see ch. 24, Foreign Economic Relations).

The Dead Sea constitutes the major mineral reservoir, its water having a salt content of 27 percent (see ch. 2, Physical Environment). The principal salts are chlorides of magnesium, sodium, calcium, and potassium, and also some magnesium bromide. The estimated reserves range from 1 billion tons of magnesium bromide to 22 billion tons of magnesium chloride. The latter is to be used as raw material for a new chemical combine under construction at Arad, near the Dead Sea and 24 miles east of Beersheba.

There are several phosphate rock deposits, with major fields located at Oron, Hazeva, and En Yahav, in the northeastern Negev. Most of the deposits can be exploited by open-pit mining. With a P_2O_5 (phos-

300

phorus pentoxide) content of 25 to 30 percent, they are rated as medium to low grade.

Deposits of low-grade copper ore with a copper content of 1.2 to 1.8 percent are located in the Timna area near Eilat. Of 20 million tons proved reserves, about 4 million tons are suitable for open-pit mining. An additional 10 million tons of possible reserves are estimated to be in the same area.

Small deposits of crude oil and natural gas have been discovered at several locations. Commercially exploitable reserves of crude oil in fields at Helez, Beror Hayil, Negba, and Kokhav, some 8 to 10 miles east and southeast of Ashqelon, are estimated to contain the equivalent of about 2 million tons of liquid fuel. The oil and gas production from these fields suffices to satisfy only about 8 percent of the country's needs. Oil prospecting is being intensified at an annual cost of about I£20 million to I£25 million.

There are no water resources for hydroelectric development. Electric power production depends upon thermal plants using imported oil.

STRUCTURE

Size and Location

Information on the structure of industry is based on an industrial census taken in 1965, and the latest available data are for 1966. In that year there were 6,631 industrial establishments employing 5 or more persons, resulting in a total employment of 172,400. About half of these enterprises employed fewer than 10 persons, and only one-tenth of the plants employed 50 or more. Seventy establishments, a little more than one in a hundred, had a labor force of 300 or more. These were primarily government-opterated mining and mineral-processing plants.

In addition, there were roughly 18,000 small workshops employing up to four persons, with a total employment of about 34,000 workers, including the owners. Industry is thus predominantly small scale, a natural consequence of the small domestic market. A meaningful breakdown of the number of plants and employees by industry branch is not available, since the census of 1965 included in its definition of industrial establishments the smallest repair and maintenance shops. Information on the defense industry has not been published.

Industrial enterprises are highly concentrated in the populated coastal plains from Acre to the Rehovot area about 12 miles southeast of Jerusalem. About 80 percent of the establishments with 75 percent of the workers were located there in 1966. The small Tel Aviv administrative district alone accounted for almost 54 percent of the firms, with about 41 percent in the city of Tel Aviv-Jaffa. Of the remaining 20 percent of the firms, about 5 percent were located in the southern part of the country, and the balance was evenly divided between the northern part and the Jerusalem area.

Ownership

Industrial ownership is divided among private individuals, the Histadrut, and public bodies. The public segment of industry is composed of companies owned by the government, the National Institutions—Jewish Agency, Jewish National Fund, and Keren Hayesod (Foundation Fund)— and by local authorities. The Histadrut segment includes cooperatives, enterprises owned by kibbutzim (collective farms or settlements), and firms wholly owned by Hevrat Ovdim, the Histadrut holding company (see ch. 13, The Governmental System; ch. 22, Labor).

In 1965 private industry, excluding owner-operated shops, accounted for about 93 percent of all establishments, or roughly 14,600, including shops with a single employee. Employment in the privately-owned establishments amounted to about 168,000 persons, or an average of less than 12 workers per plant. Private enterprise accounted for 90 percent or more of the employment in the diamond, textile, paper, and leather branches of industry.

Histadrut-affiliated enterprises totaled about 865, with 33,000 workers, or an average of about 38 workers per plant. Of these workers 48 percent were employed in plants owned by the Hevrat Ovdim, 31 percent in kibbutz industries, and 21 percent in cooperatives. These enterprises were represented in all industrial fields but were concentrated more heavily in basic metals, nonmentalic minerals, wood products (primarily plywood), machinery, and quarrying.

Publicly owned establishments other than defense plants numbered about 190, with a total employment of 19,000, or 100 employees per plant. Seventy percent of these employees worked in government companies. Public enterprises were active in all branches of industry, except diamonds and paper but were concentrated mainly in chemicals and petroleum refining, shipyards, the aviation industry, and in mining and quarrying.

These plant and employment statistics understate the role of public and Histadrut industry, because the plants in these sectors are not only larger than in the private sector but also more highly mechanized and more productive. The statistics also omit the substantial and rapidly expanding defense industry. Information on the relative importance of the three industrial segments in terms of their respective shares in equity capital or total output is lacking.

Employment and Productivity

Industrial employment, excluding construction, of about 203,800 persons in 1967 was about 2.3 times greater than in 1950 and constituted 24.6 percent of total employment. The industrial labor force had been rising steadily at an average annual rate of about 6 percent to a maximum of 227,400 in 1966 but declined the following year by nearly 24,000 as a result of the economic recession and the effects of the Six-Day War. By 1968, with the revival of the economy and accelerated industrial expansion, employment rose again and labor shortages reappeared (see ch. 22, Labor).

During the period 1950–66 the manufacturing industry absorbed about 30 percent of new employment. Many of the new workers were immigrants without previous industrial experience or training, and the general educational level of many of these was low. Intensive training programs in which the government, the army, and the Histadrut played an important role succeeded in raising the general level of skills. Nevertheless, a shortage of skilled manpower and, at times even of unskilled labor, posed a serious problem throughout the 1960's.

Output per worker in 1966 was I£31,100, more than double the value (in comparable prices) during the early 1950's. Labor productivity rose at an annual rate of about 6 percent per year since 1952, when the output per worker was at a postindependence low of I£13,-500, in response to more intensive mechanization, technological improvements, increasing plant size, better utilization of productive capacity, and a rising level of workers' skills. Productivity was also furthered by the introduction of incentive pay systems (see ch. 22 Labor). Capital per gainfully employed worker in industry and mining rose from I£6,540 in 1950 to I£20,160 in 1966 (at 1966 prices), an increase of 7 percent per year.

Industrial Organization and Structural Problems

The orgainzation of industry and some other features of the industrial structure militate against the achievement of maximum efficiency, with a consequent high cost of production. In addition to the uneconomically small size of most plants, there is a lack of specialization and only limited competition. The lack of specialization arises from the demand for a large variety of products in the small domestic market and results in an underutilization of the plants' productive capacties. It also intensifies management and distribution problems.

The lack of competition is an outgrowth of the pattern of industrial production and control. In most fields a large share of the output is concentrated in a small number of plants, and only a few firms control the bulk of the output. In the manufacturing industry, excluding diamonds, active competition affected only about 18 percent of the total industrial production in 1961. Most of the industry is effectively protected against foreign competition, although the degree of protection is gradually being reduced as a means of stimulating greater efficiency.

Many industrial companies are joined in cartels, limiting competition through agreed prices, allocation of quotas, and other restrictive measures. These cartels are subject to approval by a special public council, established by a Restrictive Practices Law enacted in 1960 and amended in 1963. Approval is granted only for cartels deemed to be in the public interest. Most of the forty approved cartels that existed in 1968 had as their declared objectives the expansion of exports, greater efficiency in production, prevention of destructive competition, and joint research. In some instances these goals were not reached, and cartelization in these instances led to higher prices in the domestic market.

DEVELOPMENT AND FINANCING

Development Assistance

Industrial development was stimulated by a Law for the Encouragement of Capital Investment, enacted in 1950 and liberalized through subsequent amendments. Under this law, intended to promote the settlement of outlying areas, approved enterprises may receive substantial cash grants and low-interest loans for buildings and equipment, as well as tax exemption, the right to accelerated depreciation of facilities for purposes of tax computation, and various other benefits for a period of several years.

Major criteria for establishing eligibility of enterprises include the proposed investment's contribution to the improvement of the trade balance, either through exports or import substitution; its contribution to employment, particularly in the development areas; and assurance of continuous orderly production of items considered essential for the economy. The benefits apply equally to domestic and foreign investors. Foreign investors may repatriate all profits and capital within 5 years and transfer their investment to other nonresidents without loss of the benefits.

The magnitude of the concession varies according to location, being greatest in priority development areas and lowest in established population centers. In the highest priority regions, the Negev and Galilee, grants and low-interest loans together amount to 80 percent of the cost of fixed assets, and the interest rate on loans is 6.5 percent, as against a regular bank rate of 10 percent (see ch. 25, Financial and Monetary System). In established areas the comparable figures are 60 percent of fixed asset costs and 9 percent interest.

Investment

Investment in manufacturing and mining has averaged about a quarter of the total gross investment and amounted to about I£5.5 billion (in 1966 prices) for the period 1950–67. The annual volume of investment rose steadily from a low of I£154 million in 1955 to I£514 million in 1964 but declined to I£264 million in 1967 because of the economic recession. In 1968 investment increased by roughly 50 percent. About two-thirds of the equity capital was derived from private sources and retained earnings. The value of industrial plants and equipment rose by an average of 13.5 percent between 1950 and 1966.

The high rate of investment was made possible in part by direct public investment in industry and by relatively low-interest loans for investment purposes provided either directly by the government or, upon its recommendation, by banks and financial institutions. Public financing accounted for about 35 percent of the investment in mining and industry between 1950 and 1966. Its share was larger in financing plants producing for export and in development area projects. The securities market is not yet sufficiently developed to serve as a significant source of industrial investment capital (see ch. 25, Financial and Monetary System).

Credit

Medium- and long-term credit for industry is provided by the Industrial Development Bank of Israel (IDBI), established in 1957 with private, public, and foreign participation; by a specialized mortgage bank, Tefahot; and by investment affiliates of three large commercial banks. The IDBI is the most important of these credit sources, and its loans constituted rougly one-fourth of the estimated gross industrial investment from 1960 to 1967. The IDBI has received loans for investment purposes from both the United States Agency for International Development and the International Bank for Reconstruction and Development (World Bank). In the first 10 years of its existence, it granted loans to industry totaling about I£900 million.

Bank credit is subject to government control, and loans are allocated to individual enterprises in amounts and at interest rates determined by their priority status. Preference is given to plants manufacturing for export or located in development areas. Bank credit to industry quadrupled between 1960 and 1967 and constituted from about 35 to more than 40 percent of the total credit extended by the bank in the years 1963 to 1966.

Availability of bank credit at the maximum legal interest of 10 percent for industrial loans has always been industry's requirements. Many establishments, therefore, particularly those in low priority categories, have borrowed on short-term notes in the bill brokerage market. The volume or industrial credit from this source averaged about 30 to 40 percent of the regular bank loans between 1963 and 1967.

PRODUCTION

In 1966, the latest year for which complete official data are available, industrial output amounted to about I£6.2 billion. It had grown rapidly since 1950, increasing by an average of about 10 percent per year. As a result of the economic recession, however, industrial progress slowed down after 1964, and output actually declined by 3 percent in 1967. The revival of the economy after the Six-Day War was accompanied by a new spurt in industrial growth. Industry was reported as booming in 1968, with an officially estimated increase of over 25 percent in output to a record volume of approximately I£8 billion.

The rapid growth in output was stimulated primarily by a strong domestic demand for manufactured goods, generated by a rapidly expanding population and by a rising standard of living. Government incentives for the expansion of production for export also played an important role. Intensive residential, business, and industrial construction activity gave a strong impetus to the production of building materials and other investment goods. After the Six-Day War, an additional stimulus to industrial growth was provided by an intensification of the government's drive for self-sufficiency in defense production.

The growth in output was accompanied by an increasing diversification. In contrast to the early 1950's, when industry was concerned mainly with the manufacture of basic consumer goods, output in 1968 comprised a broad range of products, including basic chemicals and fertilizers, rubber and plastic products, machinery, transport equipment, and such complicated items as petrochemicals, advanced electronic equipment, and small passenger jet aircraft. Defense plants were producing a variety of modern arms and ammunition. A plant for the manufacture of small jet engines, previously imported from France, was under construction in early 1969.

Despite the substantial widening of the range of products, food and textiles still constituted the major elements of output. In 1966 these two categories accounted for about I£1.4 billion and I£635 million, or some 22 and 10 percent, respectively, of the total industrial production. They were followed, in order of output value, by polished diamonds, metal products, transport equipment, wood products, chemicals, and nonmetallic mineral products. The market value of these product groups ranged from about I£525 million for diamonds to

I£322 million for nonmetallic mineral products, and totaled almost I£2.4 billion, or about 38 percent of the total output.

About 34 percent of the 1966 production was destined for direct consumption, 5 percent for investment in various branches of the economy and 16 percent for direct export (see ch. 24, Foreign Economic Relations). The remaining 45 percent constituted intermediate products, mostly building materials and agricultural supplies.

MINING AND MINERAL PROCESSING

The mining and processing of minerals in government-owned facilities have been given a high priority, because the bulk of the output of this industry is available for export. Major mining activity involes the extraction of potash and bromide from the Dead Sea; phosphate mining at Oron, southeast of Beersheba; copper production at Timna near Eilat; and salt production at Atlit, about 9 miles south of Haifa.

The extraction of potash, begun by private interests and assumed by the government after 1948, developed less rapidly than planned because of various technical difficulties. By 1968 the capacity of the plant had reached 660,000 metric tons per year, and output grew to about 600,000 metric tons. All except about 20,000 tons of this output was exported. In addition, small quantities of magnesium bromide and of sodium chloride (common salt) were produced.

Exploitation of the Oron phosphate deposits, started in 1951, has also been plagued by technical difficulties, related primarily to the enrichment of the low-grade phosphate rock. Additional problems were presented by a lack of adequate transportation facilities and by the high cost of labor because of the difficult working conditions in that part of the country. Output, however, increased to 775,000 metric tons in 1968, about 500,000 tons of which were exported. The Oron deposit is expected to be exhausted by the mid-1970's when exploitation will have to be shifted to lower-grade rock at more distant fields.

Production of chemical fertilizers is carried on by a chemical combine in Haifa. A new chemical complex was being erected in 1969 at Arad in collaboration with a United States firm. It is designed to produce about 230,000 metric tons of phosphoric acid using magnesium chloride transported from the Dead Sea by pipeline and phosphate rock from the deposit at Hazeva. This combine, planned to enter into operation by the end of 1969, is to produce concentrated chemical fertilizers, detergents, industrial chemicals, and phosphates for animal feed. By early 1969, export contracts had already been entered into for a portion of the projected output. The cost of this plant was estimated at I£100 million, and exports of its products were planned to reach US$12 million by 1971.

Also under construction in 1969 was a plant in Haifa for the production of potassium nitrate fertilizer and phosphoric acid. It will use potash from the Dead Sea, phosphate rock from the Negev, and locally produced ammonia. Planned capacity is 100,000 metric tons of potassium nitrate and about 22,000 metric tons of phosphoric acid for use by the food industry. Practically the entire output of this plant is to be exported. The cost of this plant was estimated at I£40 million, and 1971 exports at US$6 million.

CONSTRUCTION

The construction industry has played a greater role in the economy than is usual in long-established countries because of the massive investment required to provide housing for a large influx of immigrants and to develop the economy over a short period of time to the level of industrialized states. During the decade of 1956–65 it contributed about 9 percent of the net domestic product and provided employment for about 10 percent of the gainfully employed population. The annual value of new construction during this period increased by 2.5 times from approximately I£0.765 billion to about I£1.9 billion.

In 1966 building activity was adversely affected by an earlier sharp decline in immigration, by the completion or curtailment of several large development projects and by a deflationary economic policy of the government aimed at reducing the foreign trade deficit (see ch. 19, Character and Structure of the Economy). It revived in the second half of 1967 and in 1968, spurred by a resumption of industrial expasion and by new immigration in the wake of the Six-Day War. Public works initiated by the government in 1966 also helped reverse the declining trend.

During the period of 1950 to 1967, investment in construction constituted about 60 percent of total investment and amounted to more than £21 billion (in 1966 prices). Roughly half of this investment was devoted to housing; 36 percent to the construction of economic facilities; and the balance to various institutional buildings, including schools, hospitals, and government offices.

Employment in construction and public works rose from nearly 55,000 persons in 1955 to about 92,000 in 1965 but declined to only 63,000 in 1967 as a result of the building slump. Fluctuations in building activity caused temporary labor shortages, which drove wages above the level of official pay scales, and contributed to rising unemployment in the recession of 1965–67 (see ch. 22, Labor). Mechanization of the industry was not far advanced, and productivity was low by comparison with other branches of industry.

Construction has been carried out both by private interests and by public bodies. The public sector accounted for 34 to 50 perecnt of the fixed capital investment during the years 1952–1966 and for 44 percent of the investment in housing during 1955 to 1967. Its share in housing investment, however, declined from 42 percent in 1955 to 30 percent in 1967. The actual work of building public projects has been performed by private contractors.

Public construction activity included all infrastructure projects, such as water supply, electricity, highways, ports, and communication facilities; the development of mines and the construction of government-operated industrial plants; public buildings; and housing, mainly low-cost. The value of public construction rose from I£260 million in 1950 (in 1966 prices) to I£500 million in 1966.

Housing construction amounted to about 650,000 units, including some temporary buildings built between 1948 and 1967, worth approximately I£11 billion in 1966 prices. About 233,000 of the permanent units, valued at I£7 billion, were built by private enterprise, and 370,000 units, worth about I£4 billion, by public authorities. Privately built dwellings intended for the higher income groups were usually larger and better equipped than housing built by public authorities for immigrants and the underprivileged. Most housing is built for sale, with credit arrangements to ease the burden of purchase, especially for low-income families. Dwellings built for immigrants, however, are leased to the occupants.

The manufacture of building components and of prefabricated housing commenced in the midsixties. Productive capacity for prefabricated housing was 5,600 units annually in 1967, but only 2,000 units were actually produced because of the economic recession. The cost of this housing was comparable to conventionally built dwellings, but a reduction in costs was anticipated with a rise in volume and improvement in methods.

ELECTRIC POWER

All except a small fraction of the country's electricity supply is generated by the government-controlled Israel Electric Corporation (IEC) and distributed by it over a national network stretching from Metulla in the northestern tip of the country to Eilat in the south. About 4 percent of the total output is produced by some industrial enterprises and a few isolated villages for their own consumption.

In 1967 the installed capacity of IEC's three thermal stations at Haifa, Tel Aviv, and Ashdod amounted to just over 1 million kilowatts and reflected a capital investment of about I£1.25 billion (in 1966 prices) in the power industry during the period from 1950 to 1967. Virtually all the existing capacity has been built since the attainment of statehood. Plans of the IEC call for doubling the 1967 capacity in 10 years.

The production of electricity in 1967 reached about 4.6 billion kilowatt-hours. During the decade ended in that year, labor productivity in the electric power industry nearly tripled. The average number of permanent employees per million kilowatt-hours declined from 3.2 to 1.1. At the same time, fuel consumption per kilowatt-hour fell by about 10 percent.

Annual per capita consumption of electricity rose from 299 kilowatt-hours in 1948 to approximately 1.460 kilowatt-hours in 1966. Since 1960 roughly one-third of the total output has been consumed in industry and one-fourth by irrigation. The remainder has covered residential and other consumer needs.

Industrial demand for electricity is highly concentrated. At least until 1967 only seven enterprises consumed 27 percent of the total used by industry, and 10 more plants consumed an additional 12 percent. The main industrial users of electricity are the chemical, minerals, and metal industries.

By introducing a system of differential rates for power and through arrangements with large users of electricity, the IEC has been able to reduce the fluctuation of the daily demand between peak and off hours. The load factor, which expresses this fluctuation as a percentage of the average load to peak-hour load, rose steadily from 55 percent in 1954 to 72 percent in 1966, which shows a significant improvement in the utilization of available capacity.

There are no adequate water resources for significant hydroelectric power development. The existing stations and planned additions are dependent upon imported petroleum for fuel. Long-term studies of the use of nuclear power for the production of electricity have led to the conclusion that, for the time being, the cost of a nuclear station would be highly uneconomical. Research on the development of cheaper methods, however, continues, and the feasibility of building dual-purpose electric power and water desalinization plants is being investigated.

CHAPTER 22
LABOR

In 1969 Israel had a labor force of slightly over 1 million, or about one-third of an estimated total population of 2.82 million. This figure is based on the annual growth rate of the labor force, estimated by Israeli labor experts at about 4 percent.

Details reflecting characteristics of the working population show that in 1967 there were approximately 1.8 million persons of working age (14 years old and over), of whom about 926,900 constituted the civilian labor force, including some 73,600 non-Jews; the rest were in the military service, or were retired persons, housewives, and students. Of the total civilian labor force, 89.6 percent, or about 830,700 persons, were gainfully employed; the rest were unemployed. Of the gainfully employed, 24.6 percent were in industry, 24.1 percent in the public services, 13.5 percent in commerce, finance, and insurance, 12.6 percent in agriculture, 8.1 percent in personal services, 7.6 in construction, 7.3 percent in transportation, and 2.2 percent in public utilities. The relatively large proportion of workers in the public and personal services has been characterisic of the Israeli labor force, but the percentages of workers in those sectors in 1967 were not as high as those during the late 1950's.

About one-third of the labor force was skilled. Immigration was an important source of supply for this category of workers, especially in the professional and technical occupations. The government maintained recruiting services abroad to encourage immigration of scientists, engineers, and technicians.

Large-scale immigration contributed to an increase of almost 50 percent in the labor between 1955 and 1965. During that period full employment was almost maintained by vigorous economic activity, the services of government labor exchanges, and government subsidies granted to enterprises in proportion to the number of workers. The economic recession, starting late in 1965 and continuing through the Six-Day War of June 1967, precipitated nationwide unemployment, although government work-relief projects helped to check the economic social problems affecting many of the jobless. During the recession, attrition in employment was noted in several economic sectors. Since many of the public work projects were completed just prior to the recession, the attrition was especially notable in the construction sector (see ch. 19, Character and Structure of the Economy; ch. 21, Industry). Unemployment was sharply reduced with the economic recovery late in 1967; in 1968 an average of about 910,000 persons were gainfully employed.

About three-fourths of the gainfully employed labor forces in 1968 were wage and salary earners. The working conditions of about 90 percent of those workers were regulated by collective agreements covering a wide range of benefits and offering terms far more favorable than the minimum provisions contained in labor laws. Workers also benefit from the national insurance scheme and from pension funds operated by the trade unions and financed by workers' and employees' contributions (see ch. 8, Living Conditions). Wages are determined jointly by the government and by the trade unions and are adjusted to the cost of living. The amount of wages was often the subject of labor disputes, but both organized labor and individual workers have shown restraint in demanding wage raises in the presence of unemployment and the economic slowdown of 1965-67. To compensate for the absence of wage raises, the government granted supplementary allowances, tax benefits, and shorter working hours to workers in low-wage categories.

The tradition of labor organization has been strong since the period of the British Palestine Mandate (1923-48). By 1968 the labor force was almost fully organized. The overwhelming majority of unionized workers were members of the Histadrut (Histadrut Ha'ovdim Haklalit—General Federation of Labor, commonly know as Histadrut), a national-level, socialist labor organization unique to Israel, pervading the economic, political, and social life of the country. Histadrut trade unions in 1968 comprised over a million members, including their spouses, as well as persons affiliated with Histadrut through participation in its sick fund and pension plans. Histadrut's extensive economic activities have made it the country's principal employer, with about one-quarter of the labor force on its payrolls.

The influence of Histadrut in national politics derives from the composition of its governing bodies. The representative to these bodies are elected by proportional representation from lists submitted by political parties, with elections held in the same manner as the national elections. Thus, since the establishment of statehood of Israel in 1948, members of the MAPAI (see Glossary) predominated in the top echelons of the Histadrut and of the government. This relationship enabled the leadership of both organizations to resolve potential divergences between them within the councils of MAPAI (see ch. 14, Political Dynamics).

Histadrut's size and its influence in the economy, in social welfare, and in politics have made it an active partner of the government in formulating national policies, especially those governing wages, the use of manpower, and matters of social welfare. Its pervasive activities, especially those relating to the management of its economic enterprises and to the jurisdiction of social welfare schemes, have often been the subject of criticism by those top echelon Histadrut officials who represent the militant socialist parties to the left of MAPAI.

Industrial peace during the late 1960's has been relatively stable, but labor disputes and strikes have occurred, many of them in Histadrut enterprises. The controversies were often rooted in Histadrut's position as both employer and as workers' representative. Concerned with the viability and efficiency of its enterprises in a developing economy, Histadrut has not always been able to apply managerial practices embodied in the socialist labor ideology. The same considerations prevented Histadrut from responding favorably in every case to employees' demands for extended benefits and maximum job security.

THE LABOR FORCE

Participation Rates

The rate of participation in the labor force has been officially defined as the proportion of persons aged 14 years or older, who were either employed or actively seeking employment. Between 1955 and 1966 the yearly labor participation rate for the Jewish population was about 53 percent, with relatively little fluctuation from year to year. Among Arabs the participation rate was 25.3 percent in 1961, according to the latest available statistics.

Within the relatively steady rate of participation, however, changes have been noted in the percentages showing age and sex characteristics of the participants. Thus, the participation rate for men declined from 80 percent in 1955 to 76 percent in 1965. Labor experts have attributed this change mainly to the population increase in the 14 to 17 and in the 55 and older age groups, both of which tend to have low participation rates. It was noted, nevertheless, that the number of older men in the labor force has tended to increase during the 1960's.

For women, the labor participation rate rose from 26.5 to about 29.5 percent between 1955 and 1965. Most of those working were under 35 years of age. According to Israeli labor experts, this rise was due mainly to the availability of community services for working mothers, better school facilities for children, and the increasing demand for female employees in the service sector, especially in teaching, nursing, and secretarial work. In 1967 women with 9 or more years of schooling accounted for the majority, or 58.3 percent, of those at work. The participation rate was lowest among Sephardic (Middle Eastern and North African origin) Jewish women, most of whom had numerous children and few years of schooling. A growing number of younger women in this group, however, has been working or seeking work during the mid-1960's.

The economic recession of 1966–67 and the extension of the military service period for men precipitated a decline in the labor participation rate. Between these 2 years participation rates for men and women declined by 2.6 and 1.7 percent, respectively. The average labor force participation rate during 1967 was 50.4 percent compared to the average earlier rate of about 53 percent; and in 1968 it was almost the same as in 1967. Labor experts have predicted approximately the same lower rate of participation for the 1970's. The government is attempting to increase the labor participation rate by encouraging more women to work. It has established a special government committee to promote entry of women into the labor market, especially those 35 years and older. This group of women is regarded by labor experts as a source of reserve manpower.

Unemployment

Between 1961 and 1965 the yearly rate of unemployment was less than 4 percent. The rate for Arab workers was slightly higher, or about 4.6 percent. The Jewish unemployed of that period were mainly immigrants from the countries of North Africa and the Middle East. Within this group the highest unemployment rates prevailed among youths and women. At the same time, however, labor shortages existed, caused mainly by the lack of specific skills for the available job opportunities and by the uneven geographical distribution of the labor force.

The decline in immigration during the mid-1960's was reflected in diminishing activity in many economic sectors, especially in construction and in industries furnishing construction raw materals. During the first half of 1966, unemployment rose markedly, affecting mostly the coastal cities, but also the development towns. Skilled as well as unskilled workers were also affected; by 1967, skilled workers accounted for more than half of the jobless.

In late 1966 approximately 8 percent or more of the labor force was unemployed. In the construction sector alone the rate of unemployment rose to 12.7 percent from a prerecession rate of about 4.6 percent. The actual number of persons out of work in mid-1967 was estimated at about 80,000. According to official sources, more than 20,000 unemployed were assigned by the Manpower Planning Authority of the Ministry of Labor to work-relief projects, such as building schools, hospitals, bus terminals, and other public facilities.

Unempolyment began to recede early in 1968 and continued to decline throughout that year. Late in 1968 labor shortages were noted in the central regions of the country, notably in Jerusalem, Haifa, and in the Negev. The demand was greatest for skilled industrial workers in metalworking plants. Enterprises producing textile, ready-to-wear garments, and electrical and electronic equipment also had many unfilled vancanies. Government labor exchanges registered more than 25,000 job openings for unskilled workers, and also offered several thousand positions to skilled persons. The number of workers on government-relief jobs declined to 7,000.

Employment Patterns

In 1967 industry and crafts provided work for the largest number of persons, although the total of 203,800 industrial workers that year represented a more than 10 percent decline since 1966. The level of employment in industry increased slightly toward the end of 1967, but specific figures are lacking.

Construction employed 63,000 persons. This figure represents a decline in the number of employed of 16.9 percent since 1966 and of about 32 percent since 1965. In transportation and communication, the level of employment rose by 6.2 percent since 1966. Most of the 61,200 persons working in this branch of the econmy in 1967 were engaged in the inland transport of industrial and agricultural goods.

Public services employed the second largest number of workers, totaling 200,000. This economic sector included persons working for the central and local authorities of the government, for national institutions, labor organizations, political parties, educational, religious, welfare and health institutions, business and legal offices, and for city services. This sector has been only marginally affected by economic fluctuations, and the number of workers has remained relatively steady since 1965. The same has been true of personal services, which employed 66,800 workers in 1967, including domestic servants, hotel and restaurant workers, barbers and beauty salon operators, laundry workers, dry cleaners, and recreation and sport workers. Women accounted for about half of the employees in the public and private services.

Commercial, finance, and insurance companies employed 111,600 workers in 1967. Compared to the number of workers in the previous year, this figure represented a modest decline of about 1.7 percent.

There were 104,100 agricultural workers in 1967. About one-third of these worked on mixed farms (growing crops and raising animals) and on plantations growing citrus and other fruits. Mechanization and increasing productivity have accounted for a steady attrition in the employment level of this sector during the 1960's. The number of agricultural workers in 1967 represented a 3.2 percent decline from the previous year's total.

The remainder of the labor force worked in utilities (electricity, water, and sanitation). The number of workers in this sector totaled 18,500.

Data on the employment of the gainfully employed labor force show that in 1967 wage and salary earners comprised 71.2 percent of the labor force; 18.6 percent were employers, self-employed, or members of moshavim and other types of cooperatives; 6.1 percent worked in kibbutzim (collective farms or settlements); and 4.1 percent were unpaid family workers.

The most recent available data reflecting the share of white-collar workers in the labor force are for 1965. During that year administrative, managerial, executive, and clerical workers accounted for 17 percent; professional, scientific, and technical workers, for 13 percent of employed persons.

The occupational distribution of Arab workers in 1967 showed that 41.2 percent were in agriculture, 16.1 percent in construction, 15.7 percent in industry, 12 percent in services, and 8.2 percent in commerce, banking, and insurance; the remaining Arab workers were divided between transport and communications, 5.6 percent, and utilities, 1.2 percent.

Skills

From the attainment of statehood in 1948 to about 1954, the supply of skilled workers and of professional personnel was generally adequate. The high proportion of professional and technical workers and of persons who had completed secondary and higher education was characteristic of the manpower of that period. Immigrants entering between 1954 and 1957, however, came mostly from countries of the Middle East and North Africa, where they had limited opportunities for secondary education and vocational training. Among immigrants arriving after 1957, the proportion of skilled professional and technical workers was again relatively high. Moreover, graduates of Israeli secondary schools and universities began to enter the labor market. The resulting improvement in the supply of technical and professional manpower, however, was not sufficient to meet the country's needs, and shortages were noted in these categories after the mid-1960's.

According to a Ministry of Labor survey assessing the skilled manpower supply of the mid-1960's and anticipating needs for such manpower for the end of that decade, immigration represents one of the main sources of workers with high-level skills. The survey states that for some professions, the supply of qualified personnel from immigration sources equals and sometimes exceeds the output of schools, universities, and vocational training institutions. Because of the stagnation in the domestic supply of medical, engineering, transport, communication and industrial technicians, administrators, and manages, half of these workers must come from abroad in order to fill the country's needs during the 1970's.

The survey also asserts that immigrants are to fill one-third of an envisaged 60 percent increase of skilled workers in the manufacturing industry by 1970. About half of the additional technical workers needed in construction by that year are to come from abroad. In administrative and clerical skilled jobs, immigrants are to supply 25 out of every 100 additional workers by 1970.

Immigrant manpower is regarded as less important in the lower skill level and in agriculture. In the latter, 90 percent of the new entrants into the labor market by 1970 are expected to come from manpower within the country. The survey also envisages an increase in the number of unskilled workers, but states that immigration will have diminished importance as a source of supply for this category of workers.

In order to encourage the immigration of high-level professional personnel, the National Employment Service of the Ministry of Labor operates the special Employment Exchange for persons working for institutions of higher learning and research agencies abroad. The exchange has offices in London, New York, and Los Angeles to facilitate emigration to Israel of Jewish academic, scientific, and research personnel from Great Britain and the United States. In 1967 600 persons emigrated to Israel to enter positions obtained for them by the exchange. An effort is made to place most of them in the southern development areas and in the Negev.

WORKING CONDITIONS

The Ministry of Labor is responsible for the administration and enforcement of laws regulating working conditions. One of the major units of the ministry is the Employment and Absorption Division, in charge of drafting and implementing employment policies. The division supervises the Employment Service, which channels manpower to prospective employers and administers relief-work projects for the unemployed. The Labor Inspection Department enforces legislation covering working conditions through a network of labor inspectors operating from five district offices. The Labor Relations Department mediates in labor disputes and administers wage laws. The Youth and Vocational Education Department supervises apprenticeship training and organizes vocational programs for adults.

Specialized government agencies, working in conjunction with the Ministry of Labor, include the Manpower Planning Authority, organized in 1952 with the assistance of the International Labor Organization to conduct research in manpower problems and to recommend policies related to this subject to the ministry.

The Productivity Institute prepares studies on various aspects of

317

productivity and of industrial management. One of its main tasks is actively to promote productivity by offering technical advice to interested employers, distributing literature, and lectures to workers in industrial, administrative, and commercial enterprises. The institute comprises 15 professional units, each specializing in productivity problems in the respective economic sectors. The Institute of Safety and Hygiene, established in 1954, prepares programs in labor safety education, organizes plant safety education, organizes plant safety committees, and investigates industrial accidents.

The National Insurance Institute operates under the direct supervision of the minister of labor. It is headed by a council of 42 members representing employers, insured workers, and the government. The main branches of the institute correspond to the four major types of social insurance: old age and survivors pensions, workmen's compensation, maternity insurance, and family insurance (see ch. 8, Living Conditions).

Hiring and Dismissal

According to the Employment Service Law of 1959, employers must notify the local office of the government Employment Service if they wish to fill a vacancy or dismiss an employee who has worked for more than 6 days. Employers may not hire, and workers may not enter employment in most industrial or service occupations unless placement has been arranged through the Employment Service. These provisions, however, are not applicable to managerial and professional personnel and to any applicant holding degrees from an institution of higher learning. Employers may also hire relatives without resorting to the Employment Service, although they must notify the service of their intention to do so. To recruit manual workers, employers must send a letter of request to the Employment Service describing the job to be filled, and specifying the type of worker needed. If the Employment Service is unable to furnish the manpower required within a specified time, employers may recruit on their own, but the names of privately recruited persons must be submitted to the Employment Service for registration and approval.

In general, the effectiveness of the Employment Service depends on the fluctuations of the labor market. During periods of full employment the Service can provide personnel only occasionally, but it is of much assistance to workers and employers alike in times of unemployment.

Private recruitment takes place mostly by advertising or by publicizing the vacancies among employees of the enterprise. According to the Youth Employment Law of 1953, children under 14 years of age may not be hired. The law also prohibits night work for youths between 14 and 18 years of age, and stipulates that persons in this age group must work shorter working hours than other employees and must undergo a compulsory medical examination before commencing employment.

Procedures governing dismissal and resignation are subject to negotiations between workers and employers and are regulated by collective agreements. Most of these agreements stipulate that a permanent employee must be given 12 days advance notice before being dismissed; employees wishing to resign must, in turn, give the same notice period to the employer. No notice period is required for temporary or probationary workers.

Severance pay is also regulated by collective agreements, although a Severance Pay Law was promulgated in 1964 and amended in 1965 to protect workers not covered by these agreements. Severance payment provisions contained in collective agreements, however, have precedence if their provisions are more favorable to workers than those of the law.

According to the law, employers must pay severance compensation to an employee who has worked for at least 1 year or in the case of seasonal workers, for at least two consecutive seasons. To wage earners the severance compensation is paid at the rate of 2 weeks pay for every year worked; salaried employees receive 1 month's salary for every year worked. To counteract the tendency of some employers to dismiss workers just before completion of 1 year service, in order to avoid severance payment, the law stipulates that any dismissal other than for disciplinary causes before 1 year shall be regarded as evidence of the intention to avoid payment of severance compensation. A worker's right to severance pay is not affected by resignation because of ill health, maternity, relocation to join a spouse, or of moving to an agricultural settlement or a development area.

Hours of Work, Leave, and Holidays

The Hours of Work and Rest Law of 1951 provides for a 47-hour workweek, and an 8-hour workday. The law stipulates that the hours of work on the day preceding the weekly day of rest must not exceed 7 hours. Under the terms of collective agreements, however, much variation exists in the number of working hours among enterprises in the different economic sectors. In some industries and in government offices, for example, the workday is shortened by 1 hour during the summer. During the late 1960's, the average number of weekly work hours ranged from 32.5 hours in personal services, to 42.7 hours in transportation and communication. The hours of work in most industrial enterprises were from 7:00 A.M. to 3:00 P.M. or 4:00 P.M.; government offices usually worked from 7:30 A.M. to 3:00 P.M. or 3:30 P.M. According to the Employment of Women Law of 1954, women and youths between 14 and 18 years of age may not work during night hours.

Paid annual leave is granted at the rate of a minimum of 14 days for each year of continuous service, in accordance with the Annual Holidays Law of 1951. An amendment to that law, promulgated in 1965, provided that annual leave is to be granted on a graduated scale, according to length of service up to a maximum of 28 days, after 14 years of continuous employment. During the 1960's most collective agreements provided for 2 to 4 days of annual leave above the legal minimum stipulated by the 1965 amendment of the Annual Holidays Law.

There are no legal requirements for sick leave, but virtually all collective agreements contain provisions for sick pay. Most agreements call for an employer's contribution of about 2.5 percent of his monthly payroll to the Kupat Holim (Workers' Sick Fund), the country's largest health insurance group for workers, operated by the Histadrut. The fund, in turn, pays the worker 70 to 85 percent of his wages during his absence because of illness. Cash payments during illness are also provided by workers' pension and insurance funds, maintained by the Histadrut and other trade unions. In addition, some of these funds insure the workers for paid convalescent leave, which is granted by most employers under the terms of collective agreements.

Maternity leave is granted in accordance with the Employment of Women Act of 1954. Under the provisions of the act, women are entitled to 12 weeks of maternity leave with pay and, if requested, to several months in addition without pay.

Saturday is the weekly day of rest for Jews; Friday is observed by Muslims, and Sunday by Christian workers. In addition, there are 10 paid holidays, including Labor Day on May 1 and Independence Day. The latter is celebrated on dates varying according to the Jewish (lunar) calendar; in 1969 that holiday fell on April 23. The rest are major religious holidays. Non-Jewish workers are entitled to an equal number of holidays, according to their religion.

For work performed on the weekly day of rest, daily-paid workers receive 50 percent above the regular hourly rate. Employees paid by the month, however, are only granted compensatory leave, at the rate of one and a half hours' for each hour of work performed on the day of rest. Work performed on holidays is paid at rates ranging between 25 to 75 percent above the regular wage.

Wages and Benefits

An essential feature of national wage policies is the adjustment of the level of wages to the cost of living. The adjustments take place through periodic wage agreements between the trade unions and employers' organizations. This policy has been in force since 1952 when the Manufacturers' Association and the Histadrut signed a cost-of-living agreement, covering all employees whose working conditions were governed by collective agreements. The cost-of-living allowance is based on changes in the consumer's price index that is reviewed every year. The allowance is raised when the index reaches or exceeds 3 percent. According to legislation promulgated in 1964, employers must pay female workers wages equal to those of men for the same job. In the event of a dispute, an official wage collection officer may bring a decision that has the force of law.

Wage agreements signed early in 1966 provided for raises of about 8 percent in most branches of the economy. At the same time, the cost-of-living allowance was increased by about 7 percent. Because of the economic slowdown beginning late in 1965 and continuing through most of 1967, labor unions refrained from pressing for an increase in cost-of-living allowances and from demanding full implementation of collective agreements calling for wage raises in 1967.

Wage policies drafted by the Histadrut for 1968–69 reflect a continuation of the wage stabilizing trend, stipulating that in order to maintain economic stability and attain high levels of employment, wage raises during that period would be granted only in some economic sectors, and that no revisions of the cost-of-living allowances would be demanded. In return the government directed the National Insurance Institute to pay a supplement equal to the customary rise in the cost-of-living allowance to workers earning not more than I£400 a month (I£1 equals approximately US$0.285—see Glossary). Tax deductions and shorter hours of work were also granted to many workers.

Despite relatively stationary wages, increases granted in most sectors of the economy toward the end of 1967 amounted to approximately 4 percent of the monthly wage. During the second half of that year, the following average monthly wages per employee were paid in the various economic sectors: I£332 in agriculture; I£538 in industry, mining, and manufacturing; I£558 construction; I£745 in utilities; I£762 in transport and communication; I£597 in public services; and I£382 in personal services.

Data published by the Central Bureau of Statistics in 1968 show the difference between the wages of skilled and unskilled workers for 1967, without and with the cost-of-living allowance. According to these statistics, skilled agricultural workers earned a basic daily wage of I£10.54; with the addition of the cost-of-living allowance, the daily wage totaled I£15.58. Unskilled workers in agriculture received a basic daily wage of I£9.97, which rose to I£14.74 with the cost-of-living allowance. In the metalworking industry, the most skilled workers earned I£15.35, or I£22.68 with the cost-of-living

321

allowance; unskilled workers were paid I£10.20, or I£15.07 including the cost-of-living allowance. The construction industry paid a basic daily wage of I£16.64 to skilled workers and I£10.32 to unskilled laborers; with the cost-of-living allowance added, these wages totaled I£24.59 and I£15.25, respectively. Skilled carpenters earned I£16.60 a day, or I£24.53 with the cost-of-living allowance; the daily pay of unskilled laborers in this trade was I£8.86, or I£13.10 with the cost-of-living allowance. In the textile industry, an experienced female finisher was paid I£7.30 a day, or I£10.79 with the cost-of-living allowance.

In addition to the cost-of-living allowance, workers receive various kinds of supplemental payments and other benefits. End-of-year bonus payments are granted to utility workers and to those in commerce, banking, and in some manufacturing enterprises. Seniority allowances are paid by the day or month, after one year of employment. The amount of the allowance ranges from 5 to 15 agorot per day (1 agora equals approximately US$0.003), depending on the industrial branch. Wage incentive plans, based on certain production norms, are used in many manufacturing enterprises. The plans provide a premium of 1 percent of the wage for every production increase of 1 percent above the regular norm.

Many workers are entitled to other benefits in cash or kind. Heavy-duty clothing is issued to workers in most manufacturing enterprises. An allowance to purchase professional literature is granted to science and research workers. Supplementary premiums are paid to persons in hazardous occupations and to those working in areas with unfavorable climatic conditions, notably in the desert area, southeast of Beersheba. Workers living at a great distance from their jobs receive a transportation allowance or are conveyed to the work site on vehicles provided by the employer.

Additional benefits accrue to workers under the National Insurance Law of 1953, providing for old-age pensions, survivors' benefits, workmen's compensation, and family allowances (see ch. 8, Living Conditions). Trade unions also have insurance and pension funds to protect workers in the event of old age, disability, or death. Labor experts estimated during the mid-1960's that nearly three-fourths of employed persons were insured under these funds. About half of the insured persons were members of one of the seven pension funds operated by the Histadrut. The three largest of these funds are the Industrial Workers' Pension and Insurance Fund (Mivtachim), the Building Workers' Fund (Binian), and the Agricultural Workers' Fund (Haklaim). Of the three, the Mivtachim insures the largest number of persons, since it covers workers in crafts, manufacturing, and transportation, as well as seamen and civilian employees of the army. The funds provide not only pension benefits but also sick pay, supplementary cash for convalescent periods, vacation pay, and family allowances. The amounts of pension benefits are revised periodically, in accordance with the consumers' price index. Membership in a fund is voluntary, but most collective agreements provide for employer and employee contributions to the appropriate fund.

LABOR ORGANIZATION

The Histadrut

The labor movement originated in the early agricultural settlements, established by persons of varying occupational and national backgrounds, all of whom adhered to ideologies advocating communal organization and mutual aid. The Kupat Holim and the Hamashbir Hamerkazi (The Central Supplier) cooperative wholesale society, established by the members of these settlements in 1913 and 1916, respectively, became the parent organizations of the Histadrut, the country's leading labor federation. Histadrut as a trade union federation was founded in 1920 by two major labor parties of the Zionist movement, the moderate socialist Poalei Zion (Workers of Zion) and the militant Hapoel Hatzair (The Young Worker), to secure employment and provide mutual aid to immigrants. According to a constitution adopted in 1923, Histadrut's purpose is to unify and organize all labor and to deal with economic and cultural questions related to the development of a labor community in Israel. The constitution also established the basis for Histadrut's extensive role in the economy, in social welfare, and in education.

Structure and Membership

The highest authority of the Histadrut is the General Convention. Its members are elected by a direct vote of all members at national conventions, held every 4 years. All parties, except the religious ones that have their own trade unions, submit lists of candidates in these elections and are represented in the General Convention in proportion to the votes they gain.

The General Convention formulates the national policies of the Histadrut and elects the General Council, which acts as a policy-making body between national conventions. Each year the General Council in turn elects the Executive Committee whose function is to implement the policies determined by the General Convention and the General Council. The Executive Committee elects the members of the Executive Bureau, responsible for the conduct of Histadrut's daily activities. These activities are discharged through some 17 departments, each representing one of Histadrut's many functions and each headed by a member of the Executive Bureau. Of major importance is the Trade Union Department, which serves as a liaison between the national trade unions and the Executive Committee. Its principal functions include the overall supervision of national trade unions, assistance in collective bargaining, and proposal of labor legislation. Other departments are in charge of education and culture, vocational training, mutual aid and social insurance, youth and sports, Arab affairs, international relations, and finance and dues.

Local labor councils represent the local authority of the Histadrut. According to its constitution, they are the "supreme local institution" exercising authority over national trade unions and enterprise-level workers' committees in a given area. Labor councils have considerable autonomy and strong, executive power, including approval of local strikes and the use of strike funds. They also deal with disciplinary matters involving trade union members. Local labor council members are elected from party lists by a procedure similar to that governing the election of the General Convention. The labor council, in turn, elects a general secretary who is responsible for all activities of the council, including organizing nonunionized workers, establishing productivity councils composed of workers and employers, and initiating educational and vocational training programs. The local labor council is authorized to request reports covering trade unions activities in the large Histadrut enterprises and may regulate or alter these activities.

The local labor secretary of the labor council represents to the council the interests of workers in a certain trade or occupation in a certain geographical area. He is also, however, a spokesman of the local labor council to the workers in questions of general policy and in specific matters affecting the respective trades.

Most individual trade unions affiliated with Histadrut, the so-called national trade unions, are organized by trade or industry. Production workers in manufacturing enterprises are attached to the national trade unions representing branches of manufacturing. Workers in certain occupations and professional personnel are assigned to national federations or national unions that cut across industrial lines. Typical examples are the National Union of Teachers and the National Federation of Clerical Workers and Office Employees.

In 1967 the Histadrut included more than 30 national unions and federations. The largest ones were those of the clerical workers, with approximately 100,000 members and agricultural workers with about 70,000 members. The metalworkers, construction workers, and government employees' unions had approximately 50,000 members each, the food-processing workers' and teachers' union about 30,000 and 24,000 members, respectively.

Trade union activity on plant, enterprise, or office level is conducted by workers' committees. These are in charge of implementing collective agreements and performing a variety of educational, cul-

324

tural, and social services among trade union members. Depending on the size of the enterprise, its workers' committee usually comprises from five to 20 members elected by workers and employees. The committee is headed by a chairman who acts as a spokesman for the workers of the enterprise.

In 1969 there were about 1 million Histadrut members, including more than 40,000 Arab workers. The figure includes the spouses of trade union members, workers of other trade unions who participate in Histadrut's sickness and social service funds, and self-employed or nonworking persons who also wish to participate in these services, or who have joined for ideological reasons.

Histadrut union dues range from 3.0 to 4.5 percent of the total wages. In most sectors of the economy, these dues are collected by the check-off system, under which employers may withhold the dues from the wage or salary and transfer them to the trade union. According to an agreement with Histadrut, employers may also withhold so-called organization fees from nonunionized workers for the benefits that accrue to these workers from Histadrut's general social and bargaining achievement, notably health insurance. According to law, the organization fee of nonunionized workers may not exceed 1 percent of the gross wage.

Economic and Social Welfare Activities

Histadrut's economic enterprises are managed by the Hevrat Ovdim (Workers Society—also called the General Cooperative Association of Labor), a holding company in which every Histadrut member owns one share. Created originally to provide employment opportunities to immigrant workers, Hevrat Ovdim enterprises in 1967 accounted for nearly 25 percent of the national economy and employed more than 200,000 workers. Agriculture represents the largest sector of Histadrut's economic operations with about 90 percent of agricultural collectives and cooperatives (kibbutzim and moshavim) affiliated with the Hevrat Ovdim. The produce of these settlements is marketed by Tnuva (Produce), the country's largest agricultural marketing cooperative, founded by Histadrut and affiliated with Hevrat Ovdim. Histadrut also owns Solel Boneh (Road Maker and Builder), a major construction company that executed the major portion of housing construction, and road and harbor building projects since 1948. Another of its major enterprises is the Koor Company, an industrial complex of iron and steel plants and of various manufacturing enterprises. There are also a Histadrut housing company and Hamashbir Hamerkazi that is a principal supplier of agricultural collectives and of over 1,000 consumers' stores (see ch. 20, Agriculture; ch. 21, Industry; ch. 23, Domestic Trade).

Histadrut also operates Kupat Holim, the country's largest medical insurance fund, with a membership of about 1.9 million in 1967. Its budget is derived from membership dues, employers' and employees' payments, and by government grants. The Kupat Holim operates its own hospitals, clinics, convalescent homes, laboratories, and maternal and child welfare centers. Welfare and mutual aid services are discharged through seven so-called central funds, providing a variety of benefits, including retirement plans, for about a quarter of a million workers and employees.

International Affiliations

Through participation in numerous international labor organizations, the Histadrut has contributed significantly to the government's efforts to enhance Israel's image abroad.

In 1953 the Histadrut joined the International Conference of Free Trade Unions (ICFTU), after having terminated its affiliation with the Communist-dominated World Federation of Trade Unions (WFTU) in 1950. In 1966 a representative of the Histadrut served on ICFTU's Executive Board. Histadrut representatives were also included in the executive committee of several International Trade Secretariats (ITS), which had members among Histadrut trade unions. Congresses, seminars, and meetings held by the ICFTU are regularly attended by Histadrut officials.

Through its General Cooperative Association, Histadrut also maintains membership in the International Cooperative Alliance. The workers' delegate of the Israeli delegation to the International Labor Organization is provided by Histadrut. The organization's governing body and three of its permanent industrial committees include Histadrut representatives.

In addition, Histadrut maintains active relations with national trade union federations in North and South America, Africa, Asia, and Europe. During the 1960's it has especially emphasized relations with labor movements in African countries, notably with those south of the Sahara. The contacts are maintained through international labor congresses, but mainly through Histadrut's Afro-Asian Institute of Labor and Cooperative Studies in Tel Aviv. The institute offers training in labor subjects to officials and members of trade unions of African and Asian countries. Under the terms of trade union cooperation agreements, signed with the Kenya Federation of Labor and with the Tanganyika Federation of Labor, Histadrut experts were sent to establish business enterprises and consumers' unions in these countries. Histadrut offices operate in London and New York to foster cooperation with trade unions of the Western World.

Other Trade Unions

Three other labor organizations represent workers with various religious and political views. The structure of their governing bodies and their local organization resembles those of the Histadrut.

The two religious trade unions are Hapoel Ha-Mizrahi (The Workers of the Spiritual Center), the labor wing of the National Religious Party, and Poalei Agudat Israel (Workers of the Association of Israel), which represents orthodox religious workers. The two organizations have about 200,000 and 30,000 members, respectively. Both are affiliated with the Histadrut's Trade Union Department and have concluded agreements with the latter, entitling their members to use Histadrut's sick fund, its pension funds and other social services. Hapoel Ha-Mizrahi and Poalei Agudat Israel both have a voice on Histadrut's wage policy formulating councils (see ch. 14, Political Dynamics).

Hapoel Ha-Mizrahi includes some 72 affiliated agricultural settlements, operates a housing company to help build dwelling units in these settlements, and maintains a credit fund. Poalei Agudat Israel includes some 15 agricultural settlements, operates nursery schools, and maintains youth hostels.

The Histadrut Ha'ovdim Haleumit (National Labor Federation) is the trade union organization of the right-wing Herut-Liberal bloc. It has a membership of about 80,000 and operates entirely separately from the Histadrut. The federation opposes the operation of economic enterprises by trade unions, but favors workers' cooperatives. It also rejects the socialistic concept of class struggle and favors compulsory arbitration of labor disputes by the government. Medical, vocational training, and educational facilities are maintained by the federation. Its sick fund provides health insurance to some 219,000 persons, including those outside the labor movement. The federation also has a pension fund for invalidity, unemployment, and retirement, and operates a housing company for its members.

National Labor Federation members rarely constitute a majority in any enterprise or trade; they are represented, however, by members of the federation elected to the workers' committees.

EMPLOYERS' ORGANIZATIONS

The most influential employers' organization is the Manufacturers' Association, with a membership including about half of the employers in manufacturing enterprises in the private sector of the economy. Nearly all employers in the textile and pharmaceutical industries are members; membership reaches 75 to 85 percent among employers in the metal industry. Other major employers' organizations are the Merchants' Association, the Israel Farmers' Federation, and the Builders' and Building Contractors' Association.

The main function of the Manufacturers' Association is to deal with problems arising from labor relations and to represent employers' interests in negotiating collective agreements. The negotiating efforts of the association have been directed mainly toward the conclusion of industry-wide collective agreements rather than toward those that regulate working conditions in individual enterprises only. The association is headed by a Presidium, whose members represent employers in various branches of industry and are elected for two-year terms. Operations are carried out by 13 departments, including the Association's Labor Department that maintains liaison with the Ministry of Labor for the purpose of dealing with matters involving labor legislation and employer-employee relations. The department also negotiates with trade unions in the event of labor disputes and strikes and represents employers in arbitration cases. Each of the 13 departments has a policy committee, comprising elected representatives of member enterprises.

The right of management to lockout has been traditionally recognized, and the Manufacturers' Association has consistently regarded this right to be a basic prerogative of employers. Between 1960 and 1964 there were an average of five lockouts per year, but this average had declined to about two per year in 1965. In general, lockouts are invoked only as a last resort, usually in the event of a deadlock in labor disputes involving the dismissal of surplus workers or the relocation of a plant from one area to another.

LABOR RELATIONS

Labor relations are regulated by collective agreements, but disputes between employers and employees involving dismissals, production norms, and benefits are not uncommon. Many of the workers, moreover, had been independent tradesmen and artisans before immigration and often resent industrial discipline and management policies.

In accordance with its socialist ideology, Histadrut, in some of its enterprises, has given workers a share in management. This measure, however, has brought complaints by supervisors who regarded it as an impingement on their duties. Many of the workers lacked the training and experience to participate in management and felt an only moderate sense of identification with the enterprise.

Since 1952 production norms are determined by joint production committees, composed of employers' and workers' representatives. Workers' and employers' representatives of the joint production committees, however, rarely agree on the principles governing production and on the applicability of production norms to different groups of workers.

Collective Bargaining

Collective bargaining has traditionally been the principal means of regulating working conditions and labor relations. Collective agreements are negotiated on the national, industry-wide, and multiindustry-wide levels. National agreements are the most common in the manufacturing industry as well as in construction, agriculture, transport, the public services, and the liberal professions. These agreements usually stipulate that, during their duration, trade unions request no alterations or additions. In practice, however, amendments are often negotiated on the enterprise level. Industry-wide agreements are concluded between employers and workers who are nationally organized. Multiindustry-wide agreements cover one specific subject and apply to all branches of the industry.

According to the Collective Agreements Law of 1957, such agreements are legally binding. The law distinguishes between general and special agreements, the latter governing labor relations in a particular enterprise. General agreements apply to workers in a certain region or in the entire country and may be applicable to a particular branch or all branches of employment. Under the provisions of the law, the minister of labor is authorized to extend the provisions of any collective agreement to workers not represented by the parties who concluded the original agreement.

The scope of most collective agreements covers general working conditions, including hours of work, vacations, the cost-of-living allowance, and other wage supplements. They also specify procedures for the resolution of individual grievances through a plant-level labor-management committee representing workers and employers in equal numbers. If this committee deadlocks, the grievance is referred to a bipartite committee, comprised of members of the Histadrut and of the Manufacturers' Association in the community. If settlement is not reached on this level, the grievance is referred to the national committees of the two organizations. There are no labor courts in the country, but if an individual grievance is not resolved to the worker's satisfaction, he may seek recourse in the general courts.

Some collective agreements designate an arbitrator, or a board of arbitrators to resolve grievances. Agreements providing for this arrangement usually include a list of arbitrators endorsed jointly by labor and management.

A general collective agreement designed to forestall grievance problems was signed on January 10, 1967, between Histadrut and the Manufacturers' Association. The agreement calls for joint meetings of management and workers at regular intervals to discuss matters of mutual concern, provides for the establishment of a committee to study absenteeism, and to analyze the relationship between automation and layoffs. The agreement also regulates the use of medical certificates and calls for the employment of physicians and nurses in large enterprises. The agreement further provides for the more extensive use of the incentive pay system and of work norms; it contains recommendations of action to be taken if the norms are not achieved.

Labor Disputes and Strikes

Labor disputes arising between employers' and workers' organizations usually involve specific provisions of collective agreements. According to legislation promulgated in 1957, collective labor disputes are handled by the Chief Labor Relations Office of the Ministry of Labor's Labor Relations Department. Under the direct supervision of the chief labor relations officer are district labor relations officers in Jerusalem, Haifa, and Tel Aviv, who handle disputes occurring in the southern, northern, and central regions, respectively. These officers act as conciliators in meetings arranged between representatives of labor and management.

The right to strike has been established by tradition and custom. Although strikes during the 1960's have been frequent, they rarely were nation- or district-wide, and most of them involved relatively few workers. Strikes must be approved by the national trade union federations. In the case of the Histadrut, this approval is given by the Histadrut's Trade Union Department. In 1965, however, 70 percent of the strikes were not approved by Histadrut.

In 1967 there was a marked drop in the number of strike days and also in the number of workers involved in strikes as compared to 1965 and 1966. The number of strikes during that year totaled 142, involving 25,058 workers as compared to 288 strikes and lockouts, involving 90,210 workers, in 1965. Disputes over wages are the most common cause of strikes. The economic sectors most frequently affected by work stoppages in 1967 were industry and mining as well as government, commercial, and public services.

A collective agreement signed between Histadrut and the Manufacturers' Association in 1967 forbade workers to strike and management to lockout while a collective agreement is in force. The agreement stipulated, furthermore, that procedures for the settlement of disputes as provided by collective agreements must be fully exploited and that local labor councils of the trade unions must be notified if these procedures fail. If the agreement is not renewed and the workers' committee of the enterprise decides to call a strike, its decision is subject to approval of the local labor council. If the strike is approved by both the labor council and the workers of the enterprise, the council must notify management at least 5 days before the work stoppage.

Major strikes, notably those affecting several employers or all enterprises of an industry, must be approved by the appropriate national trade union federation (Histadrut or National Labor Federation). Negotiations for the renewal of a collective agreement may be initiated by the respective national trade union federation and no strikes may be called during that period. If the decision for a major strike is taken, however, the appropriate federation must notify employers 10 days before a strike affecting several enterprises and fourteen days if the strike is to be industry-wide.

To gain legal sanction for the notice period of workers to management before a strike, a bill was submitted to the Knesset in 1968, providing for a fifteen day cooling-off period before a major strike may be called. The bill also stipulated that the Ministry of Labor must be notified of such strikes.

CHAPTER 23
DOMESTIC TRADE

Government planners expect domestic trade, which in 1967 accounted for approximately 15 percent of the gross national product (GNP), to become increasingly important in the nation's economy. This expectation is based primarily on the rapid development of industry, resulting in part from a growth in demand for locally manufactured items (see ch. 21, Industry). The demand stems mainly from the increasing population and rising living standards, reflected in mounting requirements in food, durable goods, and other items to meet expanded domestic needs (see ch. 8, Living Conditions).

A prominent characteristic of domestic trade in the later 1960's was the predominance of small retail stores operated by the owner and his family, sometimes with the aid of a few hired employees. In 1967 retail outlets, with hired employees, numbered roughly 4,000, including about 350 cooperatives. The total persons engaged in retail trade numbered approximately 62,000, but only some 19,000 were hired workers. Retail sales in the same year totaled more than I£1.25 billion (I£1 equals approximately US$0.285—see Glossary). During the same period some 20,000 employees, including about 15,300 hired workers, were engaged in the wholesale trade. Togther they handled merchandise amounting to almost I£5.5 billion.

Government planners favor an economy patterned along Western lines, with emphasis on cooperative organizations for wholesale and retail trade. Special considerations, such as subsidies, loans at favorable interest rates, or protective tariffs, are given to enterprises regarded as essential for the country's economic growth. Statistics for 1967 indicate that about 24 percent of wholesale and 18 percent of retail trade was through cooperative channels (see ch. 21, Industry).

Nearly all of the domestic trade by cooperatives is carried on by the Histadrut (Histadrut Ha'ovdim Haklalit—General Federation of Labor) or its subsidiaries (see ch. 22, Labor). Affiliated with this expansive organization are most of the kibbutzim and moshavim, collective and communal agricultural settlements, started primarily by the immigrants arriving since the establishment of statehood in 1948. Agricultural trade and other activities of the organization are coordinated through its Agricultural Center, the executive body of the Agricultural Workers' Union.

Marketing is complicated by the heterogeneous origins of the immigrants who, in 1968, comprised about 57 percent of its total population (see ch. 4, Population). These foreign-born groups have varied tastes, needs, habits, and many, particularly the recent arrivals, have little buying power.

Moreover, the emphasis placed by the authorities on the development of agriculture, with its high degree of self-sufficiency, also has had an important effect on domestic trade. In 1968 over half a million people, approximately 18 percent of the country's total population, lived in rural areas and derived a living from agriculture. Many additional persons living in small towns and even in urban suburbs obtain their food and personal needs from their own gardens or local resources. Both of these groups produce almost all of their own food and make their own clothes from machine-woven textiles or by hand, knitting sweaters and baby garments. Their small cash purchases consist mainly of shoes, cloth, yarn, household utensils, some magazines, historical or religious books, and other articles to satisfy personal needs. Most of these items are available in the village marketplace or stores. The contribution of purchases by the rural population to the country's domestic trade is therefore very limited.

In urban areas the situation is quite different, with a wide variety of domestic and imported goods available in the central business districts and markets. In recent years moderate-sized department stores and modern supermarkets have begun to appear. Almost 30 percent of the population lives in the three major urban centers—Tel Aviv, Haifa, and Jerusalem—where the most important concentrations of retail and wholesale trade are found. In 1968 about 63 percent of the retail and 75 percent of the wholesale establishments employing hired workers were located in these centers.

In the major towns, such as Beersheba in the Negev, the traditional central marketplace attracts buyers and sellers from nearby communities. Bargaining between customer and merchant in order to arrive at an agreed price is the custom, as in neighboring countries throughout the Middle East. In a new settlement, established in 1968 for Bedouins, near Beersheba, space was provided for their centuries-old market.

ROLE OF GOVERNMENT

The government plays a dominant role in the regulation of domestic trade, with special attention to encouraging development and maintaining price stability. Most of the responsibility for carrying out this function devolves upon the Ministry of Commerce and Industry.

Most of the output of manufactured durable items is controlled by relatively few firms. A large proportion of these firms have formed cartels. By agreement among themselves on prices and production quotas, they are able to limit competition from other domestic firms. This practice is permissible, unless it proves to be harmful to economic progress. Under the Restrictive Trade Practices Law of 1960, amended in 1963, cartels must apply to a Public Council for approval in each case. This is granted only if it is found to be in the public interest.

In order to stimulate production and sale of locally manufactured items, the government has adopted the policy of exposing them to competition from imports. The objective is to induce manufacturers to meet this competition by introducing more efficient production methods in order to lower their operating costs and sale prices and by attracting buyers with improvements in the design and quality of manufactured products. Until 1962 practically all industrial output was protected against foreign competition by a system of import quotas and other restrictions, assuring manufacturers of a profit without considering the price of their goods on the world market. In that year restrictions were reduced and a Public Committee was set up to examine each product and advise the Ministry of Commerce and Industry on the item's status with respect to import competition. As expected, through efficiencies adopted in the manufacturing process, the output of many items increased; prices in some instances were reduced and quality improved. By the end of 1966 these restrictions were replaced by protective tariffs affecting some 85 percent of the relevant items. This procedure proved effective and, in November 1966, customs tariffs were reduced from 5 to 10 percent on various items. Further reductions were made in April 1968 by 15 percent and, in November 1968, by an additional 15 percent.

The Ministry of Commerce and Industry makes continuous attempts to guide and encourage traders and trade agents by collecting and distributing helpful information and by controlling and modernizing market procedures. To protect the consumer, ministry representatives inspect restaurants, laundries, hairdressing establishments, gas stations, and other enterprises handling consumer goods. They also check on price lists and service standards. The consumer is further protected by the ministry's Public Committee, which makes investigations designed to prevent exploitation by price-fixing groups. Violators are reported to the public prosecutors.

A staff of specialists in the ministry studies and makes recommendations regarding export and import policies, maintains commercial contacts, and conducts market researches. The ministry also contributes funds for research on commercial subjects in universities and scientific institutes, and it cooperates with the National Council for Research and Development to establish new industries. In 1968 research was under way on fibers, forest products, textiles, ceramics, rubber, and paint. In addition, an advisory service was maintained for the food industry. Planners expect these activities to benefit domestic trade, directly or indirectly.

The ministry also acts in an emergency, such as the Six-Day War of June 1967, when it took timely steps to ensure that a full supply of staple articles were available for consumers. Regional and national rationing had been planned in event of transport disruptions or serious damage to retail outlets or factories. Large stocks were stored at distributing points, whereas manpower, materials, and services were arranged for processing of food if needed. When the public became aware that food and other items were readily available, hoarding and blackmarketing tendencies were forestalled.

Representatives appointed from the Ministries of Commerce and Industry, Agriculture, and Finance constitute the Citrus Control and Marketing Board. They control 100,000 acres of citrus orchards, conclude agreements with shippers, and make other arrangements for disposing of the entire citrus crop, both on foreign and local markets. In addition, they buy all packing materials and supervise picking and crating. With governmental assistance, they finance large citrus development projects, conduct research, and give field guidance to citrus farmers.

COMPOSITION OF TRADE

Increased private consumption has resulted mainly from a fivefold increase in per capita expenditure since 1955 to approximately I£3,000 in 1967. This has caused changes in demand for various items of durable and nondurable consumer goods. At the end of 1967 most products were selling readily on the domestic market. There was a noticeable increase, however, in calls for household goods. Comparison of demands between the 1952–54 and the 1965–67 periods shows that food and beverages, gasoline, and tobacco had dropped from 40.2 to 30.5 percent of the totals and that clothing and personal effects had decreased from 10.5 to 9.1 percent. Meanwhile, housing rose from 9.7 to 14.7 percent and furniture, from 6.9 to 7.5 percent.

In 1967 expenditures for food, petroleum and petroleum products, as well as textiles and clothing, continued to head the list of retail trade items in total values of their sales, and each made substantial gains over its 1962 total. The greatest gains on a percentage basis, however, were made by household goods, kitchen utensils, and furniture. Expenditure for these items more than doubled during the 1963–67 period.

Outstanding in the category of durable goods are passenger cars, air conditioners, and television receivers. Comparing the years 1962 and 1967, these items all gained not only in numbers available and sold on the market but also in the percentages that were supplied by domestic factories or assembly plants. Radios, refrigerators, sewing machines, and gas ranges all declined in volume. Nevertheless, for some articles, increases were noted in the proportion supplied by local enterprises. For example, local increase for refrigerators was from 87.7 percent in 1962 to 96.1 percent in 1967; for sewing machines, the increase was from 59.0 to 66.0 percent. Almost all the gas and electric ranges continued to be local products. Food, beverage, and tobacco processing establishments marketed about 90 percent of their output through domestic channels. Textile and clothing plants sold about 85 percent of their production on local markets.

PRIVATE SECTOR

A large majority of the enterprises that employ hired workers are privately owned. These include retail and wholesale trade establishments. In 1967 retail outlets hiring employees numbered 4,128, and 3,749 of them, or 90.8 percent, were privately owned. Wholesale establishments numbered 2,608, and 2,216, or 84.9 percent, were privately owned. Wage earners working in the retail trade totaled 18,759, and 15,664, or 83.5 percent, were hired by private owners. Wholesale employees totaled 19,976, and 13,873, or 69.5 percent, worked for private establishments.

The private sector takes on even greater importance in the area of industrial enterprises producing items for the domestic market than it has in the retail-wholesale trade. Government sources report that in 1967 the private sector operated about 92 percent of the total industrial enterprises and employed about 73 percent of the industrial workers. In 1965, for example, almost 2,600 leather-product establishments (nearly all of them privately owned) employed some 8,000 workers. In the same year there were 3,300 carpentry shops, most of them small and owner operated.

Some groups of private farmers have formed organizations to promote their own interests. The largest among these is the Farmers' Federation, with a membership of some 7,000 citrus growers and independent farmers in about 100 villages, cultivating approximately 250,000 acres, including 55,000 acres devoted to citrus trees. Affiliated bodies include a plantation development company, several supply and marketing companies, a large citrus growers' organization, and associations for citrus, fruit, milk, and wine producers and for farm machinery owners.

Another organization is the Agricultural Union, with a membership of some 3,500 smallholders cultivating 2,500 acres. Affiliated with it are 52 villages with their own agricultural purchasing and marketing cooperatives. In addition, it has several centrally organized groups, including a purchasing body, a marketing cooperative, and an auditing and control section and, for agricultural credit purposes, it has established the Private Farmers' Fund.

The private sector of domestic commerce is encouraged and aided by numerous nongovernmental organizations. A chamber of commerce exists in each of the three principal cities: Tel Aviv (membership about 1,000), Haifa (membership 600), and Jerusalem (300). A central body in Tel Aviv coordinates their activities.

The Manufacturers' Association, organized with sections for the various industries, has about 750 enterprises on its rolls. Besides maintaining an industrial library and a permanent exhibition of Israeli industrial products, it publishes a monthly periodical in Hebrew with articles on industrial and economic subjects informative to consumers and traders.

The Merchants' Association, representing about 60 types of domestic commercial enterprises, has some 40,000 members, including hotels, restaurants, and pharmacies. It also helps new immigrants to establish their homes.

Especially important is the Artisans' and Small Manufacturers' Association, comprising about 82 trade groups and representing some 35,000 workshops. In cooperation with this association, the government has established an Artisans' Bank and an Artisans' Corporation to service the business dealings of small enterprises.

HISTADRUT

The Histadrut is preeminent among cooperative organizations associated with domestic trade, but in the overall economy it is overshadowed by private ownership. In 1968 Histadrut accounted for only 5.5 percent of the country's industrial enterprises as compared to 93 percent for the private sector. In 1965 it hired 15 percent of the total industrial workers compared to 76 percent hired by private owners. In the agricultural sector of the economy, however, Histadrut is outstandingly important through its Agricultural Center, the executive body of the Agricultural Workers' Union, operating with representatives in 550 kibbutzim and moshavim. All of Histadrut's economic activities are controlled through its General Cooperative Association of Labor, known in Hebrew as Hevrat Ovdim, affiliated with about 90 percent of the agricultural cooperatives (see ch. 22, Labor).

Under Hevrat Ovdim's direct control is the agricultural marketing cooperative called Tnuva, the Hebrew for "produce." As the largest cooperative in the country, it handles more than two-thirds of all farm produce. It also processes dairy products, fresh fruits, vegetables, meat, fish beverages, citrus juices, and similar items. Its subsidiaries, operating packing houses, cold storage plants, and warehouses, can take care of seasonal surpluses of fruits and vegetables.

On a similar status with respect to Hevrat Ovdim is the cooperative wholesale society, Hamashbir Hamerkazi, the Hebrew for "the central supplier." With about 500 subsidiary facilities, it is one of the largest commercial trading organizations in the country. It supplies more than 40 percent of the population with general consumer goods and, in addition, provides its kibbutz and moshav members with their requirements for agricultural equipment, tools, chemicals, seeds, fertilizers, and other items. It also serves as an outlet to Israeli industrial firms for farm machinery, as well as for some raw materials and technical equipment. To insure availability of suppliers, it has established numerous industrial enterprises of its own, including facilities for making soap, edible oils, shoes, textiles, rubber goods and for weaving, processing wool, refining sugar, and producing agricultural machinery.

In typical kibbutzim and moshavim, farm produce is marketed through Tnuva channels; likewise, large-scale buying is also accomplished cooperatively through Hamashbir Hamerkazi. Details of methods vary among the settlements, but usually each village has two cooperative retail stores: one is a general store where the farmers obtain their needs, such as food, kitchen utensils, textiles, hardware, and building materials; the other is a grain and feed store where food for livestock, fertilizers, seeds, and perhaps some farm equipment can be obtained.

In practice the farmer brings his produce, whether it be grain, milk, vegetables, fruit, poultry, eggs, or other items, to the village marketing cooperative, where it is weighed or otherwise measured and, in some cases, processed and packed. It is then shipped, usually by truck, along with similar produce from other farmers to the nearest Tnuva marketing facility. Credit for the value of his produce is recorded on his account in the cooperative's ledger. Debited against this account are the farmer's pro rata share of the overhead required for the cooperative's services and his expenditures for purchases to satisfy production and personal needs. Profits, if any, are distributed at the end of the harvest season or at other periods agreed upon by cooperative members.

PRICES

In 1967 prices were relatively stable, with an average index of 118.2 for the year, compared to 100 in 1964, used as a base. For consumer goods the price level rose by an average of 1.6 percent over 1966. The wholesale price index of industrial production for 1967 was 1.2 percent higher than for the previous year. The currency devaluation of November 1967 and the Six-Day War of June 1967 had little effect on this stability (see ch. 25, Financial and Monetary System).

In wholesale trading the 1.2 percent rise in the average level of

339

industrial output prices was particularly noticeable for food and chemicals. For example, chocolate prices increased in August and milk in December; during the year, basic chemical prices went up by 2 percent and detergents by 10 percent.

To maintain a stabilized price structure in view of the emergencies in 1967, the government took several prompt measures. First it avoided extra taxes on existing stocks of consumer goods as long as traders refrained from raising prices. Second, tariff rates were adjusted and, third the basic prices of bread and wheat products were pegged. Similar action was taken with respect to sugar, coffee, tea, frozen meat, rice and chocolate products, as well as fuel.

In addition, the subsidies budget, designed primarily to assist enterprises needing financial aid to compete with foreign products, was increased by 25 percent. Allocations were particularly weighted so as to aid manufacturers of oil, egg, and milk products. The customs duty on a number of basic products was adjusted to prevent price fluctuations. The purchase tax was reduced on refrigerators, radios, washing machines, electrical appliances, furniture, and gas stoves to offset the declining consumption of these durable consumer items.

In the agricultural sector of the economy, trading terms are not determined on the open market but by policies of the government. It has intervened on occasion in determining the price of farm products or items processed therefrom, as well as the price of items needed for agriculture purposes. World market developments have an influence on prices as well as local demands. For example, in 1968 flour mills bought wheat at prices fixed by a committee appointed within the Ministry of Commerce and Industry, and the 224 bakeries in the country marketed their bread at a price agreed upon by the ministry. These prices could only be maintained, however, by a subsidy of I£10 million, available in the ministry budget for the millers and bakers.

TRANSPORTATION
Roads

Transportation conditions have greatly improved since the early days of statehood when the lack of an adequate land communications network was a major factor hampering the development of domestic trade. As new immigrants arrived and new agricultural settlements were established, roads were built to connect them with the principal highways; new highways were constructed and existing roads were widened and improved (see ch. 2, Physical Environment).

By 1967 the principal trading centers were joined by some 2,500 miles of improved roads maintained by a specially designated governmental department. Of these, about 1,725 miles were main routes, and the remainder were local or feeder roads. The Eilat-Beersheba-Ashqelon highway, across the Negev desert region, is particularly important. It provides for the first time a satisfactory land route between the Gulf of Aqaba, an arm of the Red Sea, and the Mediterranean Sea. Goods are carried across it at a cost equivalent to about US$38 per ton, approximately equal to the cost on the sea route around the Cape of Good Hope but with a saving of 6 weeks in time. The land route's potential capacity is estimated by Israeli highway engineers to be about 30,000 tons per month.

Trucks carry about 93 percent of the inland freight tonnage. This includes almost all the food products and a substantial proportion of the output from stone quarries, mines, and industrial plants. Of the 47,286 trucks registered at the end of 1967, more than 15 percent were diesel powered. At the beginning of 1969 additional trucks were needed. In 1968 the Ministry of Transport and Communications stated that two-thirds of the trucks were overloaded and almost half of these exceeded the 25- to 30-percent overload authorized within the safety limit. About 400 large and medium trucks have been produced annually since 1965 by the Leyland-Ashdod plant at Ashdod, but the demand has continued, deliveries became delayed, and at the end of 1968 importation was under consideration.

Buses meet 90 percent of the demand for passenger transport. At the end of 1968 two large cooperatives, Egged and Dan, carried all except about 2 percent of the bus passengers; the rest was divided among bus companies in Tel Aviv, Nazareth, and Beersheba. In mid-1968 approximately 3,600 modern diesel-powered buses were in operation. The two large cooperatives covered about 144 million vehicle-miles from mid-1967 to mid-1968. Bus transportation is supplemented by an interurban taxi service (*sherut*), comprising in 1968 some 450 taxis, with regular stations in Tel Aviv, Haifa, and Jerusalem. Fares, routes, and schedules of buses and taxis are supervised by the Ministry of Transport and Communications.

Railways

The railway system is state owned. At the end of 1968 the trackage, almost all standard gauge, totaled 454 miles (290 miles, main line and 164 miles, branch line), connecting the principal towns. After the Six-Day War, about 220 miles of track were restored in the Gaza Strip and in Sinai. During 1968 important extensions were being added to the line in the Negev region. The 20-mile branch line from Beersheba southeast to Dimona, completed in 1965, was being continued southward 20 miles to the phosphate works at Oron. Another branch was under construction from Beersheba to Hazeva (also called Tsefa), about 40 miles southeast of Beersheba.

In fiscal year 1967/68 (April 1, 1967, to March 31, 1968), the system carried approximately 2,346,000 tons of freight, an increase of

25,000 tons over the previous year. In the same fiscal year passengers totaled 4,056,000, compared to 4,401,000 during the previous year, when operations were not interrupted by military activity. Improvements in the system underway in 1968 included an increase in the number of passenger trains and the construction of additional sidings to enable freight to be hauled directly from factory to port. Under consideration also were new air-conditioned passenger cars and a concrete-based permanent way for the main line.

Seaports

The three main ports are at Haifa, Ashdod (20 miles south of Tel Aviv), and at Eilat on the Red Sea. Operated and maintained by the government, they handled a total of 6 million tons of freight in fiscal year 1968/69, compared to 5.16 million tons during the previous year.

Haifa is the largest seaport. Its installations include a 10,000-ton floating dock and a grain silo that can unload 480 tons per hour. These modern facilities are supplemented by installations at an auxiliary harbor at the nearby mouth of the Kishon (also spelled Qishon) River in Haifa Bay, which can accommodate ships up to 3,000 tons. Both harbors handled about 3.3 million tons, or approximately 64 percent of the total for all the country's ports in fiscal year 1967/68.

The port at Ashdod started operations in 1965 and, during the fiscal year 1967/68, it handled approximately 1.5 million tons, or about 30 percent of that year's total. Its activities are expected to increase, since additional wharves and other facilities are under construction there.

Oil transportation is expected to be facilitated by the completion of a 42-inch pipeline extending approximately 160 miles northwestward from Eilat, across the Negev desert region to Ashqelon, about 10 miles south of Ashdod. Operation was scheduled to begin in late 1969. Annual capacity within 3 years is anticipated to be 20 million tons by means of floating pipelines to oil tankers anchored offshore.

The port at Eilat increased rapidly in importance after closure of the Suez Canal by Egypt in 1956 (see ch. 15, Foreign Relations). After steady expansion, the port has become the gateway for sea cargo traffic to Asia, East Africa, and Australia. The new harbor started operations in 1965, with bulk-loading equipment and other modern facilities. In fiscal year 1968/69 it handled about 6 percent of the country's total sea tonnage.

In 1967 Israeli ships carried about 45 percent of the country's total freight trade. By the end of 1967 the merchant marine, consisting of 95 vessels, had a combined capacity of 1,015,000 dead-weight tons. Two large government-controlled companies, Zim (with 57 vessels totaling 625,000 tons) and El-Yam (with 13 vessels totaling almost 284,000 tons), operated more than 75 percent of the ships and almost 80 percent of the tonnage capacity. Expansion was continuing at the end of 1967, when 15 ships totaling 600,000 tons were under construction. By the end of 1971 the merchant marine capacity was expected to exceed 2 million tons.

Air Services

The country's single international airline, the state-owned El Al, was established in 1948. It operates nine Boeing jet aircraft (to rise to 10 in early 1970), and in mid-1969 was buying two Boeing 747's, each with a capacity of more than 400 passengers. In 1967 passengers totaled 361,000, an increase of 200 percent in 6 years. Cargo traffic in 1965 was approximately 300 million ton-miles. In mid-1969 flights were being scheduled from the country's modern international airport at Lod (Lydda), 10 miles southeast of Tel Aviv, to New York, London, Copenhagen, Amsterdam, Brussels, Paris, Frankfurt, Munich, Vienna, Zurich, Geneva, Nice, Rome, Athens, Bucharest, Constanta, Istanbul, Nicosia, Tehran, Nairobi, and Johannesburg. In 1967 the line averaged 10 flights and 1,000 passengers daily.

Arkia, a subsidiary of El Al, provides internal airline service. From its headquarters at Lod airport, flights are made to fields at Haifa, Jerusalem, Mahanayim (6 miles north of Lake Tiberias), Masada (on the western shore of the Dead Sea, 30 miles east of Beersheba), and at Eilat, on the Red Sea. The line carried 180,000 passengers in 1967. Two minor lines, Chimavir and Marom, operating from a small field at Herzliya, 9 miles northeast of Tel Aviv, are used mainly for agricultural purposes, particularly crop dusting. Another line, the Monavir, operates an air taxi service.

CHAPTER 24
FOREIGN ECONOMIC RELATIONS

In the second decade of statehood, international trade became a matter of increasing priority for the government and economy of Israel. Exports increased in volume and in earnings, with industrial products setting the pace of expansion. New overseas markets were cultivated and former ones maintained. Diversification of export commodities was emphasized. Political stability and dynamic economic growth inspired an uninterrupted inflow of philanthropic and investment capital. Tourism rose sharply; so did imports, although with less favorable implications for a persisting balance of payments problem.

Foreign trade patterns were thus somewhat reflective of those challenges that confront the developing nations in their professed goal of rapidly creating a modern, industrialized society. The need to import heavy equipment, highly complex machinery, and raw materials, as well as the need to attract foreign capital, were regarded as preconditions for future growth. Overfull employment by 1969, relatively high personal incomes, and the general atmosphere of prosperity continued to increase local demand for manufactured consumer goods. These two factors, one official and directed toward the future, the other, popular and more immediate, combined to affect adversely the balance of trade by stimulating imports while reducing the quantity of products otherwise available for export.

Israel, although having avoided the hazard of relying upon a single export item, nevertheless, was subjected to the frailties of an unstable world pricing system and to a fluctuating demand for its primary export products. An additional limitation on trade expansion, one basic to Israel, has been Arab hostility with its two corollaries: a heavy defense expenditure and an inability to engage in peaceful commerce with the neighboring countries of the Middle East.

Having labored to achieve membership in the international community and having been dependent over the years upon external financial assistance, Israel continued to seek political security as well as economic self-sufficiency. Foreign trade and aid, consequently, are important both as an extension of diplomacy and as a key determinant in the growth potential of the economy as a whole.

The year 1967, distinguished by the Six-Day War and the end of a

2-year economic recession, illustrated this relationship in which rational planning and projection figures were upset by larger political factors. Full mobilization curtailed production: trade with Eastern Europe was disrupted; arms purchases abroad were intensified; and, in general, military considerations superseded economic principles. As a result, the import surplus of goods and services declined in 1967 by only US$8 million, whereas in the previous year it had been reduced by US$75 million. Sales in foreign markets of locally produced items advanced by only 7 percent as against 15 percent in 1965 and 17 percent in 1966.

The year 1968, by contrast, was more favorable for those officials associated with the program of improving the country's competitive position in world trade. Despite the economic dislocation of 1967, trade statistics for both 1967 and 1968 were still impressive when contrasted with the situation 20 years earlier. Net imports, for example, had been valued at US$251.9 million in 1949 and net exports at US$28.5 million (see fig. 7). In 1950 exports were valued at 11.7 percent of imports valued at US$300.3 million. By 1967, corresponding figures stood at US$518 million and US$735 million respectively. In 1968 Israel imports reached US$1,035 million—a 40 percent increase over 1961 imports.

THE ROLE OF GOVERNMENT

The government has had a major role in sustaining this momentum. Several steps were taken in recent years as part of an export encouragement policy. An incentive in the 1953–57 period was the Pamaz system, whereby exporters, especially of industrial products, could hold their foreign exchange in special bank deposits and use them to purchase raw materials for further production. More recently, in the early 1960's, producers of export commodities received tax rebates while benefiting from fixed high prices in the domestic market. Another category of supports was designed to reduce the individual producer's costs. This took the form of financing exports in both local and foreign currencies by supplying credit for working capital well below prevailing interest rates, by absorbing part of transportation and port costs, and by participating in the cost of foreign trade risks, publicity, and market research. The government also provided relatively easy terms of finance for investment in export projects.

Export financing has been conducted through three agencies created to make sufficient credit, usually short-term, available to exporters. The Industrial Export Fund deals solely with industrial goods whereas the Agricultural Export Fund handles all agricultural projects other than citrus. The Tourist Industry Finance Fund grants working-capital credits to tourist hotels for expansion of facilities,

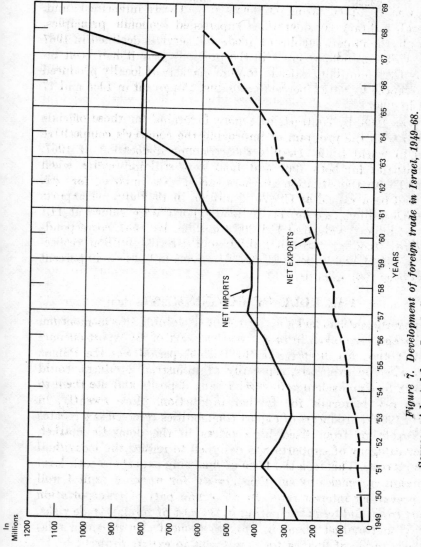

Figure 7. Development of foreign trade in Israel, 1949–68.

Source: Adapted from Israel, Central Bureau of Statistics, *Statistical Abstract of Israel, 1968*; and Israel, Ministry for Foreign Affairs, Information Division, *Facts About Israel, 1968*.

an indication of their increasing prominence as a source of revenue.

The dimensions and composition of imports were also influenced by the government. The means often employed were foreign currency control and administrative controls over imports; setting import prices; importation directly by governmental agencies; channeling import transactions toward countries with whom trade agreements already existed; and a strong customs policy imposing high duties upon imports destined for consumer consumption. The third technique, intended to cause a more efficient allocation of resources and higher productivity, stressed the maintenance of low tariffs on the import of investment goods and essential products while imposing higher tariffs on luxury goods.

In 1966, however, the Ministry of Commerce and Industry initiated a new policy aimed at the liberalization of imports in order to expose local production to the challenge of competition abroad. Customs duties were to be reduced gradually and selectively at regular intervals, one such reduction taking place in January 1969. Local industries were no longer to be protected by high tariff barriers. This policy is aimed at lower prices overseas, greater efficiency in production, improved design, emphasis upon quality manufacturing, and, ultimately, a reorganization for export by local industry. Firms adversely affected are being helped by the government to shift to more competitive lines.

An economic conference was convened in Jerusalem under the auspices of the Prime Minister's Office in 1968. Over 800 businessmen, bankers, experts, and officials, 476 of them from overseas, met at the beginning of April in order to promote the country's economic development by assisting in the improvement of the export sector. The participants pledged to undertake investments, to develop markets in their respective home countries for Israel's products, to advise exporters on design, packaging, and cost-reducing practices, and, finally, to help the export of engineering, scientific, and technical skills.

COMPOSITION OF TRADE

Exports

Total exports have risen steadily and substantially in the past two decades. During the British Mandate period and the first years of independence, agriculture was the main source of exports. Citrus fruits were especially prominent. Since then, agriculture's share in exports has declined, due in large part to the demands of a growing population (about four-fifths of agricultural produce is being consumed domestically) and also to a shift in emphasis in favor of industrial development (see ch. 20, Agriculture; ch. 21, Industry). Between 1950 and 1968 agricultural exports jumped from US$17 million to US$112 million, but their share in the total of goods exported declined from 50 percent to 19 percent.

Citrus fruits remain the largest component of agricultural exports. In 1968, US$88 million worth of citrus, in particular the Jaffa and Shamuti oranges famed for their quality, were shipped overseas, as compared with US$46 million in 1959. Citrus fruit still constituted almost 80 percent of all agricultural exports in 1968. The 1967-68 crop season, however, illustrated the vulnerability of orange exports. Disappointing prices and only moderate demand were experienced in European markets despite extensive frost damage to crop in the United States and Spain. The preliminary estimate of 1969 citrus exports was even more disappointing: US$82 million.

The export of raw cotton, begun in 1962, has grown gradually, amounting to approximately US$5 million in 1968. Another growth item is poultry produce. There has been a movement from export of eggs for direct consumption, which proved unprofitable after 1961, to export of eggs for hatching, as well as of chicks, and insemination materials. Avocadoes, melons, flowers and plants, and winter vegetables also recorded gains. Declines, by contrast, were registered in such traditional export items as bananas and potatoes.

Industry has become the leading export sector, its share in the total of goods exported rising from 50 percent in 1950 to 67 percent by 1959 to 80 percent in 1968. In terms of value, industrial export increased from roughly US$18 million in 1950 to US$480 million in 1968.

Notable increases in exports were recorded by textiles and clothing as a concerted effort was made to gain a share in the market for ladies' fashions. Similar advances were made in printing and publishing, pharmaceuticals and cosmetics, industrial machinery, communications equipment, precision instruments, kitchen and work tools, and electrical equipment. Most promising for the future, based upon 1968 figures, are clothing, up 52 percent, and copper, up 9 percent.

The export of polished diamonds holds a comparable central position in the configuration of industrial exports as citrus fruits do for the agricultural sector. Diamond sales in 1967 fell by US$7 million to US$158 million, suffering from a decline in world demand. After this brief divergence from the general upward pattern, diamond exports rose to US$194 million in 1968, providing 80 percent of the world market for medium-sized diamonds. Israel is presently second only to Belgium in international diamond production and trade.

Most of the significant price declines registered in 1967 were in standard commodities: 11 percent in potash, 7.5 percent in phosphates, 12 percent in edible oils, and 7 percent in cement. Mineral products merely maintained their previous value despite an increase in the quantities exported. In 1968, however, these commodities were included in the general resurgence of exports.

This transition from recession to recovery in the years 1967 and 1968 is perhaps best reflected in data on tourism. Receipts from tourism fell during 1967 by US$7 million (12 percent) as tension and war lessened the number of visitors. Almost 300,000 tourists visited the country that year and spent some US$52 million, excluding earnings of Israeli carriers: El Al planes and ships. The tourist industry, however, was a major beneficiary of, and contributor to, the economic upswing of 1968. There were an estimated 430,000 visitors, attracted to sites in the administered territories, such as the Wailing Wall in Jerusalem, the West Bank, the Gaza Strip, and Sinai. Income earnings from tourism reached approximately US$97 million. Transportation earnings of El Al and the merchant shipping fleet brought in about US$198 million in 1968. Thus, by 1969 tourism and transportation services had joined citrus and diamonds as the main export pillars of the economy.

The rise in tourism has been so pronounced that the government, operating through the Ministry of Development and Tourism and the Tourism Industry Development Corporation, is making a major effort at promoting this "invisible export." Somewhat parallel has been the development of an export industry for the sale of light armament, such as the "Uzi" machine gun. Precise figures are not available, but the government's net export account, generally believed to cover military exports, was about US$33 million in 1968, double the 1963 figure (see ch. 26, The Armed Forces).

Imports

One critical aspect of the economic recovery of 1968 was the great increase in imports. Net imports of goods amounted to US$1,035 million and of services to US$835 million in approximate figures, so that total imports were almost US$400 million above those for 1967, reflecting growth in every line of imports. This factor, in turn, was chiefly reponsible for a further deterioration in the balance of trade. With commodity imports rising by about US$300 milion but exports only by about US$116 million, the total deficit in trade grew by 33 percent. The disparity between imports and exports was not expected to decline in 1969.

During the first six months of 1968, 41 percent more consumer goods entered the country: imports of raw materials increased by 38 percent; investment goods by 39 percent; imports of metals more than doubled; vehicle imports rose by 121 percent; machinery and equipment, 87 percent; wood products, 54 percent; and grains, 20 percent. This sharp increase in consumer and investment goods was attributed to the replenishment of stocks and to a sudden expansion in current consumption resulting from import liberalization.

Imports of services also increased, rising from a modest US$29 million in 1950 to US$835 million in 1968. Publicity abroad and the cost of renting imported machinery, computers in particular, were significant factors in this category of costly inputs. Expenditures by the government and other public bodies have always occupied first place in imports of services, the main component being imports for military purposes. In 1968 this item embraced 42 percent of the total of service imports; the beginning of delivery in 1969 of the 50 Phantom jets ordered from the United States is likely to add substantially to such expenditures (see ch. 26, The Armed Forces).

The share of capital services in the larger category of service imports stood at US$135 million in 1968, the result of increased interest payments on the government's foreign debts, such as the maturation of State of Israel bonds. Import of insurance services was US$73 million, less than 10 percent of the total. Expenditure on travel abroad increased from US$1.3 million in 1952 to US$74 million in 1968, including Israeli spending in the occupied territories, in areas previously inaccessible to them.

Given the nature of Israel's needs, substantial import surpluses are expected to persist as a basic feature of the economy, concentration upon the export sector notwithstanding.

THE PATTERNS OF TRADE

During the Mandate period most exports from Palestine went to the United Kingdom and the Middle East. The year 1948 marked a break in this traditional pattern of trade, as dealings with Great Britain declined and those with the Arab countries ceased entirely.

Most of the country's foreign trade since independence has been conducted with the industrial countries of the West. Eighty percent of commodity imports and 72 percent of commodity exports in the 1962–67 period came from or went to the industrial countries of Western Europe and North America (see table 21).

The European Common Market has been the most important trading area, accounting for about 29 percent of commodity exports and 25 percent of imports in the 1963–67 period. Moreover, the European Economic Community's share of trade with Israel has been growing since 1948. In 1950 the member countries bought 8 percent of its total exports as compared with nearly 30 percent in 1966. During the latter year the European Economic Community (EEC) countries purchased about 40 percent of Israel's agricultural exports and 25 percent of its industrial exports.

In exporting to the EEC countries, Israel has experienced difficulty, particularly with its citrus fruits, in competing with other

Mediterranean countries that have secured special arrangements with the European Common Market. Since the Market is expected to remain the major outlet for citrus, diamonds, and other industrial exports, the government has repeatedly sought to obtain equally favorable terms and permanent membership.

Table 21. *Imports and Exports by Main Countries of Purchase and Destination, Israel, 1964–66*
(in millions of dollars)

	Imports			Exports		
	1964	1965	1966	1964	1965	1966
Europe:						
United Kingdom _____	158.8	164.1	157.8	46.0	50.1	62.2
German Federal Republic	65.7	75.1	68.7	33.3	40.0	47.3
Netherlands _____	35.1	31.9	37.8	30.2	36.6	37.1
Switzerland _____	25.3	25.3	27.8	25.8	26.3	28.0
France _____	67.9	35.0	32.8	11.8	16.0	18.8
Belgium _____	38.2	27.5	28.9	22.3	23.2	32.2
Italy _____	34.5	32.0	29.8	6.6	5.8	8.0
Finland _____	9.6	9.2	7.6	4.3	4.6	4.9
Yugoslavia _____	8.7	6.4	8.0	8.8	8.9	11.2
Sweden _____	12.1	11.4	11.4	8.1	9.7	8.0
Others _____	44.9	54.4	40.2	35.5	43.5	55.1
Total _____	500.8	472.3	450.8	232.7	264.7	312.8
America:						
United States _____	208.0	211.6	220.0	54.7	62.4	77.5
Canada _____	10.2	5.6	6.9	5.7	6.6	6.7
Others _____	10.4	15.4	21.8	6.0	5.6	6.0
Total _____	228.6	232.6	248.7	66.4	74.6	90.2
Asia:						
Japan _____	7.1	18.2	20.7	14.5	16.3	18.7
Hong Kong _____	0.2	0.4	0.7	12.7	17.1	20.9
Turkey _____	6.6	6.4	5.1	5.1	7.3	8.2
Others _____	4.7	5.0	4.3	16.2	15.7	18.0
Africa: _____	27.4	27.3	26.8	12.7	21.6	19.5

Source: Adapted from Israel, Central Bureau of Statistics, *Statistical Abstract of Israel, 1968;* and Israel, Ministry for Foreign Affairs, Information Division, *Facts About Israel, 1968.*

In 1966 the government applied formally for associate membership. As a pledge of intentions, the new liberalization policy was put into effect simultaneously. The subsequent gradual reduction of tariffs conforms to the goal of the General Agreement on Tariffs and Trade (GATT), to which Israel was admitted as a full member in 1962, and also strengthens the application for EEC membership. But even in the event that this does not materialize, Israel planners expressed hope that the economy will prove more efficient, and therefore more competitive, as a result of the lowering of barriers to imports (see ch. 25, Financial and Monetary System). Great Britain in the 1960's has been the most active single trading partner among the European Free Trade Area (EFTA) nations, having purchased US$277 million of goods while selling in return US$756 million during the 1963–67 period.

Trade relations with the countries of Eastern Europe, organized in the Council for Mutual Economic Assistance (COMECON), have reflected political developments. During the 1963–67 period, trade agreements with the Communist countries represented only 4 percent of Israel's exports and 2 percent of its imports. Prospects were improving until diplomatic relations were severed and trade canceled in the aftermath of the Arab-Israeli hostilities of 1967 (see ch. 15, Foreign Relations). Rumania has been an exception. In 1963 trade between the two countries totaled US$1.5 million; by 1966 it was US$5.2 million, and by 1967, US$10.6 million. On December 19, 1967, an agreement was signed to increase trade to US$31 million.

North America constitutes a fourth trade region and one which is increasingly prominent in the configuration of trade. During the 1963–67 period, about 16 percent of exports and 27 percent of imports went to or came from Canada and the United States. The size and purchasing power of these markets made North America an attractive outlet for Israel products. Imports from the United States during 1968 were approximately US$245 million. Almost one-third of total United States exports to Israel were agricultural: wheat, feed grains, soybeans, and corn. The countries of Central and South America, by contrast, only represented about 1.5 percent of exports and imports during the 1963–67 period.

Although trade with Asia and Africa has been modest in the past, it is expected to develop considerably in the future. The balance of trade with Asia in 1967 amounted to approximately US$75 million in exports, an increase of 16 percent over 1965, and roughly to US$31 million in imports. Japan, Hong Kong, and Turkey were the principal countries of purchase and destination. Total African trade was slightly in deficit as the need for rough diamonds and timber caused imports for the year to reach US$27.6 million, while exports totaled US$24.3 million.

A desire to promote stronger trade relations with Asia and Africa figures prominently in planning. It finds expression in two preoccupations: retaining maritime access routes and continuing the program of cooperation with developing nations that began in 1955.

Access to the Far East and Africa is facilitated by shipping to and from the southern port of Eilat and along the Red Sea water route to the Persian Gulf, then out to the Indian and Pacific Oceans. Interference with this trade route would seriously affect the country's trade potential (see ch. 3, Historical Setting).

Total exports and imports passing through Eilat in 1967 was some 300,000 tons (excluding petroleum, statistics on which are not published), and during 1968 probably reached between 350,000 and 400,000 tons. Port facilities are being expanded. The government also took steps in 1969 to purchase three super-tankers for the transportation of oil to Eilat and to construct a 42 inch pipeline between Eilat and Ashqelon on the Mediterranean coast (see ch. 2, Physical Environment).

The government is operating a modest foreign assistance program, utilizing in the process assets that it can afford: 20 years' experience in economic development, scientific proficiency, and individuals with technical, managerial skills who are prepared to volunteer for such service abroad. The government, consequently, participates in a variety of projects in over 70 countries, such as helping Iranians rebuild an area devastated by an earthquake, training police in Ethiopia and parachutists in Nepal, assisting Brazil in the development of atomic energy for peaceful uses, or training ex-soldiers in Dahomey for life in cooperative farming villages. The budget allocation to international cooperation activities was approximately US$5 million in 1967.

During the decade 1958–68 over 2,500 Israeli technicians were sent overseas to conduct training programs and to institute pilot projects. At the same time, 10,500 people from the developing countries came to Israel for specialized training. Although such efforts were aimed in the first instance at gaining goodwill and perhaps political support, the long-range hope was that these contacts, as well as participation in numerous exhibitions and trade fairs, would eventually result in greater trade between Israel and the countries of Africa, Asia, and Latin America.

Financial assistance from world Jewry is yet another major type of international transaction. This assistance has consisted mainly of private and institutional transfers, the purchase of State of Israel Bonds, and private investment. With a return to economic growth, the country became more attractive as an outlet for investment. Furthermore, the government, citing domestic political stability and the rise in the gross national product, has increasingly encouraged this type of monetary import, especially after German reparations ended in 1966.

Trade between the Arabs of the occupied territories and the Kingdom of Jordan continued even after the Arab-Israeli hostilities of June 1967. Farm exports from the Gaza Strip and the area west of the Jordan River, known as the West Bank, moving eastward across the river between July 1967 and March 1969 were worth US$35 mill-

354

ion to US$40 million. In the same period goods entering from the opposite direction were estimated at about US$7 million to US$8 million. Melons, grapes, citrus, olive oil, and tomatoes were the principal items, in terms of tonnage, flowing eastward. Israeli industry was only called upon to absorb relatively small quantities of fruit and vegetable from the West Bank in the uplands north and south of Jerusalem. Grapes, plums, and watermelons, also in small quantities, were shipped to Africa and Europe from these occupied areas. Constituting another import factor were the Arab workers of these areas employed in farming and industry (see ch. 22, Labor).

BALANCE OF PAYMENTS

Imports have consistently exceeded exports ever since statehood. A persistent deficit in the current account section of the balance of payments has therefore been a distinctive feature of the economy as well as a subject of concern for the government. The import surplus, on the one hand, has made possible a high level of capital formation, stimulating to the economy. On the other hand, finding the means to finance the import surplus has been a difficult task, its major implication being the country's ultimate economic dependence upon foreign sources of capital.

The deficit on current account reached a new and alarming high point in 1964: US$573 million, an increase of US$125 million over the previous year. Thereafter, forced domestic saving and tight import controls over consumer demands led to a partial amelioration, though not to a solution of the problem. The deficit fell in 1965 to US$520 million, and continued downward in 1966 to US$445 million. In 1967, however, because of the June hostilities, it rose again to US$532 million, and in 1968 to an unprecedented US$696 million. This deterioration in the balance on goods and services was not expected to be reversed in the short term. The minister of finance and of commerce and industry, Ze'ev Sharef, in presenting the draft budget for 1969 to the Knesset, warned that the deficit in the balance of payments was likely to increase still further, to a point where foreign currency reserves could be endangered. The deterioration in 1967 and after is attributable to increased defense expenditures abroad.

The harmful effects of this chronic deficit have been mitigated by the availability of large capital imports. The excess of imports has traditionally been compensated for by an equally persistent payments surplus of unilateral transfers and long-term capital imports. Private transfers, German restitution payments to individual Jews, and reparation payments to the Jewish state have accounted for a substantial inflow of capital. Additional sources have been United Nations technical assistance, United States grant-in-aid and loans, and World Bank loans. Thus, over the 18-year period from 1950 to 1967,

Israel was estimated to have received US$9,300 million, whereas it paid out US$1,900 million. Total capital imports in 1968 were estimated at a net figure US$606 million.

In planning for the next decade, authorities with those government agencies dealing with foreign economic relations expect the capital inflow to begin declining. They are confident, nevertheless, that the slack will be taken up by the export sector, which financed 63 percent of imports in 1968, up from 42 percent in 1958.

CHAPTER 25
FINANCIAL AND MONETARY SYSTEM

In Israel's mixed economy, the public sector includes various public and quasi-public financial institutions in addition to the government itself. The government excerises a very significant influence in the operations of all types of financial institutions, and its role in the mobilization and allocation of long-term capital has been decisive. It also has financed directly about 40 percent of total domestic investment and has controlled indirectly a large additional proportion.

There has been large public investment in agriculture, transportation, housing, and public services. Financing of industry by the public sector has been relatively minor, except in the case of factories producing for export and for industrial projects in development areas. A large proportion of commercial bank loans has not been extended at the discretion of the banks, but in accordance with directives of the government, which, together with quasi-public institutions, has made deposits with the stipulation that these deposits were to be used as the basis for loans for designated purposes.

Rapid economic growth has depended on maintenance of a high level of investment, which in turn was made possible by a large inflow of financial resources from abroad, including remittances from Jewish institutions and individuals as well as reparations and personal restitutions from West Germany. Beginning in the mid-1960's, funds for development projects have been supplied more from internal sources and less from foreign sources.

There has been a radical change in the structure of the banking system since establishment of the state of Israel in 1948. Most of the small institutions, especially the credit cooperatives, have been liquidated, and more than 75 percent of banking transactions has been concentrated in a few large institutions operating numerous branches.

The basic unit of currency is the Israeli pound (Hebrew, lira) that is divided into 100 agorot (singular agora—1 agora equals approximately US$0.003—see Glossary). There are coins for 1, 5, 10 and 25 agorot and for I£0.5 and I£1. Banknotes are issued in denominations of I£1, I£5, I£10, and I£50. Since November 1967 the official exchange rate has been I£3.50 to US$1, or I£1 equals approximately US$0.285 (see Glossary). Israeli pounds cannot be transferred into other currencies without a license from the Ministry of Finance. The proceeds from exports of certain industrial goods may be utilized by the manufacturer to import certain raw materials.

FINANCIAL INSTITUTIONS

There are three categories of financial institutions: the banking system proper that includes the central bank (the Bank of Israel) and the commercial banks; financial institutions providing mainly long-term credit; and social insurance funds and insurance companies. In 1966 the total assets of these three categories were divided as follows: banking system proper, 47 percent; financial institutions, 34 percent; social insurance funds and insurance companies, 19 percent. In addition there are credit cooperative societies that specialize in extending credit to a particular branch of the economy.

The Bank of Israel has the exclusive right to issue currency, acts as the government's fiscal agent, licenses commercial banks, and regulates and directs the flow of credit in accordance with the economic policy of the government. The three foreign banks, with offices in Tel Aviv, are the London-based Barclay's Bank, the Holland Union Bank, and the Bank Polska Dass Opieki, a Polish bank.

In 1968 there were 24 commercial banks. The three largest were Bank Leumi Le-Israel, controlled by the Zionist movement; the Israel Discount Bank; and Bank Hapoalim, controlled by the Histadrut (Histadrut Ha'ovdim Haklalit—the General Federation of Labor) (see ch. 22, Labor). These three banks accounted for approximately 70 percent of all commercial banking transactions in 1968. Their influence extends beyond commercial banking. They have subsidiary companies among the institutions providing long-term credit and, although the securities market is not yet a central factor in financing the business sector, they play a leading role in this market, both in underwriting and in trade on the stock exchange.

Most of the important financial institutions engaged in mobilization of funds for medium- and long-term investment were established by the government or by the large commercial banks. The largest group consists of mortgage banks that deal chiefly in loans to home buyers and builders; their share in the total assets of this category of financial institutions was 41 percent at the end of 1968. The Tefahot Israel Mortgage Bank is the most important in this category. The government provides a large part of its funds. About half of its mortgages are granted to municipalities for construction of schools and other public facilities.

Next in size in this group are the five industrial development banks, with 19 percent (in 1968) of the total assets of institutions providing long-term credit. The Industrial Development Bank of Israel accounts for some 80 percent of this group's assets. It was incorporated in 1957 by a joint effort of the government, the major commercial banks, the Manufacturers Association of Israel, and foreign investors. Additional capital has been provided by the Agency for International Development and the International Bank for Reconstruction and Development (commonly known as the World Bank). The majority of the Industrial Development Bank of Israel's loans has been to enterprises in the development areas, especially in the Negev. With increasing participation from other sources, the government's share of equity capital fell steadily from 93 percent in 1958 to 54 percent at the end of 1967.

Other groups of financial institutions providing long-term credit include investment companies and agricultural credit funds. The Bank of Agriculture, government-owned, is the largest of the 17 institutions lending to agriculture. The remaining institutions were set up by the various agricultural settlement organizations or by commercial banks to provide medium- and long-term farm credit.

The third category of financial institutions, social insurance funds and insurance companies, accumulate a large proportion of the domestic savings that are available for investment. Social insurance funds, including provident funds, insurance funds, and pension funds, account for about 90 percent of the total assets in this category. They are institutions established as the result of negotiations between employer and employee organizations. About five-sixths of all wage earners are members of such funds. In all of them the employers participate in the accumulation of savings funds, which are distributed to members upon retirement. Insurance companies are similar to social insurance funds in their function as savings repositories but operate on a commercial basis without regard to labor relations or considerations of social security.

INTEREST RATES

The maximum permissible rate of interest is fixed by law. The ceiling was 9 percent until 1957, when it was raised to 11 percent. Within this maximum the rates charged for a large proportion of total credit extended are specified by the government. Credit distributed by banks on the basis of funds deposited by the government and earmarked for specified purposes has been granted at rates well below the ceiling.

Price increases have tended to make the real rate of interest appreciably lower than the nominal rate. During the early years of statehood increases in the price level often exceeded the interest rate specified in loans, so that the real rate was negative. The extent to which the real rate has been negative has depended in each case on the relation between the rate of interest specified in the loan and the extent of increase in the price level during the period of the loan.

REGULATION OF CREDIT

There are three categories of short-term credit: directed credit, ordinary credit, and bill-brokerage credit. A significant proportion of short-term credit by commercial banks is granted according to guidelines laid down by the government. The purpose of this qualitative credit control is to ensure that enterprises considered essential receive sufficient credit, particularly those producing for export. During the mid-1960's credit controlled directly or indirectly by the government represented about 30 percent of all outstanding bank credit to the private sector. Ordinary credit can be extended at the discretion of the banks, but the volume is limited by the liquidity regulations of the Bank of Israel, which require commercial banks to maintain a prescribed ratio between their liabilities and their liquid assets. To control the volume of credit extended by the banks, the Bank of Israel has relied primarily on changes in this ratio.

The ceiling on interest rates and the rationing of credit to favor certain sectors of the economy gave rise to bill brokerage by which credit, mostly short-term, is extended outside the banking system. Since the commercial banks have been unable to satisfy the demand for credit at the legal rate of interest, they have served as bill brokers by negotiating loans between borrowers and lenders and transferring the borrower's note to the lender who is not a bank. In most cases the bank acts as guarantor as well as broker and receives a commission ranging from 4 to 6 percent. The lender receives the 11 percent maximum permitted by the interest rate law. Because the commission charged by the banks has not been interpreted as interest, the total charge to the borrower can be higher than the maximum legal rate by the amount of the bank's commission. The Bank of Israel has limited the volume of guarantees a bank may grant to either 3.0 times its equity capital or 1.5 times its liquid assets.

Industry, agriculture, public services, and the national institutions have received most of their short-term financing from directed and ordinary credit. The building industry and commercial enterprises have received very little directed credit and have relied mostly on ordinary credit and bill brokerage. In 1966 the volume of bill-brokerage credit was approximately two-thirds as great as the credit extended by the banks themselves to the public. In 1967 the volume dropped precipitately because of a decline in economic activity and related factors.

The government plays a decisive role in the mobilization and allocation of long-term capital. Through its control over foreign and domestic sources of borrowed capital, the government uses the financial institutions providing long-term credit as instruments for directing the flow of credit to implement national development policy.

Most of the important institutions of this type are subject to such a degree of government direction that they function as quasi-government financing agencies, even when they are not government-owned.

A considerable part of the capital inflow from abroad has been received by the government directly or by agencies subject to government direction, and a substantial part of this capital has been deposited in financial institutions that have extended loans in accordance with government instructions. The government's domination of internal sources of funds for investment derives principally from the requirement that the bulk of contractual savings, such as social insurance funds, must be invested in approved securities if contributors to these funds are to be eligible for income tax concessions. Furthermore, all new issues of securities must be authorized by the government. During the mid-1960's no new bond issues other than those of the government or government companies were permitted.

CAPITAL IMPORTS

Capital imports financed a large proportion of the investment that made possible a high economic growth rate. From 1949 through 1968 net capital imports totaled approximately US$8.1 billion—US$10.4 billion received less US$2.3 billion in payments of principal and interest. They consisted of unilateral transfers (requiring no repayment), long- and medium-term loans, and investments.

Unilateral transfers totaled US$5.4 billion, or about two-thirds of the total, and consisted of the following: institutional remittances, US$1,960 million; reparations from West Germany, US$775 million; personal restitution payments from West Germany, US$1,335 million; personal remittances, US$1,045 million; and United States government grants-in-aid, US$315 million. Institutional remittances consisted mostly of funds raised by the Jewish Agency and direct payments to numerous educational, health, welfare, and other nonprofit institutions in Israel. German reparations were paid to the state; restitution payments, in the form of lump-sum payments or annual pensions, were made to individuals or their heirs as compensation for the treatment suffered under the Nazis. Personal remittances consisted, for example, of support from relatives and pensions from abroad.

These unilateral transfers made it possible to finance the large import surplus and to accumulate substantial foreign exchange reserves. They were of decisive importance during the early years of the state, when Israel was required to absorb large numbers of immigrants and exports did not finance more than about 40 percent of imports. Foreign exchange holdings of the Bank of Israel increased from US$102 million at the end of 1958 to a peak of US$876 million at the end of August 1967 and stood at US$565 million in mid-1969.

By mid-1968 the foreign debt totaled US$1,602 million—State of Israel Bonds US$748 million (47 percent), other long- and medium-term loans US$773 million (48 percent), and short-term debt only US$81 million (5 percent). Private foreign investment amounted to approximately US$1 billion. Most State of Israel bond purchases and the bulk of foreign investment came from Jewish communities in the Western world. In the past the United States government has extended three types of loans: for purchase of surplus foods under Public Law No. 480, passed in 1954, mostly repayable in Israeli pounds; for purchase of raw materials and equipment; and for specific development projects. Other loans were extended by the World Bank, by the government of West Germany, and by private investors.

CAPITAL MARKET

The capital market is not an important source of investment capital. Personal savings are relatively low for a country with Israel's per capita income, and a large portion goes into mortgage payments for housing and into premium payments to social insurance funds. Large capital imports from abroad have reduced the importance of the capital market for financing investment. Attractive alternatives to raising funds in the capital market are available to two important sectors: Histadrut enterprises obtain funds from social insurance funds and other sources controlled by the Histadrut; and companies in the public sector have access to the government's development budget.

The capital market is primarily a bond market. A large proportion of the securities traded are public loans, either issued by the government or bearing the government's guarantee. The government dominates the bond market by requiring all new issues to have government approval and by requiring the main institutional purchasers, notably social insurance funds, to invest most of their resources in securities approved by the government.

A relatively small number of industrial and commercial firms list their shares on the Tel Aviv Stock Exchange, the only organized securities market. The number of new share issues reached a peak in 1963 and 1964, but even in those years only a small part of business investments was financed by this means. In mid-1969 the Tel Aviv Stock Exchange list published in the Jerusalem press consisted of about 70 stocks. Almost half represented banking and credit institutions; about one-third were commercial firms, and the remainder were utilities and land development enterprises.

CENTRAL GOVERNMENT BUDGET

The Ministry of Finance prepares the central government budget, which must be approved by the Knesset. The fiscal year begins April 1 and ends the next year on March 31.

In July each year the Ministry of Finance circulates to the various ministries and separate agencies specific directives relating to their budgetary preparations for the upcoming fiscal year. During September and October ministry and agency estimates are received. After consultations among the various budget officials, a final draft of the budget is prepared. It contains explanatory material and pertinent data regarding the plans and projects scheduled by each ministry and agency. It also includes comparisons with past performances and proposed allocations for new projects and programs. After study and approval of the draft by the cabinet and prime minister, it is presented by the finance minister to the Knesset for consideration.

The Knesset, as a body, does not debate the budget but transmits it to a joint subcommittee composed of the finance, foreign affairs, and security committees for discussions and possible modifications before enactment into law by the Knesset.

Improvements since 1948 and 1949, when the budget process was haphazard and data submitted were insufficient, have enabled the Knesset to exercise more effective supervision over government expenditures. The principal improvements have been in organization of the budget and in compilation of explanatory material. Altogether the expenditure section contains some 16,000 items.

The total actual expenditures are not accurately indicated in the original budget since amendments are submitted during each year for approval by the Knesset. Budgetary surveys are continuous, with the various ministers giving information regarding progress and prospects within their respective areas of responsibility.

In June 1967, as a result of the Six-Day War, the Knesset approved an amendment to the budget law, as submitted by the minister of finance, authorizing an extra I£400 million outlay for defense. He was empowered, with approval of the Knesset Finance Committee, to transfer any sum from the ordinary budget to special budgetary expenditures. In September the Knesset acted favorably on another budget measure, which provided for a supplement of I£522 million, designed mainly to finance development and encourage industrial undertakings.

Budget figures do not always include total expenditures of the public sector since many activities in this area receive only part of their funds from the government's budget. For example certain large public corporations, such as The Israel Electric Company and the Dead Sea Works (for exploitation of mineral deposits), have raised funds that are not recorded in the budget, and the Industrial Development Bank of Israel has assumed an increasing share of the financing of public investment in manufacturing and housing.

Total government expenditures rose from 42 percent of the gross national product in 1966 to 47 percent in 1967 (see table 22). Various factors have contributed to a high level of public expenditures. The scarcity of natural resources has required large capital investments to provide means of livelihood for a rapidly increasing population, and the government budget has been the main source of such financing. The geographic and political situation has required large military expenditures.

The financial burden of defense is far heavier than in most developing countries. During the decade preceding the Six-Day War of June 1967, defense expenditures amounted to about half of the ordinary budget (as distinct from the development budget). The share of defense expenditures increased substantially during and after 1967. In presenting the proposed budget for the fiscal year 1969/70, the minister of finance suggested that the final budget figure for defense might amount to 75 percent of total tax revenue, and the defense budget does not include expenditures for such purposes as border settlements, desert roads, and pipelines that are undertaken primarily because of defense considerations.

Table 22. Budget Summary, Israel, 1966-70
(in millions of Israel pounds)*

	Actual 1966-67	Actual 1967-68	Estimated 1968-69	Estimated 1969-70
Revnue:				
Taxes and fees	2,441	2,521	3,119	3,763
Income tax	(1,164)	(1,204)	(1,477)	(1,828)
Expenditure tax	(1,101)	(1,174)	(1,348)	(1,772)
Others	(176)	(143)	(294)	(163)
Borrowing	1,194	1,903	2,038	2,755
Foreign	(569)	(885)	(847)	(968)
Domestic	(625)	(1,018)	(1,191)	(1,787)
Collection of capital and interest	318	389	584	683
Other	180	627	621	649
Total	4,133	5,.440	6,362	7,850
Expenditures:				
Government offices (excluding defense)	1,368	1,439	1,327	1,638
Defense, special, and reserve budgets	1,223	1,954	2,707	3,061
Subsidies	271	365	513	549
Development projects	787	933	889	1,120
Capital and interest payments	744	882	870	1,302
Other	102	77	56	180
Total	4,495	5,650	6,362	7,850
Taxes and fees as percent of GNP	21	21	22	23
Expenditures as percent of GNP	38	47	45	49

* For value of Israeli pound, see Glossary.

Agricultural settlements, irrigation works, and electric power facilities have been financed primarily from public funds. Construction of housing and transportation facilities has relied heavily on public finance. Agriculture and housing together have consistently accounted for about half of appropriations for development projects.

Expenditures for public services are highly concentrated in education, health, and welfare. Excluding Defense the six ministries with the highest level of ordinary budget expenditures in 1968/69 were as follows: Education and Culture, I£351 million; Health, I£123 million; Labor, I£101 million; Police, I£119 million; Finance, I£87 million; and Foreign Affairs, I£72 million. The National Insurance Institute had a budget of I£56 million.

As part of the effort to control inflation, subsidies to domestic producers were almost doubled between 1966–67 and 1968–69 to prevent increases in costs from being reflected in domestic prices. Increased interest payments reflect an increasing recourse to foreign and domestic borrowing. Collection of interest exceeded I£222 million in 1968/69, reflecting the large government investment in various enterprises.

Government revenues from abroad have included grants-in-aid, West German reparations, and foreign loans. The share of revenue from abroad in total government revenue reached a peak of over one-third in 1954 and declined substantially thereafter.

TAXATION

In 1968 personal income tax rates for married persons ranged from 22.5 percent on taxable income of I£2,500 to a maximum of 62.5 percent on taxable income over I£32,500. Corporate income was subject to a company profits tax of 30 percent, plus an income tax of 25 percent of net income after deduction of the company profits tax. The effective rate of the combined taxes was therefore 47.5 percent. On dividend payments 25 percent is withheld by the paying company and remitted directly to the government with any balance to be paid by the dividend recipient.

Income tax regulations have undergone frequent changes, some of them intended as antiinflationary measures. In an effort to foster egalitarian distribution of personal income, tax rates are sharply progressive and rates are relatively high at income levels generally regarded as intermediate. Income taxes have accounted for an increasing proportion of total tax revenue, reflecting the increase in incomes and the progressive nature of the tax; in the years from 1966 to 1968 the proportion was about 50 percent, which is relatively high for developing countries but relatively low for more developed countries. Israel is classified by the World Bank as a developing country.

In addition to direct taxes on income and property, there are numerous indirect taxes, including import duties, purchase taxes, excise duties and license fees (see table 23). In 1968 customs duties accounted for 31 percent of total revenue from indirect taxes; purchase taxes, 25 percent; fuel tax, 12 percent; tobacco excise tax, 6 percent; defense stamp tax, 4 percent; and others, 22 percent. Indirect taxes fall most heavily on luxuries and semiluxuries. Purchase taxes on durable consumer goods are relatively high; for example 46 percent on musical instruments, 40.5 percent on electrical appliances, and 27 percent on photographic equipment.

Ad valorem rates predominate among import duties and range from 5 percent to 200 percent, but the majority are between 10 percent and 60 percent. Most basic food commodities, raw materials, and machinery for agricultural or industrial purposes are exempt. The highest rates are applied to nonessential foodstuffs, luxury consumer items, and manufactured goods of a type produced in Israel. Progressive reduction in the level of duties on imports began in 1966 in accordance with the government's policy to expose domestic producers to international competition in order to improve their ability to compete in world markets.

Table 23. Israeli Government Tax Revenue, by Major Category, 1967

Tax	Percent of total
Direct:	
Taxes on income	52.4
Taxes on property	3.7
Total	56.1
Indirect:	
Taxes on expenditures:	
Imports	15.4
Local production	24.3
Others	4.2
Total	43.9
GRAND TOTAL	100.0

Source: Adapted from Israel, Bank of Israel, Annual Report, 1967.

BORROWING

Heavy domestic and foreign borrowing has financed a large proportion of total government expenditures. The government has borrowed heavily from the Bank of Israel and the commercial banks, and there have been substantial purchases of government bonds by world Jewry. Various social insurance and pension funds are required to invest a large proportion of their assets in government securities and at times, between 1959 and 1968, the government has employed compulsory loans with subscriptions by all individuals and companies at a fixed percentage of the income tax due. Since 1967 the government has borrowed to cover a part of ordinary expenditures as well as development expenditures.

Total borrowing amounted to 29 percent of the budget in 1966/67 and was expected to rise to 35 percent in 1969/70. As of March 31, 1968, internal government debt totaled I£4,705 million, external debt payable in foreign currency totaled I£4,349 million, and external debt payable in Israeli pounds totaled I£819 million.

LOCAL AUTHORITIES

Local authorities include municipalities, local councils, regional councils, and area authorities. They are not homogeneous bodies because of the great difference in municipal problems. Their income and expenditures are determined largely by local conditions. Most of their income is derived from property taxes, business taxes, and fees for various services. In addition to a general grant-in-aid to the local authorities, the central government participates in financing some of their activities. Revisions in local tax rates must be approved by the central government. In 1968 the local authorities accounted for about 7.4 percent of total expenditures by the public sector.

INFLATION

Inflation has been a persisting problem. Large investment expenditures, mainly through the development budget, and increasing expenditures for defense and social services have placed more money in circulation and created more demand than the available supply of physical factors of production that could be activated by monetary expansion. From 1951 to 1954 the price level increased at a rate varying from 10 to 20 percent a year. During 1955-1966 price increases averaged 5.4 percent annually. Only the huge import surplus prevented inflation from being more severe.

Prices and wages have increased at a faster rate in Israel than among its major trading partners, and devaluation of the currency occurred in 1949, 1952, 1953, 1962, and 1967. Since November 1967, the Israeli pound equals approximately US$0.285.

The authorities attach great importance to stabilization of prices as a prerequisite for continued economic growth and, more particularly, for further expansion of traditional industrial exports, such as processed foodstuffs, textiles and clothing, phosphates and potash, and chemicals. The economic recession of 1965 to 1967 reduced inflationary pressures, and prices and wages remained fairly stable during 1967 and 1968.

Value linkage on loans originated as a reaction to inflationary pressures and the legal ceiling on the rate of interest. Rising prices meant that loans would be repaid in funds that had less purchasing power than when they were borrowed, and interest rates were prevented by the legal ceiling from rising sufficiently to compensate for this decline in purchasing power. Lenders faced the problem of preserving the real value of the principal of the loan. Consequently, bonds were sold subject to a value clause linking the principal either to the consumer price index or to the exchange rate, which meant that borrowers were required to repay a greater sum than was borrowed. Linkage to the exchange rate was abandoned after the devaluation of 1962. Linkage arrangements became increasingly important after 1955 and, by 1962, embraced nearly all long-term credit transactions since the existence of value-linking precluded the raising of long-term capital by any other means.

There has also been widespread use of value-linkage to protect against deterioration in the value of savings because of inflation. By 1967, 80 percent of the savings accumulated in social security funds were invested in value-linked securities.

Wages are linked to the consumer price index through cost-of-living allowances. The authorities have been concerned over the fact that linking wages and debts to the consumer price index creates a spiral of cost and price increases and makes stabilization more difficult to achieve. The problem has been less pressing since wages and prices became relatively stable in 1966.

SAVINGS

Savings have been discouraged by inflation. The banks provide schemes to encourage savings that permit depositors to choose among various combinations of interest rates, tax concessions, and linkage of the principal to the cost-of-living index.

A high proportion of private saving consists of payments by employers and employees to social insurance funds, most of which were initiated by the Histadrut. Employers contribute two-thirds and employees one-third. Total contributions amount to about 8 percent of the total wage bill. Since social insurance funds are required to invest half of their resources in government securities, this form of saving is an important factor in government financing. The most important component of household saving is investment in real estate, mainly in owner-occupied apartments.

Life insurance is comparatively new and saving in this form is relatively unimportant. To encourage saving through life insurance, a deduction of 25 percent of the premium is permitted in calculation of income tax. A considerable portion of interest on bonds, especially those issued by the government and by enterprises with government approval, is subject to a reduced rate of income tax as an incentive to saving.

SECTION IV. NATIONAL SECURITY

CHAPTER 26

THE ARMED FORCES

Israel has established itself as an effective military power in the Middle East. Only a small standing force is maintained, but a large, well-trained, and well-organized reserve can be mobilized rapidly and efficiently.

Popularly known as Zahal Zuq Ha-Haganah Le-Israel, the Israel Defense Forces were established by an ordinance of the Provisional Government of Israel on May 26, 1948; they are the first Jewish national forces in nearly 2,000 years. The army is organized into a number of full-strength combat brigades, with small cadres of regular personnel manning command and staff elements of reserve units to facilitate mobilization. A call-up of reserve forces could increase army strength as much as four or five times. The smallest navy and air force could also be expanded quickly, if required. The navy has several major combat vessels, and the air force has a large number of combat aircraft.

Zahal is a direct outgrowth of the Hagana (Irgan Ha-Haganah), the clandestine defense organization created during the period of the British Palestine Mandate (see ch. 3, Historical Setting). Hagana in turn has its antecedents in the Shomrim, or Guardsmen, who afforded protection to the earlier settlements. In the late 1870's, when Jews once more began to settle in Palestine, then under Ottoman rule, each village found it necessary to provide for its own self-defense. As immigration increased and settlements became more numerous, the activities of many of these local self-defense units were coordinated on an area basis. In 1907, following a large wave of immigration from Russia, the Shomrim were formed into a countrywide organization called Hashomer.

Immigration was further encouraged by the Balfour Declaration and the postwar transfer of Palestine to British administration under the Mandate. As a result of Arab disturbances in 1920 and 1921, Hagana was organized as a continuation of Jewish self-defense measures, operated and trained secretly, and smuggled arms and ammunition into the country.

A semblance of legality for some operations of the Hagana followed in the wake of the widespread Arab uprising from 1936 to 1939. British military authorities sanctioned the designation of some Hagana members as auxiliary police for the purpose of defending their settlements, and Special Night Squads were organized and trained with the assistance of then Captain Orde Wingate, a British intelligence officer who was later to become noted for his operations in Burma. In 1937–38, the Special Night Squads were instrumental in repelling attacks by guerrilla groups based in Syria.

A Jewish Legion, whose ranks included many members of Hashomer, had fought with the British against Imperial Germany in World War I; in 1944, the Jewish Brigade was formed to fight against Nazi Germany. Nearly all Palestinian Jews serving in the brigade were members of Hagana. Special groups were also organized to conduct commando, intelligence, and airborne operations. These groups were trained in Palestine with the aid of the British; known as the Palmach (Plugot Mahatz), or spearhead groups, they became the elite striking force of the Hagana.

Not everyone, however, was satisfied with Hagana's policy of self-restraint *(havlagah)*, and two rival organizations had come into being. The National Military Organization (Irgun Zvai Leumi), or Irgun, was established in 1937 and the Fighters for Freedom of Isreal (Lohamei Herut Yisrael), or LEHI, in 1941. LEHI was also known as the Stern Group, after its founder Avraham Stern, originally a member of the Irgun. These dissident groups conducted campaigns of terror, sabotage, and reprisal against British troops in Palestine in what amounted to all-out war against the Mandate Authority. The Stern Group specialized in the assassination of British and other officials. Although Hagana had the broad support of the civilian community, it was constrained from taking direct action to suppress the two dissident groups for fear of alienating some of this support and because of the common nature of the ultimate goals of all three organizations, the establishment of a national home and the creation of a sovereign Jewish state.

At the time of independence in 1948, the Hagana numbered about 45,000 members, including about 3,000 in the Palmach. The Irgun totaled less than 3,000 and the Stern Group only a few hundred. The ordinance creating Zahal had outlawed the existence of any other military organization or unit, and steps were undertaken to integrate members of the Irgun and the Stern Group into the new national forces. Both groups, however, demurred at turning in all of their arms and equipment, wishing to retain them for independent operations in Jerusalem, which was proposed to become an international zone under the United Nations Resolution of November 29, 1947.

Military unification was finally achieved, but not until a number of serious incidents had occurred. Open conflict between the rival forces broke out on June 20, 1948, when the supply ship *Altalena* arrived off Tel Aviv with 900 men and a load of arms and ammunition for the Irgun; the immediate issue was settled when a round of artillery set fire to the ship. Known members of Irgun were subsequently arrested by the Israel government. Events reached a crisis stage on September 17, 1948, when United Nations mediator Count Folke Bernadotte was assassinated in Jerusalem. Reacting quickly, the government ordered a large number of Sternists and their leaders arrested. Irgun units in Jerusalem were also ordered to surrender their arms and to disband. The elimination of dissident groups as military organizations became complete.

A difficult and certainly a more delicate problem remained to be settled. Palmach, which had developed strong political overtones, continued to operate independent of control by the newly established Israeli General Staff. Palmach maintained a separate headquarters and conducted its own recruiting and training, as it had done in earlier days. Politically, it was closely associated with the kibbutz movement for the establishment of collective settlements (see ch. 14, Political Dynamics). Palmach headquarters were finally abolished in November 1948 on orders of Minister of Defense David Ben-Gurion.

Ben-Gurion was prime minister as well as defense minister, but none of the three underground organizations—Hagana, the Irgun, or the Stern Group—was, in a political sense, committed to him as leader of his country. It was nevertheless through his stern and forceful actions that Zahal emerged as an integrated, loyal, modern defense force. He made the chief of staff of Zahal directly responsible to him as minister of defense, and thus set the pattern for future relationships between the military and the civilian arms of the government. He selected the chief of staff and operated the Ministry of Defense in such a manner that it became autonomous in all major decisions of military significance. His policies and actions were facilitated by the dual nature of his ministerial role, but that, too, set a precedent that except for a brief interlude in 1953–55, was followed until the appointment of Moshe Dayan, former chief of staff, as defense minister on June 2, 1967.

There is no written constitution, and the Basic Laws of the Knesset contain few provisions of constitutional nature relating to the armed forces (see ch. 13, The Governmental System). The president, as chief of state, has only nominal and ceremonial functions. The prime minister, as head of government, exercises the ultimate authority over the defense establishment. The minister of defense is responsible for the execution of all laws pertaining to the defense establishment; he is the actual though not the nominal commander-in-chief of the armed forces. Command is vested in the chief of staff.

Defense legislation, except the budget, must follow the prescribed legislative process. The budget bypasses action by the Knesset as a whole; after cabinet approval, it is submitted only to the Committee on Finance and the Committee on Foreign Affairs and Security, neither of which is allowed to have Arab or Communist members.

The military are an integral part of the fabric of national life. Universal military training and the reserve structure assure that virtually no citizen is left untouched by the armed forces. The armed forces are widely respected, and the people view military service as a mark of honor as well as a national duty.

Military personnel have the right to vote and to participate in political party activities; although under legislation adopted in 1958, the chief of staff and senior officers "of such ranks and in such functions as determined by law" are prohibited from being candidates for the Knesset. Among the professional officers, however, few exhibit more than a passing interest in politics, and only a relatively small number of senior officers have joined political parties. The military in Israel have refrained from intruding on political processes. They are not associated with the political philosophy of any particular party nor are they representative of any particular economic or social group. Their aims and their values appear to be no different from those of the civilian government they serve.

The military have nevertheless from the outset been influential in governmental affairs. Their influence is extended through the many retired officers and former military leaders who have been named to high posts in the government or with governmental agencies. Many have become figures of national political prominence.

Jewish military tradition is rooted in Biblical history. Joshua, who conquered Canaan, is an early hero; and David, who captured Jerusalem, is regarded by the Israelis as their greatest king and warrior. Solomon organized the first standing army and maintained a large military force.

Modern military heritage dates from the exploits of the Shomrim who guarded the early settlements. Among these were Joshua Stamper, Michael Katz, and Joseph Ben-David. Eliyahu Golomb, who died in 1945, was a member of the Hashomer and the founder and the first commander of Hagana. Especially esteemed is David Ben-Gurion, who not only was a leading figure in both Hashomer and Hagana, but also served with the British in both world wars. An outstanding heroine is Havivah Reik, who in 1944 was among a small group of volunteers that parachuted into Czechoslovakia to conduct partisan operations against the Germans; she was eventually captured and executed. Another was Hannah Szenes, who suffered the same fate in Hungary.

World War II provides the names of many others whose deeds stimulate a feeling of pride among the Israelis. Yigal Allon and Moshe Dayan participated in clandestine operations in Syria in 1941 (see ch. 18, Biographies of Selected Key Personalities). Perhaps no one is more charismatic than Dayan, who lost his eye in the Syrian campaign and was appointed minister of defense largely in response to public demand.

The basic model for the Israeli defense structure appears to have been Swiss, but from the beginning the principal foreign influence on organization and tactics was British. Israelis had become familiar with the British system during the period of the Mandate. Uniforms, even terminology, were adapted from the British.

In addition French influence has also been strong because of the predominant position France has occupied as a supplier of arms and equipment. Great Britain and the United States, as major sources of military assistance, have also been influential in training personnel to operate and maintain weapons and materiel supplied by them. Large numbers of Israelis attend service schools and specialist courses in the United States, France, and Great Britain, and senior officers make observation visits to military units and installations in various countries throughout the world.

THE ARMED FORCES AND THE NATIONAL ECONOMY

Defense Expenditures

The defense budget in Israel is a classified document. In an interview for *Bamahane* (In Camp), a weekly armed forces publication, the financial adviser to the chief of staff explained that publication of defense expenditures would jeopardize national security; he implied that enemy intelligence would benefit greatly from the information.

Although total defense expenditures are not usually revealed, reasonable inferences can be drawn from published data. The figure for the budget of the Ministry of Defense is an incomplete statement of defense costs. Additional expenditures are included in other line items in the budget, particularly those designated "special reserve," "special budgets," "general reserve," and "reserve for development expenditures." Collectively, these are referred to as "Special Reserve" by the state controller, the Ministry of Finance, and the Bank of Israel; they are counted with the Ministry of Defense Budget as defense expenditures. Reports from the state controller, however, show that the "Special Reserve" covers some civilian expenditures, and therefore it should not all be regarded as allocated for defense purposes.

Government leaders have been making increasingly explicit statements about the size of defense expenditures since the Arab-Israeli hostilities of June 1967. These statements reached a peak when the finance minister announced in May 1968 that total direct defense expenditures in the Israeli fiscal year 1968/69 (April 1, 1968–March 31, 1969) would be I£2,200 million, plus another I£100 million in indirect expenditures. At the same time he introduced a supplementary budget bill in the Knesset allocating I£500 million for security needs. He also announced that the defense budget was twice as large as that planned at the beginning of the year and was three times as much as the entire development budget.

This was the first time the government had announced the defense budget with indications of total national security costs. The sizable increases in these expenditures over the past several years and their increasing proportion of the gross national product, as stated in publications of the Central Bureau of Statistics, bear evidence that defense costs constitute a serious burden on the economy and a significant drain on foreign currency reserves (see table 24). The disadvantages resulting from a drain on foreign currency reserves are accentuated, because the country must still import major items of material, equipment, and basic raw materials for local production.

Table 24. Defense Expenditures, Israel, Fiscal Years 1964/65 to 1968/69 [1]
(in millions of Israeli pounds) [2]

	1964/65	1965/66	1966/67	1967/68	1968/69
Total budget	3,425	4,021	4,493	6,002	5,897
Defense budget [3]	752	850	984	1,384	1,907
Percent of total budget	21.9	21.4	21.9	23.1	32.3
Percent of gross national product	8.2	7.8	8.2	11.4	13.5

[1] Fiscal year (April 1–March 31).
[2] I£1 equals approximately US$0.285 (see Glossary).
[3] Does not include "Special Reserve" allocations.

Source: Adapted from Israel, Central Bureau of Statistics, *Statistical Abstract of Israel, 1968*, No. 19, p. 491.

Self-help

The country has made substantial progress in its efforts to develop and increase its own capacity for defense production. The purpose of these efforts is to reduce reliance on foreign sources and the impact of defense expenditures on the national budget. Priority is given to the manufacture of spare parts for major items of foreign origin, so as to avoid the effects of a wartime embargo; at the same time, foreign exchange is conserved and the budgetary position improved.

Plans and research towards future requirements are as much a part of the self-help program as production to meet current needs. Long-range projects are the responsibility of the Military Research and Development Authority, under the minister of defense. The authority is concerned not only with hardware but with concepts, doctrine, and techniques. It seeks to improve existing equipment, to adapt it to new uses, and to develop more effectively techniques and methods. It is also responsible for coordinating relevant research at universities and technical institutes.

Military goods are produced by Israel Military Industries and Israel Aircraft Industries. These are government-owned agencies; private civilian firms, however, many of them small workshops, also produce a number of items on a contract basis. Government shipyards, under the Ministry of Transport and Communications, are capable of building small landing craft and performing essential repair, maintenance, and overhaul on many of the larger vessels.

In October 1968, the director general of the Ministry of Defense stated that the country had already become self-sufficient in the production of ammunition, and that near self-sufficiency could be expected within a year with respect to small arms and eletronic instruments. He further stated that the total value of military exports during the preceding year was US$30 million, including ammunition, small arms, certain types of electronic instruments, and supply items such as tents and field kitchens. Another military spokesman had announced a month earlier that approximately one-third of all requirements for spare parts were then being produced locally.

Among the many items manufactured by Israel Military Industries is the Israeli-developed Uzi submachine gun; this weapon has been purchased in quantity by a number of foreign armies, including those of the Netherlands and the Federal Republic of Germany. Israel Military Industries is also responsible for the manufacture of chemicals, explosives, and optical equipment and for the modification of existing equipment to give it added flexibility and effectiveness.

Capacity for aircraft production is being expanded through the acquisition of a plant from the United States firm North American-Rockwell Standard for the manufacture of executive jet aircraft. Israel Aircraft Industries produces a jet trainer and is at work on an Israeli-designed 22-passenger transport. In addition, Israel Aircraft Industries performs most of the major repair and overhaul required and manufactures many essential spare parts and other components.

Civic Action

By virtue of their educational activities, the armed forces serve as a vast school for citizenship, and thus play a vital role in the process of nation-building. Illiteracy is the first problem attacked, and the aim is to provide every recruit with the equivalent of at least a sixth-grade education. Subjects taught include geography, history, and mathematics. Of utmost importance is Hebrew language instruction as a means of achieving greater social homogeneity among personnel of diverse origins and imbuing them with a deeper sense of national identity and unity. The armed forces also provide vocational training in skills useful upon return to civilian life.

Whereas education and training constitute the most substantial military contribution in the field of civic action, and the one with the most lasting effect, other projects and activities are nonetheless significant within a social or economic context. Military units in outlying areas, for example, often provide the inhabitants of neighboring villages with medical services and other forms of assistance. The armed forces also stand ready to assist the civilian population in the event of a natural disaster or emergency, such as might be caused by fire or flood.

The paramilitary youth organization Nahal (Noar Halutz Lochaim—Fighting Pioneering Youth) is engaged in activities of a civic action nature as well. Nahal provides agricultural assistance to settlements in frontier areas and establishes settlements of its own, thereby combining economic development of the country with border defense.

MANPOWER

In a population estimated to be 2,708,000 as of January 1, 1968, about 564,000 are Jewish males between the ages of 15 and 49. Of these, about 482,000 are considered fit for military service. Of the 63,000 non-Jewish males in that age bracket, mostly Arabs, about 41,000 could qualify; Arabs, however, are not subject to compulsory military service.

Because of their small size, the regular military forces do not constitute a serious drain on either the total population or the male labor force. In times of mobilization, however, the economy is severely strained as reserve personnel are called from their civilian occupations. The very old and the very young move in to take their places, but the efficiency of public services and the productiveness of private enterprise suffer markedly.

Universal Military Service

Under the Defense Service Law of 1949, universal military service is compulsory for both men and women. Original terms of service were set at 24 months for males between the ages of 18 and 26; 18

months for males between the ages of 27 and 29; 12 months for unmarried or childless females; these were increased to 30, 24, and 24 months respectively under amendments adopted in 1950 and 1953. Subsequent changes have been made by decree of the minister of defense. The 30-month conscription term for men was reduced to 26 months in 1963, but was returned to its former level on November 8, 1966. In May 1964, compulsory military service for women was reduced to 20 months, where it has remained. By decree of May 18, 1967, all regular personnel have been retained on active duty, and in January 1968, compulsory service for all males whose terms ended before March 31, 1969, was extended for 6 months. One of the announced purposes of the extension was to reduce the call-up of reservists.

Exemptions and deferments from compulsory military service are few. The primary basis for exemption is permanent physical disability. Exemptions may also be granted to women, mainly those of the Orthodox faith, who object on religious grounds. Others eligible for exemption or deferment include teachers and students who are taking courses in subjects deemed to be in the national interest, including medicine, engineering, agronomy, and teaching; rabbinical students are exempt upon request. Persons who are the sole support of their families may also request exemption or deferment. All requests for exemption or deferment must be acted upon by a committee within the Ministry of Defense. There are separate committees to handle each of the different categories of requests.

Young men and women must register with their local draft boards upon reaching the age of 17. They are usually inducted between the ages of 17 years and 6 months and 18 years and 6 months. The average annual intake of conscripts is about 25,000 in four approximately equal increments. Most are assigned to the army, where they comprise about two-thirds of the total strength. The air force and the navy have fewer requirements for conscripts; both have a large percentage of professionals and volunteers, and reenlistment rates are high. After completion of active duty requirements, men serve in the reserve until age 49 and childless women until age 34.

Quality and Source

Nearly all physically qualified Jewish males are inducted upon reaching military age; of the total number of persons in the population as a whole who are subject to compulsory active duty service, about 90 percent of the eligible males and as many as 50 percent of the females are actually inducted. The armed forces thus represent at any one time a cross-section of the Jewish military age group as a whole. As a consequence, the national origin of conscripts varies widely, with resultant differences in social values, attitudes, and customs.

The average conscript is generally in good physical condition, intelligent, and with a high aptitude for learning. He makes a good soldier, tough, rugged, and skillful. As a rule, he looks upon military service as no less than his expected contribution to the state. Many Shephardim are lacking in a mechanical and technical background, and many are illiterate. An explicit task of the armed forces is to produce good citizens as well as good soldiers and, in so doing, to soften ethnic distinctions, raise standards of education, and achieve a greater degree of cultural homogeneity within a nation of many diverse elements.

The career officer corps consists of a nucleus of personnel serving on a contract basis. Contracts are usually offered for terms of 3 to 5 years; they are renewable with the mutual consent of the individual and the government. Many veterans of Hagana and British service are still on active duty, but, as a group, the officer corps is young. Mandatory retirement age is 55; most retire about 10 years earlier.

Since 1948, the only source for officers has been through the enlisted ranks. The methods by which a commission may be obtained are highly competitive.

Career officers are characterized by dedication to duty and a deep sense of mission. Aggressive and tough-minded, they have proved to be able leaders and unflinching fighters. Their professional competence meets the highest standards. Almost all have had combat experience. Most enter the service with only a high school education, but many eventually achieve an opportunity to attend civilian institutions of higher learning.

Although predominantly Askenazi, the officer corps represents a wide variety of social and economic backgrounds. While enjoying high prestige as a military elite, it has not become identified with any political or other special interest group.

ORGANIZATION AND MISSION

National Level

The armed forces are headed by the chief of staff, a position that has always been held by an army officer. Under the supervision and guidance of the minister of defense, the chief of staff controls and directs all operations and activities of the armed forces. Immediately subordinate to him are the General Staff, the commanders of the navy and the air force, three area commanders, the commanders of the Military Training Command, the commanders of the Armor Corps and the Paratroop Corps, and the heads of Gadna and Nahal (see fig. 8). The chiefs of the army's administrative and technical services also report directly to the chief of staff.

The General Staff operates on behalf of all services and components of the armed forces. It is patterned basically along British lines, modified and adapted to meet local requirements and conditions.

The A (Adjutant) or Manpower Branch performs the normal personnel and administrative functions, but since 1966 it has also been responsible for handling all aspects of conscription, including registration, induction, and discharge. The I Branch is military intelligence. The G (General Staff) Branch exercises the greatest authority and influence; it formulates and develops overall plans, policies, and programs pertaining to operations and training and provides a focal point for the coordination of all General Staff activities. The Q (Quartermaster) Branch is responsible for logistical matters.

Army

The mission of the army is to provide for internal security and territorial defense. To accomplish its mission, the army relies upon a small professional cadre of officers and senior noncommissioned officers, conscripts serving a compulsory tour of duty, and a reserve that is well-organized, trained, and capable of rapid mobilization.

The Permanent Service (Sherut Qevah) is estimated to number between 12,000 and 15,000 career personnel, with about one-third being officers. The Conscript Service (Sherut Hovah) averages about 50,000 at any given moment of time. The Permanent Service and the Conscript Service together make up the Regular Service (Sherut Sadir), giving it a strength of about 65,000; actual strength depends in part on the rate of induction and the length of the compulsory term of service. At least 250,000 members of the Reserve Service (Sherut Miluim) have mobilization assignments and could be activated with 48 to 72 hours.

The army's basic combat formation is the brigade, with a strength of about 4,000. It is composed of a number of combat battalions together with supporting troops. Engineer, signal, medical, and administrative units are included in the brigade's table of organization; direct support artillery is attached. About seven brigades are maintained at full strength in the standing army; at least two of these are armored, another is airborne, and the remainder are infantry and mechanized infantry. Another 20 to 25 brigades are manned at cadre strength by career personnel, ready for immediate activation with the call-up of reserves. Armor is available to equip about one-third of the reserve brigades.

For purposes of command and control, the army is organized into

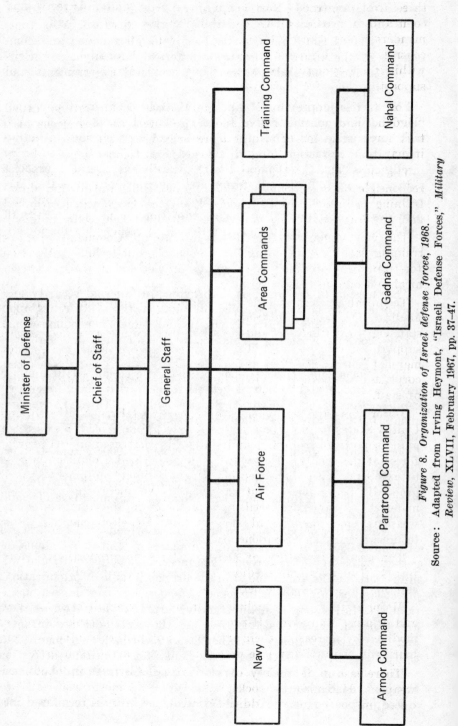

Figure 8. Organization of Israel defense forces, 1968.

Source: Adapted from Irving Heymont, "Israeli Defense Forces," *Military Review*, XLVII, February 1967, pp. 37–47.

three area commands—Northern, Central, and Southern. Each area command is further subdivided into military districts. Area commanders report directly to the chief of staff. They have operational control over all ground forces and border defense organizations within their geographical areas. They are also responsible for all supporting logistical activities.

For tactical operations, an intermediate headquarters, called "Ugdah," is organized. Its mission is to direct the operations of a task force composed of two or more brigades of the same type, or it may be a composite force of two or more combat arms.

The commanders of the Armor Corps and the Paratroop Corps are responsible for organizing and training new units and for individual training in branch service schools. For combat operations, armored and airborne units come under the control of field commanders.

The commander of the Military Training Command operates training facilities, including service schools, but technical direction for training is provided by the chiefs of the combat arms and technical and administrative services.

Technical services include the Engineer, Signal and Electronics, Medical, Ordnance, and Supply Corps. They are responsible for staff logistical functions and for providing maintenance and service support for combat units. The judge advocate general, the provost marshal general, the chief military rabbi, the director of the women's corps, and the head of Civil Defense are also responsible to the chief of staff.

Major arms and equipment are primarily of French, British, and United States origin. Some materiel dates from World War II, but most is postwar in design and similar to that used in the regular forces of the country from which it was obtained. Condition is good to excellent, with the exception of some older equipment that is gradually being phased out or replaced. An increasing amount of materiel is being produced locally, including mortars, automatic weapons, small arms, and various types of electronic and other technical items and components.

The army's inventory of armor is large in proportion to total forces, it includes both medium and light tanks, as well as armored cars and armored personnel carriers.

Major artillery pieces include guns and howitzers of varied calibers and origins. Many are self-propelled. A number of tanks have been modified by increasing their armament so that they can be used primarily in the artillery role or against hostile armed vehicles.

There is a wide variety of small arms, mortars, and automatic weapons. Machineguns, rocket launchers, and mortars are all produced in the country. Additional weapons include recoilless rifles and several types of automatic antiaircraft weapons. The army is also equipped with antitank guided missiles.

Navy

The Navy is a small force of about 3,000 personnel, the majority of whom are professionals, and about 25 vessels. It has the mission to guard the state's sovereignty in the Mediterranean and the Red Sea; to defend the national coastline and render it secure; and to protect shipping and fishing rights within territorial waters. Naval operations are complicated by the geographical separation of the two coasts and their mutual inaccessibility.

Major combat vessels include a destroyer and three submarines. Naval strength suffered a heavy blow when a destroyer was sunk off Alexandria in October 1967 and again in January 1968 when a submarine disappeared in the Mediterranean, while en route from Great Britain following delivery to an Israeli crew. Other vessels include a destroyer escort, a number of patrol and landing craft, and a submarine chaser, all of varied origin, including British, French and German.

There is no Marine Corps or naval air arm. The navy does have, however, a battalion-sized organization of marine type forces trained to conduct amphibious and commando operations.

The main naval base is at Haifa. A major operating facility at the new port of Ashdod was officially dedicated in August 1968. Minor facilities are located at Elat.

Air Force

The air force is composed of about 11,000 personnel, most of whom are volunteers. Its mission is to defend and control Israeli airspace, gain and maintain air superiority, and provide support for the army and navy.

Like the navy, the air force is subordinate to the General Staff, and the officer commanding the air force reports directly to the chief of staff. Air operations are controlled and supervised by a small Air Staff at air force headquarters in Tel Aviv.

The air force is organized into squadrons and wings, with unit equipment in each squadron, varying from about 16 to 24, depending on the type of aircraft composing it. Combat squadrons are about equally divided between interceptor and fighter-bomber squadrons. Classification is more nominal than real, however, since most aircraft can be armed for use in either role. In addition there are about three squadrons of jet trainers that can also be used for ground support. There are two transport squadrons and two helicopter squadrons.

Of the total number of aircraft, about two-thirds are jet. Most are of French origin; recent acquisitions, however, have been made also from the United States.

Paramilitary

The principal paramilitary force is called Fighting Pioneering Youth, or Nahal (Noar Halutz Lochaim), an organization that combines military service with agricultural training. Nahal's dual nature is symbolized in its insignia, a diamond-shaped shoulder patch bearing a sword and a sickle. Nahal's military mission is to serve as a first line of defense against ground attack along the borders and to prevent infiltration; a secondary mission is to assist and support the army in performing duties in the administered areas.

Nahal has an estimated total strength of about 4,000 personnel. The basic unit is the platoon, with strengths ranging from about 20 to 80 youths, depending upon assignment. A small headquarters serves as a command element for a number of platoons located in the same general area. Nahal units are assigned either to reinforce existing frontier settlements or to establish new ones in areas unsuitable for development by the civilian population. Strategic considerations are a fundamental factor in the selection of locations where Nahal units are to be stationed. Some of the new sites are later abandoned as no longer useful; others become permanent settlements. One of the goals of the Nahal program is to encourage its members to remain with an agricultural settlement upon completion of compulsory service.

The youth organization called Gadna (Gdudei Noar) has paramilitary overtones; it provides preparatory training for both Nahal and the armed forces. Boys and girls in the 14- to 17-year age group receive premilitary indoctrination and training, and training in agricultural and pioneering activities. Gadna objectives combine citizenship with physical fitness and skills and techniques helpful in the adjustment to military life. The development of such characteristics and traits as patriotism, discipline, and leadership is emphasized.

TRAINING

All training is supervised and controlled by the director of military training in G-Branch of the General Staff. Under his direction, the commander of the Military Training Command is responsible for the administrative operation of virtually all army training centers and service schools; excluded from his jurisdiction are those belonging to the Armor Corps and the Paratroop Corps. The technical aspects of training, including course curricula and content, are the responsibility of the heads of the combat arms and technical services. The navy, air force, and Nahal operate their own training facilities.

Training programs are continuous and progressive, and standards are high. Training exercises are made as realistic as possible, with combat conditions simulated through the use of live ammunition, including artillery, mortar, and small-arms fire. The tactics of mobile warfare are given major emphasis; experience is also gained in the attack of fortified emplacements and in the coordination of operations and staff functions with other arms and services. Combined arms exercises involving infantry, armor, and artillery task forces are common, and the air force participates with each of the other services in joint exercises. Another important training objective is terrain familiarization. Training is also conducted on the capabilities and limitations of material likely to be encountered in combat, using available types of such equipment.

Basic training for recruits includes instruction on small arms, scouting and patrolling, maintenance, and first aid. Recruits are also given instruction in the Hebrew language, in history, in geography, and in other subjects that contribute to their development as good citizens. Those who are illiterate receive literacy training. Recruit training is especially demanding from a physical standpoint. Recruits spend little time on the parade ground performing close order drill or the manual of arms. Instead they undergo a rugged program of obstacle courses, marches, and bivouacs. Maneuvers are ordinarily conducted over rough terrain, often at night.

The service school system is extensive, and, although many officers are still sent to foreign schools for training, most needs can be met within the country. The senior service school is the Command and General Staff College, established in 1954. A National War College was established in 1963, but was discontinued in 1966 for reasons of economy. The Command and General Staff College, a tri-service institution, conducts a 10-months' course in general staff operations, techniques, and procedures. Only outstanding officers, usually field grade, are selected to attend. They are obligated to serve for 5 years upon completion of the course.

Officer and noncommissioned officer courses are conducted by each of the combat arms and technical services. Courses at branch schools for officers of the combat arms last about 3 months; those for members of administrative and technical services are somewhat less. Shorter courses are also conducted in various individual specialties.

Premilitary training is conducted at the Reali School in Haifa and the Herzlia School in Tel Aviv. This is a program whereby high school education is provided for a select group of volunteers for military training. Upon graduation, they are inducted into the army with the rank of corporal; they are commissioned upon successful completion of the officer candidate course. About 400 were reported to be in the program in October 1968.

Another minor source for officers is the Academic Reserve Corps. This consists of a small number of conscripts who, already having been accepted for admission to college, are permitted to proceed at their own expense after completion of basic training. Their subject of study must be of special technical interest, and they must undergo a period of military training each summer. They are commissioned on graduation.

Most officers are obtained directly from among the recruits who are serving their normal compulsory tour of duty. Selection is based on a series of written competitive examinations and a continuing evaluation of the manner in which they perform their duties. After three months of basic training and 2 to 3 months of troop duty, selected individuals attend a 3-month noncommissioned officer course. They then return to branch units for another 2 to 3 months of troop duty. They next attend a 6-month officer candidate course; upon successful completion they are commissioned as reserve second lieutenants. They complete their obligatory service in this capacity, at which time they are offered contracts to remain on active duty.

Normal training for reservists consists of a consecutive 31-day period of active duty each year until the age of 40 and a 14-day period each year thereafter until the age of 49. Officers and noncommissioned officers serve an additional 7 days each year. Officers may remain in reserve status until they reach the age of 55. Emphasis during reserve training is given to individual specialization, but reservists also take part in unit training and in field exercises.

Upon induction Nahal personnel undergo a 3-month program of basic training similar to that given to other recruits. For some Nahal personnel, training begins in high school with the formation of cells from among members of youth groups with the eventual purpose to serve as nuclei for Nahal units. Conscripts inducted for regular military service may also request duty with Nahal, and any member of Nahal may transfer to the armed forces to complete his obligated service. During the period of basic training, about 15 percent of Nahal recruits are selected to take a more intensive training program as a first step towards later opportunities to become officers and noncommissioned officers in Nahal and the armed forces.

After recruit training, Nahal units are assigned for 1 year to existing villages where they receive practical training and experience in agricultural work. Military training continues, with some receiving instruction on crew-served weapons and demolitions. Service with the village is followed by 5 months of advanced military training for all physically fit males; the program includes a common course in infantry operations and specialization in one of the combat arms such as armor, artillery, or airborne. About 5 percent are selected to attend officer and noncommissioned officer candidate schools. Personnel who are not combat qualified remain with the agricultural settlements but continue to receive military training.

Israel also conducts military training for other countries, and the civic action aspects of Nahal have proved especially attractive in Latin America, Asia, and the newly developing countries of Africa. Training is conducted both in Israel and abroad. Examples include paratroop training for Nepal and the Congo (Kinshasa) and jet pilot training for Uganda. The Women's Corps has furnished advisers to the Ivory Coast; Ecuador, Bolivia, Costa Rica, Burma, and Thailand are among the countries that have received assistance in agricultural and youth programs. Youth leaders from Tanzania, Kenya, Zambia, and Malawi have visited Israel for advanced training. In all, more than 30 countries have received Israeli training and assistance in one form or another.

LOGISTICS

Responsibility for staff supervision and control over all logistical activities is centralized in the Q-Branch of the General Staff. In the army, functional responsibilities are divided among the technical services; the navy and the air force have small staffs responsible for internal logistical operations.

In general, the logistical system appears to be adequate and efficient. Its effectiveness is due principally to the high level of managerial and technical skill of the Israelis and to the widescale adoption of modern business machines and methods. Supply administration, for example, has been computerized to include requisitioning, issue, and stock control procedures.

Important handicaps are the country's continuing dependence on foreign sources for major items of combat equipment and associated spare parts. The country also depends upon the mobilization of a large share of its domestic resources to meet many of its mobilization requirements. An example is the reliance on civilian transport, including trucks, buses, and private vehicles, as well as heavy engineering construction equipment. Consideration is being given to augmenting the number of military vehicles on hand, maintaining them in reserve for purposes of emergency.

In the field, responsibility for logistical operations devolves primarily upon the area commander. He is responsible for arming and equipping the reserve forces in his area and for providing logistical support to all units coming under his control. Supply depots are located at key points to provide arms, equipment, and field rations in the event of mobilization and to furnish base support for field operations.

Equipment of all three services is maintained in excellent technical condition. Using units are well-trained and fully capable of first and some second echelon maintenance. The underlying concept for battlefield support is mobility, and mobile workshops as well as supplies accompany the combat forces.

Technical service units are attached to combat units to provide second and third echelon maintenance and service. Government factories and activities are capable of performing depot repair and maintenance, and naval vessels can be serviced and overhauled locally.

RANKS AND PROMOTION

Ranks

There are only three basic officer ranks in the Israeli armed forces: *segen* (commander of tens); *seren* (commander of hundreds); and *aluf* (commander of thousands). All other ranks are variations of these, with prefixes and suffixes to indicate relative seniority. A similar system is used for enlisted grades. Rank titles are the same for all branches of the armed forces.

The rank of *tat-aluf*, equivalent of brigadier general, was established on July 22, 1968; the existing ranks of *aluf* and *rav-aluf* were thereby upgraded one notch to major general and lieutenant general respectively.

The rank of lieutenant general is held by only one officer serving on active duty, the chief of staff. Major generals include each of the three area commanders, the commander of the Armor Corps, the chiefs of the four branches of the General Staff, and the heads of the navy and air force. The new brigadier general rank was designated for seventeen positions, including the chiefs of staff of the area commands, the assistant General Staff branch chiefs, the commandant of the Command and General Staff College, the financial adviser to the chief of staff, and the deputy commanders of the navy, air force, and Armor Corps. The military attache to the United States was also promoted to brigadier general.

United States equivalents for enlisted ranks are less exact than for officers. The two senior noncommissioned officer grades are often equated to warrant officer rank; status and functions are much alike. The lowest career noncommissioned officer rank is *samal*, or sergeant.

Promotion

Promotion is based primarily on performance, not on seniority. Basically, the same criteria are used for both officers and noncommissioned officers, including reservists. Factors considered include attendance at service schools, conduct, and special qualifications and accomplishments. Written reports and service records are closely evaluated to assure the selection of the best qualified personnel for advancement to available vacancies.

Officers are required to serve a minimum time-in-grade in order to qualify for promotion. These requirements are 1 year from second to first lieutenant, 3 years from first lieutenant to captain, and 4 years each from captain and above to the next higher rank. Promotion becomes increasingly selective among field-grade officers, and the selection rate to colonel is reported not to exceed 20 percent of those who become eligible for the first time.

PAY AND ALLOWANCES

Base pay is modest, in comparison with civilian salaries in the Israeli economy. Step increases in base pay are authorized for most personnel after a specified number of years in grade, and all are entitled to a form of additional pay for seniority. These seniority increments are computed on the basis of monthly rates established for each rank; amounts increase arithmetically at those same rates each year until prescribed maximums are reached. Accrued seniority pay is retained upon promotion, at which time additional amounts are earned at the new rate for the higher rank. Special consideration with respect to pay is given to personnel holding advanced degrees in law, medicine, engineering, and a number of other technical fields; their base pay is higher, and the value of seniority increments in most cases is also greater.

An extensive and rather complex system of bonuses and special pay supplements base pay and seniority increments. Examples of extra pay for hardship assignments include a bonus for service in the field and for sea duty. Personnel engaged in hazardous duties are also entitled to extra pay; included are parachutists, frogmen, and submariners. Bonuses are authorized for air force pilots and navigators; amounts are substantially increased for those on active flight status. Other aircrew members such as mechanics and communications specialists also receive bonuses. Career noncommissioned officers may qualify for a form of proficiency pay, based on ratings attained in examinations and tests. Other personnel eligible for extra pay include instructors at service schools and training centers. All personnel qualified in the Arabic language receive a small bonus.

Family allowances are based on the number and status of dependents, with the same rates applying to all regular personnel, regardless of rank. Children in excess of three are covered under the program of national insurance. Family allowances are also authorized for conscripts and those serving an obligated tour if they are married or are the sole family support. Amounts are determined according to need on a case-by-case basis.

Married personnel are provided with low-rent housing, or, if unavailable, a special housing allowance to help cover living expenses. Those who desire to purchase their own homes may obtain mortgages at favorable rates of interest tied to the cost-of-living index.

Other benefits include reduced income taxes, comprehensive family insurance, reduction in tuition fees for high school children, and the use by officers of military vehicles at a low monthly rental fee.

UNIFORMS AND INSIGNIA

Uniforms

Except for a typical seaman's uniform and a special dress uniform for certain categories of officers, uniforms for officers and enlisted personnel, male or female, are generally the same; insignia of rank is usually the only distinguishing feature. Uniforms for the army, navy, and the air force are also alike, in most cases differing only with respect to color.

Basic uniforms for male personnel include service dress, semidress, and combat. The service dress uniform for summer consists of a cotton shirt and slacks. Colors are olive for the army and beige for the air force; the navy has two versions, one white and one tan. For winter, the service dress uniform consists of a British-style battle jacket and trousers made of a heavy, rough-textured woolen material. Army uniforms are olive drab; the navy wears dark blue, and the air force uniform is a medium blue.

The semidress (walking-out) uniform for summer also consists of shirt and slacks but made of dacron instead of cotton. The color, beige, is the same for all three services. Winter semidress consists of a wool polyester blouse and trousers; colors are green for the army, dark blue for the navy, and blue gray for the air force.

Green combat fatigues are the same for winter and summer. Heavy winter gear is issued as needed. Windbreakers and raincoats are standard items; overcoats, parkas, and thermal underwear are also available. Paratroopers wear an olive-colored bush jacket. A leopard design camouflage suit is customarily worn by ground troops in the field.

Special dress uniforms include blue and white mess jackets. They are authorized to be worn on ceremonious and other appropriate occasions by military aides to the president, prime minister, and designated attaches serving abroad.

Headgear includes a service cap for wear with service dress and semidress uniforms and a baseball-type peaked cap for wear with fatigues. Army and air force personnel also have berets, which they usually wear in lieu of the service cap. The color of the air force beret is blue gray. For armor and artillery personnel, it is black; for paratroopers, red; for all other army personnel, khaki.

Women in the army and air force wear a summer service uniform that consists of a beige-colored, short-sleeved, hip-length jacket and a skirt. Navy personnel wear a white shirt and skirt. For winter, the uniform includes a three-quarter length jacket; jacket and skirt are olive for the army and blue for the navy and air force.

Insignia

Basic insignia for enlisted grades is a series of stripes worn diagonally on both sleeves, halfway between the shoulder and the elbow. One stripe designates a private first class; a corporal wears two stripes. Sergeants wear three stripes; a fig leaf is added to indicate the rank of sergeant first class. The same system is used for equivalent ranks in the navy, except that an anchor entwined with an olive branch is used in lieu of the fig leaf. Stripes for army and air force personnel are blue and white in color, in an alternating hashmark design; the background is khaki for the army and slate blue for the air force. Navy stripes are gold on a dark blue background.

Insignia for the two senior career, noncommissioned officer grades is composed of the Star of David encircled by a pair of olive branches. A fig leaf centered on the star indicates master sergeant (warrant officer or company sergeant major); an upright sword entwined with an olive branch indicates sergeant major (chief warrant officer or regimental sergeant major). Background colors are red for the army, blue for the air force, and gold for the navy.

Officers' insignia, worn on shoulder tabs or loops, are the same for the army and air force. Rank is designated by the use of rectangular bars for company grade officers and fig leaves for field grade officers. Both insignia are blue in color, with a red border; the figure of a white olive branch is embossed lengthwise along the bar. A single bar indicates the rank of second lieutenant; two bars represent a first lieutenant; three bars, a captain. One, two, and three fig leaves are used to indicate majors, lieutenant colonels, and colonels, respectively.

Insignia for the recently established rank of brigadier general consists of a sword crossed with an olive branch. The same device with one fig leaf indicates a major general and with two leaves, a lieutenant general, unchanged from the insignia previously worn.

Insignia for naval officers follows a conventional pattern of gold stripes worn on the sleeves and on shoulder boards. Officers of all ranks wear a gold metallic device centered just above the topmost stripe; this insignia consists of an anchor whose shank is an upright sword entwined in an olive branch.

Cap insignia for army personnel consists of a red Star of David, edged in black, with a center design of sword and olive branch. Similar but smaller devices are worn on the lapels of both collars. Air force cap insignia features a pair of wings upon which are superimposed a small star and a somewhat larger sword with olive branch. Navy cap insignia is composed of the anchor device superimposed over a large wreath formed with olive branches.

There is also a wide variety of distinctive insignia, including shoulder patches for army units and appropriate devices to indicate the general staff, combat arms, technical and administrative services, and specialist ratings.

MILITARY JUSTICE

The administration of military justice was based originally on Hagana law, which, by decree of the Ministry of Defense, was adopted to serve as Army Law. Hagana, however, had been an underground volunteer force, and its code of military justice was found to be inadequate or inappropriate for legally established national forces based on compulsory service. After numerous amendments, the Army Law was replaced by a new and comprehensive Military Justice Law, which was enacted on June 21, 1955, and became effective on January 1, 1956.

The Military Justice Law is divided into 10 parts, containing a total of 546 sections or clauses. It embraces the entire range of legal matters affecting personnel subject to its jurisdiction. Under its provisions, a separate and independent system of military courts is established; military offenses are defined, with maximum authorized punishments specified in each case; pretrial, trial, appeal procedures, and rules of evidence are described in detail.

Military law applies to military personnel serving on a voluntary or compulsory basis, reservists on active duty, civilian employees of the armed forces, and certain other civilians engaged in defense-related activities, as determined by the minister of defense. Persons in each of these categories may also be tried by military courts for nonmilitary offenses, unless otherwise directed by the attorney general.

That part of the law pertaining to offenses contains a total of 93 clauses. The first of these enumerates those acts that constitute treason, stating that any guilty person is liable to the death penalty if the offense was committed during a period of actual fighting. Offenses for which life imprisonment may be imposed are mutiny and mass rape committed by three or more military personnel. Typical examples of other authorized punishments include 2 years for absence without leave and 1 year for disorderly conduct in public. Absence without leave for 21 consecutive days is presumed to be evidence of the intent element in desertion, the penalty for which may be imprisonment up to 15 years.

Courts-martial of first instance include district courts, naval courts, field courts, and a special court. The special court has jurisdiction over officers above the rank of lieutenant colonel and any person charged with an offense punishable by death. District, naval, and field courts have judicial power and competence in all other cases.

The basic type of court-martial is the district court; it is composed of three members, at least two of whom must be officers. A naval court-martial may be convened at sea when the vessel is not expected to return to coastal waters for at least 21 days and when the commander deems an earlier trial is necessary in the interest of discipline; a naval court consists of three members, including at least one officer. The establishment of field courts may be authorized by the minister of defense in times of actual fighting; composition is the same as for district courts. Power to convene field courts is normally not vested in any commander below the rank of major. The special court may comprise either three or five members, the majority in each case being officers.

The composition of each court of first instance must include at least one member who is a legally qualified military judge. No member may be of lower rank than the accused, and a private has the right to request that at least one be of his own rank. The accused may act as his own defense counsel or elect to be represented by another military person who has agreed to do so or by a civilian lawyer authorized to practice before courts-martial. Any judgment may be appealed within 15 days; appeals in the case of a death sentence are automatic, regardless of action by the defendant.

Appeals from conviction or punishment are decided by a court-martial, empaneled from membership on the Military Court of Appeals. An appeal court-martial usually has three members; there are five for cases involving the death penalty. The president of the Military Court of Appeals is appointed by the president of the state on the recommendation of the chief of general staff and approval of the minister of defense. Appeal judges number not less than 21; they are appointed by the chief of staff on the recommendation of the president of the appeal court.

Personnel below the rank of lieutenant colonel charged with an offense, the penalty for which does not exceed 3 years' imprisonment, are subject to disciplinary trial in lieu of court-martial. Disciplinary trials are conducted by unit commanders; for the purposes of the code of military justice, unit commanders not below the rank of lieutenant colonel are termed senior disciplinary officers, and those not below the rank of captain are termed junior disciplinary officers. If the accused is also an officer, the disciplinary officer must be at least two ranks his senior. Types of punishment that may be imposed by disciplinary officers include warning, reprimand, forfeiture of pay, fines, detention or confinement, and reduction in rank for personnel in the grade of sergeant first class or below. Persons arraigned before a junior disciplinary officer may request trial by a senior disciplinary officer, and those arraigned before a senior disciplinary officer may request trial by court-martial.

DISCIPLINE, MORALE, AND WELFARE SERVICES
Discipline

Military discipline is characterized by informality in relationships between officers and enlisted men and an apparent lack of concern for such exterior symbols as smartness on the parade ground and military appearance and bearing. Enlisted men customarily address officers by their first names or nicknames, a practice that has its origins in the Bible and in the days of the underground Hagana, and saluting is a casual and rather infrequent gesture. Little attention is devoted to military drills and ceremonies, and uniform regulations are not always strictly enforced.

Discipline and morale are nevertheless excellent. Responsibility and lines of authority are clearly defined, and prompt obedience to orders is expected. The quality of leadership is high, and professionalism is a hallmark. The average conscript understands why he is in uniform; he is inclined therefore to look upon military service as a national obligation. His basic amenability to military discipline is continually reinforced through troop information and education sessions, at which he is encouraged to bring up problems for discussion.

Military service does not hold great attraction for the Israeli conscript, and disciplinary problems are by no means unknown. On the contrary, military authorities have found it necessary to take several steps towards stricter enforcement of disciplinary measures. In a September 1968 interview, the chief of staff cited the need for improvements in personal appearance and highway discipline. An Israeli government source reports that summary courts have been established to handle military traffic violations on the spot; the same source further reports that a special drive to round up deserters accounted for "all but 1 percent."

Morale

One of the principal factors favoring morale is the opportunity that military service affords for education and training. Conscripts receive literacy training and instruction in basic academic subjects, and many are able to progress through high levels of classes. They also acquire skills that are useful upon their return to civilian life. A number of higher ranking officers are selected to attend colleges or universities at government expense and with full pay, and both officers and enlisted men may qualify to attend service schools and training courses abroad.

Morale-building activities include a wide variety of recreational services and facilities; most are provided by Shekem, an organization that combines commissary, post exchange, and special services functions. Permanent shops and mobile canteens offer numerous items for sale at discount prices, ranging from food and refreshments to household articles. Libraries and bookmobiles are among the other services available. Armed forces publications include several periodicals and journals, and there is an armed forces radio service. Movies are shown frequently, and military entertainment troupes present programs of music, drama, and variety. Physical conditioning and athletics are emphasized, with facilities provided for both individual and team sports, including football, basketball, and volleyball.

Military personnel enjoy an excellent diet; rations are high in quality and more than adequate in quantity. Meat is frequently served twice a day. Refrigerated trucks serve troops stationed in isolated garrisons with meat, fruits, and vegetables, as well as ice. Field messes for officers and enlisted men serve the same food. Kosher food is assured under an ordinance adopted in 1948.

Another stimulant to morale is provided in the form of efficiency prizes; these are awarded to service personnel or civilian employees of the armed forces for suggestions that result in monetary savings or improvement in operations.

Among the factors adversely affecting morale, the principal complaint has been low pay; pay is still considerably below comparable civil service levels, despite recent increases in several forms of special pay. Other conditions with implications for morale include the extension of military service and the widespread deployment of troops in the occupied areas. A pay raise in the first case has helped to ameliorate the situation; in the second, telephone service has been extended to distant locations so that personnel may now keep in touch with home, and air transportation is furnished for those going on leave.

Welfare Services

In addition to special housing, insurance, and educational benefits, military persons receive free medical care and treatment and social welfare services. Personnel with a physical disability rating of 19 percent or more are entitled to a pension and continued medical treatment; those with a lower rating receive a one-time payment. Widows are granted a pension, with the amount increasing in the event there are dependent children.

One of the government's most important services is an extensive program to assist veterans in readjustment to civilian life. Ministry of Defense guidance offices in Tel Aviv, Haifa, and Beersheba provide information on educational and job opportunities and conduct tours of schools, factories, and business firms. Many veterans are integrated into the civil service system. The civilian economy has a great absorptive capacity, but this program concerned with conversion from military to civilian status greatly eases the transition for returning veterans.

AWARDS AND DECORATIONS

The method commonly used to accord recognition to individuals for outstanding acts or services is the device known as Mentioned in Dispatches. Early in 1969, however, the Knesset had under consideration a proposal submitted by the minister of defense to establish a new system of awards and decorations to honor individual acts of heroism or bravery. The proposed decorations would be awarded in three classes: for extreme valor in the face of the enemy, for valor in battle, and for valor not in battle.

In 1949, the Knesset made a one-time Hero of Israel award to a small group who had distinguished themselves for valor in the War of Independence. The decoration consists of a ribbon only; there is no accompanying medal. It was awarded to 12 persons, four posthumously; the last recipient to serve on active duty was Commodore Ben-Nun, commander of the navy, who retired on January 1, 1966. The proposed new decorations would be retroactive to holders of the Hero of Israel as well as to those Mentioned in Dispatches.

Campaign ribbons are authorized under regulations prescribed by the Ministry of Defense. In order of precedence, they include the War of Independence Campaign Ribbon for those who served on active duty from February 1, 1948, to March 10, 1949; the Sinai Campaign Ribbon for those who served on active duty from October 29 to November 6, 1956; and the Six-Day War Campaign Ribbon for those who performed a minimum of 24 hours' consecutive service during the period of June 5–11, 1967.

Military service performed before the State of Israel was established is indicated by a series of small metal devices worn on the War of Independence Campaign Ribbon. Devices are authorized for service with the British in World War II, participation in the defense of Jerusalem, and service as a member of Palmach.

CHAPTER 27
PUBLIC ORDER AND INTERNAL SECURITY

The enforcement of law and the maintenance of public order and safety are the responsibility of the Israel Police Force, a national organization under the centralized control and direction of the minister of police. Its immediate forerunner was the Palestine Police Force, and the Police Ordinance of 1926 is still the principal law governing police operations and functions. The new national force came into being in 1948, during the War of Independence, with a minimum of resources, having inherited few personnel and little equipment from its predecessor organization. It has since developed into a highly effective and efficient organization, well regarded by the people.

Headed by the inspector general of police, the force is organized into three territorial commands and a separate Frontier Force. Formerly known as the Border Guard, the Frontier Force has the mission to prevent infiltration at the borders by hostile elements and to assist in the protection and defense of border settlements. The three district commandants and the officer commanding the Frontier Force are directly subordinate to the inspector general.

English law was gradually introduced during the period of the British Mandate to replace penal codes based on Ottoman law and to establish a system of civil courts patterned after the British (see ch. 13, The Governmental System). The Law and Administration Ordinance of 1948 revalidated Palestinian law that was in force on May 14, 1948, and subsequent Israeli laws have continued to follow the English model.

The law has been modified on numerous occasions to bring it into conformity with the organizational structure of the new Israeli government, and much of it has been codified. There have been a number of important changes, but none has altered the fundamental character of the law or its method of application. The law has also been augmented by legislation dealing with specific subjects, such as crimes against humanity and matters that had no relevance under British administration.

A major principle of criminal law and procedure is the presumption that an accused is innocent until proven guilty. Except under clearly defined circumstances, warrants are required for arrest, and a person detained must be brought before a magistrate within 48 hours. Release may be obtained on a writ of habeas corpus or on bail, set by the court. If charges have not been filed within 90 days, a detained person must be released unconditionally.

Other principles include the right to public trial, with the accused present. The accused also has the right to be represented by counsel and, if he cannot afford his own, counsel will be provided at government expense. During the trial, the accused may remain silent or he may testify under oath in his own behalf. Trials are conducted by a court consisting of one or more judges; the jury system was never applied in Palestine and it has not been adopted in Israel. The accused has a right to appeal all or a part of the verdict and sentence adjudged by the court.

Civil criminal codes are administered by the attorney general through a court structure established by the Judges Law of 1953 and the Courts Law of 1957. These laws contained little that was new or different from the existing system (see ch. 13, The Governmental System). The military code is the responsibility of the minister of defense in accordance with the Military Justice Law of 1955 (see ch. 26, The Armed Forces). The minister of defense also supervises and directs the activities of military courts and tribunals established to enforce the Defense (Emergency) Regulations of 1945 and the Prevention of Infiltration (Offenses and Jurisdiction) Law of 1954.

The penal system was formerly under the jurisdiction of the police force; it became a separate organization in 1946. There are six major prisons in which a total of 1,534 persons were confined at the end of 1967. The relatively small prison population is due in part to the widespread use of fines as the principal form of punishment; moreover, where imprisonment is imposed, the sentence is often suspended.

Crime rates for felonies and misdemeanors, as measured by the number of cases resulting in formal charges, have leveled off since about 1965, but rates represented by the number of offenses brought to police attention have continued to increase. In 1967 felony and misdemeanor charges totaled nearly 100,000; this represents a rate of about 36 per thousand population. Over three-fourths of the total were offenses against property; almost 8,000 were crimes against the person, and about the same number constituted offenses against public order and the administration of lawful authority. A 1967 amnesty law was instrumental in reducing the number of cases brought before the courts and in effecting the release of certain prisoners.

Except for East Jerusalem and an adjacent area, which was unified with West Jerusalem under Israeli municipal administration, territory occupied in the Six-Day War of June 1967 is under military government control. A military governor heads each of the four districts comprising the occupied areas: the Golan Heights, the West

Bank, the Gaza Strip and North Sinai, and South Sinai. The Military Government Department of the General Staff coordinates and supervises military government activities. Proclamations and orders are enforced through a system of military courts, whose judgments are subject to review only by the military commander.

THE POLICE FORCE

Organization and Functions

Police authority in both urban and rural areas is concentrated in a single, national force, comprising a total of approximately eleven thousand personnel. Primary duties include the prevention and detection of crime, the apprehension and prosecution of offenders, the maintenance of public order, and the protection of persons and property. A separate prison service is charged with responsibility for the safe custody of prisoners. Both the police force and the prison service are under the direct supervision and control of the minister of police (see fig. 9)

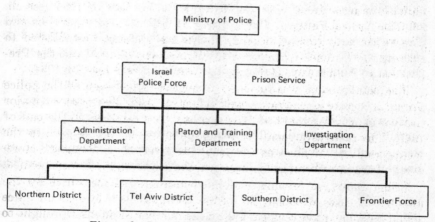

Figure 9. Israeli police and prison organization.

Source: Adapted from Israel, Central Office of Information, Prime Minister's Office, *Israel Government Yearbook, 5728 (1967–68)*, pp. 265, 266.

Heading the police force is the inspector general of police. He commands the force and is responsible for its administration, disposition, and operations. National headquarters, located in Tel Aviv, comprises a staff divided into three major departments: Patrol and Training, Administration, and Investigation. The Patrol and Training Department exercises staff supervision over patrol and traffic operations and all police training. Functions of the Administration Department include personnel, pay and finance, communications, supply, and buildings and property. The Investigation Department is composed of an Investigation Division, a Special Division, and a Criminal Identification Division. The inspector general also has advisers for planning and operations, public relations, and legal affairs.

Operating forces are organized into four major subordinate commands, including three police districts and the Frontier Force. Districts are further subdivided into subdistricts, stations, and posts. The organization of district staffs generally follows the national headquarters' pattern, except there is no training branch. The Northern District, with headquarters in Nazareth (20 miles southeast of Haifa), comprises the Haifa Port Unit and six subdistricts, including one for the occupied northern sector of the West Bank (called Samaria by Israel). The Tel Aviv District has four subdistricts, including one for occupied Gaza and Northern Sinai. The Southern District, with headquarters in Jerusalem, comprises the Lod Airport Unit (ten miles southeast of Tel Aviv) and five subdistricts, including one for the occupied southern sector of the West Bank (called Judaea by Israel).

A small coast guard operates under the supervision of the Northern District's Haifa Port Unit. Coast guard duties are to insure compliance with port rules, to guard against infiltration, to enforce fishing regulations, and to keep the bathing beaches free of navigation. Like the Frontier Force, the coast guard in time of war comes under military command.

Personnel

In a force of approximately 7,600 at the end of 1966, there were about 700 officers and 2,700 noncommissioned officers. Ranks are generally comparable to those in the armed forces (see table 25). The inspector general of police (*mefakeach klali*) holds a rank equivalent

Table 25. Ranks, Israel Police Force, 1969

Rank	Police equivalents	Military equivalents
Mefakeach Klali	Inspector General	Major General
Nitzav	Commander	Brigadier General
Nitzav-Mishneh	Assistant Commander	Colonel
Sgan-Nitzav	Chief Superintendent	Lieutenant Colonel
Rav-Pakad	Superintendent	Major
Pakad	Chief Inspector	Captain
Mefakeach	Inspector	First Lieutenant
Sgan-Mefakeach	Deputy Inspector	Second Lieutenant
Rav Samal	Sergeant Major	Sergeant Major
Samal Rishon	Sergeant	Sergeant
Samal Sheni	Corporal	Corporal
Rav Shoter	Lance Corporal	Lance Corporal

Source: Adapted from Israel, Ministry for Foreign Affairs, Information Division, *Facts About Israel, 1968.*

to that of major general. The next highest police rank, commander (*nitzav*), is equivalent to brigadier general; it is held by the district commandants and the department heads at national headquarters. Chiefs of staff divisions and the officer commanding the Frontier Force are assistant commanders (*nitzav-mishneh*), equivalent in rank to colonel.

Police strength increased to about 8,700 by the end of 1967, and by November 1968, it had risen to slightly over 11,000 personnel, including about 1,000 recruited from the administered areas. In commenting on the figures for 1968, however, the minister of police indicated that the police force was confronted with a serious manpower drain and that, if it continued, he would recommend that police service be made compulsory.

Except for the Frontier Force, the police have in the past relied on a system of volunteers. Conscripts have been used in the Frontier Force for a number of years and the reenlistment rate is high, with about 40 percent electing to remain in service. Aside from conscript losses, however, personnel turnover from other causes has been fairly large within the police force as a whole. In 1966, for example, including 240 conscripts who completed their border guard service, the police force lost a total of 771 personnel. Some were retired and a few lost their lives in the line of duty, but there were also 308 resignations and 101 dismissals. In 1968, personnel losses from all causes reached a total of about 1,500, the largest number in the history of the police force.

In January 1969, it was announced that several hundred women conscripts would be assigned to duty with the police force to help ease the police manpower shortage; the women would remain under military jurisdiction, but would be placed under police control for operations and training. The announcement also cited the activities of Arab terrorist organizations and stated that the women police would be assigned to patrol duty in the country's three largest cities with the primary mission of preventing sabotage attempts.

Training

Training for both the border police and the regular police is conducted at the National Police Training Depot, located at Shefar-am (12 miles east of Haifa). Facilities, orgininally built and used by the British, are old, but well maintained. In December 1967, there were 550 trainees for the regular police and 130 for the Frontier Force; training is conducted separately.

The Frontier Force course comprises a total of 12 weeks of instruction, followed by 2 weeks of unit training. Citizenship and physical conditioning are emphasized along with professional subjects. Study of the Hebrew language is mandatory. Military training is basically along infantry lines, including small arms, scouting and patrolling, guard duty, weapons and equipment maintenance, and first aid; a major portion of the military phase is conducted at night.

Recruits for the regular police undergo a 5 months' course of instruction. The course includes the usual citizenship and military training and specialized training in law, investigation, traffic control, and other aspects of police operations.

Courses are also provided for officers, noncommissioned officers, and officer candidates. Officer courses vary in length according to purpose; they are designed mainly for refresher and specialist training. The 6-month noncommissioned officers' course offers advanced military and police training; the art of leadership is stressed. Attendance, although voluntary, is a prerequisite to promotion; trainees are selected by a board of officers. An officer candidate course, lasting 9 months, is open to noncommissioned officers in the grade of sergeant or sergeant major. Applicants must be recommended by a district commandant; final selection is made by a board of officers.

Specialist training includes an investigators' course lasting 10 weeks; trainees are noncommissioned officers and other enlisted personnel with 5 to 7 years' service. Specialized training is also provided in a wide range of other professional and technical skills. Subjects taught include photography, fingerprinting, ballistics, criminal identification, and record-keeping.

Higher ranking officers attend the Senior Officers' College, where they receive instruction in national policy, staff operations, criminology, and sociology. Senior officers are also encouraged to attend universities and other civilian institutions, with support and assistance furnished by the government.

Public Attitudes, Morale, and Discipline

The police enjoy the confidence and respect of the public, and morale and discipline are considered excellent. Attitudes of the public have changed notably since 1948, when the police were first organized. The police were a symbol of the persecution and oppression from which many had fled, and inadequate personnel and deficiencies in leadership and training contributed to popular distrust. As the quality and effectiveness of the police force improved, however, fears and suspicions were gradually overcome.

The police force has developed into an organization characterized by loyalty, devotion to duty, and high standards of professional competence. Morale remains excellent, despite a shortage of manpower and the increased burden of added responsibilities. Relatively low pay adversely affects morale, however, and personnel retention is a major problem; many of the best qualified personnel, especially among senior officers, are attracted by the opportunities available in the civilian economy.

Steps have been taken to ameliorate this situation, and in April 1969, it was announced that police of all ranks serving in the occupied areas would be granted a special monthly increment of I£100 (I£1 equals approximately US$0.285—see Glossary). It was also announced that Frontier Force officers in the grade of chief inspector and higher would be entitled to a field bonus on the same basis as army personnel; a "technical alert" bonus, ranging from I£60 per month for a chief inspector to I£85 for a commander, was authorized for those not performing duty in occupied areas. At the same time, a bonus of I£55 monthly was offered to all personnel through the grade of inspector who agreed to 5-year contracts.

Discipline is strict. It is administered in accordance with the provisions of the Police Ordinance of 1926, as amended in 1963. Personnel charged with violating police rules and regulations are tried before a court of discipline appointed by the inspector general of police. The court is composed of three police officers senior in rank to the accused. Maximum punishments are imprisonment for not more than 2 years, a fine not to exceed 3 months' pay, or both. A sentence in excess of 3 months' imprisonment requires confirmation by the minister of police; all other sentences, including fines, must be confirmed by the inspector general of police. The reviewing authority in each case has the power to mitigate the sentence or reverse the judgment and find the accused innocent.

CRIMINAL LAW AND PROCEDURE

Criminal Law

The principal basis for criminal law is the Criminal Code Ordinance of 1936. Effective on January 1, 1937, it specifically repealed the Ottoman Penal Code and a long list of related ordinances; it further provided for the law to be interpreted in accordance with the practices and principles prevailing in England. Originally comprisin a total of 391 sections, the code has subsequently been amended a number of times; its 44 chapters contain detailed provisions on such subjects as criminal responsibility, offenses, and punishments.

The law presumes every person to be mentally sound until proved otherwise. Ignorance of the law is no excuse, unless knowledge of the law constitutes an explicit element of the offense. A child under the age of 9 is not criminally responsible for any act or omission and, if under the age of 12, he can be held criminally responsible only if it can be proved that he had the capacity to distinguish right from wrong at the time he committed the offense.

An offense is defined as any act, attempt, or omission punishable by law. Offenses are classified in three categories: felonies, misdemeanors, and contraventions. A felony is an offense that is punishable, without proof of previous conviction, with death or with imprisonment for more than 3 years. Under a 1966 amendment, the definition of a contravention was expanded to include any offense that is punishable with imprisonment for not more than a month or with a fine not exceeding I£200; maximum penalties in each case had been much lower. A misdemeanor is any offense that is not a felony or a contravention.

Major revisions to the law have dealt mainly with degree or method of punishment. Treason is the only offense under the Criminal Code for which the death penalty may be imposed, and that only as an alternative to life imprisonment during a period of armed hostilities. Capital punishment for murder has been replaced with a mandatory sentence to life imprisonment. Courts may not impose a punishment greater than that provided by law; except where the punishment is mandatory, they may impose any lesser sentence. In cases where a person is convicted of more than one offense, sentences are to be served concurrently, unless the court rules otherwise. Courts are also empowered to impose conditional or suspended sentences in lieu of imprisonment.

Flogging as a punishment has been abolished and collective punishments may no longer be imposed. Provisions originally designed to halt the wave of child marriages accompanying large-scale immigration have been changed to make it a criminal offense to marry a female below the age of 17 rather than 18, except where authorized by a district court under special circumstances. The law relating to bigamy has been modified to provide that no person shall be convicted of that offense if a previous marriage has been legally dissolved on the basis that a spouse is mentally incapable of participating in divorce or annulment proceedings, is missing and can reasonably be presumed dead, or has been absent without a trace for a period of 7 years. In another amendment, the offense of bribery has been extended to include those who offer bribes to public employees as well as to public employees who accept them.

Major new legislation in the field of criminal law includes the Punishment of Nazis and Nazi Collaborators Law of 1950, the Crime of Genocide (Prevention and Punishment) Law of 1950, and the Prevention of Infiltration Law of 1954. Offenders under all three laws are subject to heavy punishment, including the death penalty.

The nature of the offense determines the court having original jurisdiction. Magistrate courts are competent to try contraventions and misdemeanors; district courts are competent to try felonies. The Supreme Court, acting as a court of first instance, has special authority with respect to writs of habeas corpus and mandamus and to conduct retrials in criminal matters under specified conditions. Both the Supreme Court and the district courts hear appeals from lower courts. The competence of municipal courts is limited to petty offenses and offenses violating municipal bylaws and regulations (see ch. 13, The Governmental System).

Offenses committed by civilians against the Defense Regulations of 1945, most of which were still in effect in 1969, are tried by military courts composed of three commissioned officers. Their judgments were final until 1963, when the right of appeal was granted under an amendment to the Military Justice Law; the Appeal Court-Martial was designated as the appellate authority. Persons charged with offenses against the Prevention of Infiltration Law are tried by a military court consisting of a single officer; appeals are heard by a court composed of three officers.

Criminal Procedure

Various laws pertaining to judicial proceedings in criminal cases were consolidated and revised under the Criminal Procedure Law of 1965. Legislation had become highly fragmented, and adoption of the new law marked a major advance in the codification of legal principles. For the most part, the existing system was retained; the opportunity was taken, however, to introduce a number of reforms and to resolve outstanding conflicts and contradictions. Effective on January 15, 1966, the new law consists of 228 sections divided into seven chapters. Subjects covered include general provisions with regard to application of the law, pretrial and trial procedure, and appeal. The law supplements the Courts Law of 1957, which prescribes the composition, jurisdiction, and functioning of the court system and provides in detail for appellate remedies and procedures.

Under the law, no person may be brought to trial for an act constituting an offense for which he has previously been acquitted or convicted, except if the act caused the death of another person, in which case he may be tried for that offense regardless of whether or not he was earlier convicted of any other offense constituted by the act. Unless otherwise provided by law, no person may be brought to trial for felony punishable by death or life imprisonment if a period of 20 years has elapsed since the offense was committed. Time limitation for the prosecution of other felonies is 10 years; it is 5 years in the case of a misdemeanor and 1 year in the case of contravention. Limitation on the enforcement of penalties in the case of felony is 20 years from the date when the period for appeal expired, when final judgment on appeal was rendered, or when enforcement was suspended, whichever comes last. Statutes of limitation for offenses under the Nazis and Nazi Collaborators Law and the Genocide Law were abolished in 1966.

As a general rule, warrants are required for arrests and searches. A person may be arrested without a warrant if there is reason to suspect that he has committed a felony or is a fugitive from justice, if he is apprehended in the act of committing an offense, and in other special circumstances defined in the Criminal Procedure (Arrests and Searches) Ordinance of 1924. A person so arrested must be brought before a judge within 48 hours; the judge may order his release, with or without bail, or may authorize further detention for a period up to 15 days. Authorization for detention may be renewed for an additional 15-day period, but any further extension requires the approval of the attorney general.

Unless detained for an offense punishable by death or life imprisonment, a person who has been arrested may request release on bail, whether or not a formal charge has been entered against him. Bail may consist of personal recognizance, cash deposit, surety bond, or any combination thereof. A person held in custody must be released unconditionally if no charges have been filed against him within 90 days; he must also be released without condition if trial has not commenced within 60 days or if it has not been concluded within 1 year from the date on which a statement of charge was filed. Only a judge of the Supreme Court may order an extension of these time limitations.

Any person is entitled to communicate information on his arrest to a friend or relative and to a lawyer as soon as possible. In felony cases, arrests may be kept secret for reasons of national security upon written request from the minister of defense or for the sake of investigation upon written request from the inspector general of police. Requests are valid for periods not exceeding 48 hours; they may be renewed so long as the total does not exceed 7 days.

Proceedings begin with the filing of a statement of charge; the state acts as plaintiff, and police officers or state attorneys designated by the attorney general conduct the prosecution. Where an accused is not represented by counsel, counsel is appointed by the court at state expense if the accused is charged with an offense punishable by imprisonment for 10 years or more, if he is under the age of 16 and being tried as an adult offender, or if he is deaf, dumb, or blind. Defense counsel may also be provided at state expense if the accused is without adequate means or if there is reason to believe that he may be mentally ill.

The accused pleads to the facts alleged in the indictment; he is not called upon to make a plea of guilt or innocence with respect to the charge itself. In pleading, the defendant may remain silent or he may admit or deny any or all of the alleged facts; he may also plead additional facts. During the hearing, a defendant may testify under oath in his own behalf, in which case he is subject to cross-examination or he may make a statement upon which he may not be examined; he also has the choice to remain silent.

Hearings are conducted according to the rules of evidence established by the Evidence Ordinance of 1924. English common law applies on any point not covered by the ordinance or in other legislation. Fundamental is the provision that all persons are competent to give evidence in all cases, except that a husband or wife or a parent or child may not be compelled to testify against each other in criminal cases. Confessions are admissible as evidence only if the prosecution presents sufficient evidence that they were given freely and voluntarily. Other provisions of the Evidence Ordinance deal with *res gestae*, the value of oral testimony, the credibility of witnesses, proof of documents, and evidence taken abroad. Under a 1936 amendment, testimony of a single witness does not require corroboration in criminal cases.

Verdict of the court must be in writing, together with reasons therefor. If the defendant is convicted, the prosecutor may then present evidence relating to punishment, including any record of previous convictions. The defendant is also permitted to submit evidence in mitigation. Following the pronouncement of sentence, the court explains to the accused the appellate remedies open to him.

The time limit for appeals is 45 days; appeal is automatic where a death sentence has been imposed, regardless of action by the accused. Grounds of appeal must be stated and, if insufficient, the court may order that a more detailed statement be made. Appeals may be dismissed for lack of grounds. New evidence is rarely taken by an appellate court; its decisions are ordinarily based on evidence already presented to the lower court, although it may reach different conclusions as to the facts or the law.

THE PENAL SYSTEM

The prison service is responsible for the safe custody of prisoners and the administration and execution of prisoner rehabilitation programs. The prison service is headed by a commissioner of prisons, who is assisted by a staff that includes branches responsible for administrative, security, and training functions. Originally a part of the police force, the prison service was given independent status by the Prisons Ordinance of 1946.

Within the limits of the security precautions necessary to protect both the prisoner and the public, the primary objective in the treatment of prisoners is to assist them to become productive members of normal society. To this end, there are extensive programs for vocational training and social rehabilitation. The process begins at a classification and observation station where prisoners are examined by a number of social workers and specialists as well as physicians.

The prisoners are given tests to determine their aptitude for learning various trades.

Civilian specialists are employed to teach courses in carpentry, printing and bookbinding, tailoring, and shoemaking. Among a number of items produced in prisons are clothes, shoes, and other articles for use of the prison service and other government agencies. Prisoners engaged in productive work receive token wage payments. Short-term prisoners are used mostly for maintenance duties, food preparation, and work in laundry and cleaning plants.

Prison facilities were built by the British in the 1930's. They consist of converted fortresses characterized by thick walls and small windows with bars and surrounded by a barbed wire fence. Small farms and workshops are usually located within the prison compound. The larger cities and towns have facilities where persons under arrest may be held in custody for short periods of time, usually no more than a few days.

Total prison capacity is rated at 1,507, not including facilities for observation and classification. The number of persons confined in penal institutions at the end of 1966 totaled 1,656; it dropped to 1,534 at the end of 1967, mainly as the result of an amnesty law under which a number of prisoners gained their release (see table 26).

Table 26. Data on Persons Confined in Israeli Prisons, 1965–67

Persons confined	Year		
	1965	1966	1967
Convicted persons	3,332	4,032	5,805
Jews	(2,588)	(3,160)	(3,980)
Others	(744)	(872)	(1,825)
Detained persons	562	683	937
Jews	(377)	(408)	(545)
Others	(185)	(275)	(392)
Total receptions	3,894	4,715	6,742
End of year total	1,487	1,656	1,534

Source: Adapted from Israel, Central Bureau of Statistics, *Statistical Abstract of Israel, 1968.*

Prisons are located at Maasiyahu (near Lod, 10 miles southeast of Tel Aviv), Tel Mond (about 20 miles northeast of Tel Aviv), Ramla (11 miles southeast of Tel Aviv), Damoun (in the hills east of Haifa), Bet Hashitta (about 12 miles southwest of Lake Tiberias), and Neve Tirza (near Lod). The facility at Maasiyahu is the only one to have been established since the new state of Israel came into being. In 1968, construction was reported underway on a new maximum security prison for long-term convicts at a location south of Beersheba.

The prison at Maasiyahu is reported to be the most progressive institution; it is a minimum security facility where the inmates actually participate to some extent in prison administration. Capacity is 248 prisoners. Tel Mond, with a capacity of 220, is another prison where education and vocational training are emphasized. Inmates are youthful offenders between the ages of 14 and 21; many are habitual offenders.

Two of the most overcrowded prisons are those at Ramla and Bet Hashitta. Ramla has a capacity of 429; it is used primarily for infiltrators and persons sentenced to more than 5 years' imprisonment. It also has a section for prisoners in transit or awaiting trial. Bet Hashitta, with a capacity of 230, is for prisoners sentenced to less than 5 years; its inmates are considered among the most unresponsive to treatment and rehabilitation.

Prisoners at Damoun include those with sentences under 3 years and Arabs and Druzes who are less than 20 years old. Its capacity is 300. Neve Tirza is a prison for women, with a capacity of 80. Because the prisoners are all ages and all types, it is difficult to organize groups suitable for vocational training.

All prison terms in excess of 6 months are reviewed by a Release Board consisting of a district court judge as the presiding officer, the commissioner of prisons or his representative, and a doctor or educator appointed by the minister of justice. On the board's recommendation, a person who has served a minimum of two-thirds of his sentence may be released on parole. The minister of police has parole authority over prisoners with sentences of 3 to 6 months.

INCIDENCE OF CRIME

In 1965, the police dealt with 152,371 felonies and misdemeanors; in 1966 the number was 173,924. These figures represent a rate of about 59 per thousand total population in 1965 and about 65 per thousand in 1966. Investigation resulted in the filing of formal charges in about 60 percent of the cases in each of the 2 years. The remainder were dismissed for lack of sufficient evidence or on the basis that no public interest would be served by prosecution. The number of felonies and misdemeanors brought to police attention reached 200, 000 in 1968, a rate of about 70 per thousand population.

Felony and misdemeanor charges numbered 56,146 in 1960; the number rose to 89,956 in 1965 and 99,709 in 1967 (see table 27). In 1960, the rate per thousand population was about 26; by 1965 it had increased to about 35 per thousand, where it appears to have leveled off.

Offenses against property constitute by far the majority of criminal offenses and their number has continued to increase, both absolutely

Table 27. Offenses Recorded by Israel Police Force, 1965–67

Offenses	1965	1966	1967
Against public order and administration of lawful authority	7,834	7,267	7,845
Against the person	10,102	9,537	7,749
Murder	(29)	(30)	(29)
Attempted murder	(35)	(35)	(30)
Manslaughter	(50)	(53)	(44)
Assault with bodily harm	(7,822)	(7,270)	(6,046)
Others	(2,166)	(2,149)	(1,600)
Against morality	1,894	1,932	1,766
Against property	64,481	72,306	77,861
Robbery	(47)	(75)	(66)
Housebreaking	(16,183)	(19,476)	(22,627)
Thefts	(40,417)	(44,478)	(47,552)
Others	(7,834)	(8,277)	(7,616)
Fraud and forgery	4,092	4,493	3,259
Other offenses	1,553	1,469	1,229
Total	89,956	97,004	99,709
Rates per thousand population	35	37	36

Source: Adapted from Israel, Central Bureau of Statistics, *Statistical Abstract of Israel, 1968.*

and at a faster rate in relation to other categories. By contrast, the number of offenses against the person has diminished.

Convictions in 1966 totaled 24,534 persons. Of these, 19,194 were adults, including 14,243 Jews and 4,951 non-Jews. Juvenile offenders numbered 5,340, of whom 4,483 were Jews and 857 others. The overall adult rate was 12.3 per thousand; for Jewish adults, it was 10 per thousand. The juvenile rate was also 10 per thousand.

The total number of criminal cases in all categories entered before the courts during 1967 was 209,188 (see table 28). The sharp decline from the 237,553 cases introduced in 1966 was due mainly to the Pardon Law of 1967. The effects of that law are also reflected by a much lower rate of court actions per thousand population and a substantial drop in the number of cases pending at the end of the year.

The Pardon Law was adopted on July 12, 1967, becoming effective 2 days later. The law provided amnesty for persons convicted of a wide range of crimes committed before June 5, 1967; persons electing to initiate or continue with an appeal could waive the pardon by filing written notice to that effect within 30 days from the law's effective date. The law also provided for a stay in proceedings against persons under prosecution and for dropping charges against those not yet brought to trial. Exceptions to the law included offenses carrying a punishment of imprisonment for 10 years or more and offenses under

Table 28. Criminal Court Cases, Israel, 1965–67

Court Cases	1965	1966	1967
Supreme Court _____	505	552	453
District courts _____	5,419	4,611	4,167
Magistrates' courts _____	130,776	150,053	126,227
Municipal courts _____	81,403	77,074	74,018
Juvenile courts _____	5,257	5,263	4,323
Total cases entered _____	223,360	237,553	209,188
Rates per thousand population _____	86	89	75
Pending at end of year _____	31,109	33,733	16,906

Source: Adapted from Israel, Central Bureau of Statistics, *Statistical Abstract of Israel*, 1968, pp. 569–570.

the Nazis and Nazi Collaborators Law, the Genocide Law, and laws concerning national security.

LAW IN ADMINISTERED AREAS

Military government in the administered areas became effective immediately upon entry of Israeli troops. Under the provisions of Proclamation No. 1, the Israel Defense Forces assumed responsibility for security and the maintenance of public order; a curfew was imposed, and public gatherings prohibited. Proclamation No. 2 stated that the law in areas under military control was to consist of the law in force at the time, together with proclamations and orders issued by the military commander. Proclamation No. 3, still in effect in mid-1969, prescribed in detail the legal principles and procedures to be followed in the administration of justice; it contains a total of 74 clauses dealing with offenses and their punishment, arrests and searches, military courts, criminal procedure, and special security regulations.

Under Proclamation No. 3, the death penalty may be imposed upon any person over the age of 17, who has been convicted of willfully causing death or conducting sabotage against military installations. A person found guilty of carrying arms, ammunition, or explosives is liable for a maximum punishment of life imprisonment; anyone convicted on a charge of illegal possession of any of these items, or other military equipment, such as uniforms and insignia, may be sentenced to imprisonment for as long as 10 years. Imprisonment for a term of 15 years may be imposed for the collection of military information. Offenses for which a punishment is not otherwise provided in laws or regulations carry a penalty of up to 5 years' imprisonment, a fine of not more than I£4,000, or both.

The law is administered by a system of military courts. Military courts may consist of either a single judge or a panel of three judges. A judge sitting alone, or the president of a court of three judges, must be an officer with legal training.

411

Military courts are competent to try any offense defined in the orders and proclamations of the military commander; they may also try offenses against the local criminal law. Dual jurisdiction protects against double jeopardy in the case of a person accused of an act or omission that constitutes an offense against both military and local law. A court composed of three judges may impose any sentence, including the death penalty; a single judge may not impose a sentence of imprisonment for more than 2 years or a fine of more than I£13,000.

To convict, a three-man court must reach a unanimous verdict; if there is dissent, the accused must be acquitted. Findings of guilt by a court of three judges must be confirmed by the military commander; verdicts of a single judge are subject to the commander's review, but they do not require confirmation. In either case, the military commander has a complete range of options; he may confirm the verdict and sentence; he may quash them and acquit the accused; he may uphold the verdict and mitigate the sentence; or he may order a retrial.

A convicted person has the right of appeal to the military commander; this is the only appellate remedy. Otherwise, criminal procedures are generally similar to those provided under Israeli law. Powers of arrest and search are vested in military personnel and in members of the Israel Police Force assigned to military government duties.

BIBLIOGRAPHIES

Section I. Social
RECOMMENDED SOURCES

Abramov, S.Z. "The Danger of a Religious Split in Jewry," *Midstream*, October 1966, 3–13.

Antonius, George. *The Arab Awakening.* London: Hamish Hamilton, 1938.

Appelbaum, Shimon. *Archaeology in Israel.* (Israel Today Series, No. 10.) Jerusalem: Israel Digest, 1967.

Arian, Alan. *Ideological Change in Israel.* Cleveland: Case Western Reserve University Press, 1968.

Avni-Segre, Dan. "Israel: A Society in Transition," *World Politics*, XXI, No. 3, April 1969, 346–365.

Badi, Joseph. *Religion in Israel Today: The Relationship Between State and Religion.* New York: Bookman Associates, 1959.

Baker, Henry E. *The Legal Systems of Israel.* Jerusalem: Israel Universities Press, 1968.

Bentwich, Joseph. *Education in Israel.* Philadelphia: Jewish Publication Society of America, 1965.

Bentwich, Norman. "Religious Stirrings in Israel," *Contemporary Review*, CCXII, May 1968, 241–247.

Braham, Randolph L. *Israel: A Modern Education System.* Washington: U.S. Department of Health, Education and Welfare, Office of Education, 1966.

Brutzkus, Eliezer. *Physical Planning in Israel: Problems and Achievements.* Jerusalem: Mifal Hashichpul, 1964.

Cantril, Hadley. *The Pattern of Human Concerns.* New Brunswick: Rutgers University Press, 1965.

Casper, Bernard M. *Religious Life.* (Israel Today Series, No. 24.) Jerusalem: Israel Digest, 1965.

Cressey, George B. *Crossroads: Land and Life in Southwest Asia.* Philadelphia: J.P. Lippincott, 1960.

Davis, Moshe (ed.). *Israel: Its Role in Civilization.* New York: Harper and Brothers, 1956.

Eisenstadt, S.N. "Israel." In Arnold M. Rose, *The Institutions of Advanced Societies.* Minneapolis: University of Minnesota Press, 1958.

_____. *Israeli Society.* New York: Basic Books, 1967.

Elston, D.R. *Israel: The Making of a Nation.* London: Oxford University Press, 1963.

Epstein, Isidore. *Judaism: A Historic Presentation.* Baltimore: Penguin Books, 1959.

Falk, Z.W. "Religious Law and the Modern Family in Israel." Pages 235–254 in J.N.D. Anderson (ed.), *Family Law in Asia and Africa.* New York: Praeger, 1967.

Fein, Leonard J. *Israel: Politics and People.* Boston: Little and Brown, 1967.

Fisch, Harold. "Faith in Israel," *Commentary,* XLVII, No. 2, February 1969, 64–67.

Fisher, William Bayne. *The Middle East: A Physical, Social, and Regional Geography.* London: Methuen, 1956.

Freudenheim, Yehoshua. *Government in Israel.* Dobbs Ferry: Oceana Publications, 1967.

Glueck, Nelson. *The River Jordan.* New York: McGraw-Hill, 1968.

Goldberg, Harvey. "Acculturation, Continuity and Youth in an Israel Immigrant Village." Unpublished master's thesis, Department of Social Relations, Harvard University, 1967.

_____. "Elite Groups in Peasant Communities: A Comparison of Three Middle Eastern Villages," *American Anthropologist,* LXX, No. 4, August 1968, 718–731.

Goode, William J. *World Revolution and Family Patterns.* Glencoe: The Free Press, 1963.

Herskovits, Melville J. "Who are the Jews?" In Louis Finkelstein (ed.), *The Jews: Their History, Culture, and Religion,* II. New York: Harper and Brothers, 1955.

Herzl, Theodor. *The Jewish State.* Tel Aviv: Newman, 1959.

Israel. Central Bureau of Statistics. *Statistical Abstract of Israel, 1966,* No. 17. Jerusalem: Government Press, 1966.

_____. *Statistical Abstract of Israel, 1968,* No. 19. Jerusalem: Government Press, 1968.

Israel. Ministry for Foreign Affairs. Information Division. *Facts About Israel, 1968.* Jerusalem: Publication Services Division, Israel Program for Scientific Translations, 1968.

_____. *Facts About Israel, 1969.* Jerusalem: Publication Services Division, Israel Program for Scientific Translations, 1969.

Israel. Ministry of Health. *Health Services in Israel.* (Ed., M.D., Gruskha.) Jerusalem: Government Press, 1968.

Israel. Ministry of Religious Affairs. *Moslem Religious Life in Israel.* Jerusalem: Government Press, 1968.

"Israel." Pages 101–116 in *International Encyclopedia of the Social Sciences,* XI. New York: Macmillan, 1968.

Jacobs, Louis. *Principles of the Jewish Faith: An Analytical Study.* London: Vallentine, 1964.

Johnston, Scott D. "Election Politics and Social Change in Israel," *Middle East Journal,* XVI, No. 3, Summer 1962, 309–327.

"Judaism." Pages 272–281 in *International Encyclopedia of the Social Sciences,* VIII. New York: Macmillan, 1968.

Kaufmann, Yehezkel. *The Religion of Israel.* Chicago: University of Chicago Press, 1959.

Khouri, Fred J. *The Arab-Israeli Dilemma.* Syracuse: Syracuse University Press, 1968.

Klieman, Aaron S. "Britain's War Aims in the Middle East in 1915," *Journal of Contemporary History,* III, July 3, 1968, 237–251.

Koenig, Samuel. "Israeli Culture and Society," *American Journal of Sociology,* LVIII, July 1952–May 1953, 160–166.

Kolack, Shirley M., and Kolack, Sol. "Can Israel Surmount Its Internal Problems?," *Trans-Action,* V, No. 4, 1968, 40–43.

Kreitler, Hans, and Kreitler, Shulamith. "Crucial Dimensions of the Attitude Toward National and Supra-National Ideals: A Study on Israeli Youth," *Journal of Peace Research* (Oslo), No. 2, 1967, 107–124.

Krivine, David. *Housing in Israel.* (Israel Today Series, No. 17.) Jerusalem: Israel Digest, 1965.

————. *Transport and Communications.* (Israel Today Series, No. 28.) Jerusalem: Israel Digest, 1964.

Laquer, Walter Z. *The Road to Jerusalem.* New York: Macmillan, 1968.

Louvish, Misha. *The Challenge of Israel.* Jerusalem: Israel Universities Press, 1968.

Margalith, Haim. "Enactment of a Nationality Law in Israel," *American Journal of Comparative Law,* II, 1953, 63–66.

Matras, Judith. *Social Change in Israel.* Chicago: Aldine Publishing Company, 1965.

Orni, Efraim, and Efrat, Elisha. *Geography of Israel.* (2d ed., rev.) Jerusalem: Israel Program for Scientific Translation, 1966.

Pryce-Jones, David. *Next Generation: Travels in Israel.* New York: Holt, Rinehart, and Winston, 1964.

Rabin, Chaim. *The Revival of Hebrew.* (Israel Today Series, No. 5.) Jerusalem: Israel Digest, 1958.

Rejwan, Nissim. "Semites: An Essay in Definition," *New Middle East* (London), No. 6, March 1969, 44–48.

Rosenfeld, Henry. "Change, Barriers to Change and Contradictions in the Arab Village Family," *American Anthropologist,* LXX, August 1968, 732–752.

Safran, Nadav. *The United States and Israel.* Cambridge: Harvard University Press, 1963.

415

Schwarz, Walter. *The Arabs in Israel.* London: Faber and Faber, 1959.

Selzer, Michael. *The Outcasts of Israel.* (An Oriental Israel Pamphlet.) Jerusalem: The Council of the Sephardi Community, 1965.

Shuval, Judith T. "Emerging Patterns of Ethnic Strain in Israel," *Social Forces,* XL, 1962, 323-330.

Talmon, J.L. "Israel Among the Nations: Reflections on Jewish Statehood," *Commentary,* XLV, No. 6, June 1968, 32-51.

Talmon, Yonina. "The Family in a Revolutionary Movement—The Case of the Kibbutz in Israel." Chapter 13 in M.F. Nimkoff (ed.), *Comparative Family Systems.* Boston: Houghton Mifflin, 1965.

Tamuz, Benjamin (ed.). *Art in Israel.* New York: International Publication Service, 1966.

von Imhoff, Christoph. *Israel: die zweite Generation.* Stuttgart: Deutsch Verlags Anstalt, 1966.

Weiner, Herbert. *The Wild Goats of Ein Gedi.* New York: Doubleday, 1961.

Weingrod, Alex. *Reluctant Pioneers: Village Development in Israel.* Ithaca: Cornell University Press, 1966.

Weintraub, Dov, and Shapiro, Miriam. "The Traditional Family in Israel in the Process of Change: Crisis and Continuity," *British Journal of Sociology,* XIX, September 1968, 284-299.

Zenner, Walter P. "Ambivalence and Self-Image Oriental Jews in Israel," *Jewish Journal of Sociology,* V, 1963, 214-223.

OTHER SOURCES USED

Adler, Joshua. *Philosophy of Judaism.* New York: Philosophical Library, 1960.

Alport, E.A. "The Integration of Oriental Jew into Israel," *World Today,* XXIII, No. 4, 1968, 153-159.

Amiran, D.H.K., and Shahar, A. "The Towns of Israel: The Principles of Their Urban Geography," *Geographical Review,* LI, 1961, 348-369.

"Arab and Jews: Intermarriage Reviewed," *Jerusalem Post,* December 16, 1968, 16.

Avidor, M. *Education for a Growing Nation.* (Israel Today Series, No. 1.) Jerusalem: Israel Digest, 1964.

Avnery, Uri. *Israel Without Zionists: A Plea for Peace in the Middle East.* New York: Macmillan, 1968.

Bachi, R. "A Statistical Analysis of the Revival of Hebrew in Israel," *Scripta Hierosolymitana,* III, 1956, 178-247.

Badeau, John S. *The American Approach to the Arab World.* New York: Harper and Row, 1968.

Bernadotte, Folke. *To Jerusalem.* London: Hodder and Stoughton, 1951.

Blanc, Haim. "Druze Particularism: Modern Aspects of an Old Problem," *Middle Eastern Affairs*, III, 1952, 314–321.

Boehm, Yohanan. *The Making of Music*. (Israel Today Series, No. 12.) Jerusalem: Israel Digest, 1964.

Bonne, Batsheva. "The Samaritans: A Demographic Study," *Human Biology*, XXXV, 1963, 61–89.

Buber, Martin. *Israel and Palestine*. (Trans. from German by Stanley Goodman.) (The East and West Library.) New York: Farrar, Strauss and Young, 1952.

Cantineau, Jean. "Remarques sur les parlers de sedentaires syro-libano-palestiniens," *Bulletin de la Societe de Linguistique de Paris*, XL, 1939, 80–88.

Carpenter, Roswell D. *Forest Utilization in Israel: Report to the Government of Israel*. Tel Aviv: United States of America Operations Mission to Israel, 1959.

Chejne, Anwar G. "Arabic: Its Significance and Place in Arab-Muslim Society," *Middle East Journal*, XIX, 1965, 447–470.

Chomsley, W. *Hebrew: The Eternal Language*. Philadelphia: n.pub., 1957.

The Christian Science Monitor, July 13, 1968.

Cohen, Gerda L. "Family Planning in Israel," *Midstream*, XXII, June 1966.

Cohen, Percy. "Ethnic Group Differences in Israel," *Race*, IX, 1968, 303–310.

Eisenstadt, S.N. *Ethnic and Cultural Pluralism in Israel*. (Report of the 30th meeting of the International Institute of Differing Civilizations, Ethnic and Cultural Pluralism in Intertropical Countries, held in Lisbon on April 15–18, 1957.) Brussels: n.pub., 1957.

Elath, Eliahu. "Arabs and Jews in Israel," *New Outlook*, II, No. 2, 1968, 28–33.

Etzioni, Amitai. "The Functional Differentiation of Elites in the Kibbutz," *American Journal of Sociology*, LXIV, No. 4, January 1959, 476–487.

Falah, Salman H. "Druze Communal Organization in Israel," *New Outlook*, X, No. 3, 1967, 40–44

Ferguson, Charles A. "Diglossia," *Word*, XV, 1959, 325–340.

———. *Myths About Arabic*. (Ed., R.S. Harrell.) (Monograph Series on Language and Linguistics, No. 12.) Washington: Georgetown Press, 1960.

Fine, Morris, and Himmelfarb, Milton (eds.). *American Jewish Year Book, 1968*, LXIX. New York: American Book-Stratford Press, 1968.

Finkelstein, Louis (ed.). *The Jews: Their History, Culture, and Religion* (3d ed.) 2 vols. New York: Harper and Brothers, 1960.

Fisher, Yona, et al. *Art.* (Israel Today Series, No. 35.) Jerusalem: Israel Digest, 1966.

Friedlander, Saul. "New Moral Values for Israel?," *New Middle East* (London), No. 7, April 1969, 17–20.

Friedmann, Georges. *The End of the Jewish People?* Garden City: Doubleday, 1967.

Gaster, Theodor H. *Customs and Folkways of Jewish Life.* New York: Apollo Books, 1955.

Geismar, Ludwig L. "Ideology and the Adjustment of Immigrants," *Jewish Social Studies*, XXI, No. 3, July 1959, 155–164.

Gillon, Philip, et al. *Science.* (Israel Today Series, No. 30.) Jerusalem: Israel Digest, 1964.

Glubb, Sir John B. *Britain and the Arabs.* London: Hodder and Stoughton, 1959.

Glueck, Nelson. *Rivers in the Desert.* London: Weidenfeld and Nicolson, 1959.

Goldberg, Harvey. "FBD Marriage and Demography Among Tripolitanian Jews in Israel," *Southwestern Journal of Anthropology*, XXIII, 1967, 176–191.

Goldschmidt, Elisabeth, et al. 'Changing Marriage Systems in the Jewish Communities of Israel," *Annals of Human Genetics*, XXIV, 1960, 191–204.

Goshen-Gottstein, Esther R. "Courtship, Marriage and Pregnancy in Geula," *Annals of Psychiatry and Related Disciplines* (Israel), No. 1, 1966, 43–65.

Gothelf, Yehuda (ed.). *Israel Today: A New Society in the Making.* Tel Aviv: Ihud Olami, 1967.

Great Britain. British Naval Intelligence Division. *Palestine and Transjordan.* (Geographical Handbook Series.) London: Mis Majesty's Stationery Office, 1942.

Groen, J.J. "Historical and Genetic Studies on the Twelve Tribes of Israel and Their Relation to the Present Ethnic Composition of the Jewish People," *Jewish Quarterly Review*, LVIII, 1967, 1–13.

Halderman, J.W.(ed.)"The Middle East Crisis: Test of International Law," *Law and Contemporary Problems*, XXXIII, Winter 1968.

Halevi, H.S. "Divorce in Israel," *Population Studies*, X, pt. 2, November 1956, 184–192.

Hertzberg, A. (ed.) *The Zionist Idea.* Garden City: Doubleday, 1959.

Howard, Harry N. *The King-Crane Commission.* Beirut: Khayats, 1963.

Hurewitz, J.C. *Diplomacy in the Near and Middle East.* Princeton: Van Nostrand, 1956.

Irvine, Elizabeth E. "Children in the Kibbutzim: Thirteen Years After," *Journal of Child Psychology and Psychiatry*, VII, Nos. 3 and 4, 1966, 167–178.

Israel. Central Office of Information. Prime Minister's Office. *Israel Government Yearbook 5728 (1967–68)*. Jerusalem: Government Press, 1968.

Israel. Prime Minister's Office. National Council for Research and Development. *Aims, Structure and Work*. (Prepared by the Bureau of Scientific Liaison.) Jerusalem: Hathyia Press, 1968.

————. "Financing of Research in Israel from United States Government Sources." (Survey conducted and prepared under the direction of Moshe Eshel.) Jerusalem: Government Press, December 1968 (mimeo.).

————. *Scientific Research in Israel, 1968*. (Prepared by the Center of Scientific and Technological Information.) Tel Aviv: A. Yarom Press, 1968.

Jacobs, N.J. "The Literary Scene in Israel Today," *Books Abroad*, XXVIII, No. 1, Winter 1954, 21–25.

Jaffe, Eliezer D. "Correlates of Differential Placement Outcome for Dependent Children in Israel," *Social Service Review*, XLI, December 1967, 390–400.

Kanovsky, Eliyahu. "Problems of Integration in Israel," *American Journal of Economics and Sociology*, XXVI, July 1967, 329–336.

Karmon, Yehuda. "The Drainage of the Huleh Swamps," *Geographical Review*, L, 1960, 169-193.

Kohansky, Mendel. "Reform Judaism Meets in Israel," *Midstream*, November 1968, 54–61.

Labes, Emmanuel. *Handbook of the Moshav: An Introduction to Israel's Cooperative Farm Village*. (2d ed.) Jerusalem: Haikar Haoved and the Youth and Hechalutz Department of the World Zionist Organization, 1962.

Lilienthal, Alfred M. *What Price Israel*. Chicago: Henry Regnery, 1953.

Meeker, Oden. *Israel: Ancient Land, Young Nation*. New York: Scribners, 1968.

Meged, M. "The Jewish Intellectual in Israel," *Commentary*, XXI, No. 1, January 1961, 28–33.

"The Mineral and Water Resources of Israel," *Israel Economic Forum*, VI, No. 3, 1954.

Muhsam, H.V. "Sedentarization of the Bedouin in Israel," *International Social Science Journal*, XI, 1959, 539–549.

Nardi, Sulamith Schwartz. *Women in Israel*. (Israel Today Series, No. 13.) Jerusalem: Israel Digest, 1964.

The New York Times, January 13, 1969.

Noss, John B. *Man's Religions*. New York: Macmillan, 1956.

Noy, Dov. *Folktales of Israel*. (Folktales of the World.) Chicago: University of Chicago Press, 1963.

Nutting, Anthony. *The Arabs*. New York: Potter, 1965.

Nuttonson, M.Y. "Agroclimatology and Crop Ecology of Palestine and Transjordan and Climatic Analogues in the United States," *Geographical Review*, XXXVII, 1947, 436–456.

Oakes, Paul E., and Savidor, M. *Israel Railways: Report to the Government of Israel.* Tel Aviv: United States of America Operations Mission to Israel, 1958.

Petuchowski, Jacob J. *Zion Reconsidered.* New York: Twayne Publishers, 1966.

Prittie, Terence. *Israel: Miracle in the Desert.* London: Pall Mall Press, 1967.

Raphaeli, Nimrod. "Military Government in the Occupied Territories," *Middle East Journal*, XXIII, No. 2, Spring 1969, 177–190.

Regling, Dietrich. *Die Bahn der drei Meere* (Railroads of the Three Seas). Studien in Arbeit beim List Institut, Basel, No. 1.) Tubingen: J.C.B. Mohr, 1963.

Sachar, Abram. *A History of the Jews.* (5th ed.) New York: Alfred A. Knopf, 1964.

St. John, Robert. *Israel.* (Life World Library Series.) New York: Time, Inc., 1965.

Schweid, Eliezer. *Modern Hebrew Literature.* (Israel Today Series, No. 30.) Jerusalem: Israel Digest, 1964.

Sedych, Andrei. *This Land of Israel.* (Trans., Elizabeth Reynolds Hapgood.) New York: Macmillan, 1967.

Shakov, Zara. *The Theater in Israel.* New York: Herzl Press, 1964.

Shapiro, Harry L. *The Jewish People: A Biological History.* Paris: United Nations Educational, Scientific and Cultural Organization, 1960.

Shuval, Judith T. *Immigrants of the Threshold.* New York: Atherton Press, 1963.

Solente, Christiane. "Attitudes israeliennes a l'egard du probleme de la minorite arabe," *L'Afrique et l'Asie*, LII, 1960, 29–42.

Spencer, Charles. "Sculptures in the Sun," *Ariel* (Jerusalem), No. 12, 1965.

Stock, Ernest. *Israel on the Road to Sinai, 1949–1956.* Ithaca: Cornell University Press, 1967.

Storrs, R. *The Memoirs of Sir Ronald Storrs.* New York: G.P. Putnam's Sons, 1937.

Strizower, Schifra. "The 'Bene-Israel' in Israel," *Middle Eastern Studies*, II, 1966, 123–143.

Teller, Judd. "Modern Hebrew Literature of Israel," *Middle East Journal*, VII, No. 2, Spring 1953, 182–195.

United Nations. Statistical Office of the United Nations. Department of Economic and Social Affairs. *Statistical Yearbook, 1967.* New York: United Nations Publishing Service, 1968.

U.S. Department of Agriculture. *Research Around the World*. Jerusalem: Israel Program for Scientific Translation, n.d.

U.S. Department of State. International Scientific and Technological Affairs. *International Science Notes*, No. 21, January 1969.

Walter Reed Army Medical Center. Walter Reed Army Institute of Research. *Israel*. (Health Data Publications.) Washington: February 1969.

Weiner, Herbert. "Exercise in Hasidism," *Midstream*, April 1967, 27–47.

Weingrod, Alex. "Administered Communities: Some Characteristics of New Immigrant Villages in Israel," *Economic Development and Cultural Change*, XI, 1962, 69–84.

———. *Israel: Group Relations in a New Society*. London: Praeger, 1965.

Section II. Political
RECOMMENDED SOURCES

Antonovsky, Aaron. "Classification of Forms, Political Ideologies, and the Man in the Street," *Public Opinion Quarterly*, XXX, Spring 1966, 109–119.

Arian, Alan. *Ideological Change in Israel*. Cleveland: Case Western Reserve University Press, 1968.

Baker, Henry E. *The Legal System of Israel*. Jerusalem: Israel Universities Press, 1968.

Cantril, Hadley. *The Pattern of Human Concerns*. New Brunswick: Rutgers University Press, 1965.

Daniel, Jean. "The Voices I Heard," *Atlas*, XVII, April 1969, 17–22. (Trans. from *Le Nouvel Observateur* [Paris].)

Eisenstadt, S.N. "Israeli Identity: Problems in the Development of the Collective Identity of an Ideological Society," *Annals of the American Academy of Political and Social Science*, CCCLXX, March 1967, 116–123.

Etyan, Walter. *The First Ten Years*. London: Weidenfeld and Nicolson, 1958.

Fein, Leonard J. *Israel: Politics and People*. Boston: Little and Brown, 1967.

Freudenheim, Yehoshua. *Government in Israel*. Dobbs Ferry: Oceana Publications, 1967.

Guttman, Louis, "Whither Israel's Political Parties?," *Jewish Frontier*, XXVII, December 1961, 14–18.

Halpern, Ben. *The Idea of the Jewish State*. Cambridge: Harvard University Press, 1961.

The International Who's Who, 1968–1969. (32d ed.) London: Europa Publications, 1968.

Israel. Central Office of Information. Prime Minister's Office. *Israel Government Yearbook 5728 (1967–68)*. Jerusalem: Government Press, 1968.

Israel. Ministry for Foreign Affairs. Information Division. *Facts About Israel, 1968*. Jerusalem: Publication Services Division, Israel Program for Scientific Translations, 1968.

Johnston, Scott D. "Election Politics and Social Change in Israel," *Middle East Journal*, XVI, No. 3, Summer 1962, 309–327.

_____. "Major Party Politics in a Multi-Party System: The MAPAI Party of Israel," *Il Politico*, XXX, June 1965, 331–347.

Kimche, David, and Bawley, Dan. *The Sandstorm*. New York: Stein and Day, 1968.

Kraines, Oscar. *Government and Politics in Israel*. Boston: Houghton Mifflin, 1961.

Kreitler, Hans, and Kreitler, Shulamith. "Crucial Dimensions of the Attitude Toward National and Supra-National Ideals: A Study on Israeli Youth," *Journal of Peace Research* (Oslo), No. 2, 1967, 107–124.

Louvish, Misha. *The Challenge of Israel*. Jerusalem: Israel Universities Press, 1968.

Oren, Nissan. "The Origins of the Israel Foreign Ministry," *Public Administration in Israel and Abroad, 1968*, No. 9, 1969.

Peretz, Dagan (ed.). *Who's Who in Israel, 1956*. Tel Aviv: P. Mamut, 1956.

Perlmutter, Amos. "The Israeli Army in Politics: The Persistence of the Civilian Over the Military," *World Politics*, XX, July 1968, 606–643.

Peters, S. "Politics and Terrorism in Israel," *Newsletter*, LII, March 31, 1969, 3–5.

Ribalow, Harold U. (ed.) *Fighting Heroes of Israel*. New York: The New American Library, 1967.

Rosetti, Moshe. *The Knesset: Its Origins, Forms and Procedures*. Jerusalem: Israeli Government Press, 1966.

Safran, Nadav. *The United States and Israel*. Cambridge: Harvard University Press, 1963.

Shaul, Moshe Ben (ed.). *Generals of Israel*. (Translated from Hebrew by I. Hanoch.) Tel Aviv: Hadar Publishing Company, 1968.

Stock, Ernest. *Israel on the Road to Sinai, 1949–1956*. Ithaca: Cornell University Press, 1967.

Talmon, J.L. "Israel Among the Nations: Reflections on Jewish Statehood," *Commentary*, XLV, No. 6, June 1968, 32–51.

Zidon, Asher. *Knesset: The Parliament of Israel*. New York: Herzl Press, 1967.

(Various issues of the following periodical were used in the preparation of this section: *Keesing's Contemporary Archives* [London], January 1, 1955–April 16, 1969.)

OTHER SOURCES USED

Assaf, Michael. "The Arabic Press in Israel," *Gazette* [Leiden] (Special Issue on "Israel"), VII, No. 1, January 1961.

Avnery, Uri. *Israel Without Zionists: A Plea for Peace in the Middle East*. New York: Macmillan, 1968.

Avni-Segre, Dan. "Israel: A Society in Transition," *World Politics*, XXI, No. 3, April 1969, 346–365.

Badi, Joseph. *The Government of the State of Israel.* New York: Twayne Publishers, 1963.

Balstan, Hayim. "ITIM and Experiment in National News Agency Reporting," *Gazette* [Leiden] (Special Issue on "Israel"), VII, No. 1, January 1961.

Ben-Gurion, David. *Israel: Years of Challenge.* London: Anthony Blond, 1964.

Bernstein, Marver H. *The Politics of Israel: The First Decade of Statehood.* Princeton: Princeton University Press, 1957.

Buber, Martin. *Israel and Palestine.* (Trans. from German by Stanley Goodman.) (The East and West Library.) New York: Farrar, Strauss and Young, 1952.

Draper, Theodore. *Israel and World Politics.* New York: Viking Press, 1967.

Dunner, Joseph. *The Republic of Israel.* New York: McGraw-Hill, 1950.

Eban, Abba. *Voice of Israel.* (2d ed., rev.) New York: Horizon Press, 1969.

Eilemers, J.E. "Some Sociological Comments on Mass Communications in Israel," *Gazette* [Leiden] (Special Issue on "Israel"), VII, No. 1, January 1961.

Eisenstadt, S.N. *Israeli Society.* New York: Basic Books, 1967.

Etzioni, Amitai. "Alternative Ways to Democracy: The Example of Israel," *Political Science Quarterly*, LXXIV, June 1959, 196–214.

————. "The Functional Differentiation of Elites in the Kibbutz," *American Journal of Sociology*, LXIV, No. 4, January 1959, 476–487.

Europa Publications. *Europa Year Book, 1968.* London: Europa Publications, 1968.

Gervasi, Frank. *The Case for Israel.* New York: Viking Press, 1967.

Gruenfeld, Walter. "Press Advertising in Israel," *Gazette* [Leiden] (Special Issue on "Israel"), VII, No. 1, January 1961.

Harkabi, Y. *Fedayeen Action and Arab Strategy.* (Adelphi Papers, No. 53.) London: Institute for Strategic Studies, 1968.

Israel. Central Bureau of Statistics. *Statistical Abstract of Israel, 1968*, No. 19. Jerusalem: Government Press, 1968.

Israel. Ministry of Information. *Newspapers and Periodicals Appear in Israel, 1966.* Jerusalem: Government Press, 1967.

"Israel Labor: Mapam Alignment," *Israel Digest*, XII, February 7, 1949, 4–6.

Johnston, Scott D. "Communist Party Politics in Israel." Pages 105–120 in *Studies on Asia, 1964.* Omaha: University of Nebraska Press, 1964.

Khouri, Fred J. *The Arab Dilemma.* Syracuse: Syracuse University Press, 1968.

Kimche, Jon. *The Unromantics.* London: Weidenfeld and Nicolson, 1968.

Kramer, Elchanan. "The Development of the Evening Press in Israel," *Gazette* [Leiden] (Special Issue on "Israel"), VII, No. 1, January 1961.

Lankin, Doris. *Israel Today: The Legal System.* Jerusalem: Israel Digest, 1964.

Lazar, David. "Teachers and Guides in Israeli Journalism" *Gazette* [Leiden] (Special Issue on "Israel"), VII, No. 1, January 1961.

Mao Tse-tung. *Selected Works.* 4 vols. Peking: Foreign Language Press, 1961.

Melkman, J. "The Information Center," *Gazette* [Leiden] (Special Issue on "Israel"), VII, No. 1, January 1961.

"Notes of the Month," *Israel Economist*, XXV, No. 4, April 1969, 96.

Pearlman, Moshe (ed.). *Ben Gurion Looks Back.* New York: Simon and Schuster, 1965.

Peaslee, Amos J. *Constitutions of Nations*, II. (3d ed., rev.) The Hague: Martinus Nijhoff, 1966.

Pines, Dan. "The Press of the Histadrut," *Gazette* [Leiden] (Special Issue on "Israel"), VII, January 1961.

Rivkin, Arnold, "Israel and the Afro-Asian World," *Foreign Affairs*, XXXVII, April 1959, 486–495.

Rouleau, Eric. "L'Etat d'Israel Auquel Nous Revions N'est Pas Encore Ne," *Le Monde*, April 17–23, 1969, 5.

Sachar, Abram. *A History of the Jews.* (5th ed.) New York: Alfred A. Knopf, 1964.

Seligman, Lester C. *Leadership in a New Nation: Political Development in Israel.* New York: Atherton Press, 1964.

Stevens, Georgiana G. (ed.) *The United States and the Middle East.* Englewood Cliffs: Prentice-Hall, 1964.

Stock, Ernest. "The Press of Israel: Its Growth in Freedom," *Journalism Quarterly*, XXXI, Fall 1954, 481–490.

Talmi, Ephraim. "Periodicals for Children and Teenagers," *Gazette* [Leiden] (Special Issue on "Israel"), VII, January 1961.

Taylor, Alan R. *Prelude to Israel: An Analysis of Zionist Diplomacy, 1897–1947.* New York: Philosophical Library, 1959.

U.S. Department of Labor. Bureau of Labor Statistics. *Labor Law and Practice in Israel.* (BLS Report No. 315. Washington: GPO, 1967.

United States Information Service. Office of Policy and Research. *Communist Propaganda Organizations and Activities in the Near East and South Asia during 1967.* Washington: GPO, 1967.

Warsoff, Louis A. "Citizenship in the State of Israel: A Comment," *New York University Law Review*, XXXIII, June 1958, 857–861.

Weinrub, Bernard D. "Broadcasting to Israel," *Public Opinion Quarterly*, XX, Fall 1956, 501–514.

Wigoder, Geoffrey. "Radio in Israel," *Gazette* [Leiden] (Special Issue on "Israel"), VII, No. 1, January 1961.

World Radio-Television Handbook, 1968. (22d ed.) Hellerup: World Radio-Television Handbook Company, 1967.

Yadin, Yigael. "Communication in Ancient Israel," *Gazette* [Leiden] (Special Issue on "Israel"), VII, No. 1, January 1961.

Yagol, Yona. "On Dissemination of News and Information in the Kibbutzim," *Gazette* [Leiden] (Special Issue on "Israel"), VII, No. 1, January 1961.

Zak, Moshe. "The Contemporary Press of Israel," *Gazette* [Leiden] (Special Issue on "Israel"), VII, No. 1, January 1961.

Zinder, Harry. "Television in Israel," *Gazette* [Leiden] (Special Issue on "Israel"), VII, No. 1, January 1961.

(Various issues of the following periodicals and newspapers were used in the preparation of this section: *The Christian Science Monitor*, February 28, 1969–March 29, 1969; *The Jerusalem Post*, 1967–1969; *The National Observer*, March 3, 1969–April 15, 1969; *The New York Times*, July 1, 1966–April 15, 1969; and *The Observer* (London), March 3, 1969–March 31, 1969.)

Section III. Economic
RECOMMENDED SOURCES

Fein, Leonard J. *Israel: Politics and People.* Boston: Little and Brown, 1967.

Halevi, Nadav, and Klinov-Malul, Ruth. *The Economic Development of Israel.* (Praeger Special Studies in International Economics and Development.) New York: Praeger, published in cooperation with the Bank of Israel, 1968.

Horowitz, David. *The Economics of Israel.* New York: Pergamon Press, 1967.

Israel. Central Bureau of Statistics. *Statistical Abstract of Israel,* 1968, No. 19. Jerusalem: Government Press, 1968.

Israel. Central Office of Information. Prime Minister's Office. *Israel Government Yearbook 5728 (1967–68).* Jerusalem: Government Press, 1968.

———. *Israel Government Yearbook 5729 (1968–69).* Jerusalem: Government Press, 1969.

Israel. Investment Authority. *Israel Investor's Manual.* Jerusalem: Government Press, 1968.

Israel. Ministry for Foreign Affairs. Information Division. *Facts About Israel, 1968.* Jerusalem: Publication Services Division, Israel Program for Scientific Translations, 1968.

———. *Facts About Israel, 1969.* Jerusalem: Publication Services Division, Israel Program for Scientific Translations, 1969.

Israel. Ministry of Agriculture. Agriculture and Settlement. Planning and Development Center. *Outline of the Five Year Plan for Israel's Agriculture, 1966–7/1970–1.* Tel Aviv: Hakiryia, 1967.

Israel. Prime Minister's Office. Economic Planning Authority. *Israel Economic Development: Past Progress and Plan for the Future.* Jerusalem: Government Press, 1968.

Kanovsky, Eliyahu. *The Economy of the Israeli Kibbutz.* (Harvard Middle East Monograph Series.) Cambridge: Harvard University Press, 1966.

Laufer, Leopold. *Israel and the Developing Countries: New Approaches to Cooperation.* New York: The Twentieth Century Fund, 1967.

Mundlak, Yair. *Long-Term Projections of Supply and Demand for*

Agricultural Products in Israel, I: General View and Summary. Jerusalem: Falk Project for Economic Research in Israel, Faculty of Agriculture, the Hebrew University, May 1964.

Orni, Efraim, and Efrat, Elisha. *Geography of Israel*. (2d ed., rev.) Jerusalem: Israel Program for Scientific Translations, 1966.

Remba, Oded. "The Real State of Israel's Economy—and the Prospect Ahead," *New Middle East* (London), No. 5, December 1968, 44–50.

Schaar, Stuart H. *Patterns of Israeli Aid and Trade in East Africa*. (American Universities Field Staff Reports Services, East Africa Series, VII, No. 1.) New York: AUFS, 1968.

U.S. Department of Labor. Bureau of Labor Statistics. *Labor Law and Practice in Israel*. (BLS Report No. 315.) Washington: GPO, 1967.

U.S. Department of State. Agency for International Development. Statistics and Reports Division. Office of Program and Policy Coordination. *Near East and South Asia: Economic Growth and Trend*. Washington: GPO, 1967.

Weingrod, Alex. *Reluctant Pioneers: Village Development in Israel*. Ithaca: Cornell University Press, 1966.

Zweig, F. "The Jewish Trade Union Movement in Israel," *Jewish Journal of Sociology*, I, April 1959, 23–42.

OTHER SOURCES USED

The American-Israel Chamber of Commerce and Industry, Inc. *Economic Horizons Yearbook and Trade Directory, 1969*. New York: American-Israel Chamber of Commerce and Industry, 1969.

American-Israel Economic Horizons, XX, No. 5, December 1968–January 1969.

Ben-David, Joseph. "Professionals and Unions in Israel," *Industrial Relations*, V, October 1965, 48–68.

Derber, Milton. "Plant Labor Relations in Israel," *Industrial and Labor Relations Review*, XVII, October 1963, 51–72.

_____. "Worker Participation in Israeli Management," *Industrial Relations*, III, October 1963, 39–59.

The Economist Intelligence Unit, Ltd. *Quarterly Economic Reviews: Annual Supplement, Israel*, 1968.

_____. *Quarterly Economic Reviews: Israel*, No. 3, August 1968.

_____. *Quarterly Economic Reviews: Israel*, No. 4, November 1968.

_____. *Quarterly Economic Reviews: Israel*, No. 1, February 1969.

_____. *Quarterly Economic Reviews: Israel*, No. 2, May 1969.

Friedmann, Georges. "The Histadrut Paradox," *Midstream*, XIII, April 1967, 3–12.

Hoffman, Gail. *The Land and People of Israel*. Philadelphia: J. P. Lippincott, 1960.

Horne, Arner. "The Economic Scene in Israel," *Midstream*, May 1967.

"Import Liberalization." *Israel Investors' Report*, October 1968.

International Monetary Fund. *International Financial Statistics*, XXII, No. 1, January 1969.

Israel. Bank of Israel. *Annual Report, 1967*. Jerusalem: Government Press, 1968.

————. *Bulletin*, No. 31. Jerusalem: Government Press, 1969.

Israel. Bank of Israel (Bank Leumi Le-Israel B.M.). *Review of Economic Conditions in Israel* (Special Issue), No. 62. Jerusalem: Government Press, September 1968.

Israel. Central Bureau of Statistics. *Monthly Foreign Trade Statistics* (Jerusalem), XIX, No. 7, 1968.

Israel. Ministry for Foreign Affairs. Information Division. *Facts About Israel, 1964–65*. Jerusalem: Publication Services Division, Israel Program for Scientific Translations, 1965.

Israel. Ministry of Agriculture. *Israel Agriculture: Autumn News Letters, 1968*. Jerusalem: Government Press, 1968.

————. *Israel Agriculture: Facts and Figures*. Jerusalem: Government Press, 1968.

Israel. Ministry of Commerce and Industry. Programme for Industrial Development. *Second Outlook, 1965–1970*. Jerusalem: Hatchiya Printing Press, n.d.

The Israel Economist, XXIV, No. 9, July–September 1968.

"Israel's War Boom," *Economist*, CCXXX, No. 6542, January 11, 1969.

The Jerusalem Post (Weekly Overseas Edition), No. 390, April 1968.

Jewish Agency. Economic Division. Department of Immigration and Absorption. *The Israel Yearbook, 1968*. Tel Aviv: Israel Yearbook Publications, 1968.

Labes, Emmanuel. *Handbook of Moshav: An Introduction to Israel's Cooperative Farm Village*. (2nd ed.) Jerusalem: Haikar Haoved and the Youth and Hechalutz Department of the World Zionist Organization, 1962.

Louvish, Misha. *The Challenge of Israel*. Jerusalem: Israel Universities Press, 1968.

Meir, Ziona. *The Labour Movement in Israel*. (Israel Today Series, No. 20.) Jerusalem: Israel Digest, 1965.

Pockier, Sewer. "Israel Trade with the Socialist Bloc," *New Outlook*, XI, No. 7, September 1968.

Sheskin, Arhey. "Post-War Economics of the West Bank," *New Outlook*, XI, No. 8, October 1968.

Smith, Hanoch. "Israel's Employment Potential," *Israel Economist*, XXV, January 1969, 12–14.

Trager, Frank N. *Marxism in Southeast Asia*. Stanford: Stanford University Press, 1959.

U.S. Department of Commerce. *International Commerce*. Washington: GPO, January 1969.

U.S. Department of Commerce. Bureau of International Commerce. *Basic Data on the Economy of Israel*. (OBR 66–79.) Washington: GPO, 1966.

_____. *Establishing a Business in Israel*. (OBR 68–25.) Washington: GPO, 1968.

Weitz, Raanan, and Kokakh, Avshalom. *Agricultural Development: Planning and Implementation—An Israeli Case Study*. New York: Praeger, 1968.

Willner, Dorothy. *Nation-Building and Community in Israel*. Princeton: Princeton University Press, 1969.

(Various issues of the following periodical were used in the preparation of this section: Israel, Bank of Israel, *Bulletin* [Jerusalem], 1964–66.

Section IV. National Security
RECOMMENDED SOURCES

Baker, Henry E. *The Legal System of Israel.* Jerusalem: Israel Universities Press, 1968.

Bayne, E. A. *Economics of a Victor.* (American Universities Field Staff Reports Service, Southwest Asia Series, XVI, No. 2.) New York: AUFS, 1966.

Eaton, J. W. *Prisons in Israel.* Pittsburgh: University of Pittsburgh Press, 1964.

Freudenheim, Yehoshua. *Government in Israel.* Dobbs Ferry: Oceana Publications, 1967.

Halpern, Ben. "The Role of the Military in Israel." In John J. Johnson (ed.), *The Role of the Military in Underdeveloped Countries.* Princeton: Princeton University Press, 1962.

Heiman, Leo. "Israel's Home Defense," *Ordinance,* LII, November-December 1967, 252–257.

Heymont, Irving. "The Israeli Career Officer Corps," *Military Review,* XLVII, October 1968, 13–19.

_____. "Israeli Defense Forces," *Military Review,* XLVII, February 1967, 37–47.

_____. "The Israeli Nahal Program," *Middle East Journal,* XXI, Summer 1967, 314–324.

Hurewitz, J. C. *Middle East Politics: The Military Dimension.* New York: Praeger, 1969.

_____. "The Role of the Military in Society and Government in Israel." In Sydney Nettleton Fisher (ed.), *The Military in the Middle East.* Columbus: Ohio State University Press, 1963.

Israel. Central Bureau of Statistics. *Statistical Abstract of Israel, 1968,* No. 19. Jerusalem: Government Press, 1968.

Israel. Central Office of Information. Prime Minister's Office. *Israel Government Yearbook 5728 (1967–68).* Jerusalem: Government Press, 1968.

Israel. Ministry for Foreign Affairs. Information Division. *Facts About Israel, 1968.* Jerusalem: Publication Services Division, Israel Program for Scientific Translations, 1968.

Marshall, S. L. A. *Sinai Victory.* New York: William Morrow, 1958.

The Military Balance, 1968–1969. London: Institute for Strategic Studies, 1968.

Pearlman, Moshe. *The Army of Israel.* New York: Philosophical Library, 1950.

Perlmutter, Amos. "The Israeli Army in Politics: The Persistence of the Civilian Over the Military," *World Politics,* XX, July 1968, 606–643.

Safran, Nadav. "Israel Today: A Profile," *Headline Series,* No. 170, April 1965.

Shamgan, Meir. "The Law in the Areas Held by the Israel Defense Forces." In *Public Administration in Israel and Abroad, 1967.* Jerusalem: n.pub., 1968.

Shoemaker, R. L. "The Arab-Israeli War," *Military Review,* XLVIII, August 1968, 56–59.

U.S. Department of Defense. *Military Uniforms.* (DOD Pam 1–14.) Washington: GPO, 1959.

OTHER SOURCES USED

Bayne, E. A. *The Arab-Israeli War of 1967.* (American Universi- York: Israel Office of Information, October 1957.

Bayne, E. A. *The Arab-Israeli War of 1967.* (American Universities Field Staff Reports Service, Southwest Asia Series, XVI, No. 4.) New York: AUFS, 1967.

Cramer, James. *The World's Police.* London: Cassell, 1964.

Heiman, Leo. "Firepower in Sinai," *Ordinance,* LIII, November-December 1968, 273–277.

_____. "The Israeli Reserve Force: An Ancient Concept in Modern Form," *National Guardsman,* XX, August 1966, 14–20.

_____. "War in the Middle East: An Israeli View," *Military Review,* XLVII, September 1967, 56–76.

Israel. Central Office of Information. Prime Minister's Office. *Israel Government Yearbook, 5718 (1957–58).* Jerusalem: Government Press, 1958.

Israel. Laws, Statutes, etc.
The Laws of Palestine, I and II. London: Waterlow and Sons, 1934.
"Military Justice Law, 5715–1955." (Reprint from *Laws of the State of Israel,* IX.) Jerusalem: Government Press, n.d.
Ordinances, Regulations, Rules, Orders, and Notices: Annual Volume for 1936. Jerusalem: Government Press, December 1936.

Kimche, David, and Bawley, Dan. *The Sandstorm.* New York: Stein and Day, 1968.

Kraines, Oscar. *Government and Politics in Israel.* Boston: Houghton Mifflin, 1961.

Reagan, J. F. "Air Power Over Sinai," *Ordinance*, LII, November–December 1967, 258–259.

Safran, Nadav. *The United States and Israel.* Cambridge: Harvard University Press, 1963.

Time, XCII, No. 17, October 25, 1968, 97–98.

GLOSSARY

agora (plural, agorot)—An Israeli coin. 1 agora equals approximately US$0.003 (see currency). One hundred agorot equal one Israeli pound.

Agudat Israel—A small political party founded in 1912. Commonly referred to as Agudah, its members are mostly Orthodox Jews who favor a religious state.

Ahdut Ha-Avoda—Hebrew for Unity of Labor, a left-wing socialist party, commonly called Ahdut. It started as a non-Marxist group in MAPAM (q.v.), later joined with MAPAI (q.v.), but withdrew and became autonomous in 1954. It favors industrialization and is actively engaged in maintaining and improving workers' living standards.

Al Fatah—An abbreviated version of the Arabic words Harakat al Tahrir al Falastin (Movement for Liberation of Palestine). Initials of the Arabic words, HTF, are reversed to FTH and pronounced "fatah" (conquest). The name is given to an Arab activist movement, members of which oppose existence of Israel. Created in the mid-1950's, mainly with Syrian backing, it is the largest and most effective Arab guerrilla group.

aliyah (plural, aliyot)—From the Hebrew word meaning "ascent" or "going up," applied to the idea of the Jewish return to Israel and generally to the waves of immigration to Palestine and to the state of Israel.

Ashkenazi (plural, Ashkenazim)—A member of one of the two major divisions of Jews, the Ashkenazi and Sephardi (q.v.). The term Ashkenazi is generally applied to Yiddish-speaking Jews from Eastern European and sometimes from northern and central European countries. It is frequently applied also to descendants of Jews who formerly lived in Germany.

bagrut—The terminal examination given after the completion of secondary school.

COMECON—Council for Mutual Economic Assistance, founded in 1949 by representatives of European Communist nations. Members: Bulgaria, Czechoslovakia, East Germany, Hungary, Poland, Romania, and the Soviet Union. Observers: Cuba, North Korea, North Vietnam, People's Republic of China, and Yugoslavia. The

Mongolian People's Republic was admitted in 1962. Headquarters is in Moscow.

currency—Basic unit, the Israeli pound (I£), is divided into 100 agorot (singular, agora—*q.v.*); alternatively up to December 31, 1959, the pound was divided into 1,000 prutoth (singular, prutah). There are coins of 1, 5, 10, 25, 50 (0.5 pound), and 100 (1 pound) agorot. Banknotes are issued in denominations of I£1, I£5, I£10, and I£50. Backed by gold and foreign exchange, the currency is relatively stable. The amount in circulation in 1968 was covered by approximately 15 percent in gold and 85 percent in foreign exchange. A par value of I£3.50 per US$1, or exchange rate of I£1 equals approximately US$0.285, was agreed on November 19, 1967.

Diaspora—Literally dispersion. Term is commonly applied to the settling of scattered colonies of Jews outside Palestine after the Babylonian exile (ending in 536 B.C.), or to the area outside Palestine settled by Jews, or sometimes to the Jews living outside Palestine.

dunam—Unit of land, used in regions included in the former Ottoman Empire. It varies in size from country to country; in Israel it equals approximately 0.25 acre.

EFTA—European Free Trade Area. Established in 1960, it is designed to bring about free trade between member countries in industrial goods and an expansion of trade in agricultural products. In 1968 member countries were: Austria, Denmark, Norway, Portugal, Sweden, Switzerland, and the United Kingdom. Headquarters is in Geneva, Switzerland.

Eretz Yisrael—Hebrew phrase meaning "The Land of Israel."

ETZEL—See Irgun Group.

Fatah—See Al Fatah.

fedayeen—Plural of fedayee, a member of an Arab commando group, especially one operating against Israel.

Fertile Crescent—Term used frequently by geographers and historians when referring to the semicircle of fertile land stretching from Palestine on the Mediterranean Sea around the Syrian Desert, north of Arabia to the Persian Gulf.

Gadna—Abbreviation for Gedudei Noar, literally "youth battalions." This name has been given to a paramilitary youth organization for boys and girls that provides them with an elementary military training program. Formations are held weekly and on holidays for Israeli schoolchildren between the ages of fourteen and eighteen.

GAHAL—Acronym for the Hebrew, Gush Herut-Liberalim, literally Freedom-Liberal Bloc, also known as the Herut-Liberal Bloc, a political coalition group, created in 1965 by combination of the Liberal and Herut (*q.v.*) parties.

GATT—General Agreement on Tariffs and Trade, drafted in 1946, is designed to ease trade barriers and establish rules of fair trade. In 1969 parties to the agreement numbered 66 nations. Headquarters is in Geneva, Switzerland.

General Federation of Labor—See Histadrut Ha'ovdim Haklalit.

General Zionists—One of the three main parties of the World Zionist Organization (*q.v.*). The largest until 1933, it included many non-party Zionists and various middle-class groups. In 1961 it united with the liberal-oriented Progressives to form the Liberal party.

Hagana (literally, Defense)—Abbreviation for Irgun Ha-Haganah. The Jewish defense organization formed in 1919–20 by volunteers in early Jewish communities as home guards for protection against hostile bands. It became the military arm of the Jewish Agency (*q.v.*) and went underground during the British Palestine Mandate period (1923–48), when it was declared illegal. Along with the Jewish Brigade, which fought with the Allied forces in World War II, it formed the nucleus of the Israeli defense forces established in 1948.

Hamashbir Hamerkazi—Hebrew for "the central supplier." The Cooperative Wholesale Society, Limited, which is Histadrut's (*q.v.*) principal supplier for agricultural collectives and consumers' stores.

Ha'olam Hazeh—Hebrew for "this world," an independent political reform movement that started in 1965. It is also known as the New Force. It advocates a written constitution for the state and a firm separation of church and state.

Hapoel Ha-Mizrahi—Hebrew for "the workers of the spiritual center," an orthodox religious, labor Zionist political party. In 1956 it joined certain other political religious groups to form the National Religious party.

Hapoel Hatzair (The Young Worker)—A moderate organization with non-Marxist doctrine. It merged in 1929 with Ahdut Ha-Avoda (*q.v.*) to form MAPAI (*q.v.*).

Hashomer Hatzair—Hebrew for the "young watchman," a Marxist socialist organization of Zionist youths. In the early years of statehood it was an important segment of MAPAM (*q.v.*).

Haskalah—Derived from Hebrew *sechel*, meaning "understanding" or "intelligence." An intellectual and enlightenment movement in the 18th and 19th centuries among eastern European Jewish intellectuals. They were attempting to acquaint the Jewish people with European and Hebrew languages, as well as with secular education and culture to supplement study of the Talmud (*q.v.*).

Herut (literally Freedom)—A political party generally associated with extreme right-wing groups on most issues. It developed from the Zionist Revisionist movement and from the Irgun Group (*q.v.*).

Hevrat Ovdim—Hebrew for "workers society," commonly called the General Cooperative Association of Labor. A holding company of Histadrut (*q.v.*) that manages all of its economic enterprises.

Histadrut Ha'ovdim Haklalit—General Federation of Labor, commonly known as Histadrut. Founded in 1920, this national-level organization by 1969 comprised about 1 million members and accounted for about 90 percent of the Israeli labor force; it is also the nation's largest single employer, its direct employment accounting for about 25 percent of the labor force. Histadrut performs many economic and welfare services in addition to trade union activities, leadership of Histradrut is generally drawn from the MAPAI party (*q.v.*).

Histadrut Ha'ovdim Haleumit—Federation of the National Worker, also known as the National Labor Federation. The trade union organization of the right-wing Herut-Liberal bloc; membership about 80,000 in 1968.

hora—A popular folk dance, generally regarded as the Israeli national dance.

Irgun Group—In Hebrew, Irgun Zvai Leumi (National Military Organization). Established in 1937 as an underground Jewish extremist organization known as ETZEL (*q.v.*), derived from the pronounced initials of its Hebrew name. A more extreme group, known as the Stern Gang (*q.v.*), broke away from it in 1939. Both groups were especially active in 1944 against the British Palestine Mandate Administration. Both maintained several thousand armed men until all Israeli forces were integrated in June 1948.

Israel Workers' List—See RAFI.

Israeli pound—See currency.

Jewish Agency—Representing the World Zionist Organization (*q.v.*) and working in close cooperation with the government, it seeks to promote the development of Israel through the unity of the Jewish people, encourages immigration of Jews into the country, organizes their immigration, helps them get started, and assists in their social and economic integration.

Keren Hayesod—Foundation Fund. Established to collect contributions from Jews on a worldwide basis, to finance immigration and settlement.

kibbutz (plural, kibbutzim)—An Israeli collective farm or settlement, cooperatively owned and operated by its members and organized on a communal basis. Communal care is provided for children.

Knesset—The State of Israel's parliament, a unicameral legislative body, elected by universal suffrage for 4-year terms. It may decide to hold new elections before the end of its term.

Kupat Holim—Workers Sick Fund, administered by Histadrut it is the country's largest medical insurance fund. It operates its own hospitals, clinics, laboratories, and other related facilities.

LEHI—Acronym for Lohamei Herut Yisrael, literally Fighters for Israel's Freedom, a former resistance and political organization, created in 1939. It is commonly known as the Sternists or the Stern Gang (q.v.).

Levant—Name given to countries on the eastern shores of the Mediterranean, from western Greece to western Egypt.

MAKI—Acronym for Mifleget Ha Kommunisti Yisraeli—The Israeli Communist party, or the Communist Party of Israel. Founded in 1919, it is anti-Zionist in doctrine, and ideologically it closely follows Soviet Union leadership.

MAPAI—Acronym for Mifleget Poalei Eretz Yisrael—Workers' Party, Land of Israel, also known as the Israel Workers' party or the Israel Labor party. It is a socialist-oriented political group, deriving substantial support from cooperative agricultural villages. In 1968 and 1969 it combined with two other labor groups, RAFI (q.v.) and MAPAM (q.v.), to form the Israel Labor party.

MAPAI-Histadrut—Combination of the MAPAI (q.v.) and Histadrut Ha'ovdim Haklalit (q.v.), political and labor organizations, respectively.

MAPAM—Acronym for Mifleget Poalim Meuchedet—United Workers' Party. Founded in 1948, it is a left-wing, socialist-Zionist political party. Membership is derived mainly from urban workers and professional groups. The party was among the first to favor agricultural collectives.

Mifleget Poalim Meuchedet—See MAPAM.

Mishnah—The first part of the Talmud (q.v.), consisting of a collection of traditions and decisions developed chiefly by rabbis before A.D. 200.

Mizrahi—Abbreviated combination of Merkaz and Ruhani, meaning Spiritual Center, a term applied to a moderately Orthodox Zionist political group. It is concerned with the maintenance and extension of orthodox religious tradition in state law and with the maintenance of religious institutions.

moshav (plural, moshavim)—A cooperative smallholder's settlement of individual farms in Israel. Individuals own their farms and personal property. Work is organized collectively, equipment is used cooperatively, and produce is marketed jointly.

moshav ovdim (plural, moshavei ovdim)—A workers' cooperative settlement of small farm holders. Individual units are independent, but are worked cooperatively.

moshav shitufi—A collective smallholder's settlement that combines the economic features of a kibbutz (*q.v.*) with the social features of a moshav (*q.v.*). Farming is done collectively and profits are shared equally. Each family lives in its own household, as in the moshav.

moshava (plural, moshavoth)—A settlement or colony of independent farmers in Israel who own and work their own land.

Nahal—An abbreviated version of Noar Halutz Lochaim (Pioneer Fighting Youth), a paramilitary youth organization that includes both boys and girls. Nahal groups participate part-time in agricultural work during their military service that includes assignment for almost a year to suitable villages. There, under military discipline, they continue military training and receive practical experience in farming.

New Communist List—See RAKAH.

Palestine Liberation Force (PLF)—Military arm of the Palestine Liberation Organization (*q.v.*). Organized, trained, and equipped by Egyptians in the early 1950's, it was defeated by Israeli forces in the Six-Day War of June 1967, but under Egyptian pressure it reportedly merged with Egyptian-controlled organizations and specialized in mine-planting and rocket-launching activities in Israeli occupied territory, particularly in the Gaza Strip.

Palestine Liberation Organization (PLO)—A group composed mainly of Palestinian refugees, apparently based in the Gaza Strip (many born in Gaza) and extensively financed by Arab League countries. Its military arm is the Palestine Liberation Force. The organization leaders state that they oppose a negotiated settlement of the Middle East issue unless unspecified rights to Palestinians are guaranteed. Nevertheless, it cooperated in 1968 with the Al Fatah (*q.v.*) because of pressure from Egypt and other Arab countries and because of an avowed conviction that the anti-Israel guerrilla movement should be unified as similar operations were carried on in Cuba and Algiers.

Palmach—Abbreviation for Plugot Mahatz, striking forces. In British Palestine and in the early years of the state of Israel, it was a commando section of the Jewish military forces. Organized in 1941 to provide the Hagana (*q.v.*) with a mobile force, it consisted of young men mostly from kibbutzim (*q.v.*), who took military training while working part-time at farming, serving in cooperation with the British army, without pay or uniforms. Many high-ranking officers in the modern Israeli military forces once served in the Palmach.

P.L. 480—Public Law No. 480—The Agricultural Trade Development and Assistance Act of 1954, approved by the 83d Congress of the United States on July 10, 1954. It was designed to increase the consumption of United States agricultural commodities in foreign countries, to improve foreign relations of the United States.

Poalei Agudat Israel—Poalei Agudat is Hebrew for Workers of the Association. Hence, Workers of the Association of Israel, an extremist political party with orthodox religious and labor elements, advocating land pioneering and protection of workers' rights according to Jewish scriptural teaching.

Poalei Zion—Hebrew for Workers of Zion, a Zionist political organization founded in 1907 with a moderate socialistic platform.

Popular Front for the Liberation of Palestine (PFLP)—Formed from a merger in 1967 of several small Arab activist groups. Based in Beirut, it has training camps scattered throughout Palestinian refugee villages in Lebanon.

RAFI—Acronym for Reshimat Poalei Yisrael, literally The Israel Workers' List (also known as the Israel Labor List), created in 1965 when David Ben-Gurion and many of his supporters broke away from MAPAI (*q.v.*).

RAKAH—Acronym for the Hebrew Reshima Kommunistit Hadasha, literally New Communist List. Created in 1965, it is an offshoot from the Israeli Communist Party, MAKI (*q.v.*), when it broke up into two factions.

Reshima Kommunistit Hadasha—See RAKAH.

Reshimat Poalei Yisrael—See RAFI.

Revisionists—Established in 1925 as a fourth important group in the World Zionist Organization (*q.v.*), led by Vladimir Jabotinsky, who opposed Dr. Chaim Weizmann's policy of cooperation with British Palestine Mandate authorities.

Sabra (plural, Sabras or Tsabarim)—From Hebrew word meaning "a prickly pear," but adapted to mean a native-born Israeli.

seker—Terminal examination of the primary school cycle.

Sephardi (plural, Sephardim)—A member of the occidental branch of European Jews of Middle East and African origin, but settling early in Spain and Portugal; later they spread to Greece, the Levant (*q.v.*), England, the Netherlands, and the Americas. They tend to speak Ladino or Arabic.

sharav—Hot winds from Sinai desert, also known as *hamsin*, its Arabic name.

Shiah—The group of Muslims comprising one of the two major branches of Islam; it originated as a party holding Ali, the son-in-law of Mohammed, as his legitimate successor.

Shiite—A Muslim belonging to the Shiah (*q.v.*) branch of Islam.

Solel Boneh—Hebrew for Road Maker and Builder; a major building and power company owned by the Histadrut Ha'ovdim Haklalit (*q.v.*).

Stern Gang—A small but vigorously militant underground group conventionally named after its leader, Abraham Stern, formally known as Lohamei Herut Yisrael (Fighters for Israel's Freedom), sometimes identified by the acronym LEHI (*q.v.*). It broke away from the Irgun Group (*q.v.*) in 1939 and opposed the plan for partition of Palestine between Jews and Arabs proposed by the United Nations in 1947.

Sunni—The group of Muslims constituting one of the two major branches of Islam. They adhere to the orthodox traditions of old Arabian custom and early Islamic practice and acknowledge the first four caliphs as rightful successors of Mohammed.

Sunnite—A Muslim belonging to the Sunni (*q.v.*) branch of Islam.

Talmud—The body of Jewish civil and canonical law incorporated with commentary in the Hebrew Mishnah (*q.v.*).

Tnuva—Hebrew for "produce." The agricultural cooperative marketing agency of Histadrut Ha'ovdim Haklalit (*q.v.*). It handles the produce of the kibbutzim and moshavim and is the largest in the country.

Torah—The first five books of the Old Testament collectively, often called The Pentateuch, or Law of Moses. The term was also used in designating certain religious groupings, known in the 1950's as the Torah Religious Front.

Transjordan—Formerly Transjordania, a kingdom in northwest Arabia, east of Palestine and the Jordan River. Capital was Amman. The name Jordan, in full, the Hashimite Kingdom of Jordan, was adopted after the 1948 Armistice between Israel and the Arab states, when Jordan gained territory west of the Jordan River.

UNESCO—United Nations Educational, Scientific and Cultural Organization, a specialized agency of the United Nations.

United Workers' Party—See MAPAM.

UNRWA—United Nations Relief and Works Agency for Arab Palestinian refugees in the Near East.

Workers' Party—See MAPAI.

World Zionist Organization—Founded in 1897 at the First Zionist Congress called by Theodor Herzl at Basel, Switzerland. The movement, named after Mount Zion in Jerusalem, was designed to establish in Palestine a national home for Jews scattered throughout the world. Its efforts are devoted primarily to promoting unity of the Jewish people, raising funds, as well as supporting welfare activities among them. In 1929 it established the Jewish Agency (*q.v.*), which directed construction projects in Palestine

444

and, as a representative of World Jewry, it maintained liaison with the British Palestine Mandate authorities.

yeshiva—(*yeshivot*, plural) A school for advanced study of the Talmud (*q.v.*). The term is also used to denote an Orthodox Jewish rabbinical seminary or college; it is sometimes used to denote a Hebrew-English day school providing both secular and religious instruction.

Yiddish—A Germanic language spoken by Jews chiefly in Eastern, northern, and central Europe and in areas to which Jews from these regions have migrated. It is basically a High German dialect containing elements of Hebrew, Russian, and Polish, and it is commonly written in Hebrew characters.

Yishuv—The Jewish community in Palestine, before statehood. Also used in referring to the period between 1900 and 1948.

Youth Aliyah—An organization, founded in 1934, that brings children and young people to Israel from all parts of the world to rehabilitate and educate them. It has brought in and cared for approximately 25,000 from 80 different countries, and they have been established at 46 new villages.

Zahal—Abbreviation for Zva Ha-Haganah Israel, literally "Israel Defense Force."

Zionist Organization—See World Zionist Organization.

INDEX

French influence: 233, 373, 381
French language: 117, 225, 228, 236
Frontier Force: 397, 400, 401, 403

Gadna: 159, 380, 383
GAHAL: 10, 193, 194, 227, 249, 259
Galilee, Sea of: *See* Tiberias, Lake
Gaza Strip: 14
Gaza Strip and North Sinai: 399, 400
Gazit: 229
General Agreement on Tariffs and Trade (GATT): 352
General Federation of Labor: *See* Histadrut
General Zionist party: 115
Genocide Law: 405, 411
George, David Lloyd: 39
Gerizim, Mount: 147
German language: 224, 226
Germany: 68, 277, 361; West Germany, 11, 212, 213, 216, 352
Ghor: 15
Givatayim: 66
Godik theater: 135
Golan Heights: 398
Golomb, Eliyahu: 372
Gotthelf, Jehua: 225
government (*see also* chapter 13, and budget, cabinet, Knesset, political parties): 49, 166
Government Press Office: 221, 222, 235
government role: 275; agriculture, 276, 295, 340; credit and finance, 279, 360; development planning, 281; domestic trade, 334; industry, 277, 299–300
Great Britain (*see also* British influence): 213, 216, 233, 252, 253; Palestine Mandate, 41–42, 115, 155
Greece: 218
Greek Orthodox community: 70, 152
Green, Nathaniel: 225
Greenberg, Uri Zvi: 133
Gross National Product: 273

Haaretz: 225, 227
Habibi, Emile: 196
Habimah theater: 134
Hadassah Women's Zionist Organization: 126, 127
Hadera: 66
Hadera River: 14
Hagana: 42, 46, 369, 391
Haifa: District, 25, 27; municipal

theatre, 134–135; port, 25, 26, 342, 400; population, 65, 66, 92; sanitation, 105; University College, 128
Haim, Paul Ben: 136
Halevy, Joseph: 138
Hamashbir Hamerkazi: 323, 339
Hamis'har: 229
Hamodia: 228
hamulas: 92
Hanukah: 32
Ha'olam Hazeh: party, 87, 193, 197; periodical, 229, 247
Hapoalim, Bank: 358
Hapoel Ha-Mizrahi: 327
Hapoel Hatzair: party, 323; periodical, 229
Hashefela: *See* Shephela
Hashomer Hatzair youth group: 195, 369
Hasidism: 131, 149
Haskalah movement: 72
Hatzofe: 225, 228
Hayom: 225, 227
Hazaz, Hayyim: 133
Health, Ministry of: 104, 107, 365
health insurance: 107, 109, 325–326
Hebrew language: 71, 86, 117, 128, 162, 376, 401; press, 224
Hebrew Language Academy: 139
Hebrew University of Jerusalem: 42, 125, 126, 127, 184, 234
Hebrew University-Hadassah Medical Center: 108, 139, 140
Hehalutz movement: 260
Herut party: 192, 247, 259
Herut-Liberal Bloc: *See* GAHAL
Herzl, Theodore: 35, 154, 244
Herzlia School: 384
Herzliya: 66
Hess, Moses: 36
Hevrat Ovdim: 302, 325, 338
Hibbat Zion: 36
Hijaz Railway: 24
Histadadrut: 10, 42, 59, 183, 246, 260, 267, 323–326; education, 115, 117, 124, 128; funds, 322, 358, 362; industry and trade, 302, 333, 338; influence, 198, 274–275, 312; labor agreements, 278, 321; publishing, 227, 234; theatre, 135
Histadrut Ha'ovdim Haleumit: 327
holidays: 320
Holon: 66
holy days in Judaism: 148

Hope-Simpson Royal Commission: 44
Horowitz, David: 265
hospitals: 108
housing: 102, 308, 336, 388
Hubermann, Bronislav: 136
Hula, Lake: 15, 22
Hungary: 237
Hussein, Abdulla: 38, 39, 43
Hussein, Faisal: 39, 40
Hussein Ibn Ali, Sharif: 38, 39

Immigrant Absorption, Ministry for: 182, 199
immigration (*see also aliyot*): 38, 50, 51, 215, 273; employment, 311, 316; sources, 57–62, 68
imports: 276, 280, 300, 347, 350
income taxes: 365
Independence Proclamation: 164, 165, 240
Independent parties: 247, 248
India: 68
industry (*see also* chapter 21): 305, 346, 358, 359
inflation: 340, 365, 367
Information, Central Office of: 222, 235
insignia, military: 390
interest rates: 304, 305, 359, 368
Interior, Ministry of the: 179
intermarriage: 70, 84, 85, 97
International Bank for Reconstruction and Development: 305, 359
international labor organizations: 326
international organizations, membership in: 164, 210, 216
Iran: 354
Iraq: 26, 68, 215
Irgun Group: 43, 370, 371
irrigation: 276, 285, 286–288, 296–297, 310
Islam: 70, 151
Israel, ancient: 30
Israel, Bank of: 266, 358, 360
Israel, State of: 1, 48, 210
Israel Aircraft Industries: 375
Israel Discount Bank: 358
Israel Electric Corporation: 309
Israel Exploration Society: 142
Israel Institute of Technology: *See* Technion
Israel Labor party: 228, 248, 261, 268
Israel Military Industries: 375
Israel Museum: 139, 142
Israel Philharmonic Orchestra: 136

Israel Society for Biblical Research: 139
Italy: 233, 352
Izraelskie Noviny i Kurier: 225, 228

Jabotinsky, Vladimir: 43, 195
Jaffa: 26, 66
Janco, Marcel: 138
Jarring, Gunnar: 205
Jerusalem: 18, 20, 48, 66, 92, 172, 208; District, 25, 27, 65; holy city of Islam, 151; Old City, 185; sanitation, 23, 105; ultra-Orthodox Jews, 149
Jerusalem Post: 225, 228
Jewish Agency (*see also* Hagana): 42, 50, 102, 111, 182, 199
Jewish Brigade: 370
Jewish National Fund: 42, 183, 287, 289
Jewish Resistance Movement: 46
Jewish Telegraphic Agency: 230
Jews (*see also* Ashkenazic Jews, immigration, Sephardic Jews, ultra-Orthodox Jews): 55, 62–63, 67, 77, 145
Jezreel, Valley of: *See* Esdraelon, Plain of
Johnson, Lyndon B.: 216
Johnston, Eric, plan: 52
Jordan, Hashimite Kingdom of: 6, 14, 15, 43, 46, 54, 354
Jordan Rift Valley: 13, 15
Jordan River: 14, 15, 20, 52
Judaea: ancient, 15, 32; modern, 400
Judaism: 144–151
Judges Law: 175
judicial review: 176
jury trial: 398

Kahana, Aharon: 138
Kaminsky, Joseph: 136
Karaites: 146, 147
kashrut: 148
Katz, Michael: 372
Kefar Blum: 18, 20
Keren Hayesod: *See* Foundation Fund
kibbutzim (*see also* moshavim): 38, 79, 92, 94, 103, 290, 291, 339
King-Crane Commission: 40
Kinneret, Lake: *See* Tiberias, Lake
Kishon, Ephraim: 162
Kishon River: 14, 20, 342
Kitchener, Horatio H.: 38

National Insurance Institute: 184, 318, 365
National Physics Laboratory: 141
National Religious party: 196, 251
national security: 161; censorship, 221, 222; costs, 374; secret arrests, 406
national unity: 5, 8, 37, 40, 68, 86, 114, 129, 132, 161, 221, 241, 242
National Water Carrier: 23, 157
Nationality Law: 178, 205
natural gas: 301
navy: 369, 377, 380, 382
Nazareth: 25, 27, 66
Nazi Collaborators Law: 178, 404, 405, 411
Negev: 14, 23, 24, 300, 341
Negev, Institute for Higher Education in the: 128
Negev Institute for Arid Zone Research: 141
Nepal: 354
Netanya: 66
Netherlands: 352
Neturei Karta: 77, 149, 240
Neve Tirza prison: 409
New Force: See Ha'olam Hazeh
newspapers: 221, 223–230
Nobel Prize: 256
North American-Rockwell Standard: 375
Northern District: 25, 27, 65
nuclear power: 140, 310; nonproliferation treaty, 215
nutrition: 101

occupied territories: See Six-Day War
Ohel Theater Company: 134
Omer: 226, 227
opera: 136
Oriental Jews: See Sephardic Jews
Orthodox Judaism (see also ultra-Orthodox Jews): 149
Ottoman Penal Code: 403

Padahzur, David: 225
"Pale of Settlement": 35
Palestine Mandate: See Great Britain
Palestinian Arabs: See Arabs, Palestinian
Palestinian Liberation Organization: 206
Palmach: 256, 370, 371

Palumbo, David: 138
Pamaz system: 346
Pardon Law: 410
Paris Peace Conference: 40–41
Partos, Oedoen: 136
Paul VI, Pope: 213
Peel Commission: 44
pensions: 170, 322, 394
periodicals: 228
Petah Tigra: 66
petroleum: 16, 301; pipelines, 25–27, 342, 354
Pharisees: 146
phosphates: 16, 307
Pinsker, Leo: 36, 243
Poalei Agudat Israel party: 77, 192, 196, 327; newspaper, 228
Poalei Zion party: 189, 323
Poland: 58, 68, 233
Polish language: 225, 228
Police, Ministry of: 181, 365
police force: 241, 399–403, 412
political parties (see also chapter 14): 8, 37, 42, 77, 114, 115, 172, 174, party system, 242, 247
population (see also chapter 4): 27, 43, 79; employment, 311, 313; family size, 92; military service, 376
population, non-Jewish (see also Arabs, Palestinian): 69, 77, 291, 311; literacy, 129
ports and harbors: 26, 342
potash: 307
poultry: 294, 295, 296
power sources: See electric power; nuclear power; petroleum; solar energy
president: 167
press associations: 229
Prevention of Infiltration Law: 398, 404, 405
prime minister: 168, 202–204
prison system: 182, 398, 399, 407, 408
private industry: 302, 337
Progressive Judaism: 149
Protestants: 70, 116, 152
Provisional Council of State: 165
Public Committee: 335
public housing: 102

Qarn River: 14
Qishon River: See Kishon River

Rabin, Yitzhak: 53, 268

radio (see also Kol Israel Broadcasting Authority): 222, 230, 394
radio sets: 221, 232
RAFI: 191, 192, 261, 263
railroads: 24, 25, 341
rainfall: 19, 20, 286
RAKAH: 189, 196
Ramat Gan: 66
Ramla: 25, 27, 409
ranks, military: 387
Reali School: 384
recurring issues: 197, 205–208; national identity, 143, 151, 153, 154, 253
Reform Judaism: 35–36, 149
refugee problem: 12, 46, 48, 52, 56, 124, 212, 217
Rehovot: 66
Reik, Havivah: 372
religion (see also chapter 11): 155
Religious Affairs, Ministry of: 123, 150
religious courts: 177
Religious Discrimination, League for Prevention of: 251
religious parties: 77, 195
religious schools: 125, 130; public, 114, 116
religious trade unions: 327
research: agricultural, 285, 287; biblical, 139; commerce and trade, 141, 336; desalinization, 141, 310; medicine and science, 139–41; military, 300, 375; U.S. aided, 132
Research and Development, National Council for: 132, 139, 140
research institutes: 109, 127, 128
reserves, military: 377, 385
Reshumot: 166
Restrictive Practices Law: 304
retail stores: 333
Riad, Abdel Munim: 206
Rishon Le Zion: 66
roads and highways: 25, 26, 340
Rogoff Medical Research Institute: 109
Roman Catholics: 70, 116, 152
Rosenblum, H.: 226
Rotem, Zvi: 226
Rothschild, Edmond: 36, 59
Rothschild, James A. de: 172
Rothschild, Lionel Walter: 39
Rothschild Memorial Group: 232
Rumania: 241, 217, 237, 270, 353;

Rumanian language periodicals, 224, 226, 228, 229
rural areas: 79, 92, 94, 103, 245, 290, 291, 334, 383
Russia (see also Soviet Union): 58, 244

sabotage: 411
Sabras: 56, 67, 162; literature, 134; political values, 250, 251; social structure, 78, 97
Safety and Hygiene, Institute of: 318
Samaria: 15; West Bank, 398–399, 400
Samaritans: 69, 147
Samuel, Herbert: 41
sanitation: 104, 107
Saphir, Joseph: 259
Sapir, Pinhas: 270
savings: 368
Schatz, Boris: 137
Schocken, Gershom: 225
schools (see also religious schools): 42, 72, 150; art, 137; drama, 135; journalism, 229; music, 135; public secular, 114, 116
sculpture: 138
securities market: 358, 361, 362, 365
Sedom: 19, 20
Sephardic Jews: 49, 56, 67–69, 89, cultural tradition, 131, 313; education, 80, 113, 251; political attitudes, 250; social structure, 78, 83, 85, 92, 157
Severance Pay Law: 319
Shalom, Shin: 133
Shalom of Safad: See Moskowitz, Shalom
Shamir, Moshe: 133
Shamosh, Juriah: 225
Sharef, Ze'ev: 355
Sharett, Moshe: 202, 210, 211
Shaw Royal Commission: 44
Shazar, Shneur Zalman: 139, 211, 270
She'arim: 228
Shekem: 394
Shem, Jehiel: 138
Shephela: 15
shipping: 375
Shlonsky, Avraham: 133
Shomrim: 369, 372
sickness funds: 110
Six-Day War: 6–7, 54, 205, 270, 336, 395; consequences, 155, 242, 295; occupied territories, 16, 54, 184, 207,

Voice of America: 237
Volcani Institute: 140, 141
voting: 172–175, 192, 243, 372

wages, salaries, pay: 81, 100, 170, 172,
279, 329, 321, 367; military and
police, 388, 394, 402
Wailing Wall: 33, 48, 150, 350
water supply (*see also* desalinization
of sea water, irrigation): 11, 23,
104, 287
Wechsler, Jacob: 138
Weizmann, Chaim: 37, 39, 40, 45, 49,
166, 209
Weizmann Institute of Science: 49,
76, 128, 139, 264
Weizmann Rehabilitation Center: 109
welfare programs: 110
West Bank: *See* Samaria
Wilner, Meir: 196
Wingate, Orde: 370
women: 129, 148, 229, 409; education,
80, 126–128; employment, 313–314,
equal rights, 82, 91, 159, 319, 321;
family status, 94–96; fertility, 63;
military service, 129, 376, 377, 390,
401; teachers, 125, 129
Women's International Zionist Organization: 193, 197
Woodhead Commission: 44

World Bank: *See* International Bank
for Reconstruction and Development
World War II: 45, 83–84, 370
World Zionist Organization: 4, 37, 38,
41, 42, 44, 50, 115, 182, 199

Yadin, Yigael: 142
Yafo: *See* Jaffa
Yarqon River: 14, 20
Yedidyah, S.: 225
Yediot Achronot: 226, 228
Yediot Chadashot: 226, 228
Yemenites: 133, 137, 138, 215
yeshivot schools: 123, 150
Yiddish language: 67, 71, 73, 135;
newspapers, 225, 228
Yizhar, S.: 133
youth: 228, 317; crime, 409, 410
Youth Aliyah: 183
youth organizations (*see also* Nahal):
111, 383

Zahal: 369, 371
Zait, Meir: 226
Zaritsky, Joseph: 137
Zealots: 2, 33
Zim shipping company: 342
Zionism (*see also* World Zionist Or-
ganization): 35, 37, 42
Zor: 15
Zouia, M.: 225

PUBLISHED AREA HANDBOOKS